THIRSTY MERMAIDS

Kat Leyh

GALLERY 13

NEW YORK   LONDON   TORONTO   SYDNEY   NEW DELHI

GALLERY 13

An Imprint of Simon & Schuster, Inc.
1230 Avenue of the Americas
New York, NY 10020

First Gallery 13 hardcover edition February 2021

GALLERY 13 and colophon are trademarks of Simon & Schuster, Inc.

For information about special discounts for bulk purchases,
please contact Simon & Schuster Special Sales at 1-866-506-1949
or business@simonandschuster.com.

The Simon & Schuster Speakers Bureau can bring authors to your live event.
For more information or to book an event, contact the Simon & Schuster Speakers Bureau
at 1-866-248-3049 or visit our website at www.simonspeakers.com.

Manufactured in the United States of America

1   3   5   7   9   10   8   6   4   2

Library of Congress Cataloging-in-Publication Data is available.

ISBN 978-1-9821-3357-3
ISBN 978-1-9821-3359-7 (ebook)

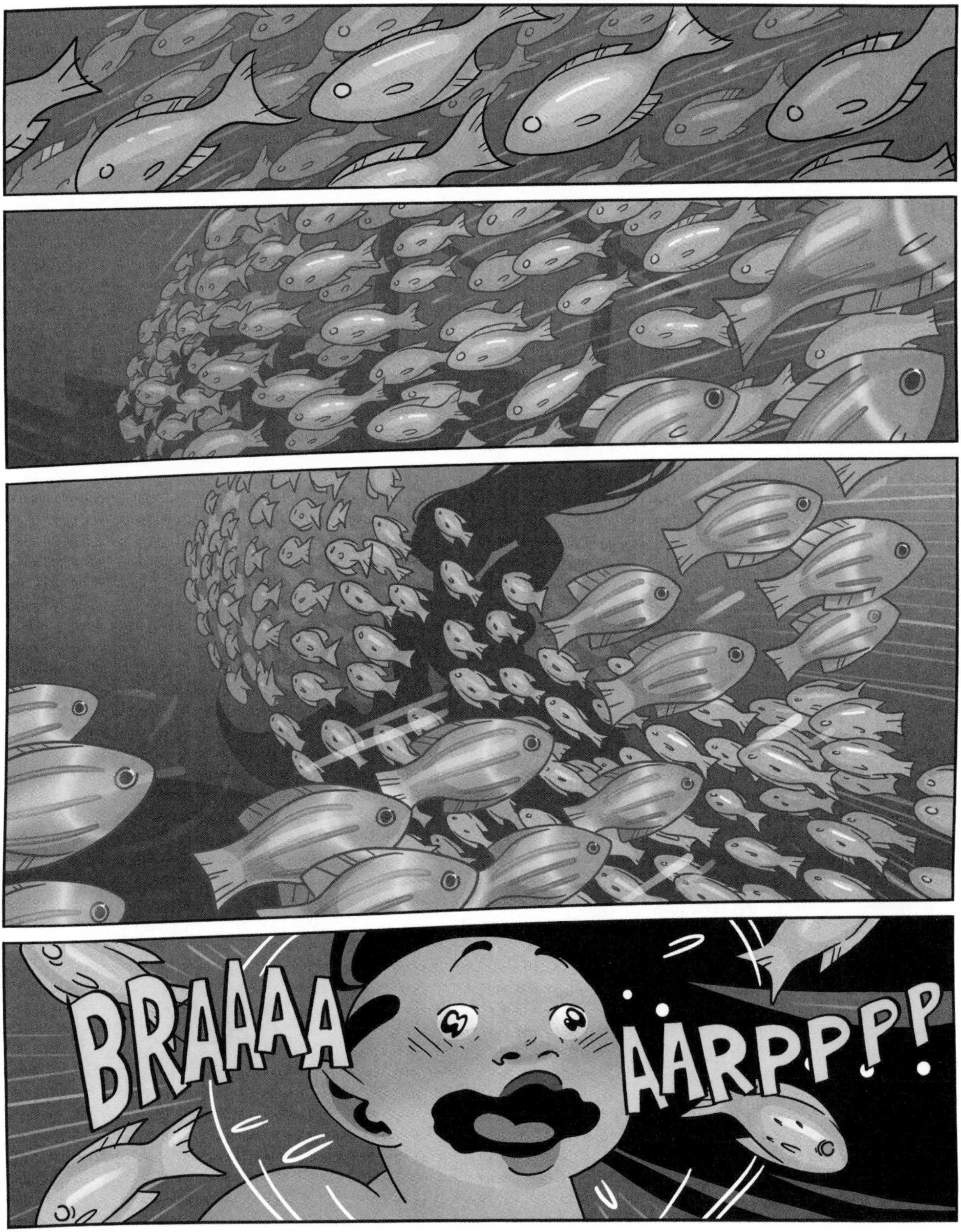
BRAAAA AARPPPP

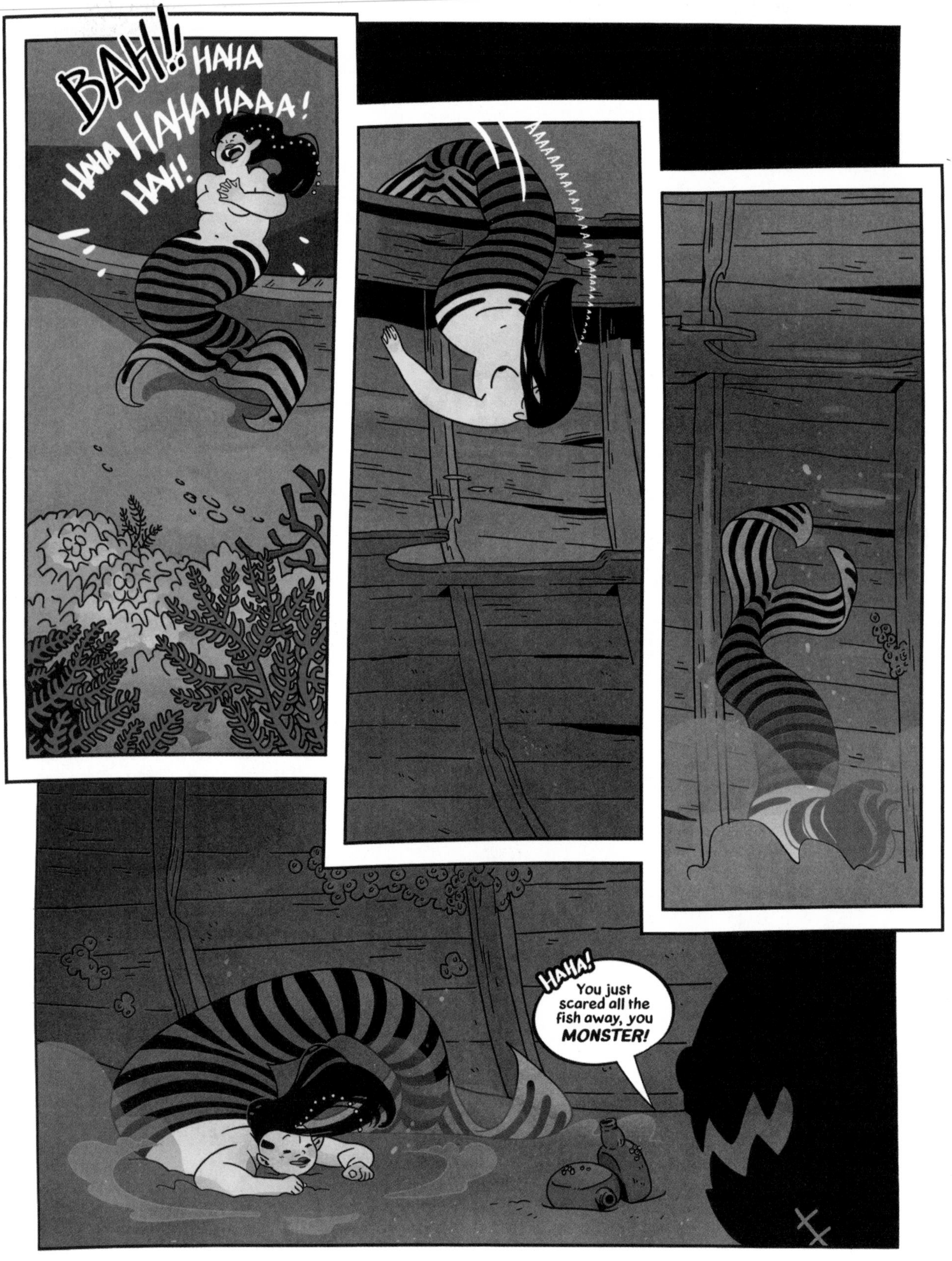
BAH!! HAHA
HAHA HAHA HAAA!
HAH!
AAAAAAAAAAAAAAAAAAAAAAAAA
HAHA! You just scared all the fish away, you MONSTER!

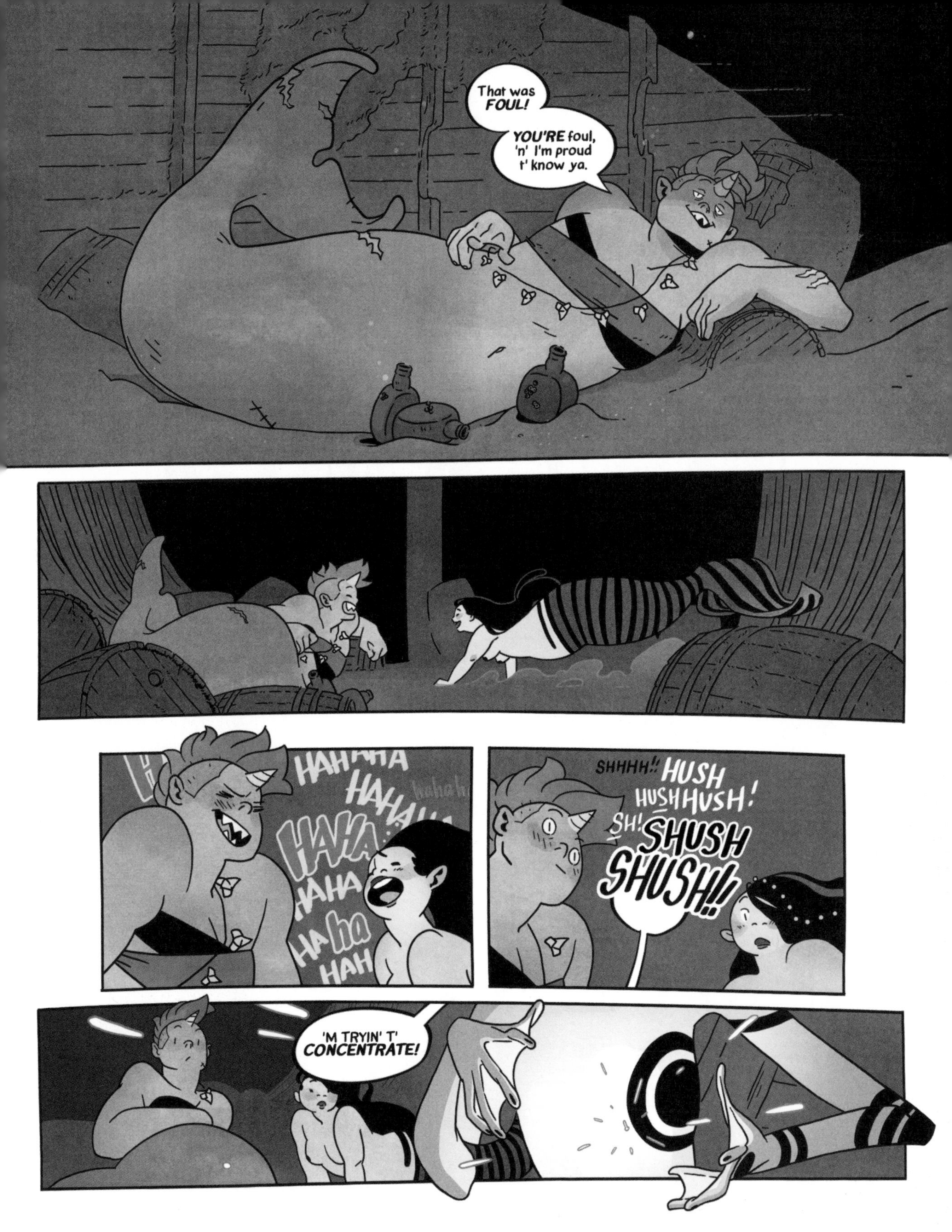
That was FOUL!
YOU'RE foul, 'n' I'm proud t' know ya.
HAHAHA HAHAHA HAHA HAHA HAha HAH
SHHHH!! HUSH HUSH HUSH! SH! SHUSH SHUSH!!
'M TRYIN' T' CONCENTRATE!

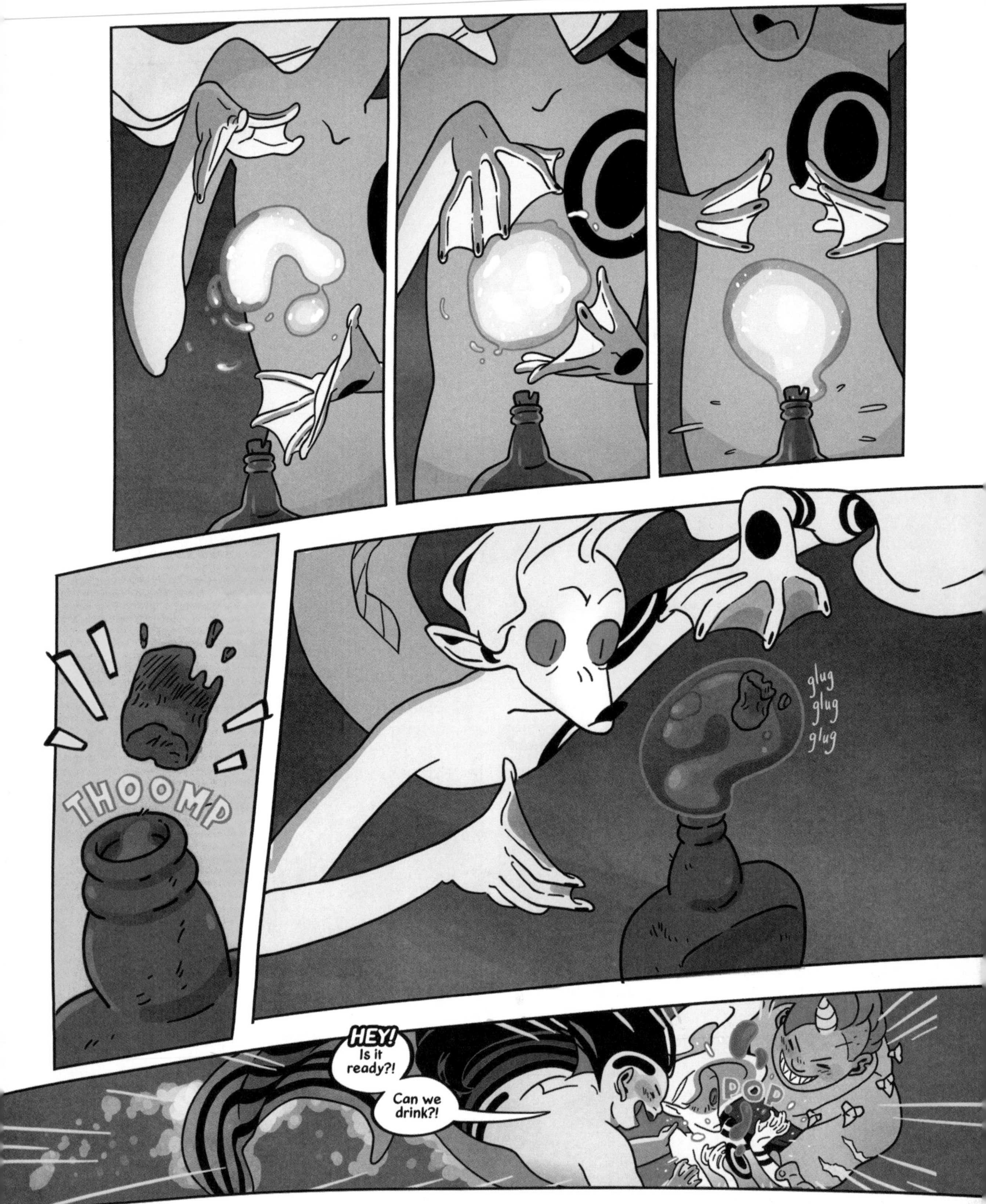
THOOMP
glug
glug
glug
HEY!
Is it ready?!
Can we drink?!
POP

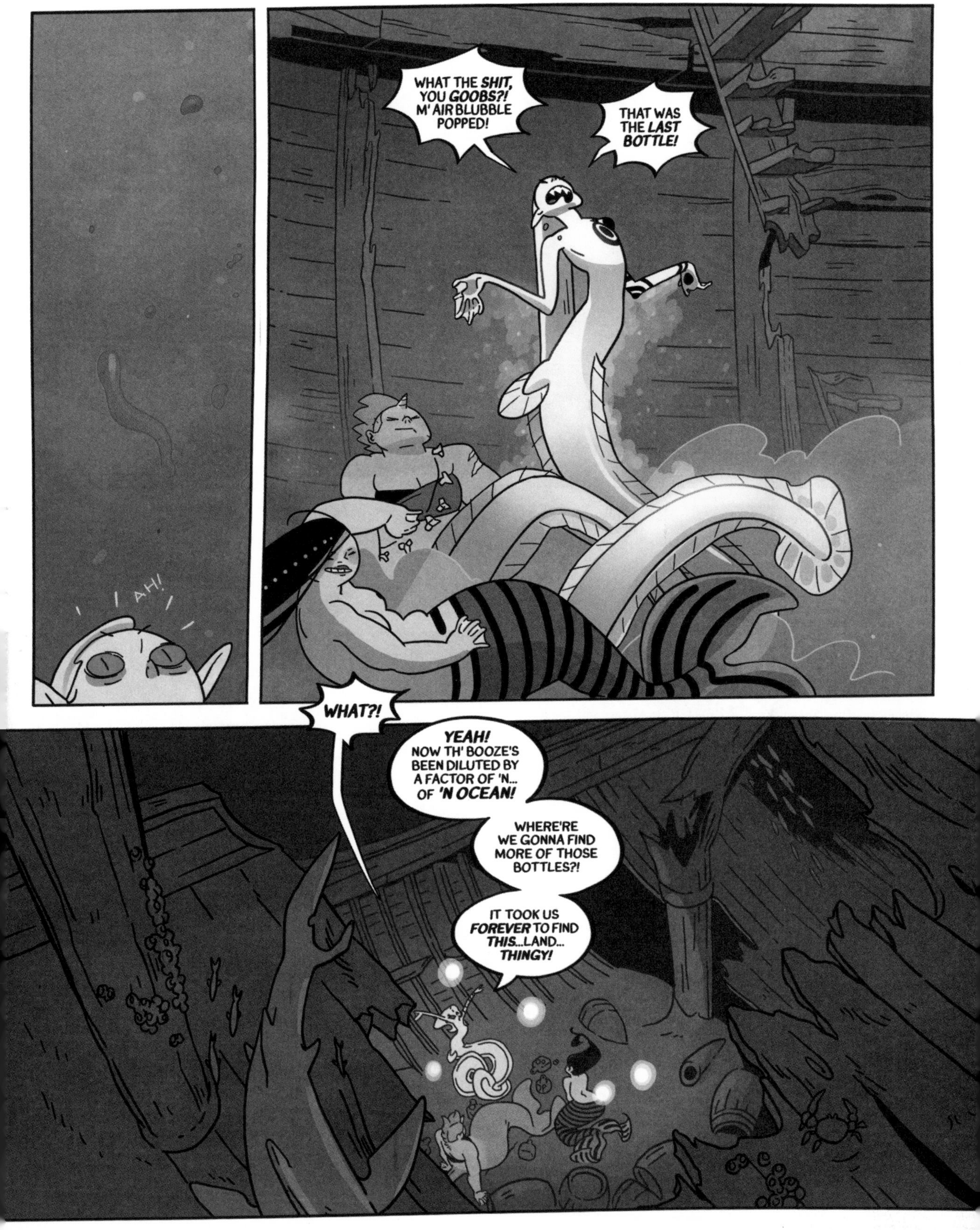
AH!
WHAT THE SHIT, YOU GOOBS?! M' AIR BLUBBLE POPPED!
THAT WAS THE LAST BOTTLE!
WHAT?!
YEAH! NOW TH' BOOZE'S BEEN DILUTED BY A FACTOR OF 'N... OF 'N OCEAN!
WHERE'RE WE GONNA FIND MORE OF THOSE BOTTLES?!
IT TOOK US FOREVER TO FIND THIS...LAND... THINGY!

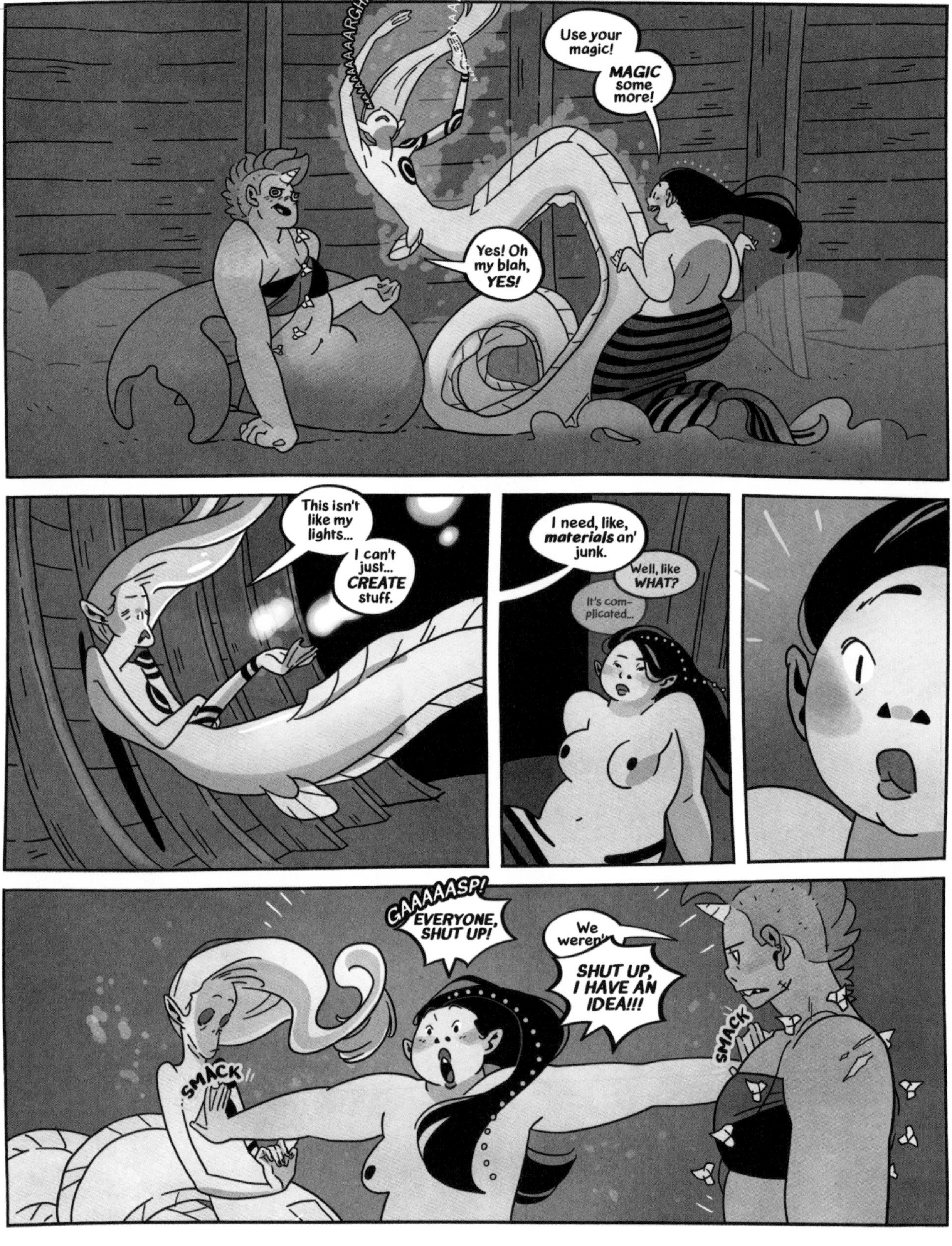
AAAAAAAAAAAAARGHH
Use your magic!
MAGIC some more!
Yes! Oh my blah, YES!
This isn't like my lights...
I can't just... CREATE stuff.
I need, like, materials an' junk.
Well, like WHAT?
It's complicated...
GAAAAASP!
EVERYONE, SHUT UP!
We weren'
SHUT UP, I HAVE AN IDEA!!!
SMACK
SMACK

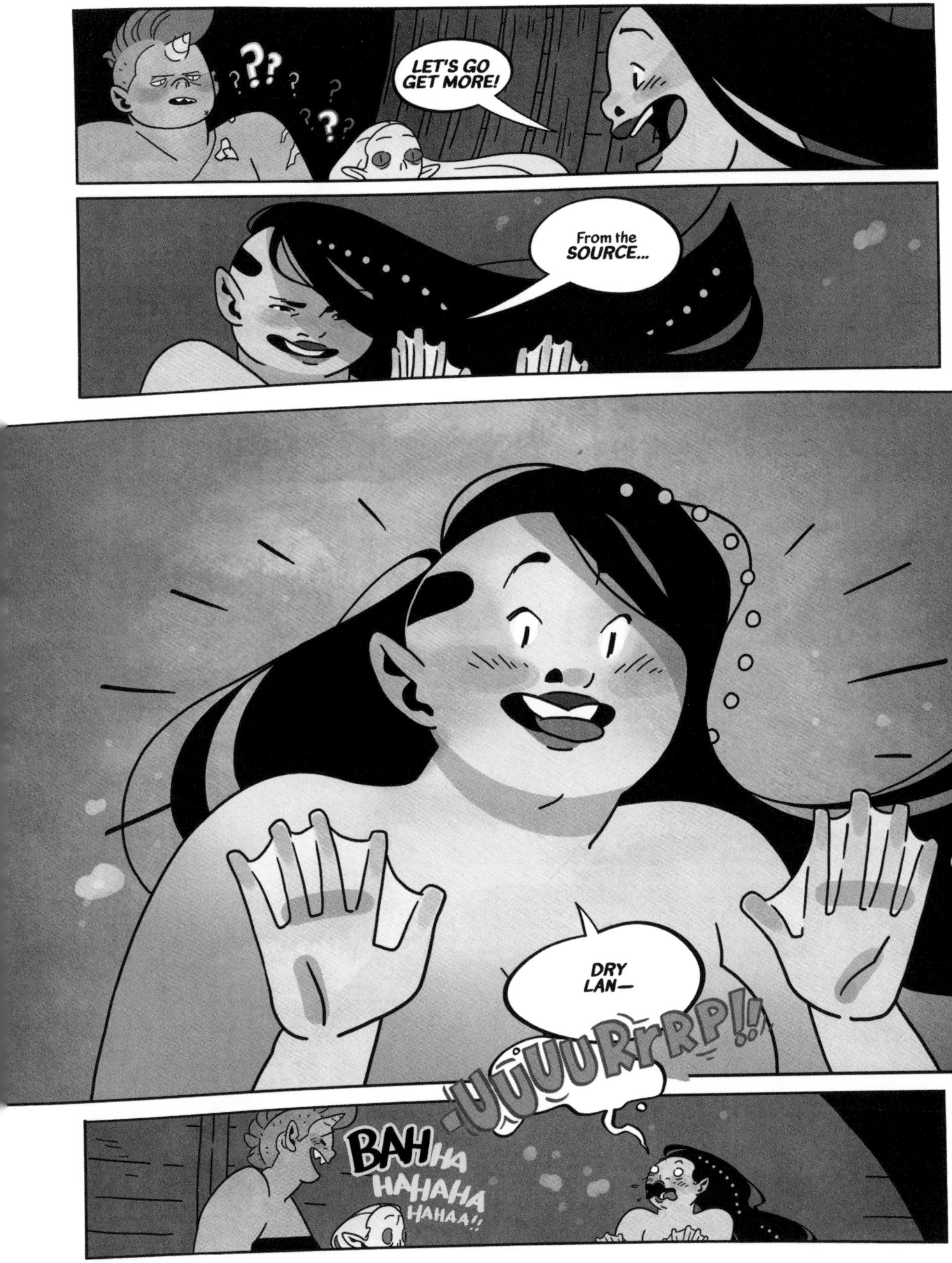
??
LET'S GO GET MORE!
From the SOURCE...
DRY LAN—
-UUUURrrRP!!
BAHHA HAHAHA HAHAA!!

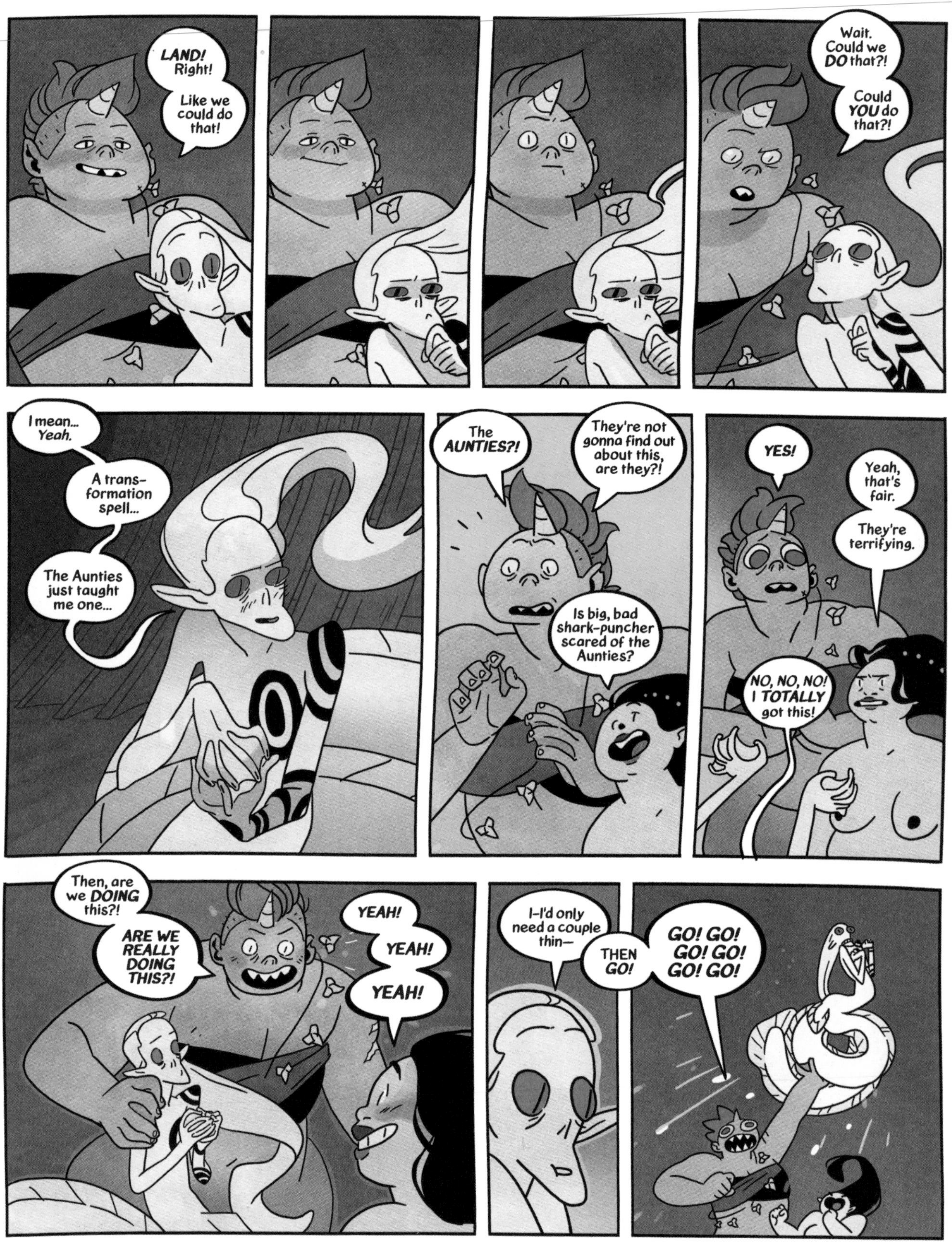
LAND! Right!
Like we could do that!
Wait. Could we DO that?!
Could YOU do that?!
I mean... Yeah.
A trans-formation spell...
The Aunties just taught me one...
The AUNTIES?!
They're not gonna find out about this, are they?!
Is big, bad shark-puncher scared of the Aunties?
YES!
Yeah, that's fair.
They're terrifying.
NO, NO, NO! I TOTALLY got this!
Then, are we DOING this?!
ARE WE REALLY DOING THIS?!
YEAH!
YEAH!
YEAH!
I-I'd only need a couple thin—
THEN GO!
GO! GO! GO! GO! GO! GO!

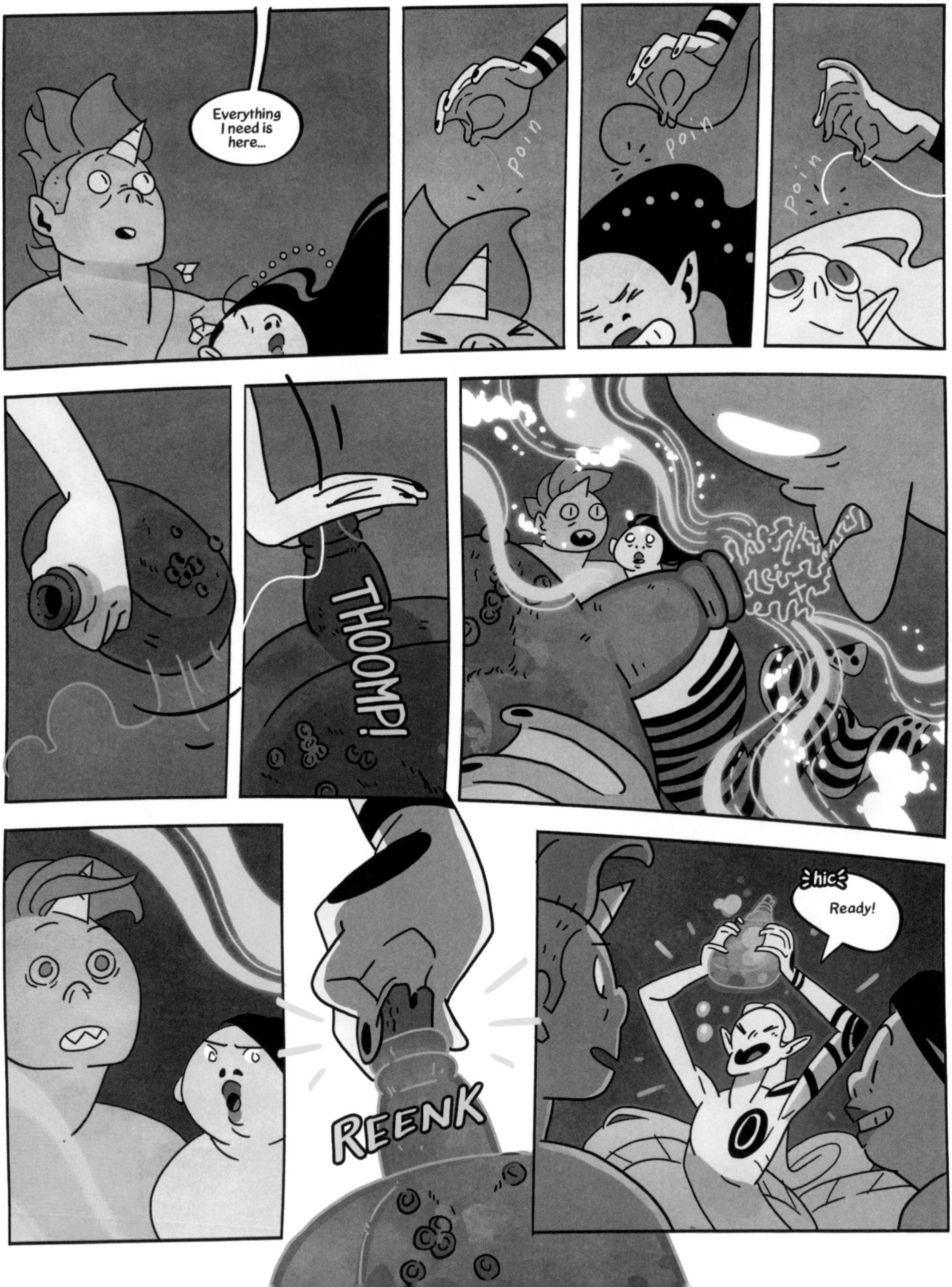
Everything I need is here...
poin
poin
poin
THOOMP!
REENK
hic
Ready!

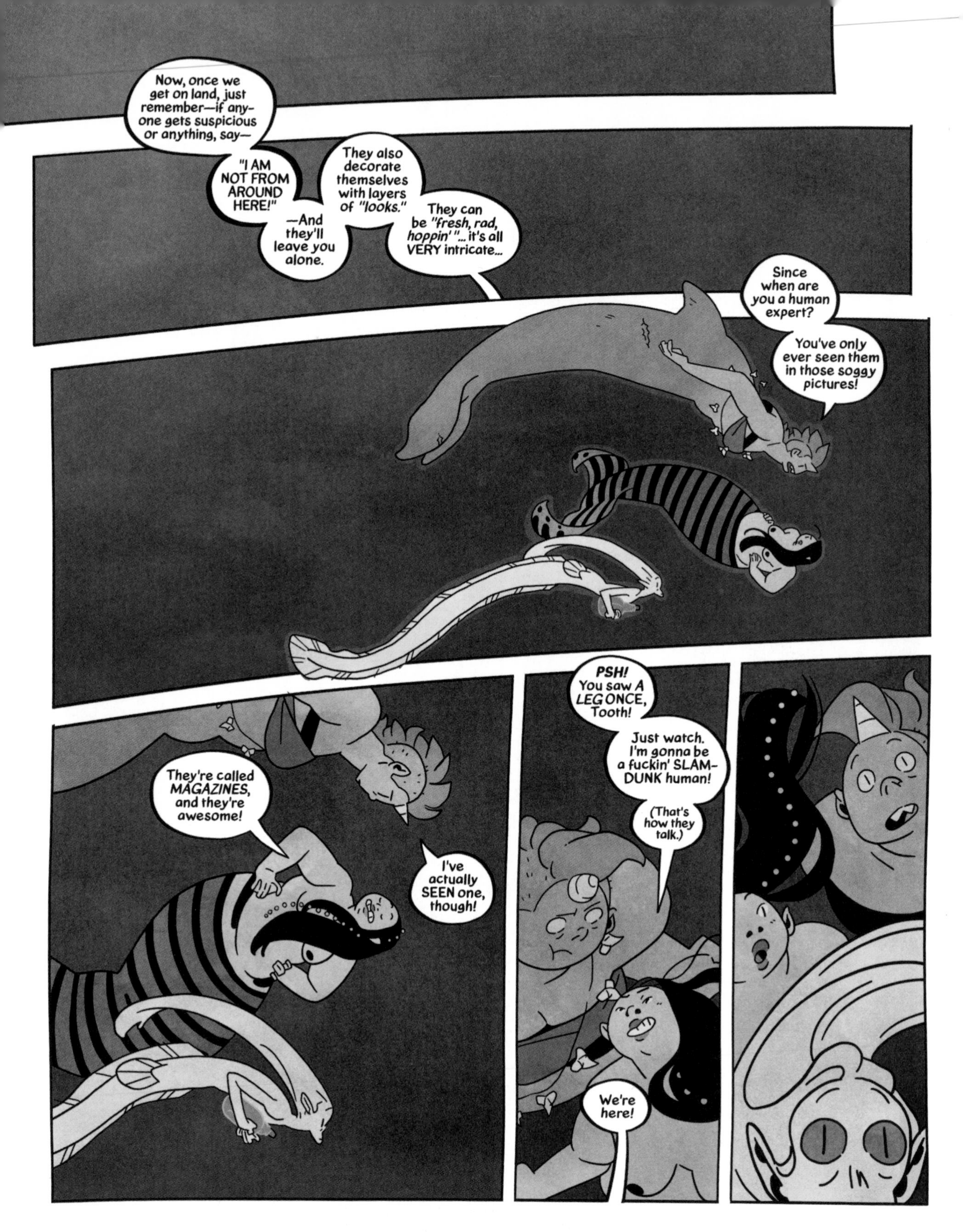
Now, once we get on land, just remember—if anyone gets suspicious or anything, say—
"I AM NOT FROM AROUND HERE!"
—And they'll leave you alone.
They also decorate themselves with layers of "looks."
They can be "fresh, rad, hoppin' "... it's all VERY intricate...
Since when are you a human expert?
You've only ever seen them in those soggy pictures!
They're called MAGAZINES, and they're awesome!
I've actually SEEN one, though!
PSH! You saw A LEG ONCE, Tooth!
Just watch. I'm gonna be a fuckin' SLAM-DUNK human!
(That's how they talk.)
We're here!

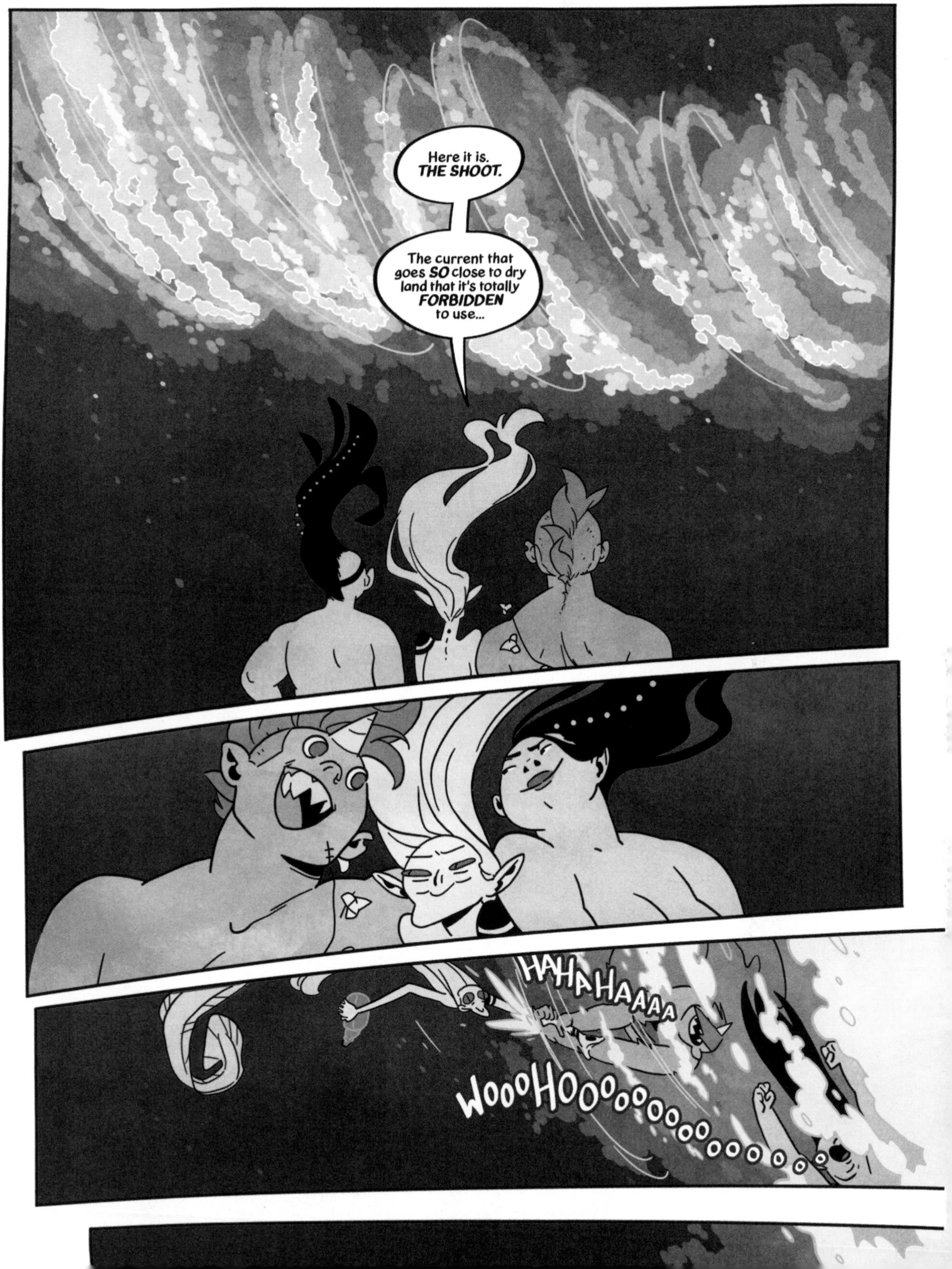
Here it is. THE SHOOT.
The current that goes SO close to dry land that it's totally FORBIDDEN to use...
HAHAHAAAA
WOOOHOOOOOOOOOOOOOOO

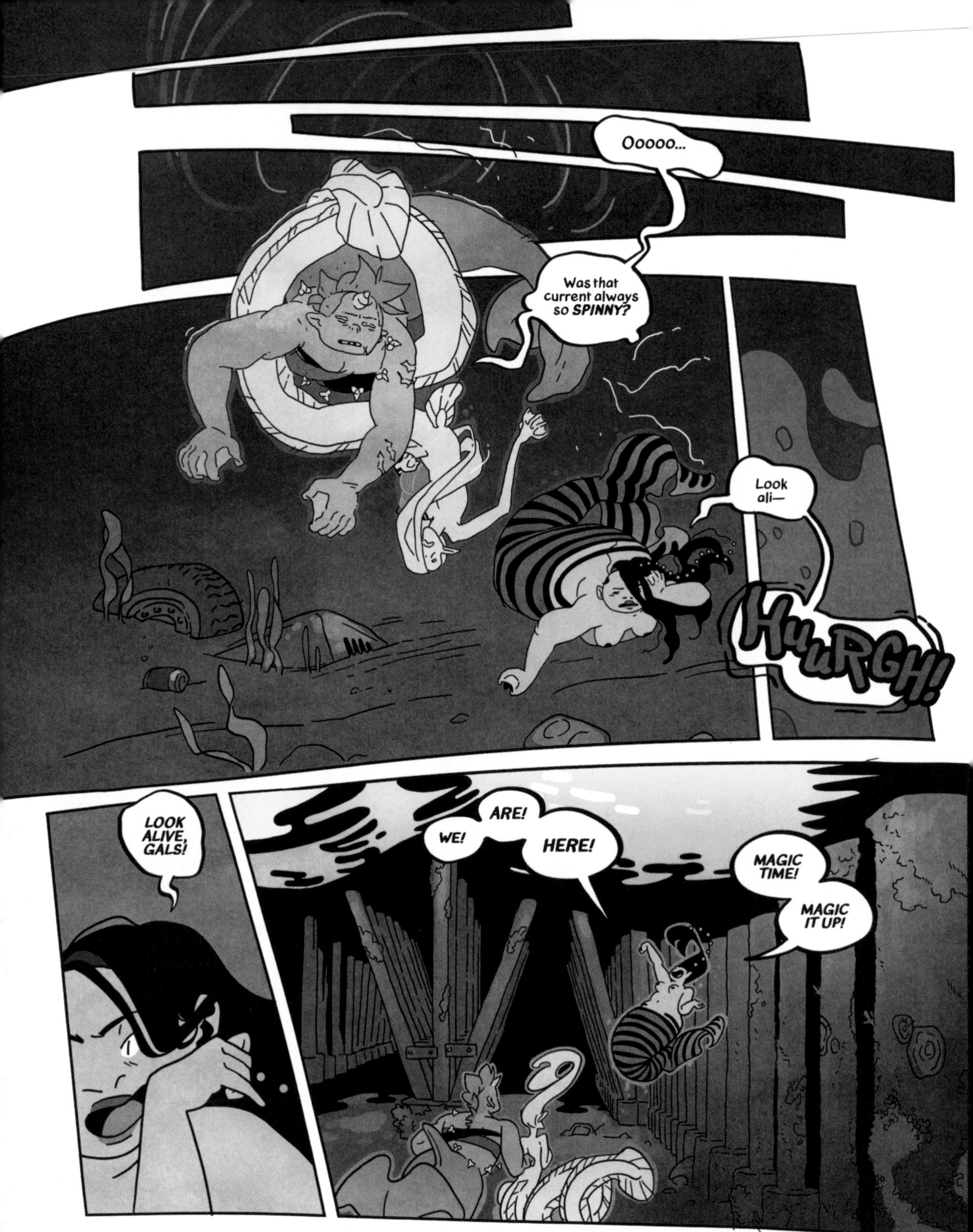
Ooooo...
Was that current always so *SPINNY?*
Look ali—
HUURGH!
LOOK ALIVE, GALS!
WE!
ARE!
HERE!
MAGIC TIME!
MAGIC IT UP!

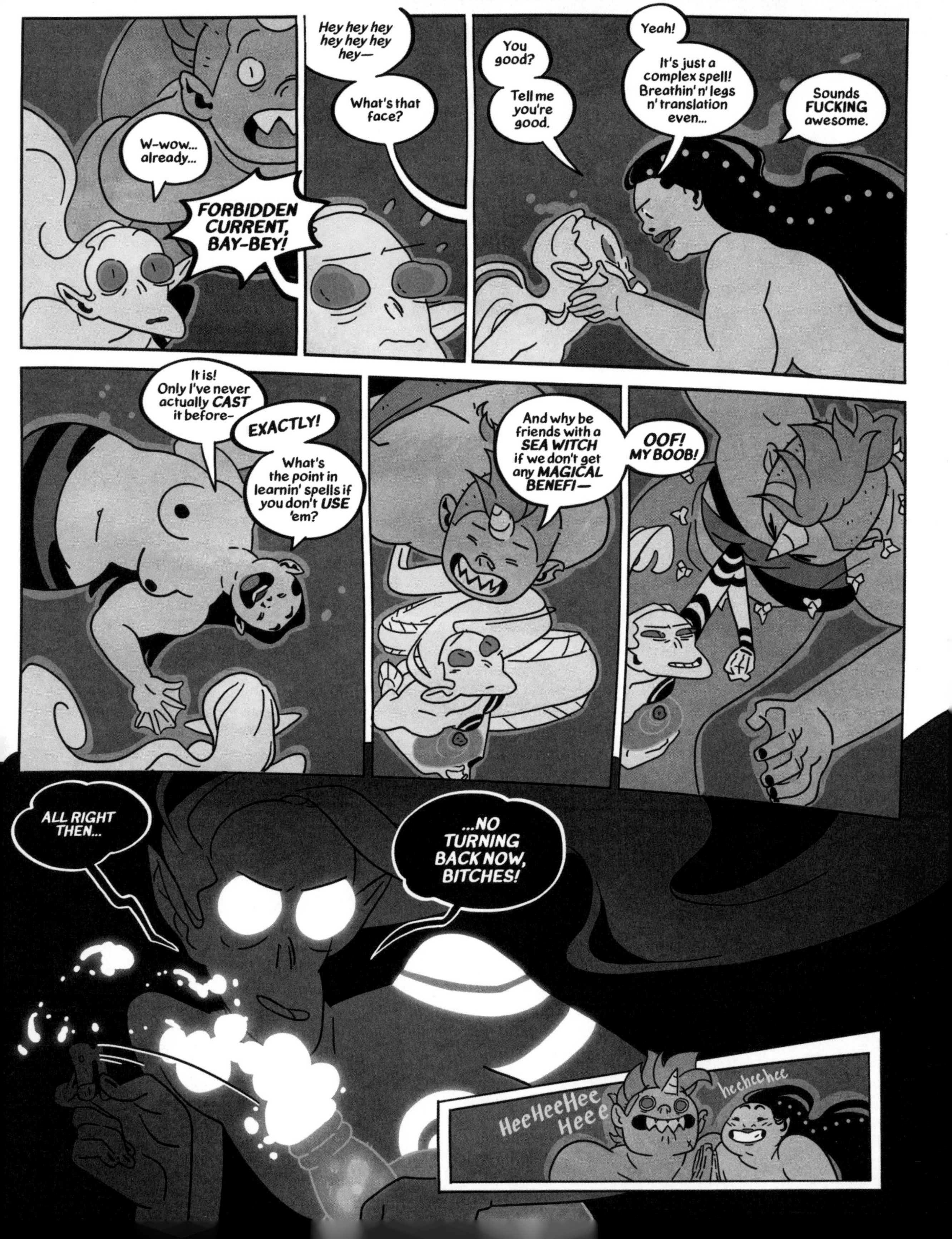
W-wow... already...
FORBIDDEN CURRENT, BAY-BEY!
Hey hey hey hey hey hey hey—
What's that face?
You good?
Tell me you're good.
Yeah!
It's just a complex spell! Breathin' n' legs n' translation even...
Sounds FUCKING awesome.
It is! Only I've never actually CAST it before-
EXACTLY!
What's the point in learnin' spells if you don't USE 'em?
And why be friends with a SEA WITCH if we don't get any MAGICAL BENEFI—
OOF! MY BOOB!
ALL RIGHT THEN...
...NO TURNING BACK NOW, BITCHES!
HeeHeeHee Heee
heeheehee

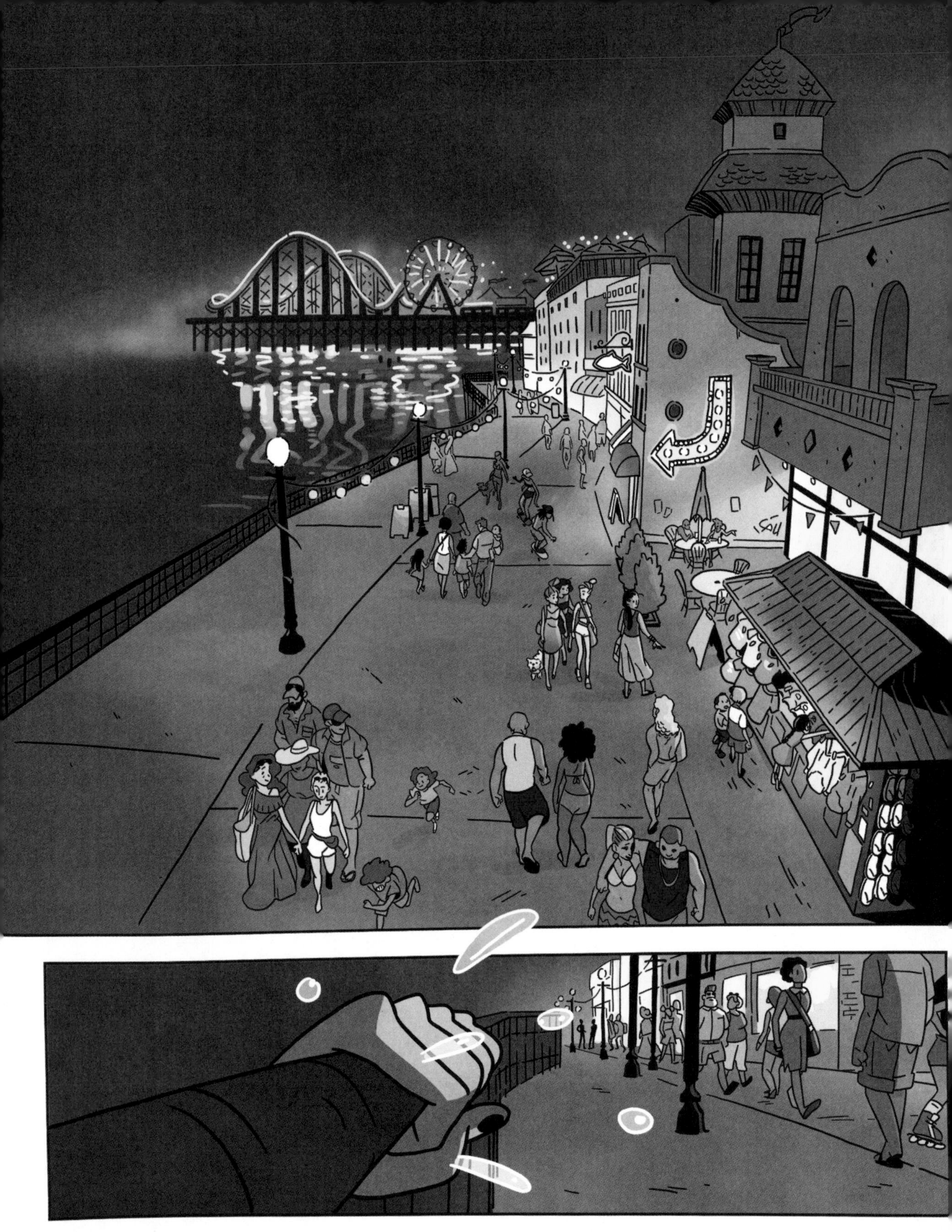

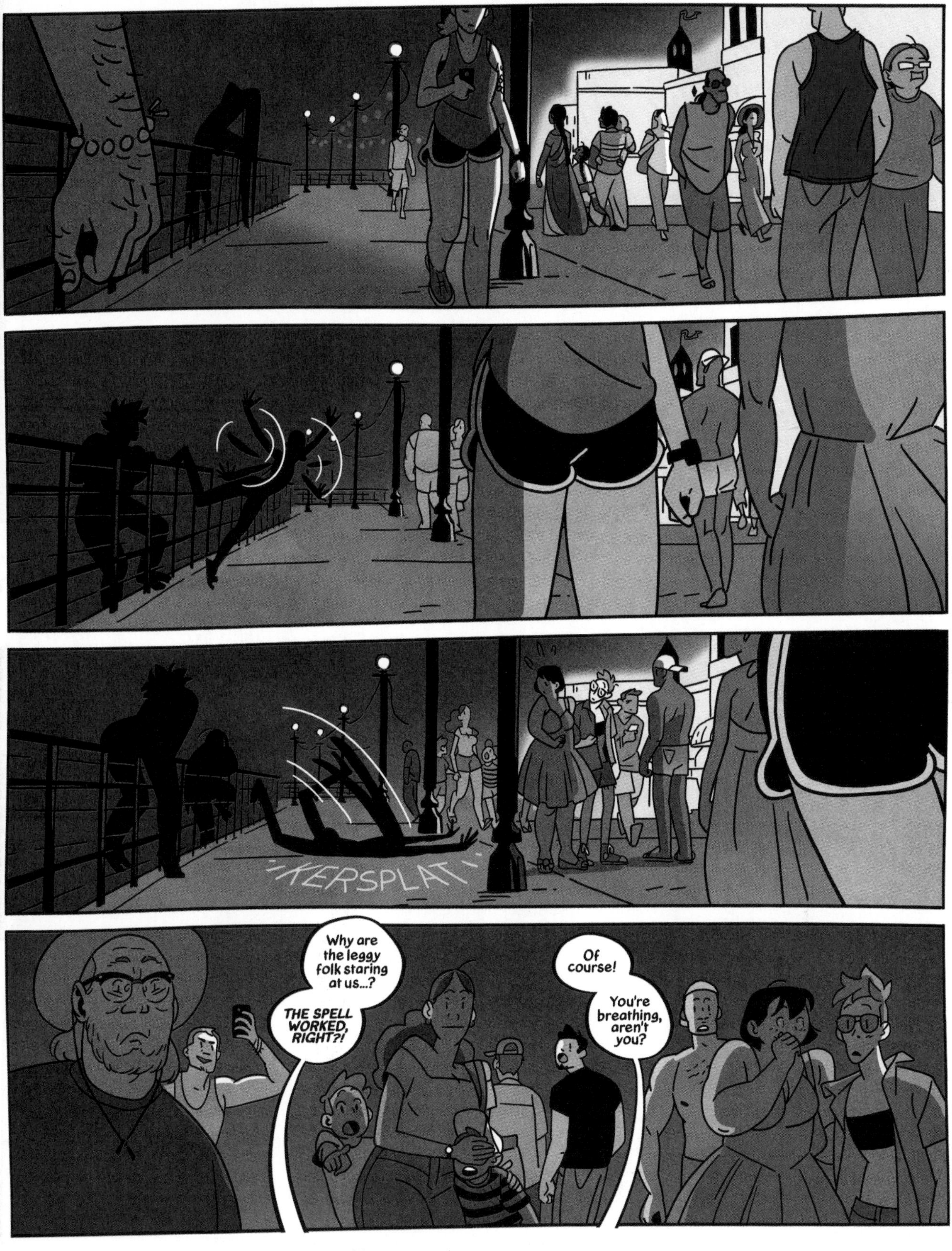
KERSPLAT
Why are the leggy folk staring at us...?
THE SPELL WORKED, RIGHT?!
Of course!
You're breathing, aren't you?

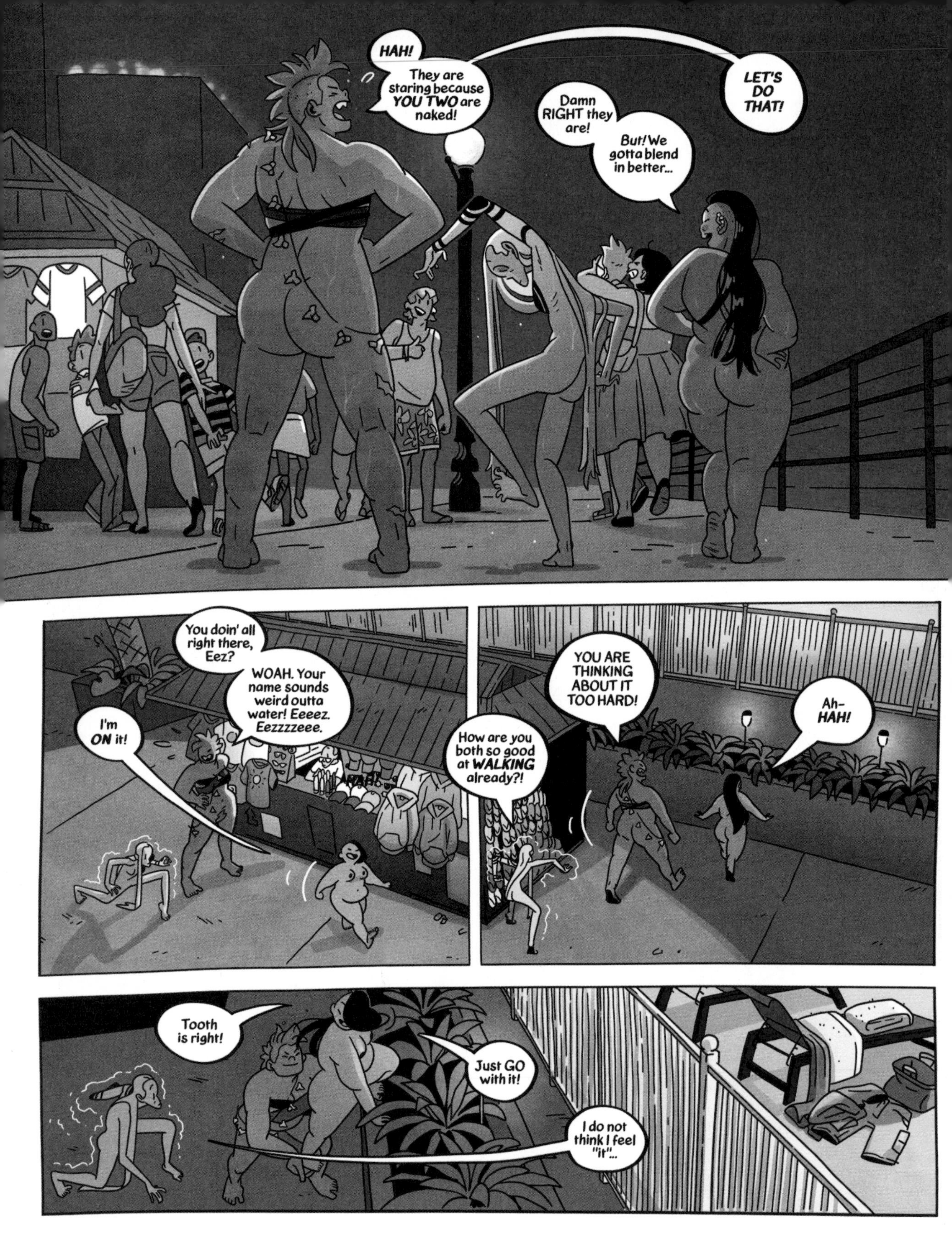

HAH!
They are staring because **YOU TWO** are naked!
Damn RIGHT they are!
But! We gotta blend in better...
LET'S DO THAT!
You doin' all right there, Eez?
WOAH. Your name sounds weird outta water! Eeeez. Eezzzzeee.
I'm **ON** it!
YOU ARE THINKING ABOUT IT TOO HARD!
How are you both so good at **WALKING** already?!
Ah-**HAH!**
Tooth is right!
Just GO with it!
I do not think I feel "it"...

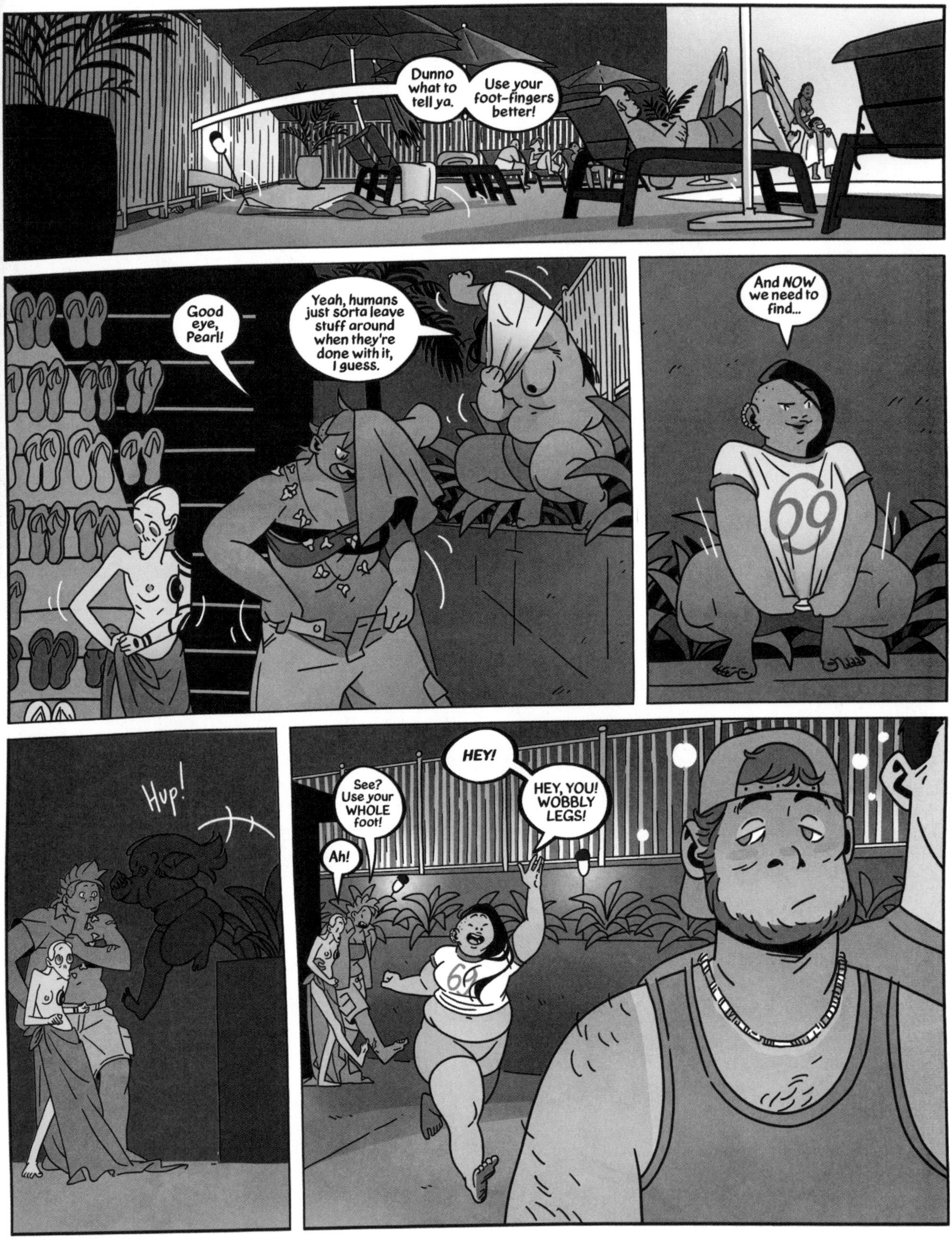
Dunno what to tell ya.
Use your foot-fingers better!
Good eye, Pearl!
Yeah, humans just sorta leave stuff around when they're done with it, I guess.
And NOW we need to find...
Hup!
See? Use your WHOLE foot!
Ah!
HEY!
HEY, YOU! WOBBLY LEGS!

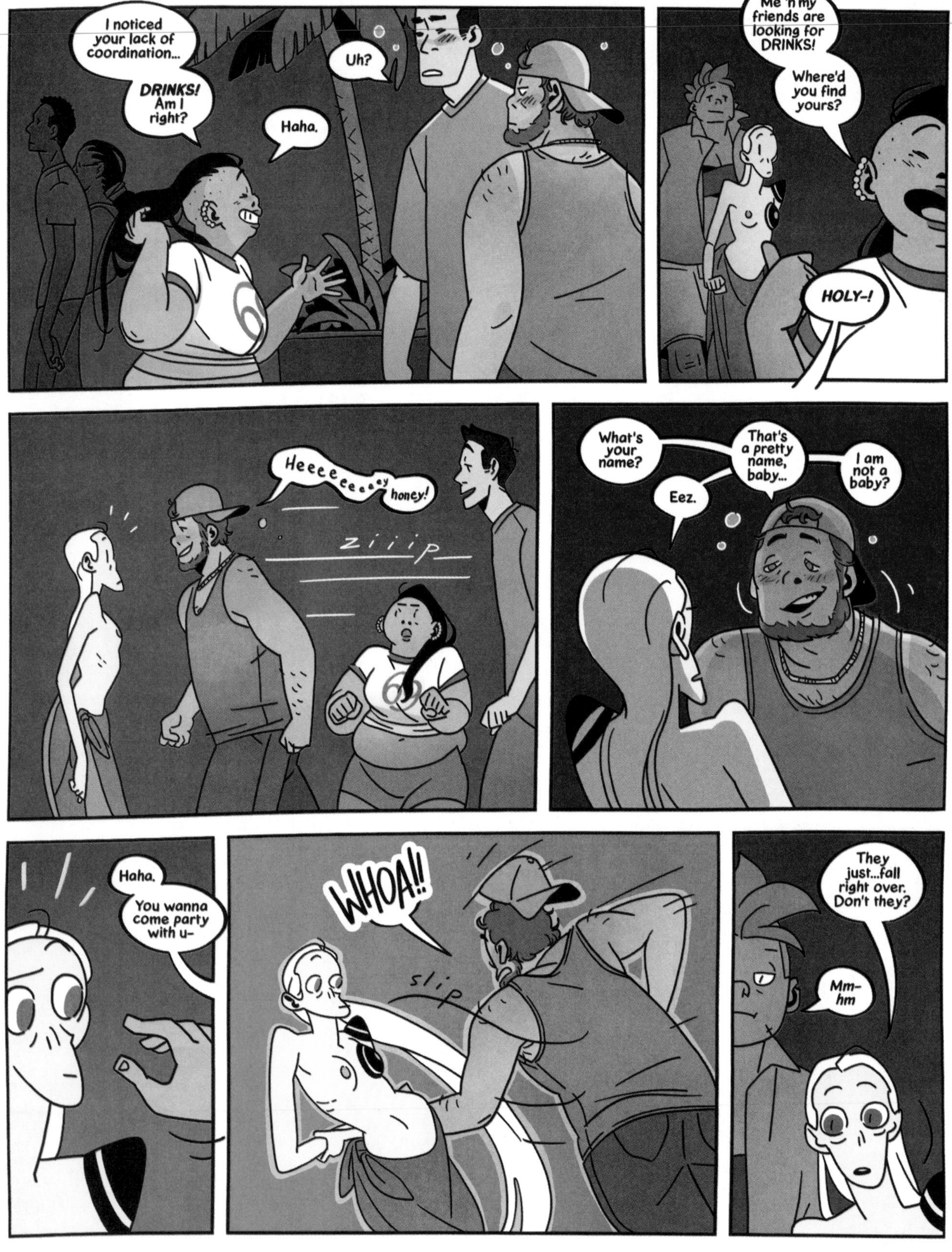
I noticed your lack of coordination...
DRINKS! Am I right?
Uh?
Haha.
Me 'n my friends are looking for DRINKS!
Where'd you find yours?
HOLY-!
Heeeeeeeeeey honey!
ziiip
What's your name?
Eez.
That's a pretty name, baby...
I am not a baby?
Haha.
You wanna come party with u-
WHOA!!
slip
They just...fall right over. Don't they?
Mm-hm

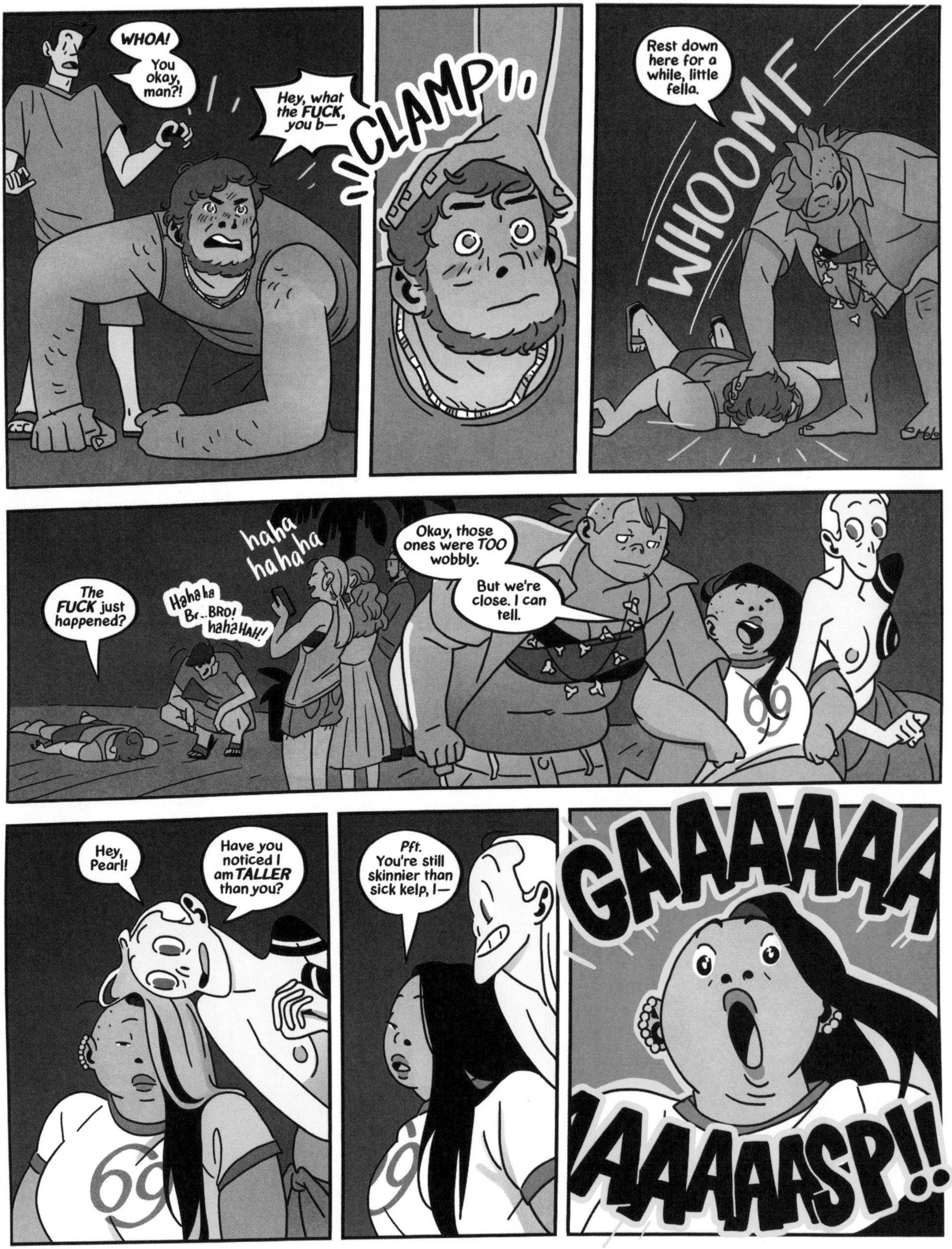

WHOA!
You okay, man?!
Hey, what the FUCK, you b—
CLAMP
Rest down here for a while, little fella.
WHOOMF
The FUCK just happened?
Hahaha Br... BRO! hahaHAH!
haha hahaha
Okay, those ones were TOO wobbly.
But we're close. I can tell.
Hey, Pearl!
Have you noticed I am TALLER than you?
Pft. You're still skinnier than sick kelp, I—
GAAAAAAAAAAAAASP!!

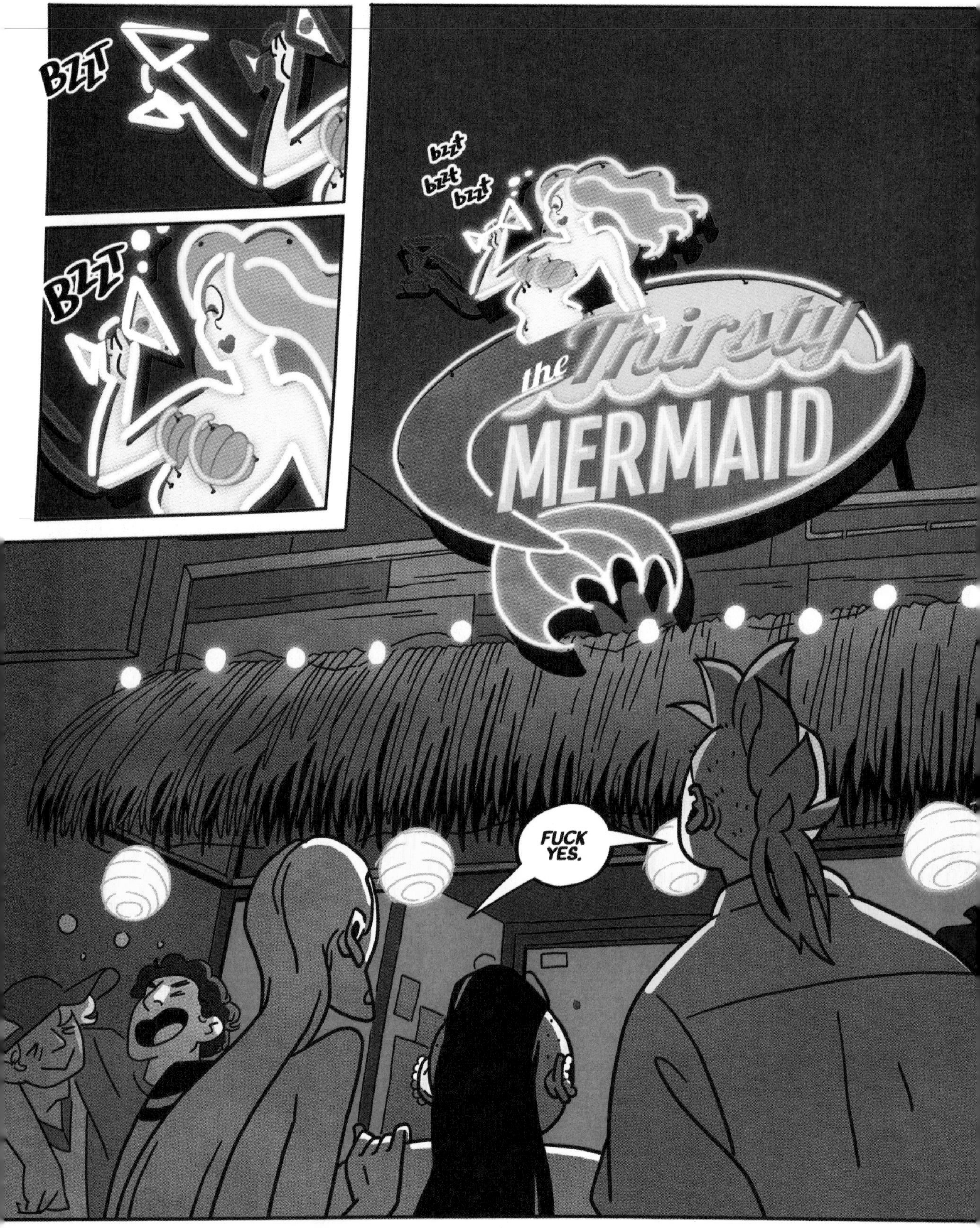
BZZT
BZZT
bzzt
bzzt
bzzt
the Thirsty MERMAID
FUCK YES.

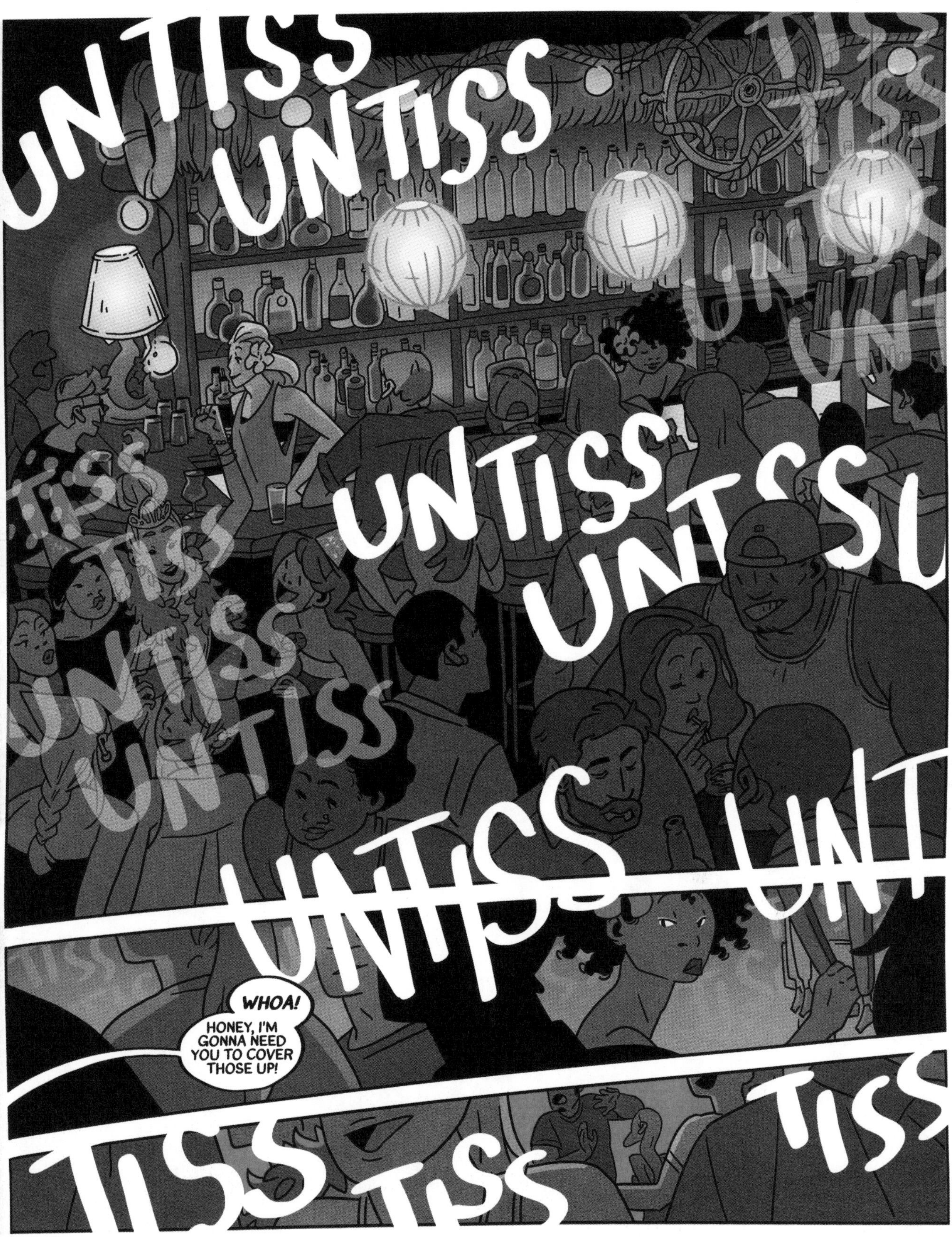
UNTISS
UNTISS
UNTISS
UNTISS
UNTISS UNT
WHOA!
HONEY, I'M GONNA NEED YOU TO COVER THOSE UP!
TISS TISS TISS

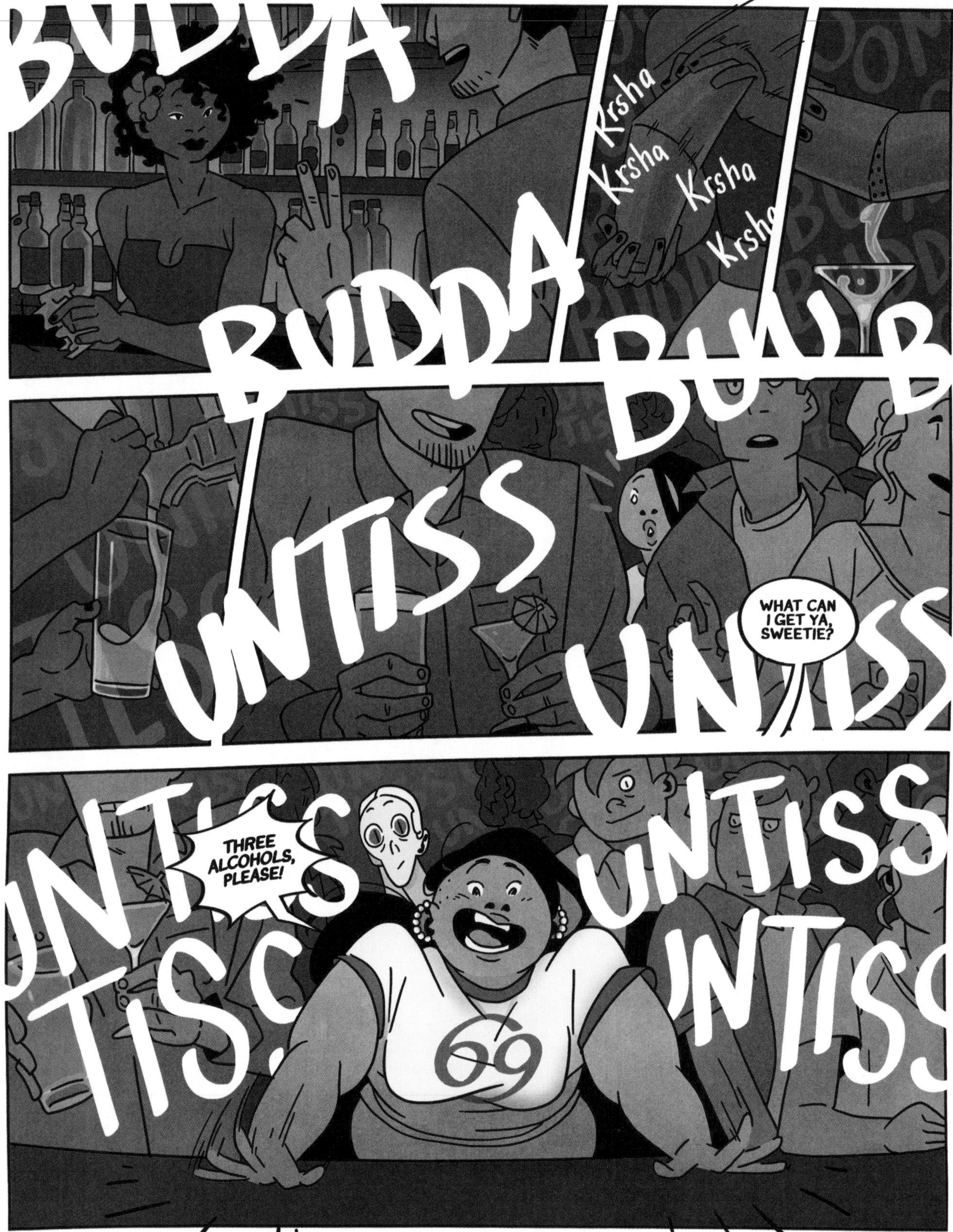
BUDDA
Krsha
Krsha
Krsha
Krsha
BUDDA
UNTISS
WHAT CAN I GET YA, SWEETIE?
THREE ALCOHOLS, PLEASE!
UNTISS
UNTISS

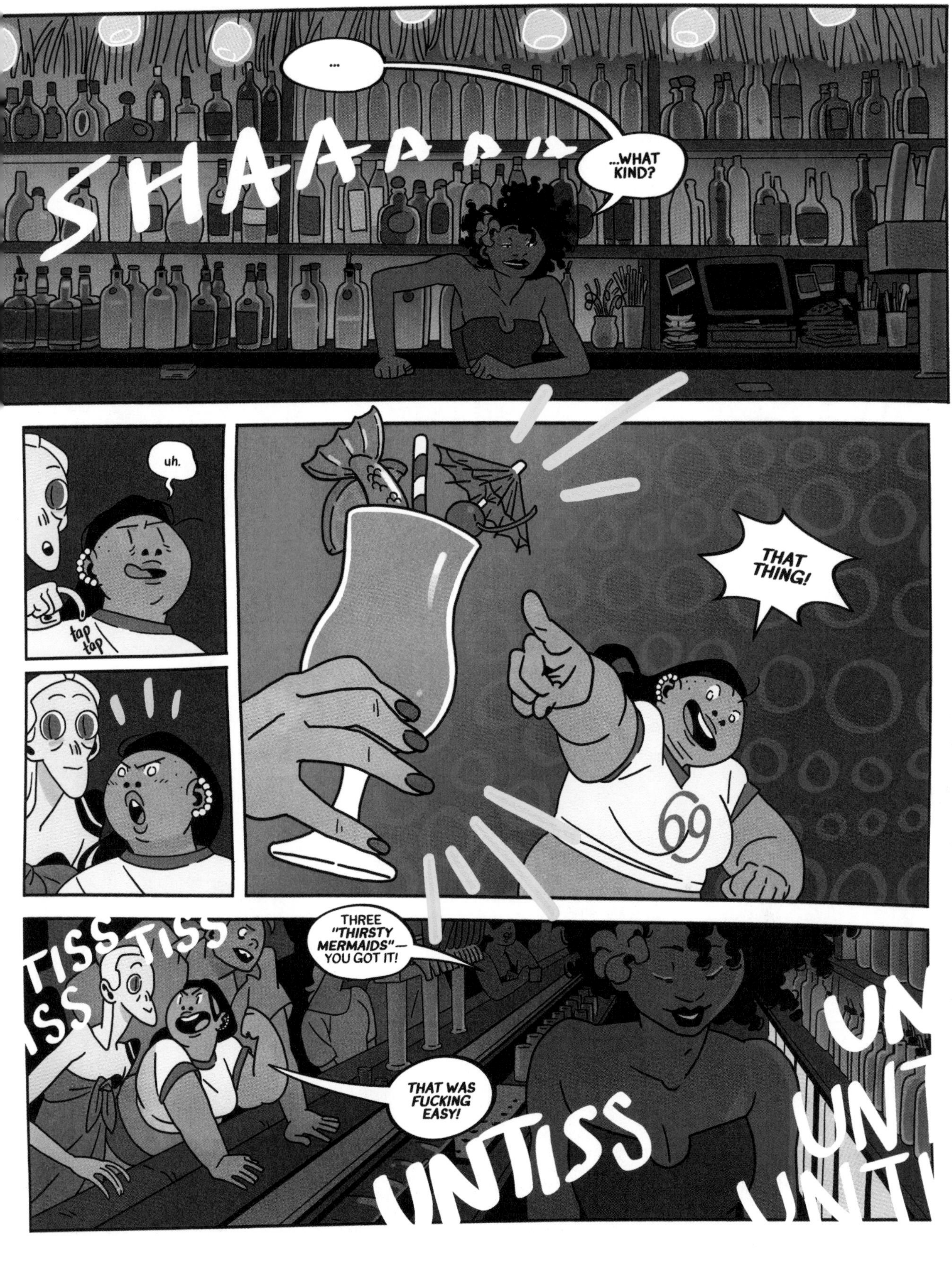
...
SHAAAAA
...WHAT KIND?
uh.
tap tap
THAT THING!
THREE "THIRSTY MERMAIDS"—YOU GOT IT!
TISS TISS
TISS
TISS
THAT WAS FUCKING EASY!
UNTISS
UN
UN-
UNTI

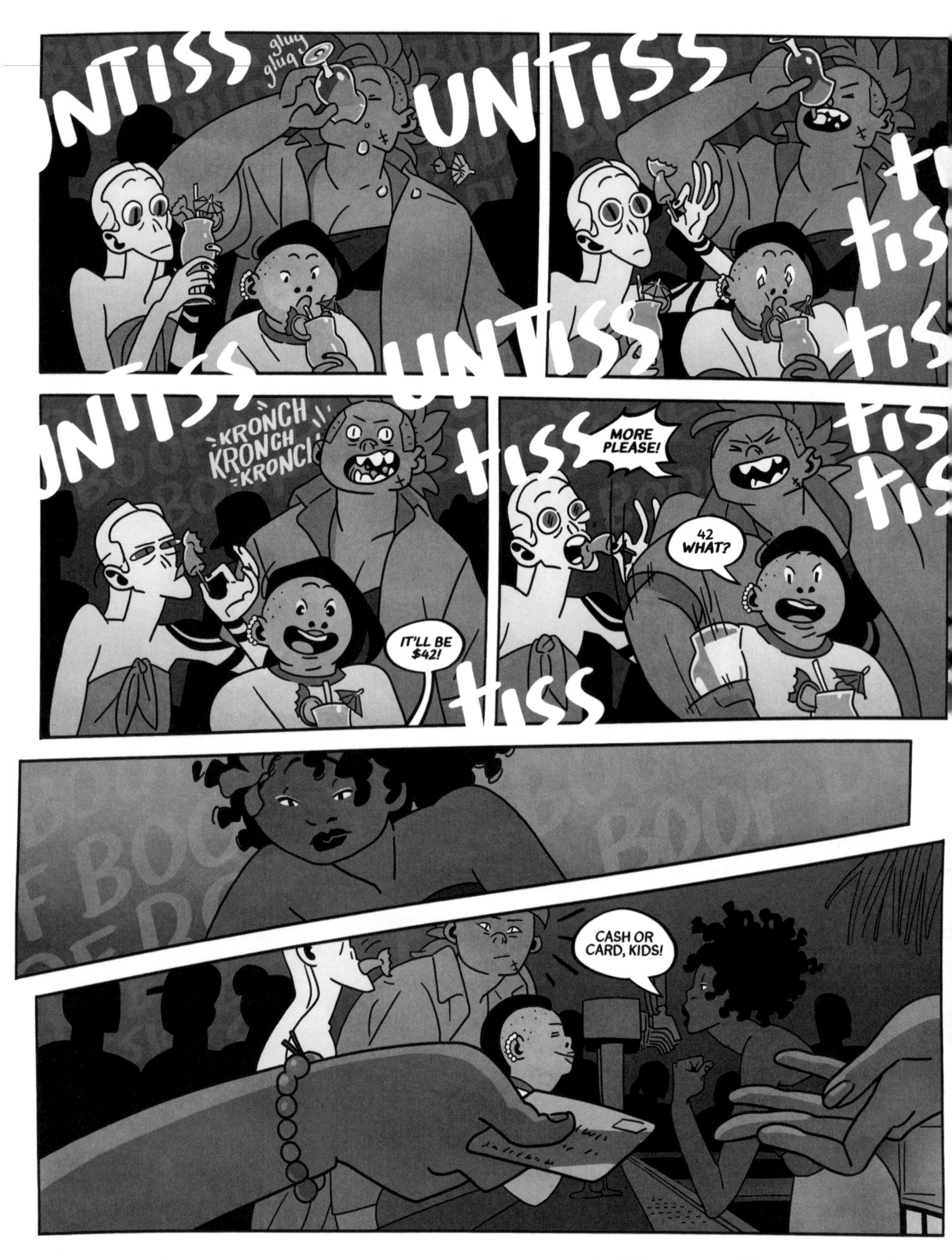

UNTISS
glug glug
UNTISS
UNTISS
UNTISS
tiss tiss tiss
UNTISS
KRONCH KRONCH KRONCH
IT'LL BE $42!
tiss
MORE PLEASE!
42 WHAT?
tiss tiss
tiss
CASH OR CARD, KIDS!

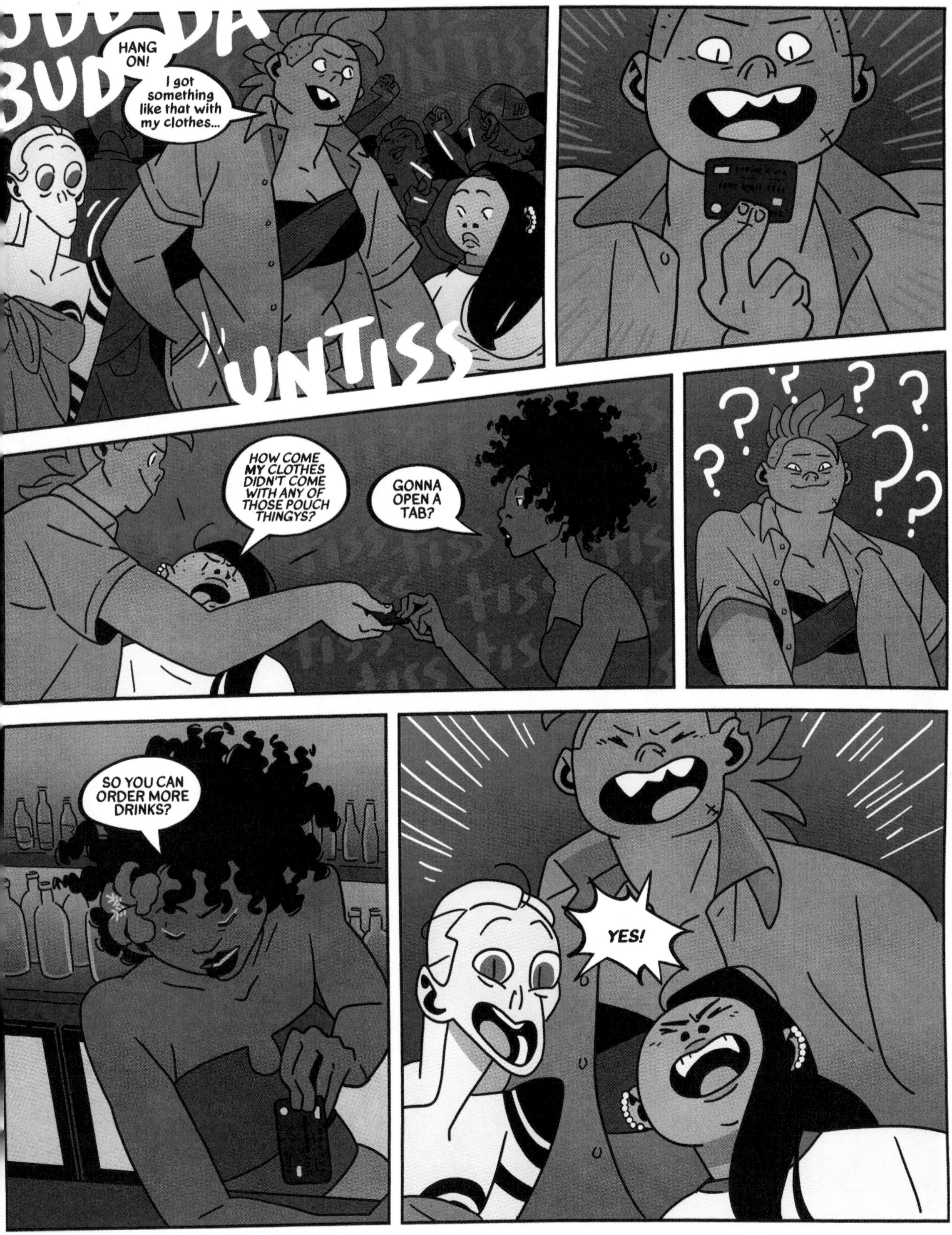
BUD DA BUD
HANG ON!
I got something like that with my clothes...
UNTISS
HOW COME MY CLOTHES DIDN'T COME WITH ANY OF THOSE POUCH THINGYS?
GONNA OPEN A TAB?
SO YOU CAN ORDER MORE DRINKS?
YES!

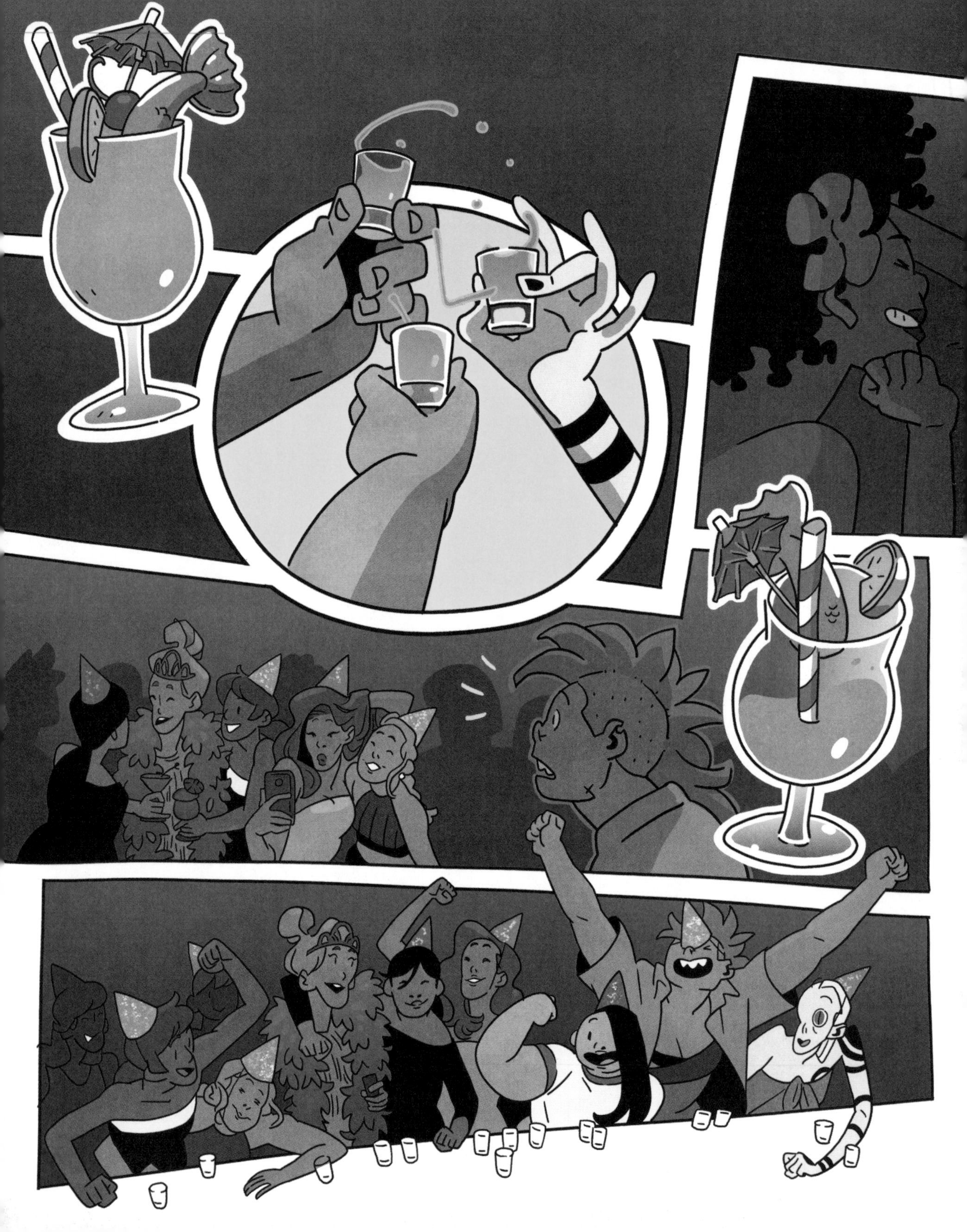

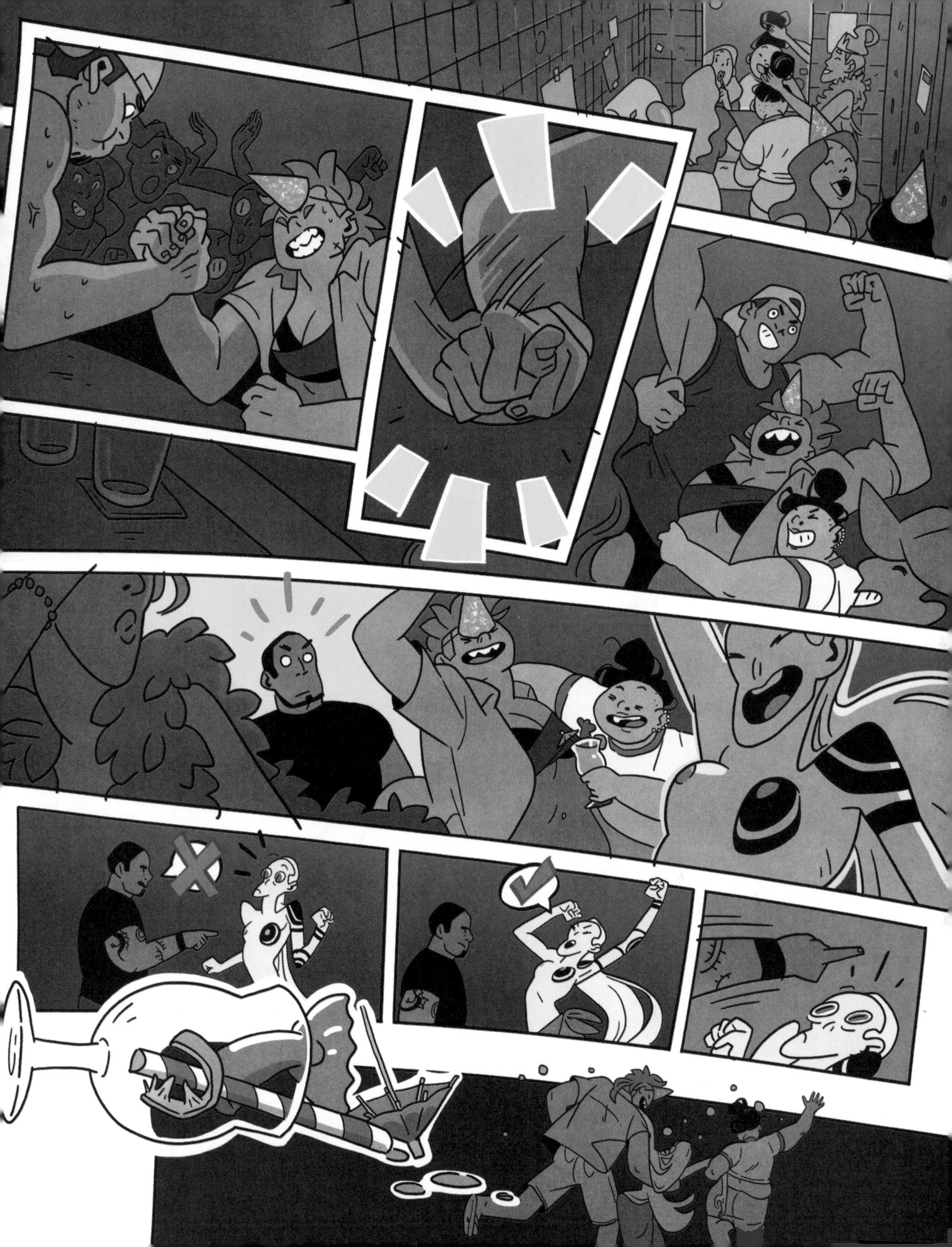

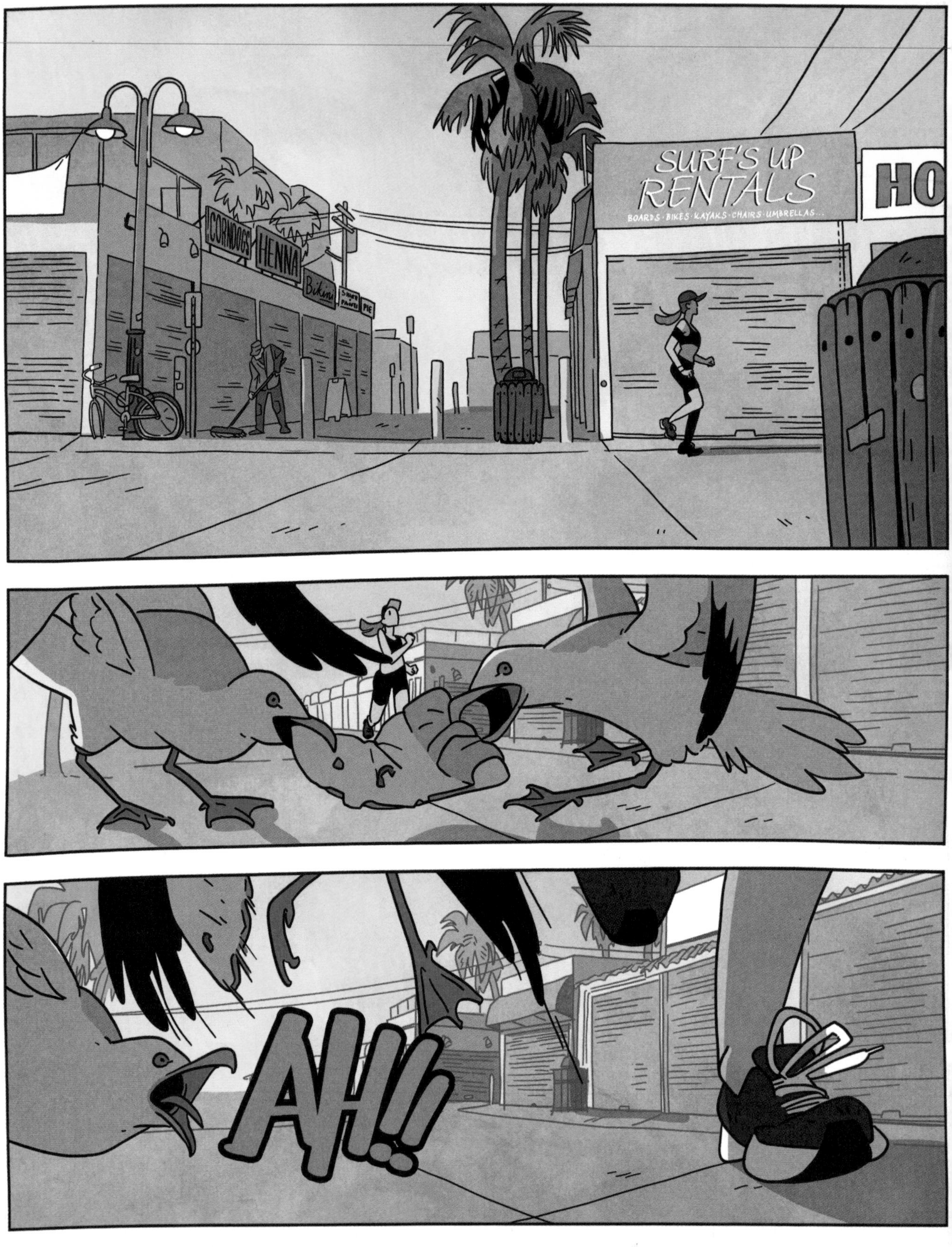
CORNDOGS
HENNA
Bikini
PIE
SURF'S UP
RENTALS
BOARDS · BIKES · KAYAKS · CHAIRS · UMBRELLAS...
AH!!

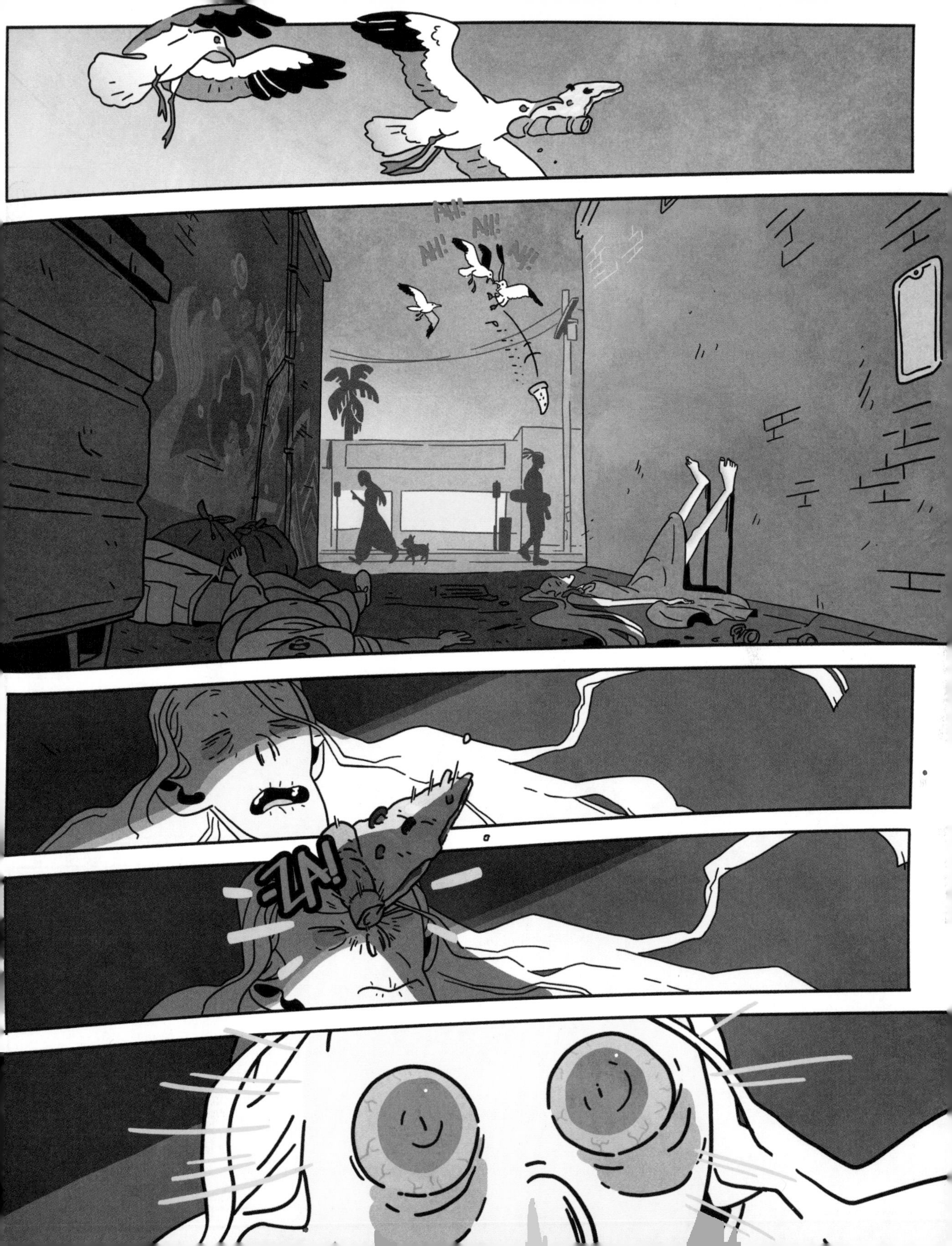

AH!
AH!
AH!
AH!
-ZA!

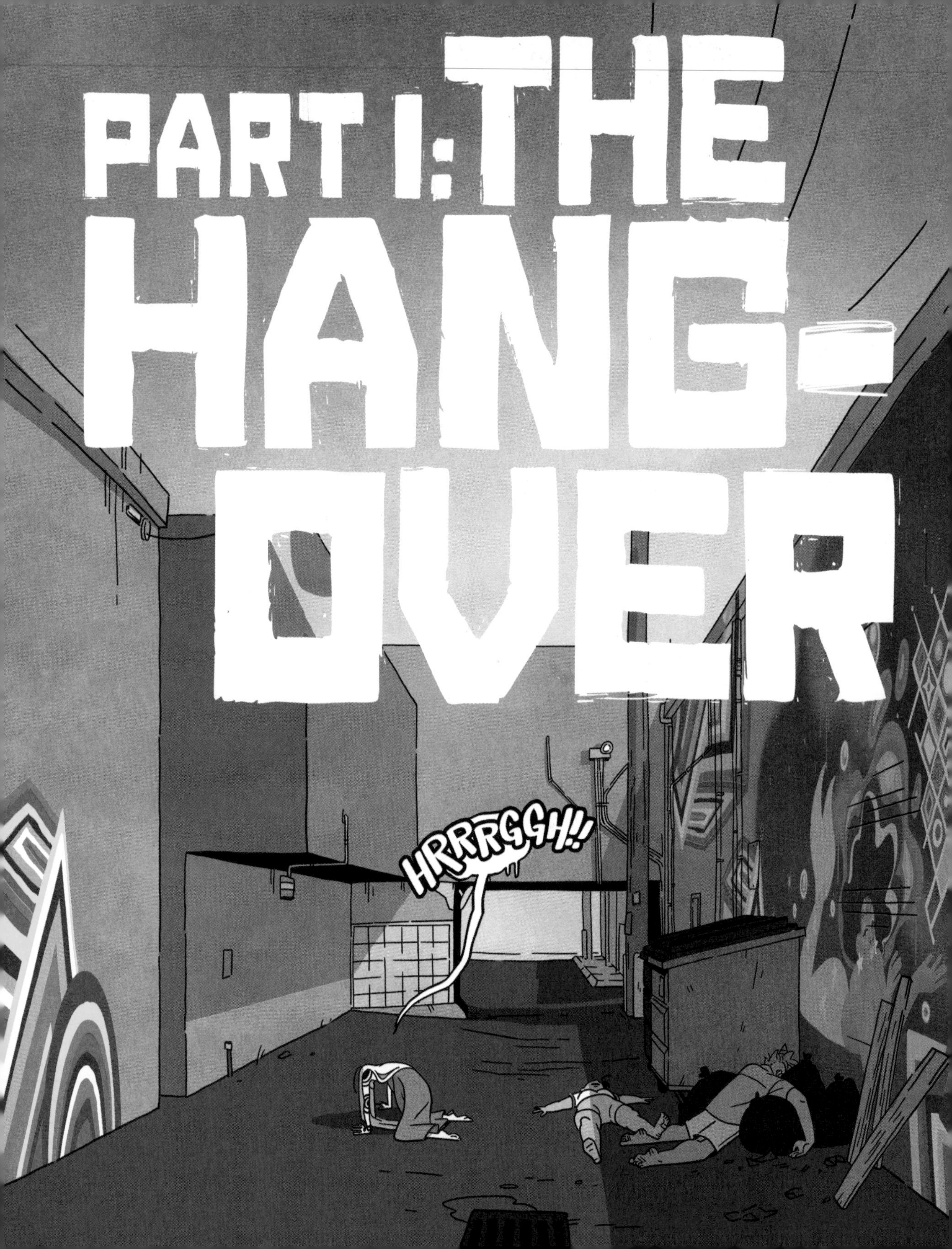
PART 1: THE HANG-OVER
HRRRGGH!!

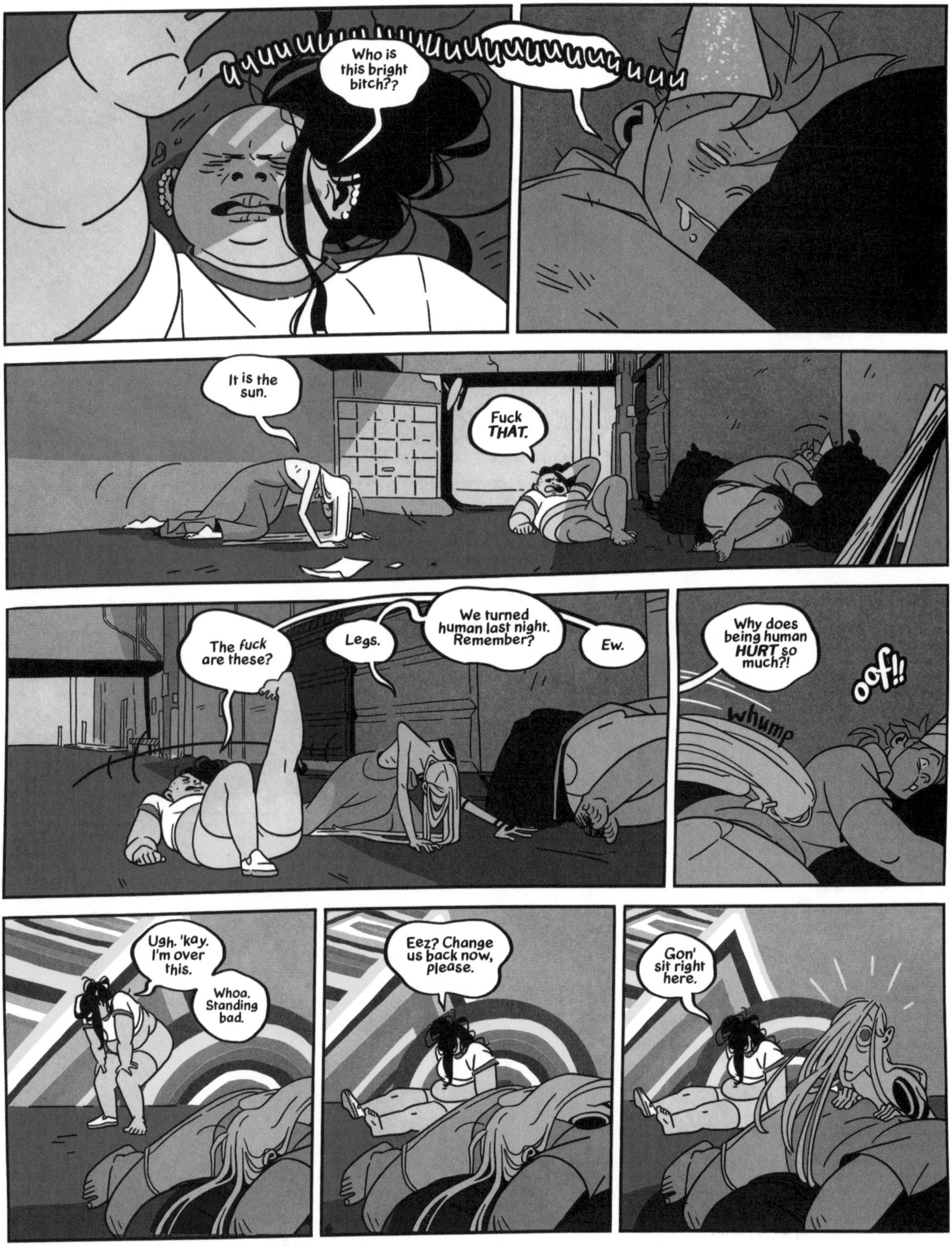
uuuuuuuuuuuuuuuuuuuuuuuuuuuuu
Who is this bright bitch??
It is the sun.
Fuck THAT.
The fuck are these?
Legs.
We turned human last night. Remember?
Ew.
Why does being human HURT so much?!
oof!!
whump
Ugh. 'kay. I'm over this.
Whoa. Standing bad.
Eez? Change us back now, please.
Gon' sit right here.

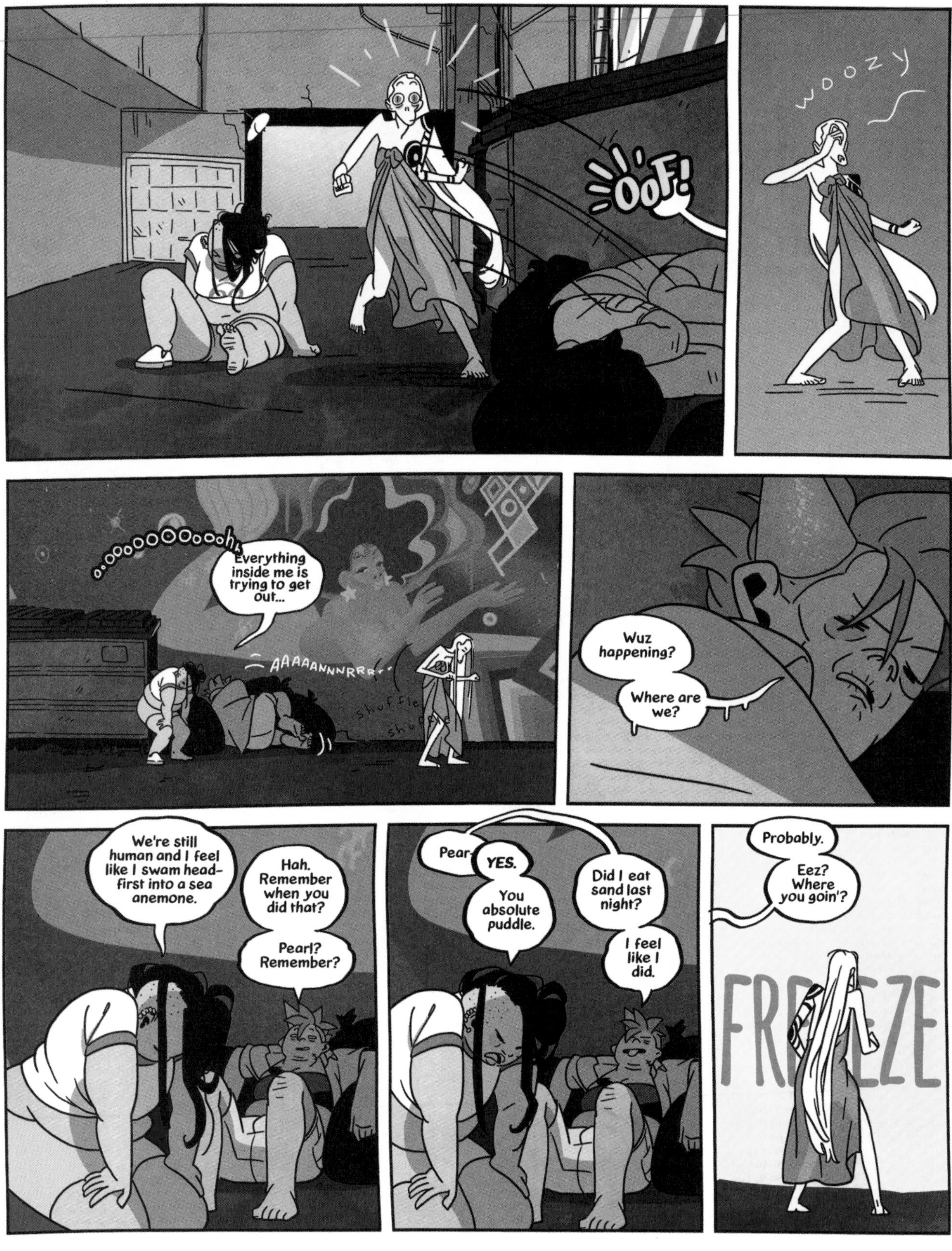
OOF!
WOOZY
o.ooooOOOOooo.h
Everything inside me is trying to get out...
AAAAANNNRRR
shuffle shuffle
Wuz happening?
Where are we?
We're still human and I feel like I swam head-first into a sea anemone.
Hah. Remember when you did that?
Pearl? Remember?
Pear-
YES.
You absolute puddle.
Did I eat sand last night?
I feel like I did.
Probably.
Eez? Where you goin'?
FREEZE

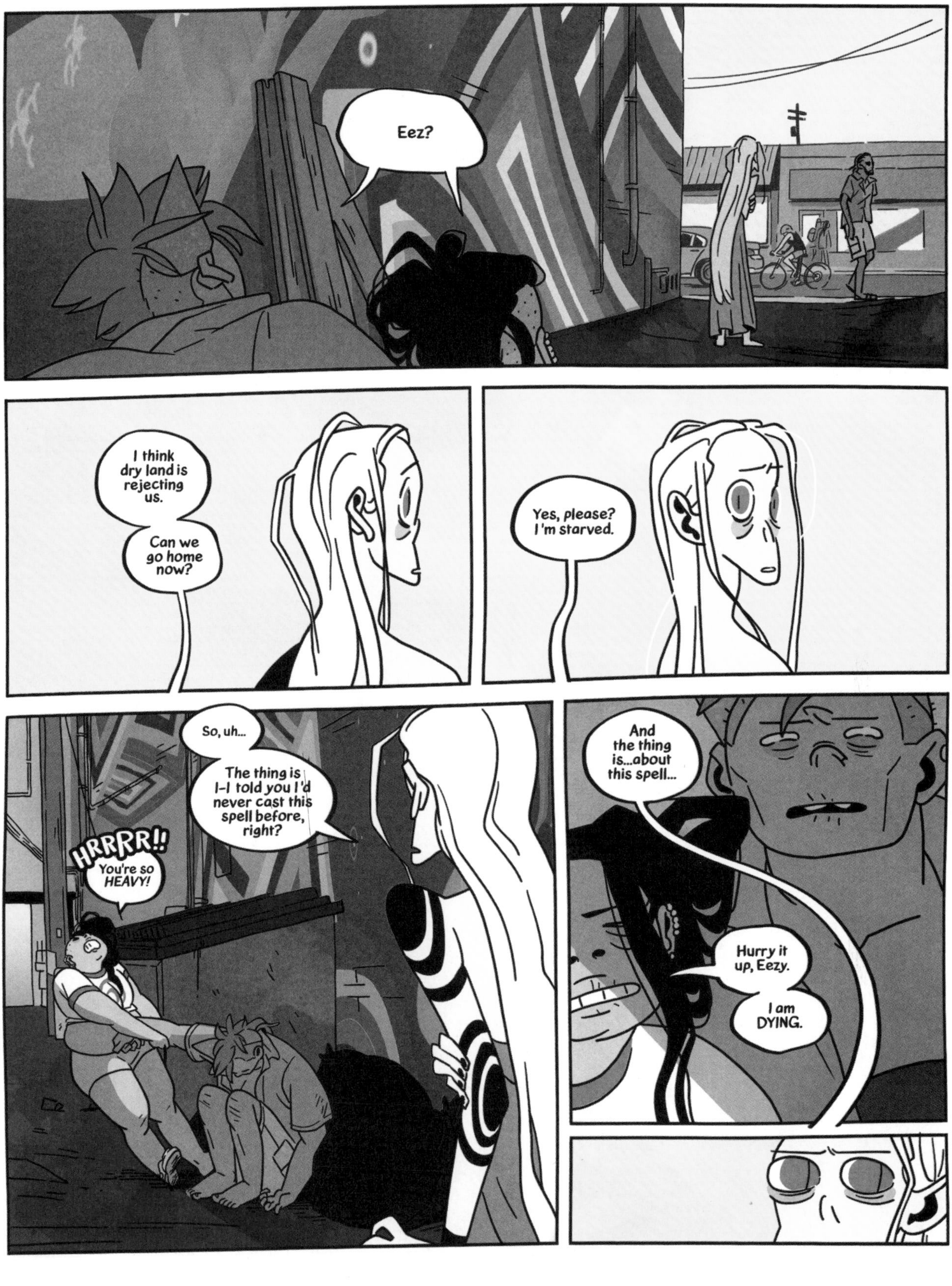
Eez?
I think dry land is rejecting us.
Can we go home now?
Yes, please? I'm starved.
So, uh...
The thing is I-I told you I'd never cast this spell before, right?
HRRRR!! You're so HEAVY!
And the thing is...about this spell...
Hurry it up, Eezy.
I am DYING.

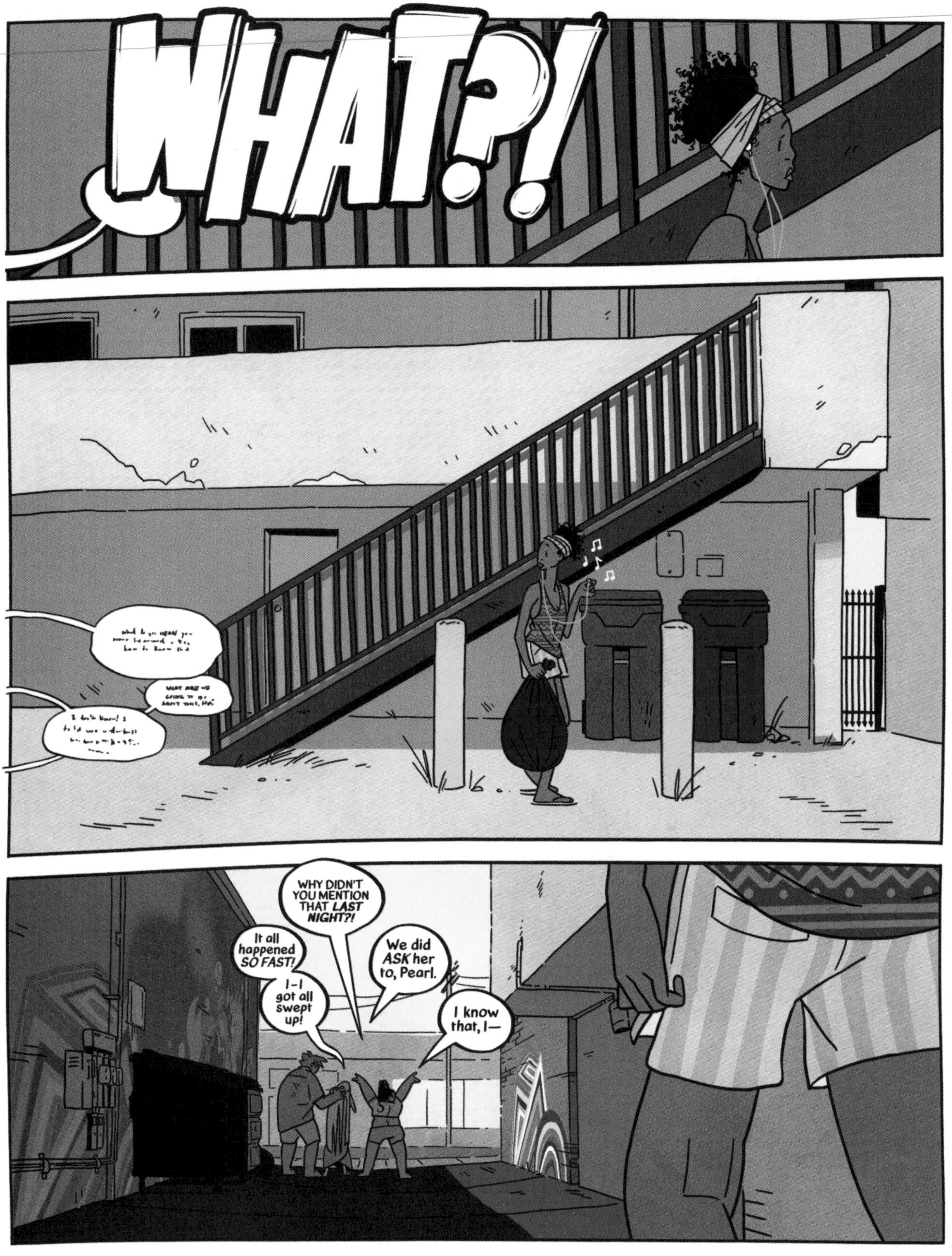
WHAT?!
WHY DIDN'T YOU MENTION THAT LAST NIGHT?!
It all happened SO FAST!
I-I got all swept up!
We did ASK her to, Pearl.
I know that, I—

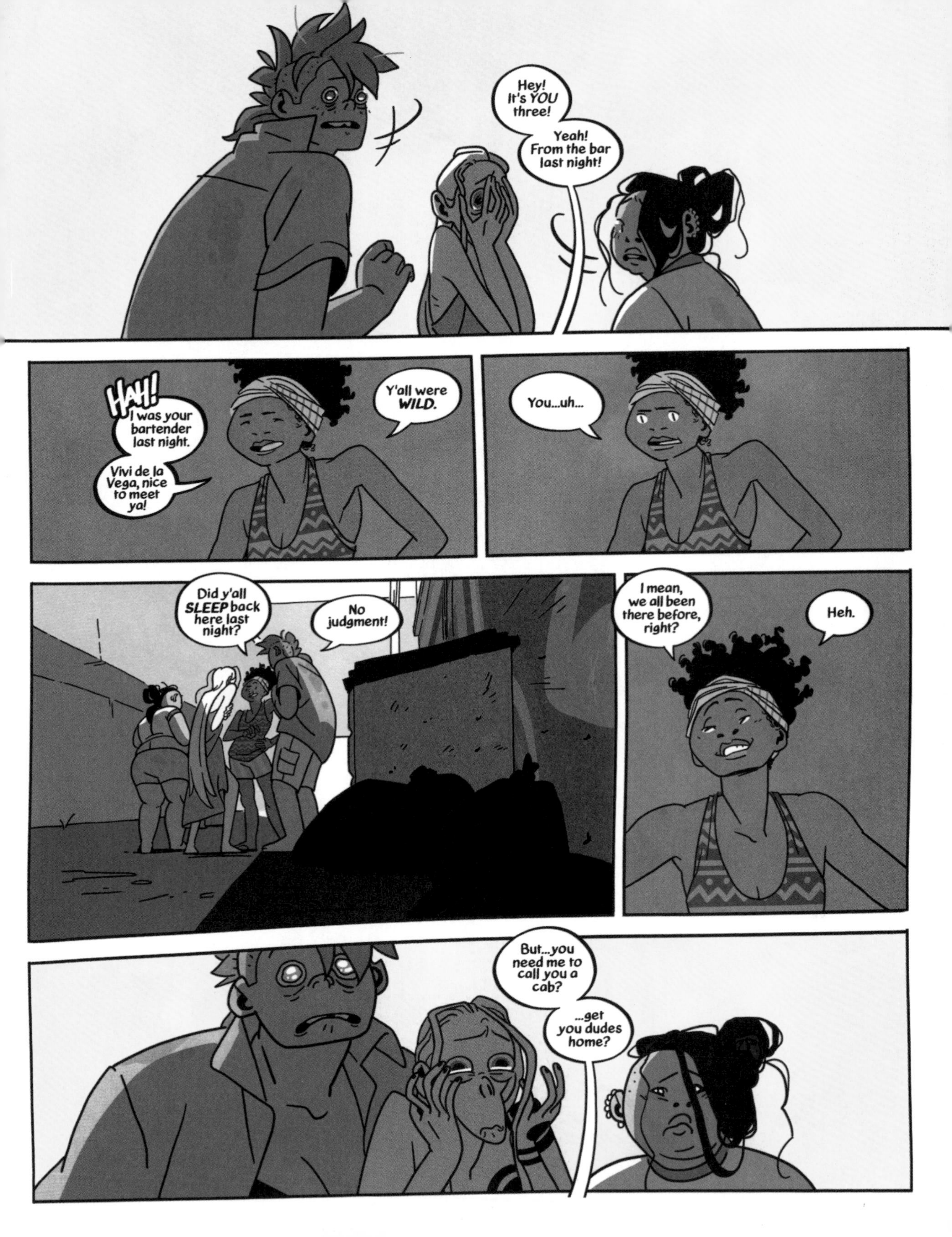
Hey! It's YOU three!
Yeah! From the bar last night!
HAH! I was your bartender last night.
Vivi de la Vega, nice to meet ya!
Y'all were WILD.
You...uh...
Did y'all SLEEP back here last night?
No judgment!
I mean, we all been there before, right?
Heh.
But...you need me to call you a cab?
...get you dudes home?

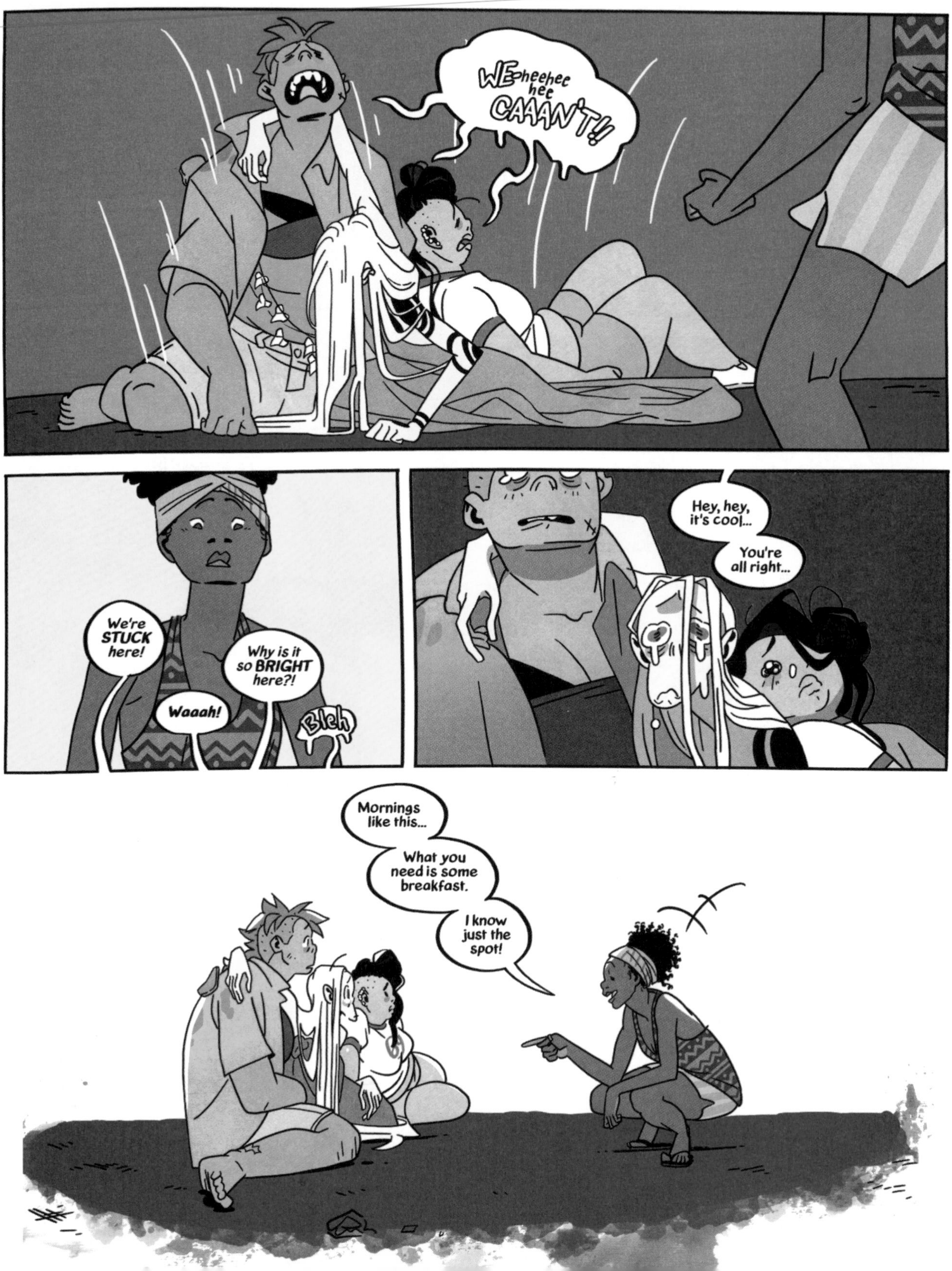
WE-heehee hee CAAAN'T!!
We're STUCK here!
Waaah!
Why is it so BRIGHT here?!
Bleh
Hey, hey, it's cool...
You're all right...
Mornings like this...
What you need is some breakfast.
I know just the spot!

Hang tight! I gotta grab better shoes!

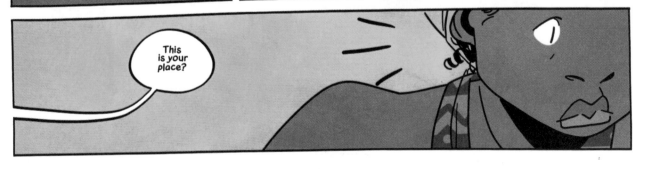

This is your place?

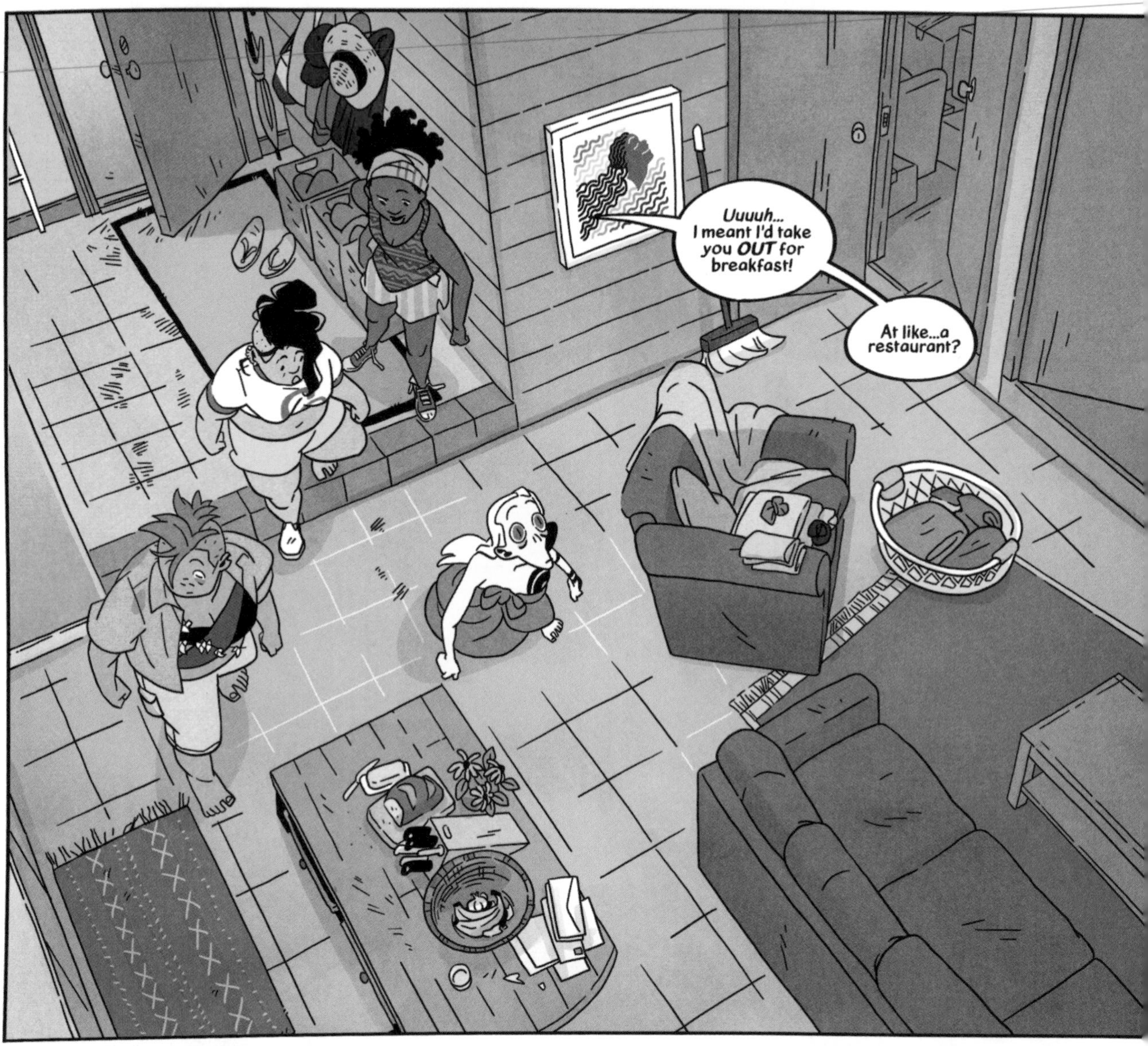
Uuuuh... I meant I'd take you OUT for breakfast!
At like...a restaurant?

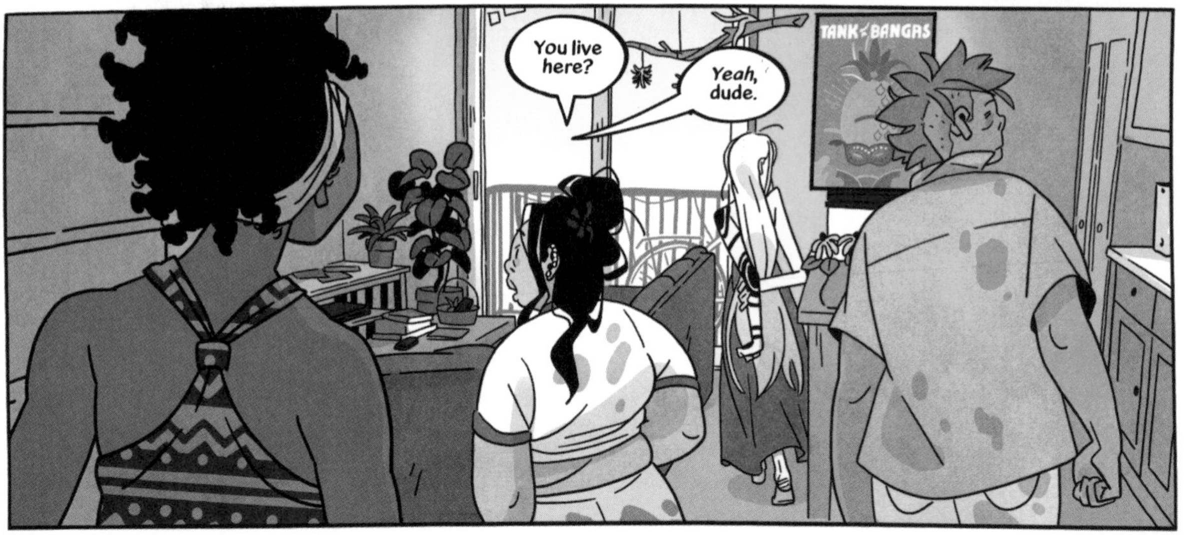
TANK ⚡ BANGAS
You live here?
Yeah, dude.

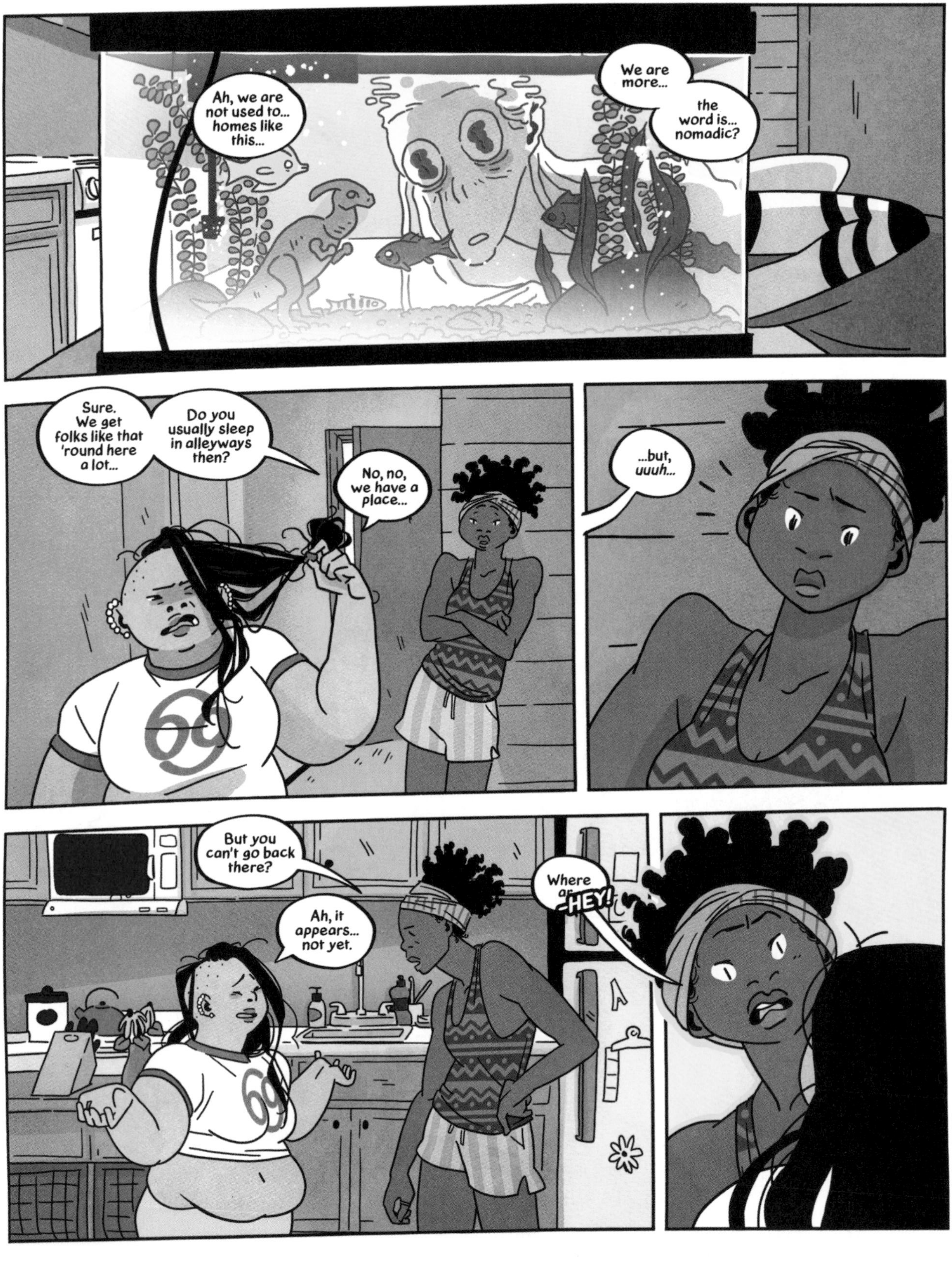

Ah, we are not used to... homes like this...
We are more...
the word is... nomadic?
Sure. We get folks like that 'round here a lot...
Do you usually sleep in alleyways then?
No, no, we have a place...
...but, uuuh...
But you can't go back there?
Ah, it appears... not yet.
Where ar—
HEY!

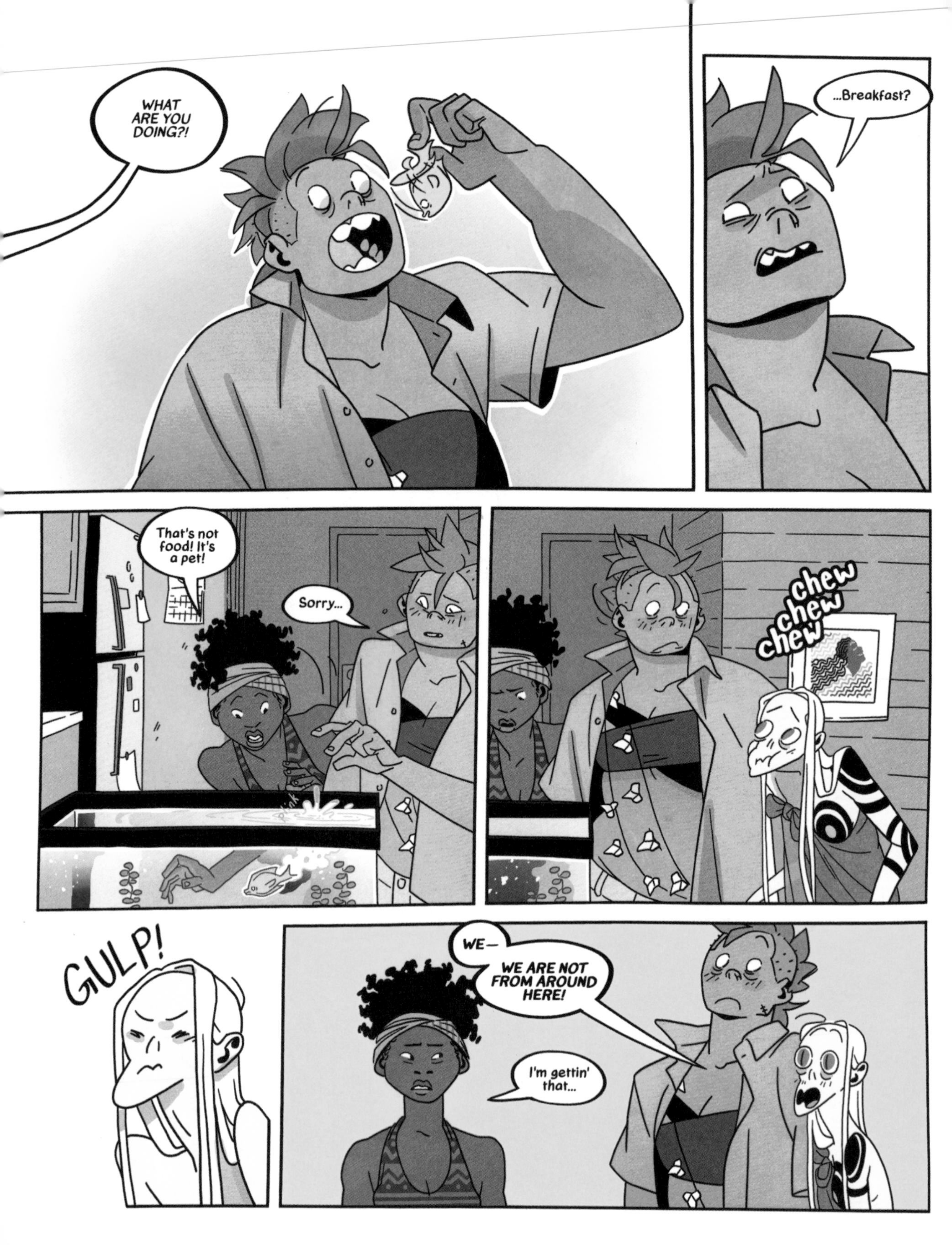

WHAT ARE YOU DOING?!
...Breakfast?
That's not food! It's a pet!
Sorry...
chew chew chew
GULP!
WE—
WE ARE NOT FROM AROUND HERE!
I'm gettin' that...

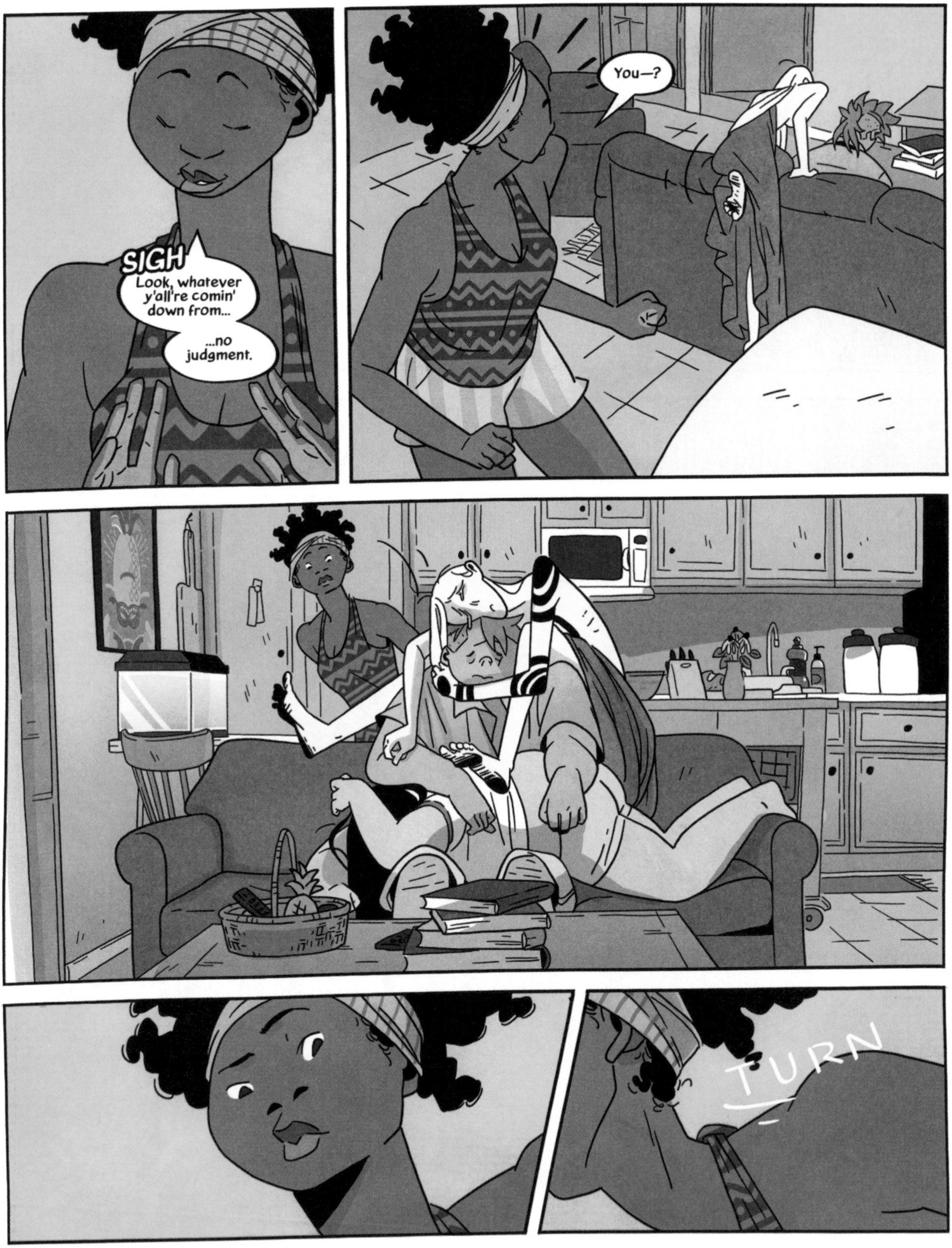
SIGH
Look, whatever y'all're comin' down from...
...no judgment.
You—?
TURN

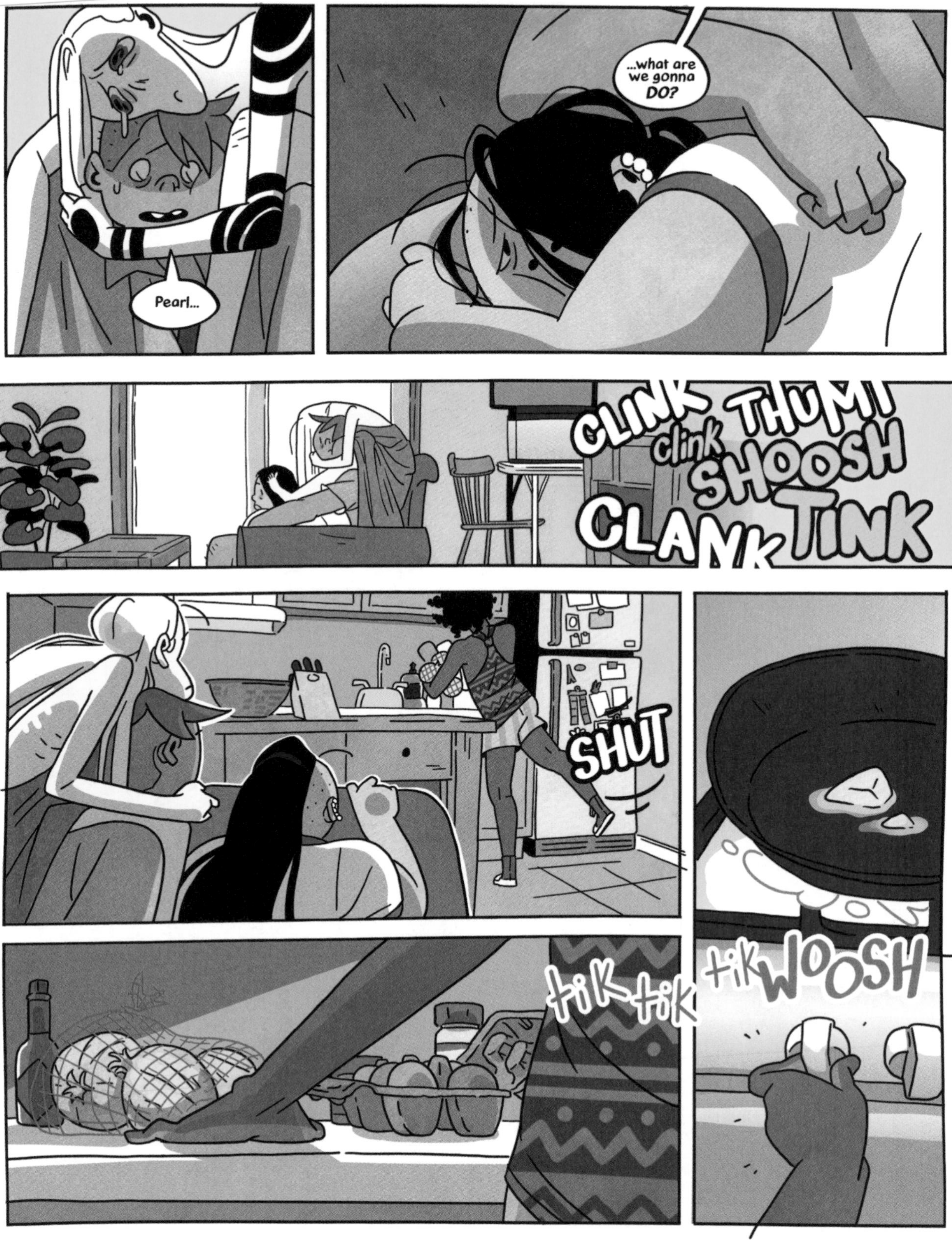
Pearl...
...what are we gonna DO?
CLINK clink THUMP SHOOSH
CLANK TINK
SHUT
tik tik tik WOOSH

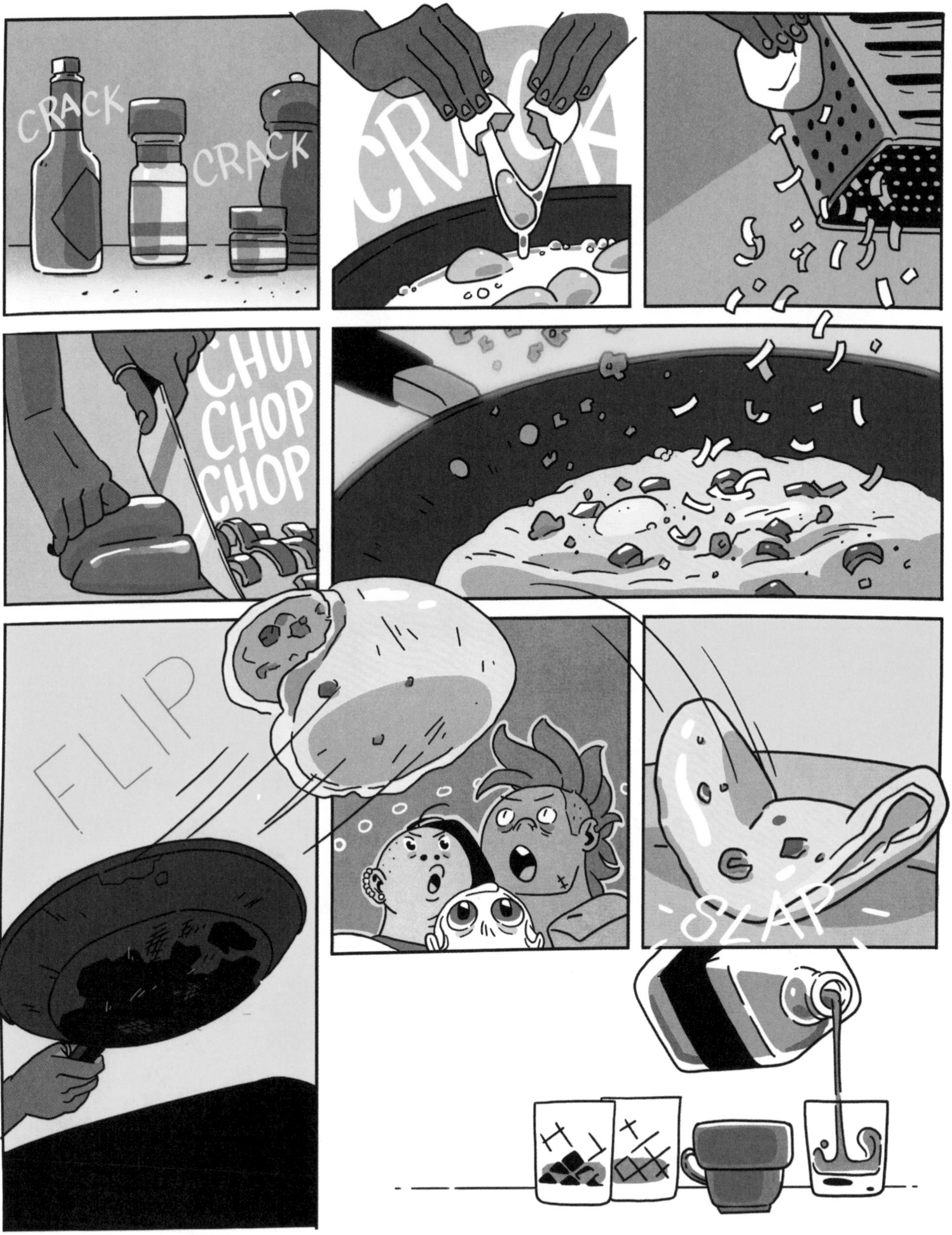
CRACK
CRACK
CRACK
CHOP
CHOP
CHOP
FLIP
SLAP

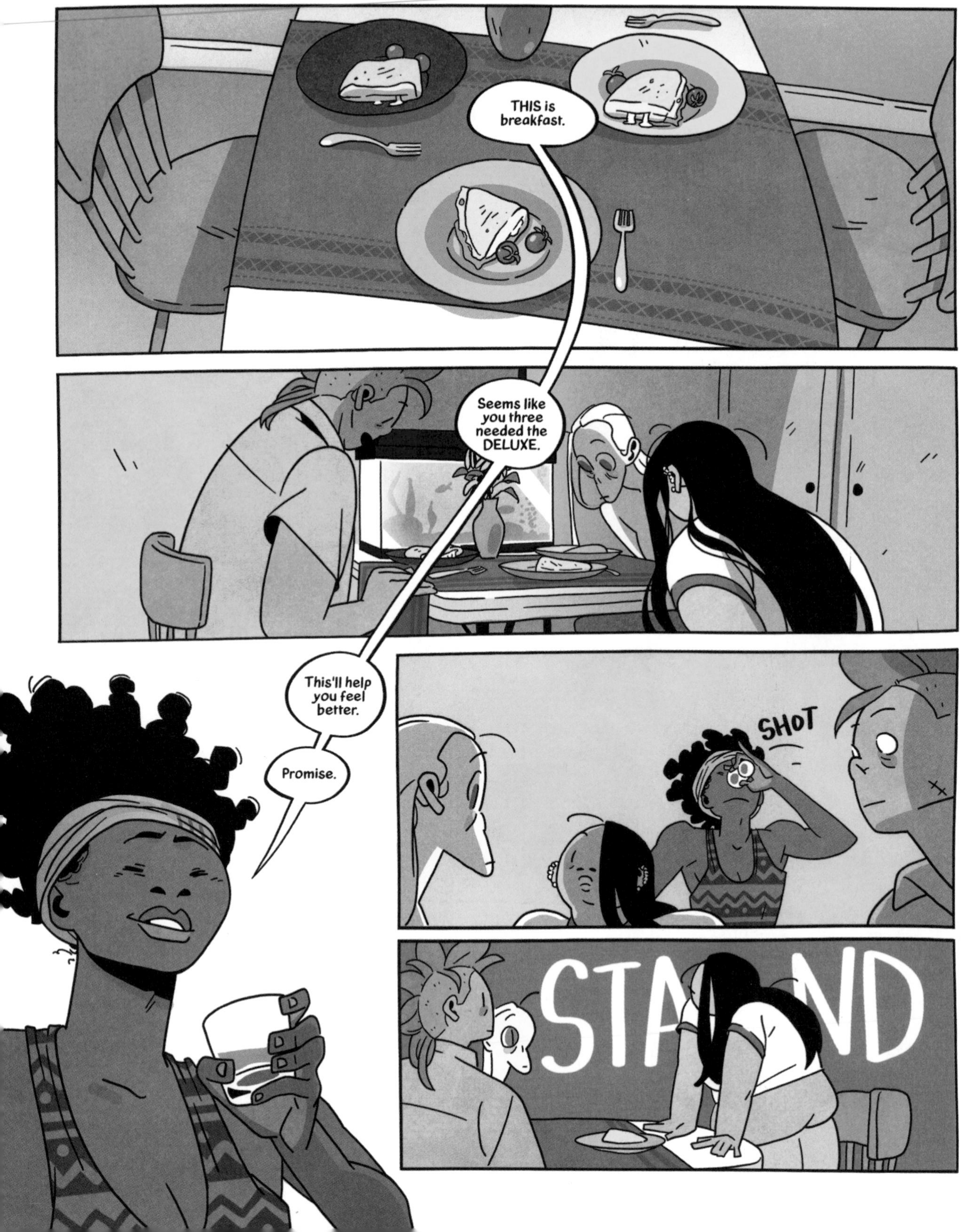
THIS is breakfast.
Seems like you three needed the DELUXE.
This'll help you feel better.
Promise.
SHOT
STAND

gulp

WE—

—are mermaids.

...usually.

We—

HULLP!!

Up until yesterday.

Eez turned us human, but—

—I only **JUST LEARNED** the spell!

I don't know how to **BREAK** it!

This is our first time as humans, and—

—I'm sure you can imagine—

—we're feeling pretty dried out.

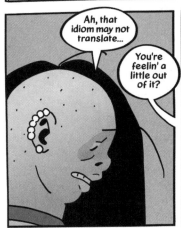

Ah, that idiom may not translate...

You're feelin' a little out of it?

"Out of it."

YES!

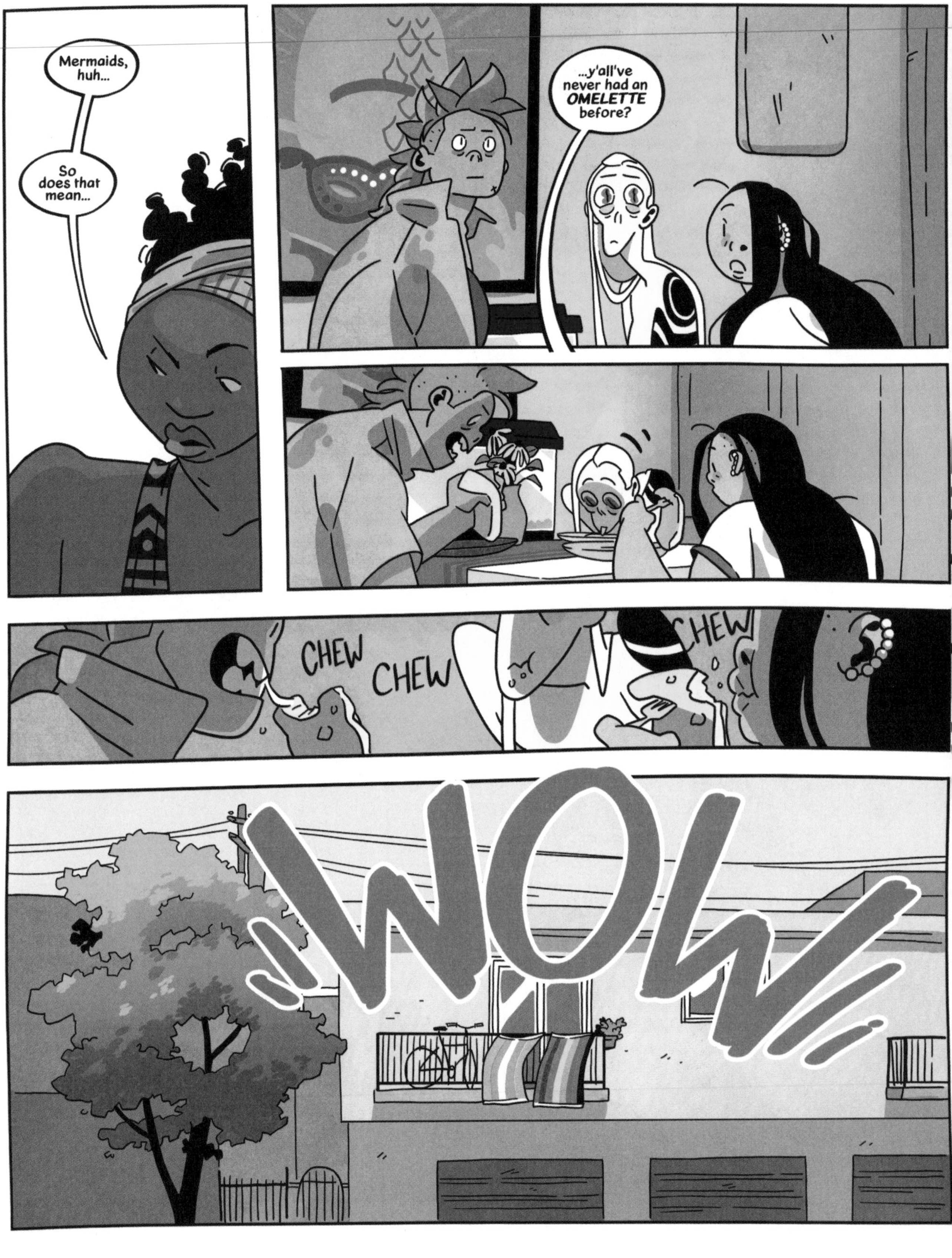
Mermaids, huh...
So does that mean...
...y'all've never had an **OMELETTE** before?
CHEW
CHEW
CHEW
WOW

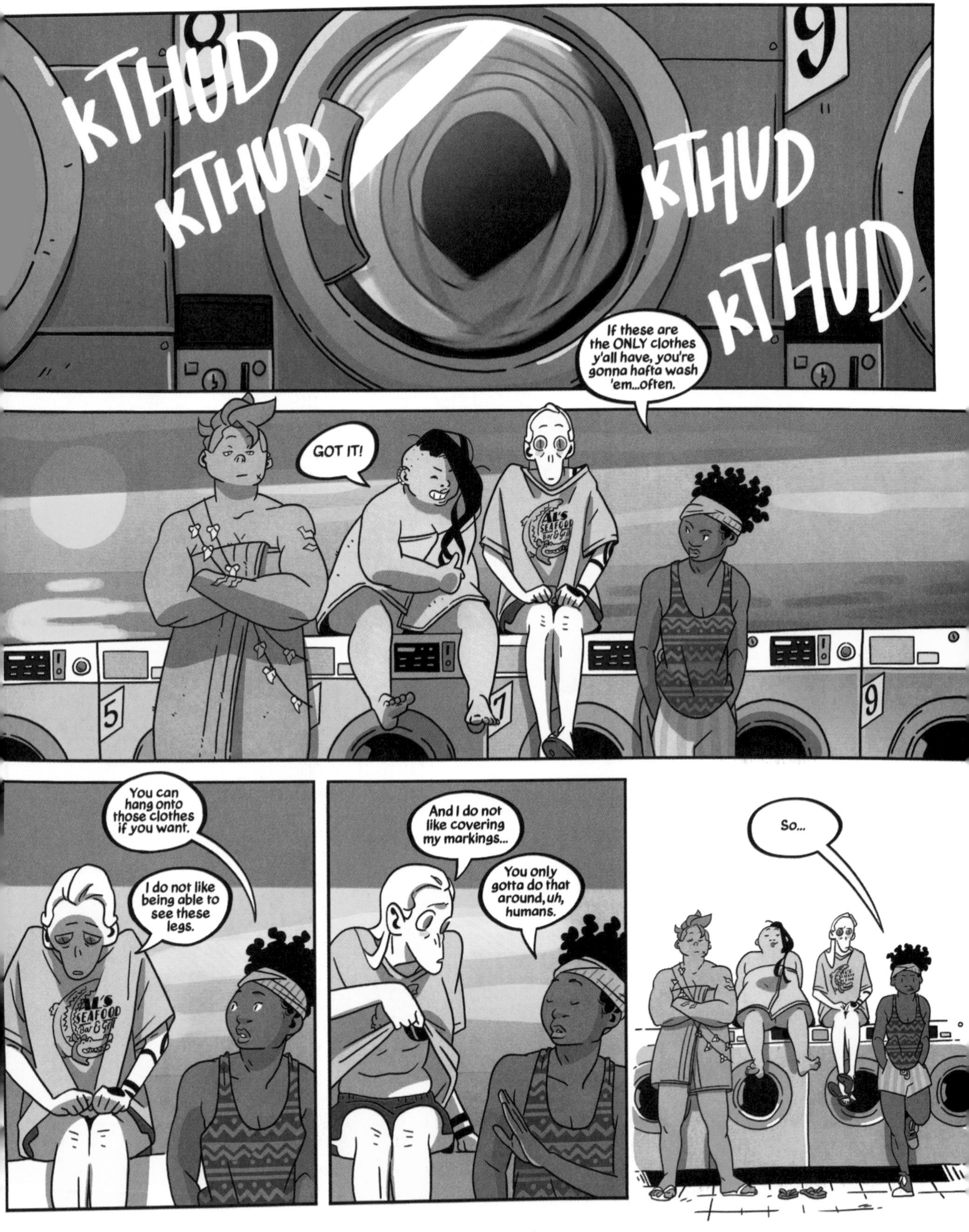
kTHUD kTHUD
kTHUD kTHUD
If these are the ONLY clothes y'all have, you're gonna hafta wash 'em...often.
GOT IT!
You can hang onto those clothes if you want.
I do not like being able to see these legs.
And I do not like covering my markings...
You only gotta do that around, uh, humans.
So...

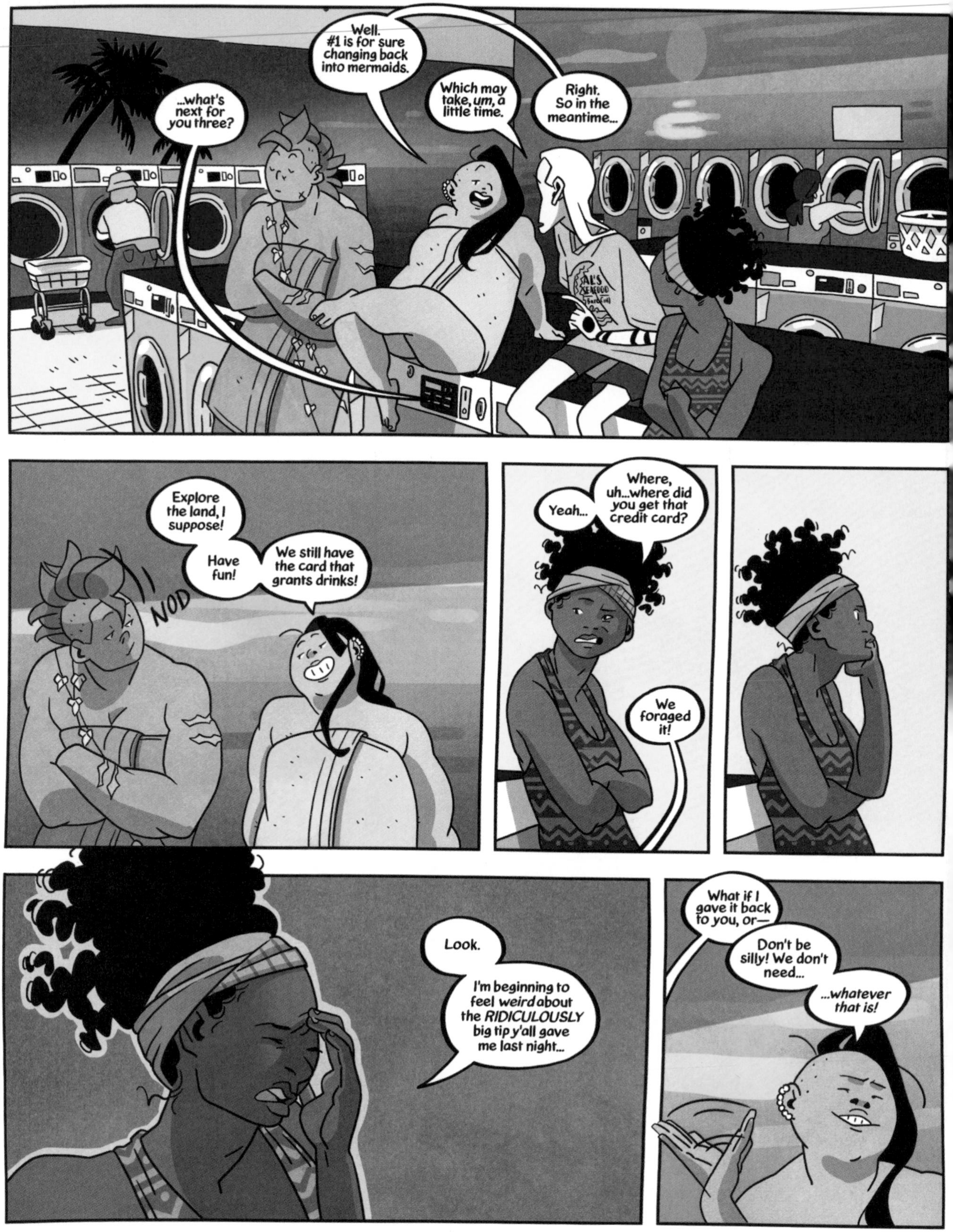
...what's next for you three?
Well. #1 is for sure changing back into mermaids.
Which may take, *um*, a little time.
Right. So in the meantime...
AL'S SEAFOOD
Explore the land, I suppose!
Have fun!
We still have the card that grants drinks!
NOD
Yeah...
Where, uh...where did you get that credit card?
We foraged it!
Look.
I'm beginning to feel *weird* about the *RIDICULOUSLY* big tip y'all gave me last night...
What if I gave it back to you, or—
Don't be silly! We don't need...
...whatever that is!

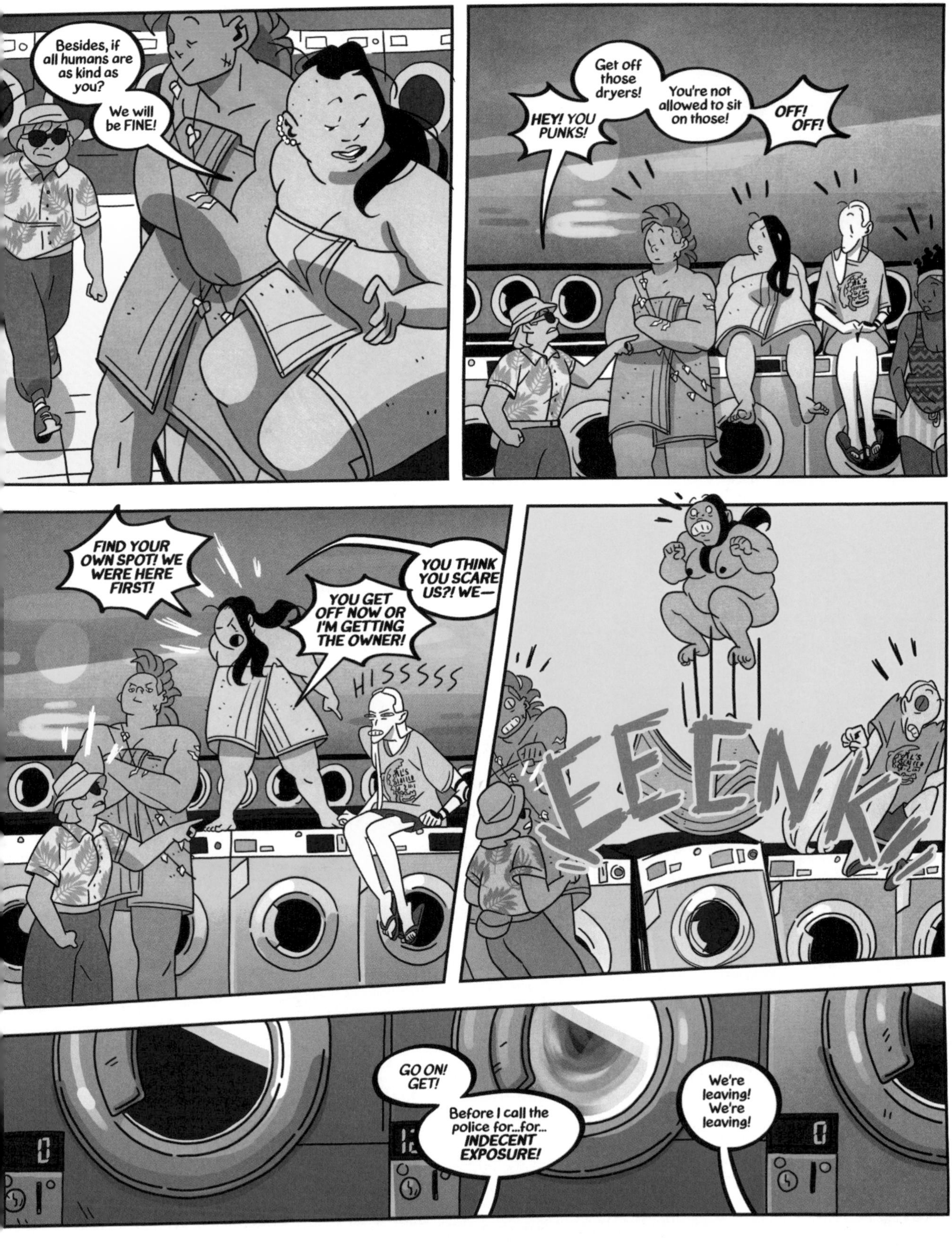
Besides, if all humans are as kind as you?
We will be FINE!
HEY! YOU PUNKS!
Get off those dryers!
You're not allowed to sit on those!
OFF! OFF!
FIND YOUR OWN SPOT! WE WERE HERE FIRST!
YOU GET OFF NOW OR I'M GETTING THE OWNER!
YOU THINK YOU SCARE US?! WE—
HISSSSS
EEENK!
GO ON! GET!
Before I call the police for...for... INDECENT EXPOSURE!
We're leaving! We're leaving!

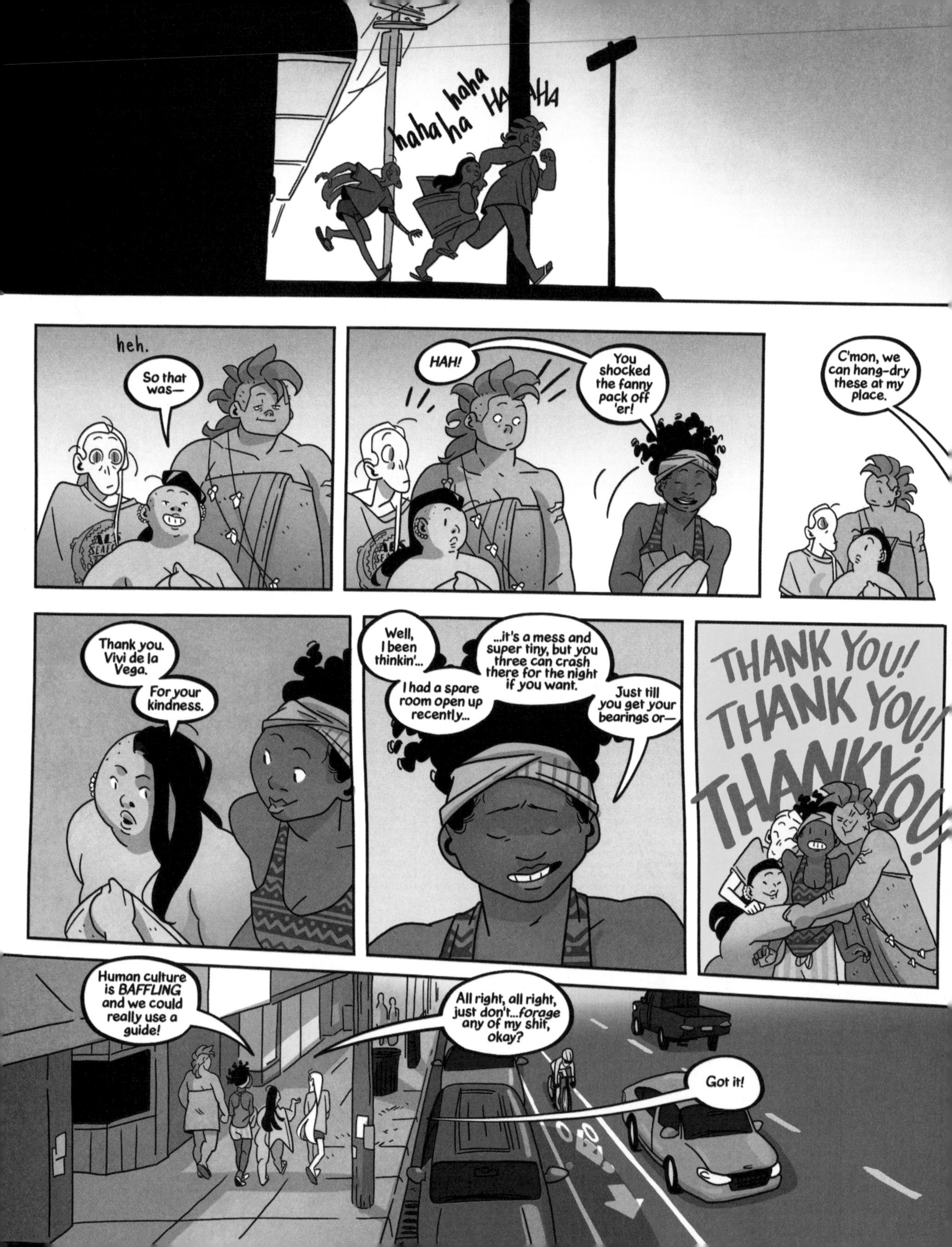

haha haha haha HAHAHA
heh.
So that was—
HAH!
You shocked the fanny pack off 'er!
C'mon, we can hang-dry these at my place.
Thank you. Vivi de la Vega.
For your kindness.
Well, I been thinkin'...
I had a spare room open up recently...
...it's a mess and super tiny, but you three can crash there for the night if you want.
Just till you get your bearings or—
THANK YOU! THANK YOU! THANK YOU!
Human culture is *BAFFLING* and we could really use a guide!
All right, all right, just don't...*forage* any of my shit, okay?
Got it!

THE NEXT DAY...

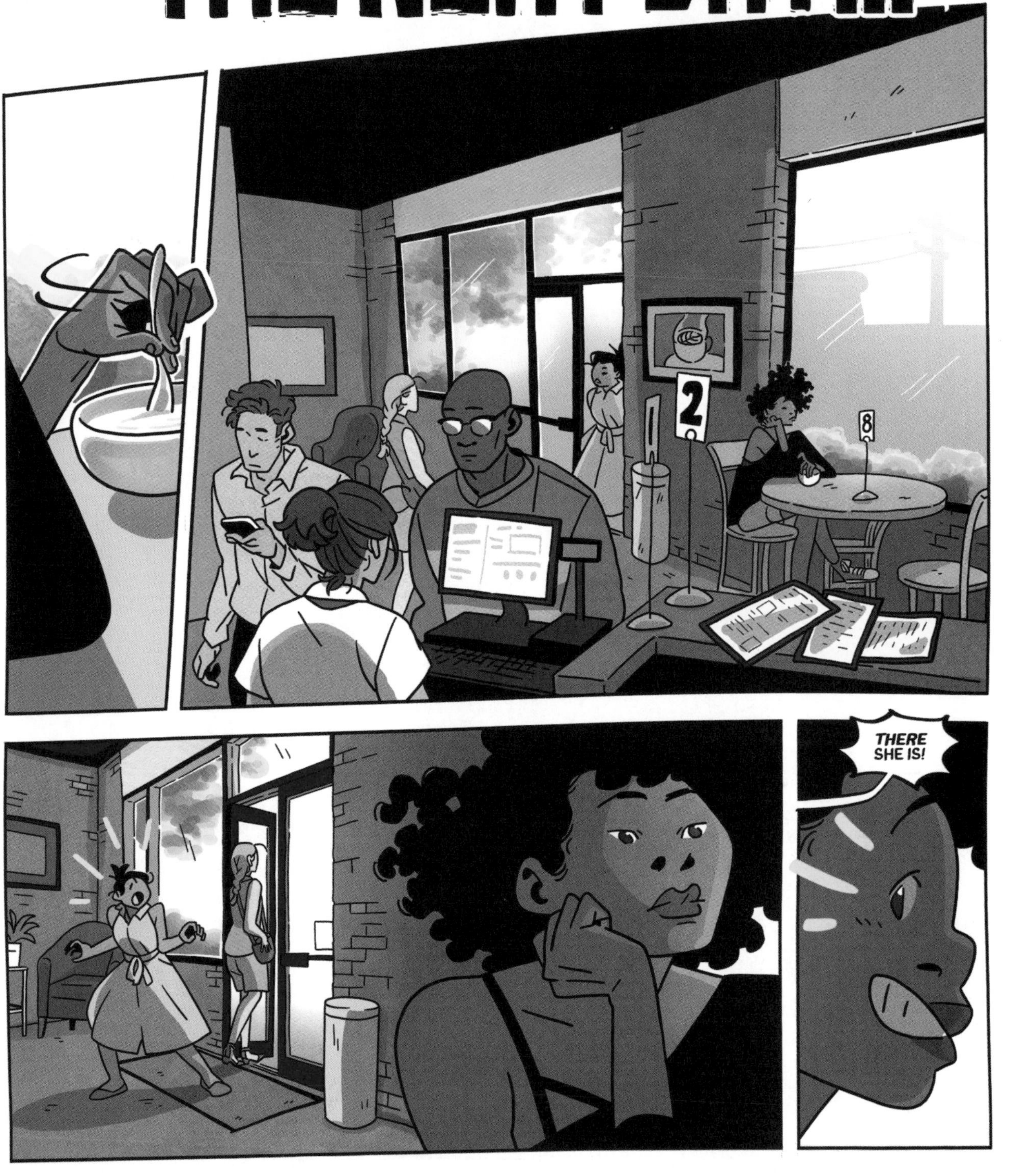
2
8
THERE SHE IS!

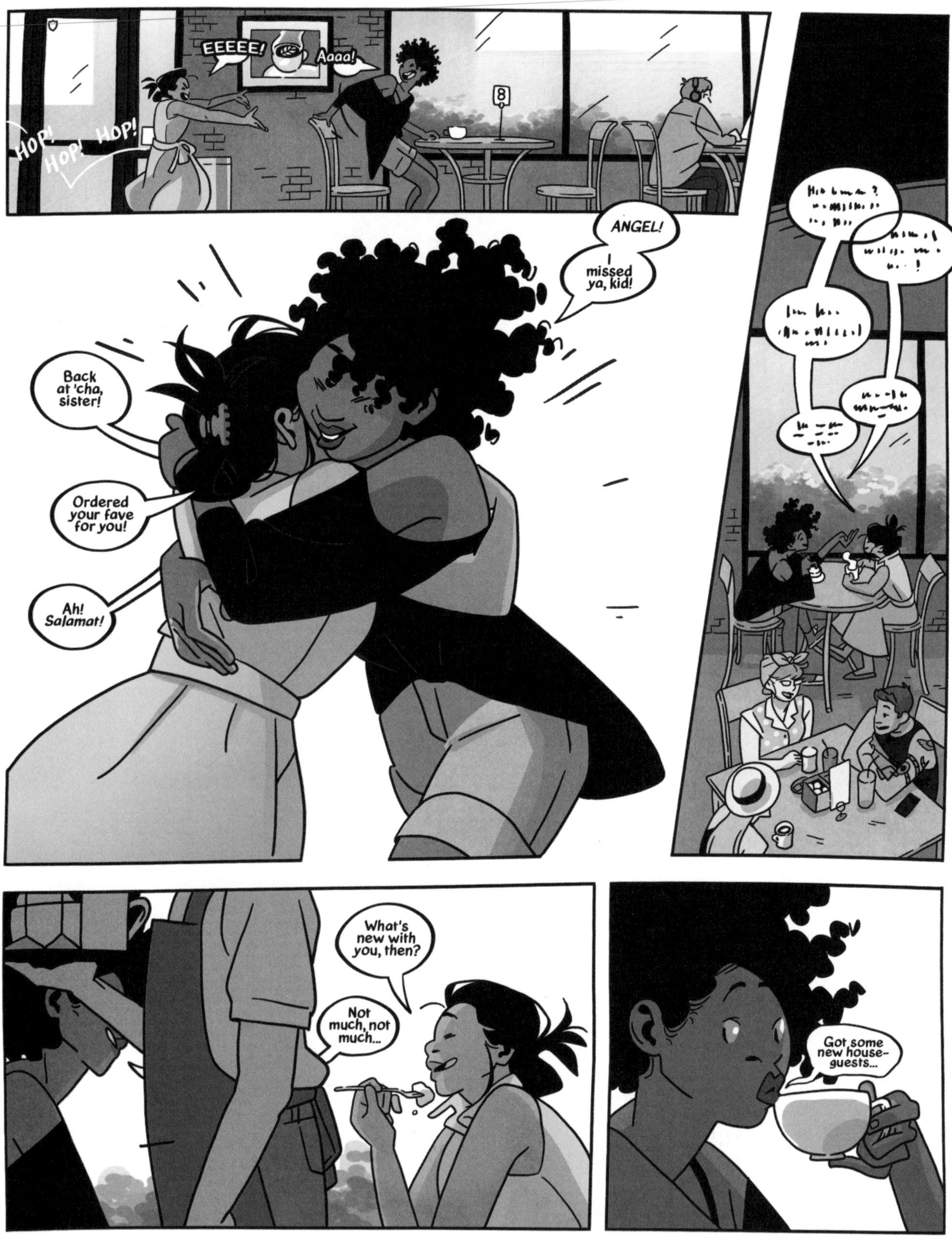
HOP! HOP! HOP!
EEEEE!
Aaaa!
ANGEL!
I missed ya, kid!
Back at 'cha, sister!
Ordered your fave for you!
Ah! Salamat!
What's new with you, then?
Not much, not much...
Got some new house-guests...

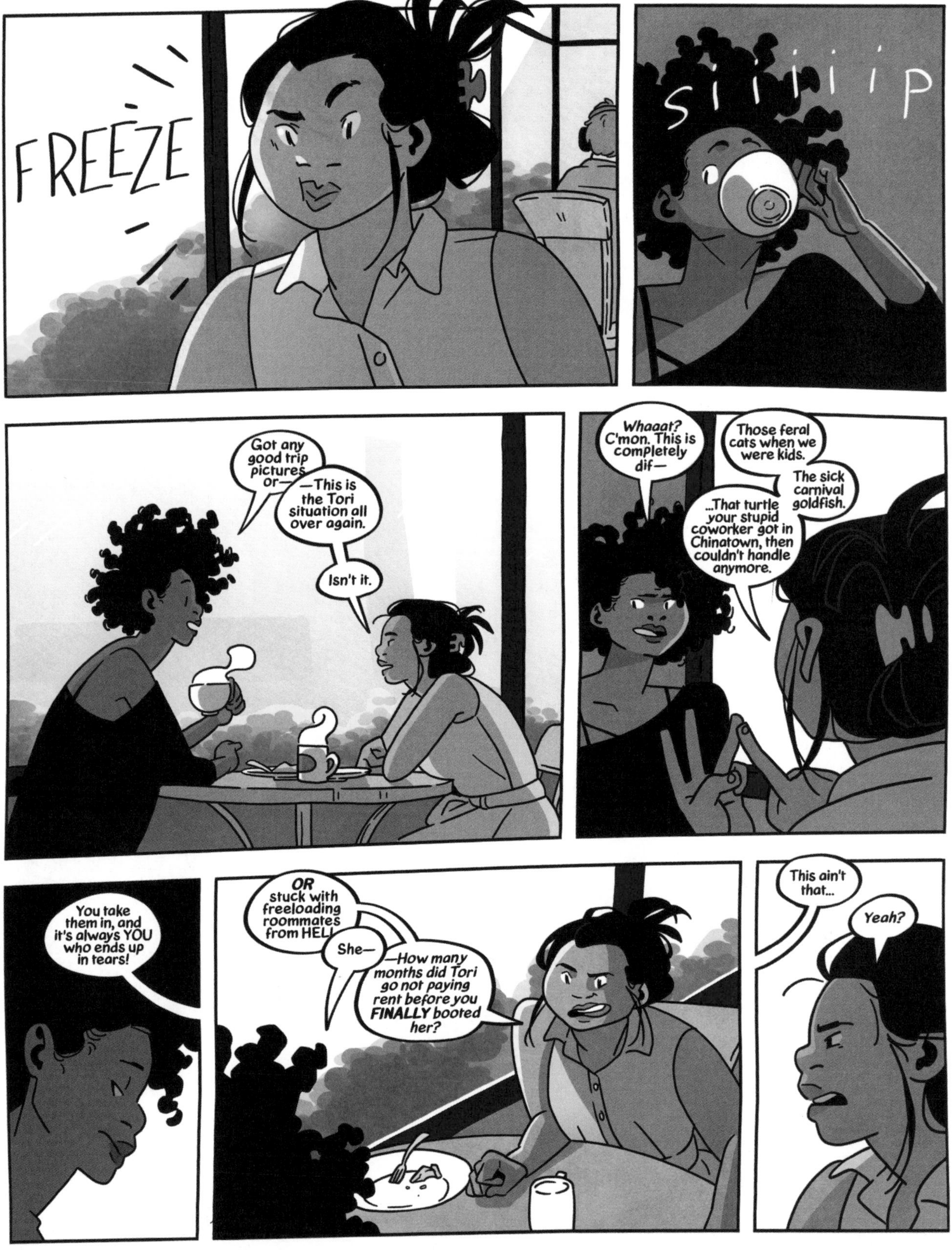
FREEZE
siiiiip
Got any good trip pictures or—
—This is the Tori situation all over again.
Isn't it.
Whaaat? C'mon. This is completely dif—
Those feral cats when we were kids.
The sick carnival goldfish.
...That turtle your stupid coworker got in Chinatown, then couldn't handle anymore.
You take them in, and it's always YOU who ends up in tears!
OR stuck with freeloading roommates from HELL
She—
—How many months did Tori go not paying rent before you FINALLY booted her?
This ain't that...
Yeah?

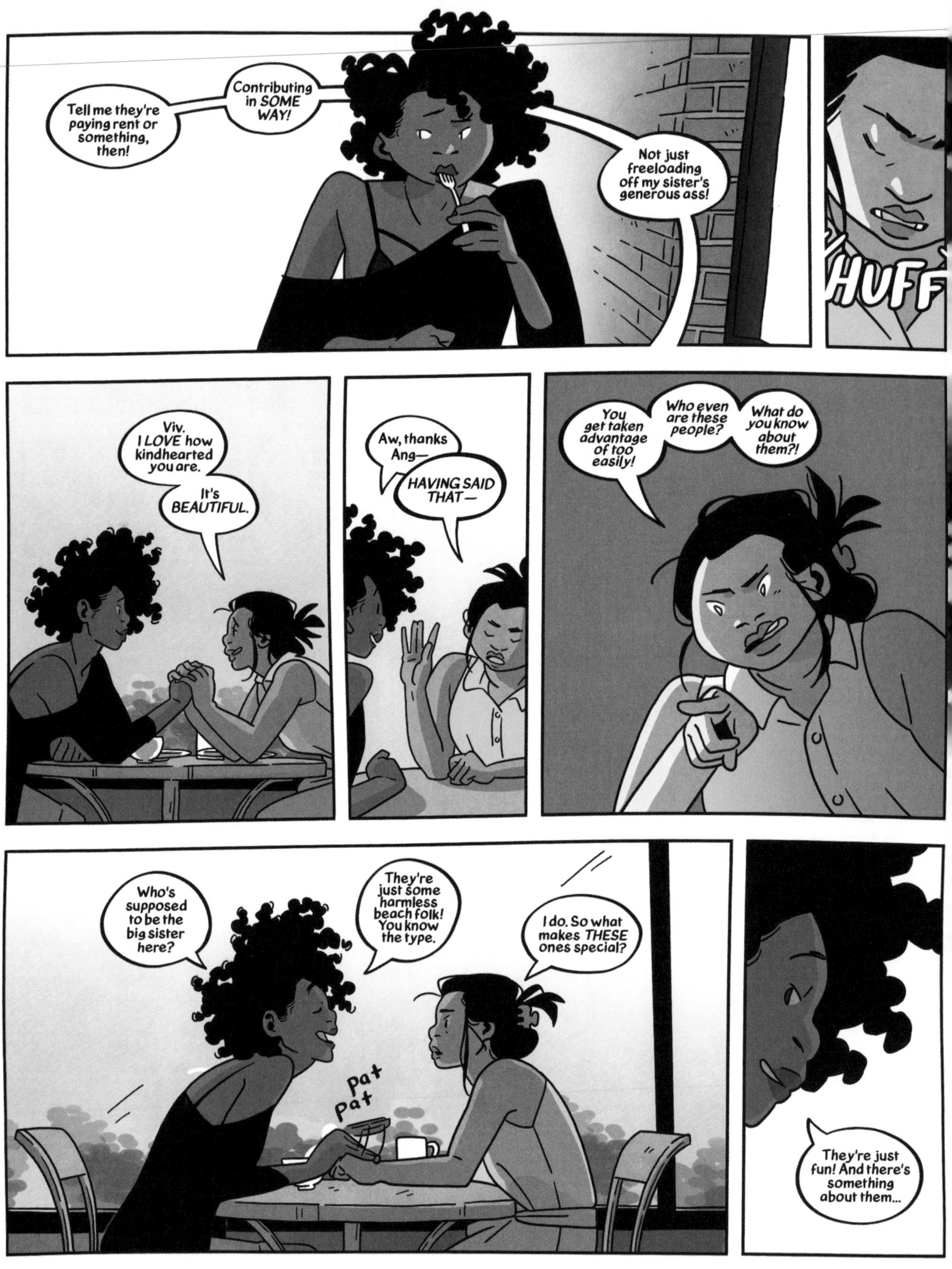

Tell me they're paying rent or something, then!
Contributing in SOME WAY!
Not just freeloading off my sister's generous ass!
HUFF
Viv. I LOVE how kindhearted you are.
It's BEAUTIFUL.
Aw, thanks Ang—
HAVING SAID THAT—
You get taken advantage of too easily!
Who even are these people?
What do you know about them?!
Who's supposed to be the big sister here?
They're just some harmless beach folk! You know the type.
pat pat
I do. So what makes THESE ones special?
They're just fun! And there's something about them...

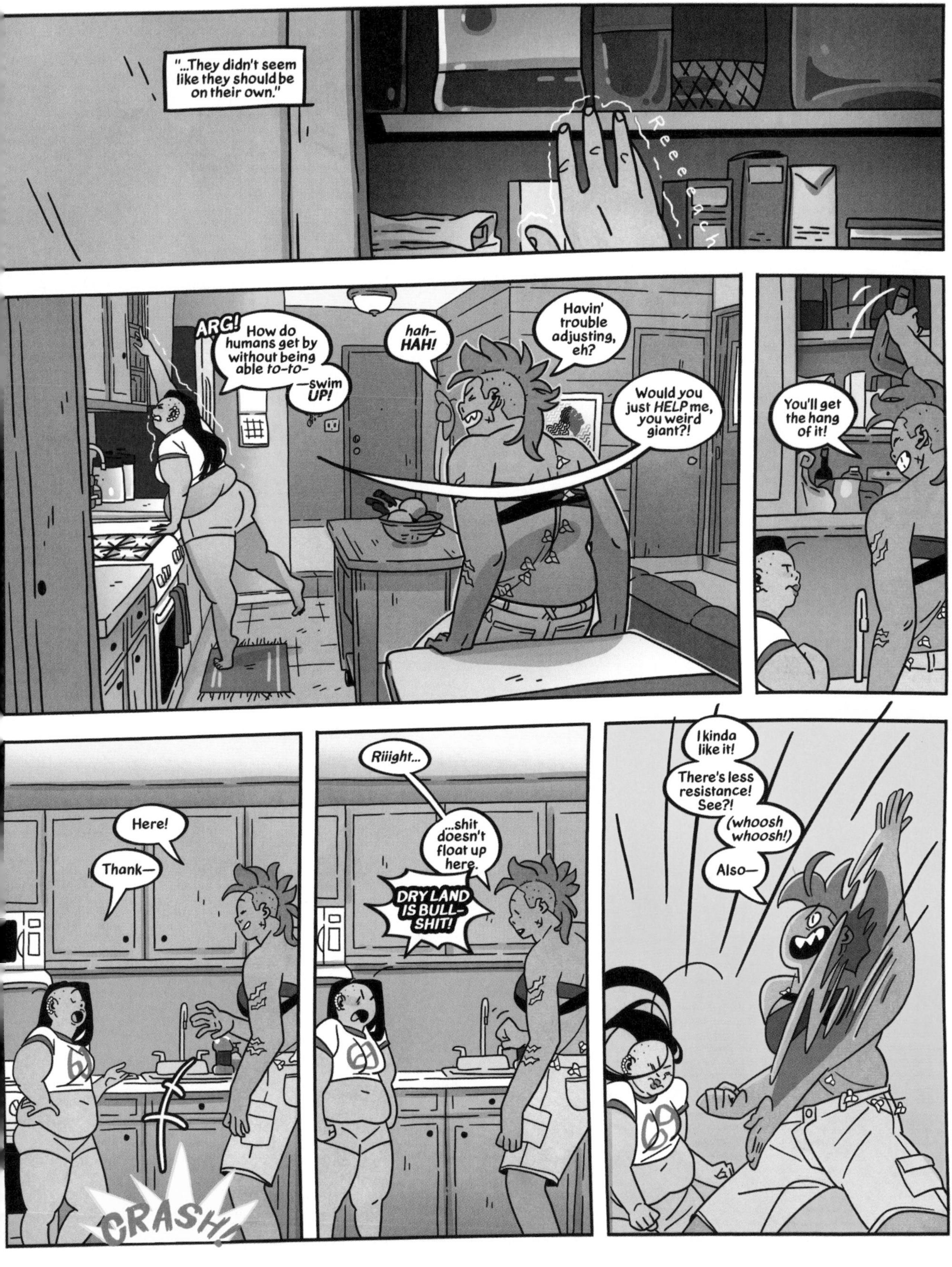
"...They didn't seem like they should be on their own."
Reeeeach
ARG!
How do humans get by without being able *to-to-*
—swim *UP!*
hah-*HAH!*
Havin' trouble adjusting, eh?
Would you just *HELP* me, you weird giant?!
You'll get the hang of it!
Here!
Thank—
CRASH!
Riiight...
...shit doesn't float up here.
DRY LAND IS BULL-SHIT!
I kinda like it!
There's less resistance! See?!
(whoosh whoosh!)
Also—

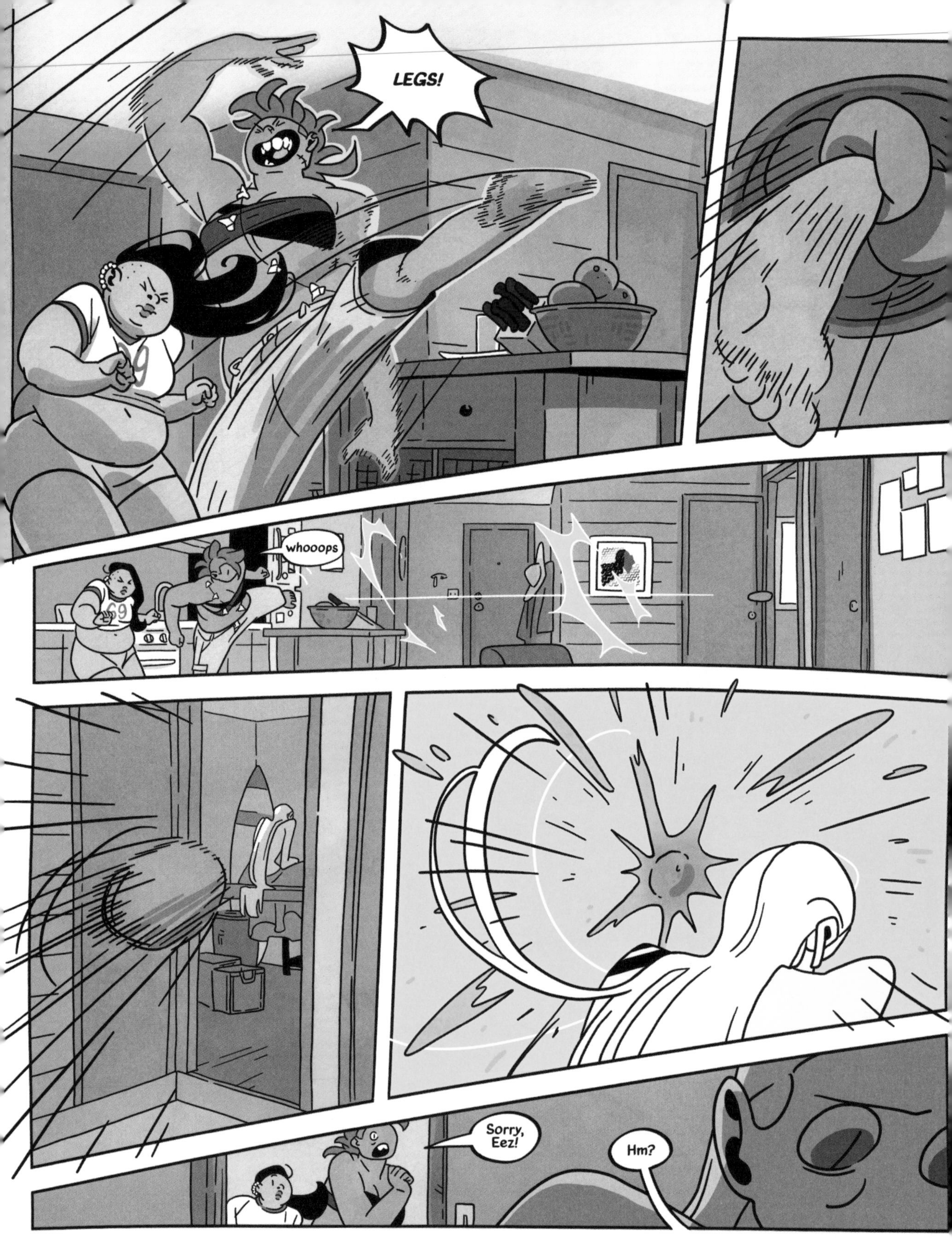
LEGS!
whoooops
Sorry, Eez!
Hm?

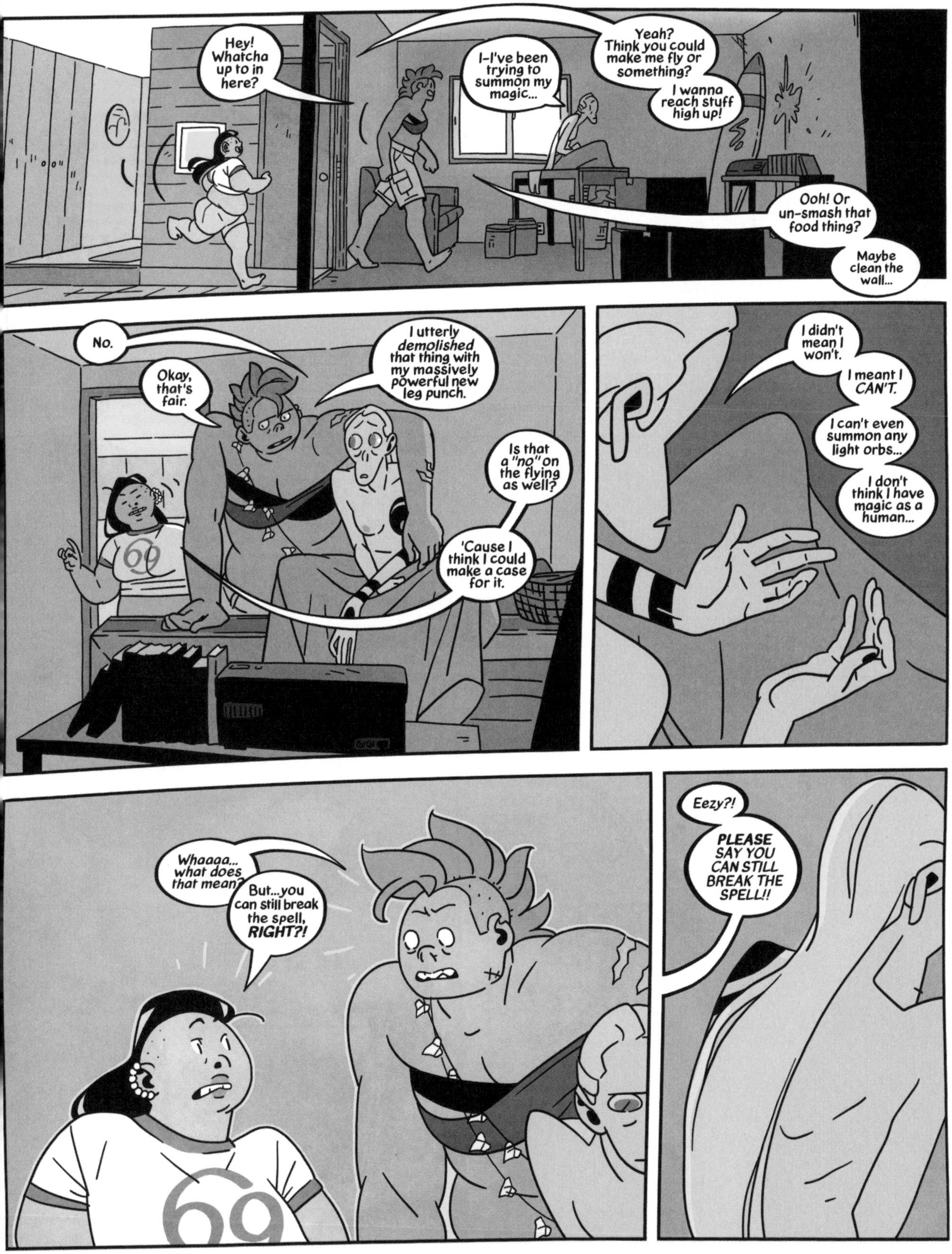
Hey! Whatcha up to in here?
I-I've been trying to summon my magic...
Yeah? Think you could make me fly or something?
I wanna reach stuff high up!
Ooh! Or un-smash that food thing?
Maybe clean the wall...
No.
Okay, that's fair.
I utterly *demolished* that thing with my massively powerful new leg punch.
Is that a *"no"* on the flying as well?
'Cause I think I could make a case for it.
I didn't mean I won't.
I meant I *CAN'T.*
I can't even summon any light orbs...
I don't think I have magic as a human...
Whaaaa... what does that mean?
But...you can still break the spell, ***RIGHT?!***
Eezy?!
PLEASE SAY YOU CAN STILL BREAK THE SPELL!!

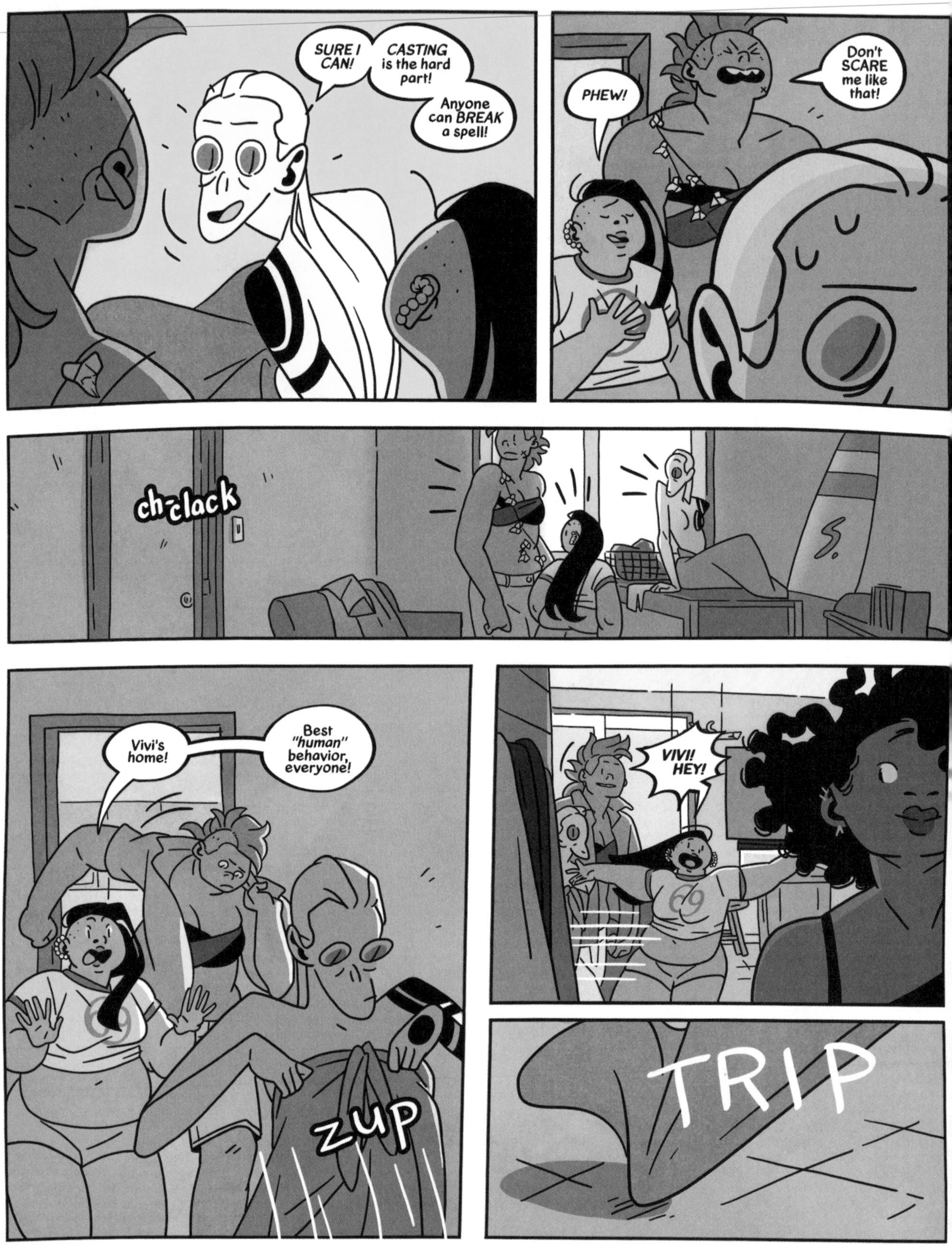
SURE I CAN!
CASTING is the hard part!
Anyone can BREAK a spell!
PHEW!
Don't SCARE me like that!
ch-clack
Vivi's home!
Best "human" behavior, everyone!
zup
VIVI! HEY!
TRIP

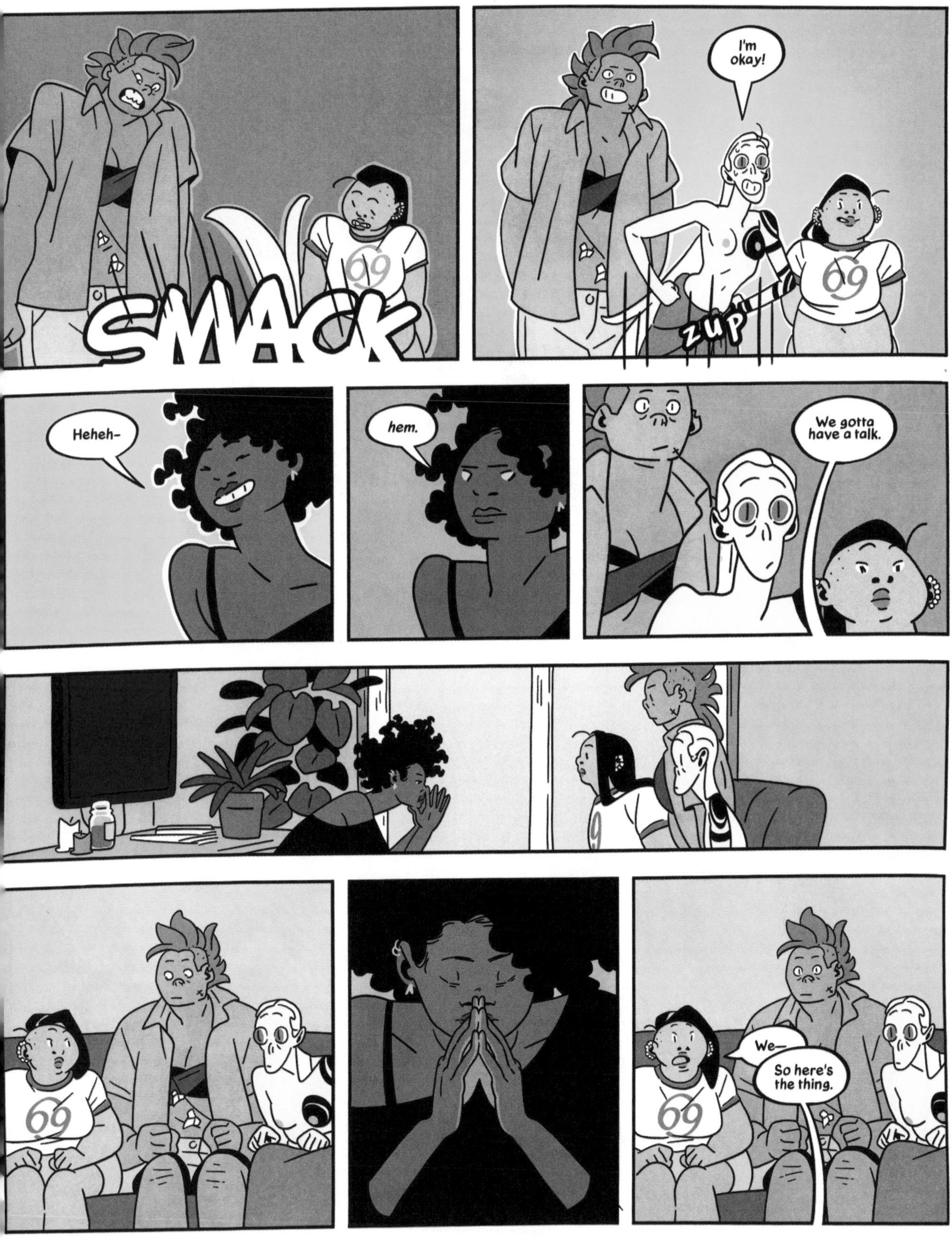
SMACK
I'm okay!
zup'
Heheh-
hem.
We gotta have a talk.
We—
So here's the thing.

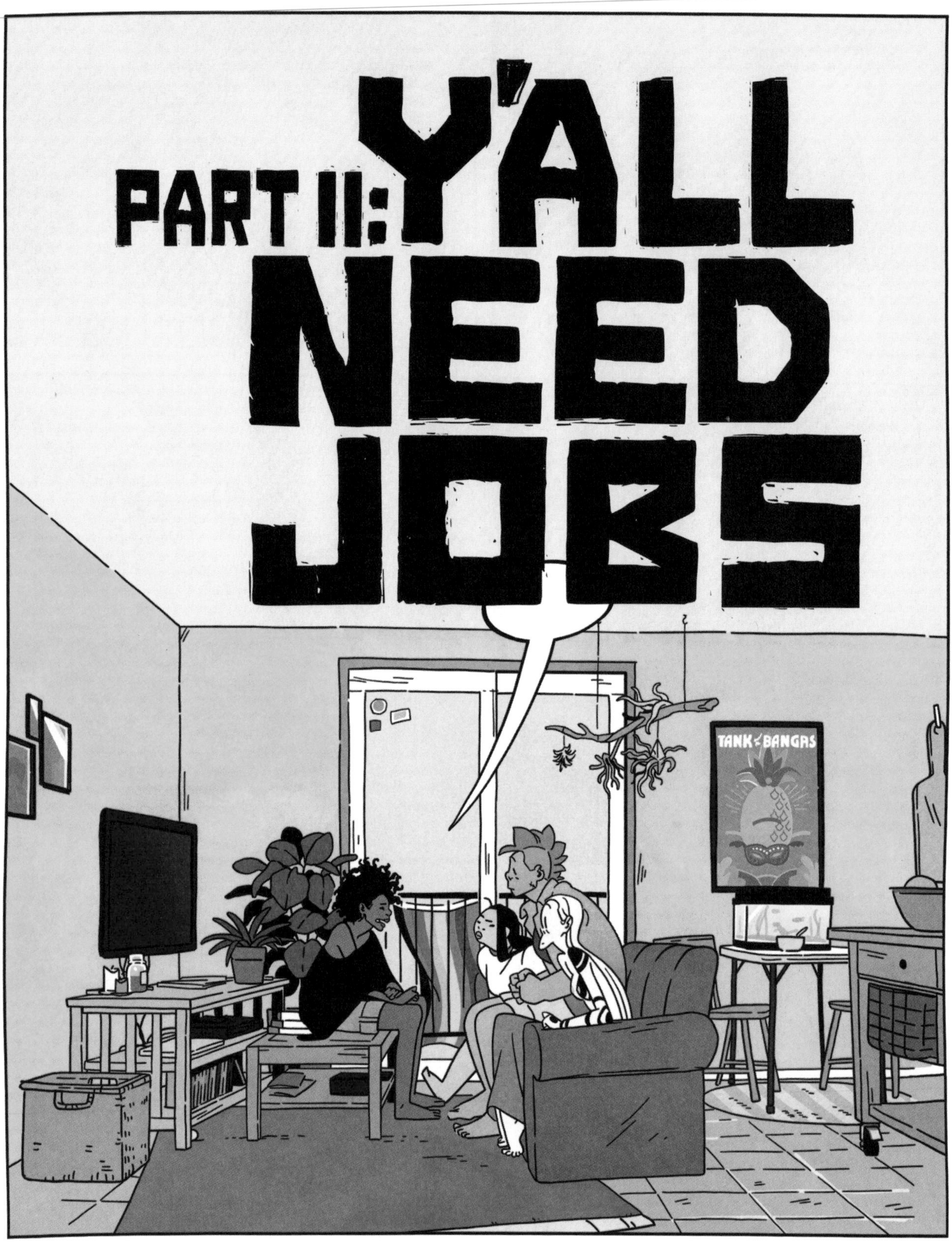
PART II: Y'ALL NEED JOBS
TANK & BANGAS

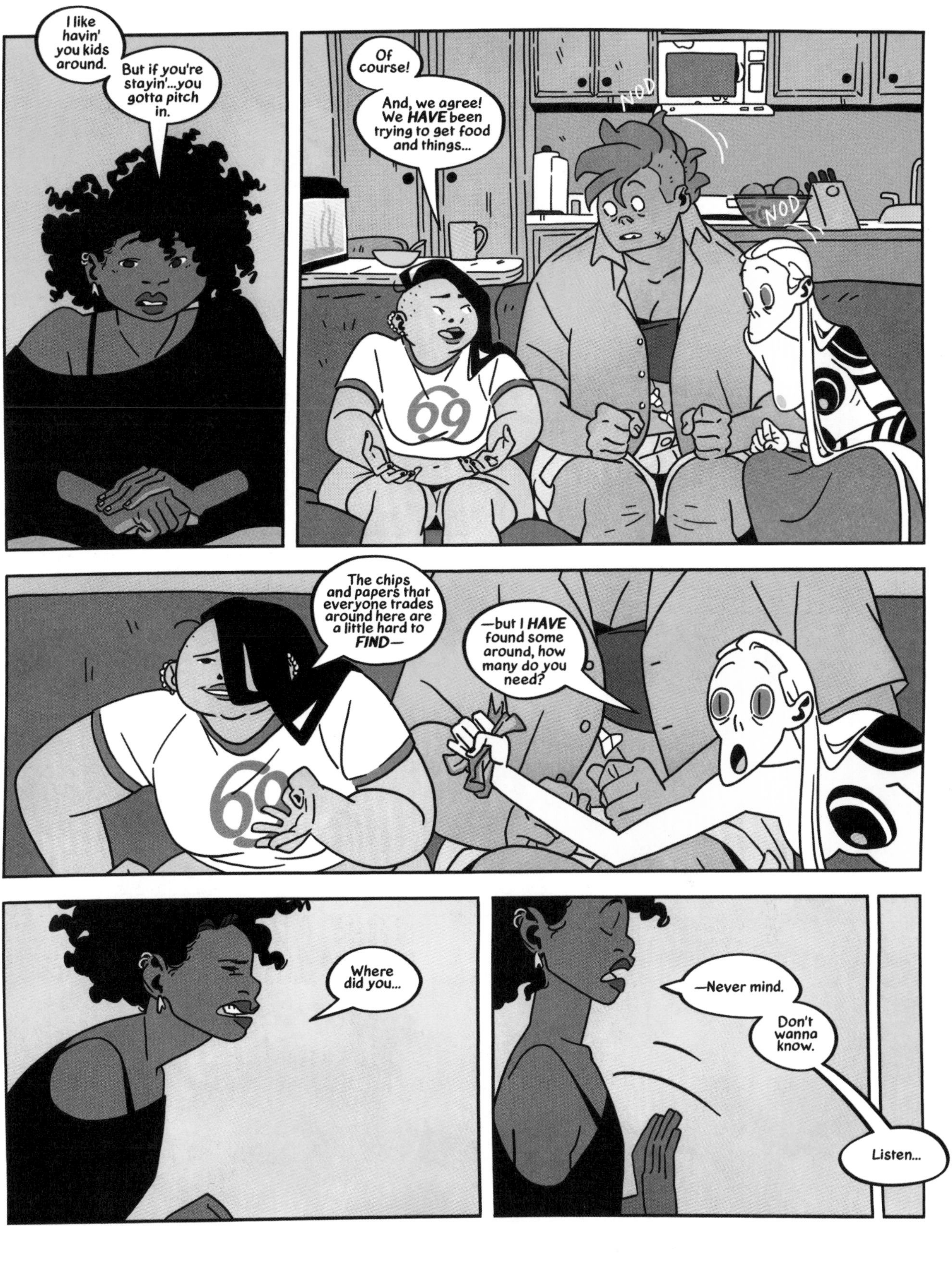
I like havin' you kids around.
But if you're stayin'...you gotta pitch in.
Of course!
And, we agree! We HAVE been trying to get food and things...
NOD
NOD
The chips and papers that everyone trades around here are a little hard to FIND—
—but I HAVE found some around, how many do you need?
Where did you...
—Never mind.
Don't wanna know.
Listen...

THEN VIVI EXPLAINS CAPITALISM TO THE MERMAIDS...

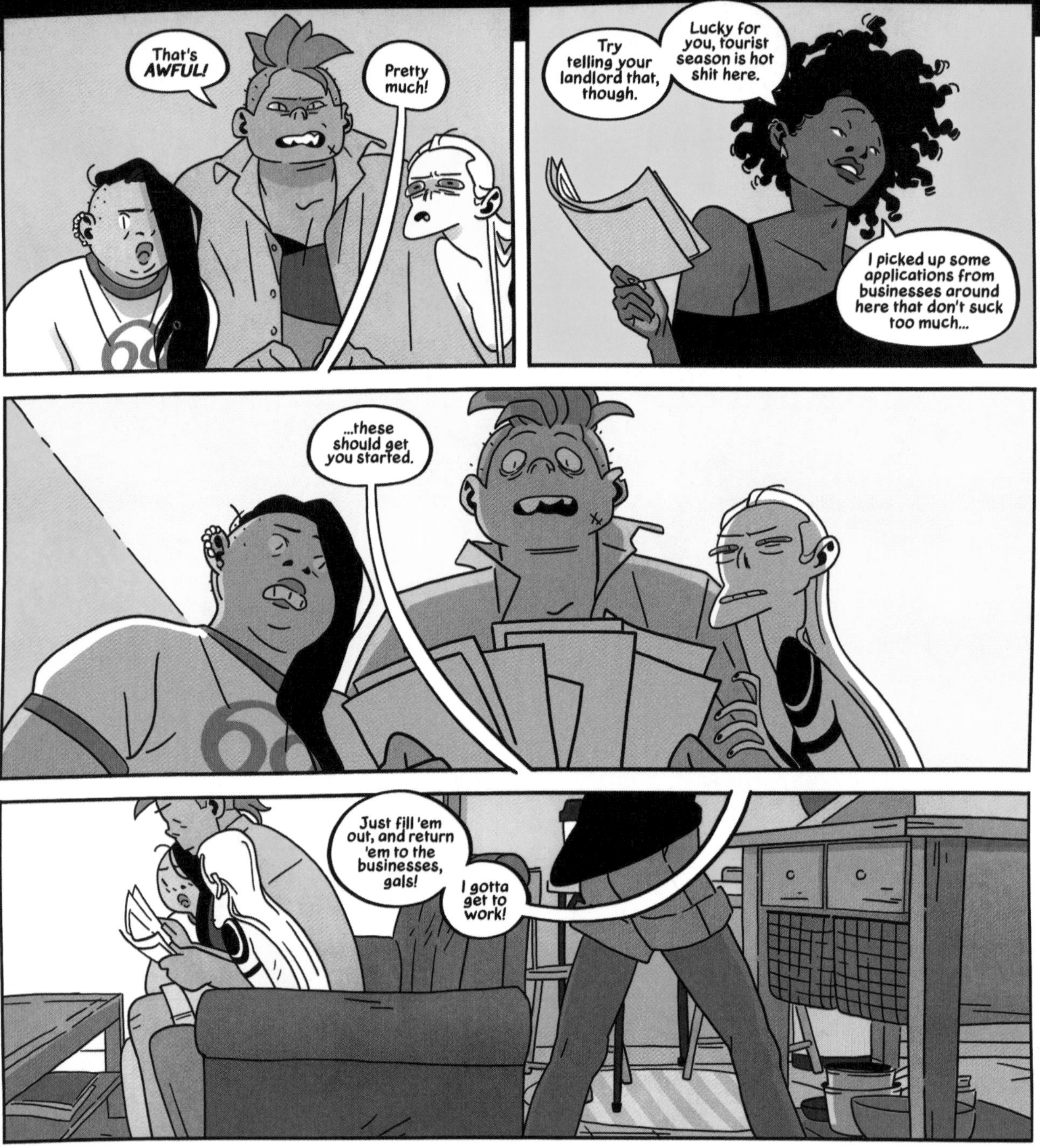
That's AWFUL!
Pretty much!
Try telling your landlord that, though.
Lucky for you, tourist season is hot shit here.
I picked up some applications from businesses around here that don't suck too much...
...these should get you started.
Just fill 'em out, and return 'em to the businesses, gals!
I gotta get to work!

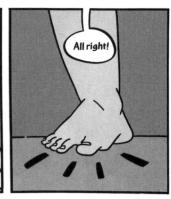

All right!

LISTEN UP, BITCHES!

This is gonna be FUN.

We're gonna get the most out of this human thing—

—OR SO HELP ME!

TOOTH! Me 'n' you are gonna get some jobs or whatever!

See how these leggies really DO!

And Eezy, you give your all to breaking this DAMN SPELL!

NOW!

Let's take a look at these...

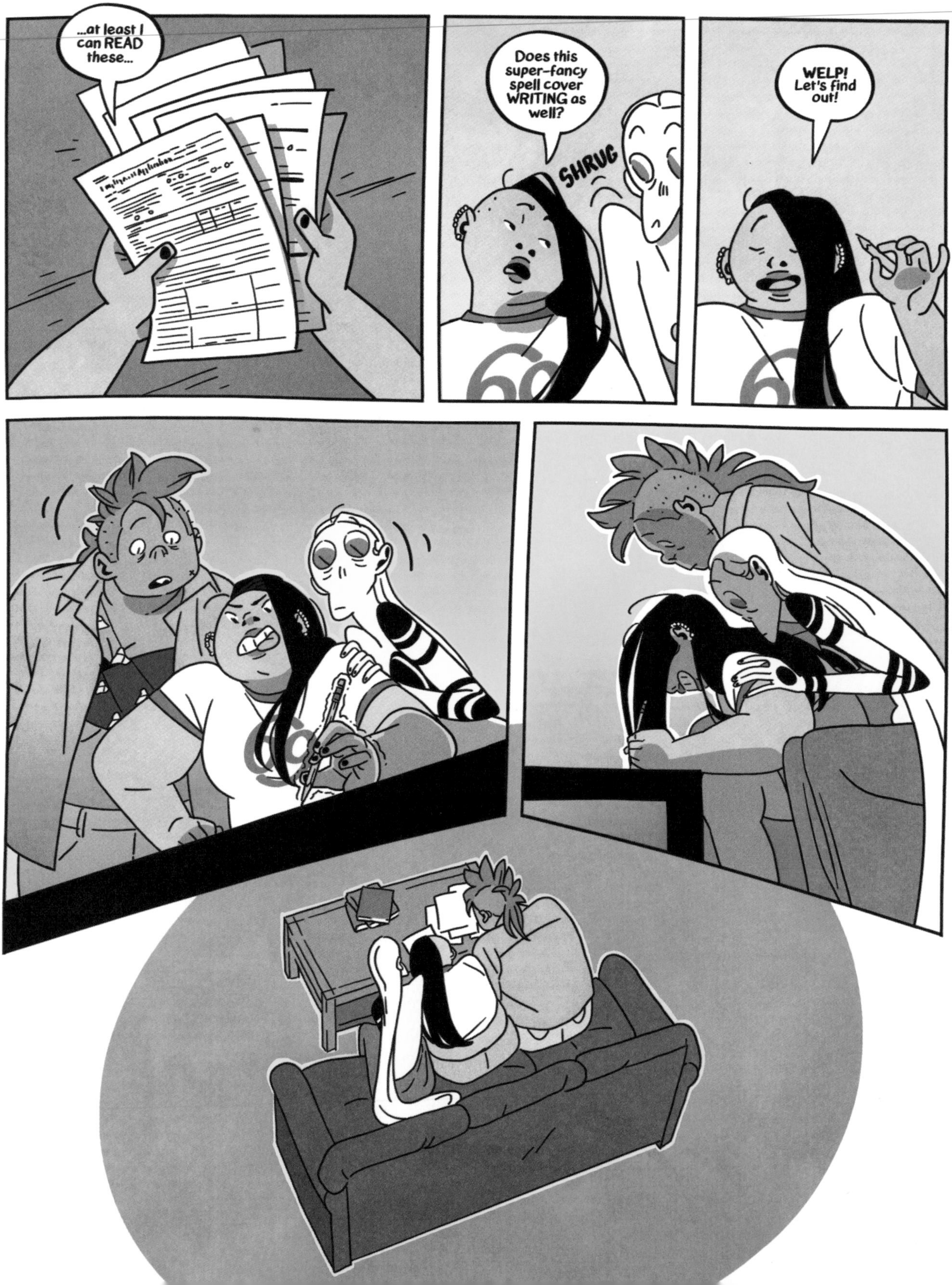
...at least I can READ these...
Does this super-fancy spell cover WRITING as well?
SHRUG
WELP! Let's find out!

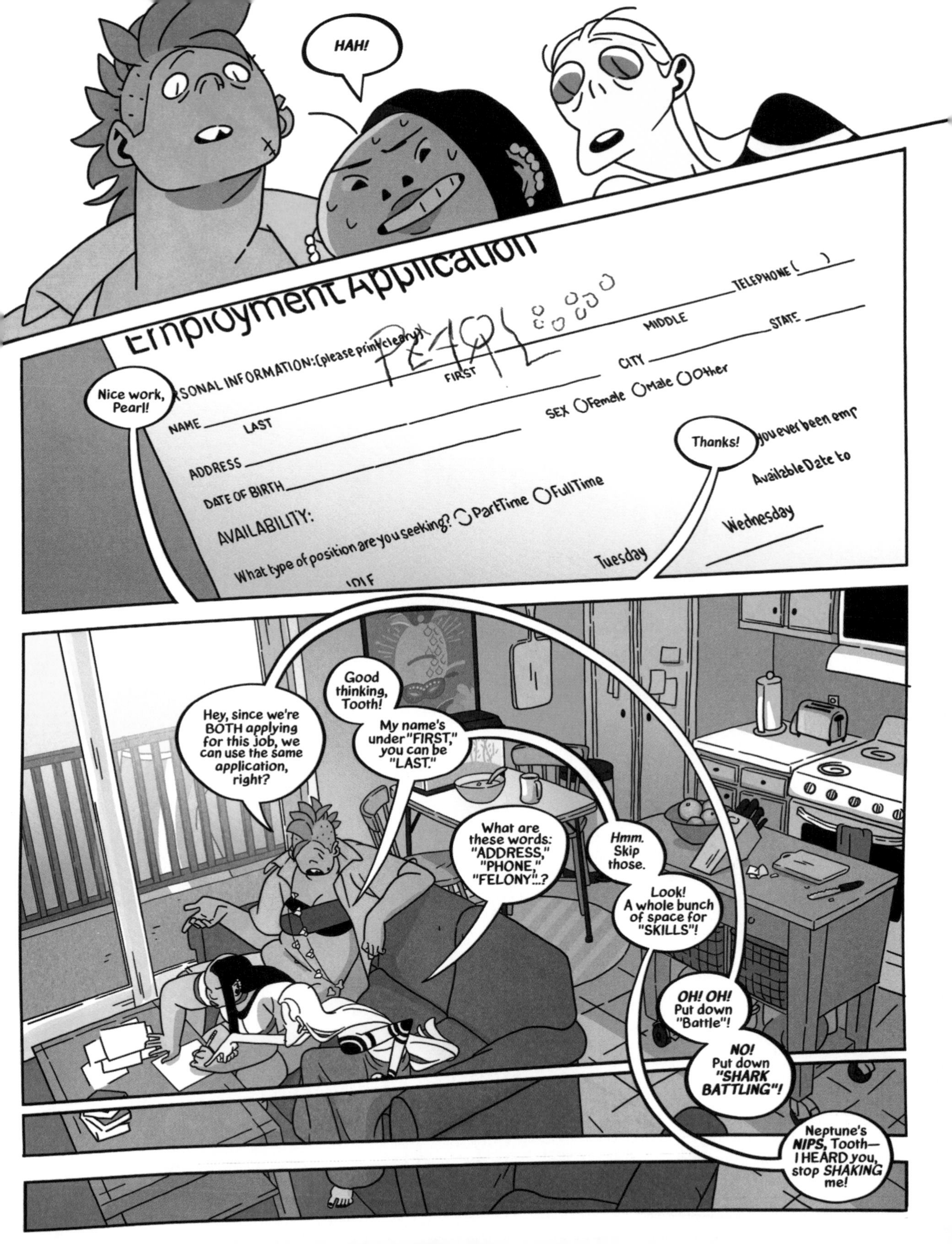
HAH!
Employment Application
PERSONAL INFORMATION: (please print clearly)
PEARL
NAME
FIRST
MIDDLE
LAST
TELEPHONE ( )
CITY
STATE
SEX Female Male Other
ADDRESS
DATE OF BIRTH
AVAILABILITY:
What type of position are you seeking? PartTime FullTime
Available Date to
Tuesday
Wednesday
Nice work, Pearl!
Thanks!
Hey, since we're BOTH applying for this job, we can use the same application, right?
Good thinking, Tooth!
My name's under "FIRST," you can be "LAST."
What are these words: "ADDRESS," "PHONE," "FELONY"...?
Hmm. Skip those.
Look! A whole bunch of space for "SKILLS"!
OH! OH! Put down "Battle"!
NO! Put down "SHARK BATTLING"!
Neptune's NIPS, Tooth—I HEARD you, stop SHAKING me!

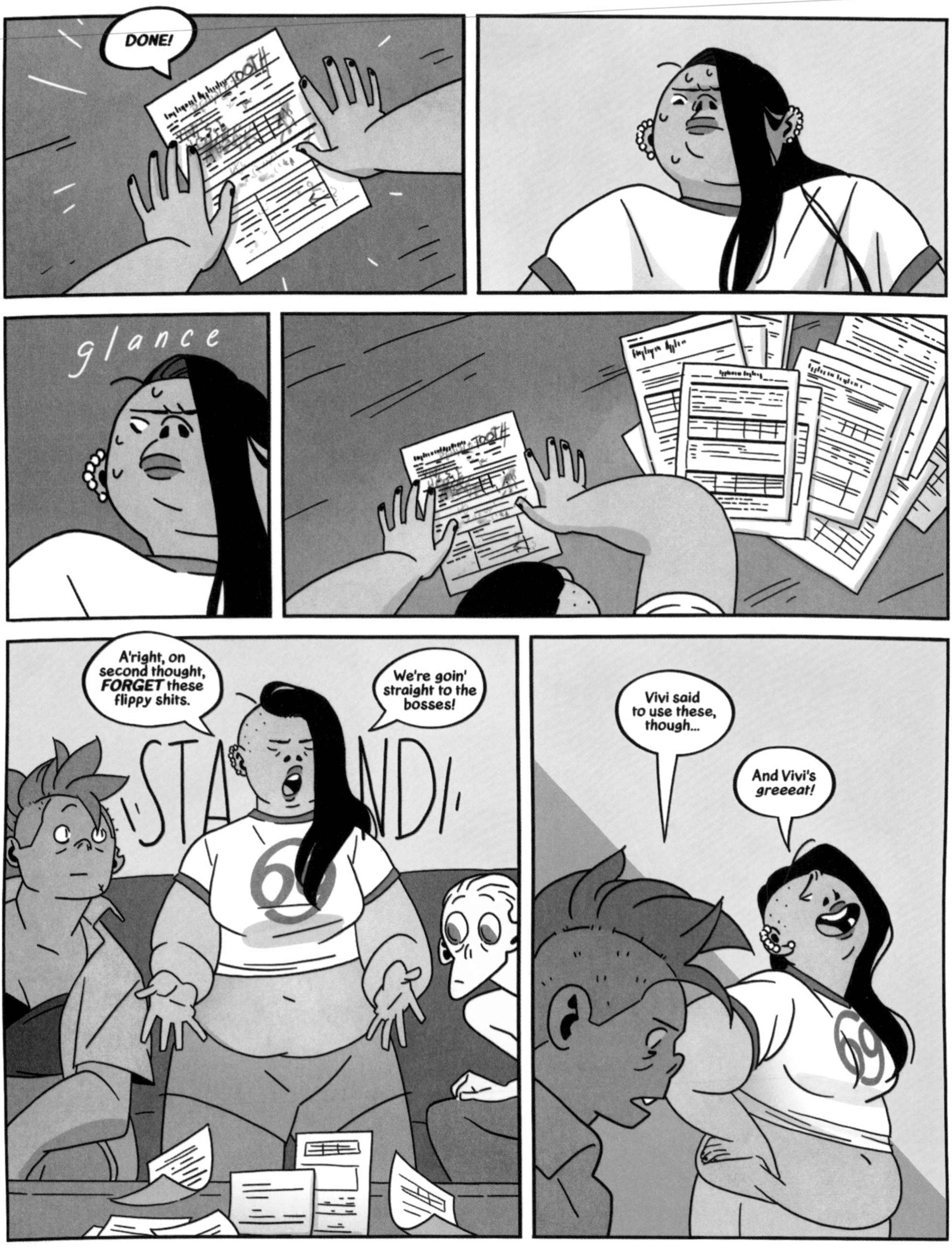
DONE!
glance
A'right, on second thought, **FORGET** these flippy shits.
STAND
We're goin' straight to the bosses!
Vivi said to use these, though...
And Vivi's *greeeat!*

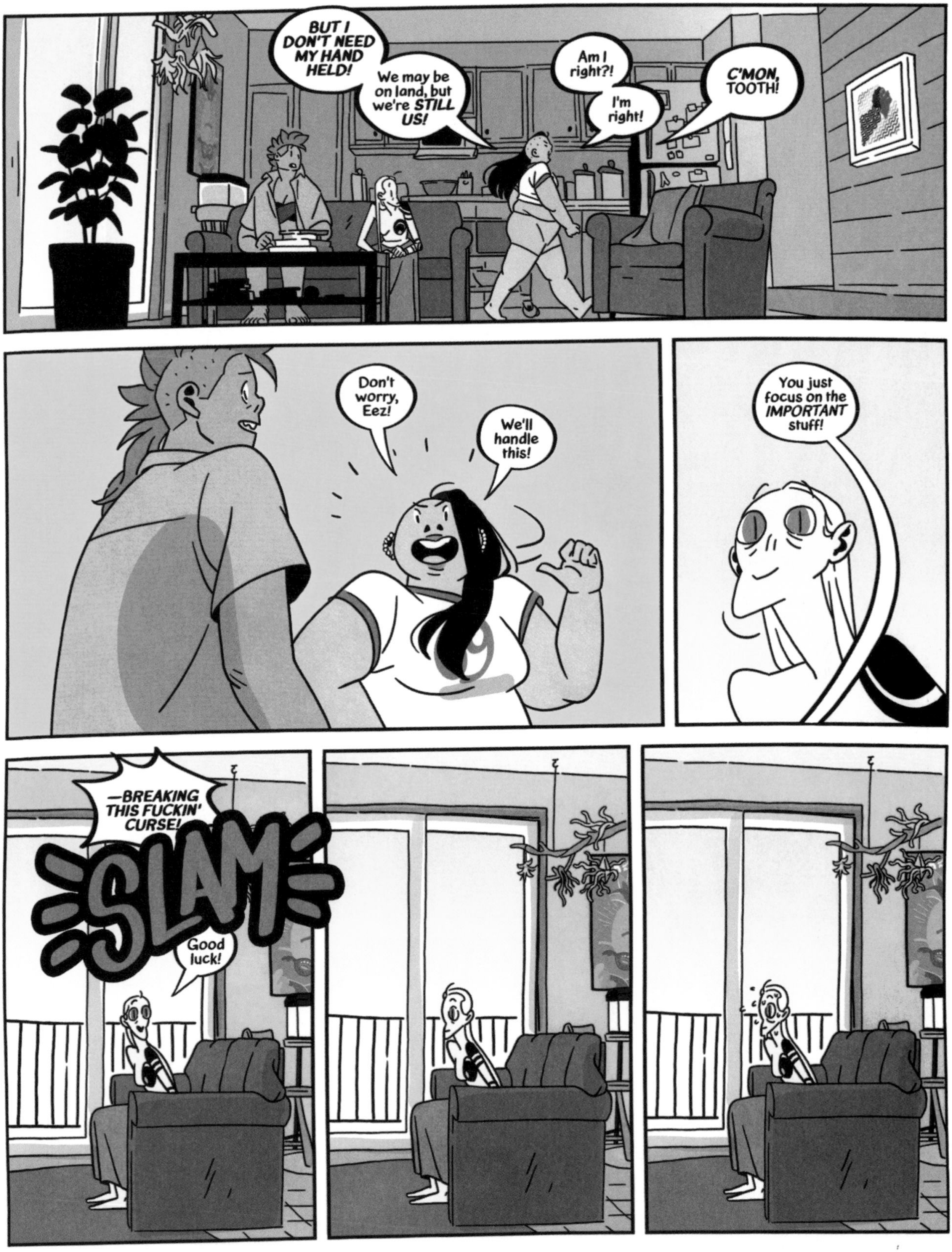
BUT I DON'T NEED MY HAND HELD!
We may be on land, but we're STILL US!
Am I right?!
I'm right!
C'MON, TOOTH!
Don't worry, Eez!
We'll handle this!
You just focus on the IMPORTANT stuff!
—BREAKING THIS FUCKIN' CURSE!
SLAM
Good luck!

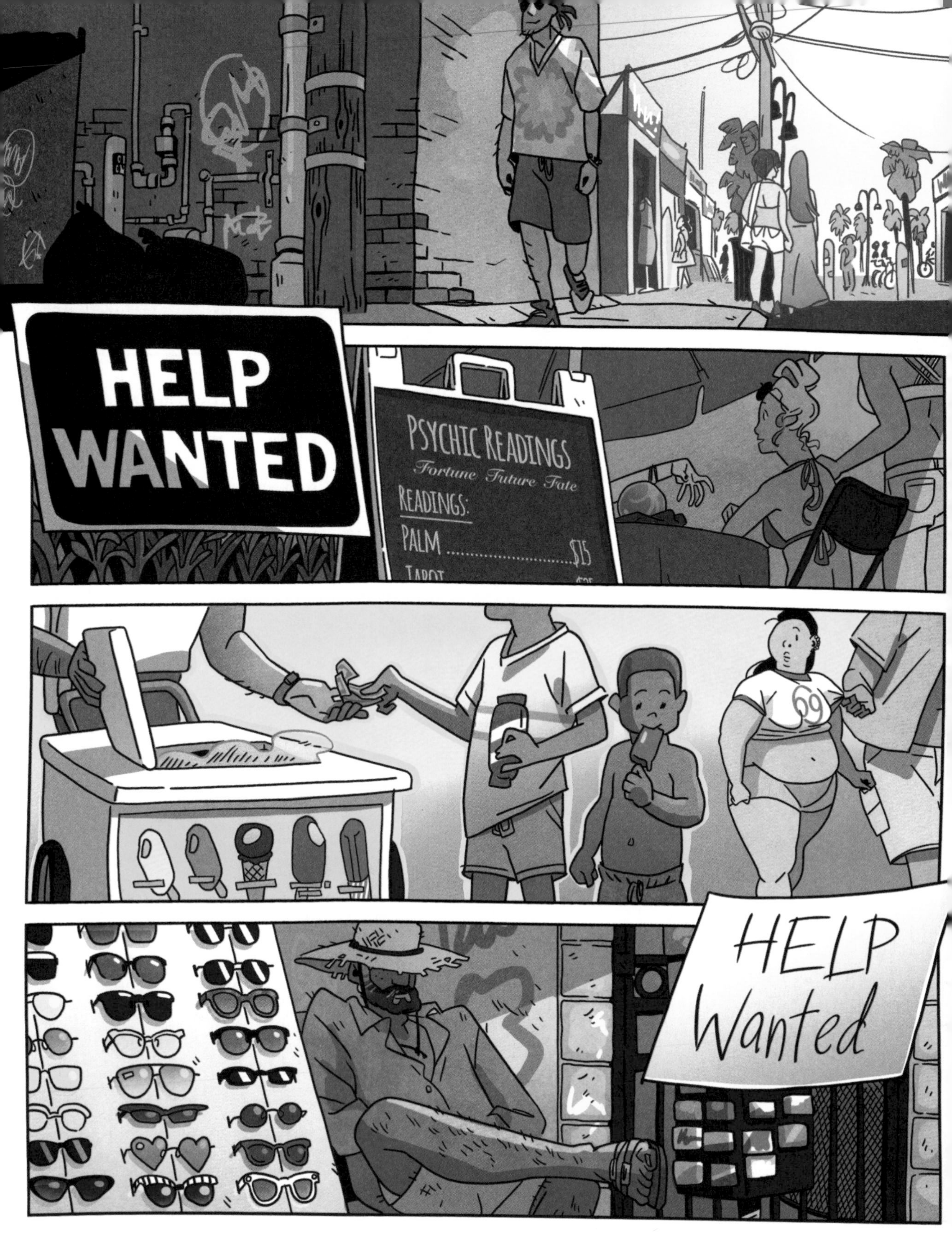

HELP WANTED
PSYCHIC READINGS
Fortune Future Fate
READINGS:
PALM $15
HELP Wanted

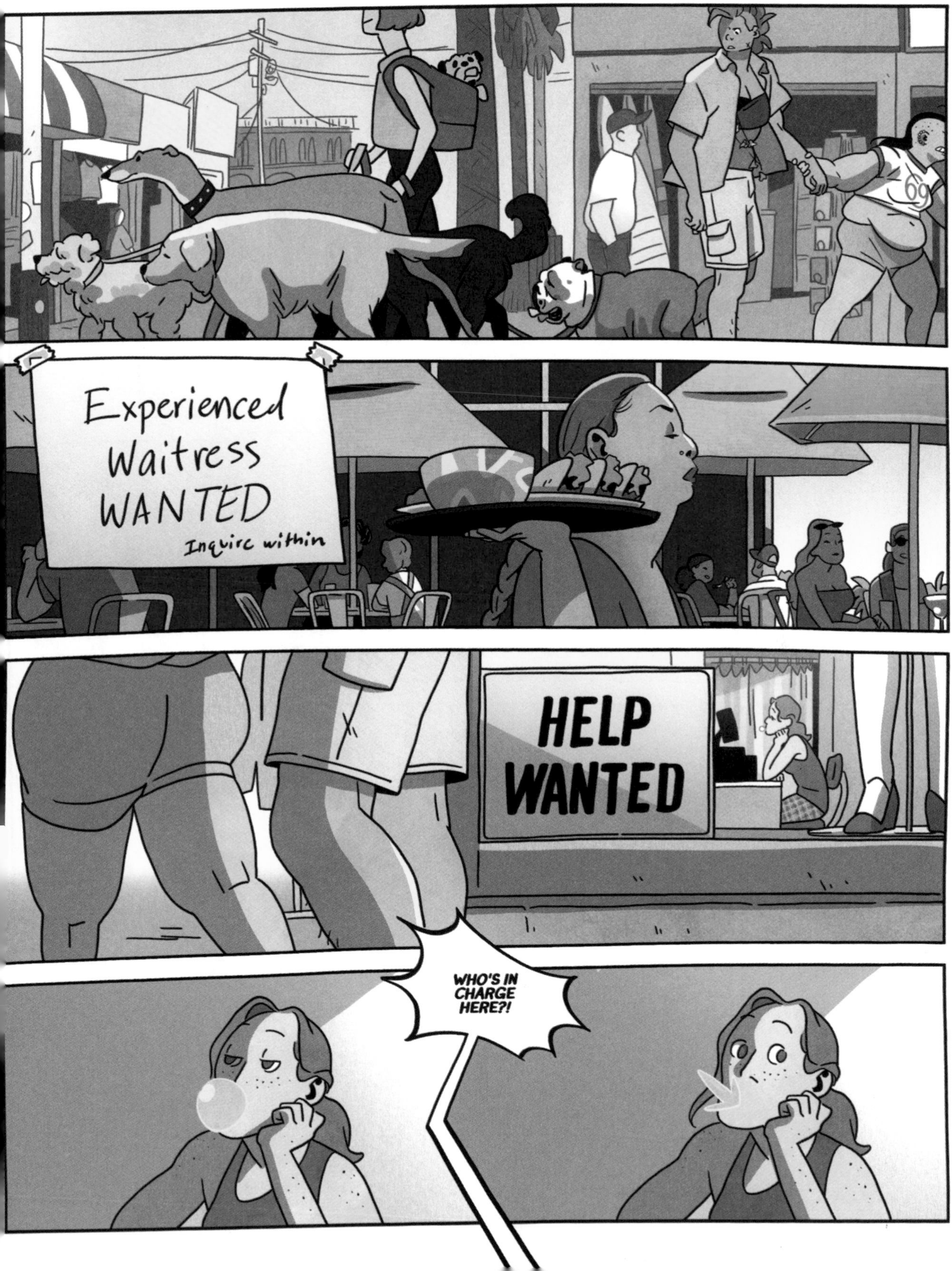
Experienced Waitress WANTED
Inquire within
HELP WANTED
WHO'S IN CHARGE HERE?!

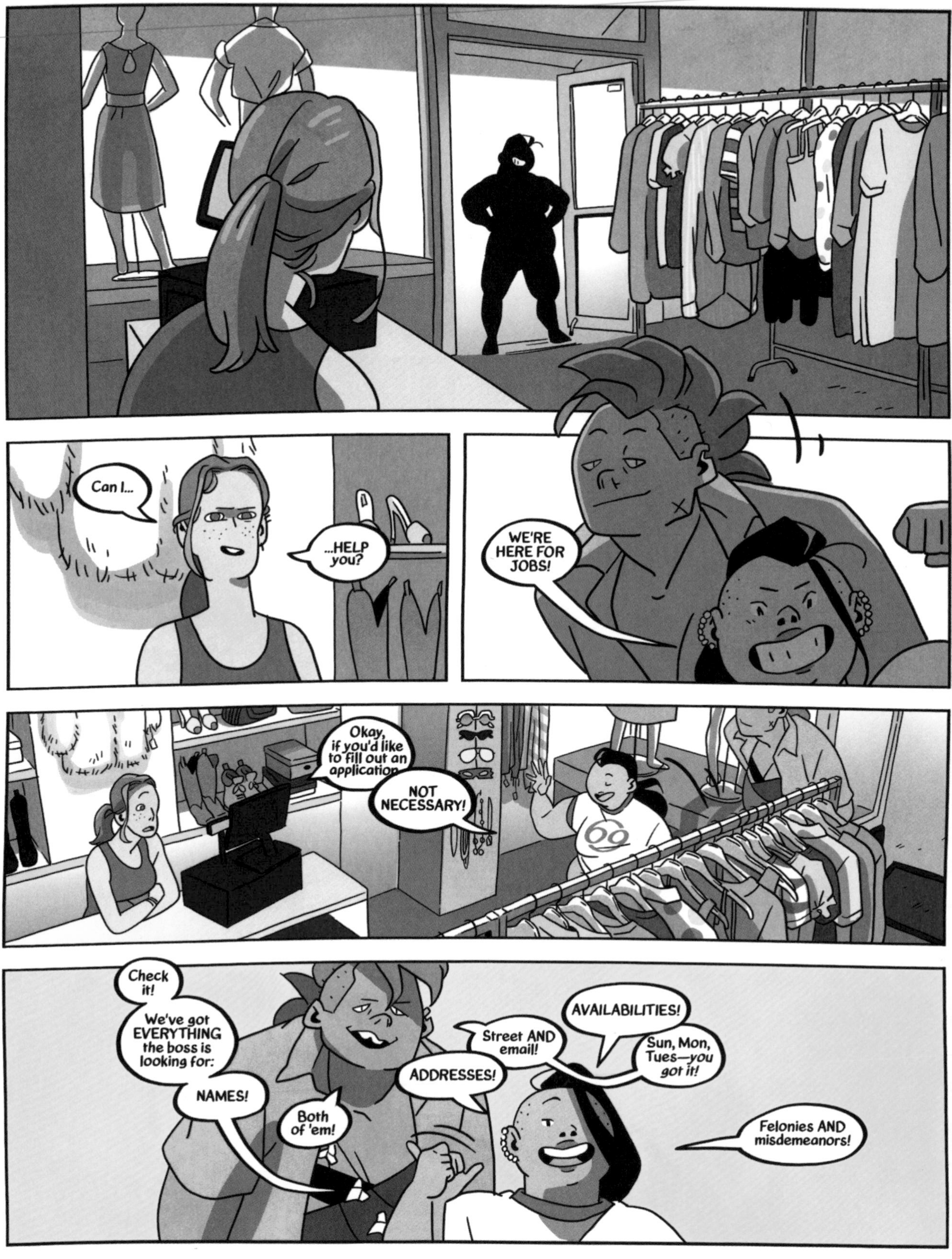
Can I...
...HELP you?
WE'RE HERE FOR JOBS!
Okay, if you'd like to fill out an application
NOT NECESSARY!
Check it!
We've got EVERYTHING the boss is looking for:
NAMES!
Both of 'em!
ADDRESSES!
Street AND email!
AVAILABILITIES!
Sun, Mon, Tues—*you* got it!
Felonies AND misdemeanors!

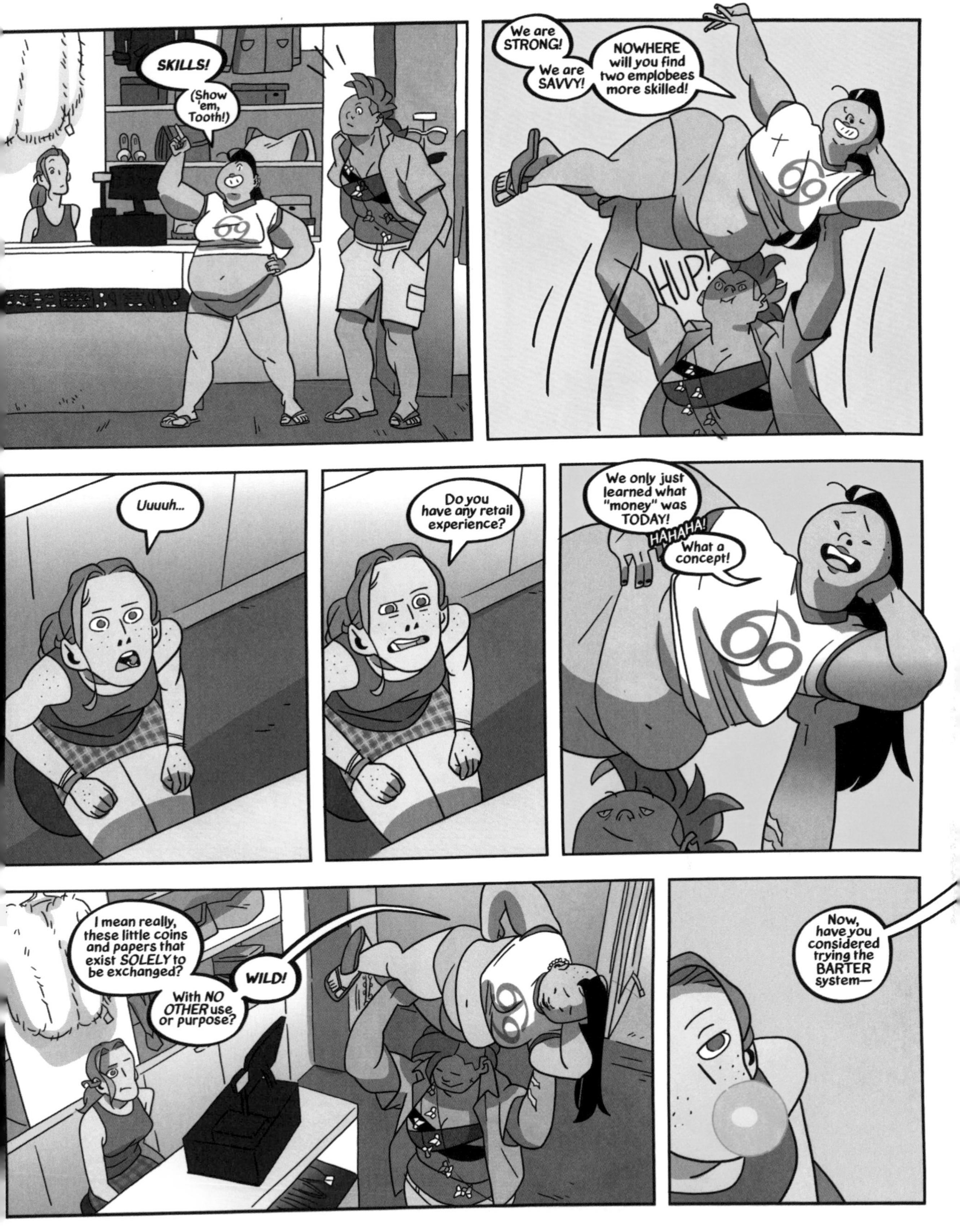
SKILLS!
(Show 'em, Tooth!)
We are STRONG!
We are SAVVY!
NOWHERE will you find two emplobees more skilled!
HUP!
Uuuuh...
Do you have any retail experience?
We only just learned what "money" was TODAY!
HAHAHA!
What a concept!
I mean really, these little coins and papers that exist SOLELY to be exchanged?
With NO OTHER use or purpose?
WILD!
Now, have you considered trying the BARTER system—

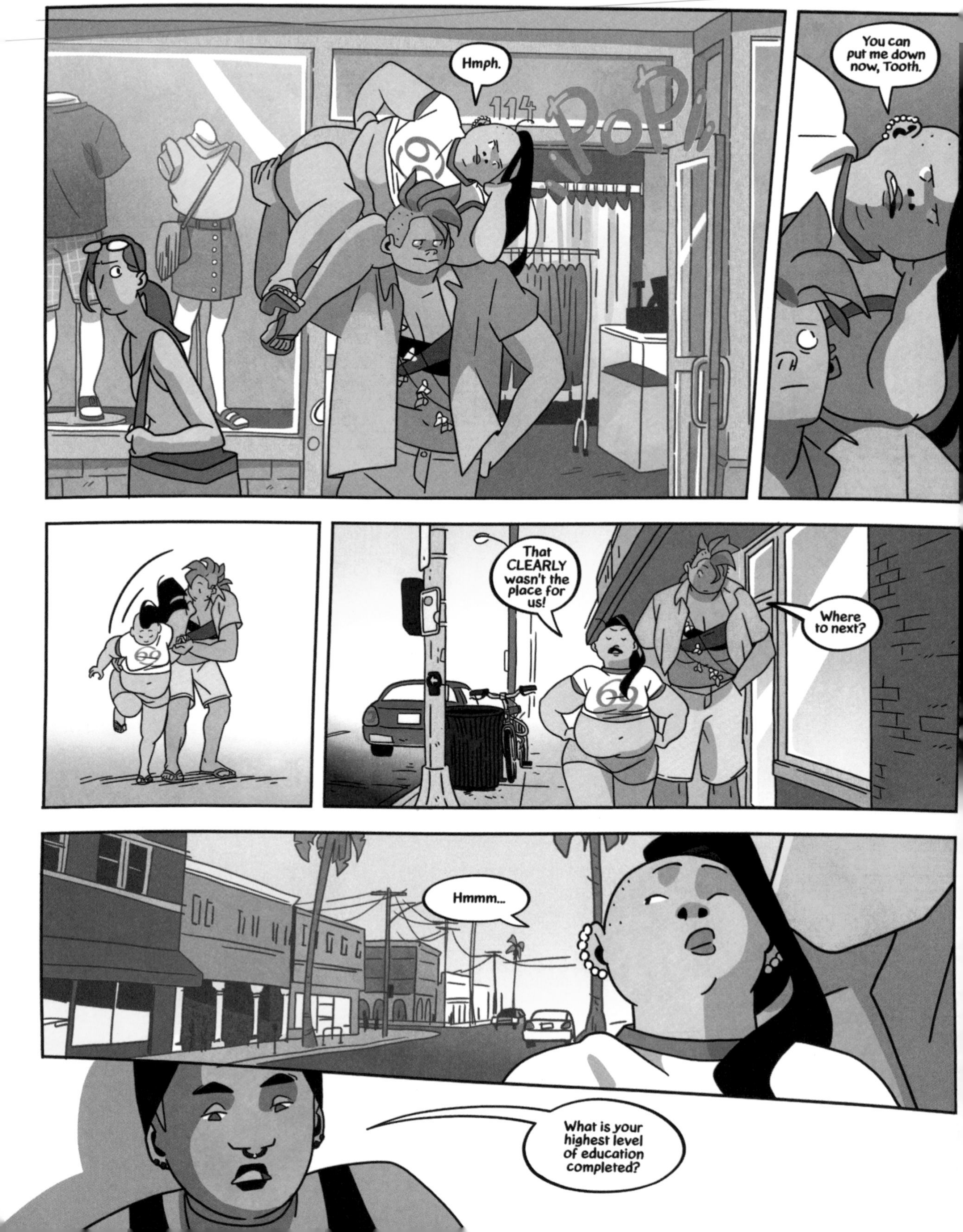
Hmph.
114
POP!
You can put me down now, Tooth.
That CLEARLY wasn't the place for us!
Where to next?
Hmmm...
What is your highest level of education completed?

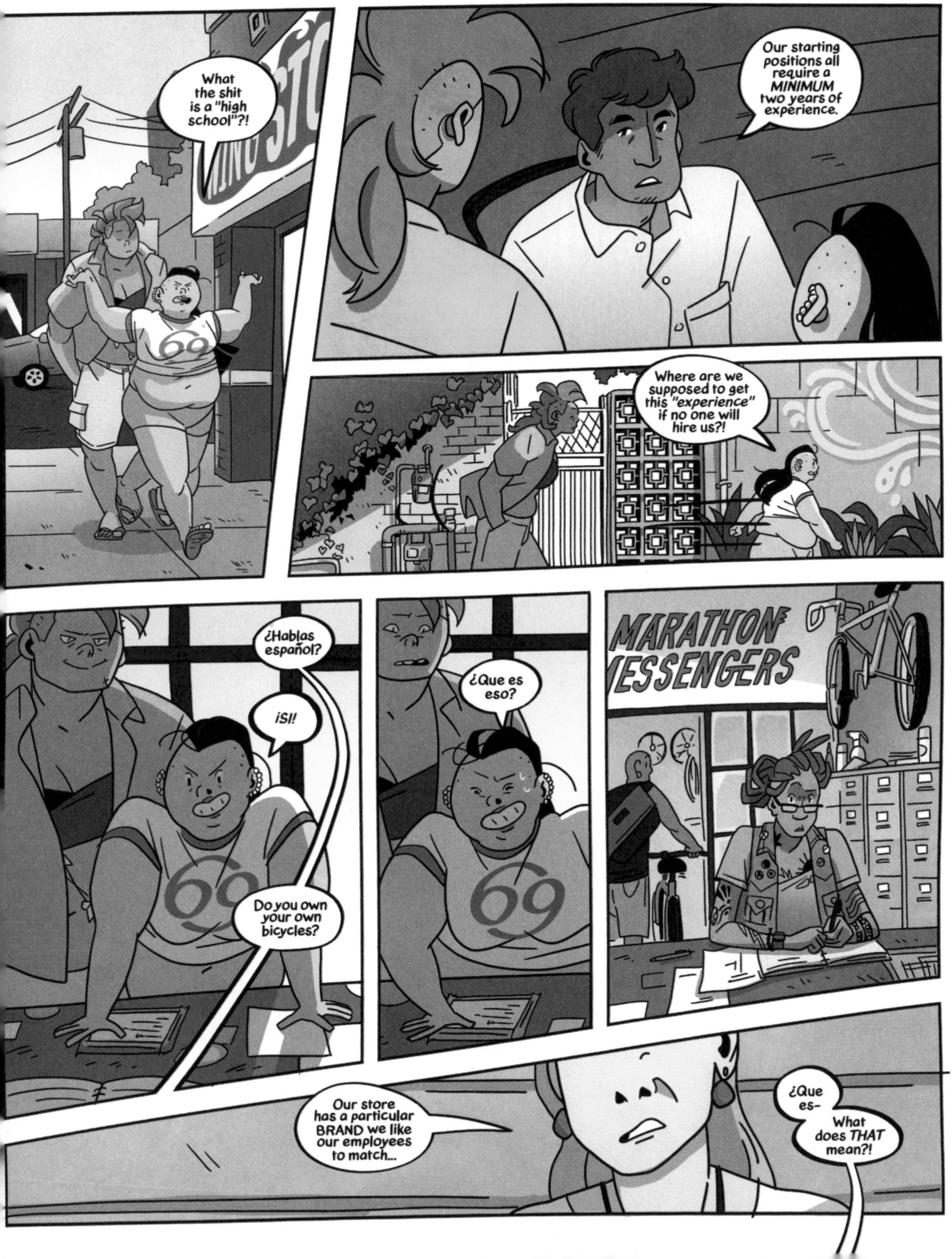

MING STO
What the shit is a "high school"?!
Our starting positions all require a MINIMUM two years of experience.
Where are we supposed to get this "experience" if no one will hire us?!
¿Hablas español?
¡SI!
Do you own your own bicycles?
¿Que es eso?
MARATHON MESSENGERS
Our store has a particular BRAND we like our employees to match...
¿Que es-
What does THAT mean?!

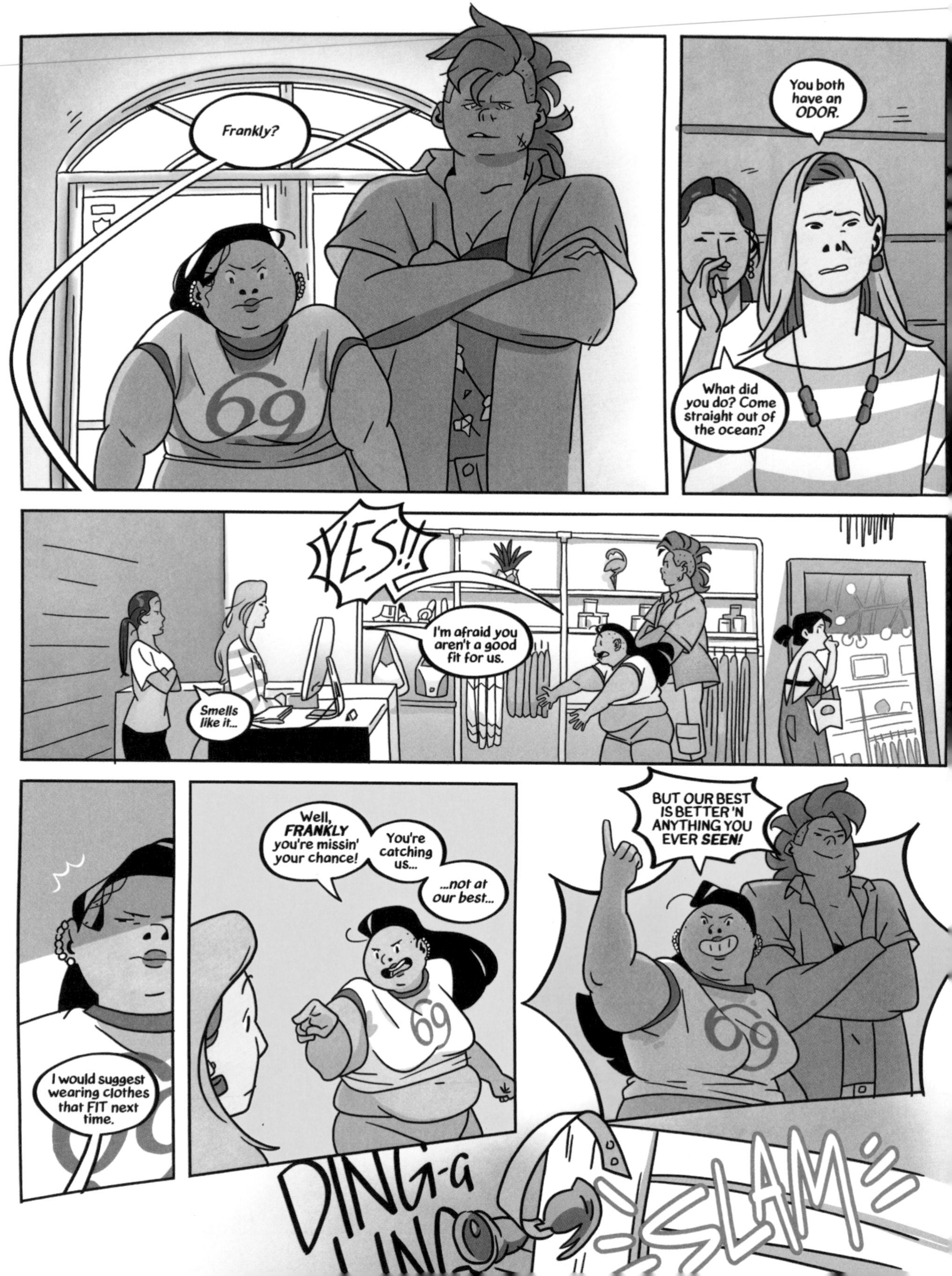

Frankly?
You both have an ODOR.
What did you do? Come straight out of the ocean?
YES!!
I'm afraid you aren't a good fit for us.
Smells like it...
I would suggest wearing clothes that FIT next time.
Well, FRANKLY you're missin' your chance!
You're catching us...
...not at our best...
BUT OUR BEST IS BETTER 'N ANYTHING YOU EVER SEEN!
DING-G
SLAM

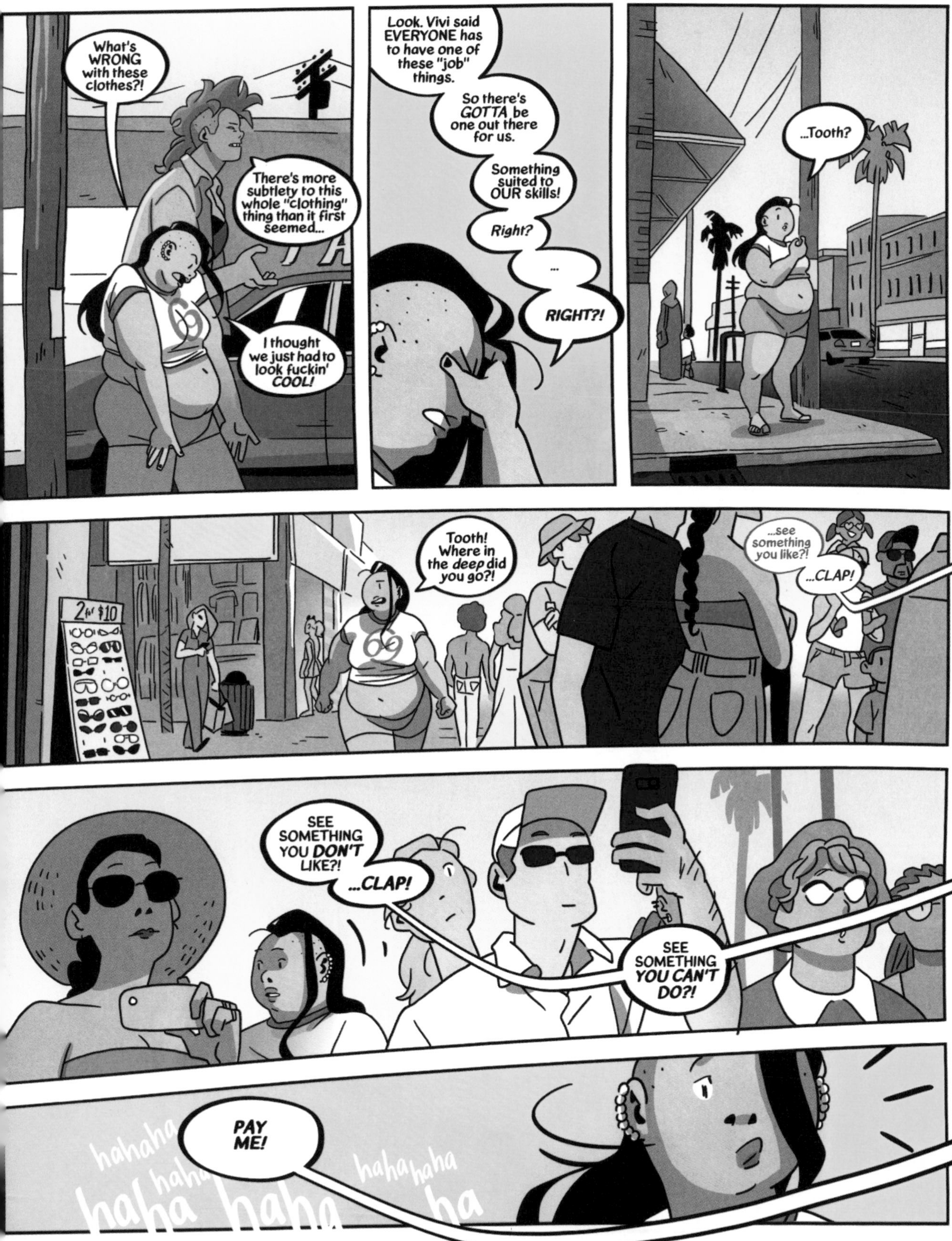
What's WRONG with these clothes?!
There's more subtlety to this whole "clothing" thing than it first seemed...
I thought we just had to look fuckin' COOL!
Look. Vivi said EVERYONE has to have one of these "job" things.
So there's GOTTA be one out there for us.
Something suited to OUR skills!
Right?
...
RIGHT?!
...Tooth?
2 for $10
Tooth! Where in the deep did you go?!
...see something you like?!
...CLAP!
SEE SOMETHING YOU DON'T LIKE?!
...CLAP!
SEE SOMETHING YOU CAN'T DO?!
PAY ME!
hahaha haha haha haha haha haha ha

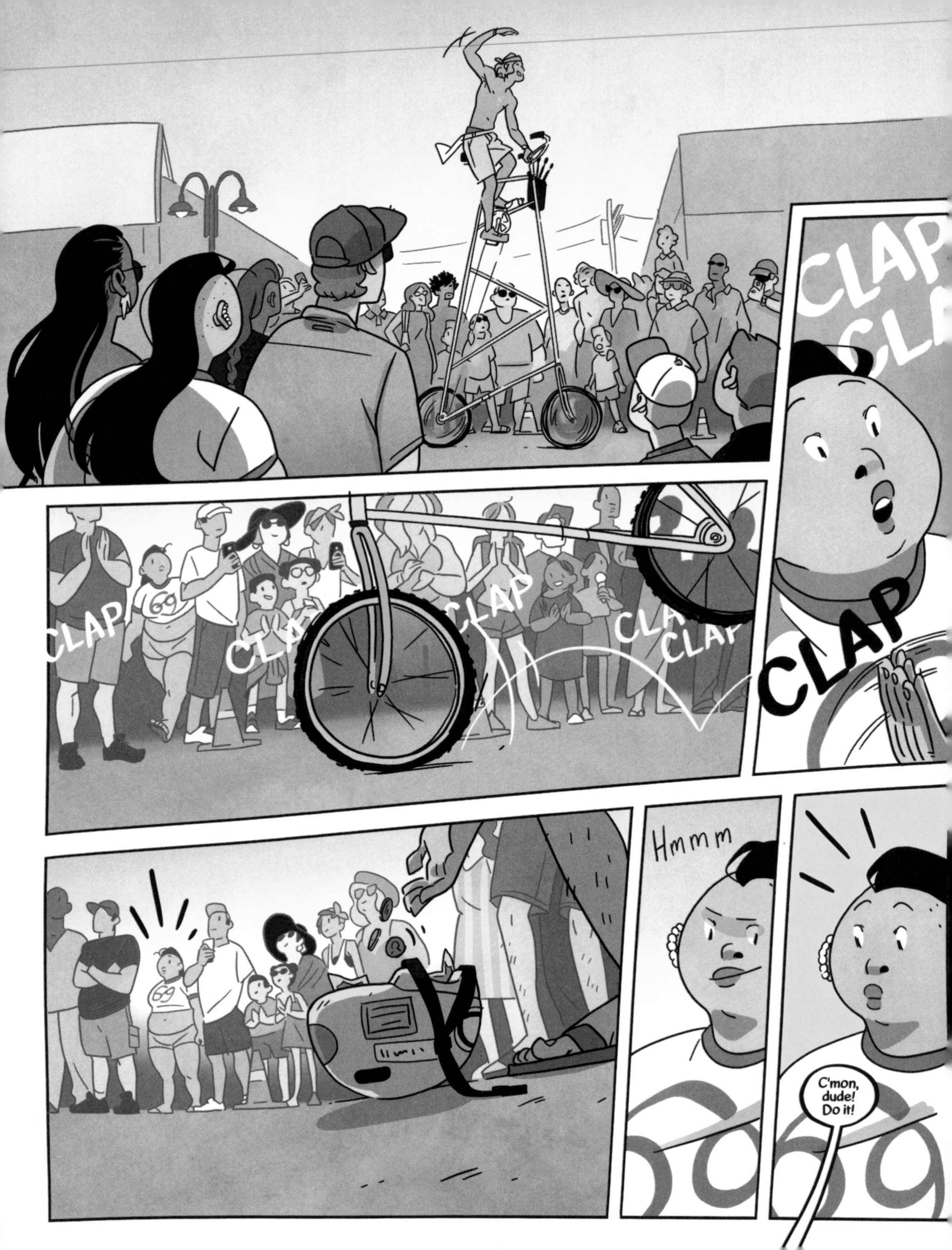
CLAP
CLAP
CLAP
CLAP
CLAP
CLAP
CLAP
Hmmm
C'mon, dude! Do it!

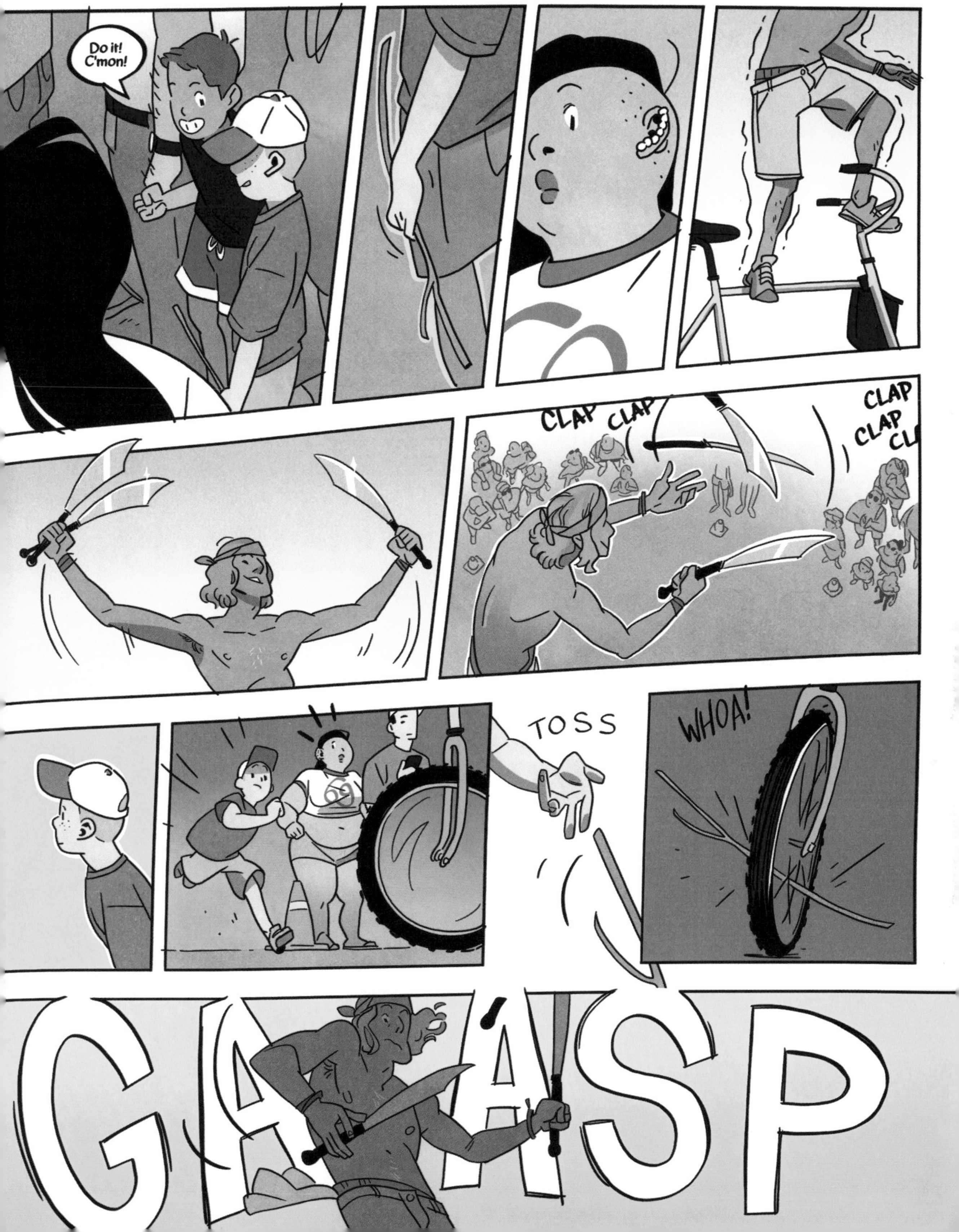
Do it! C'mon!
CLAP CLAP
CLAP
CLAP
TOSS
WHOA!
GASP

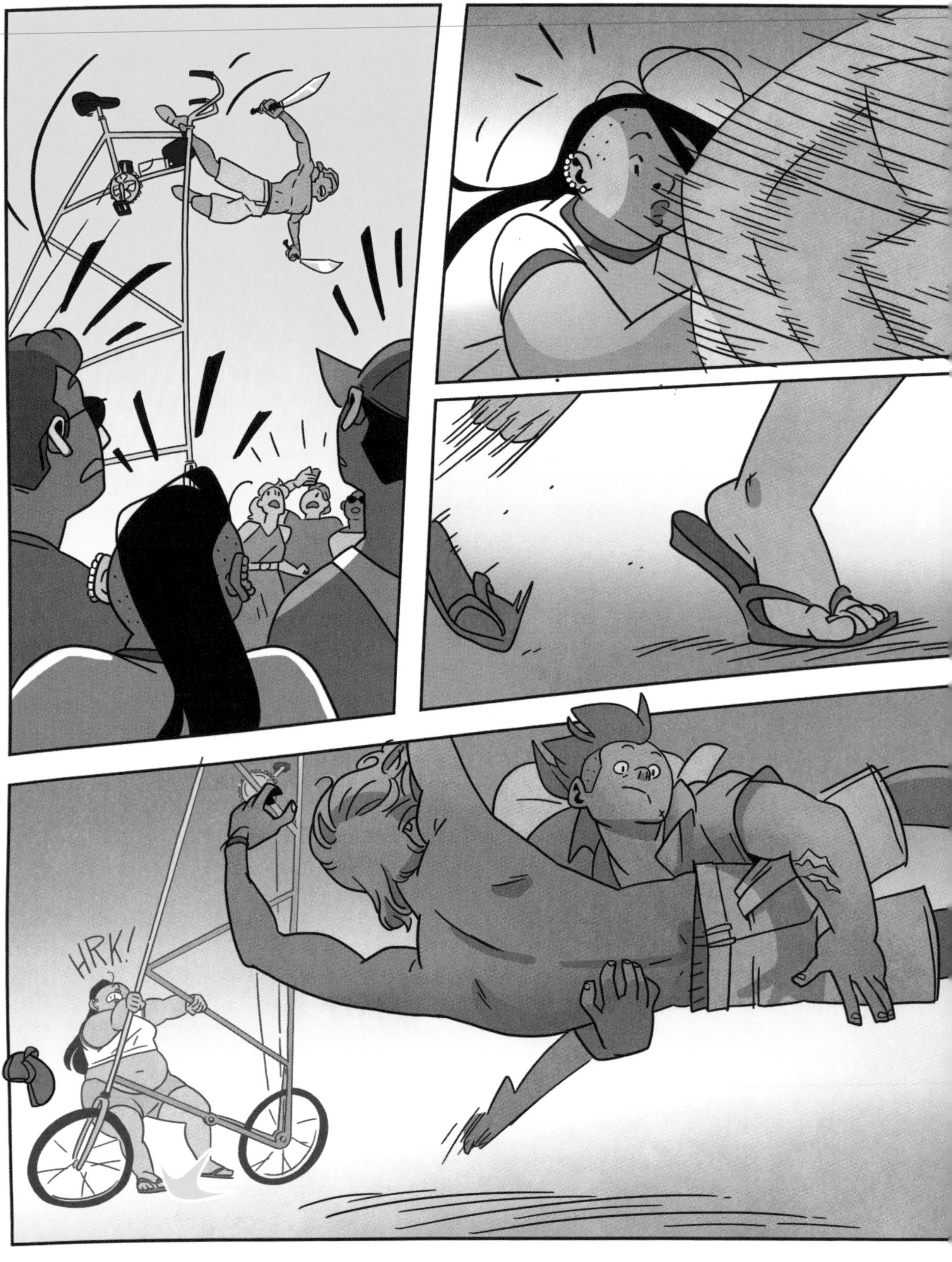
HRK!

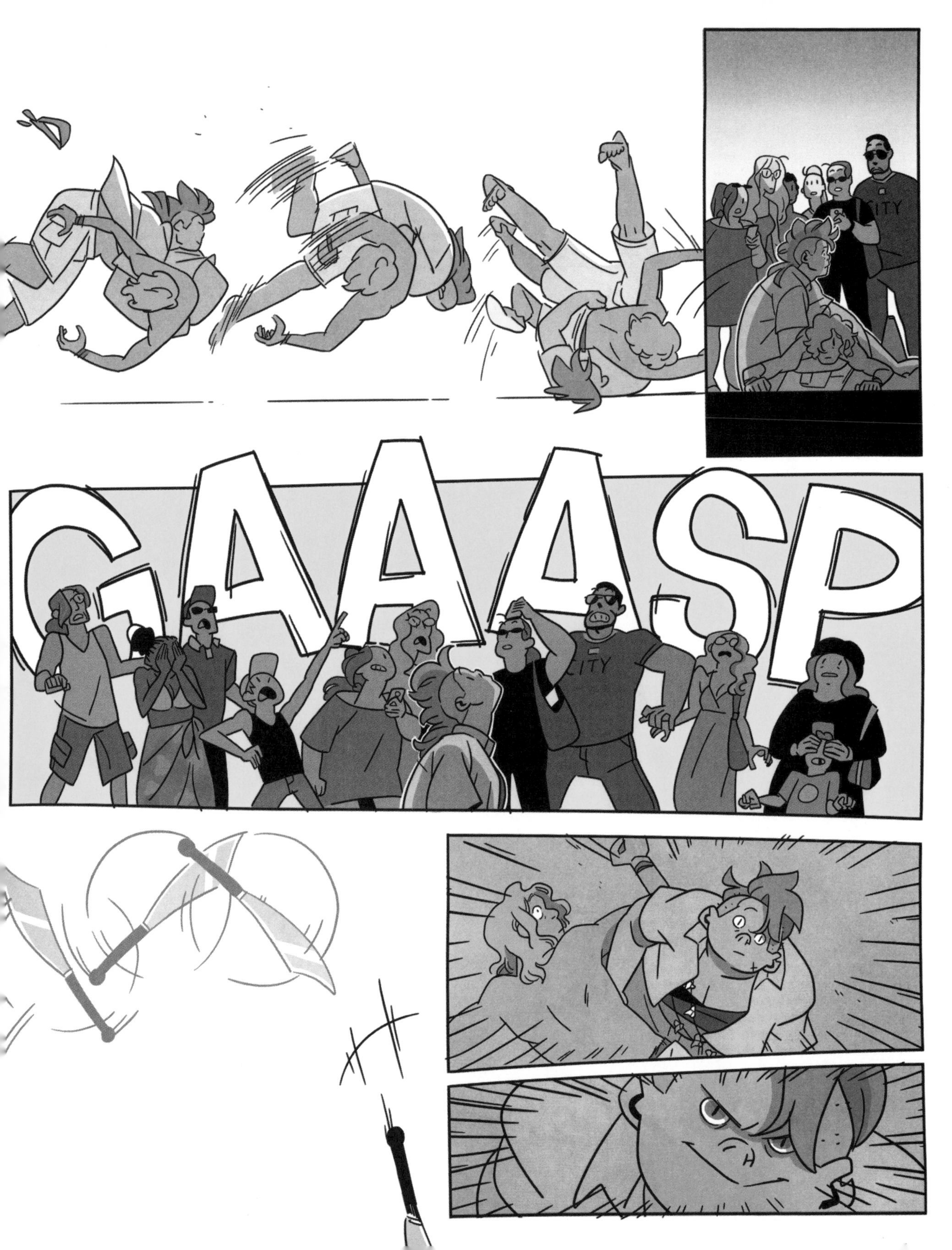
GAAASP
CITY

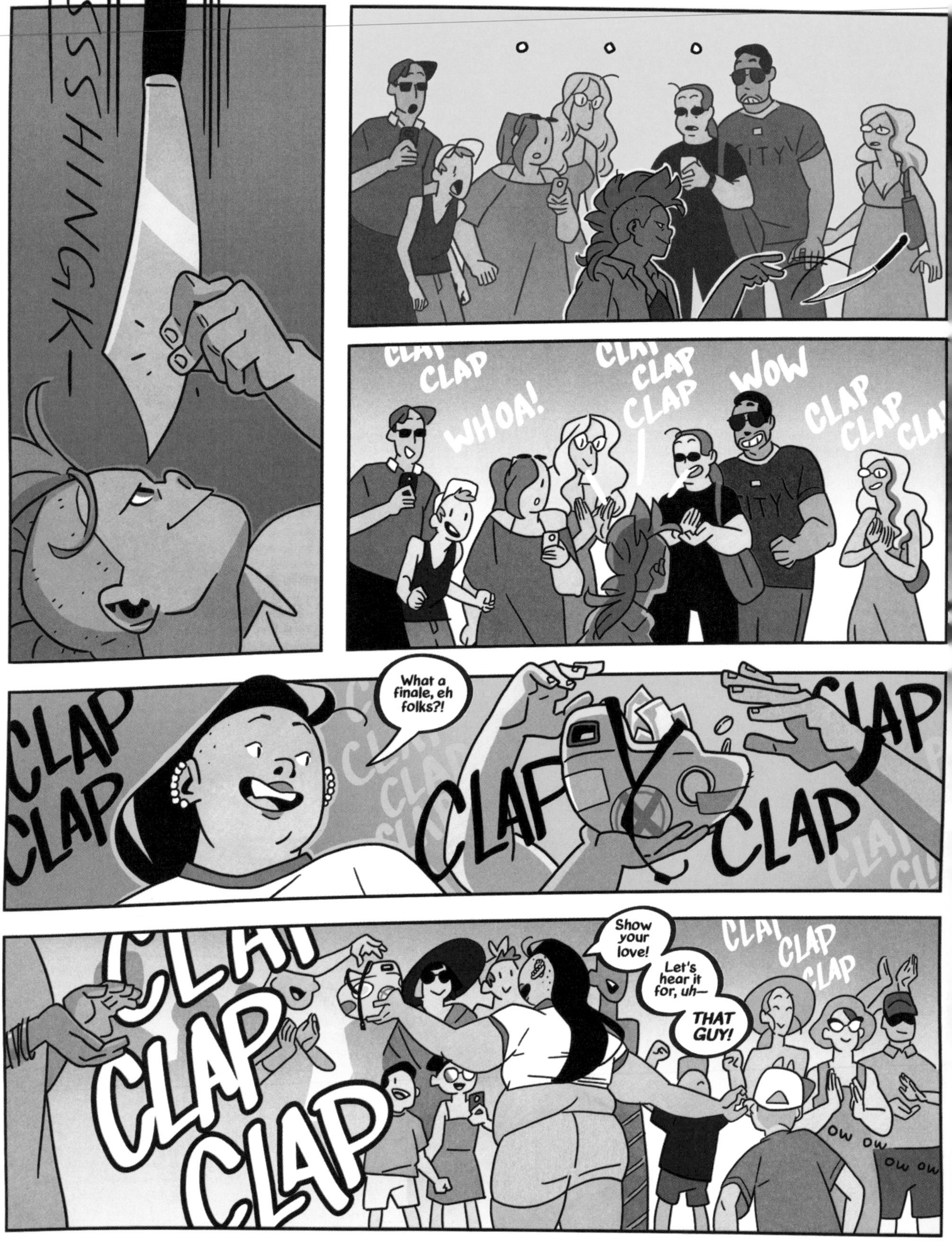
SSSHINGK—
WHOA!
CLAP CLAP
CLAP CLAP CLAP
WOW
CLAP CLAP
What a finale, eh folks?!
CLAP CLAP
CLAP
CLAP
CLAP
Show your love!
Let's hear it for, uh—
THAT GUY!
CLAP CLAP
CLAP CLAP
OW OW
OW OW

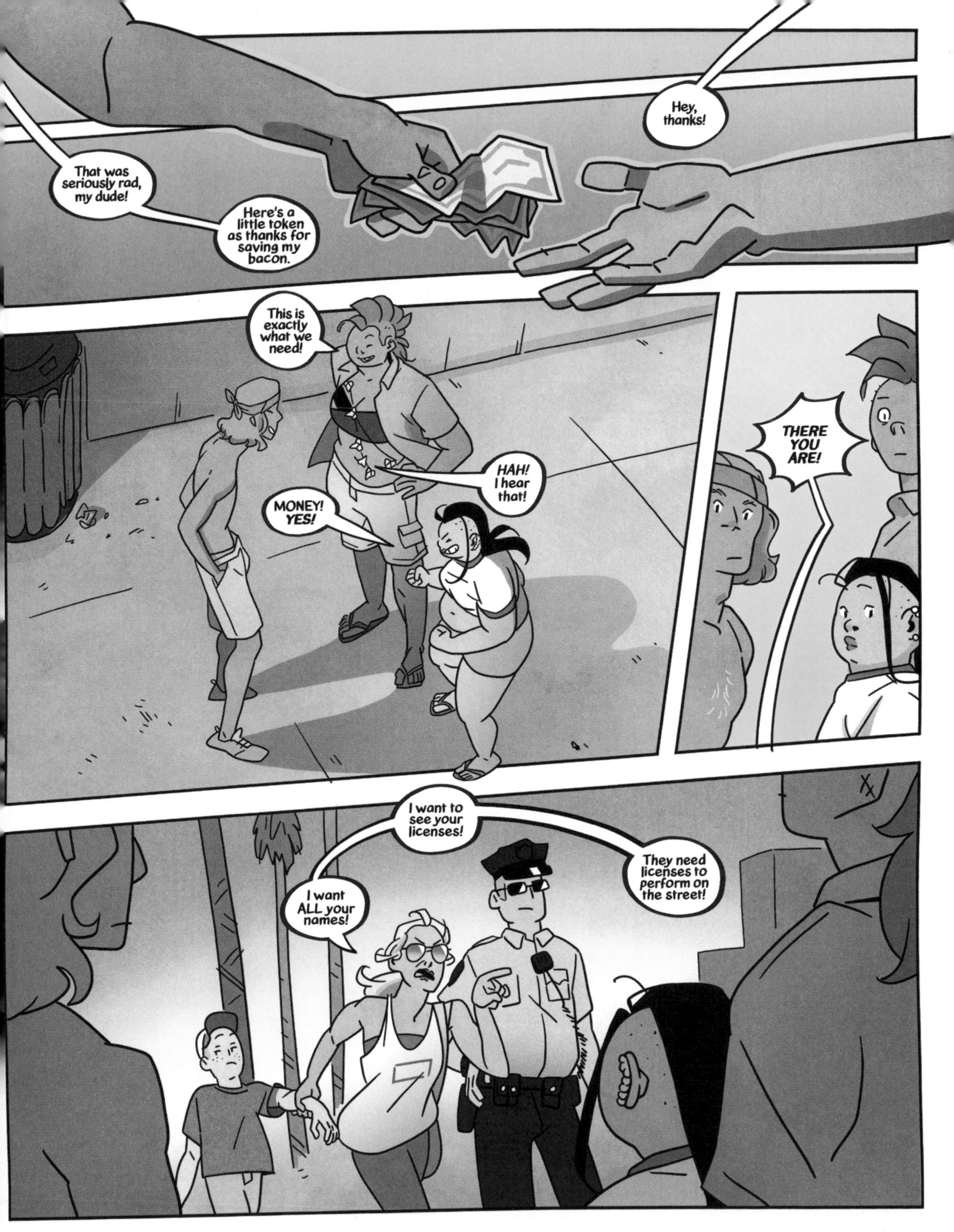
That was seriously rad, my dude!
Here's a little token as thanks for saving my bacon.
Hey, thanks!
This is exactly what we need!
HAH! I hear that!
MONEY! *YES!*
THERE YOU ARE!
I want to see your licenses!
I want ALL your names!
They need licenses to perform on the street!

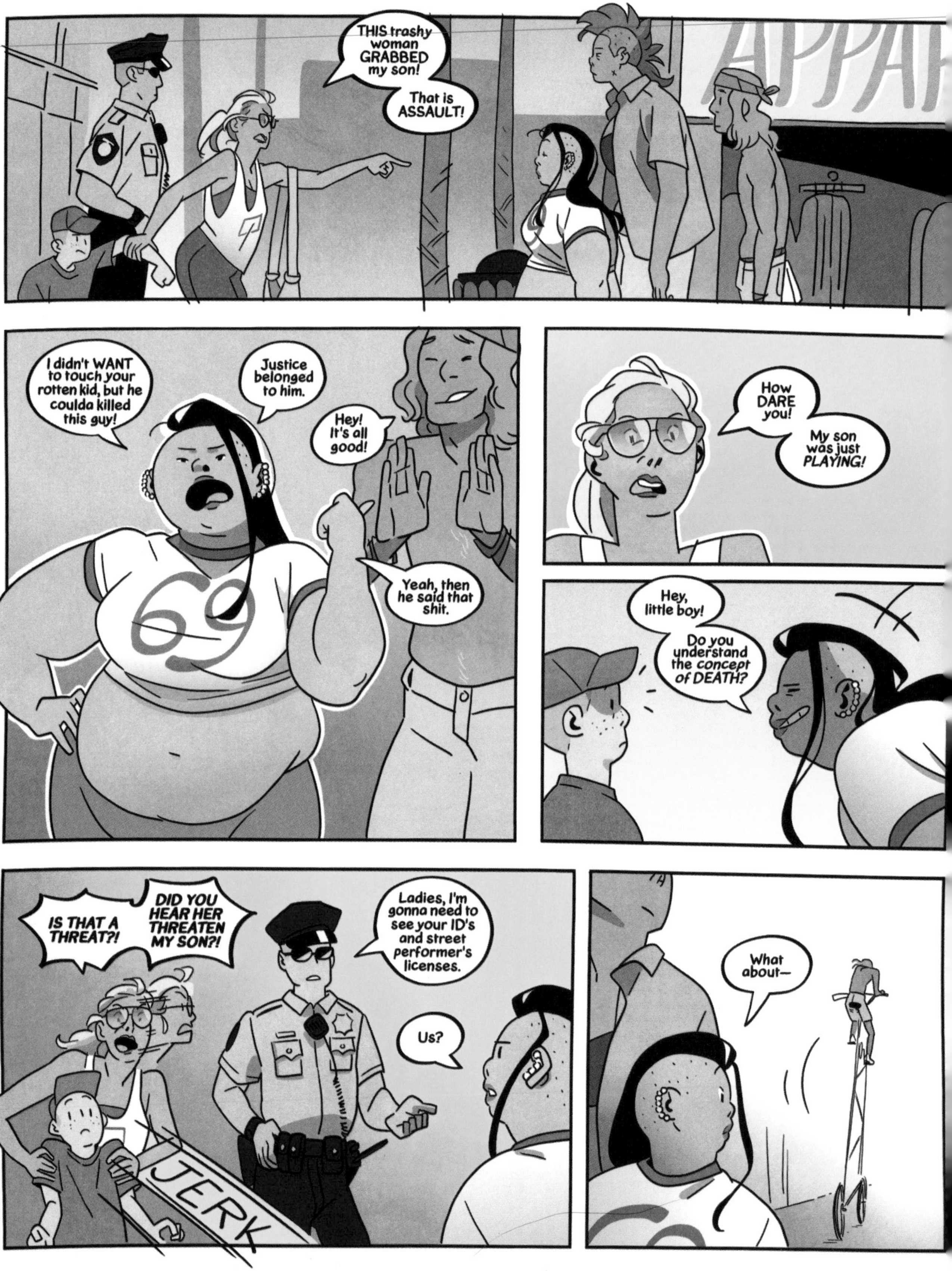
THIS trashy woman GRABBED my son!
That is ASSAULT!
APPAR
I didn't WANT to touch your rotten kid, but he coulda killed this guy!
Justice belonged to him.
Hey! It's all good!
Yeah, then he said that shit.
69
How DARE you!
My son was just PLAYING!
Hey, little boy!
Do you understand the concept of DEATH?
IS THAT A THREAT?!
DID YOU HEAR HER THREATEN MY SON?!
Ladies, I'm gonna need to see your ID's and street performer's licenses.
Us?
JERK
What about—

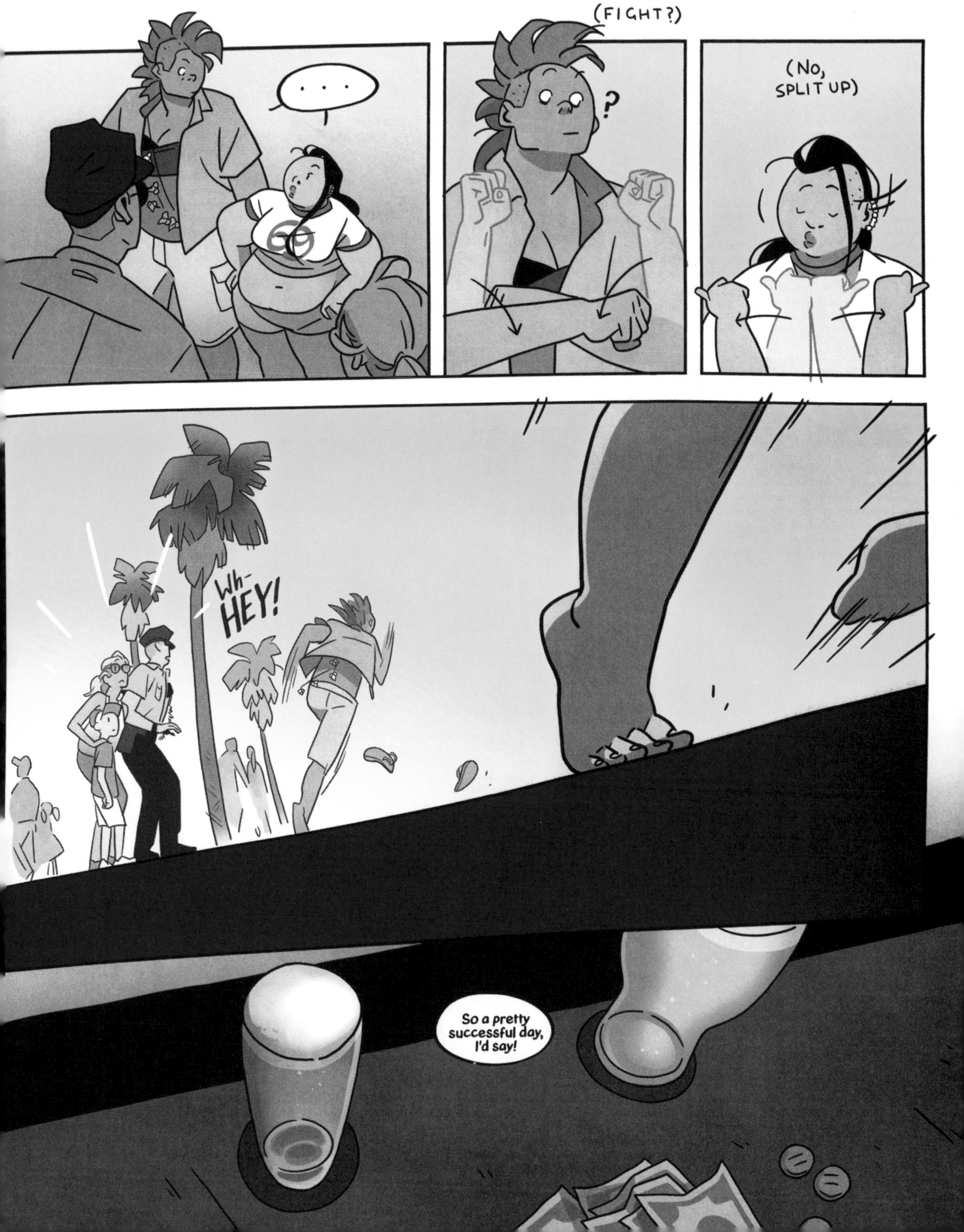
. . .
(FIGHT?)
?
(No, SPLIT UP)
Wh-HEY!
So a pretty successful day, I'd say!

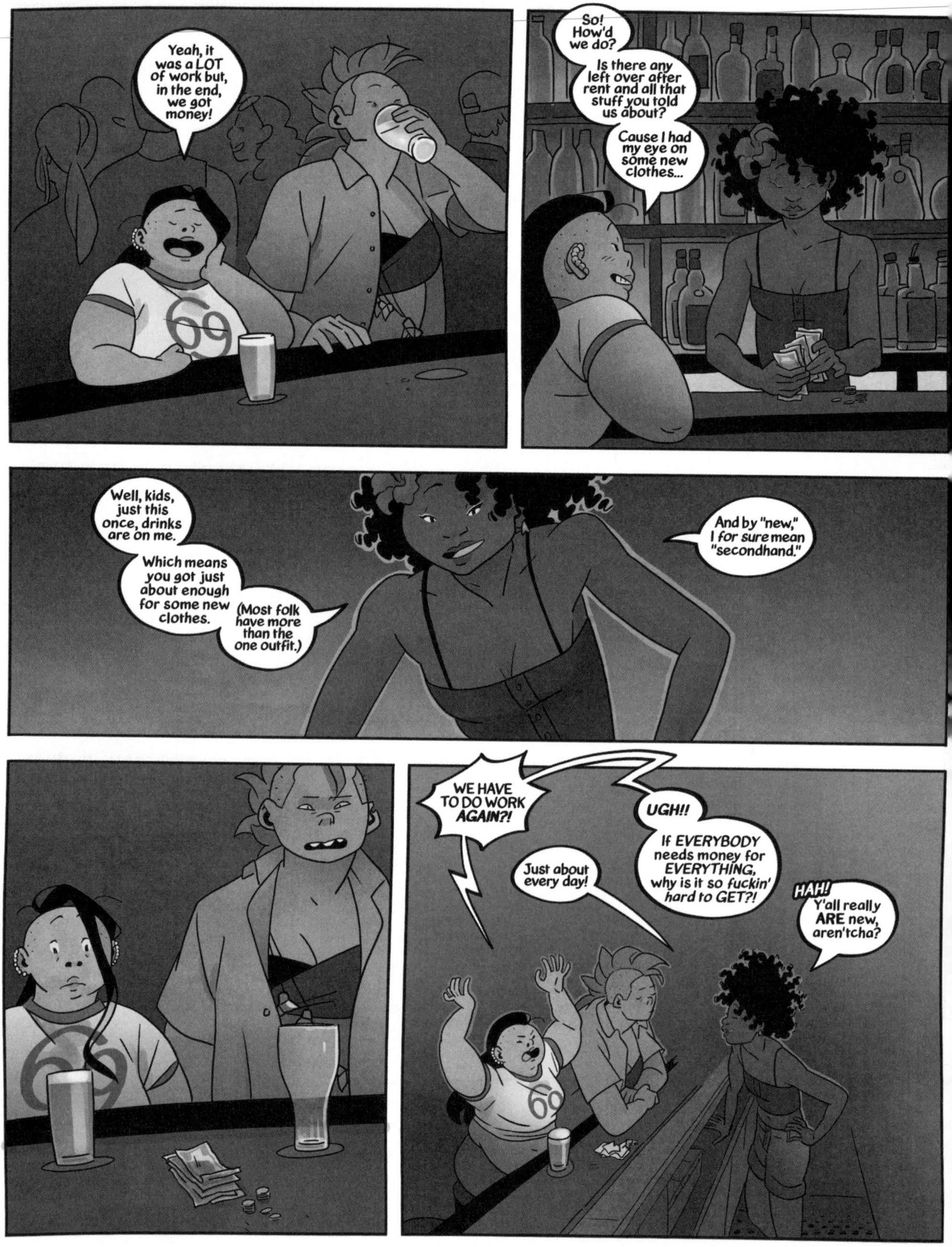
Yeah, it was a LOT of work but, in the end, we got money!
So! How'd we do?
Is there any left over after rent and all that stuff you told us about?
Cause I had my eye on some new clothes...
Well, kids, just this once, drinks are on me.
Which means you got just about enough for some new clothes.
(Most folk have more than the one outfit.)
And by "new," I for sure mean "secondhand."
WE HAVE TO DO WORK AGAIN?!
UGH!!
If EVERYBODY needs money for EVERYTHING, why is it so fuckin' hard to GET?!
Just about every day!
HAH!
Y'all really ARE new, aren'tcha?

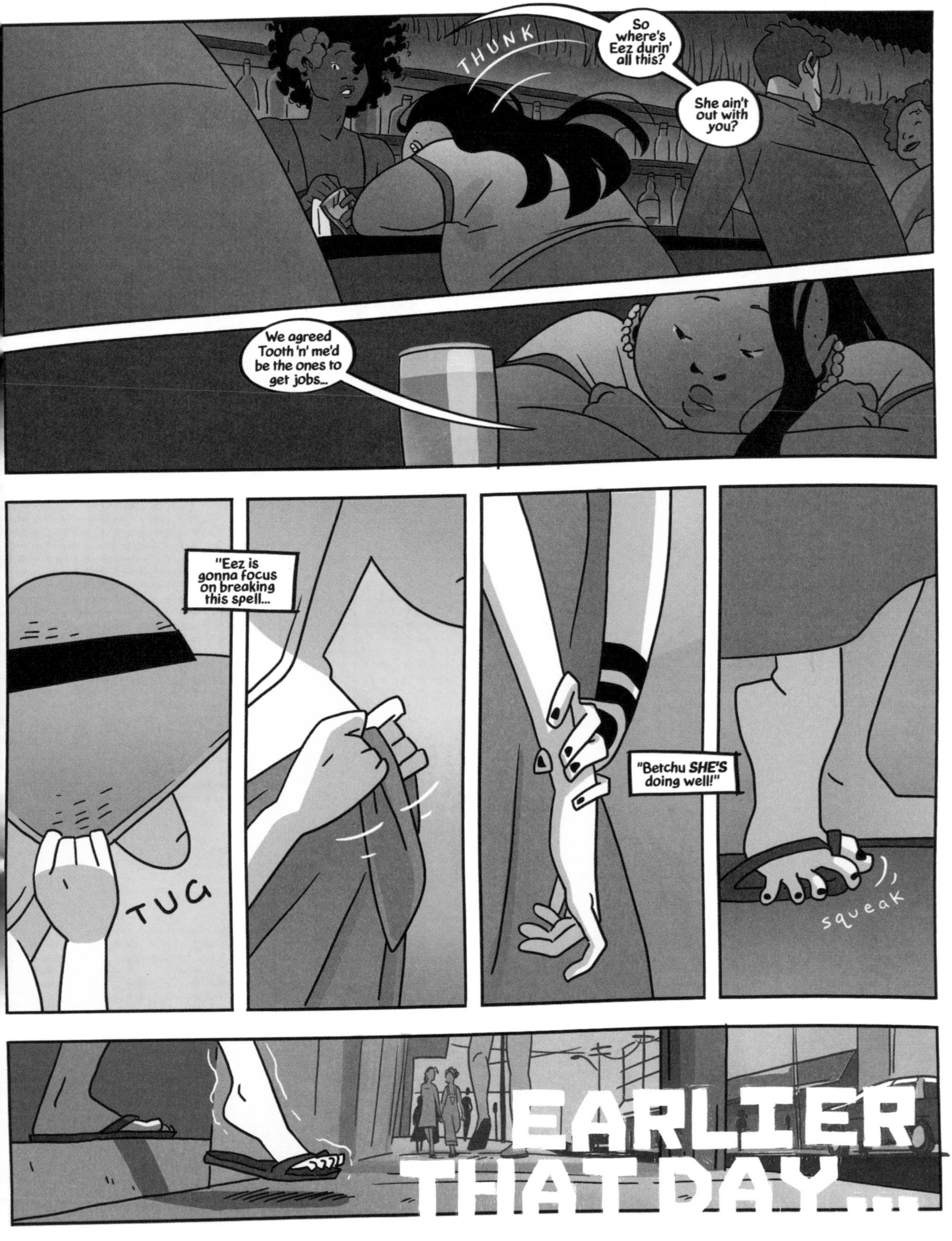
THUNK
So where's Eez durin' all this?
She ain't out with you?
We agreed Tooth 'n' me'd be the ones to get jobs...
"Eez is gonna focus on breaking this spell...
TUG
"Betchu SHE'S doing well!"
squeak
EARLIER THAT DAY...

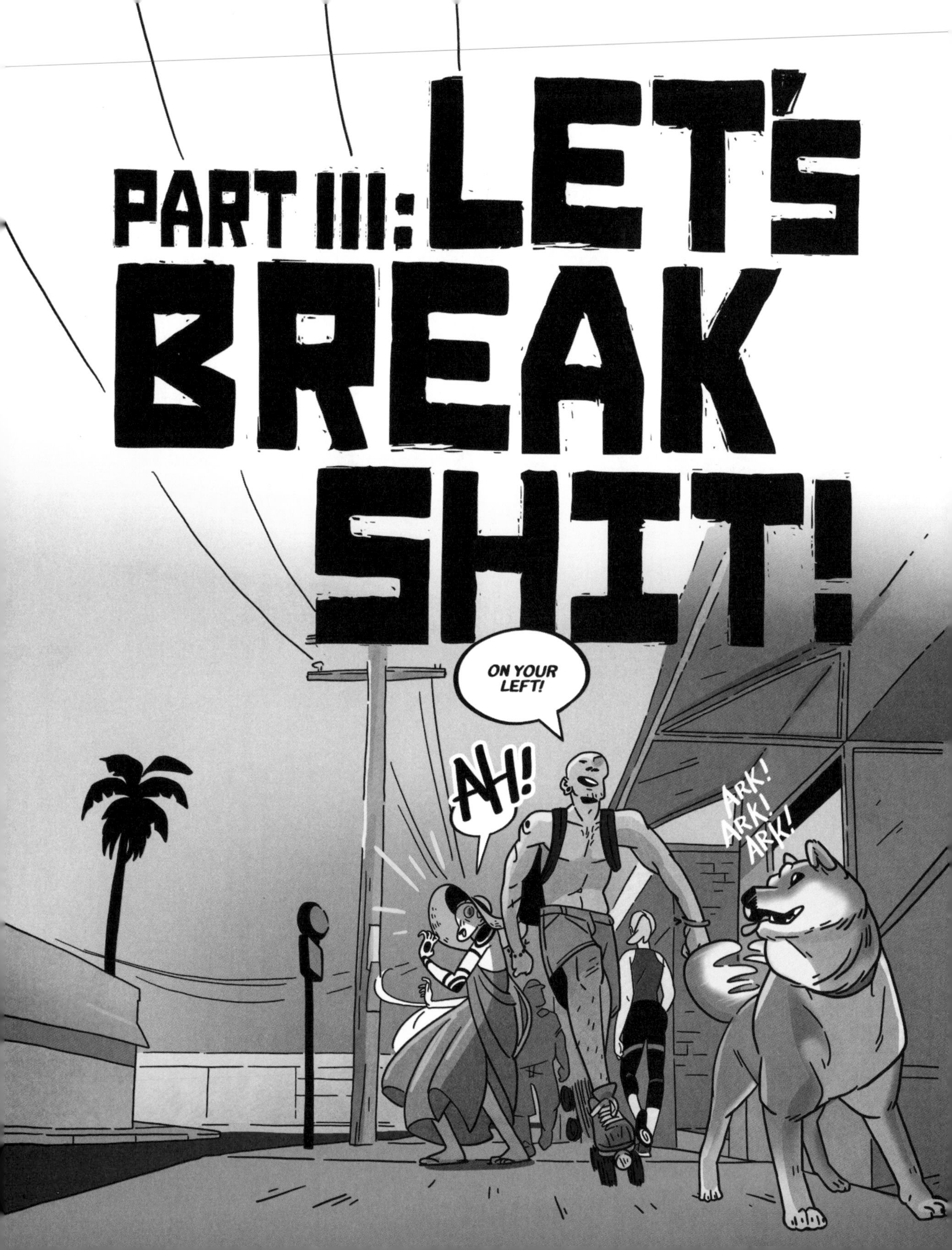
PART III: LET'S BREAK SHIT!
ON YOUR LEFT!
AH!
ARK! ARK! ARK!

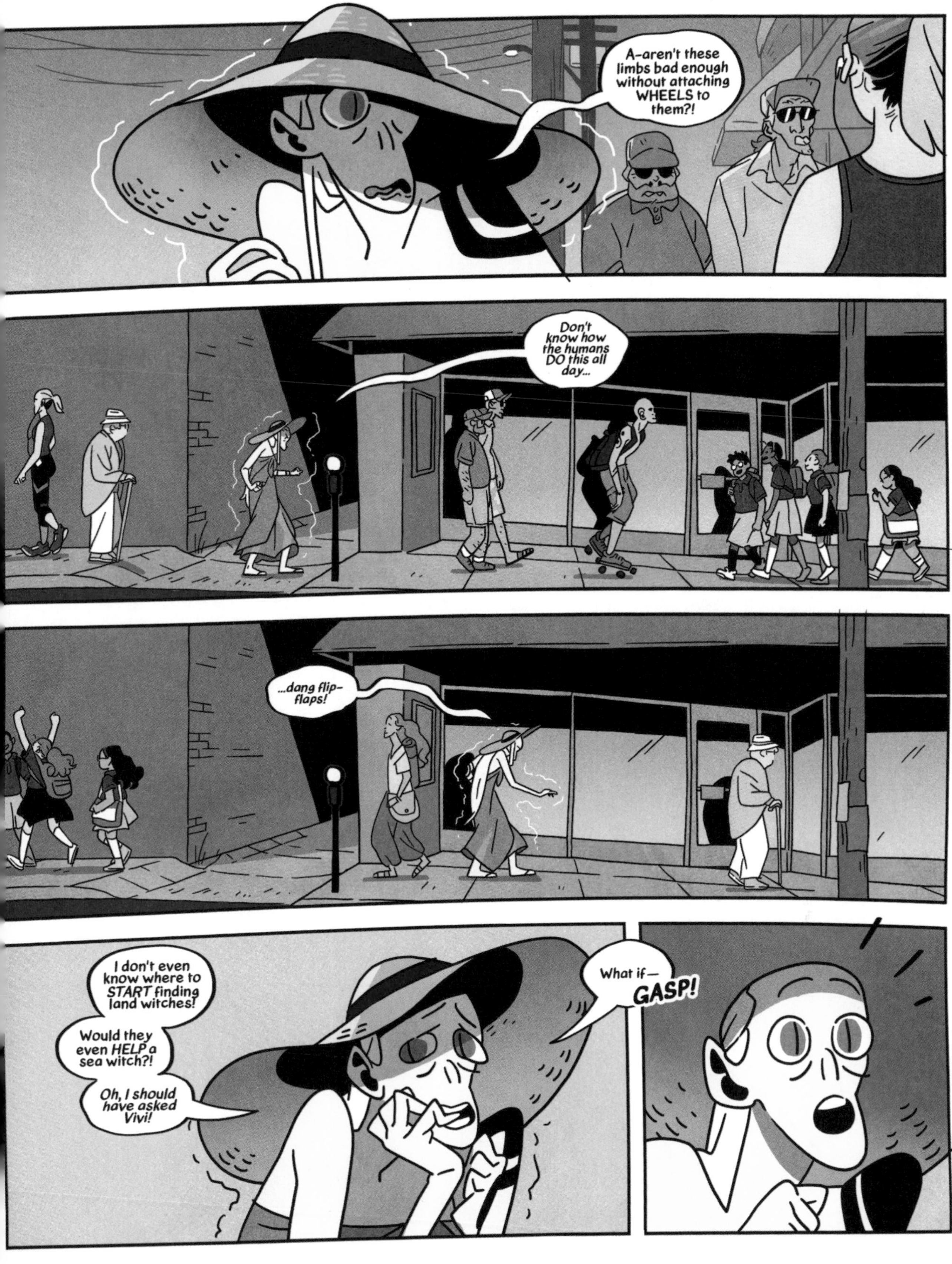

A-aren't these limbs bad enough without attaching WHEELS to them?!
Don't know how the humans DO this all day...
...dang flip-flaps!
I don't even know where to START finding land witches!
Would they even HELP a sea witch?!
Oh, I should have asked Vivi!
What if—
GASP!

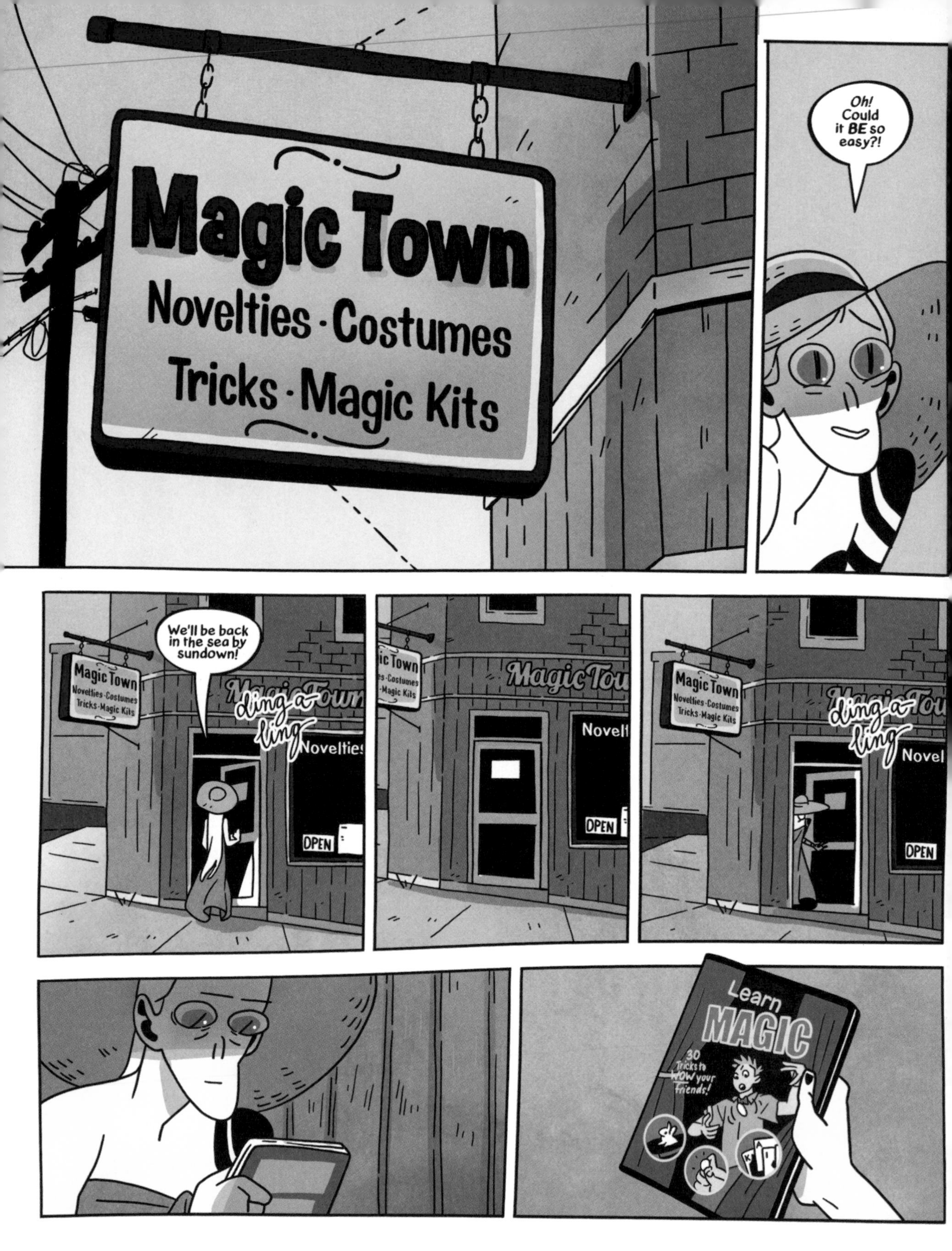

Magic Town
Novelties · Costumes
Tricks · Magic Kits
Oh! Could it BE so easy?!
We'll be back in the sea by sundown!
Magic Town
ding-a-ling
Novelties
OPEN
Magic Town
Novelt
OPEN
ding-a-ling
OPEN
Learn MAGIC
30 Tricks to WOW your Friends!

or not.

PSYCHIC READINGS
Fortune Future Fate

READINGS:
PALM $15
TAROT $35
CRYSTAL BALL $40

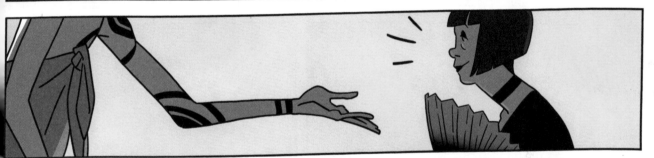

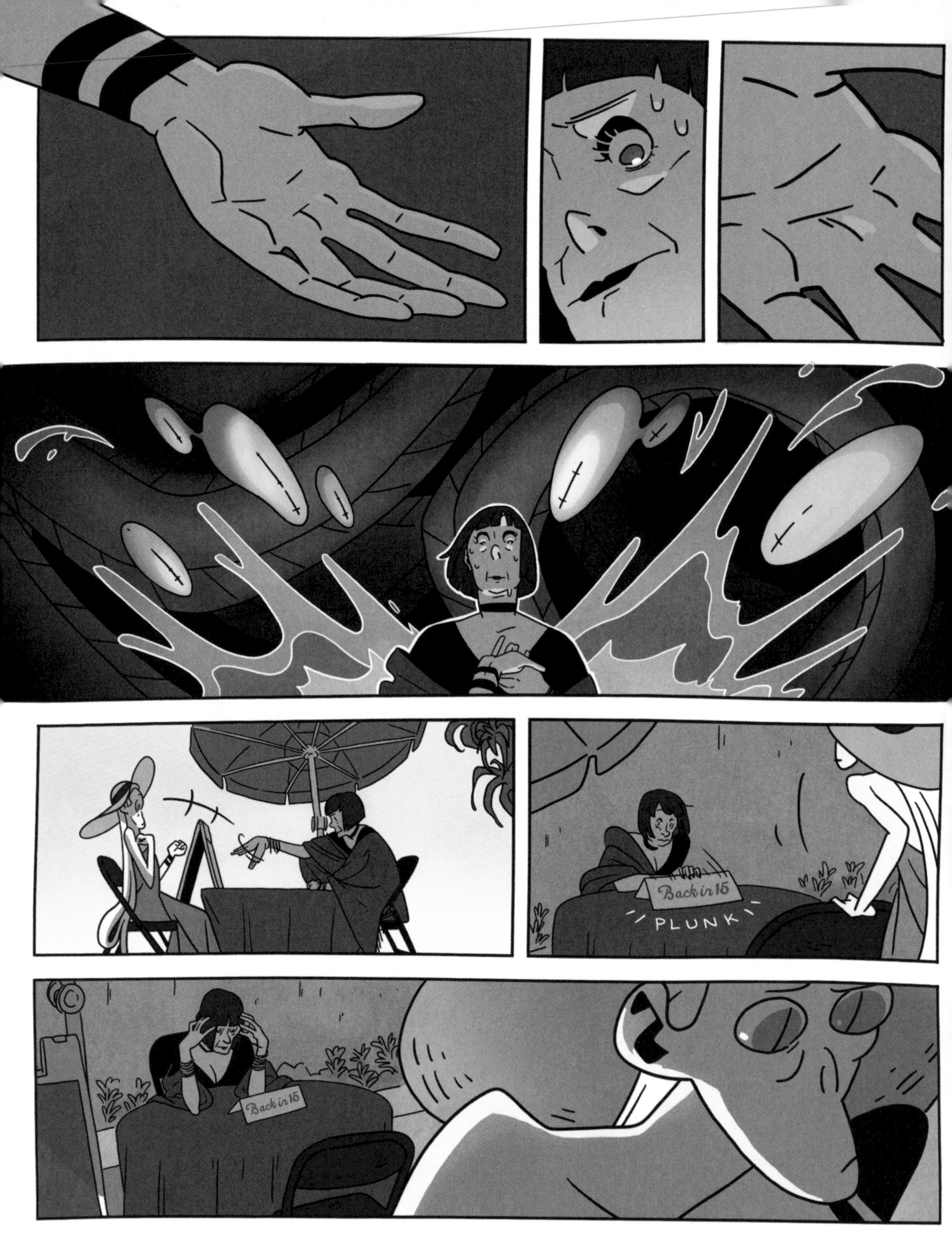
Back in 15
PLUNK
Back in 15

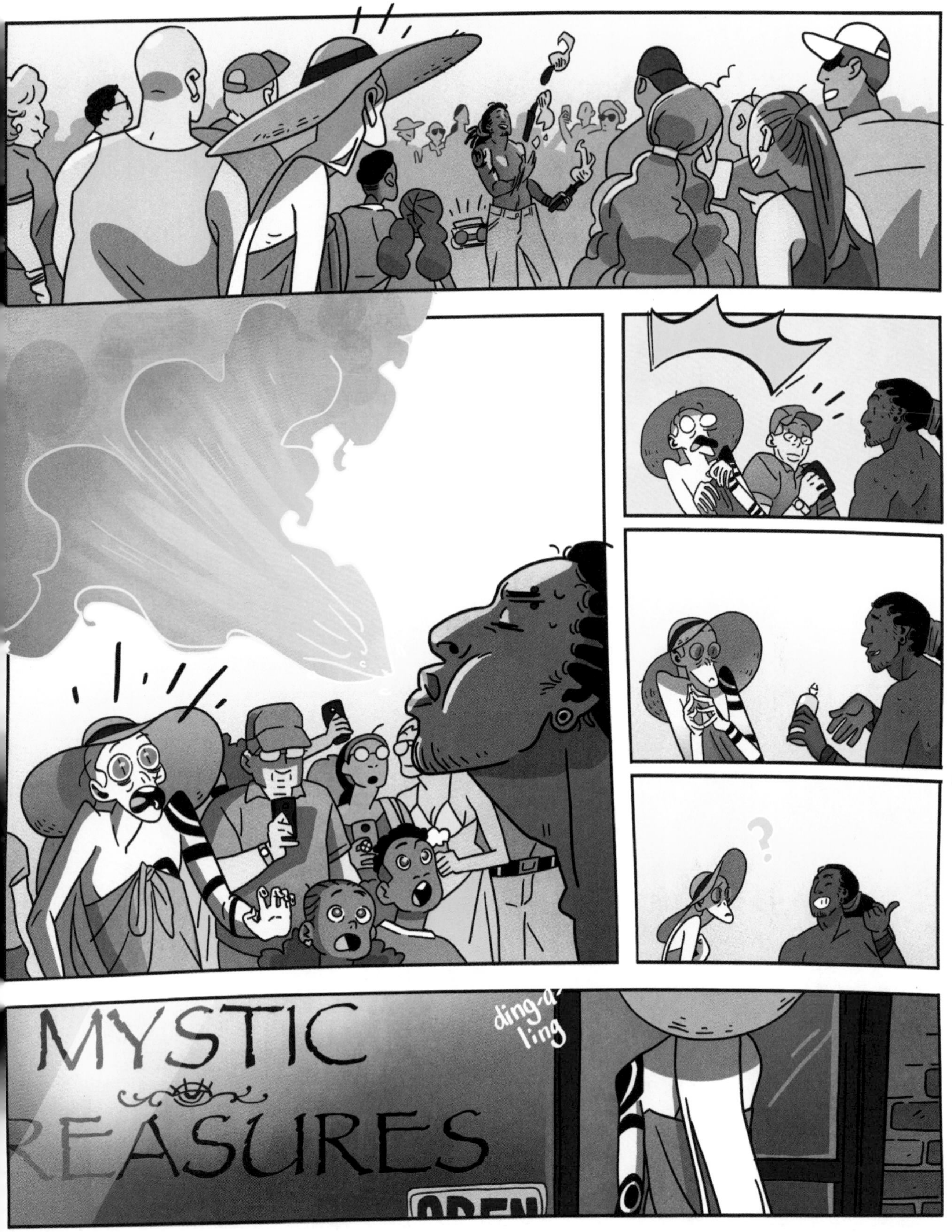
?
MYSTIC
TREASURES
ding-a-ling
OPEN

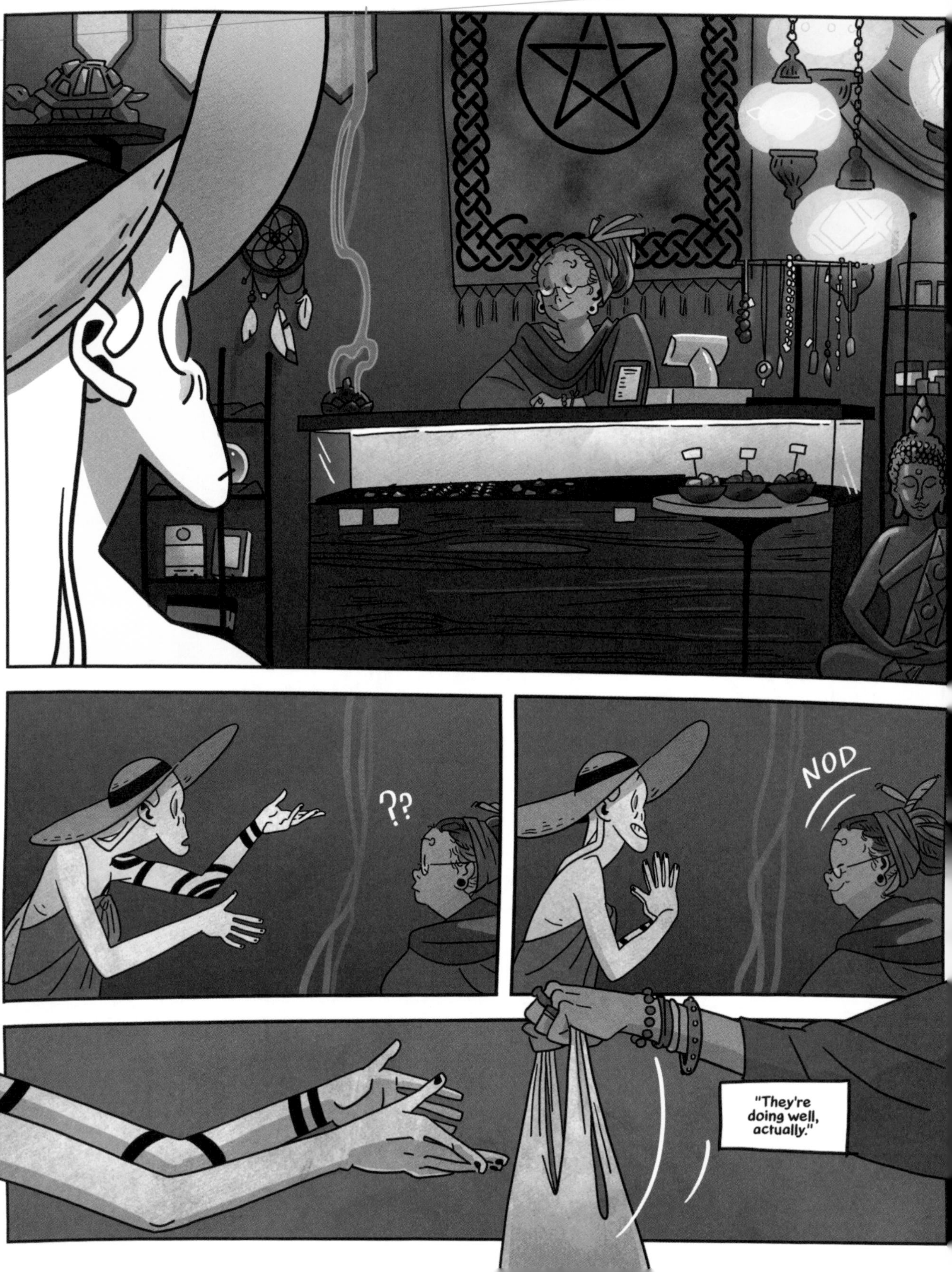
??
NOD
"They're doing well, actually."

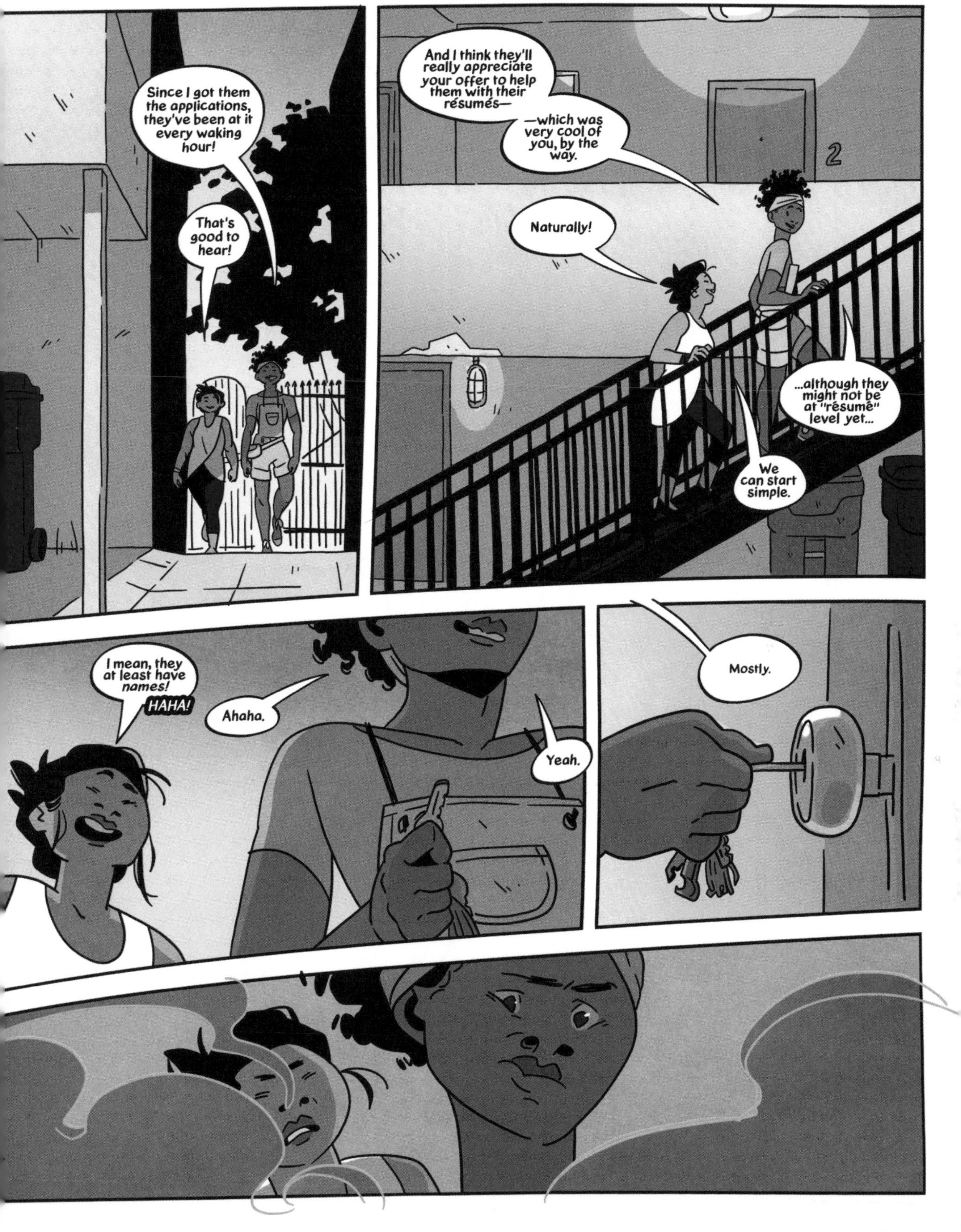

Since I got them the applications, they've been at it every waking hour!
That's good to hear!
And I think they'll really appreciate your offer to help them with their résumés—
—which was very cool of you, by the way.
Naturally!
...although they might not be at "résumé" level yet...
We can start simple.
I mean, they at least have names!
HAHA!
Ahaha.
Yeah.
Mostly.

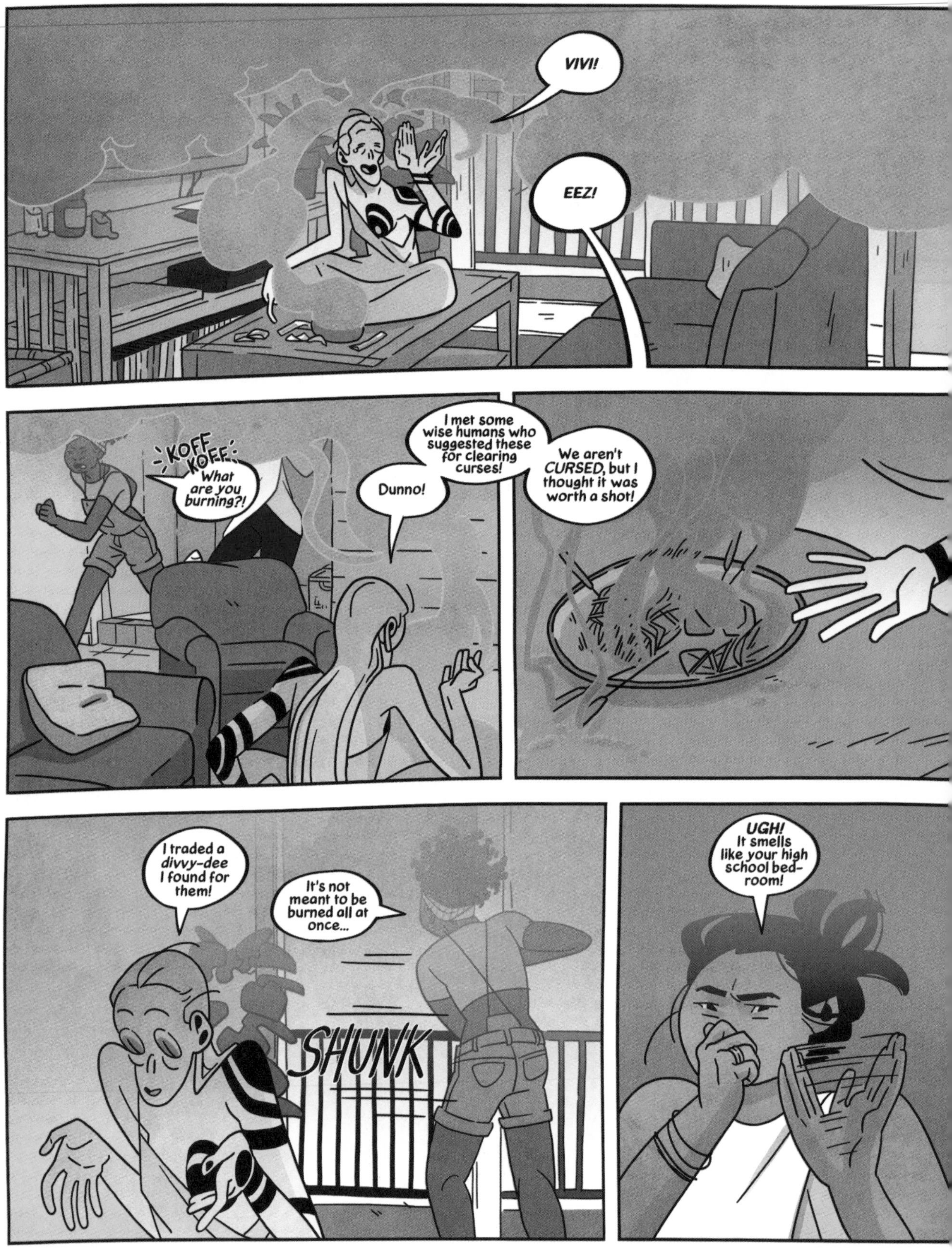
VIVI!
EEZ!
KOFF KOFF
What are you burning?!
Dunno!
I met some wise humans who suggested these for clearing curses!
We aren't CURSED, but I thought it was worth a shot!
I traded a divvy-dee I found for them!
It's not meant to be burned all at once...
SHUNK
UGH! It smells like your high school bed-room!

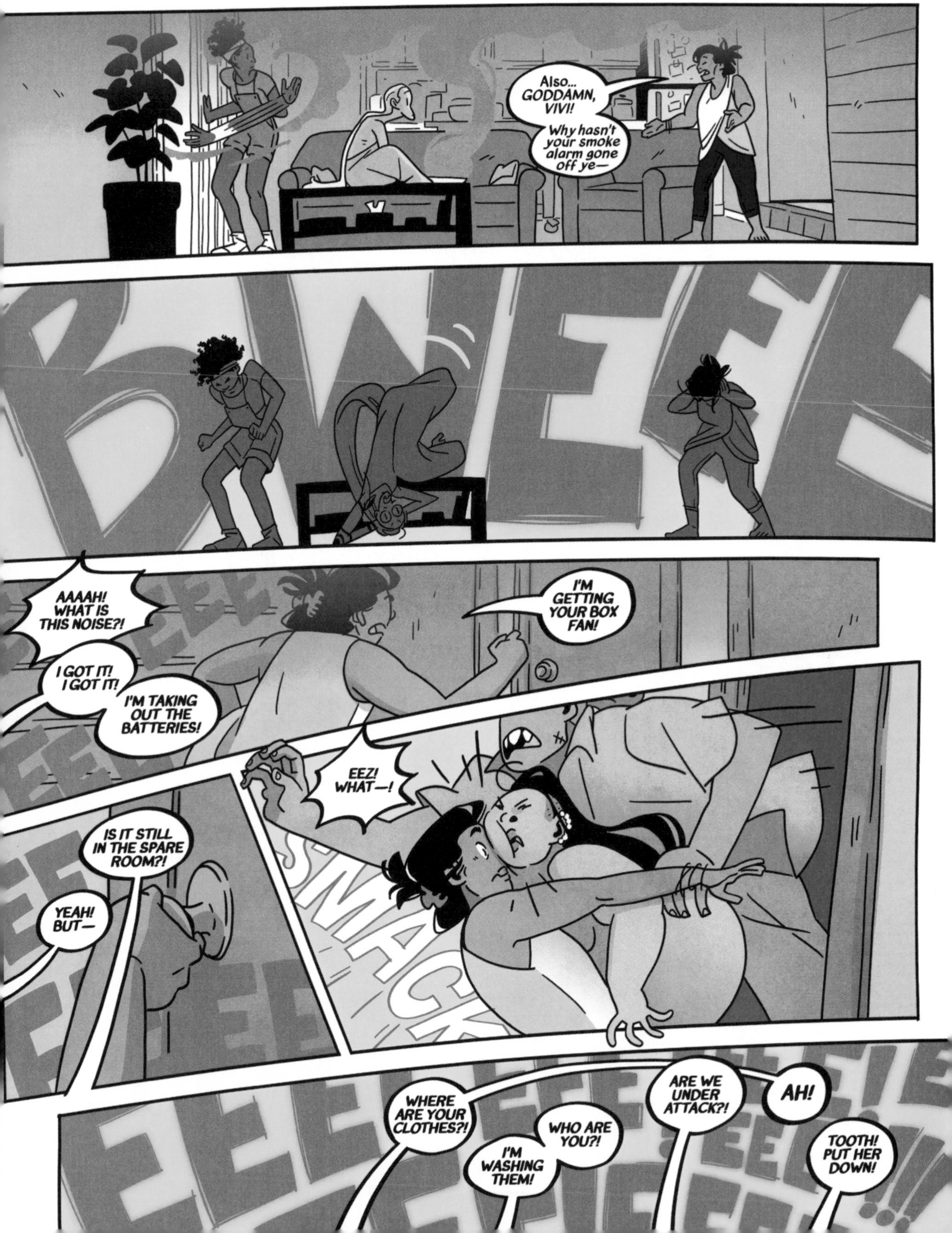
Also... GODDAMN, VIVI!
Why hasn't your smoke alarm gone off ye—
AAAAH! WHAT IS THIS NOISE?!
I'M GETTING YOUR BOX FAN!
I GOT IT! I GOT IT!
I'M TAKING OUT THE BATTERIES!
EEZ! WHAT—!
IS IT STILL IN THE SPARE ROOM?!
YEAH! BUT—
SMACK
WHERE ARE YOUR CLOTHES?!
I'M WASHING THEM!
WHO ARE YOU?!
ARE WE UNDER ATTACK?!
AH!
TOOTH! PUT HER DOWN!

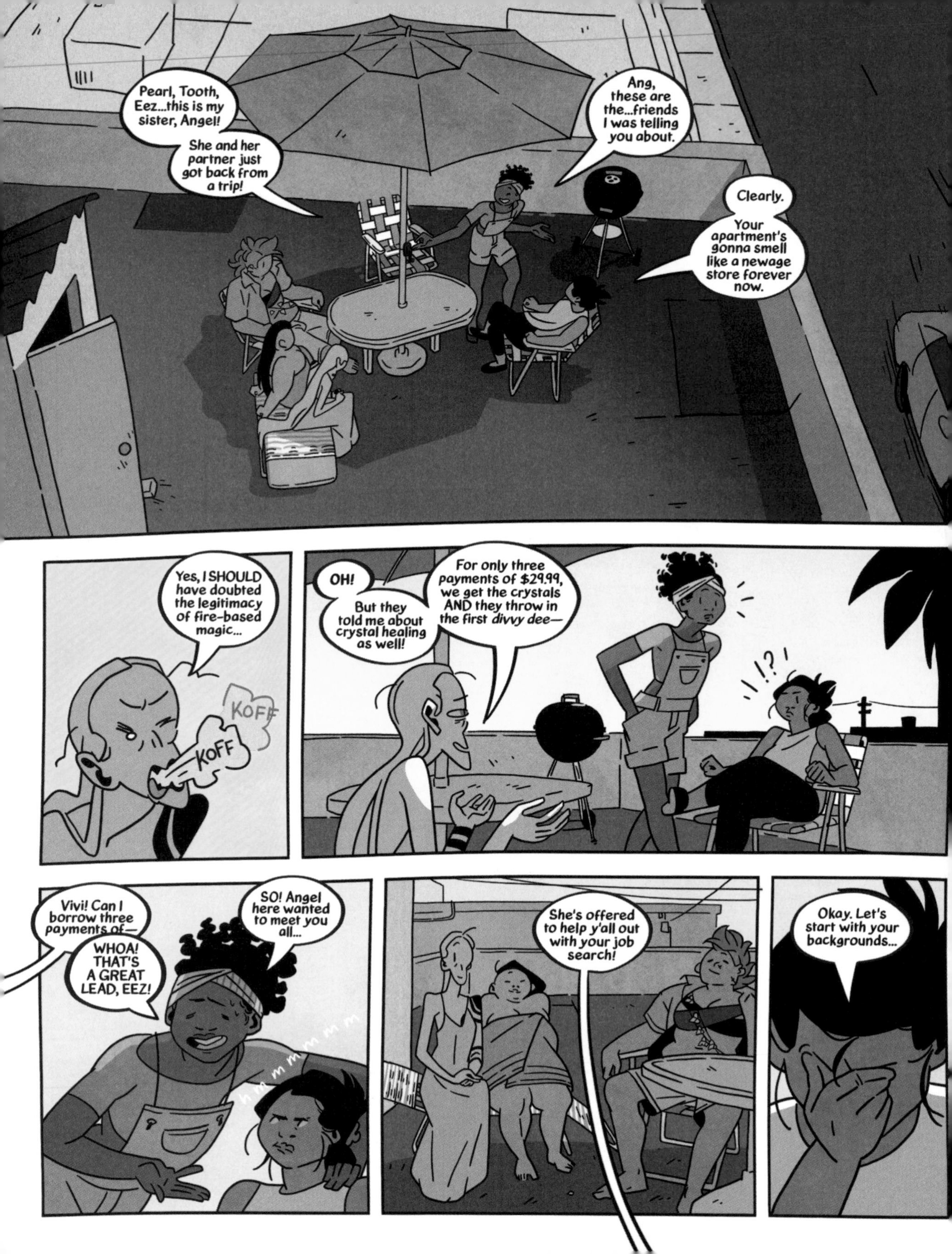
Pearl, Tooth, Eez...this is my sister, Angel!
She and her partner just got back from a trip!
Ang, these are the...friends I was telling you about.
Clearly.
Your apartment's gonna smell like a newage store forever now.
Yes, I SHOULD have doubted the legitimacy of fire-based magic...
KOFF
KOFF
OH!
But they told me about crystal healing as well!
For only three payments of $29.99, we get the crystals AND they throw in the first *divvy dee*—
!?
Vivi! Can I borrow three payments of—
WHOA! THAT'S A GREAT LEAD, EEZ!
SO! Angel here wanted to meet you all...
hmmmmmmm
She's offered to help y'all out with your job search!
Okay. Let's start with your backgrounds...

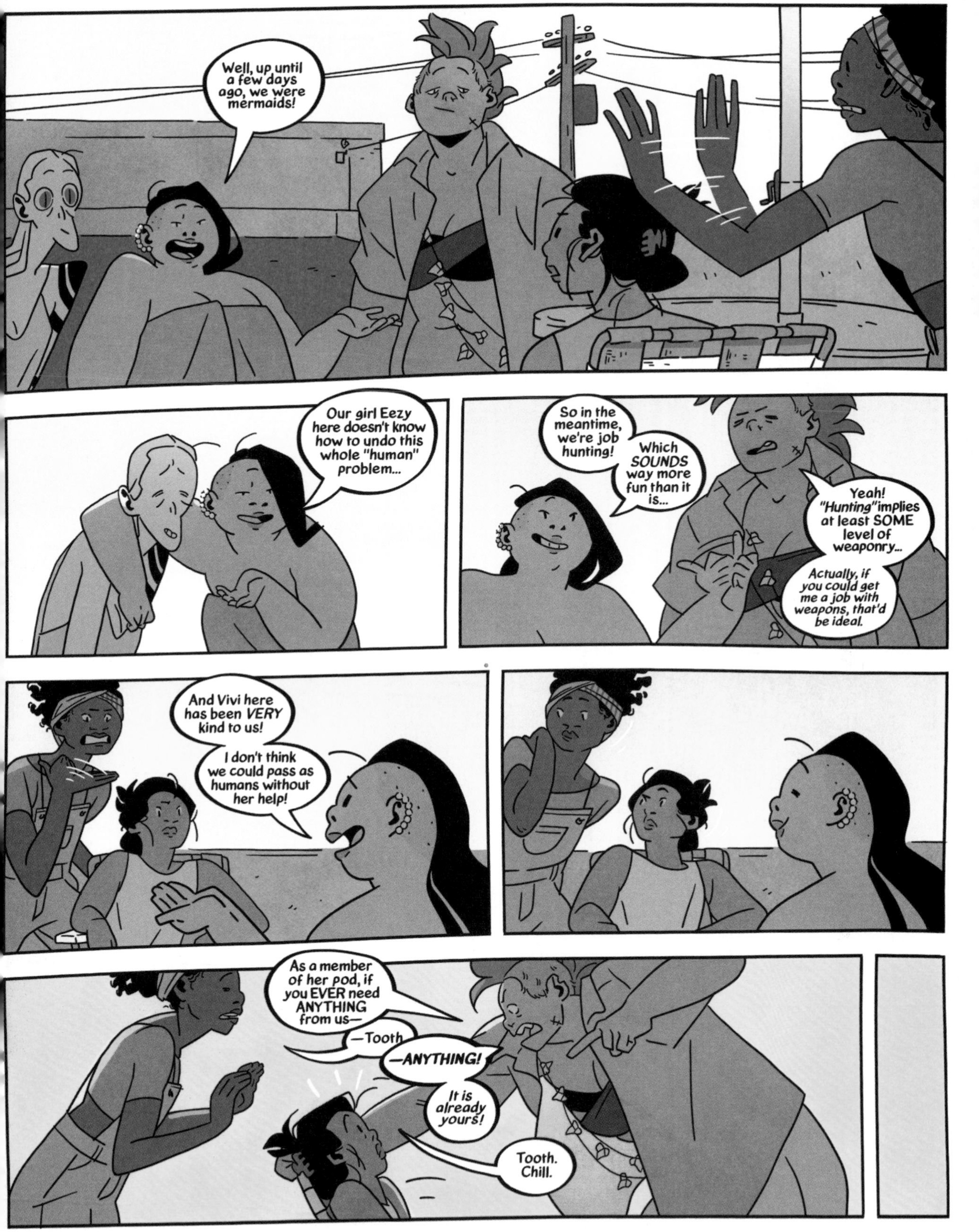
Well, up until a few days ago, we were mermaids!
Our girl Eezy here doesn't know how to undo this whole "human" problem...
So in the meantime, we're job hunting!
Which SOUNDS way more fun than it is...
Yeah! "Hunting" implies at least SOME level of weaponry...
Actually, if you could get me a job with weapons, that'd be ideal.
And Vivi here has been VERY kind to us!
I don't think we could pass as humans without her help!
As a member of her pod, if you EVER need ANYTHING from us—
—Tooth
—ANYTHING!
It is already yours!
Tooth. Chill.

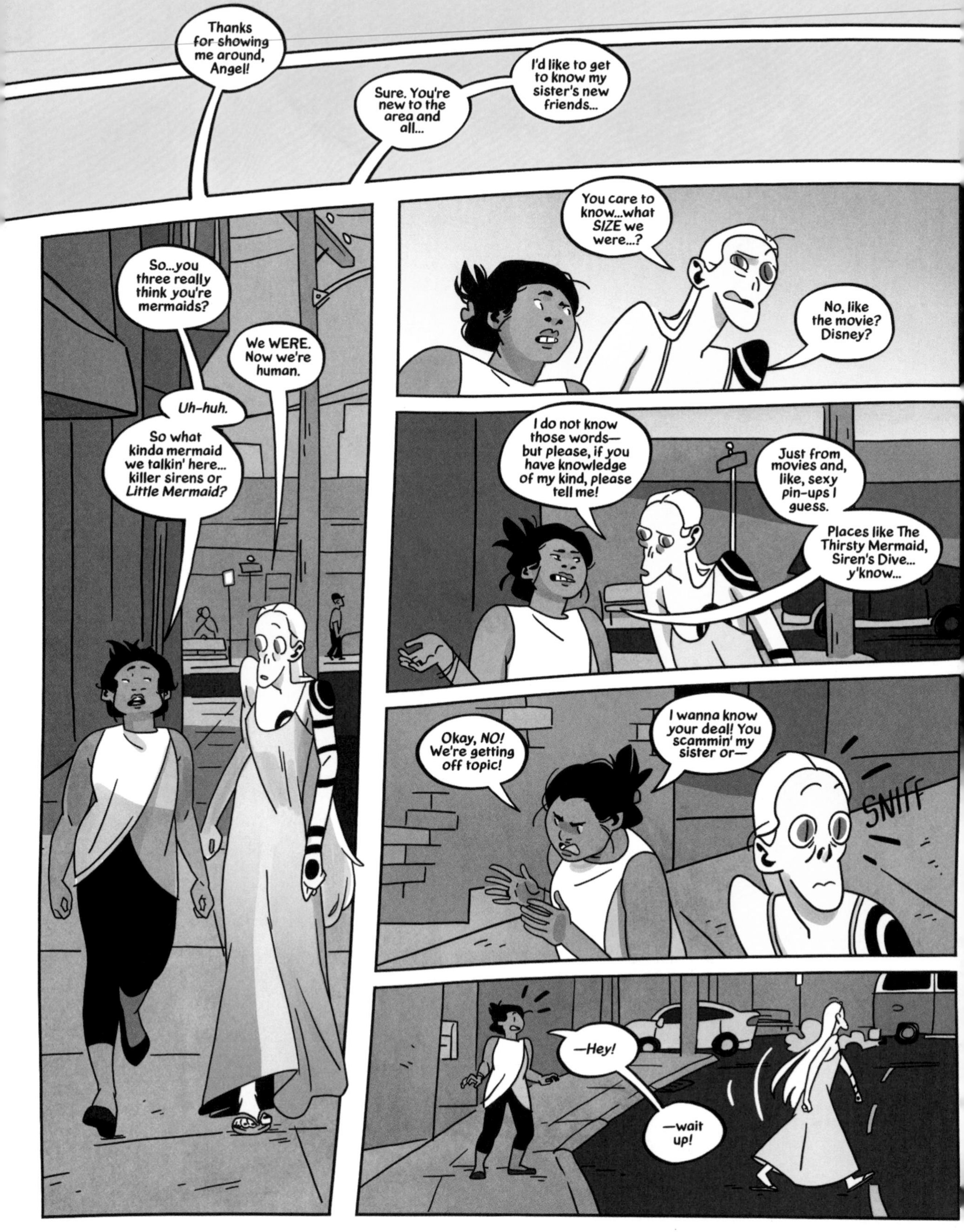

Thanks for showing me around, Angel!
Sure. You're new to the area and all...
I'd like to get to know my sister's new friends...
So...you three really think *you're* mermaids?
We WERE. Now we're human.
Uh-huh.
So what kinda mermaid we talkin' here... killer sirens or *Little Mermaid?*
You care to know...what *SIZE* we were...?
No, like the movie? Disney?
I do not know those words— but please, if you have knowledge of my kind, please tell me!
Just from movies and, like, sexy pin-ups I guess.
Places like The Thirsty Mermaid, Siren's Dive... y'know...
Okay, *NO!* We're getting off topic!
I wanna know your deal! You scammin' my sister or—
SNIFF
—Hey!
—wait up!

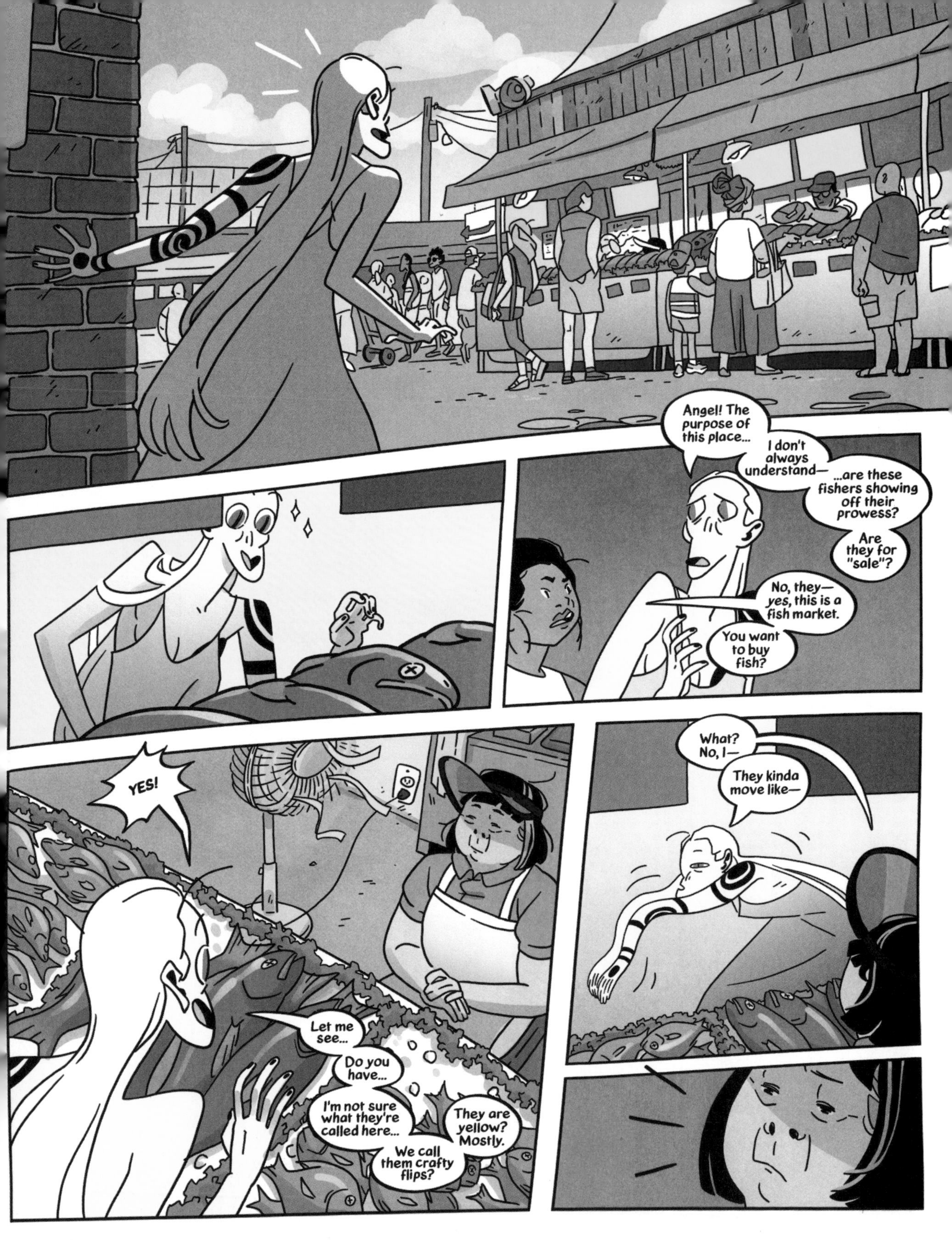
Angel! The purpose of this place...
I don't always understand—
...are these fishers showing off their prowess?
Are they for "sale"?
No, they—yes, this is a fish market.
You want to buy fish?
YES!
Let me see...
Do you have...
I'm not sure what they're called here...
They are yellow? Mostly.
We call them crafty flips?
What? No, I—
They kinda move like—

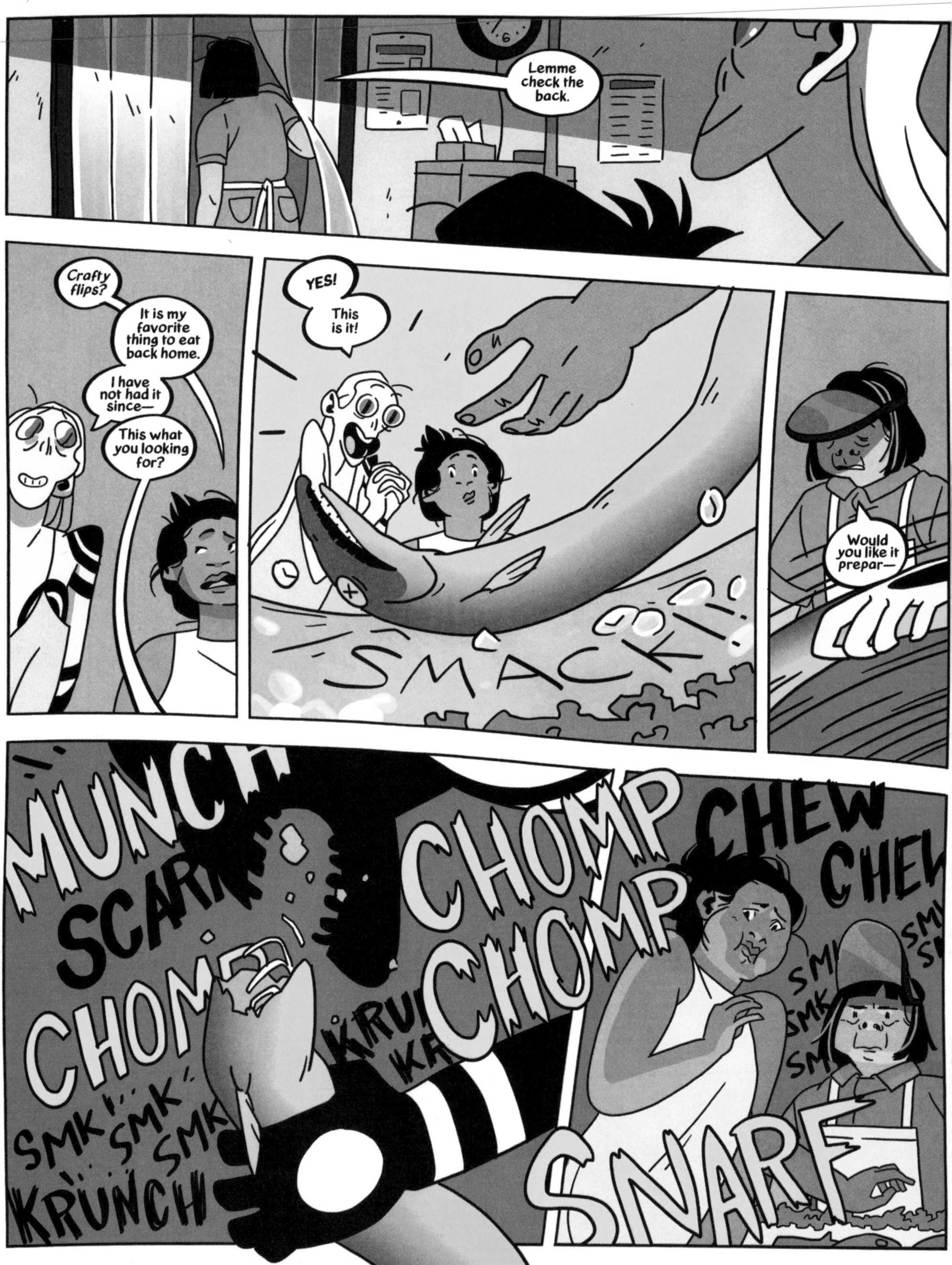

Lemme check the back.
Crafty flips?
It is my favorite thing to eat back home.
I have not had it since—
This what you looking for?
YES!
This is it!
SMACK
Would you like it prepar—
MUNCH
SCARF
CHOMP
CHOMP
CHOMP
CHEW
CHEW
KRUN
KRU
SMK
SMK
SMK
KRUNCH
SNARF

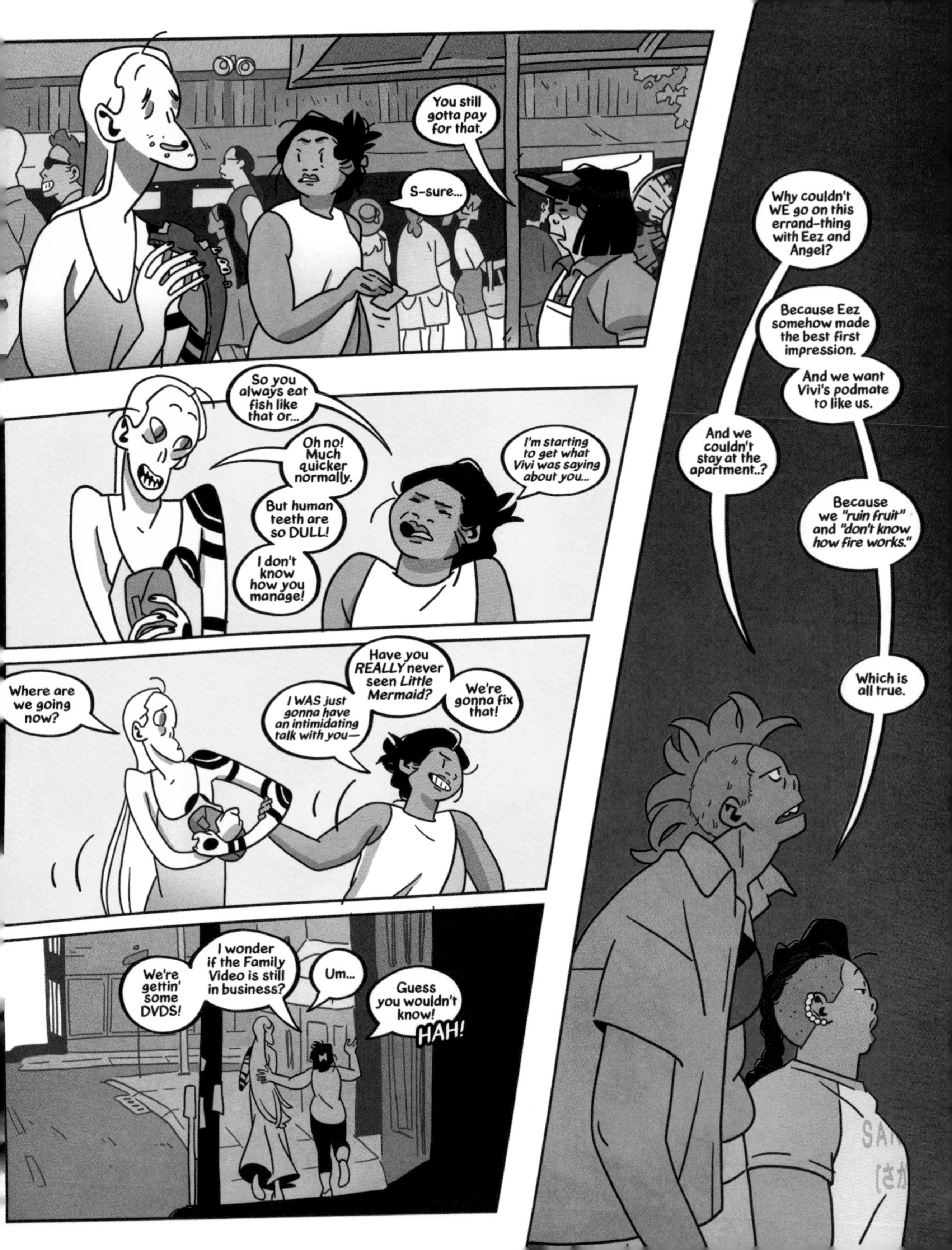
You still gotta pay for that.
S-sure...
So you always eat fish like that or...
Oh no! Much quicker normally.
But human teeth are so DULL!
I don't know how you manage!
I'm starting to get what Vivi was saying about you...
Where are we going now?
I WAS just gonna have an intimidating talk with you—
Have you REALLY never seen Little Mermaid?
We're gonna fix that!
We're gettin' some DVDS!
I wonder if the Family Video is still in business?
Um...
Guess you wouldn't know!
HAH!
Why couldn't WE go on this errand-thing with Eez and Angel?
Because Eez somehow made the best first impression.
And we want Vivi's podmate to like us.
And we couldn't stay at the apartment..?
Because we "ruin fruit" and "don't know how fire works."
Which is all true.

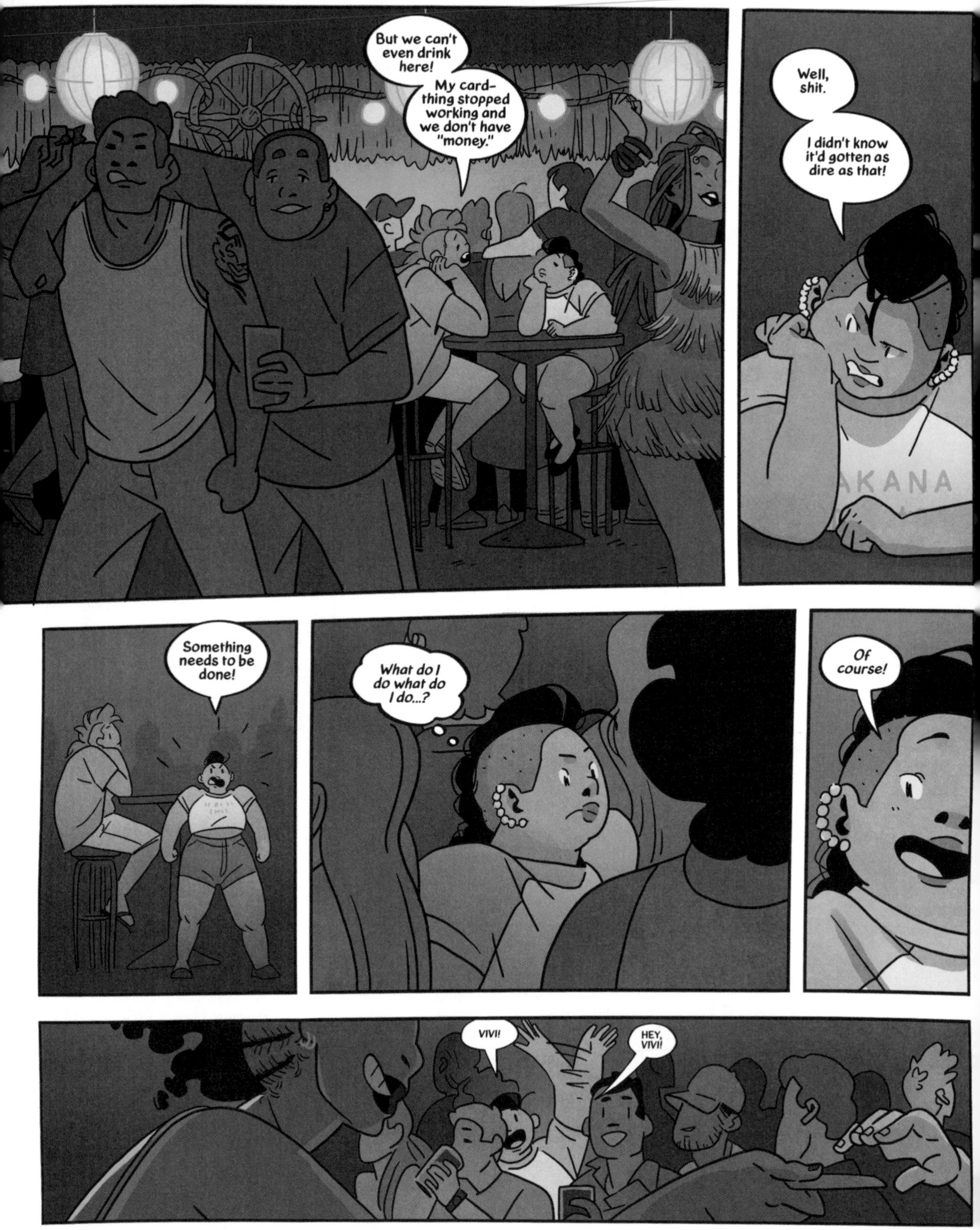
But we can't even drink here!
My card-thing stopped working and we don't have "money."
Well, shit.
I didn't know it'd gotten as dire as that!
AKANA
Something needs to be done!
What do I do what do I do...?
Of course!
VIVI!
HEY, VIVI!

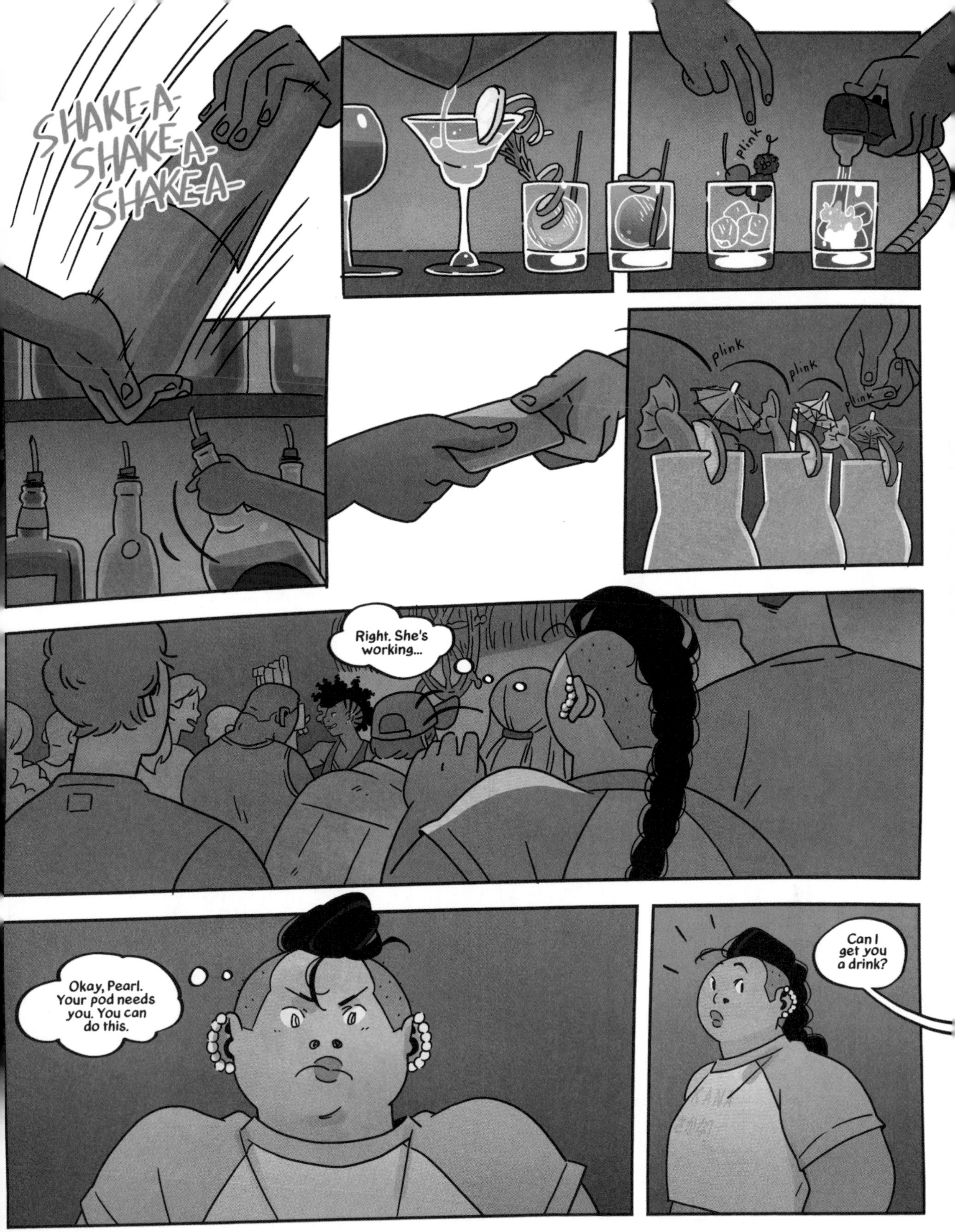
SHAKE-A-
SHAKE-A-
SHAKE-A-
plink
plink
plink
plink
Right. She's working...
Okay, Pearl. Your pod needs you. You can do this.
Can I get you a drink?

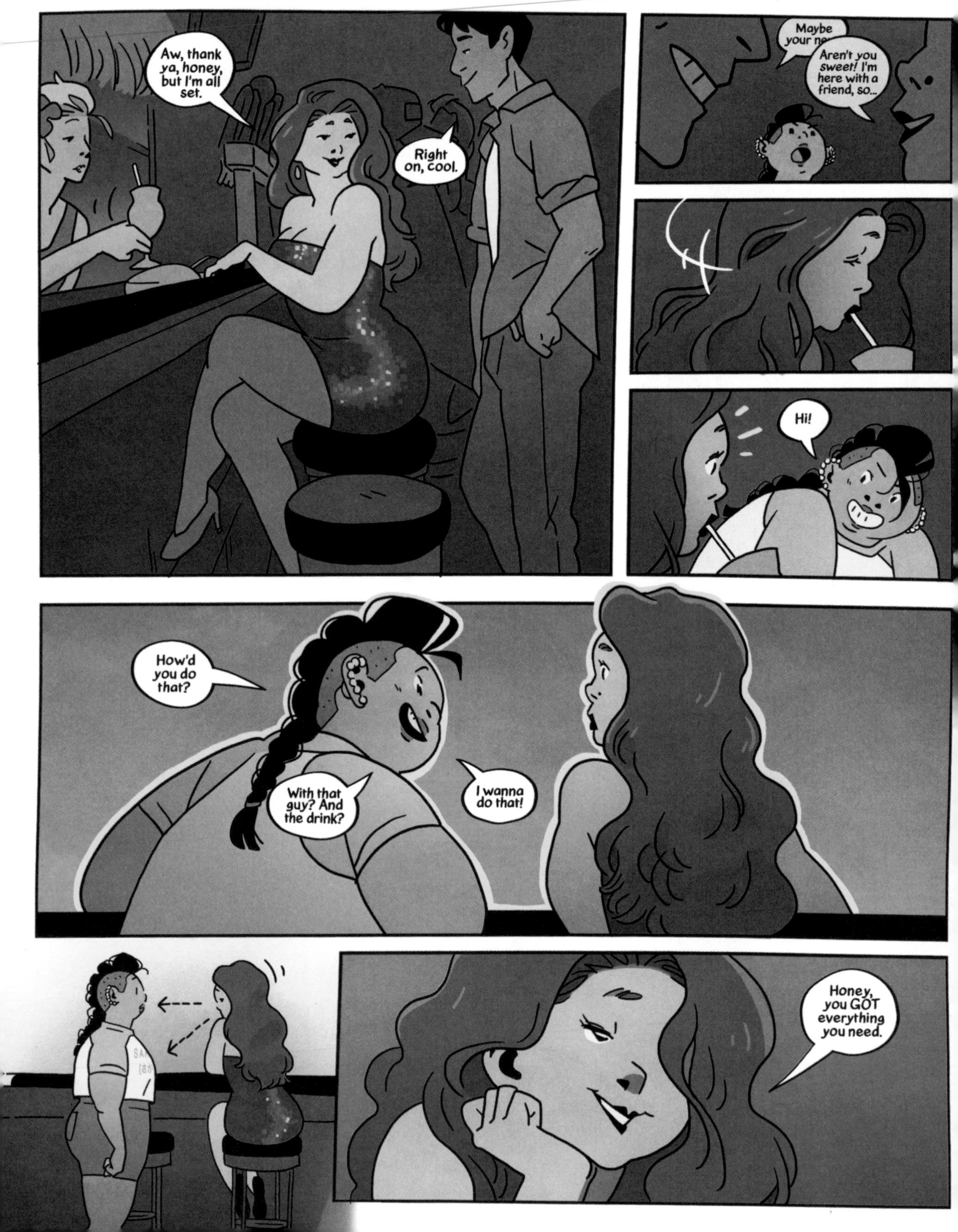
Aw, thank ya, honey, but I'm all set.
Right on, cool.
Aren't you sweet! I'm here with a friend, so...
Hi!
How'd you do that?
With that guy? And the drink?
I wanna do that!
Honey, you GOT everything you need.

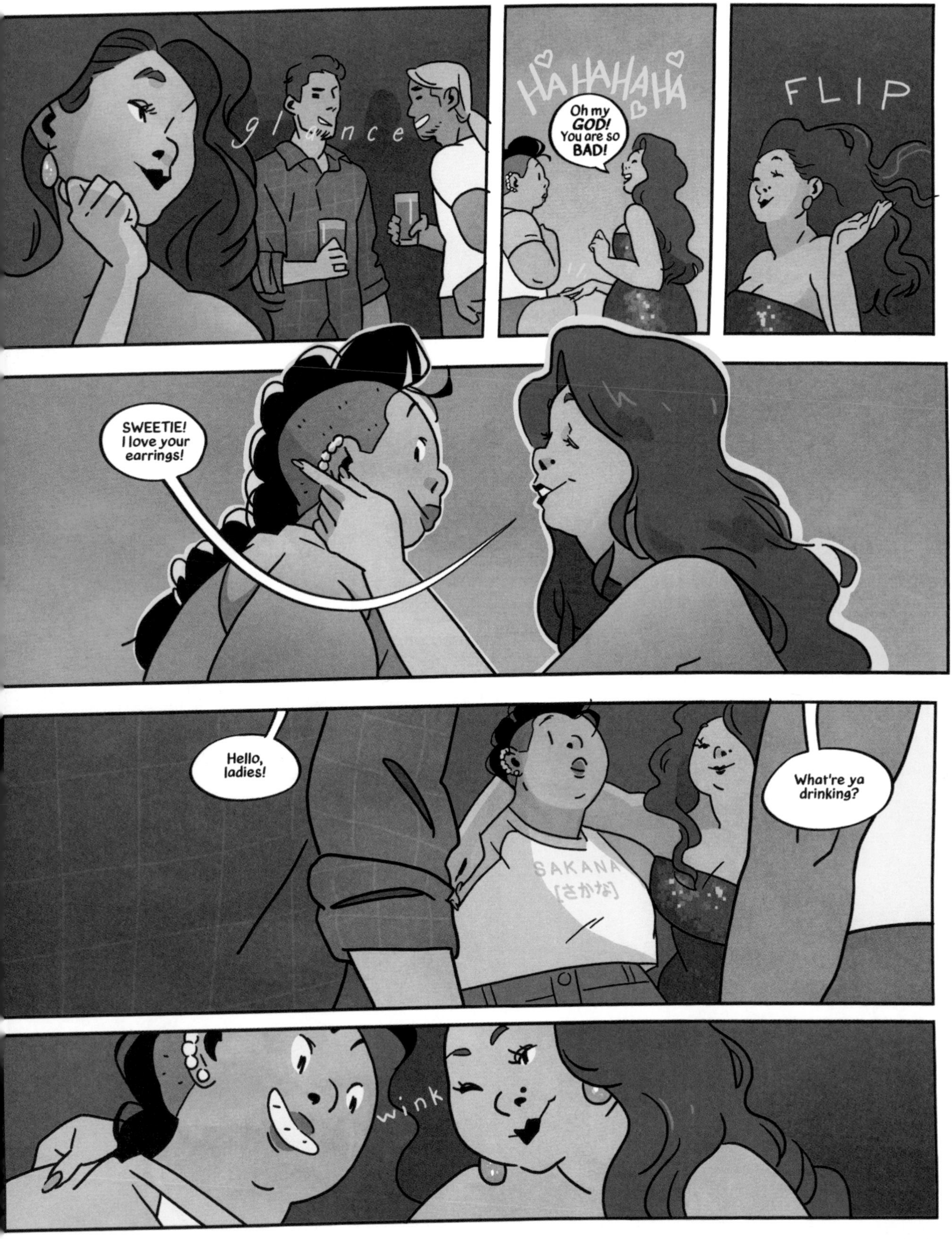
glance
HAHAHAHA
Oh my GOD! You are so BAD!
FLIP
SWEETIE! I love your earrings!
Hello, ladies!
What're ya drinking?
SAKANA [さかな]
wink

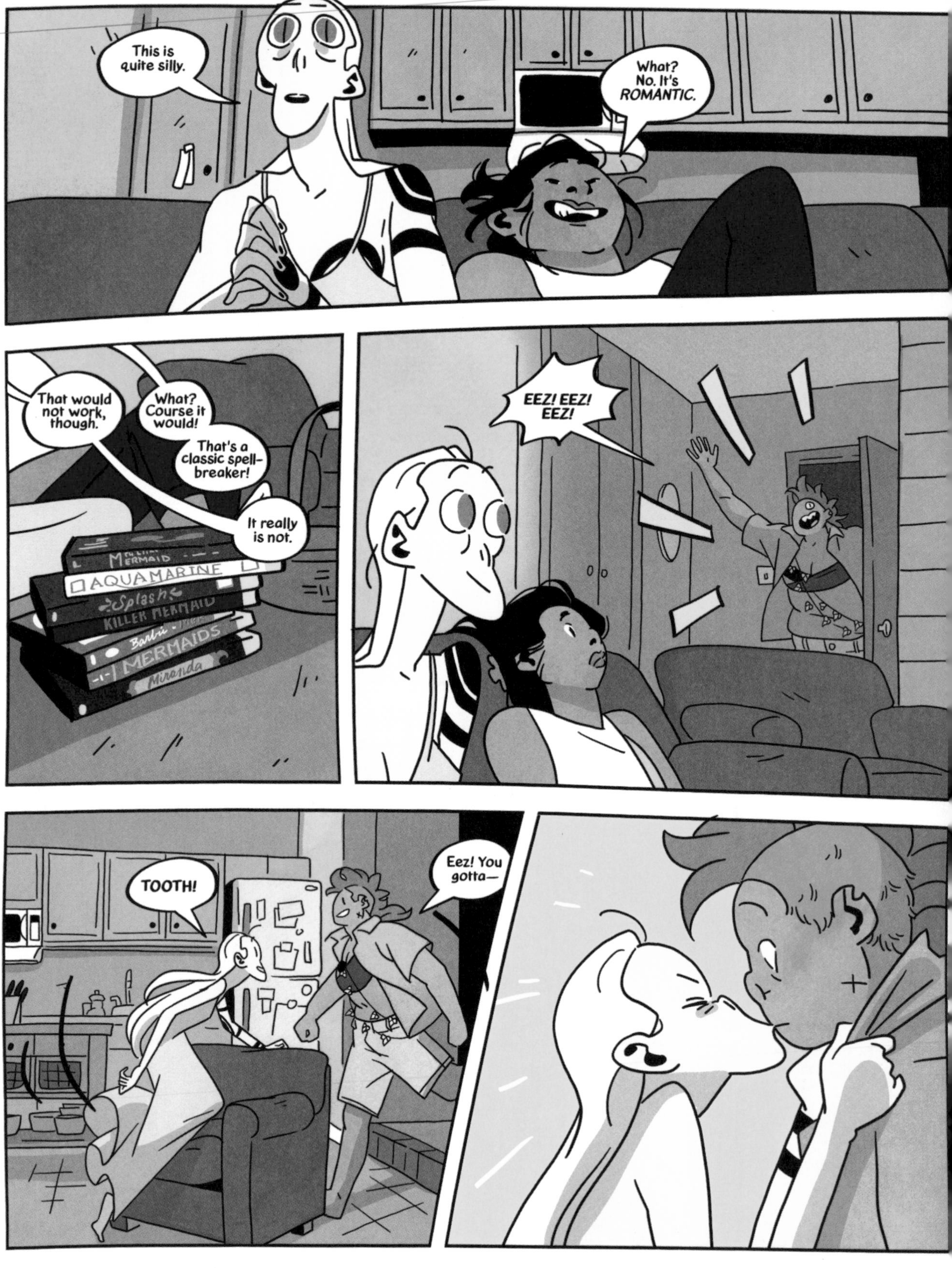
This is quite silly.
What? No. It's ROMANTIC.
That would not work, though.
What? Course it would!
That's a classic spell-breaker!
It really is not.
AQUAMARINE
Splash
KILLER MERMAID
Barbie
MERMAIDS
Miranda
EEZ! EEZ! EEZ!
TOOTH!
Eez! You gotta—

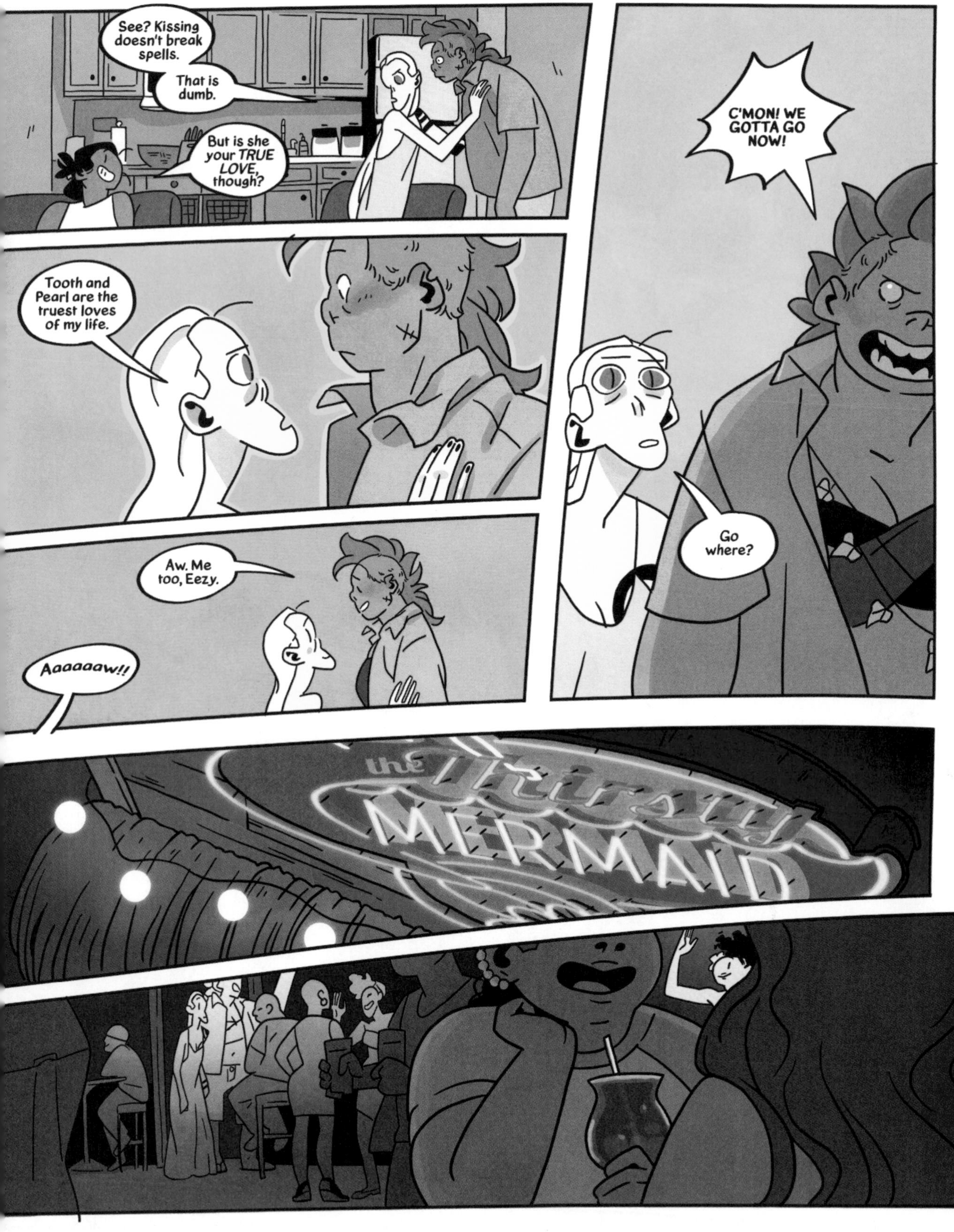
See? Kissing doesn't break spells.
That is dumb.
But is she your *TRUE LOVE,* though?
Tooth and Pearl are the truest loves of my life.
Aw. Me too, Eezy.
Aaaaaaw!!
C'MON! WE GOTTA GO NOW!
Go where?
the Thirsty MERMAID

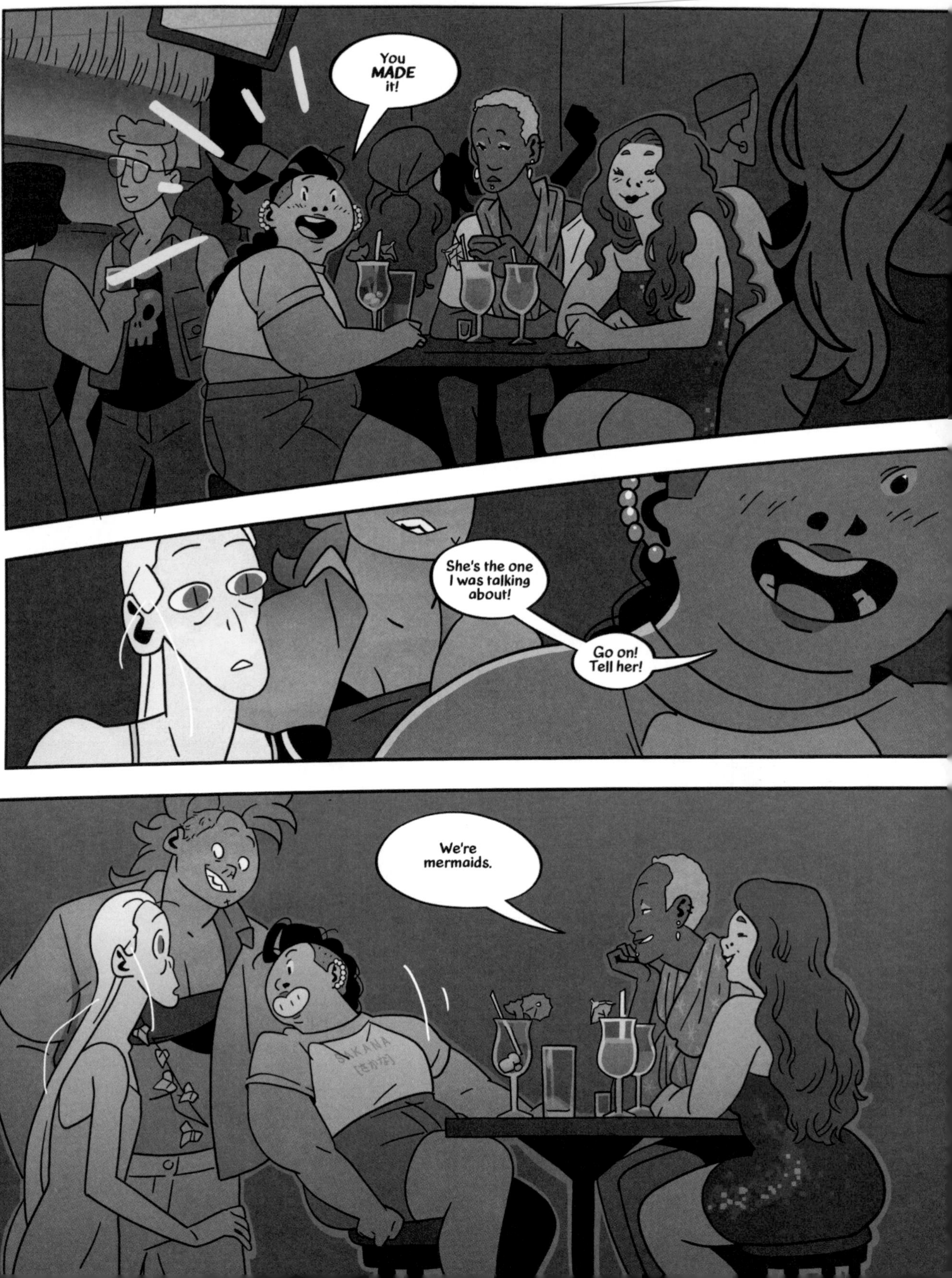
You MADE it!
She's the one I was talking about!
Go on! Tell her!
We're mermaids.

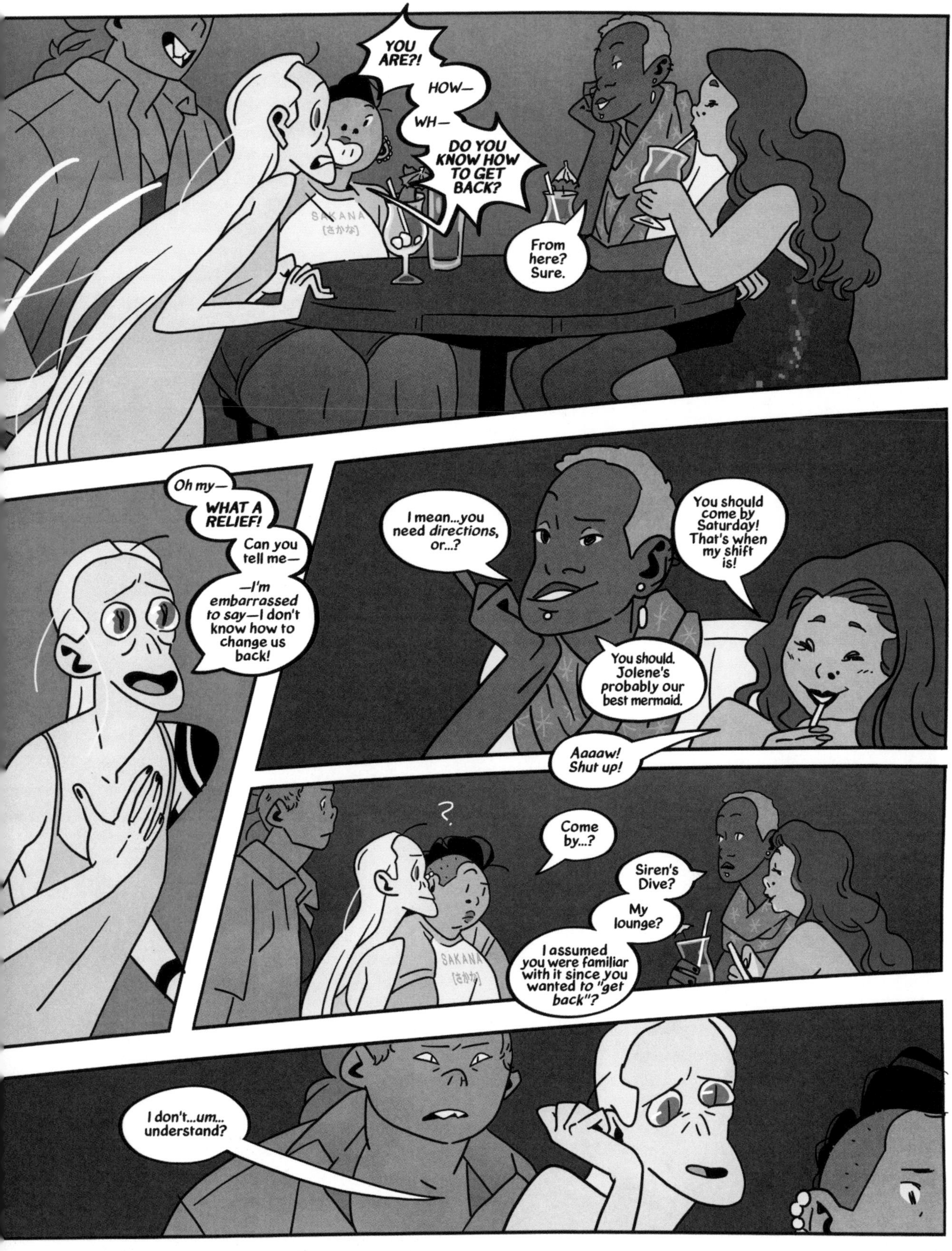
YOU ARE?!
HOW—
WH—
DO YOU KNOW HOW TO GET BACK?
SAKANA [さかな]
From here? Sure.
Oh my—
WHAT A RELIEF!
Can you tell me—
—I'm embarrassed to say—I don't know how to change us back!
I mean...you need directions, or...?
You should come by Saturday! That's when my shift is!
You should. Jolene's probably our best mermaid.
Aaaaw! Shut up!
?
Come by...?
Siren's Dive?
My lounge?
I assumed you were familiar with it since you wanted to "get back"?
SAKANA [さかな]
I don't...um... understand?

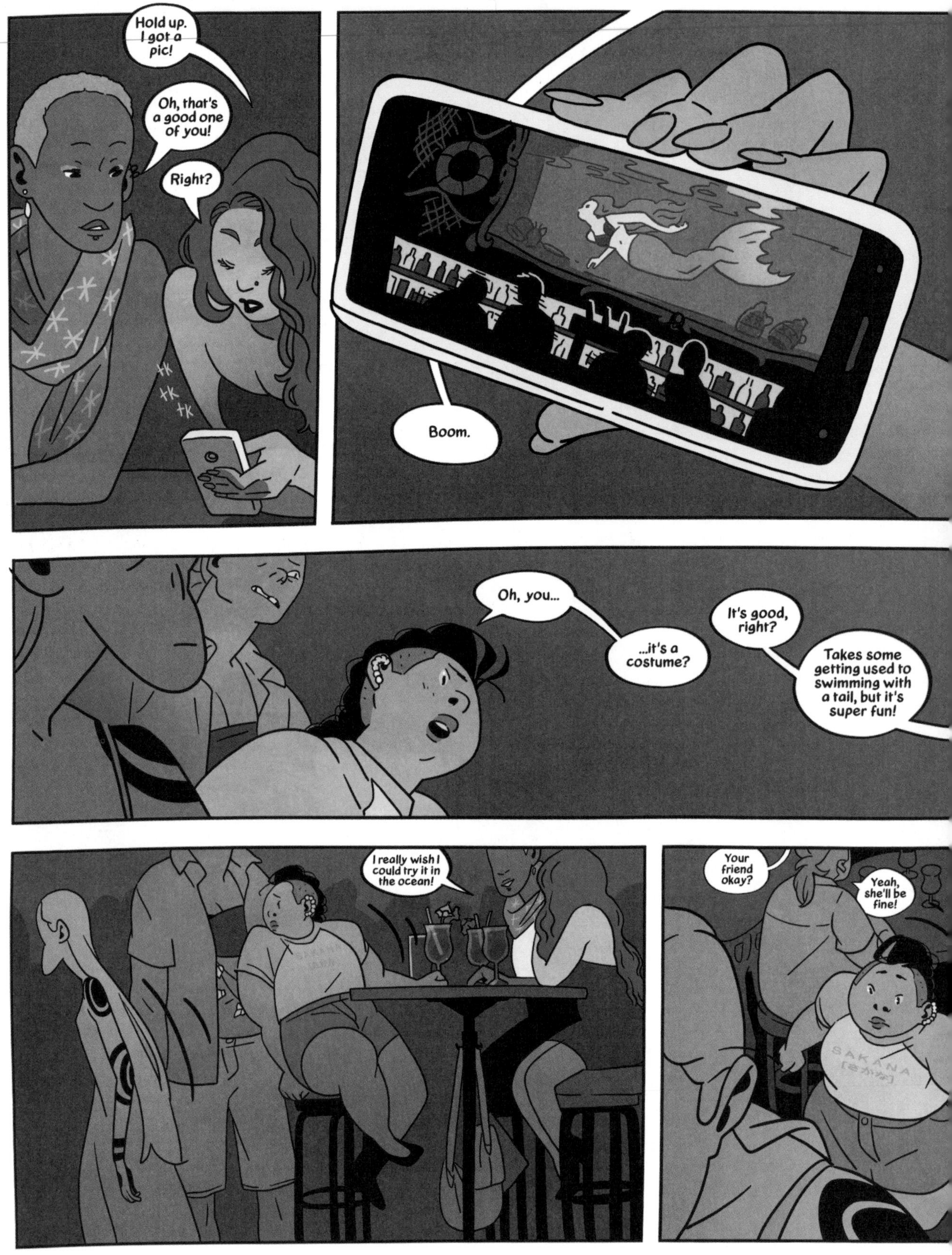
Hold up. I got a pic!
Oh, that's a good one of you!
Right?
Boom.
Oh, you...
...it's a costume?
It's good, right?
Takes some getting used to swimming with a tail, but it's super fun!
I really wish I could try it in the ocean!
Your friend okay?
Yeah, she'll be fine!

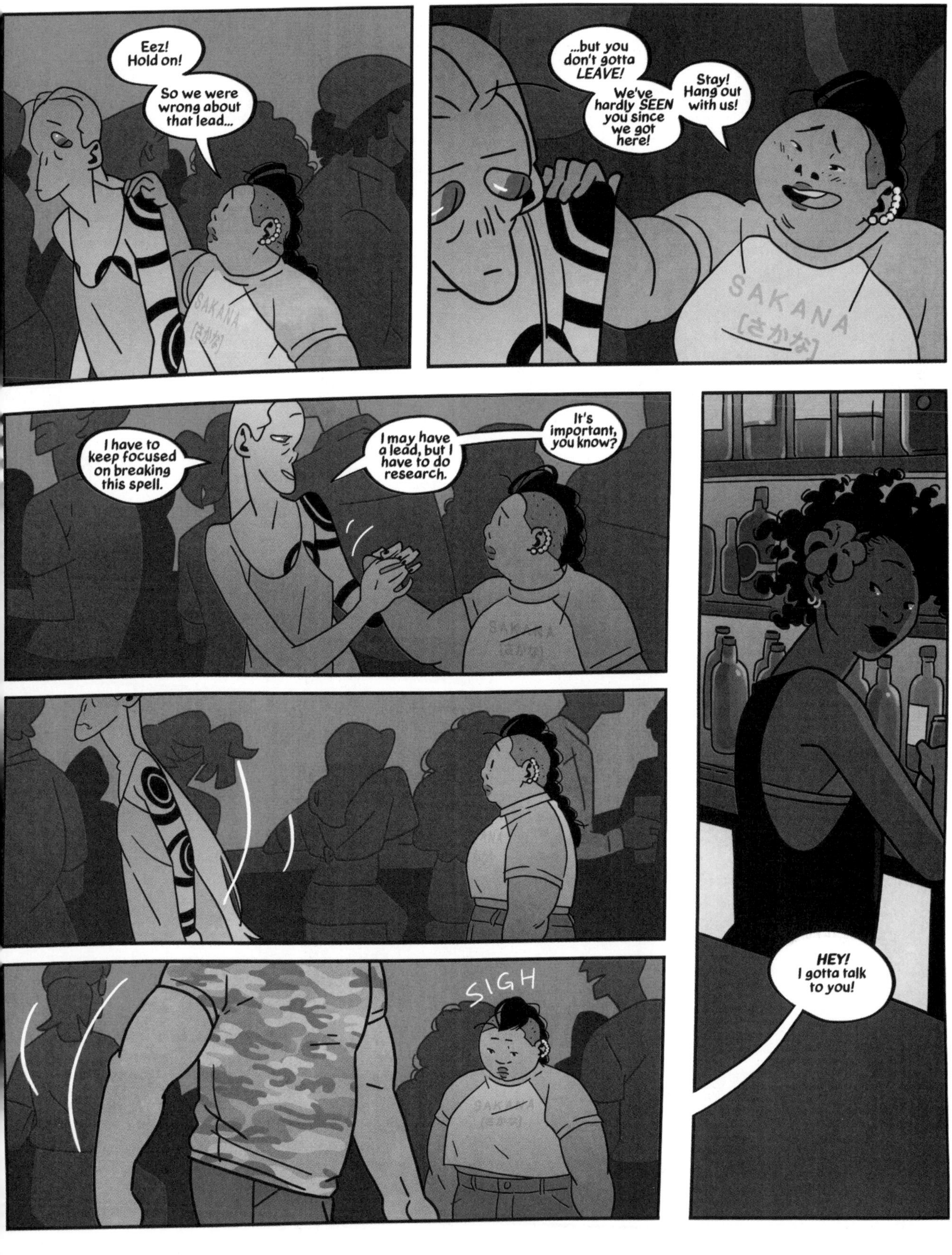
Eez! Hold on!
So we were wrong about that lead...
SAKANA [さかな]
...but you don't gotta LEAVE!
We've hardly SEEN you since we got here!
Stay! Hang out with us!
SAKANA [さかな]
I have to keep focused on breaking this spell.
I may have a lead, but I have to do research.
It's important, you know?
SIGH
HEY! I gotta talk to you!

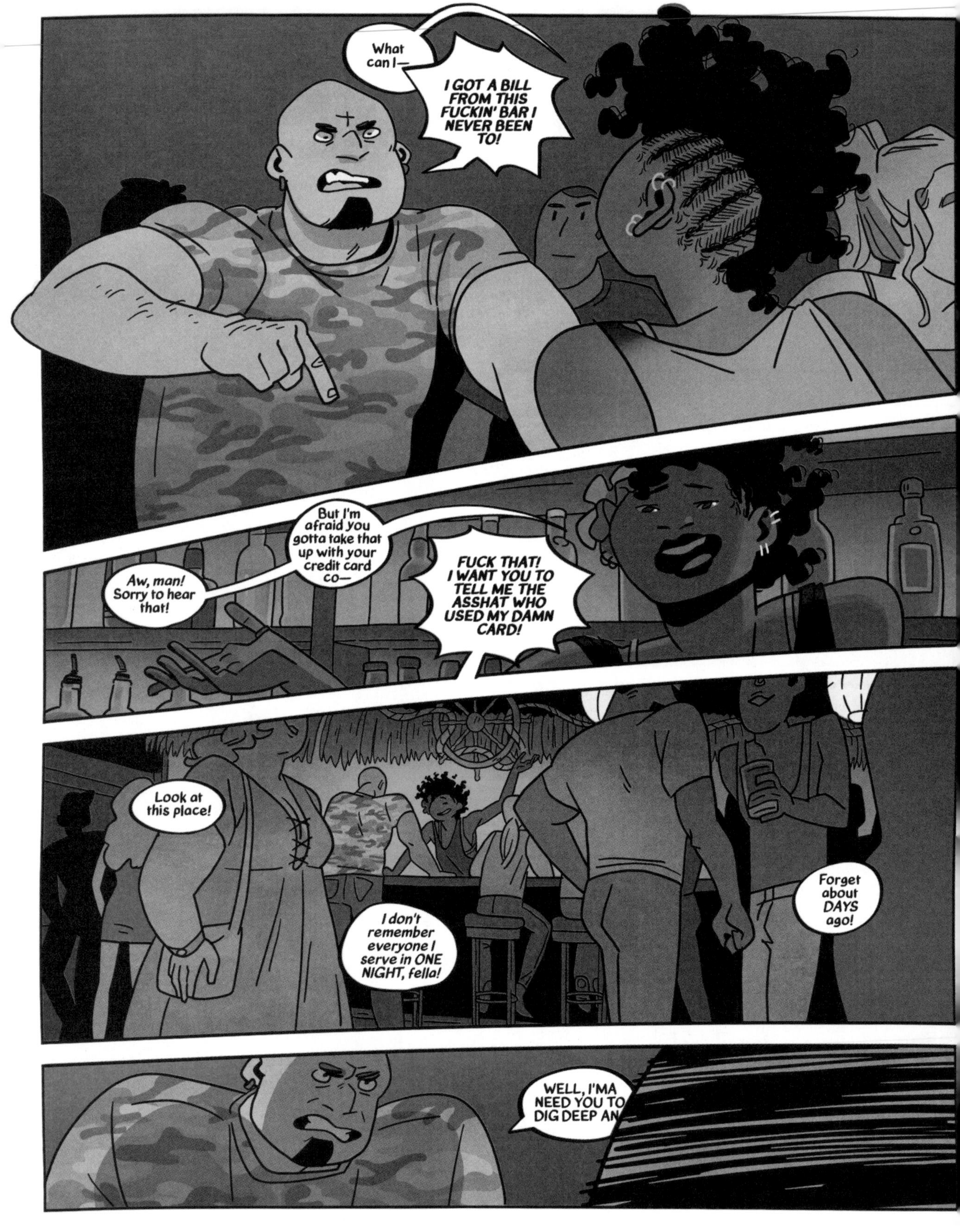
What can I—
I GOT A BILL FROM THIS FUCKIN' BAR I NEVER BEEN TO!
Aw, man! Sorry to hear that!
But I'm afraid you gotta take that up with your credit card co—
FUCK THAT! I WANT YOU TO TELL ME THE ASSHAT WHO USED MY DAMN CARD!
Look at this place!
I don't remember everyone I serve in ONE NIGHT, fella!
Forget about DAYS ago!
WELL, I'MA NEED YOU TO DIG DEEP AN

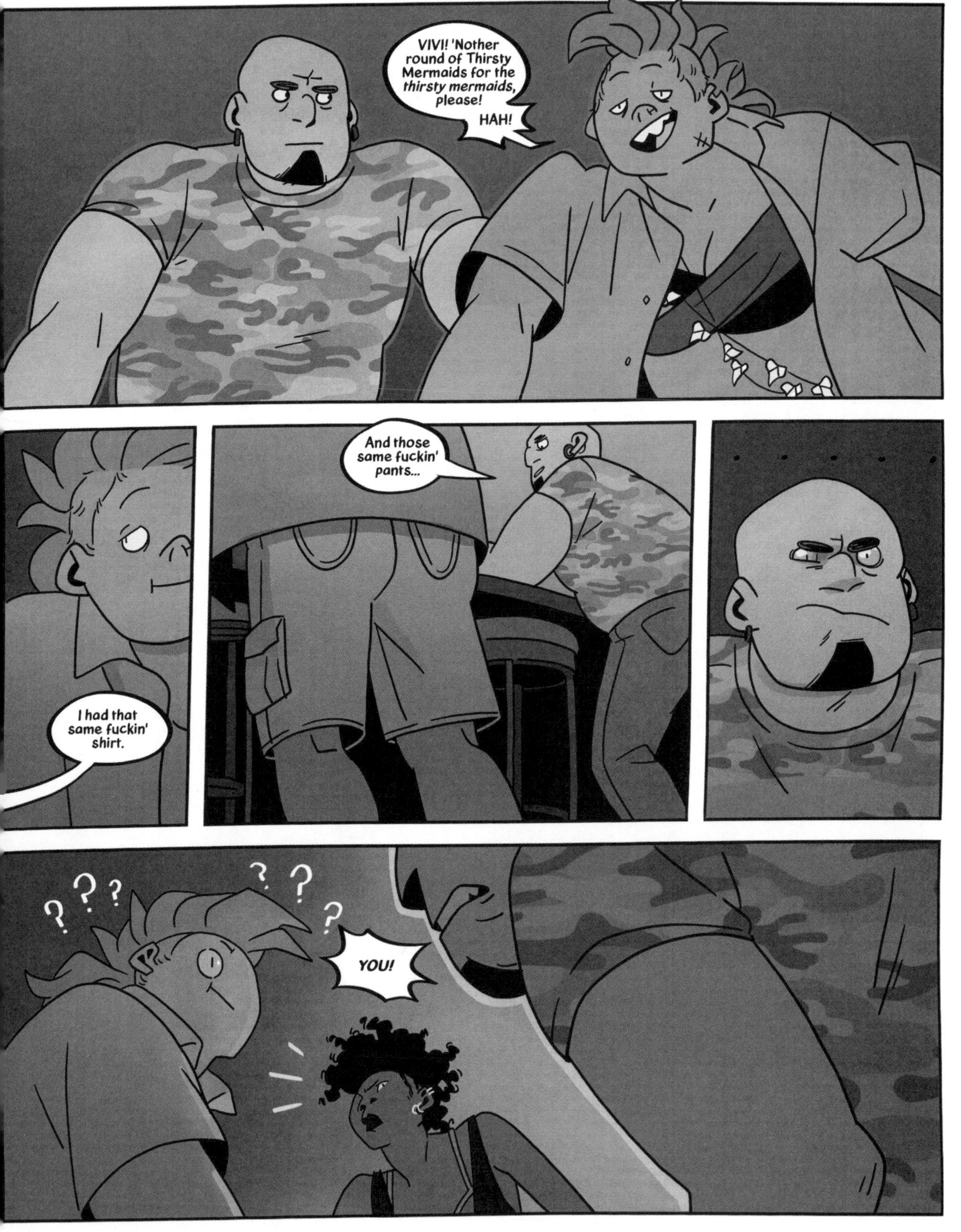
VIVI! 'Nother round of Thirsty Mermaids for the *thirsty mermaids,* please!
HAH!
I had that same fuckin' shirt.
And those same fuckin' pants...
???
???
YOU!

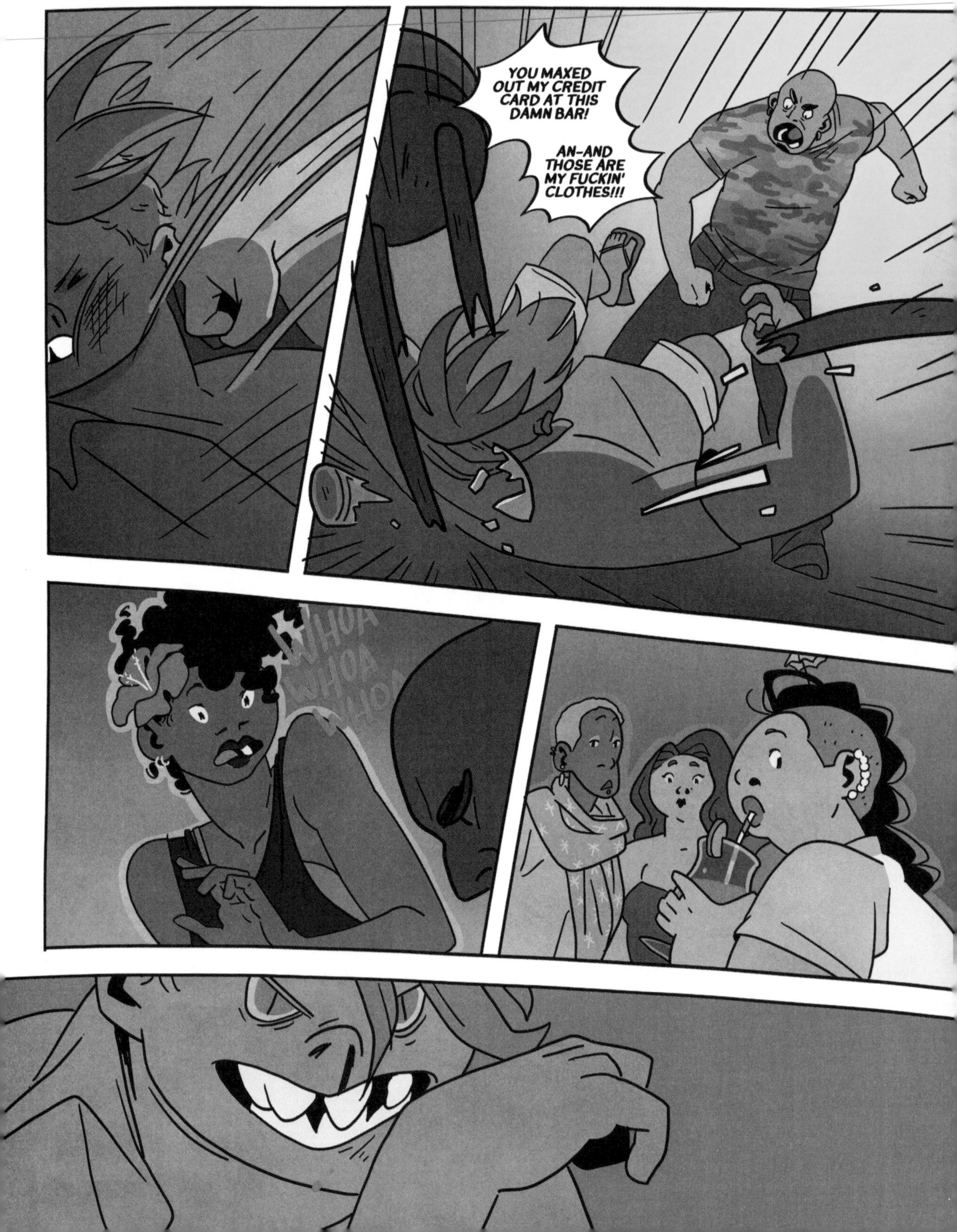
YOU MAXED OUT MY CREDIT CARD AT THIS DAMN BAR!
AN-AND THOSE ARE MY FUCKIN' CLOTHES!!!
WHOA WHOA WHOA

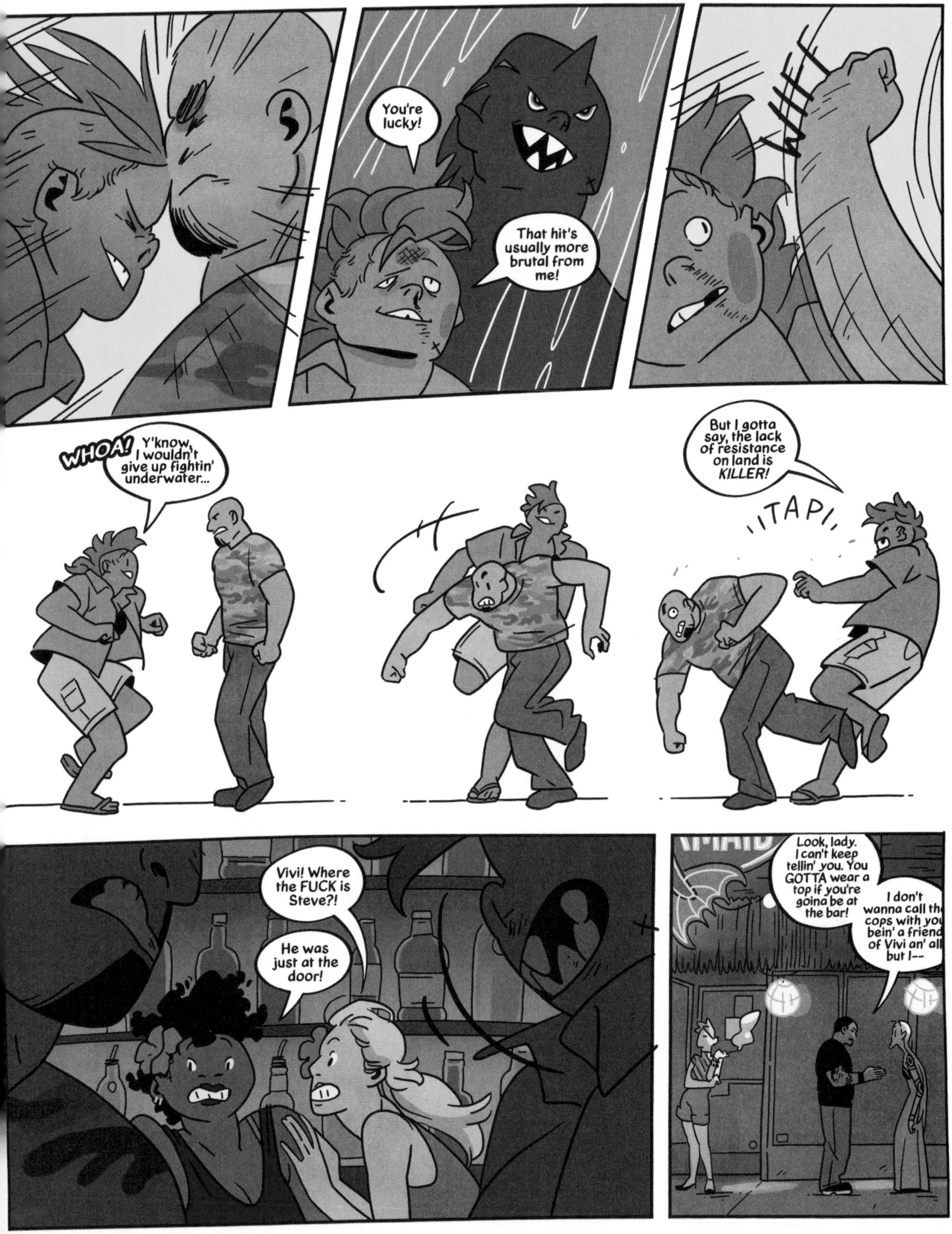
You're lucky!
That hit's usually more brutal from me!
WHIFF
WHOA!
Y'know, I wouldn't give up fightin' underwater...
But I gotta say, the lack of resistance on land is KILLER!
TAP!
Vivi! Where the FUCK is Steve?!
He was just at the door!
Look, lady. I can't keep tellin' you. You GOTTA wear a top if you're goina be at the bar!
I don't wanna call the cops with you bein' a friend of Vivi an' all but I--

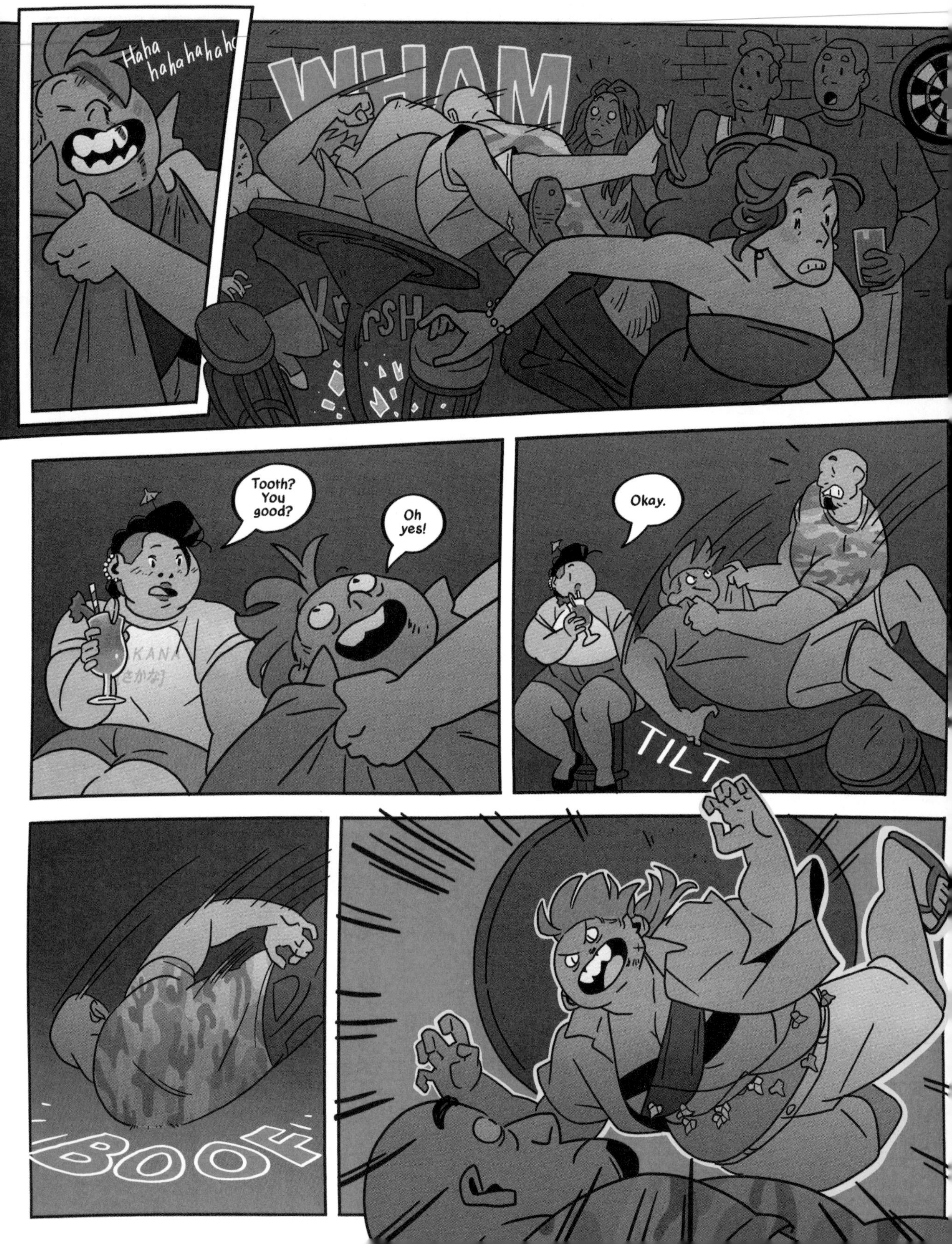

Haha hahahahaha
WHAM
KrrrsH
Tooth? You good?
Oh yes!
SAKANA
さかな
Okay.
TILT
BOOF

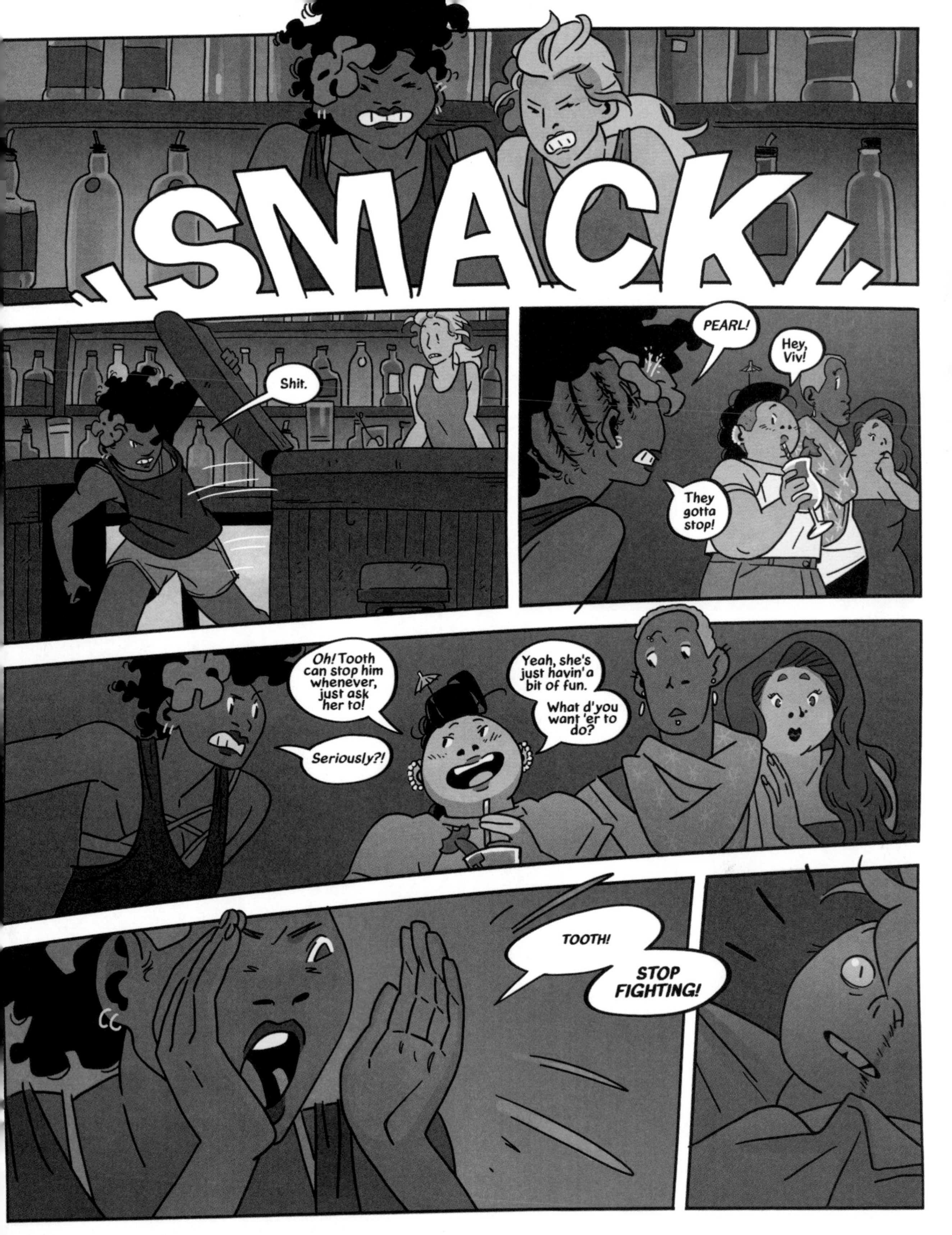
SMACK
Shit.
PEARL!
Hey, Viv!
They gotta stop!
Oh! Tooth can stop him whenever, just ask her to!
Seriously?!
Yeah, she's just havin' a bit of fun.
What d'you want 'er to do?
TOOTH!
STOP FIGHTING!

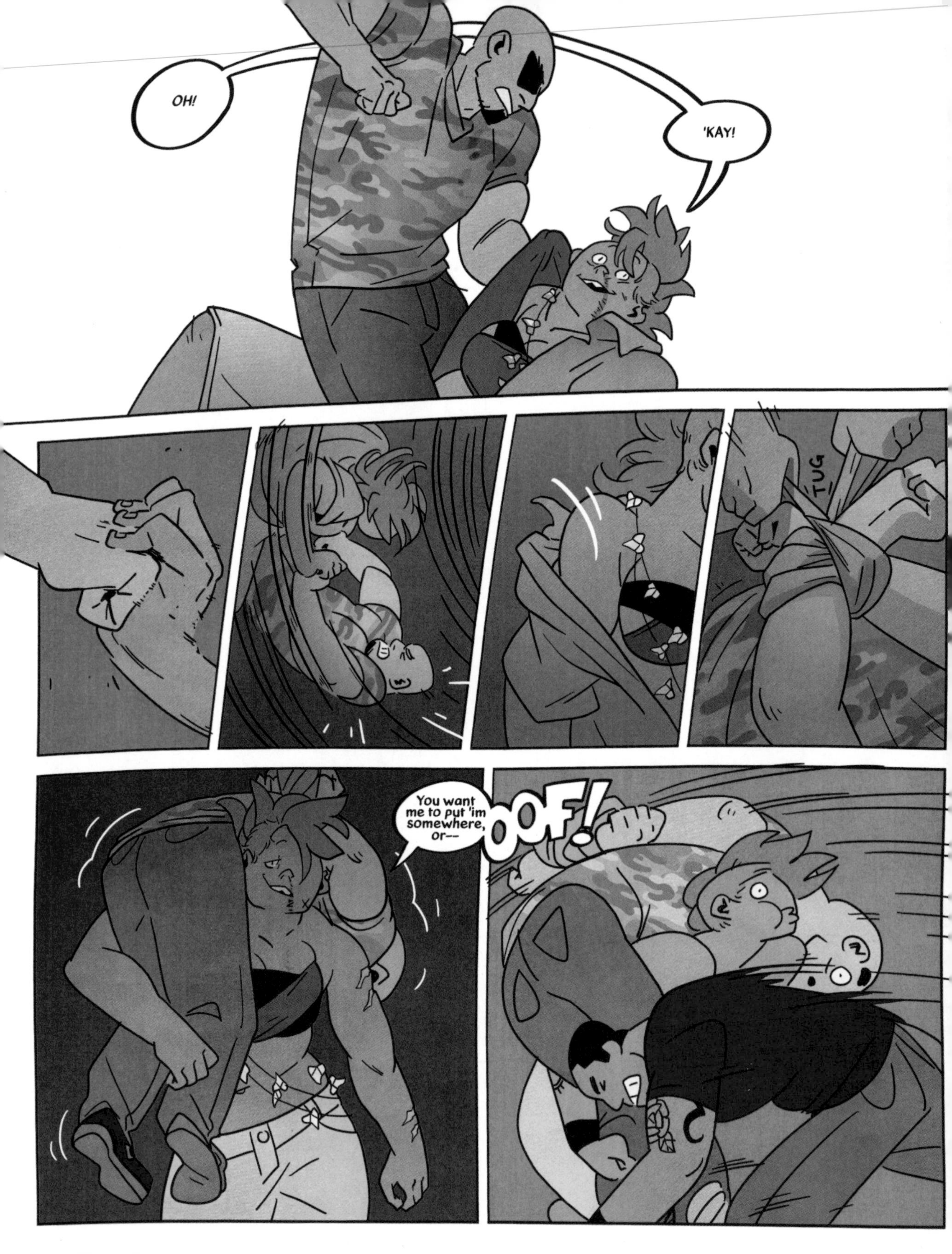

OH!
'KAY!
TUG
You want me to put 'im somewhere, or--
OOF!

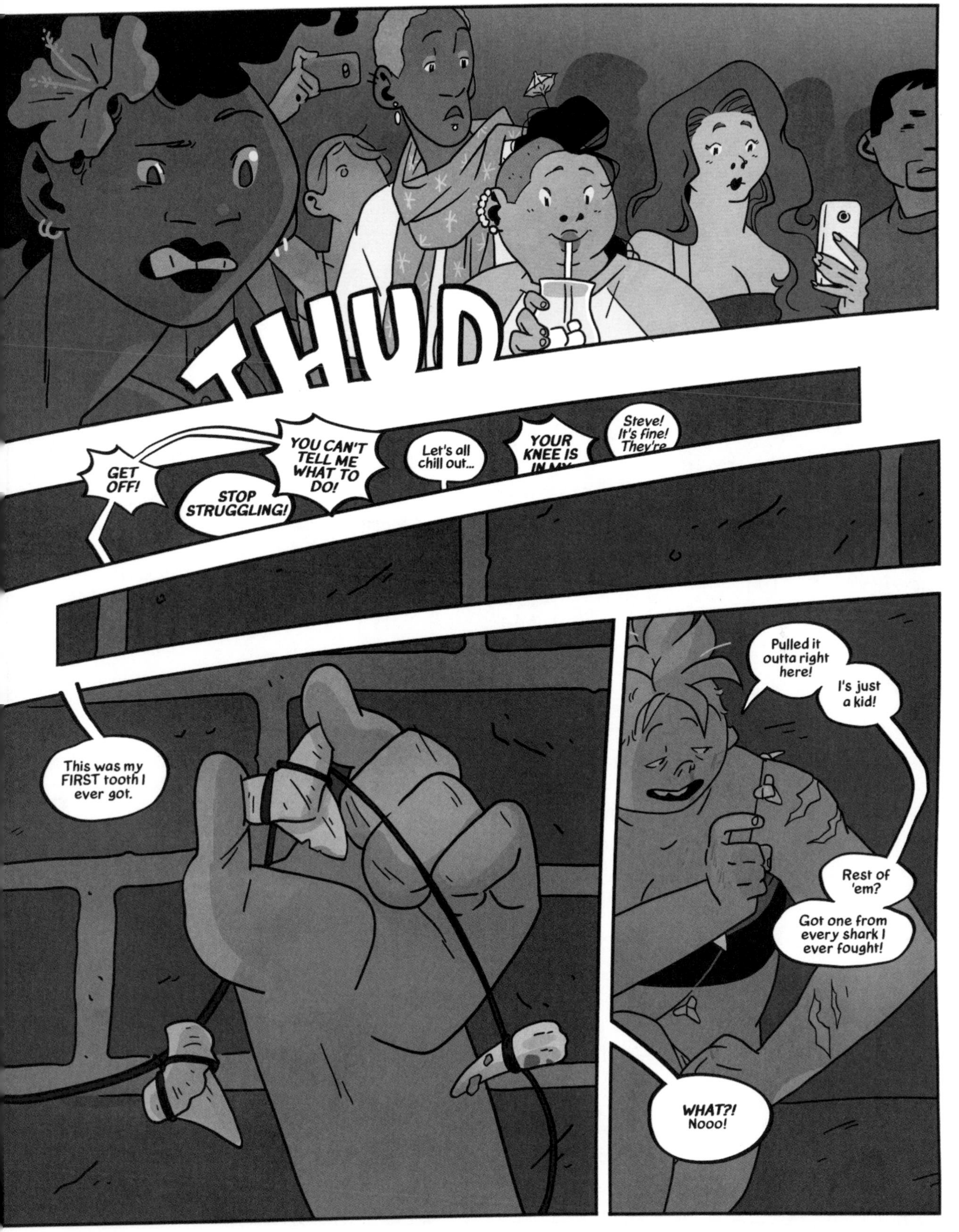
THUD
GET OFF!
STOP STRUGGLING!
YOU CAN'T TELL ME WHAT TO DO!
Let's all chill out...
YOUR KNEE IS
Steve! It's fine! They're
This was my FIRST tooth I ever got.
Pulled it outta right here!
I's just a kid!
WHAT?! Nooo!
Rest of 'em?
Got one from every shark I ever fought!

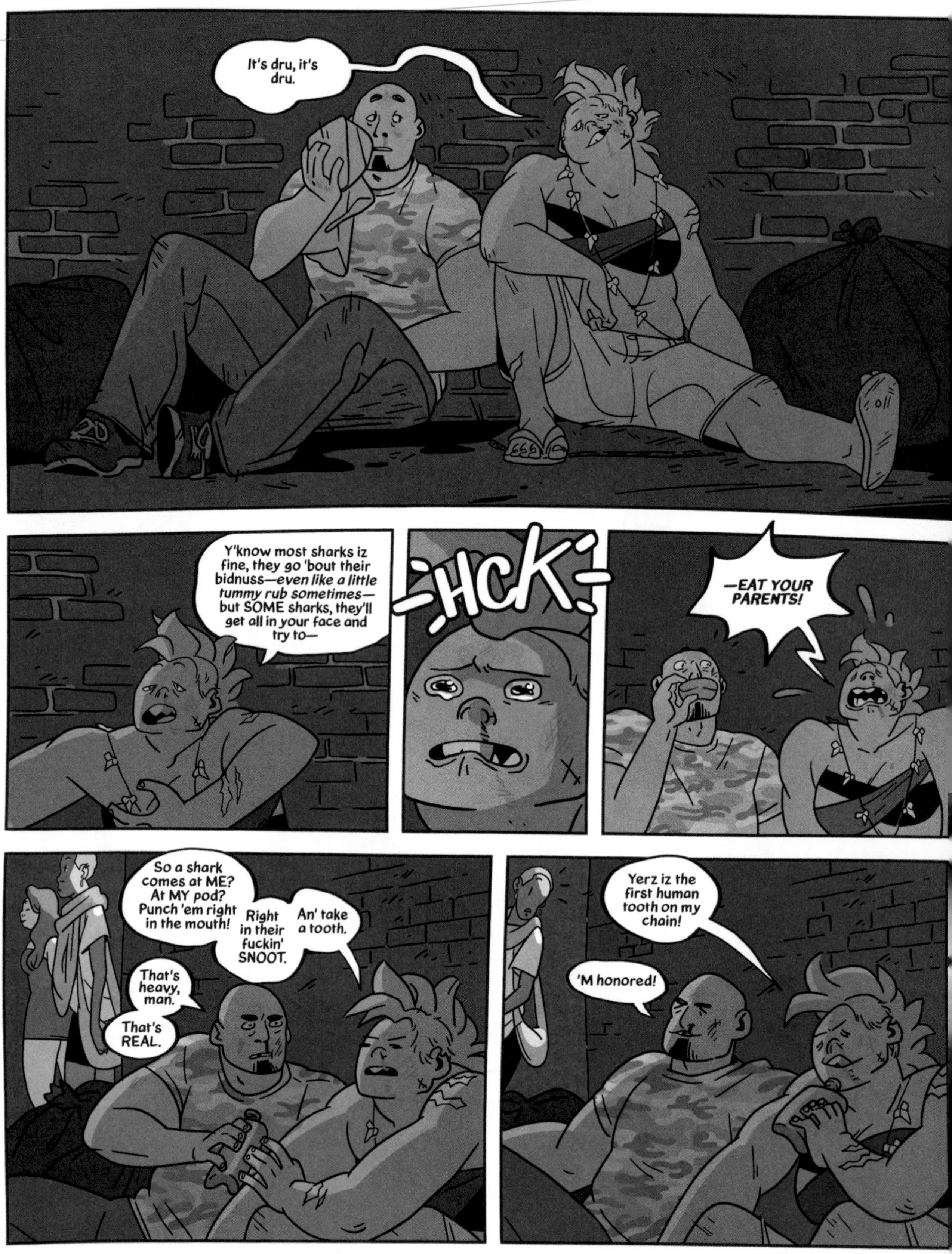
It's dru, it's dru.
Y'know most sharks iz fine, they go 'bout their bidnuss—*even like a little tummy rub sometimes*—but SOME sharks, they'll get all in your face and try to—
HCK
—EAT YOUR PARENTS!
So a shark comes at ME? At MY *pod*? Punch 'em right in the mouth!
Right in their fuckin' SNOOT.
An' take a tooth.
That's heavy, man.
That's REAL.
Yerz iz the first human tooth on my chain!
'M honored!

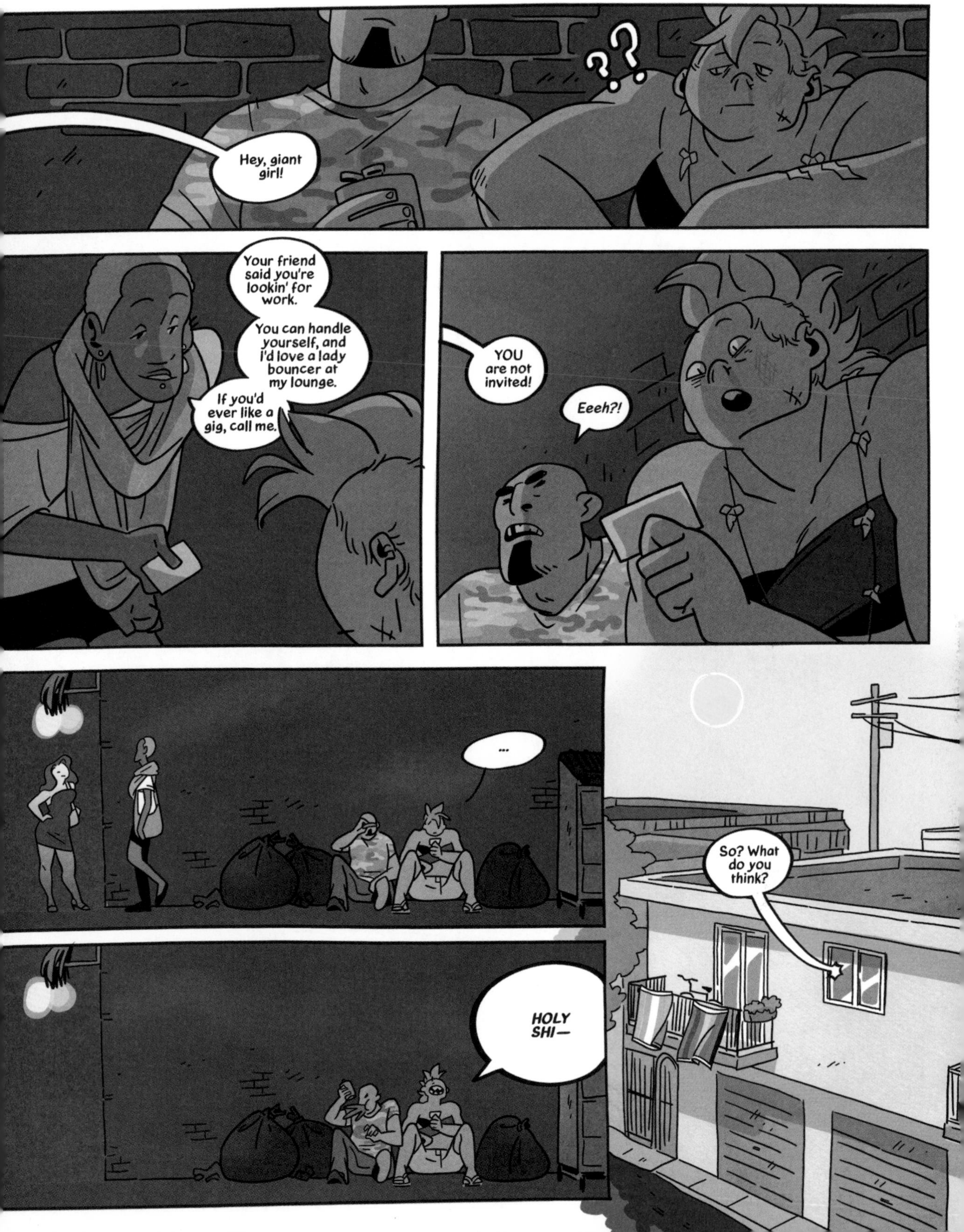

Hey, giant girl!
Your friend said you're lookin' for work.
You can handle yourself, and I'd love a lady bouncer at my lounge.
If you'd ever like a gig, call me.
YOU are not invited!
Eeeh?!
...
HOLY SHI—
So? What do you think?

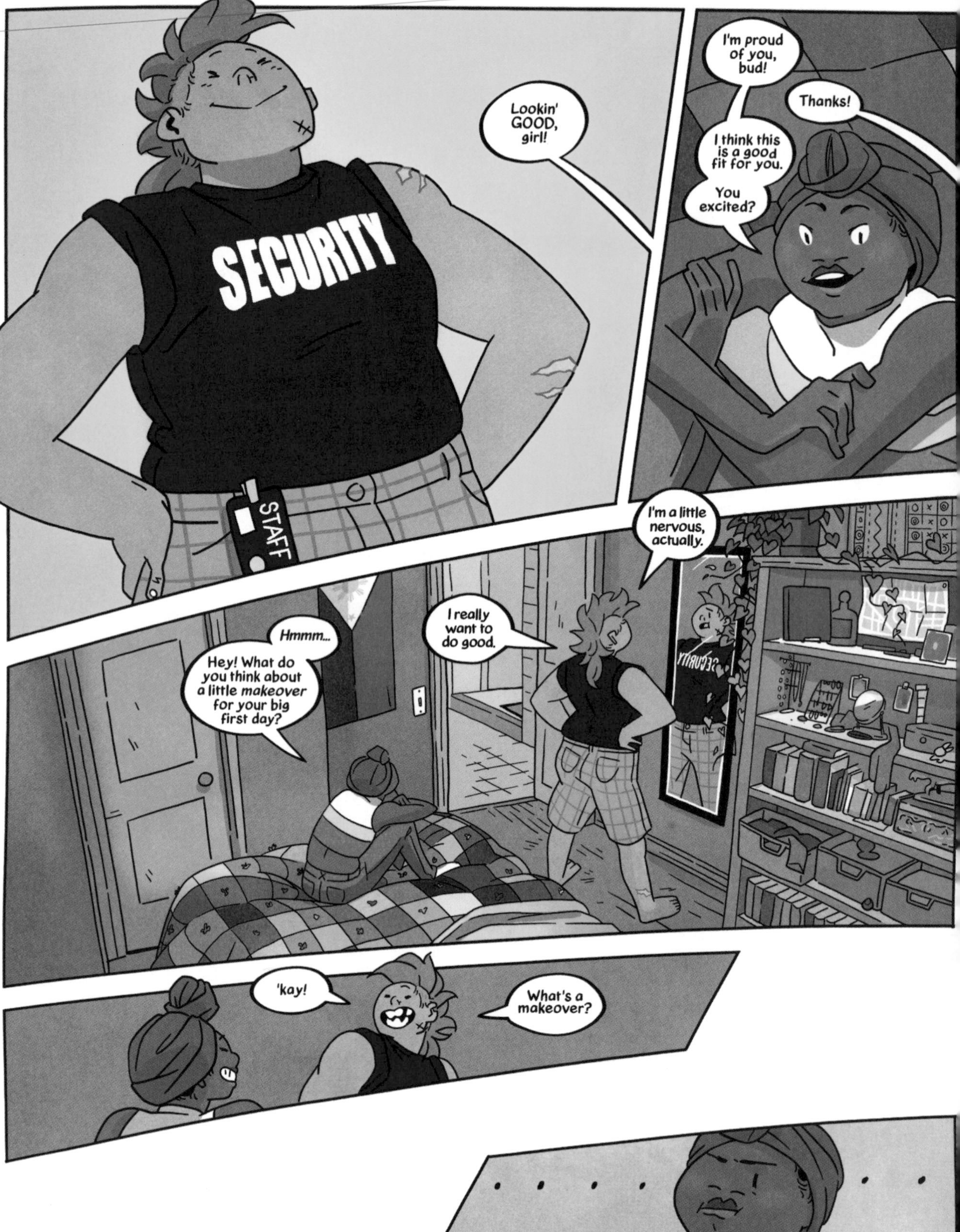
SECURITY
STAFF
Lookin' GOOD, girl!
I'm proud of you, bud!
Thanks!
I think this is a good fit for you.
You excited?
I'm a little nervous, actually.
I really want to do good.
Hmmm...
Hey! What do you think about a little *makeover* for your big first day?
'kay!
What's a makeover?
. . . . . .

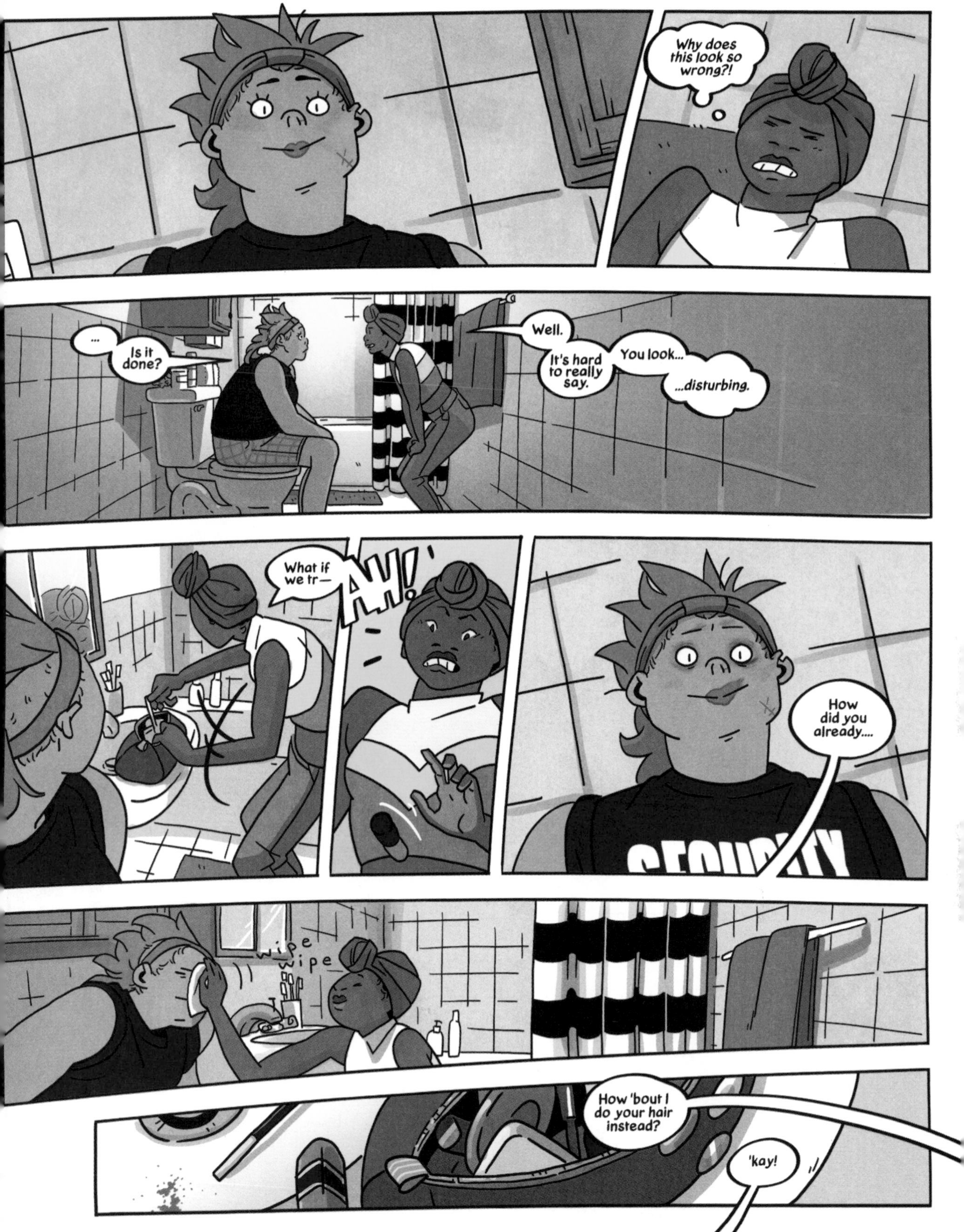
Why does this look so wrong?!
...
Is it done?
Well.
It's hard to really say.
You look...
...disturbing.
What if we tr—
AH!
How did you already....
SECURITY
wipe wipe
How 'bout I do your hair instead?
'kay!

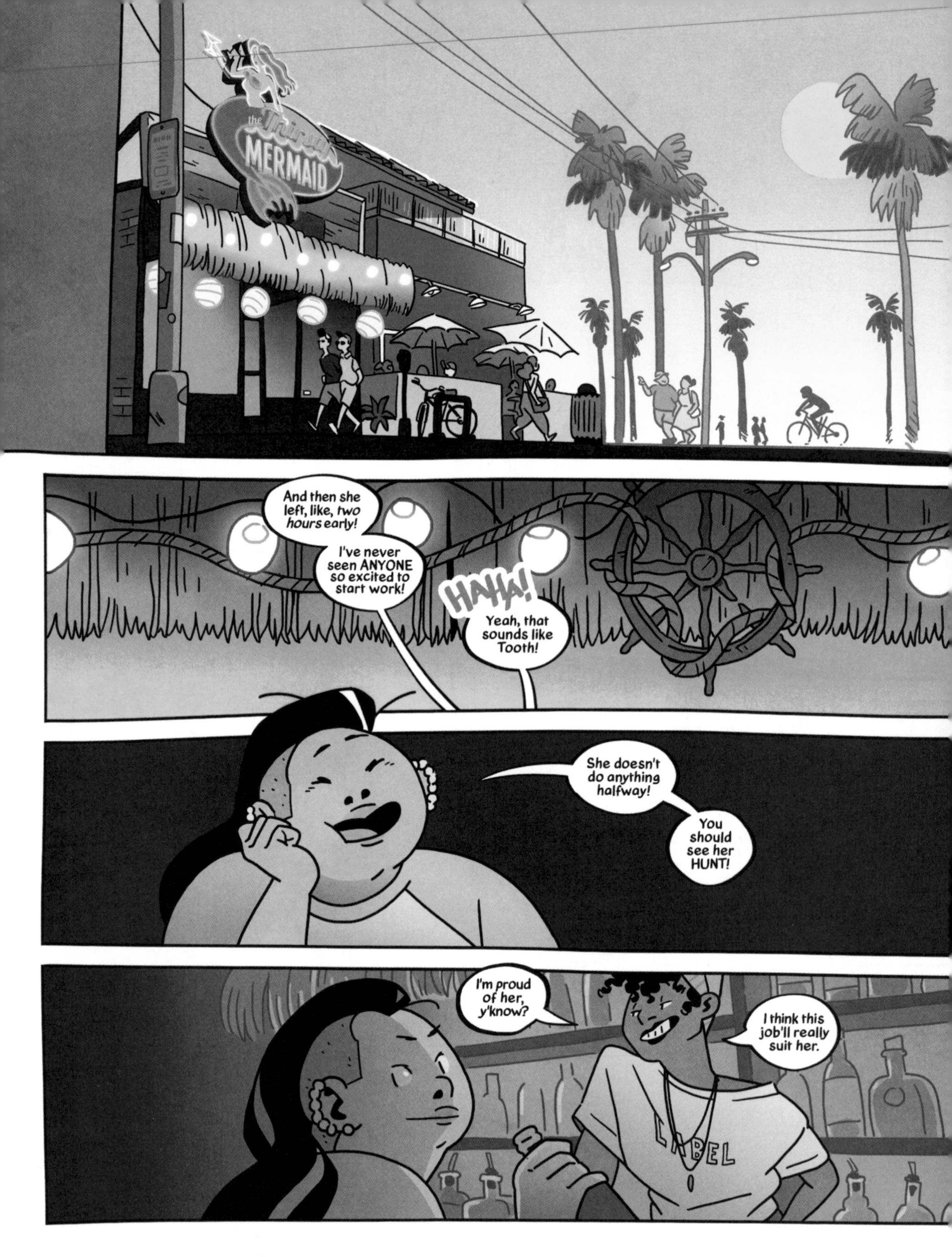
the Thirsty MERMAID
And then she left, like, two hours early!
I've never seen ANYONE so excited to start work!
HAHA!
Yeah, that sounds like Tooth!
She doesn't do anything halfway!
You should see her HUNT!
I'm proud of her, y'know?
I think this job'll really suit her.
LABEL

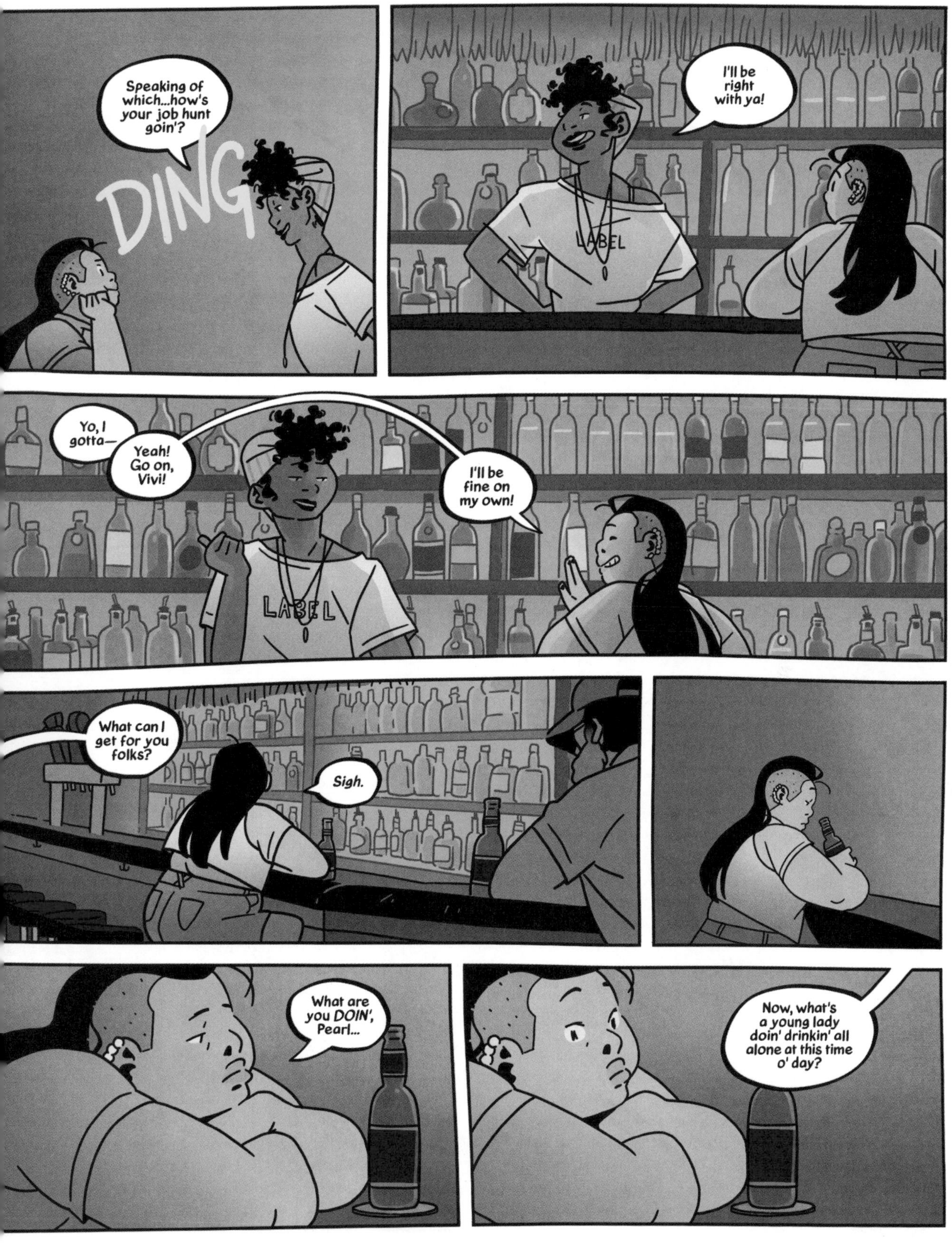
Speaking of which...how's your job hunt goin'?
DING
I'll be right with ya!
Yo, I gotta—
Yeah! Go on, Vivi!
I'll be fine on my own!
What can I get for you folks?
Sigh.
What are you DOIN', Pearl...
Now, what's a young lady doin' drinkin' all alone at this time o' day?

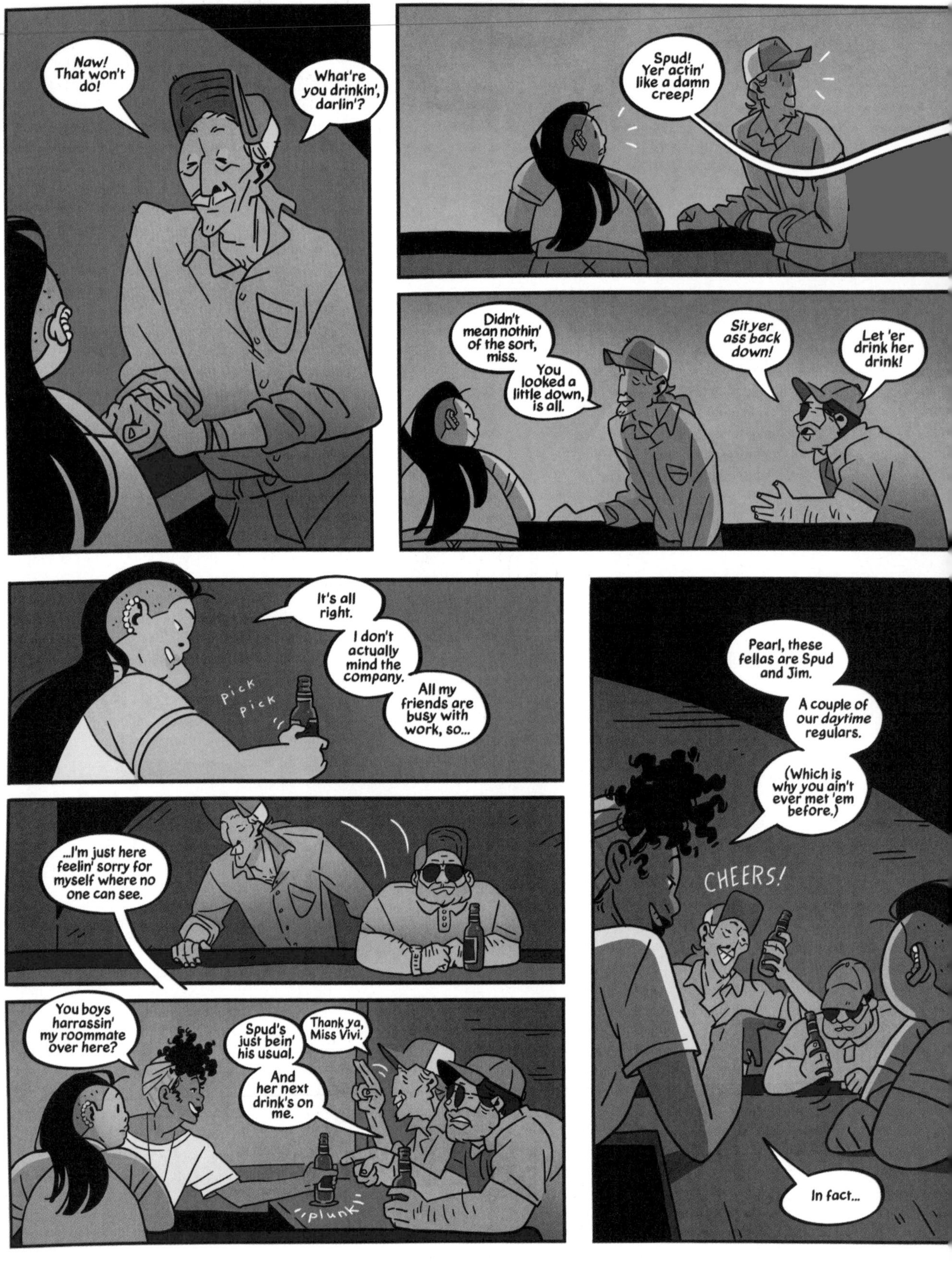
Naw! That won't do!
What're you drinkin', darlin'?
Spud! Yer actin' like a damn creep!
Didn't mean nothin' of the sort, miss.
You looked a little down, is all.
Sit yer ass back down!
Let 'er drink her drink!
It's all right.
I don't actually mind the company.
All my friends are busy with work, so...
pick pick
...I'm just here feelin' sorry for myself where no one can see.
You boys harrassin' my roommate over here?
Spud's just bein' his usual.
Thank ya, Miss Vivi.
And her next drink's on me.
plunk
Pearl, these fellas are Spud and Jim.
A couple of our *daytime* regulars.
(Which is why you ain't ever met 'em before.)
CHEERS!
In fact...

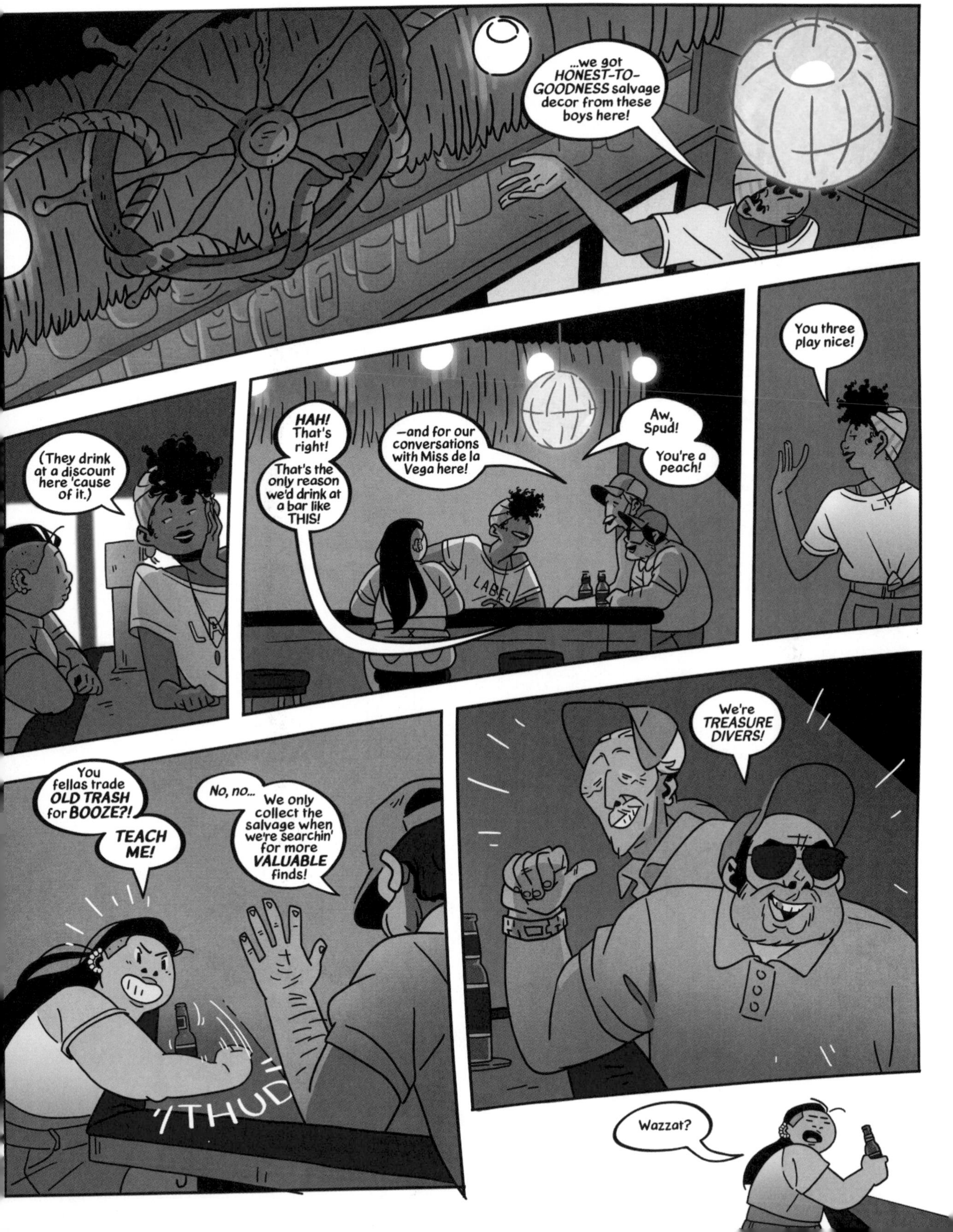
...we got HONEST-TO-GOODNESS salvage decor from these boys here!
(They drink at a discount here 'cause of it.)
HAH! That's right!
That's the only reason we'd drink at a bar like THIS!
—and for our conversations with Miss de la Vega here!
Aw, Spud!
You're a peach!
You three play nice!
You fellas trade OLD TRASH for BOOZE?!
TEACH ME!
THUD
No, no... We only collect the salvage when we're searchin' for more VALUABLE finds!
We're TREASURE DIVERS!
Wazzat?

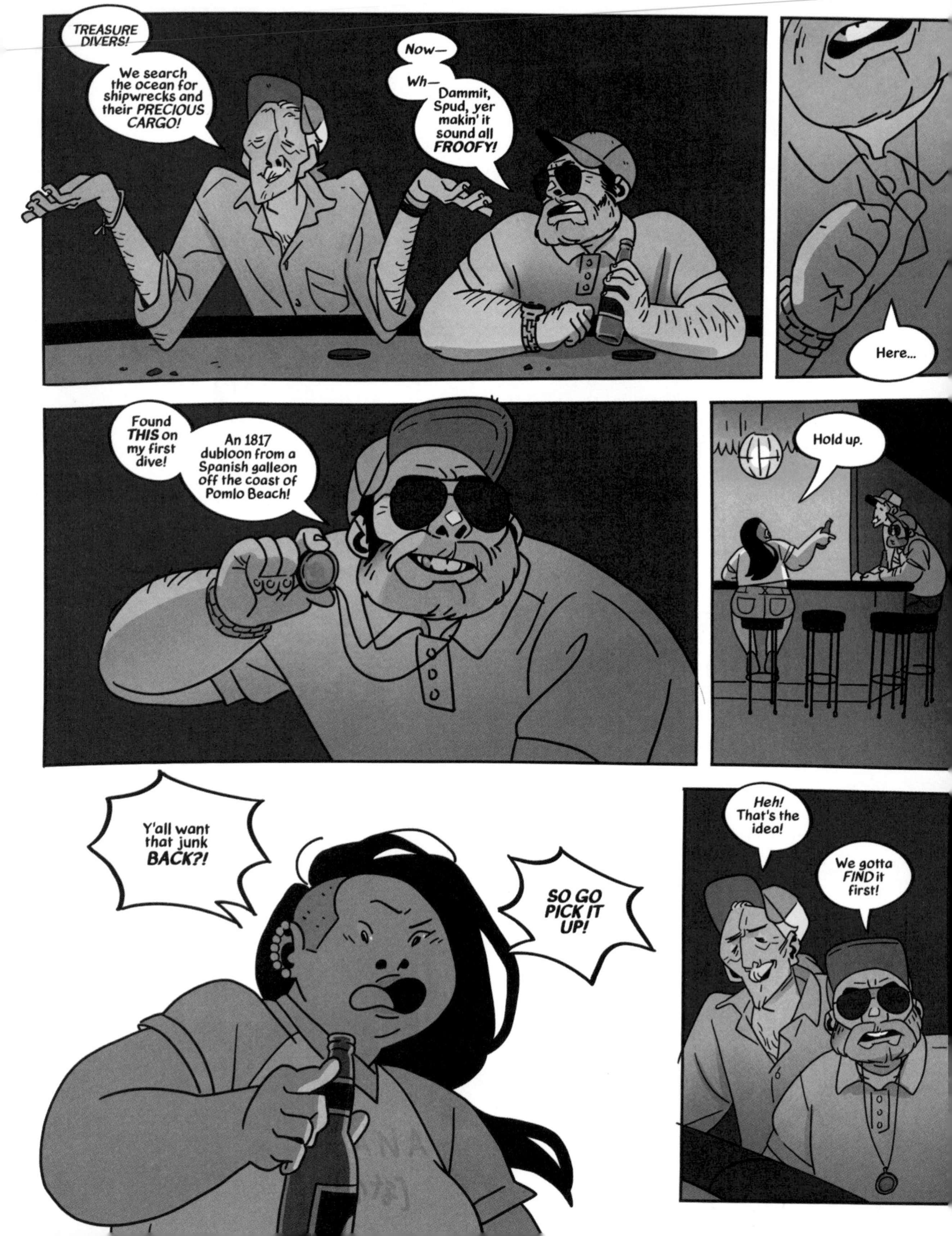
TREASURE DIVERS!
We search the ocean for shipwrecks and their PRECIOUS CARGO!
Now—
Wh—
Dammit, Spud, yer makin' it sound all FROOFY!
Here...
Found THIS on my first dive!
An 1817 dubloon from a Spanish galleon off the coast of Pomlo Beach!
Hold up.
Y'all want that junk BACK?!
SO GO PICK IT UP!
Heh! That's the idea!
We gotta FIND it first!

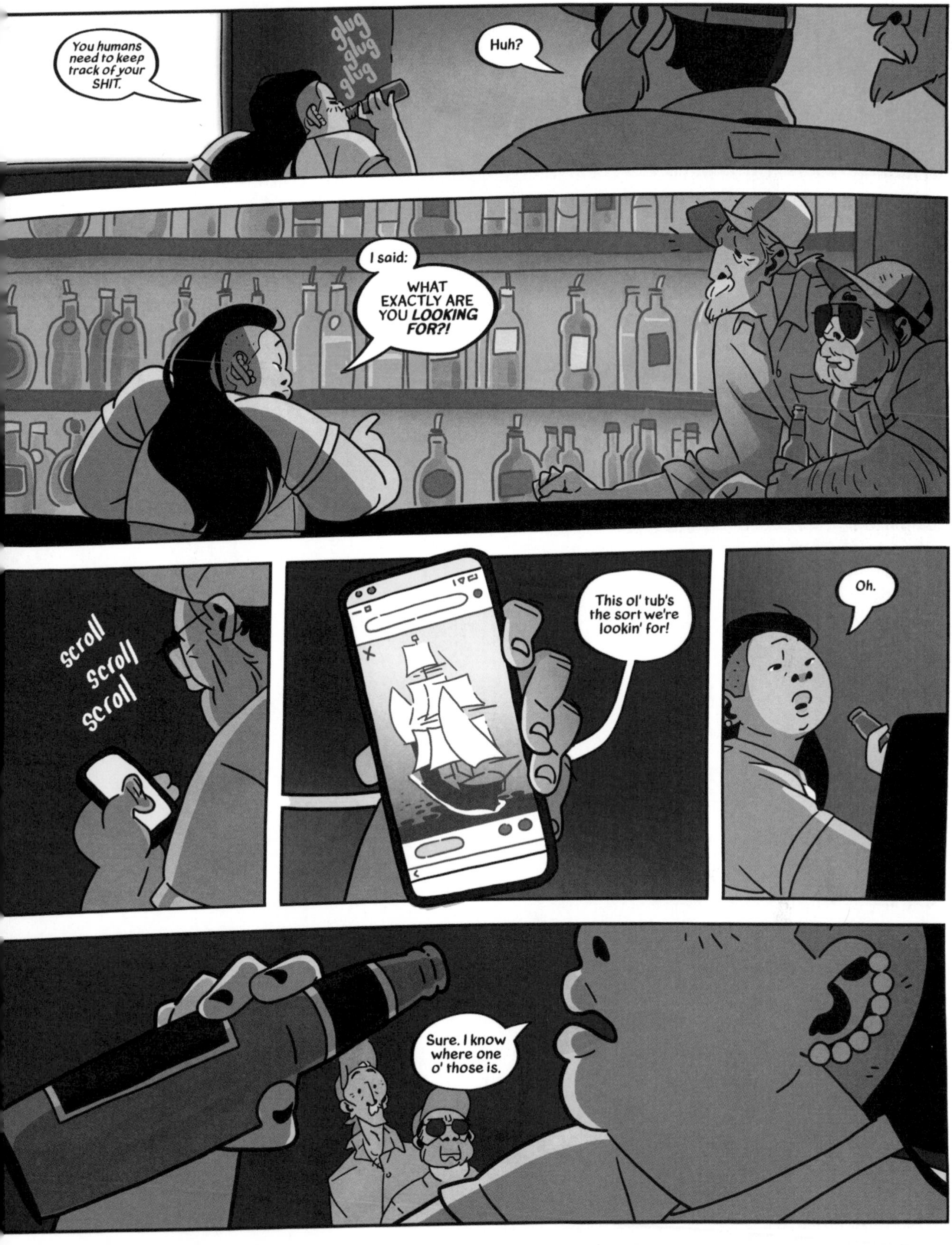
You humans need to keep track of your SHIT.
glug glug glug
Huh?
I said:
WHAT EXACTLY ARE YOU LOOKING FOR?!
scroll scroll scroll
This ol' tub's the sort we're lookin' for!
Oh.
Sure. I know where one o' those is.

PART IV: THE TUB

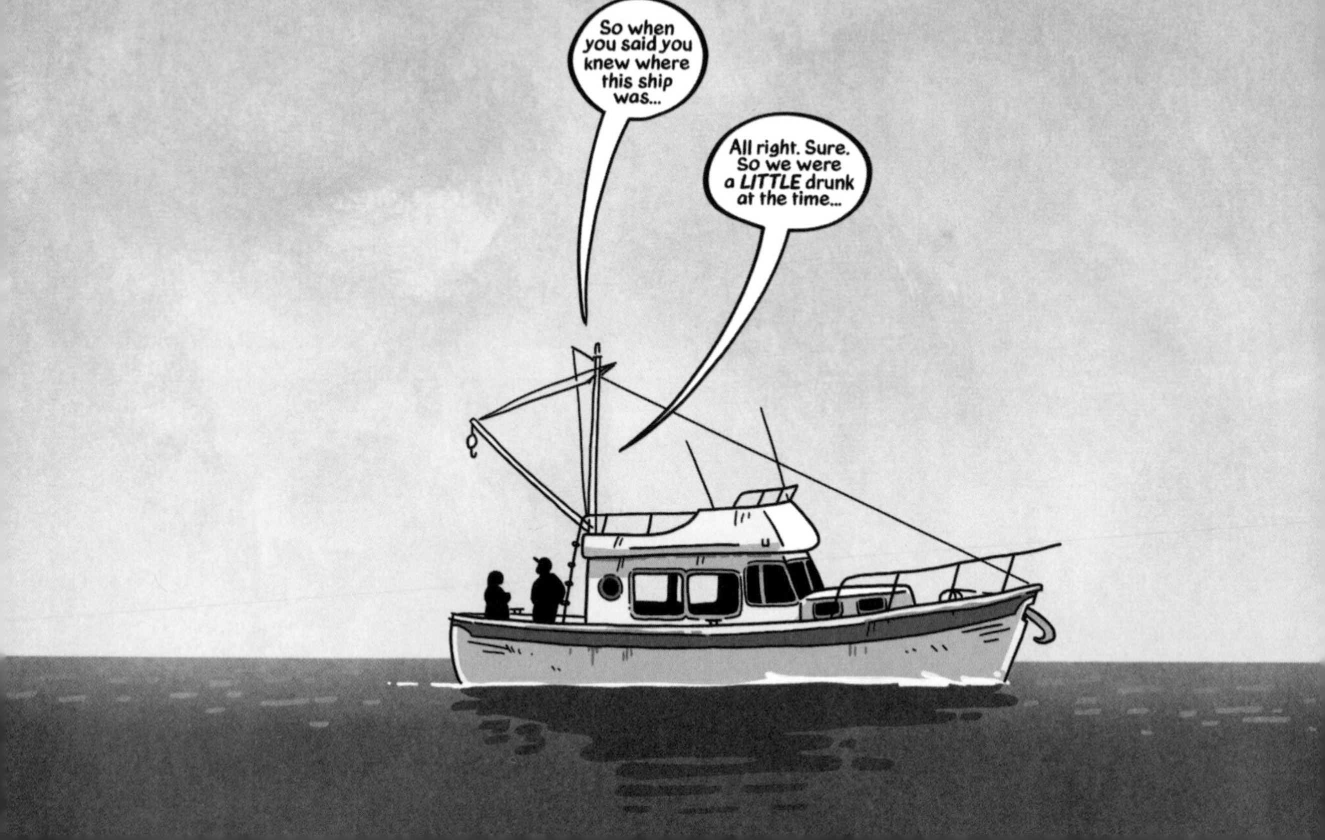

So when you said you knew where this ship was...
All right. Sure. So we were a *LITTLE* drunk at the time...

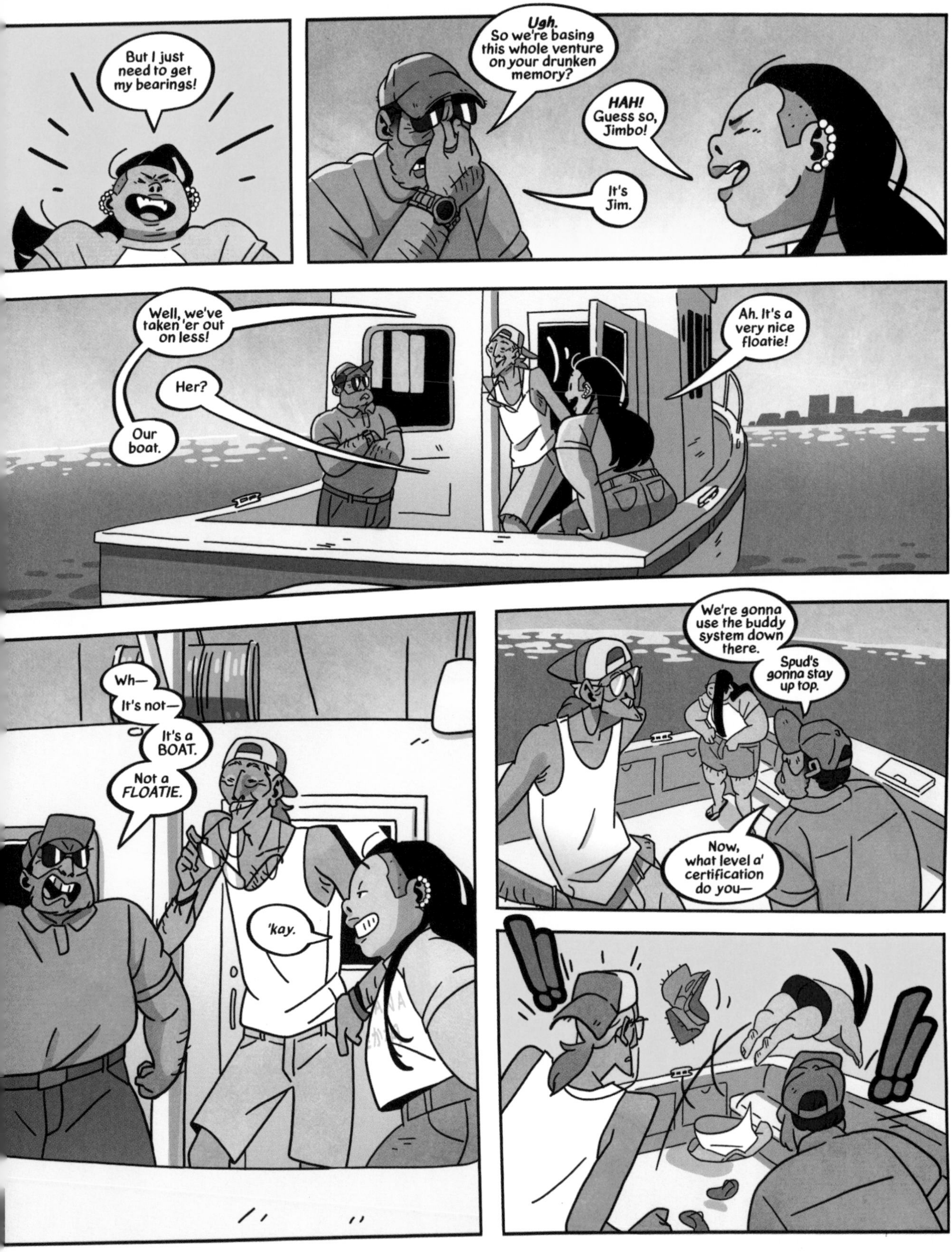
But I just need to get my bearings!
Ugh. So we're basing this whole venture on your drunken memory?
HAH! Guess so, Jimbo!
It's Jim.
Well, we've taken 'er out on less!
Her?
Our boat.
Ah. It's a very nice floatie!
Wh—
It's not—
It's a BOAT.
Not a FLOATIE.
'kay.
We're gonna use the buddy system down there.
Spud's gonna stay up top.
Now, what level a' certification do you—

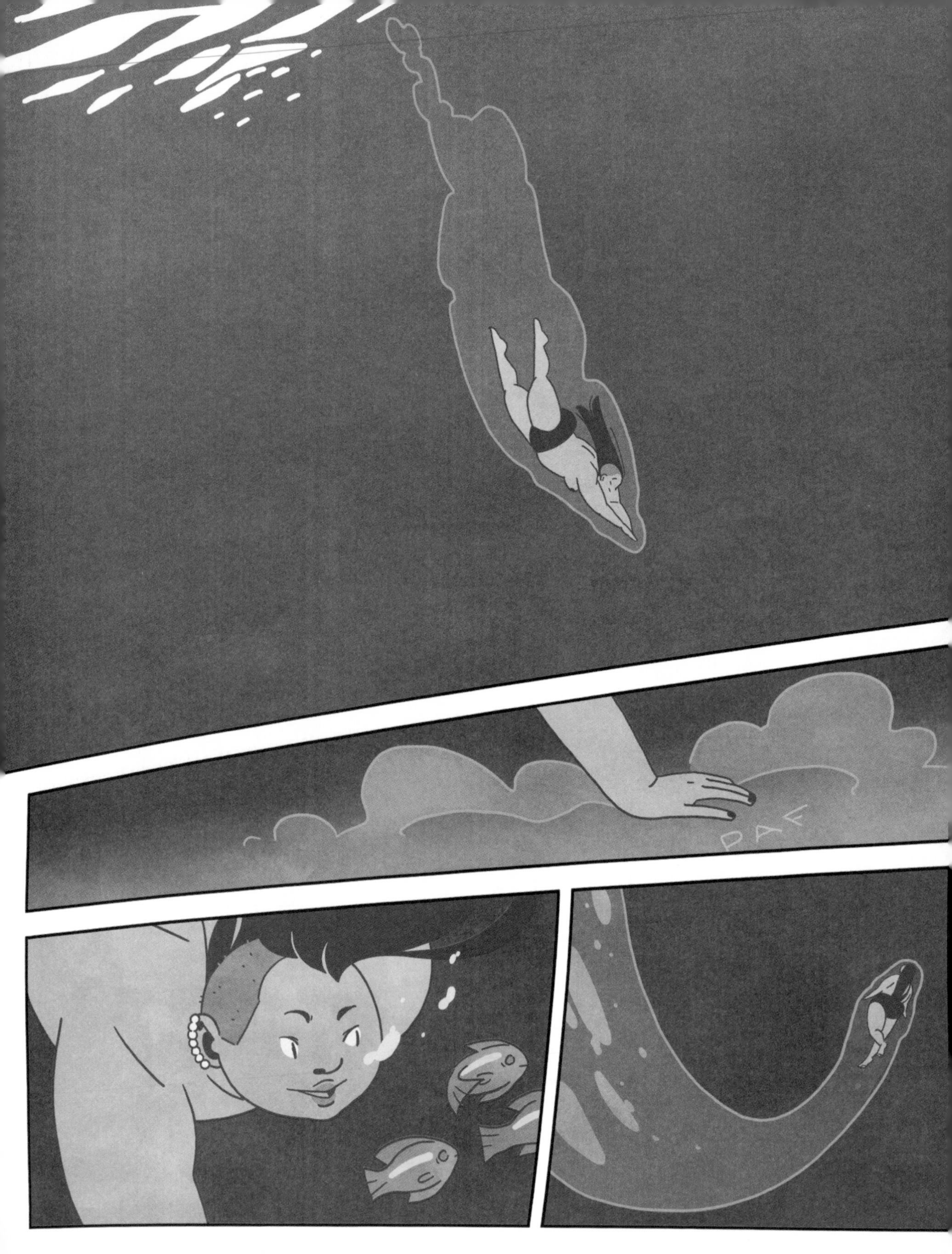
PAF

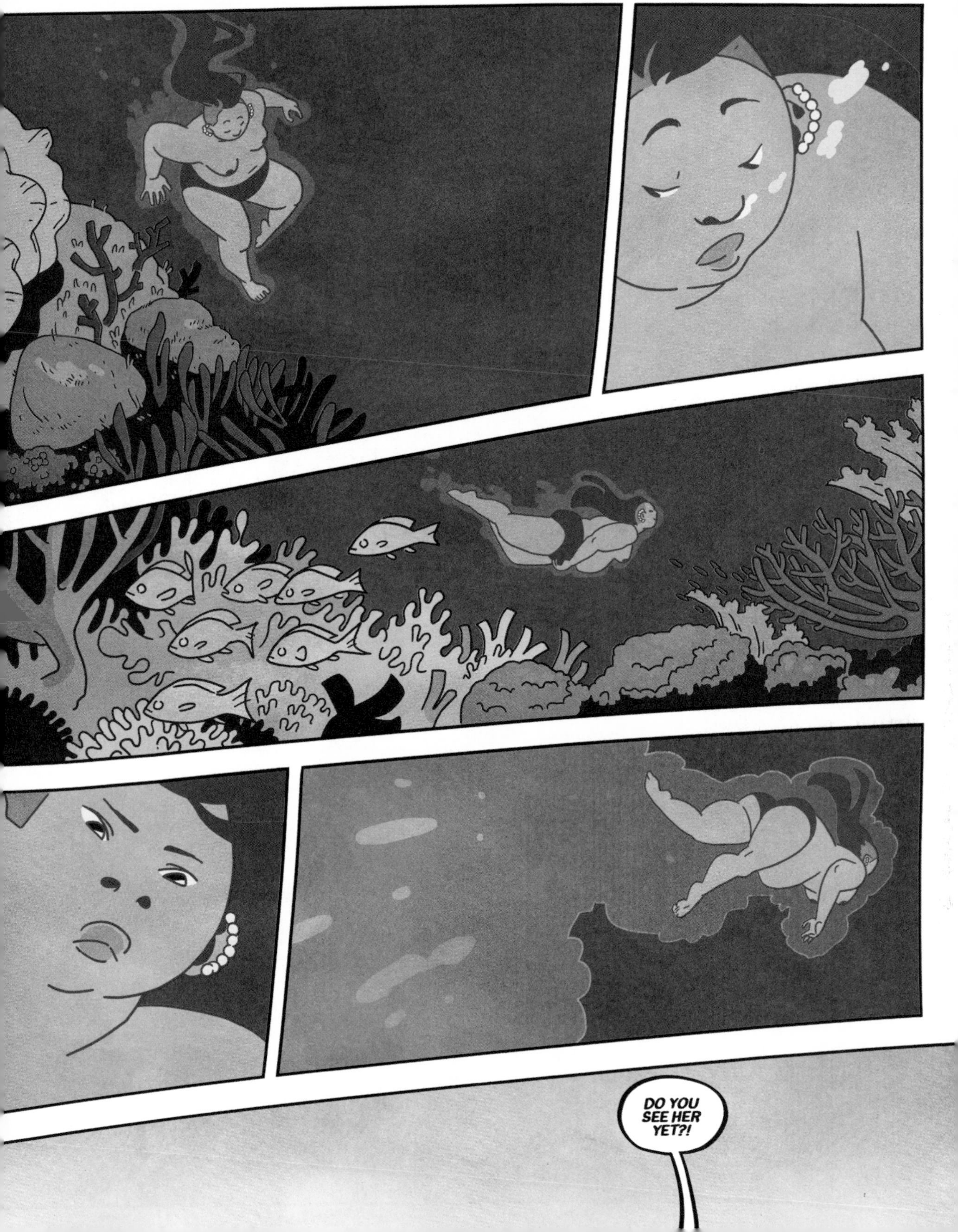
DO YOU SEE HER YET?!

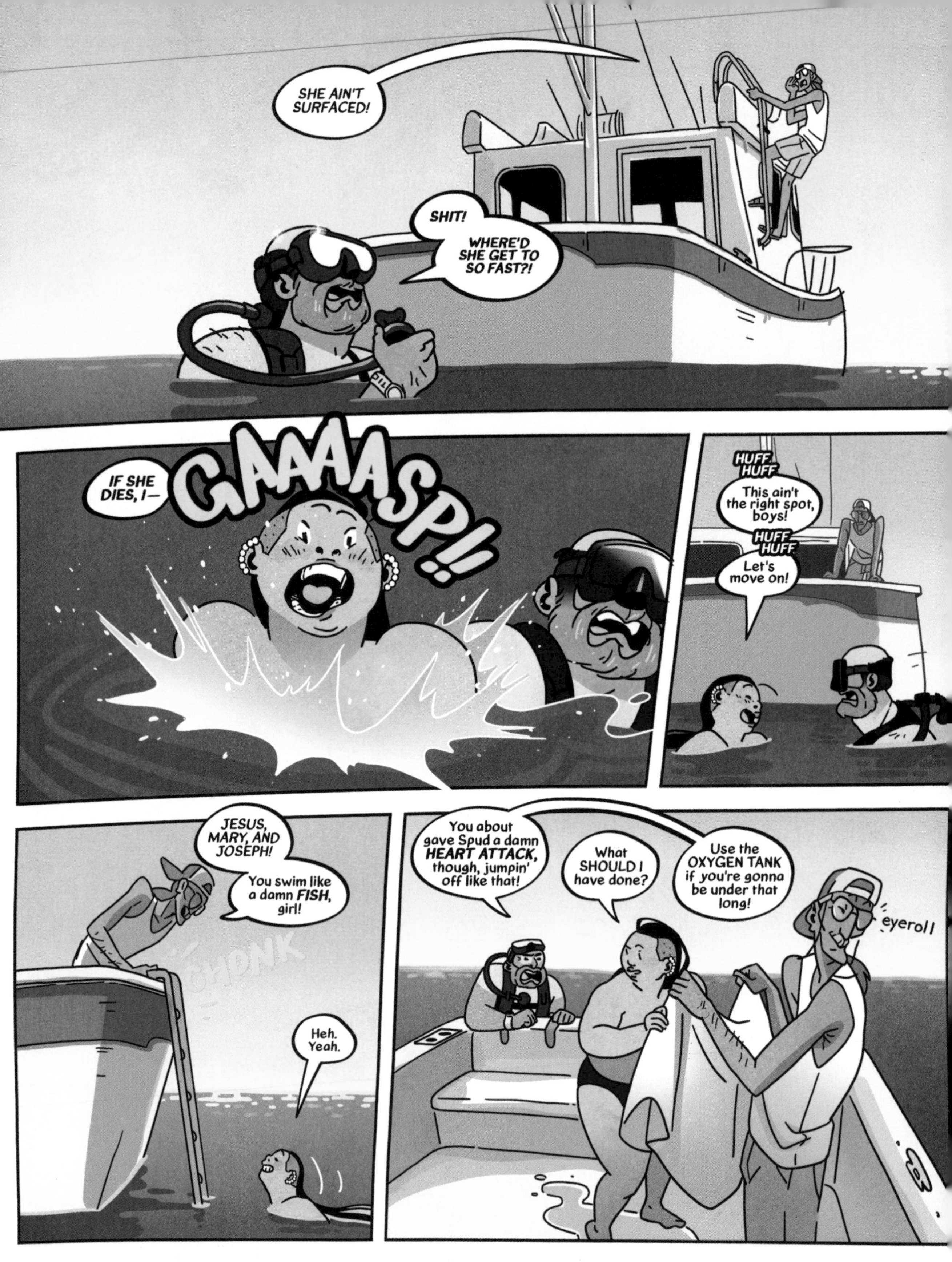
SHE AIN'T SURFACED!
SHIT!
WHERE'D SHE GET TO SO FAST?!
IF SHE DIES, I—
GAAAASP!!
HUFF HUFF
This ain't the right spot, boys!
HUFF HUFF
Let's move on!
JESUS, MARY, AND JOSEPH!
You swim like a damn FISH, girl!
CHONK
Heh. Yeah.
You about gave Spud a damn HEART ATTACK, though, jumpin' off like that!
What SHOULD I have done?
Use the OXYGEN TANK if you're gonna be under that long!
eyeroll

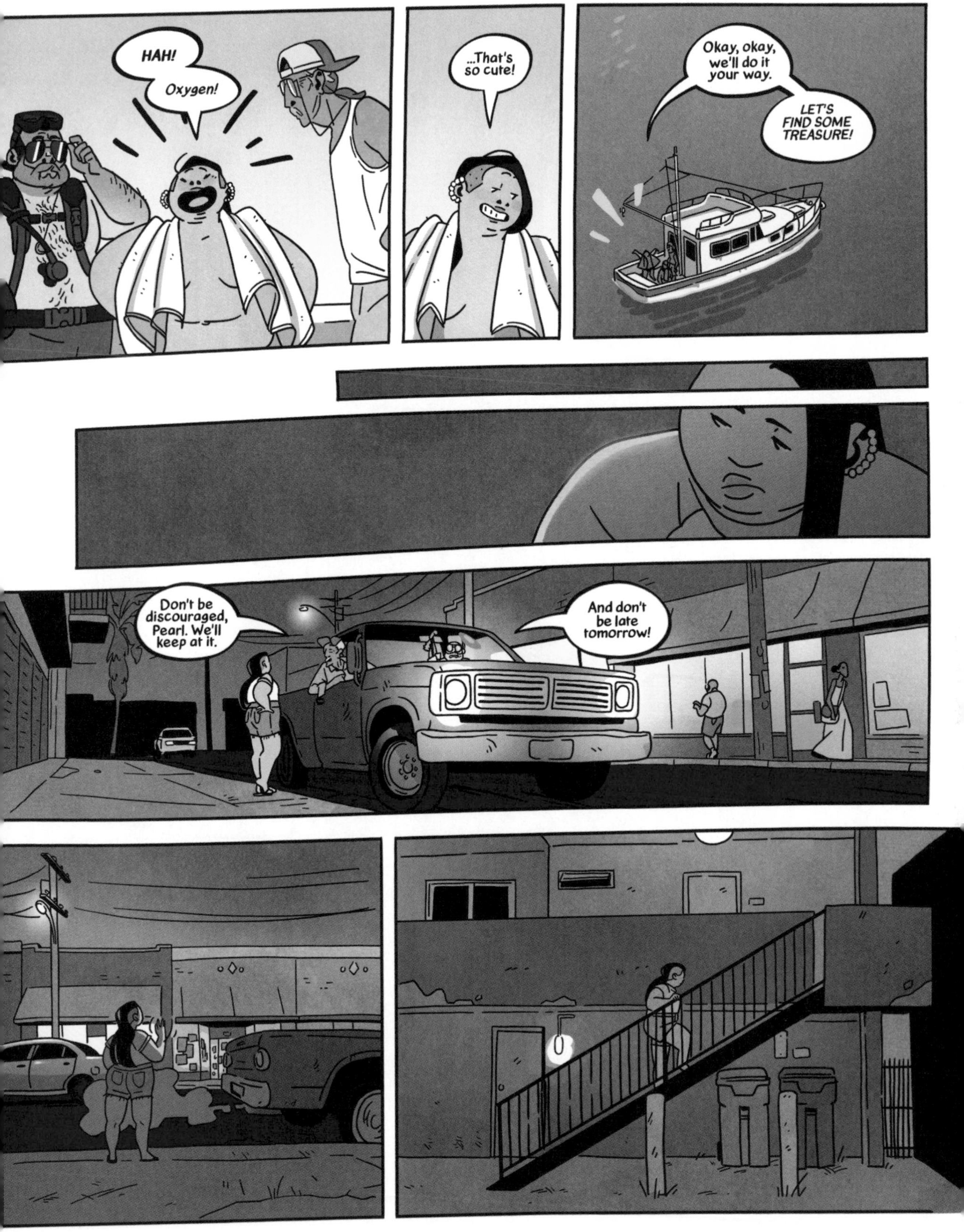
HAH!
Oxygen!
...That's so cute!
Okay, okay, we'll do it your way.
LET'S FIND SOME TREASURE!
Don't be discouraged, Pearl. We'll keep at it.
And don't be late tomorrow!

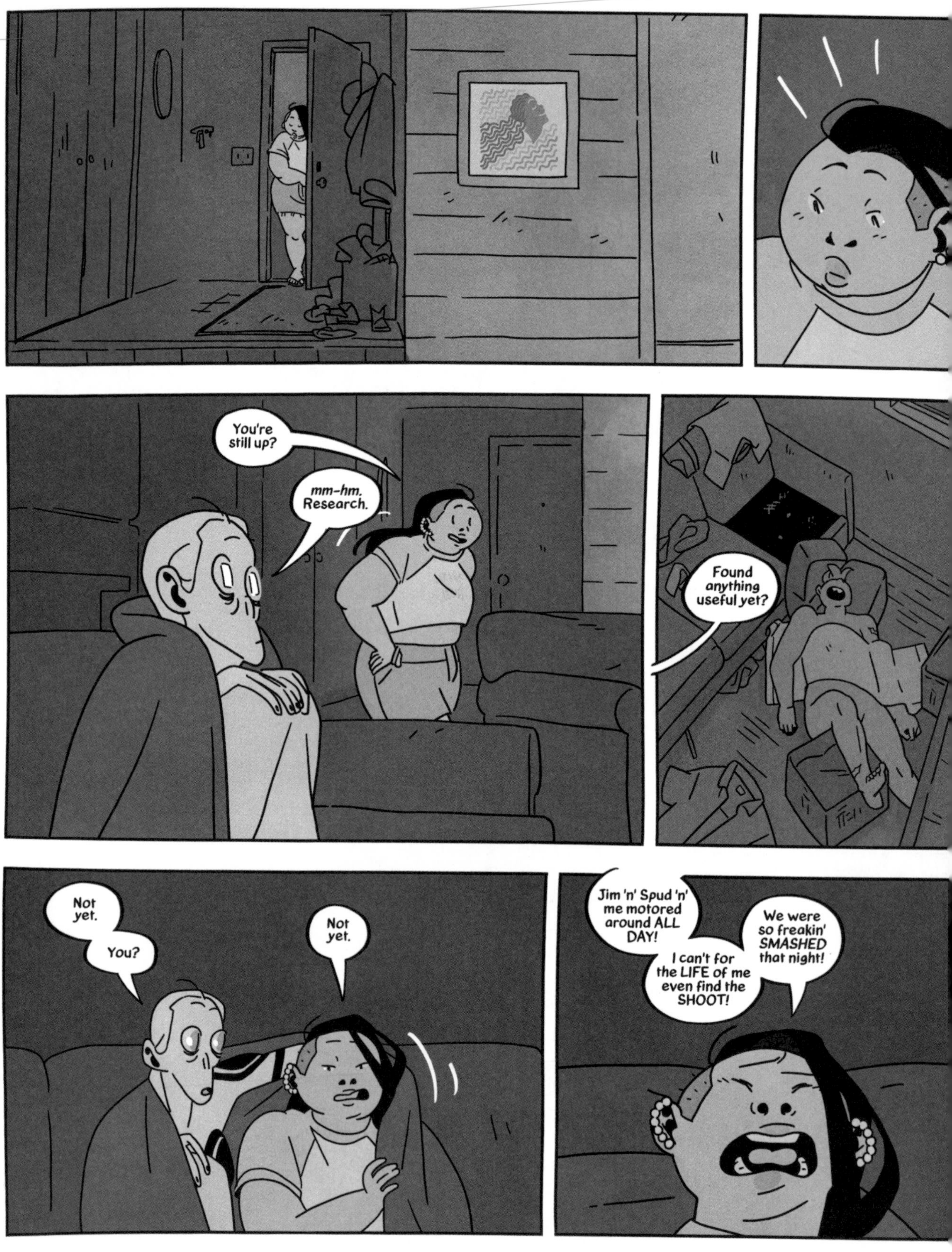
You're still up?
mm-hm. Research.
Found anything useful yet?
Not yet.
You?
Not yet.
Jim 'n' Spud 'n' me motored around ALL DAY!
I can't for the LIFE of me even find the SHOOT!
We were so freakin' SMASHED that night!

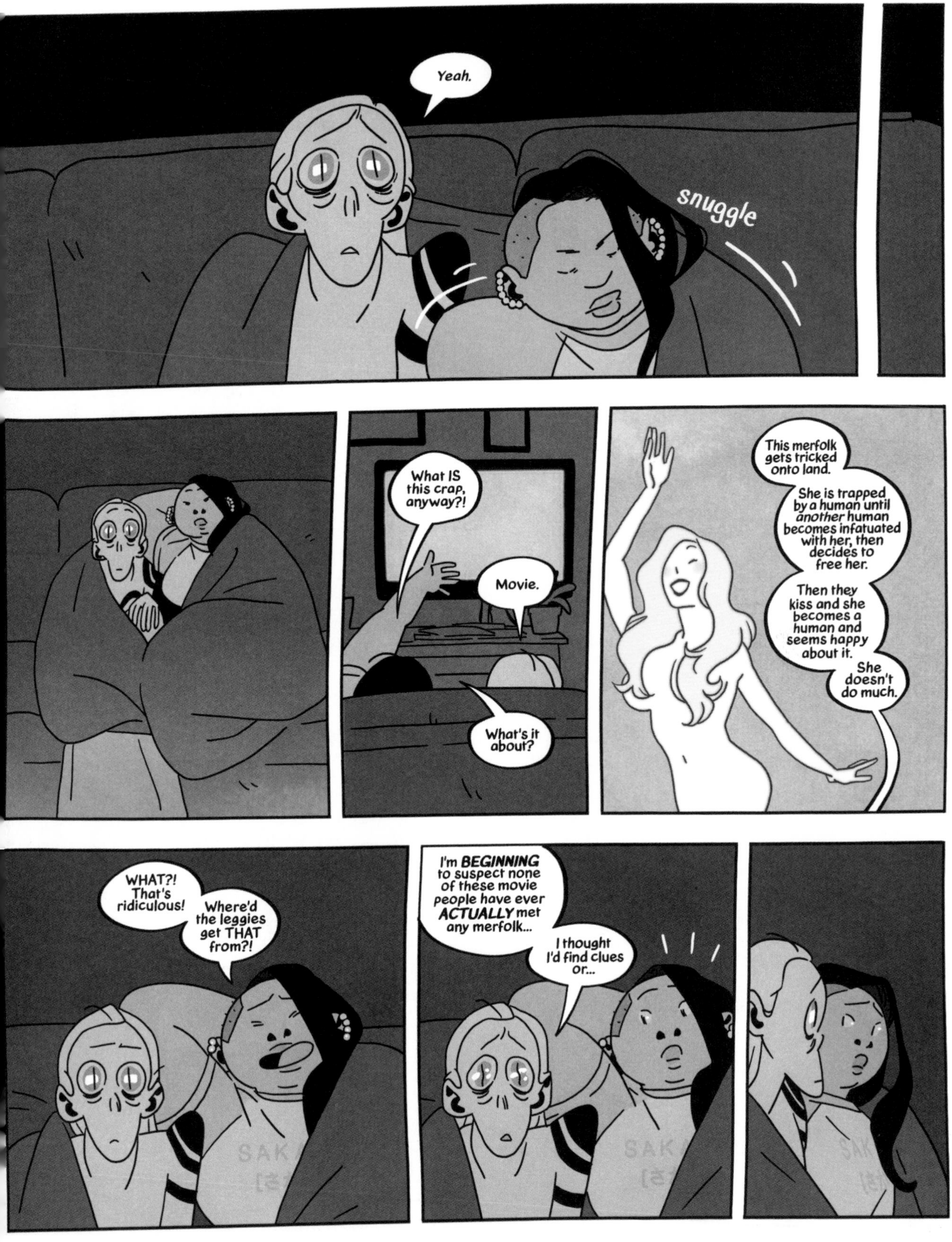
Yeah.
snuggle
What IS this crap, anyway?!
Movie.
What's it about?
This merfolk gets tricked onto land.
She is trapped by a human until another human becomes infatuated with her, then decides to free her.
Then they kiss and she becomes a human and seems happy about it.
She doesn't do much.
WHAT?! That's ridiculous!
Where'd the leggies get THAT from?!
I'm BEGINNING to suspect none of these movie people have ever ACTUALLY met any merfolk...
I thought I'd find clues or...

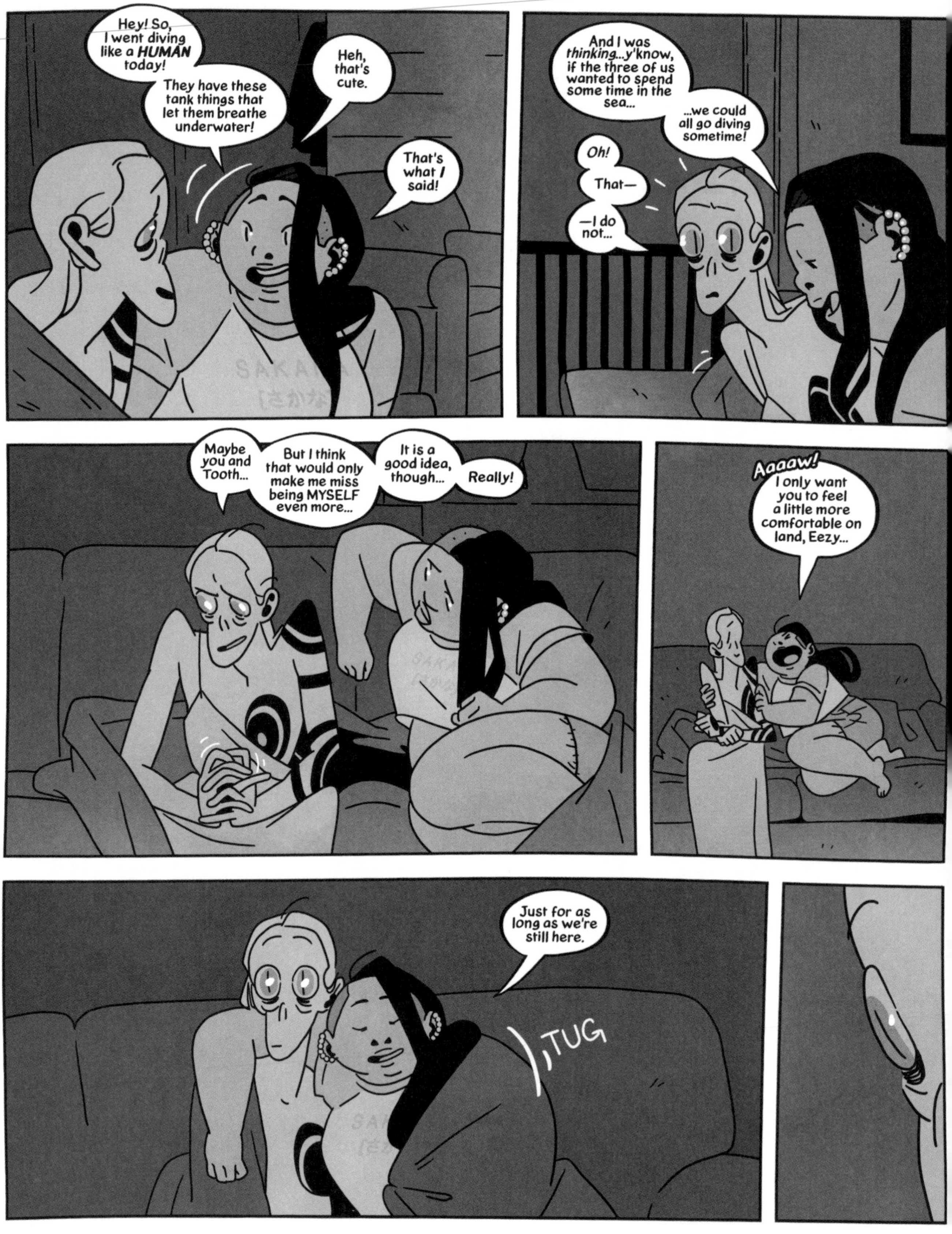
Hey! So, I went diving like a HUMAN today!
They have these tank things that let them breathe underwater!
Heh, that's cute.
That's what I said!
SAKA
And I was thinking...y'know, if the three of us wanted to spend some time in the sea...
...we could all go diving sometime!
Oh!
That—
—I do not...
Maybe you and Tooth...
But I think that would only make me miss being MYSELF even more...
It is a good idea, though...
Really!
Aaaaw!
I only want you to feel a little more comfortable on land, Eezy...
Just for as long as we're still here.
TUG

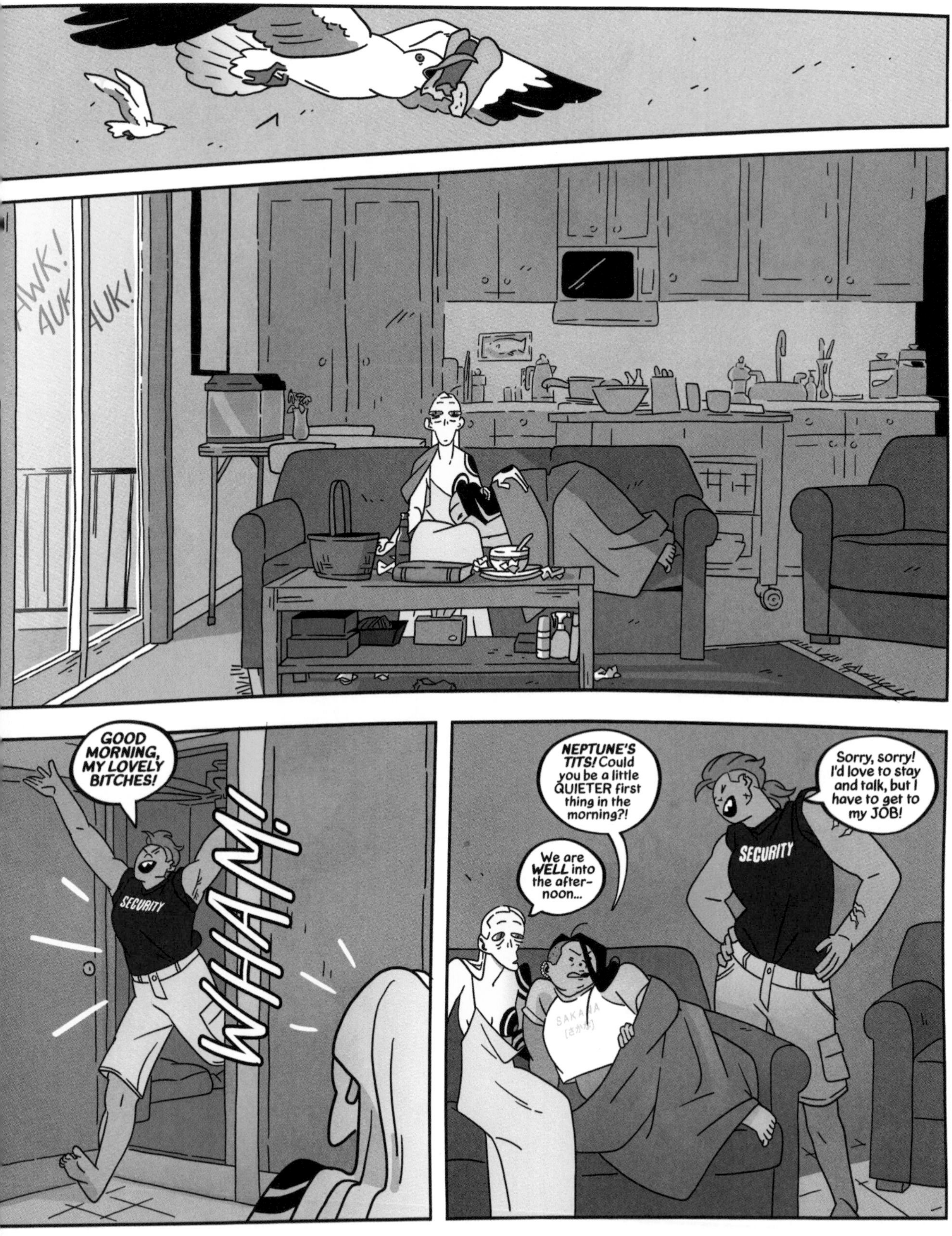
HAWK! AUK! AUK!
GOOD MORNING, MY LOVELY BITCHES!
WHAM!
NEPTUNE'S TITS! Could you be a little QUIETER first thing in the morning?!
We are WELL into the afternoon...
Sorry, sorry! I'd love to stay and talk, but I have to get to my JOB!
SECURITY
SECURITY
SAKANA
[さかな]

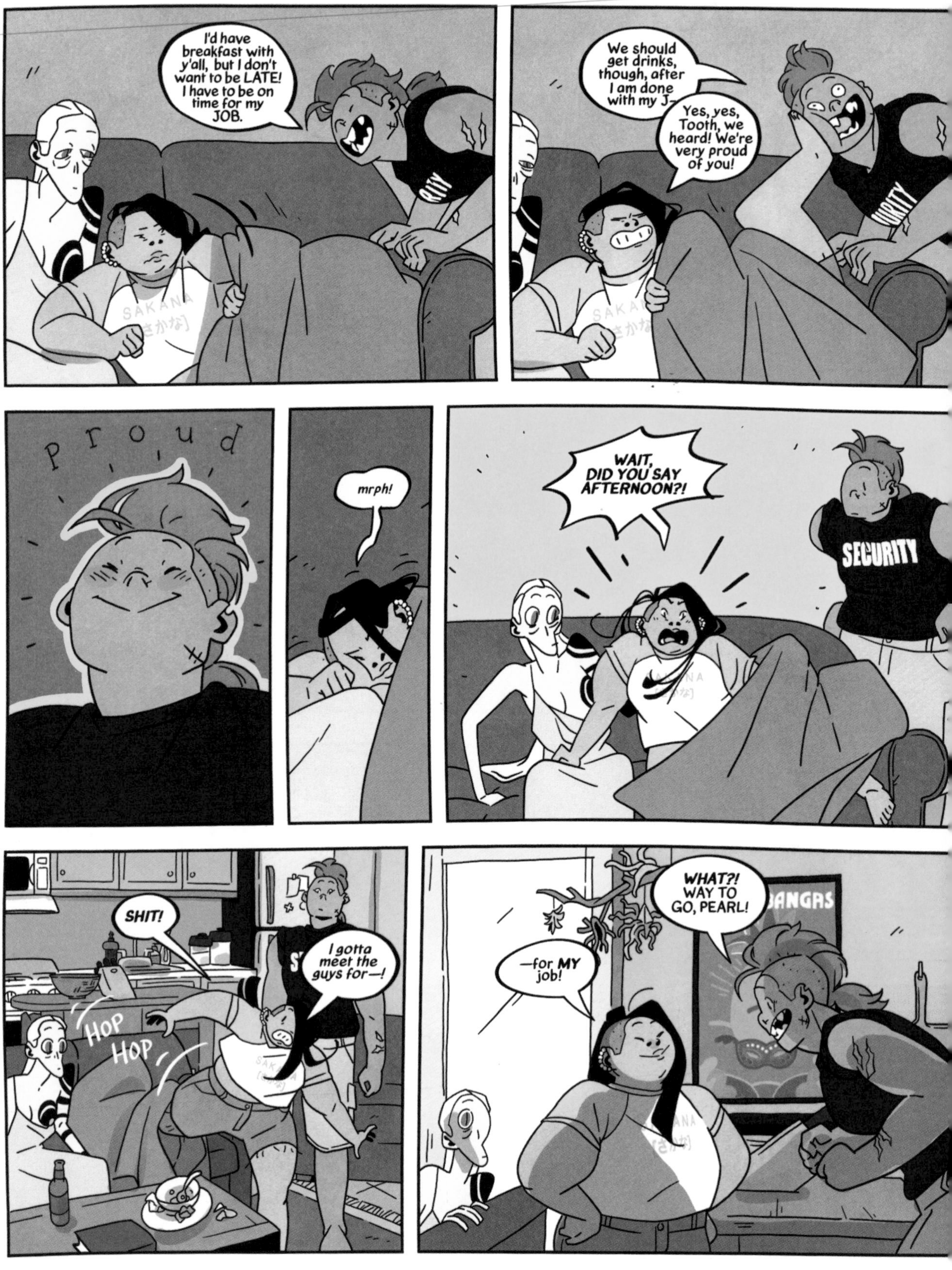
I'd have breakfast with y'all, but I don't want to be LATE! I have to be on time for my JOB.
SAKANA [さかな]
We should get drinks, though, after I am done with my J—
Yes, yes, Tooth, we heard! We're very proud of you!
proud
mrph!
WAIT, DID YOU SAY AFTERNOON?!
SECURITY
SHIT!
I gotta meet the guys for—!
HOP HOP
WHAT?! WAY TO GO, PEARL!
—for MY job!
BANGAS

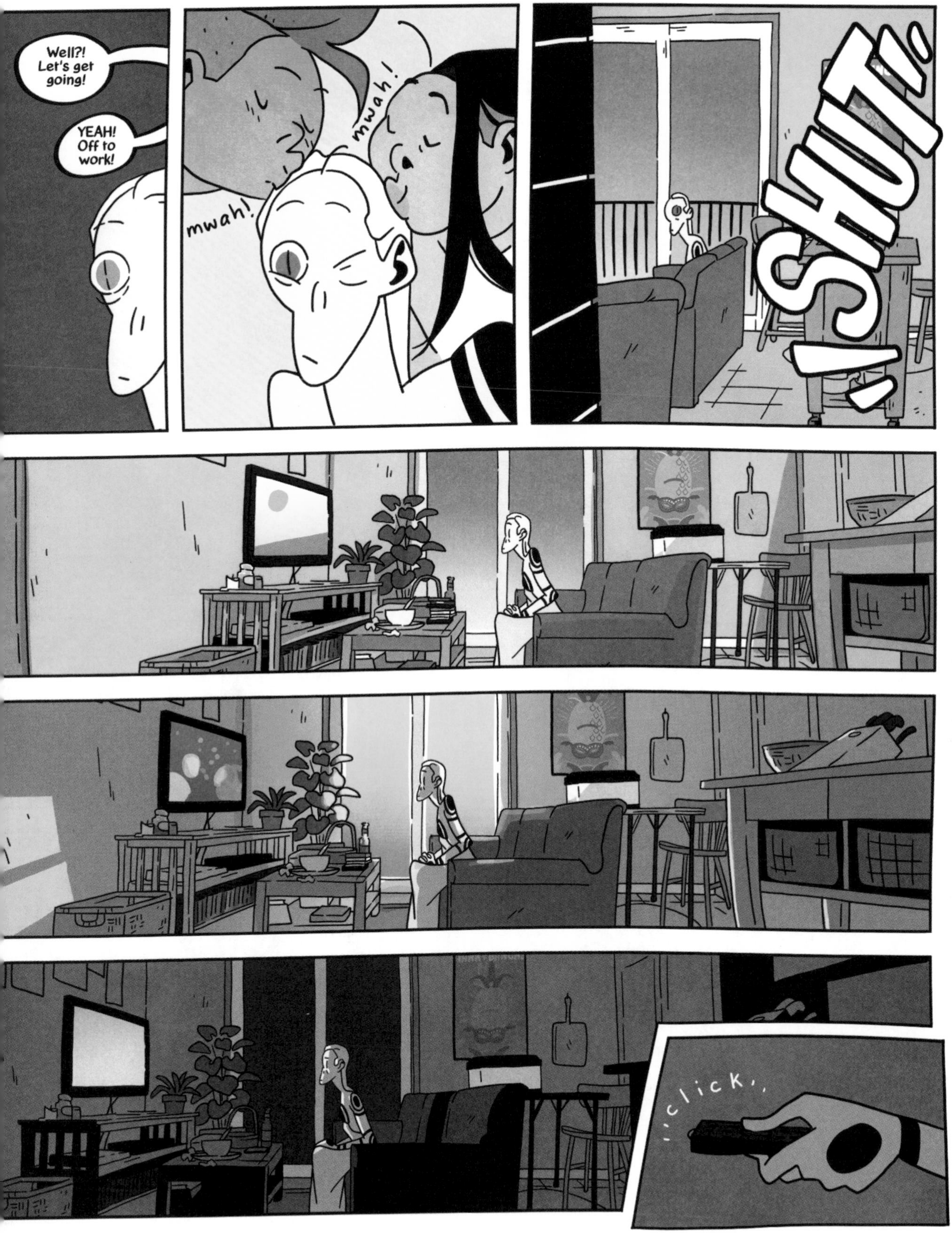

Well?! Let's get going!
YEAH! Off to work!
mwah!
mwah!
SHUT!
click

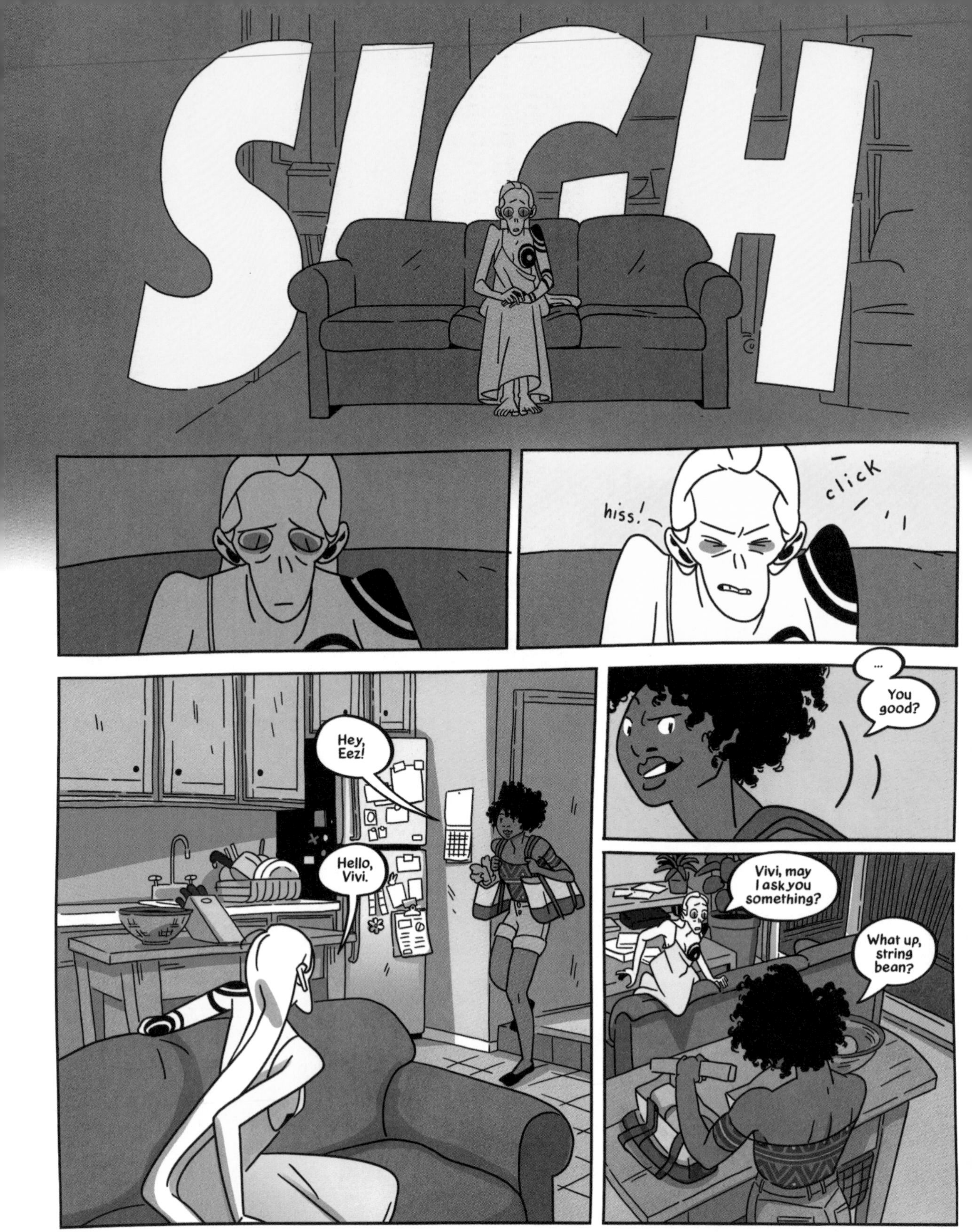
SIGH
hiss!
click
Hey, Eez!
Hello, Vivi.
...
You good?
Vivi, may I ask you something?
What up, string bean?

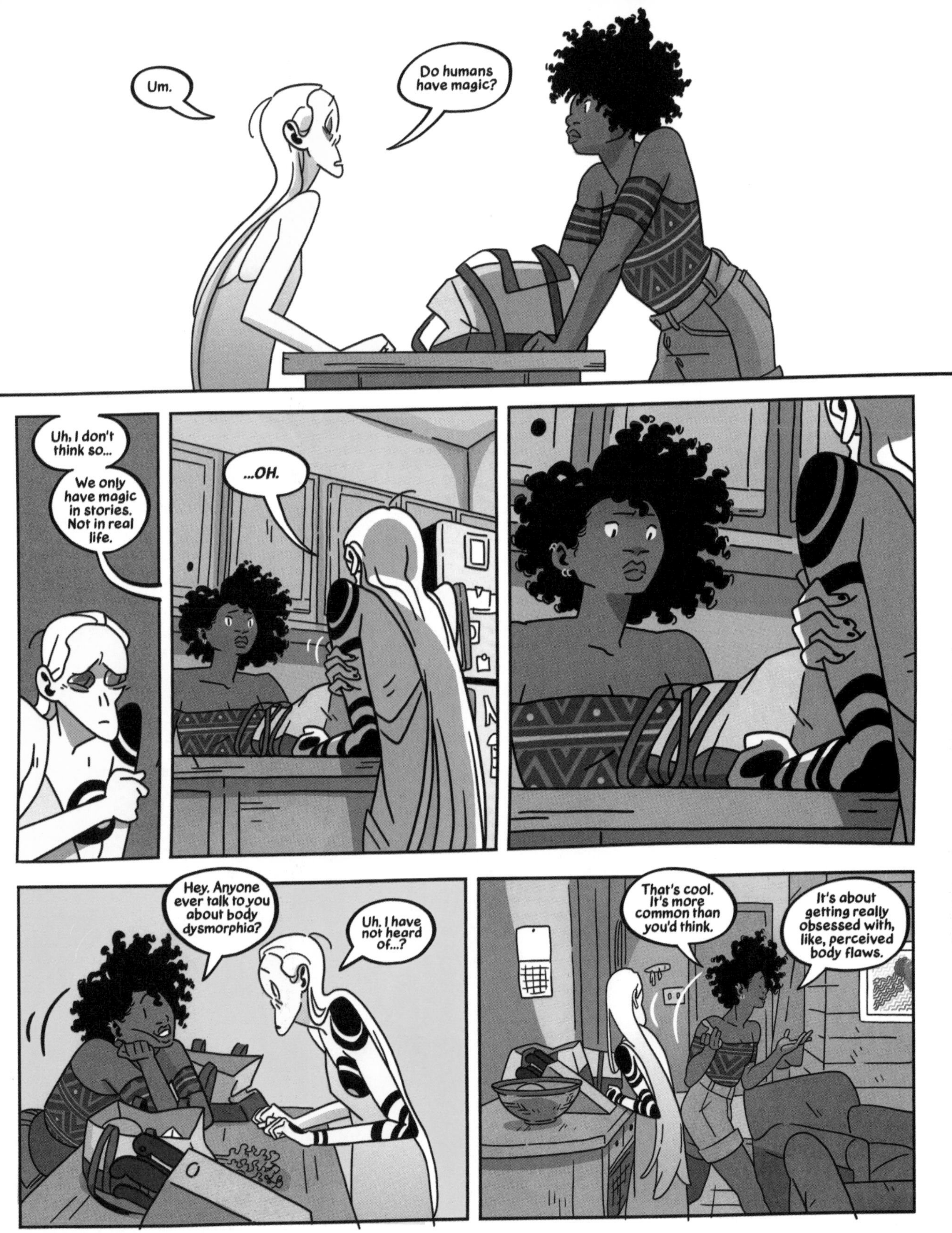
Um.
Do humans have magic?
Uh, I don't think so...
We only have magic in stories. Not in real life.
...OH.
Hey. Anyone ever talk to you about body dysmorphia?
Uh. I have not heard of...?
That's cool. It's more common than you'd think.
It's about getting really obsessed with, like, perceived body flaws.

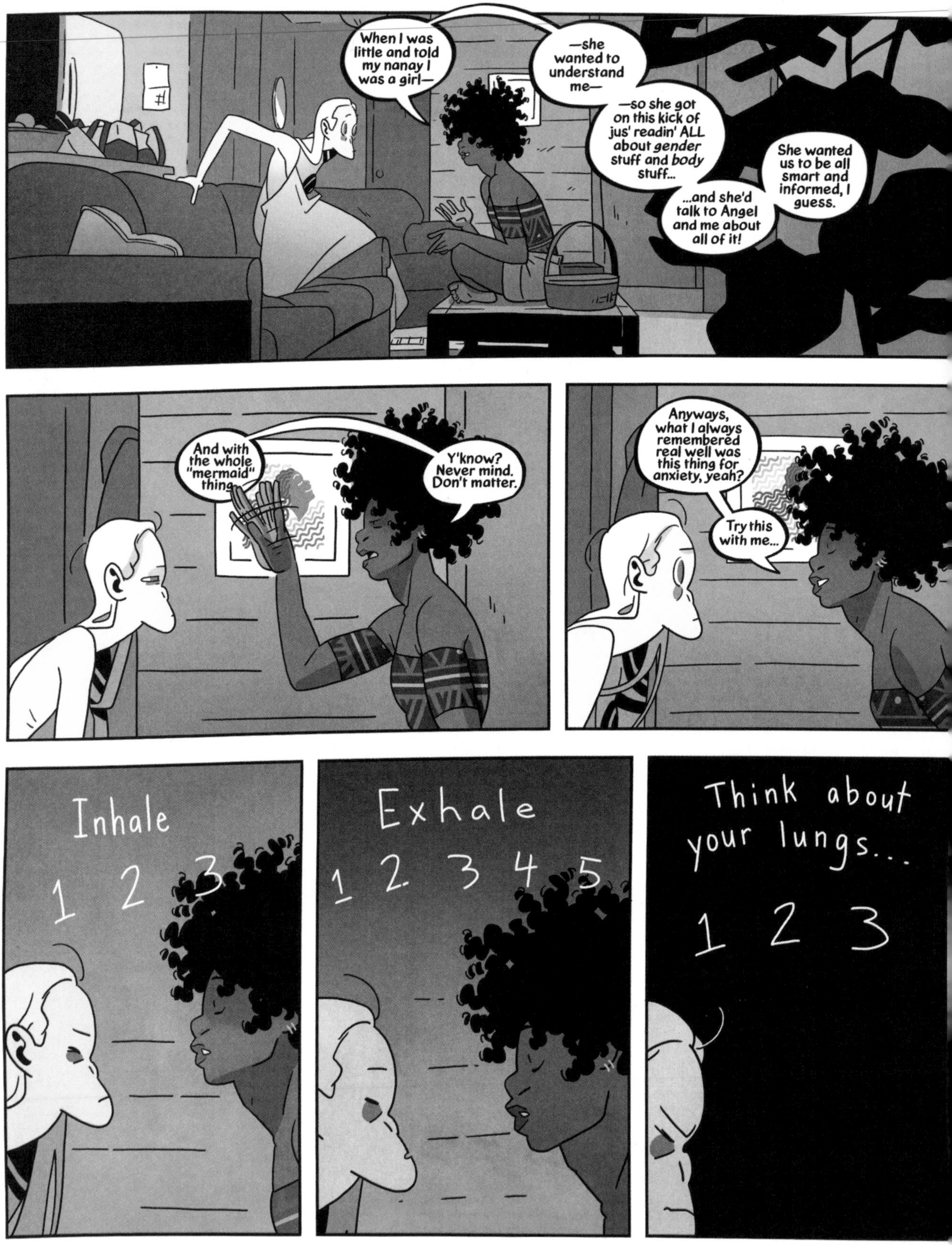
When I was little and told my nanay I was a girl—
—she wanted to understand me—
—so she got on this kick of jus' readin' ALL about *gender* stuff and *body* stuff...
...and she'd talk to Angel and me about all of it!
She wanted us to be all smart and informed, I guess.
And with the whole "mermaid" thing
Y'know? Never mind. Don't matter.
Anyways, what I always remembered real well was this thing for anxiety, yeah?
Try this with me...
Inhale
1 2 3
Exhale
1 2 3 4 5
Think about your lungs...
1 2 3

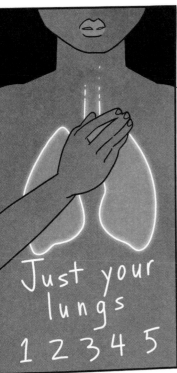

Just your lungs
1 2 3 4 5

Just focus on what you can control in this moment...
1   2   3

sigh

Thank you for sharing this wisdom, Vivi.

SLUMP

...but I do not take comfort in my human lungs.

...

Hey! You got me curious!

What's mermaid life like?

Tell me about magic!

MerFOLK. We are not all little girls.

Right!

Well, ALL merfolk have a little magic.

Usually only a small amount...

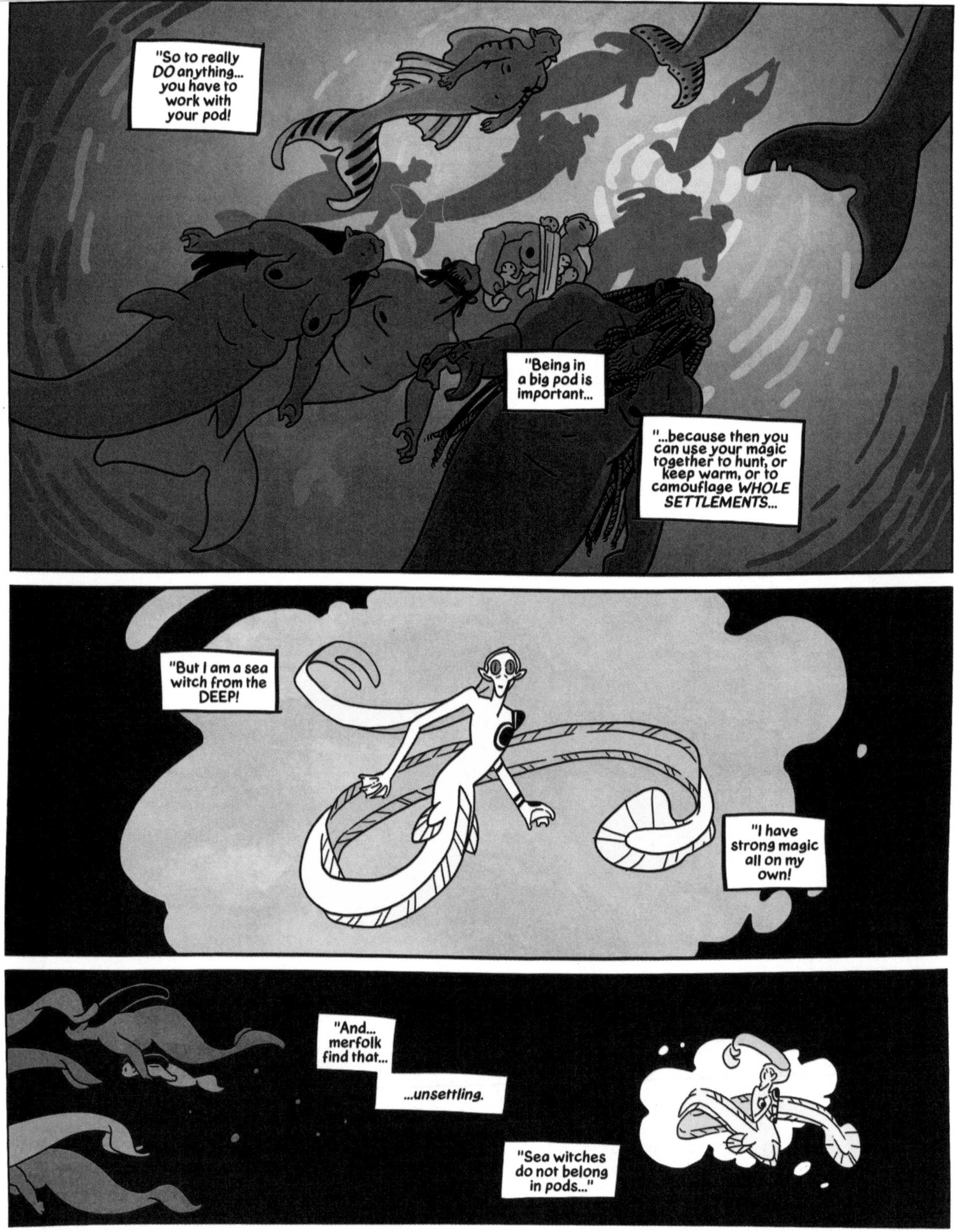
"So to really DO anything... you have to work with your pod!
"Being in a big pod is important...
"...because then you can use your magic together to hunt, or keep warm, or to camouflage WHOLE SETTLEMENTS...
"But I am a sea witch from the DEEP!
"I have strong magic all on my own!
"And... merfolk find that...
...unsettling.
"Sea witches do not belong in pods..."

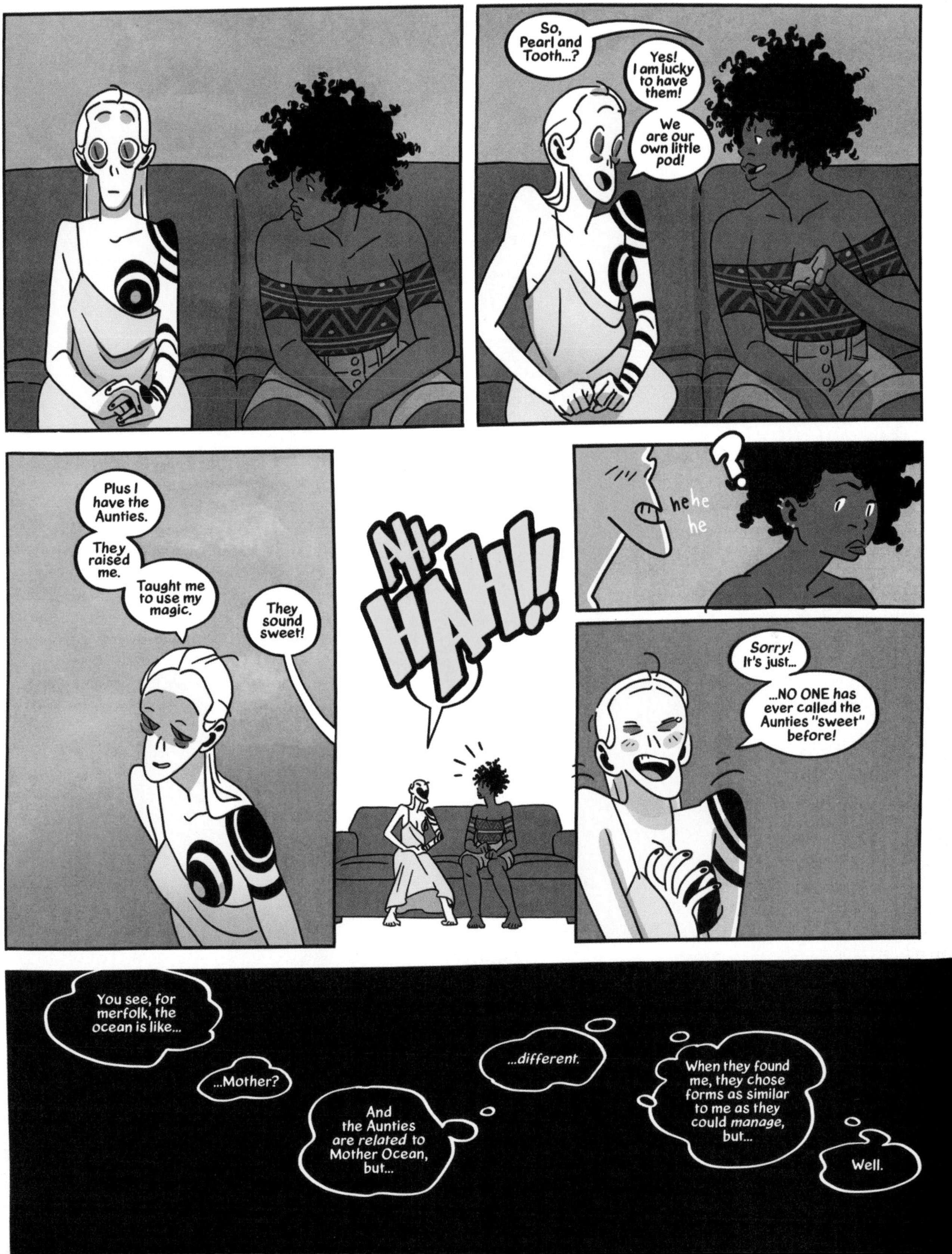
So, Pearl and Tooth...?
Yes! I am lucky to have them!
We are our own little pod!
Plus I have the Aunties.
They raised me.
Taught me to use my magic.
They sound sweet!
AH-HAH!!
hehe he
?
Sorry! It's just...
...NO ONE has ever called the Aunties "sweet" before!
You see, for merfolk, the ocean is like...
...Mother?
And the Aunties are *related* to Mother Ocean, but...
...*different.*
When they found me, they chose forms as similar to me as they could *manage*, but...
Well.

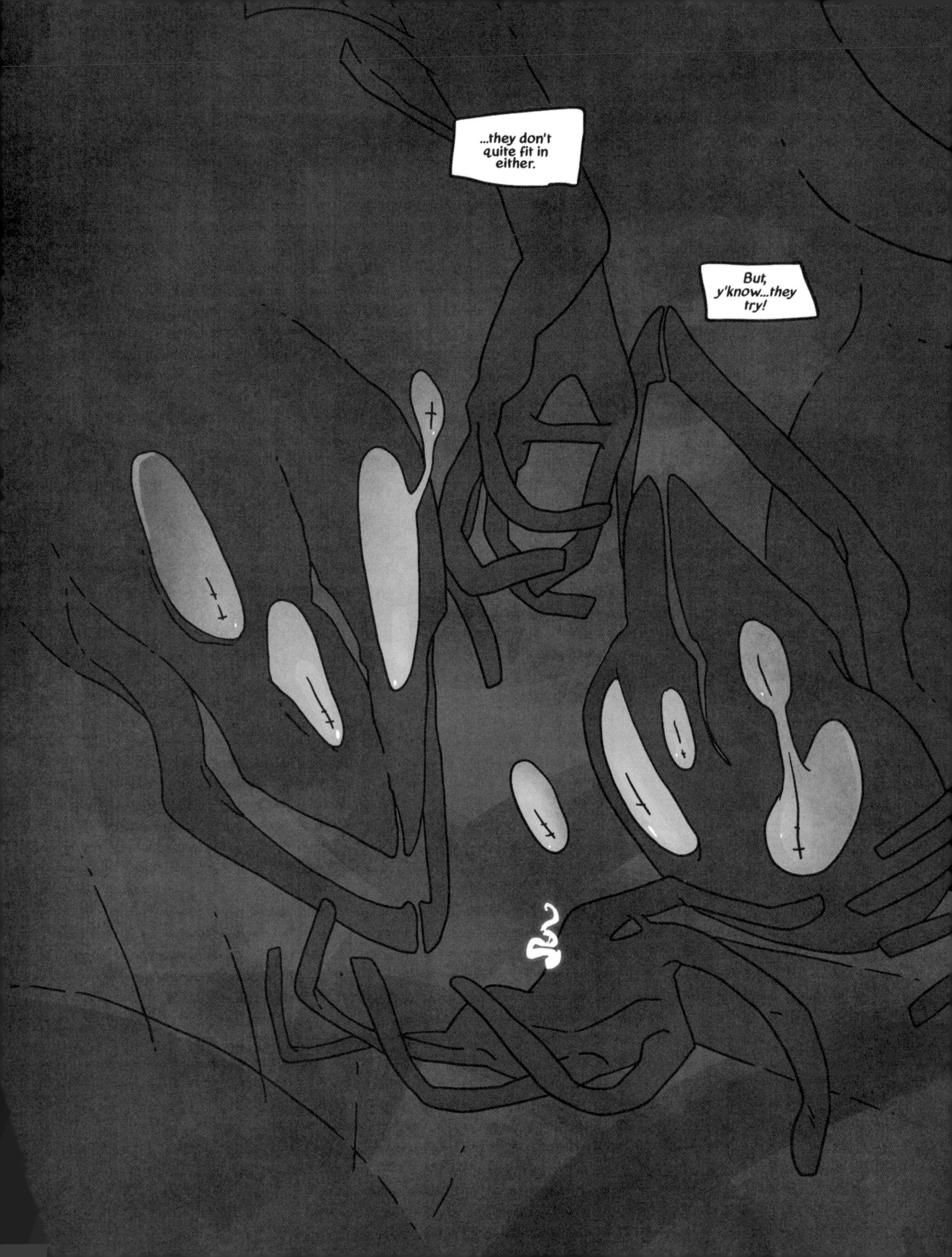
...they don't quite fit in either.
But, y'know...they try!

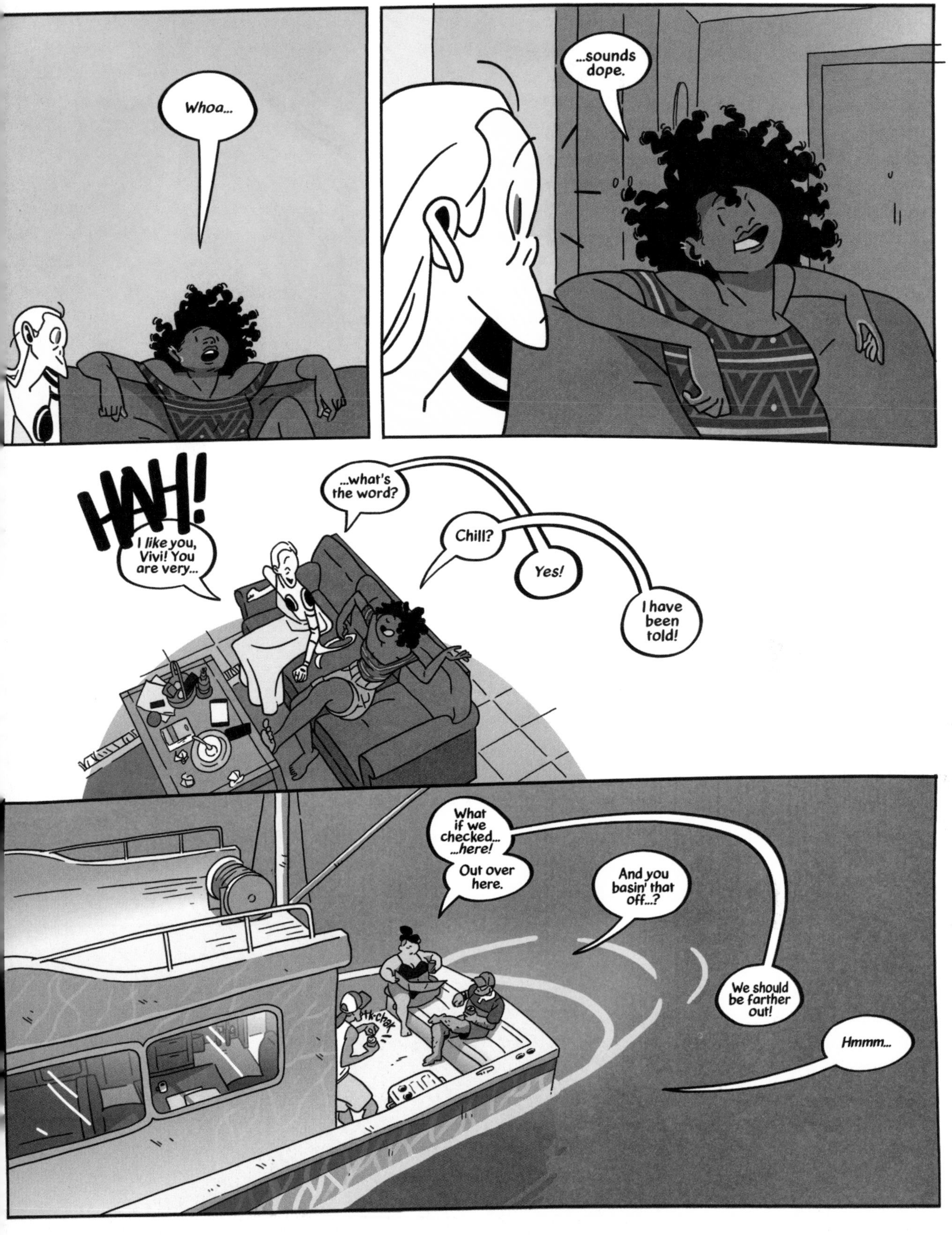
Whoa...
...sounds dope.
HAH!
I like you, Vivi! You are very...
...what's the word?
Chill?
Yes!
I have been told!
What if we checked... ...here!
Out over here.
And you basin' that off...?
We should be farther out!
Hmmm...
tk-chak

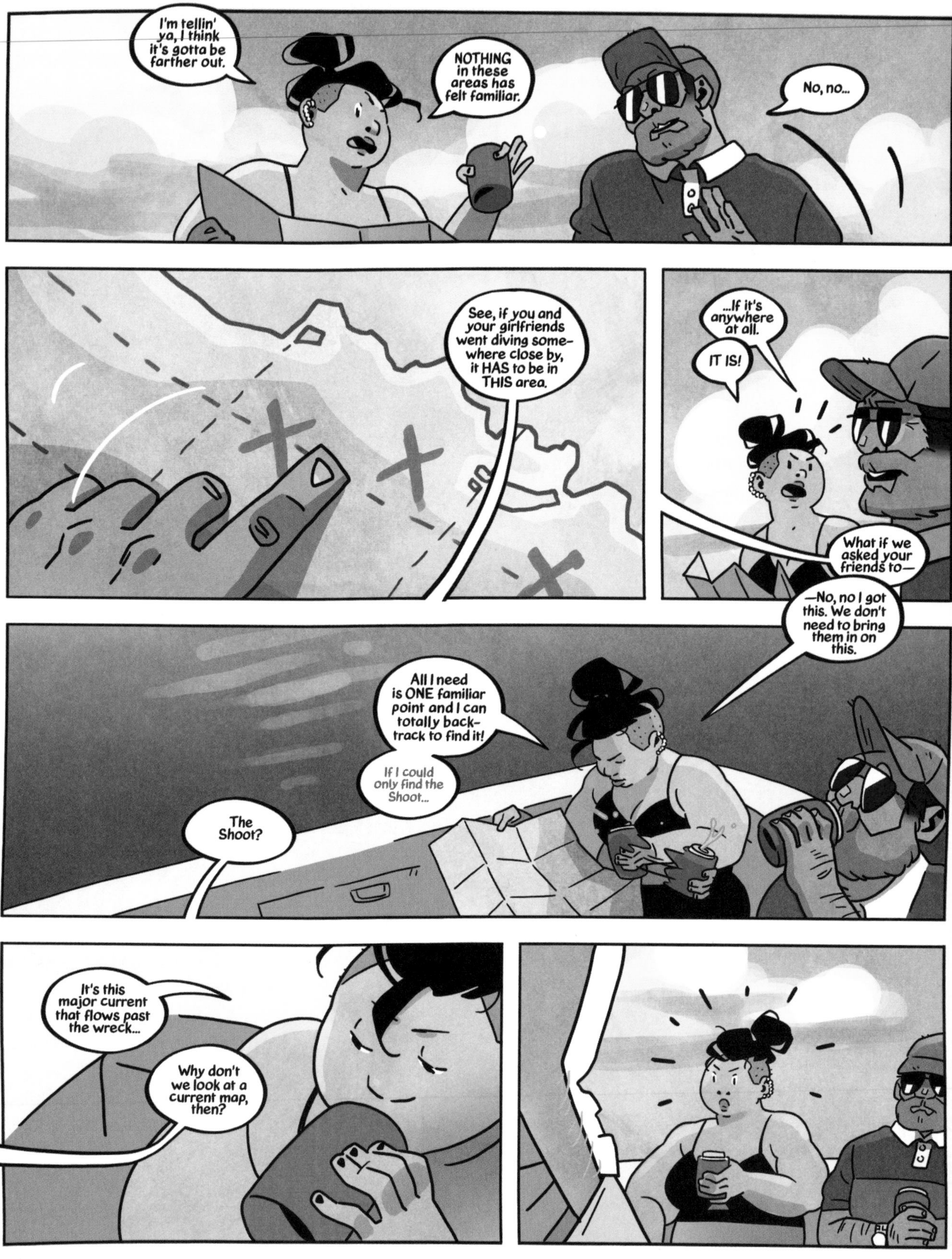
I'm tellin' ya, I think it's gotta be farther out.
NOTHING in these areas has felt familiar.
No, no...
See, if you and your girlfriends went diving some-where close by, it HAS to be in THIS area.
...If it's anywhere at all.
IT IS!
What if we asked your friends to—
—No, no I got this. We don't need to bring them in on this.
All I need is ONE familiar point and I can totally back-track to find it!
If I could only find the Shoot...
The Shoot?
It's this major current that flows past the wreck...
Why don't we look at a current map, then?

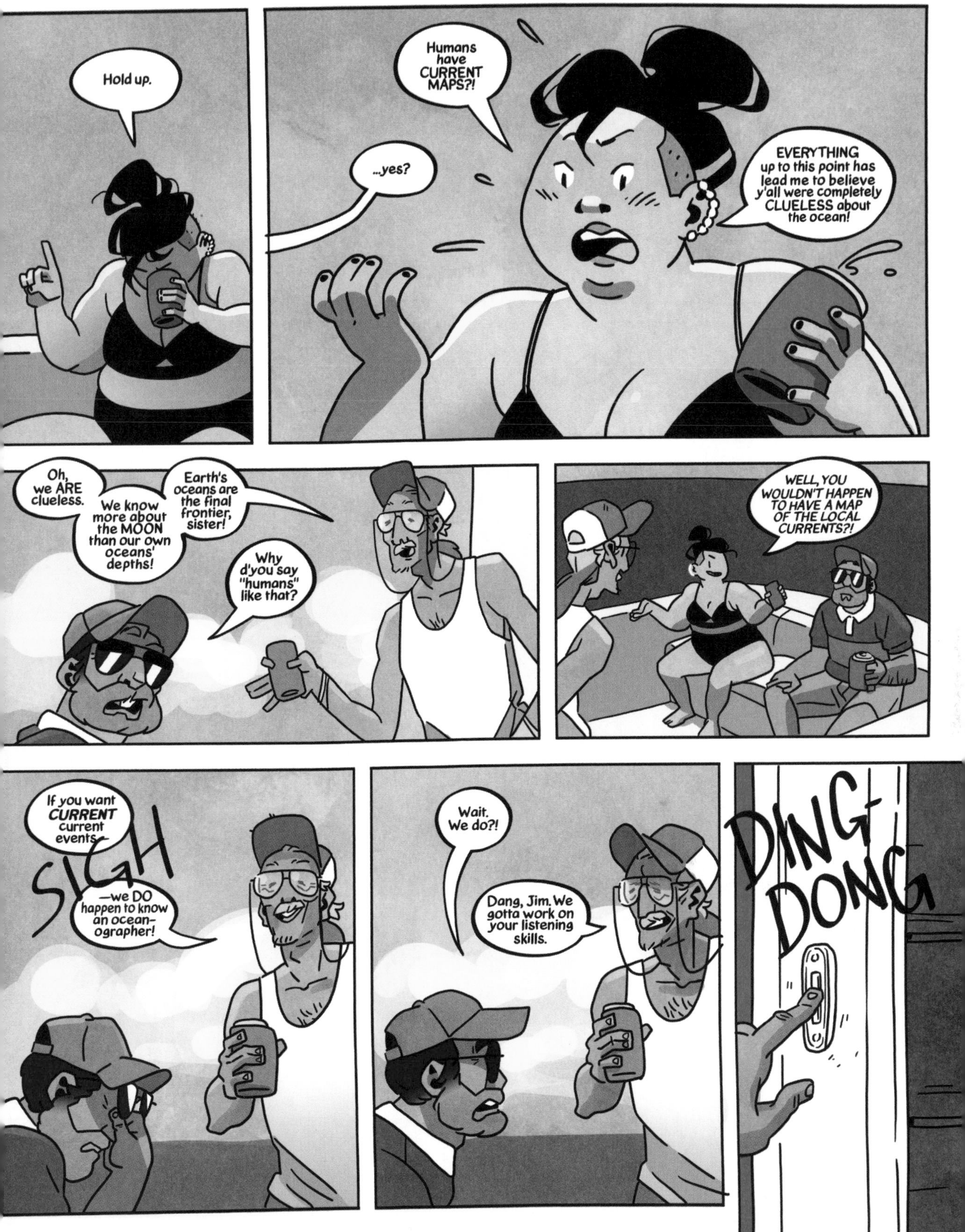
Hold up.
Humans have CURRENT MAPS?!
...yes?
EVERYTHING up to this point has lead me to believe y'all were completely CLUELESS about the ocean!
Oh, we ARE clueless.
We know more about the MOON than our own oceans' depths!
Earth's oceans are the final frontier, sister!
Why d'you say "humans" like that?
WELL, YOU WOULDN'T HAPPEN TO HAVE A MAP OF THE LOCAL CURRENTS?!
If you want CURRENT current events—
SIGH
—we DO happen to know an ocean-ographer!
Wait. We do?!
Dang, Jim. We gotta work on your listening skills.
DING DONG

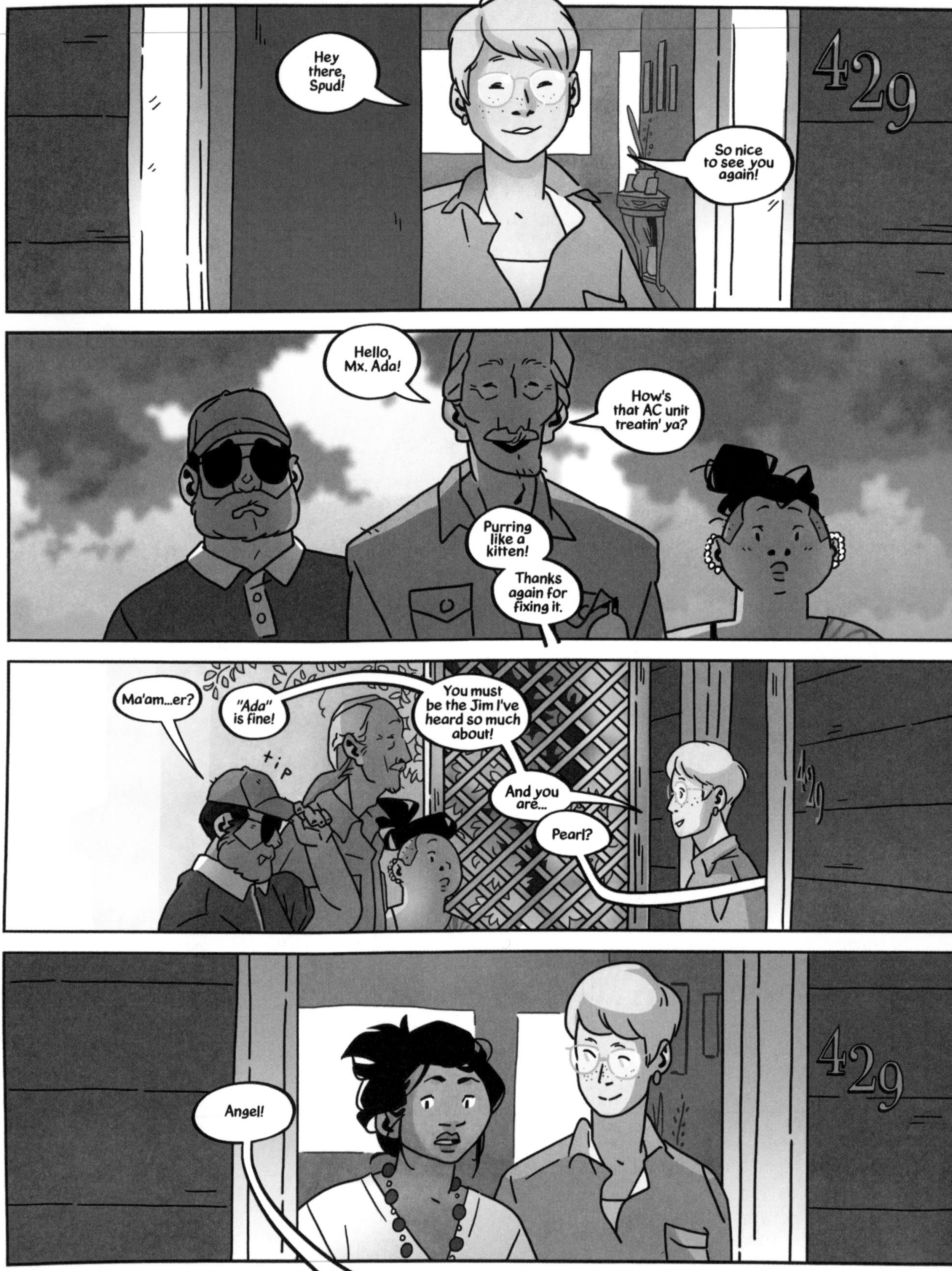

Hey there, Spud!
So nice to see you again!
429
Hello, Mx. Ada!
How's that AC unit treatin' ya?
Purring like a kitten!
Thanks again for fixing it.
Ma'am...er?
"Ada" is fine!
You must be the Jim I've heard so much about!
tip
And you are...
Pearl?
429
Angel!
429

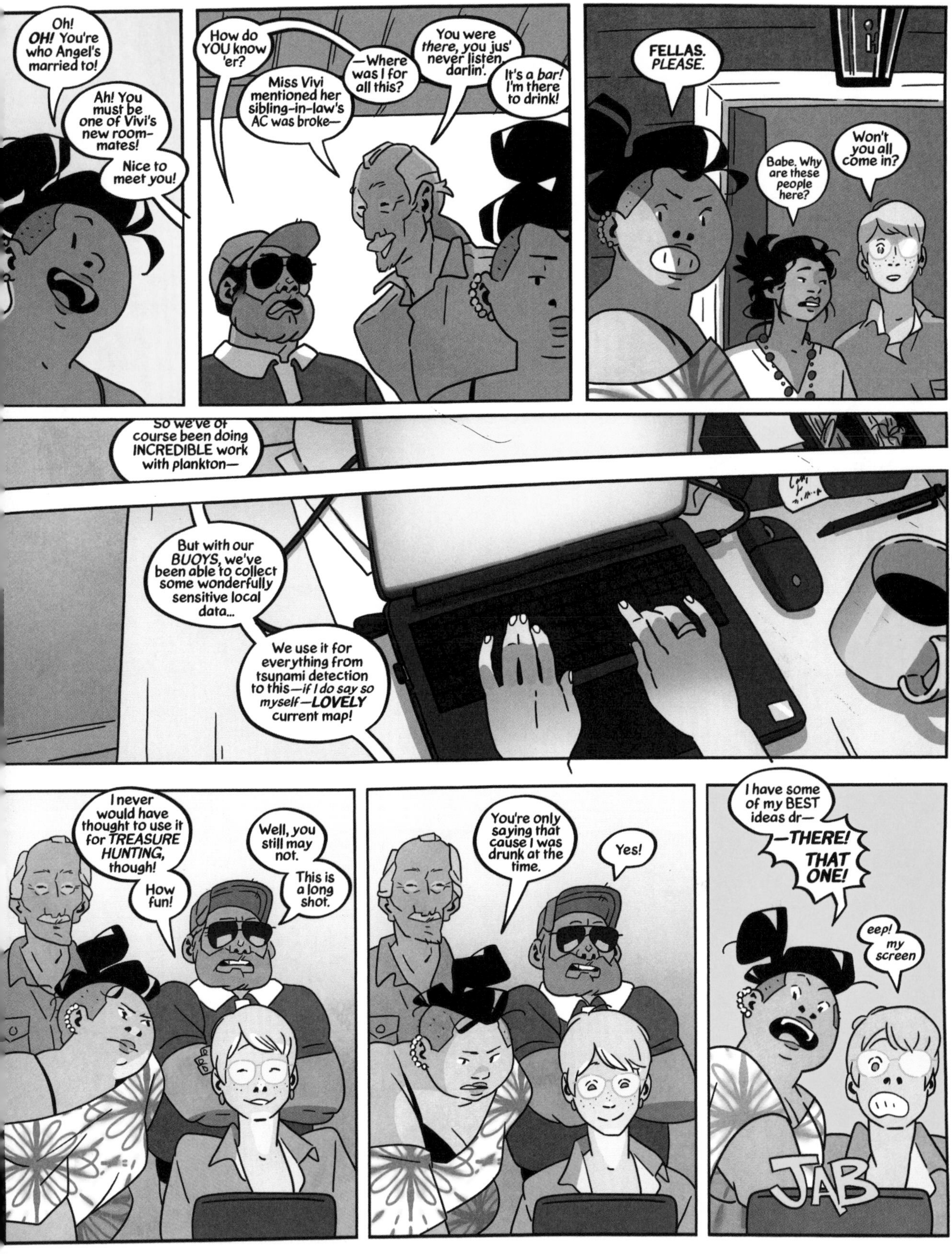

Oh! OH! You're who Angel's married to!
Ah! You must be one of Vivi's new room-mates!
Nice to meet you!
How do YOU know 'er?
Miss Vivi mentioned her sibling-in-law's AC was broke—
—Where was I for all this?
You were there, you jus' never listen, darlin'.
It's a bar! I'm there to drink!
FELLAS. PLEASE.
Babe. Why are these people here?
Won't you all come in?
So we've of course been doing INCREDIBLE work with plankton—
But with our BUOYS, we've been able to collect some wonderfully sensitive local data...
We use it for everything from tsunami detection to this—if I do say so myself—LOVELY current map!
I never would have thought to use it for TREASURE HUNTING, though!
How fun!
Well, you still may not.
This is a long shot.
You're only saying that cause I was drunk at the time.
Yes!
I have some of my BEST ideas dr—
—THERE! THAT ONE!
eep! my screen
JAB

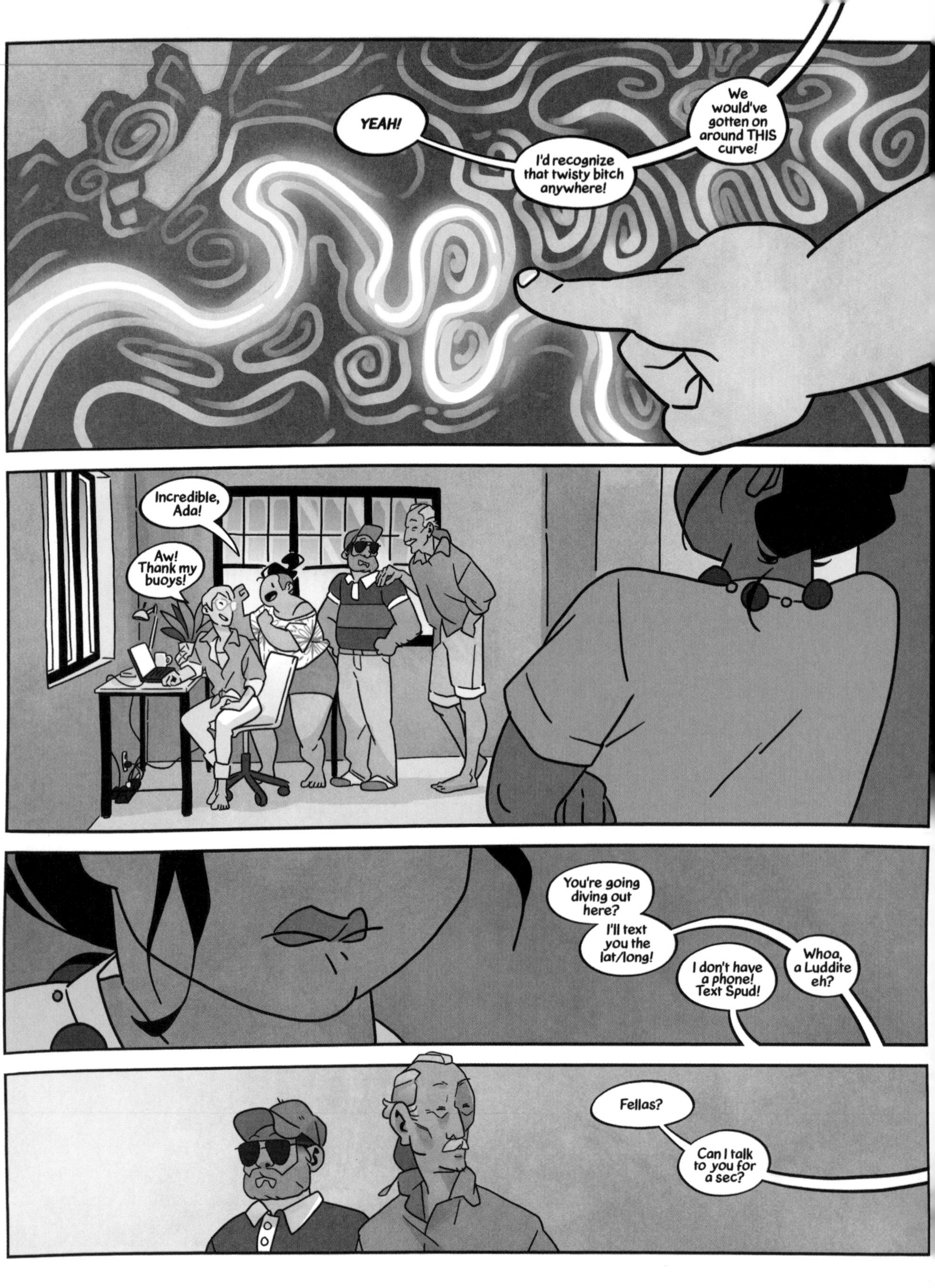
YEAH!
I'd recognize that twisty bitch anywhere!
We would've gotten on around THIS curve!
Incredible, Ada!
Aw! Thank my buoys!
You're going diving out here?
I'll text you the lat/long!
I don't have a phone! Text Spud!
Whoa, a Luddite eh?
Fellas?
Can I talk to you for a sec?

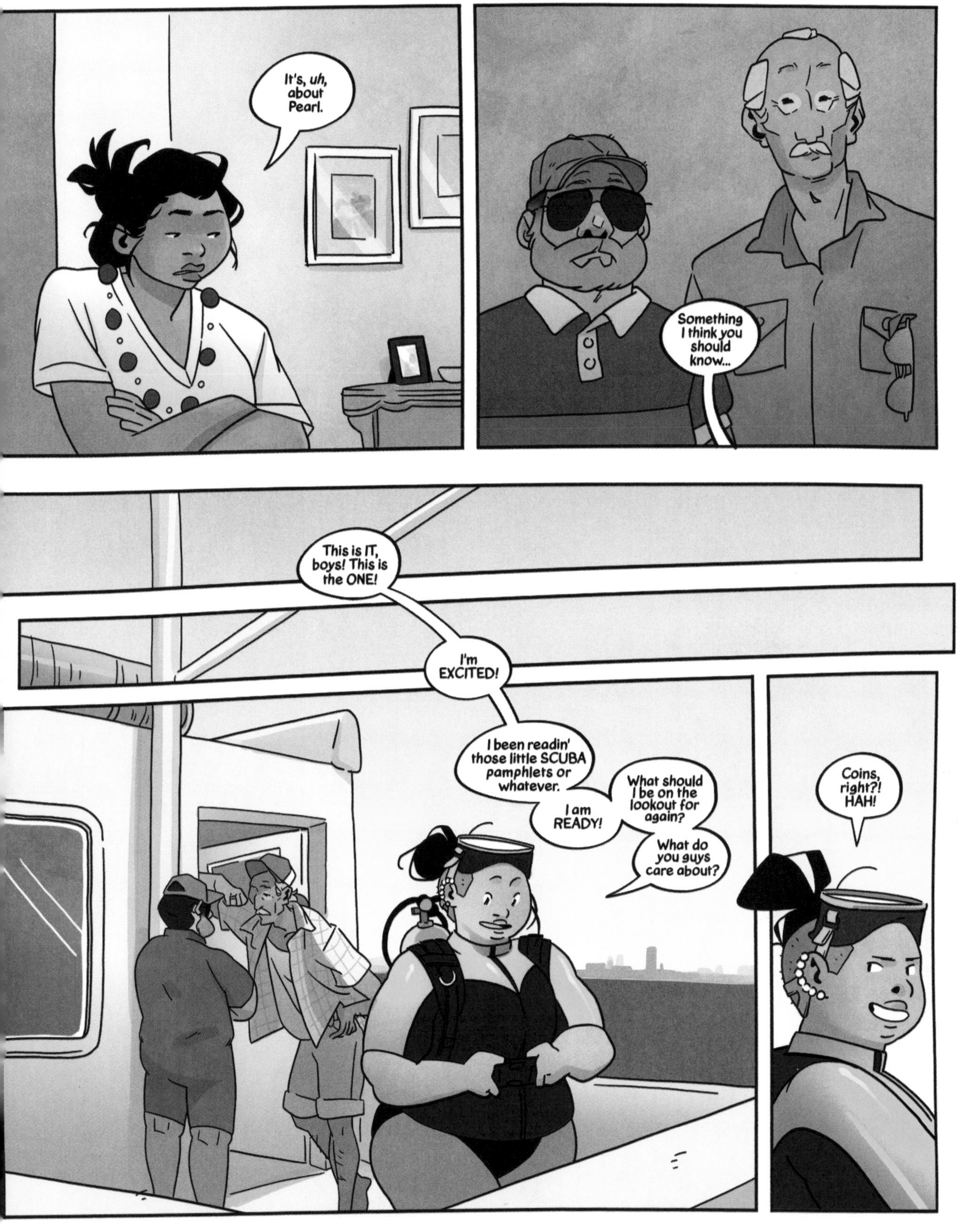
It's, *uh*, about Pearl.
Something I think you should know...
This is IT, boys! This is the ONE!
I'm EXCITED!
I been readin' those little SCUBA pamphlets or whatever.
I am READY!
What should I be on the lookout for again?
What do you guys care about?
Coins, right?! HAH!

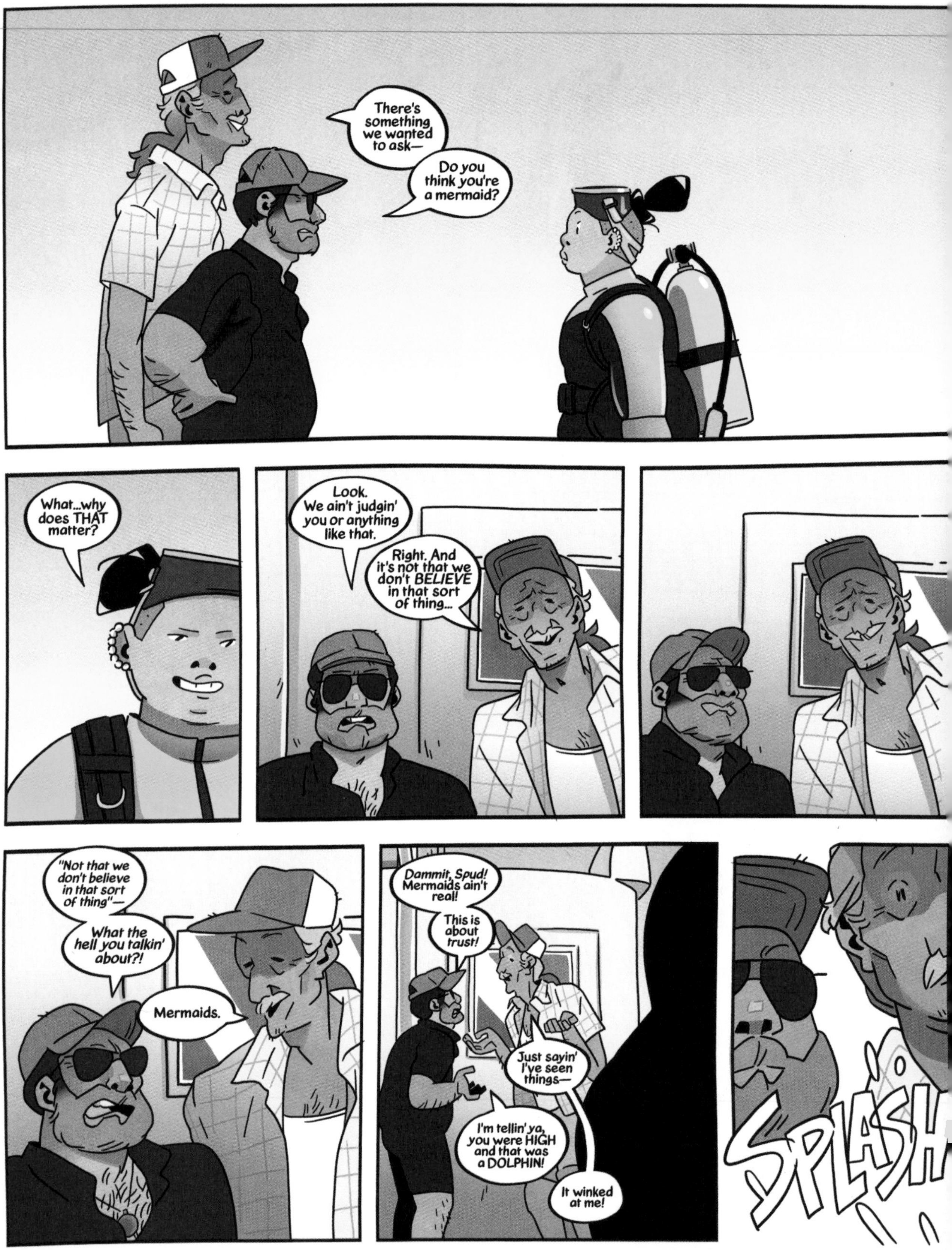
There's something we wanted to ask—
Do you think you're a mermaid?
What...why does THAT matter?
Look. We ain't judgin' you or anything like that.
Right. And it's not that we don't BELIEVE in that sort of thing...
"Not that we don't believe in that sort of thing"—
What the hell you talkin' about?!
Mermaids.
Dammit, Spud! Mermaids ain't real!
This is about trust!
Just sayin' I've seen things—
I'm tellin' ya, you were HIGH and that was a DOLPHIN!
It winked at me!
SPLASH

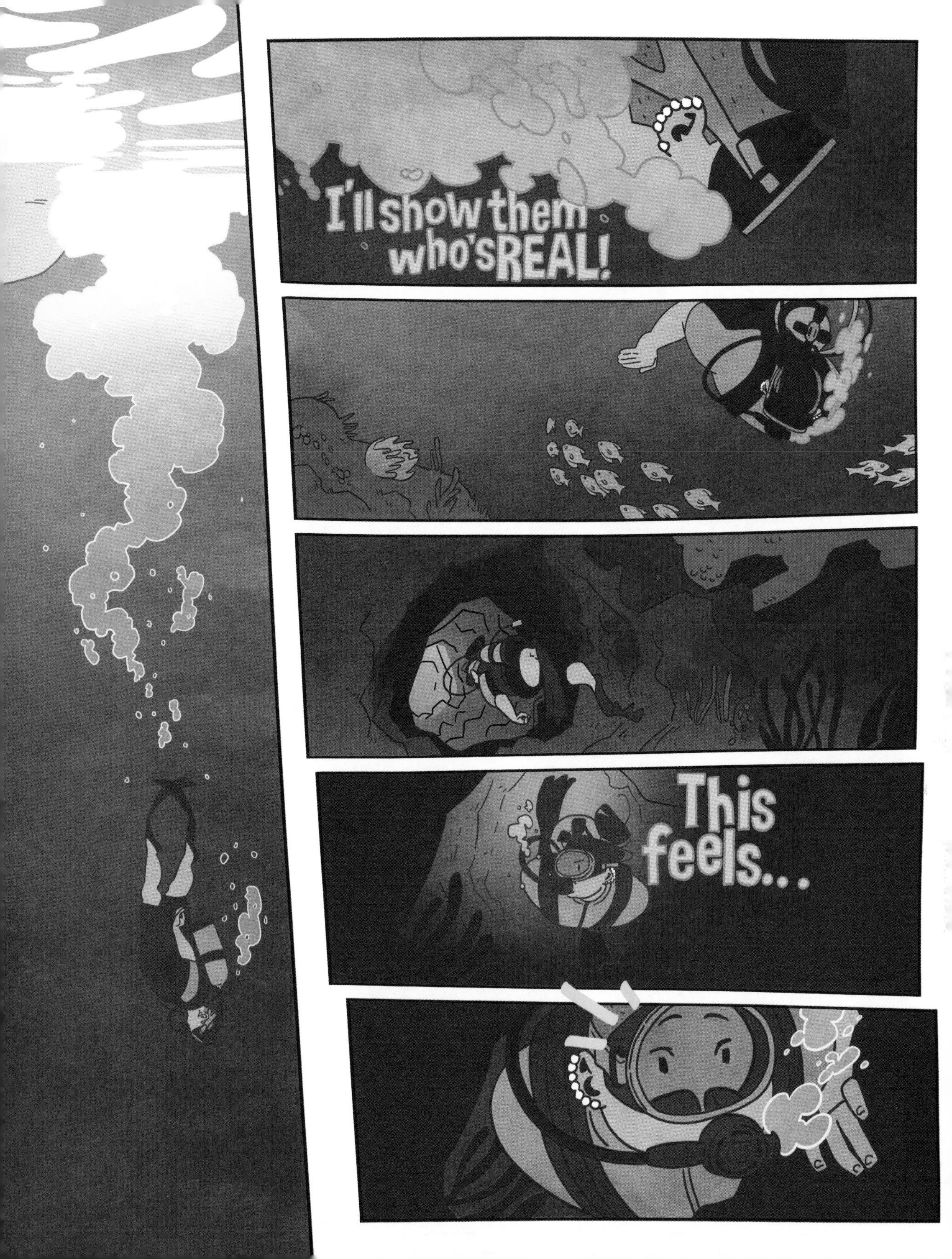

I'll show them who's REAL!
This feels...

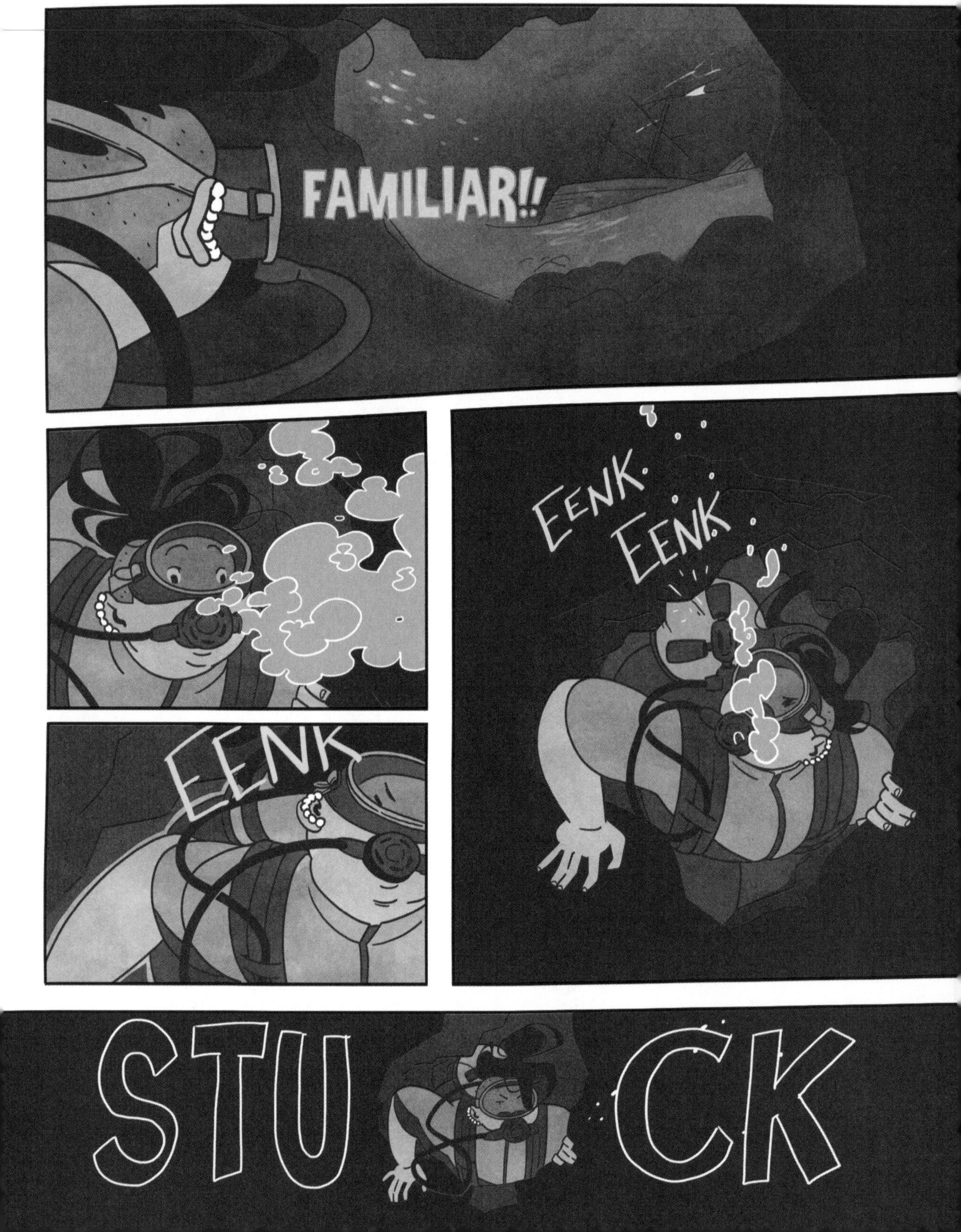
FAMILIAR!!
EENK
EENK
EENK
STU CK

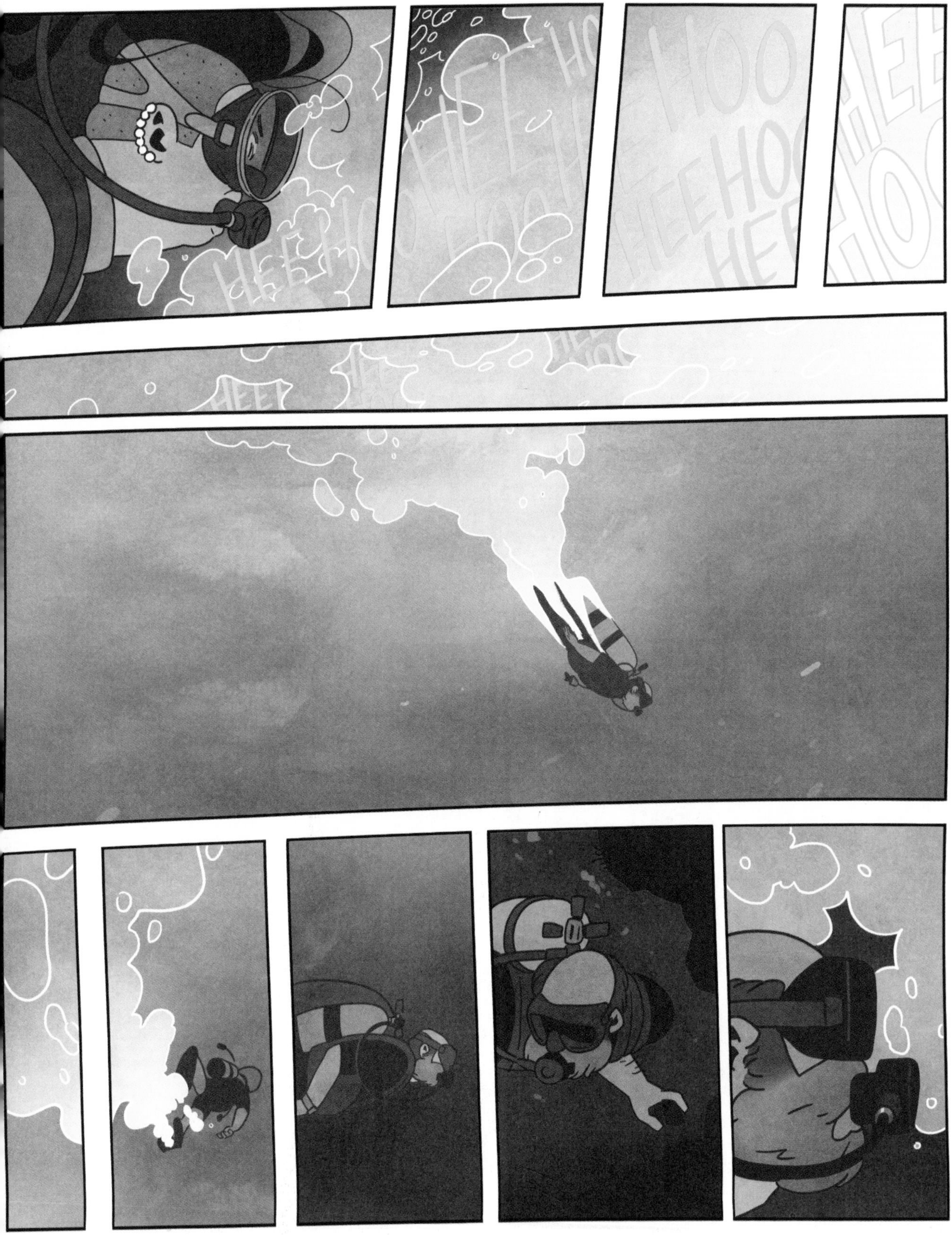
HEE HOO
HEE HOO
HEE HOO
HEE HOO
HEE HOO
HEE
HEE HOO
HEE
HEE
HEE HOO

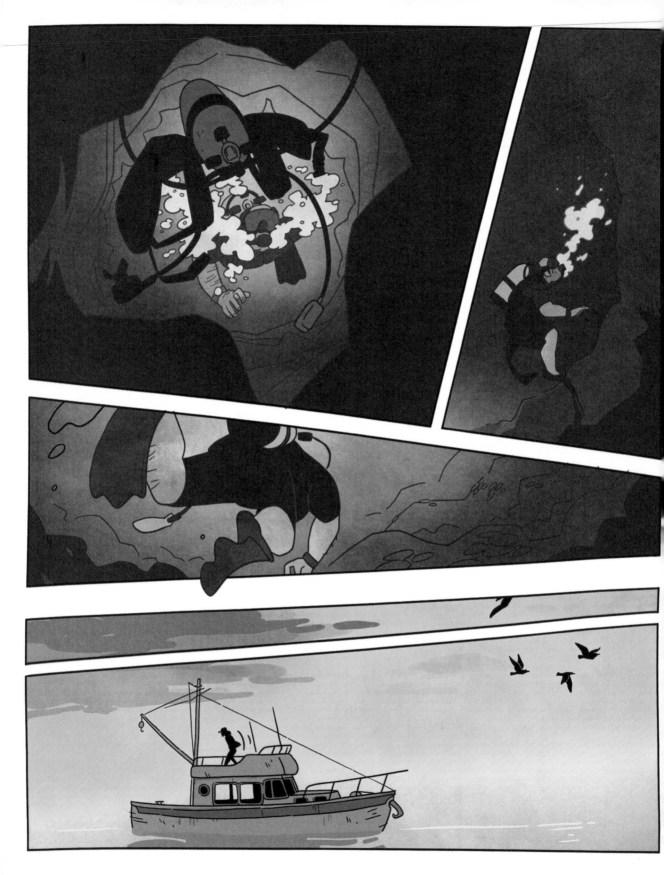

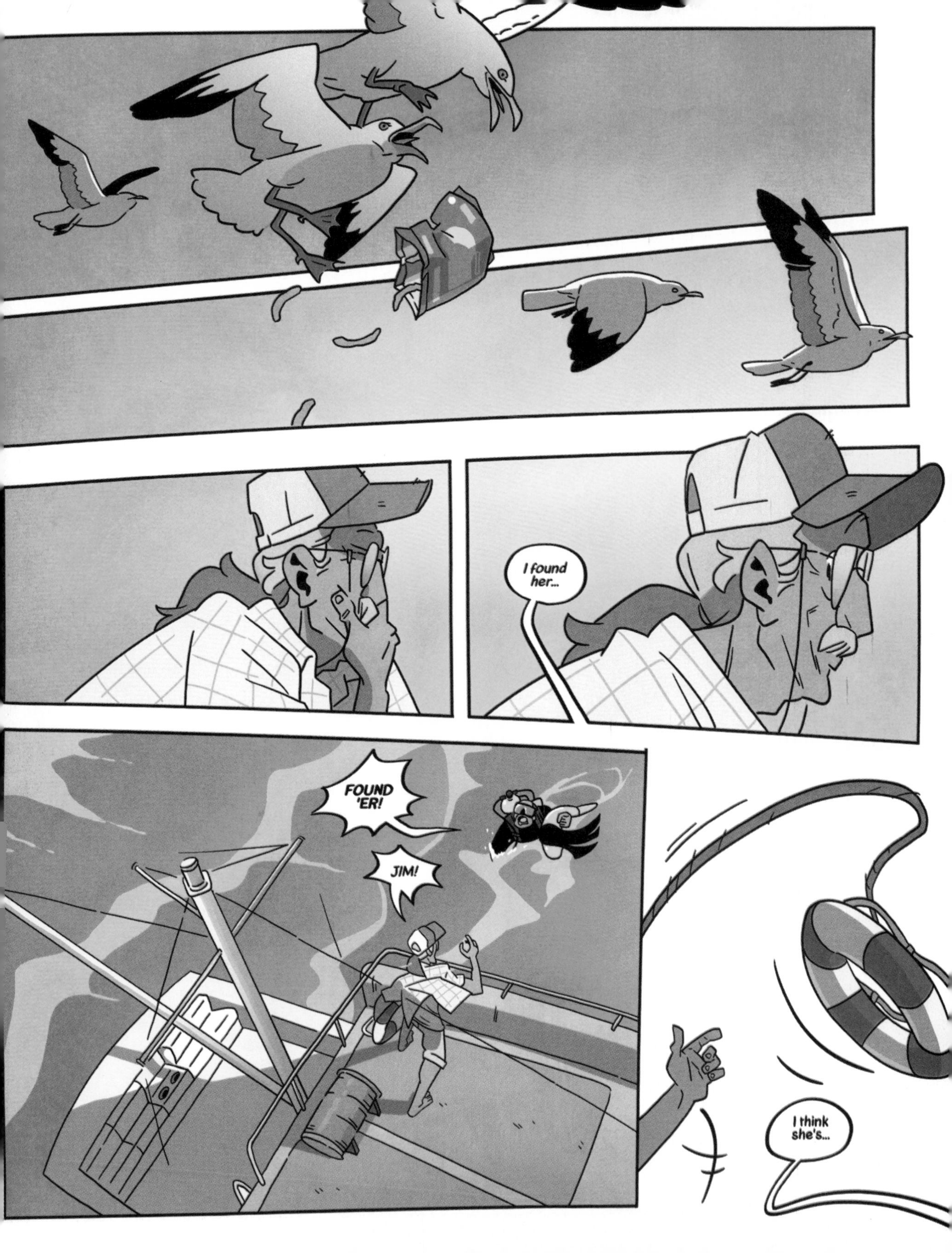
I found her...
FOUND 'ER!
JIM!
I think she's...

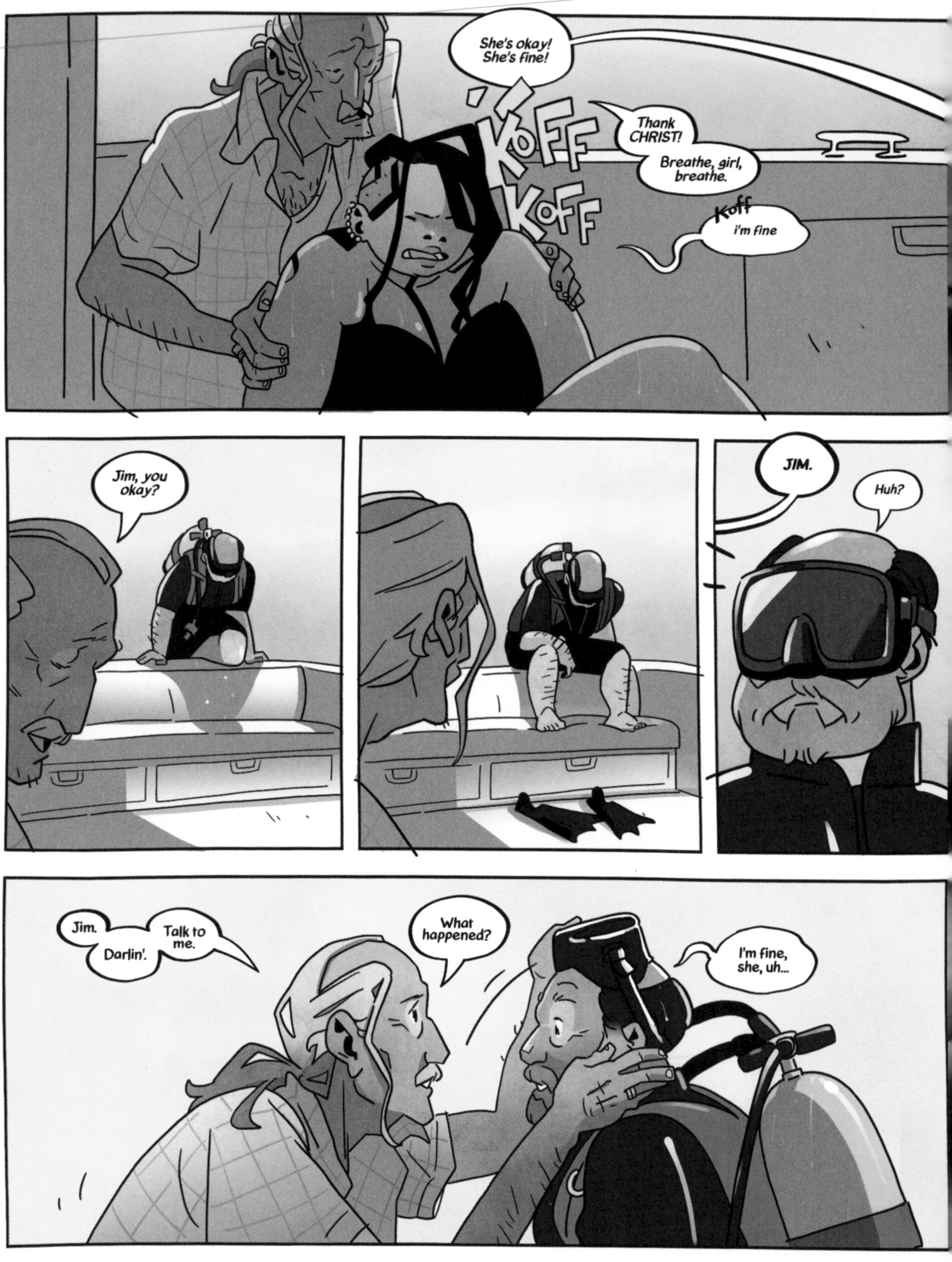
She's okay! She's fine!
KOFF KOFF
Thank CHRIST!
Breathe, girl, breathe.
Koff i'm fine
Jim, you okay?
JIM.
Huh?
Jim.
Darlin'.
Talk to me.
What happened?
I'm fine, she, uh...

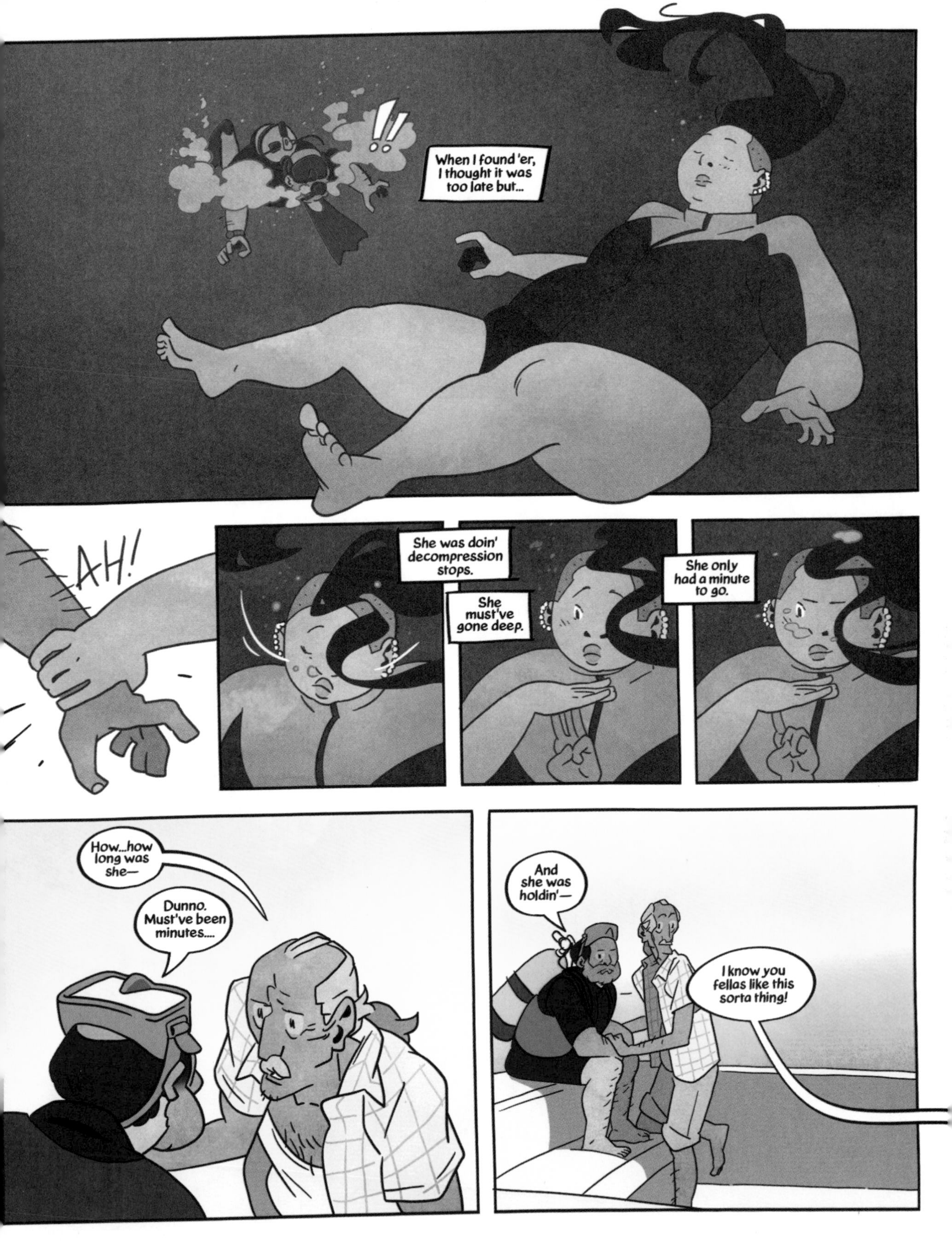
!!
When I found 'er, I thought it was too late but...
AH!
She was doin' decompression stops.
She must've gone deep.
She only had a minute to go.
How...how long was she—
Dunno. Must've been minutes....
And she was holdin'—
I know you fellas like this sorta thing!

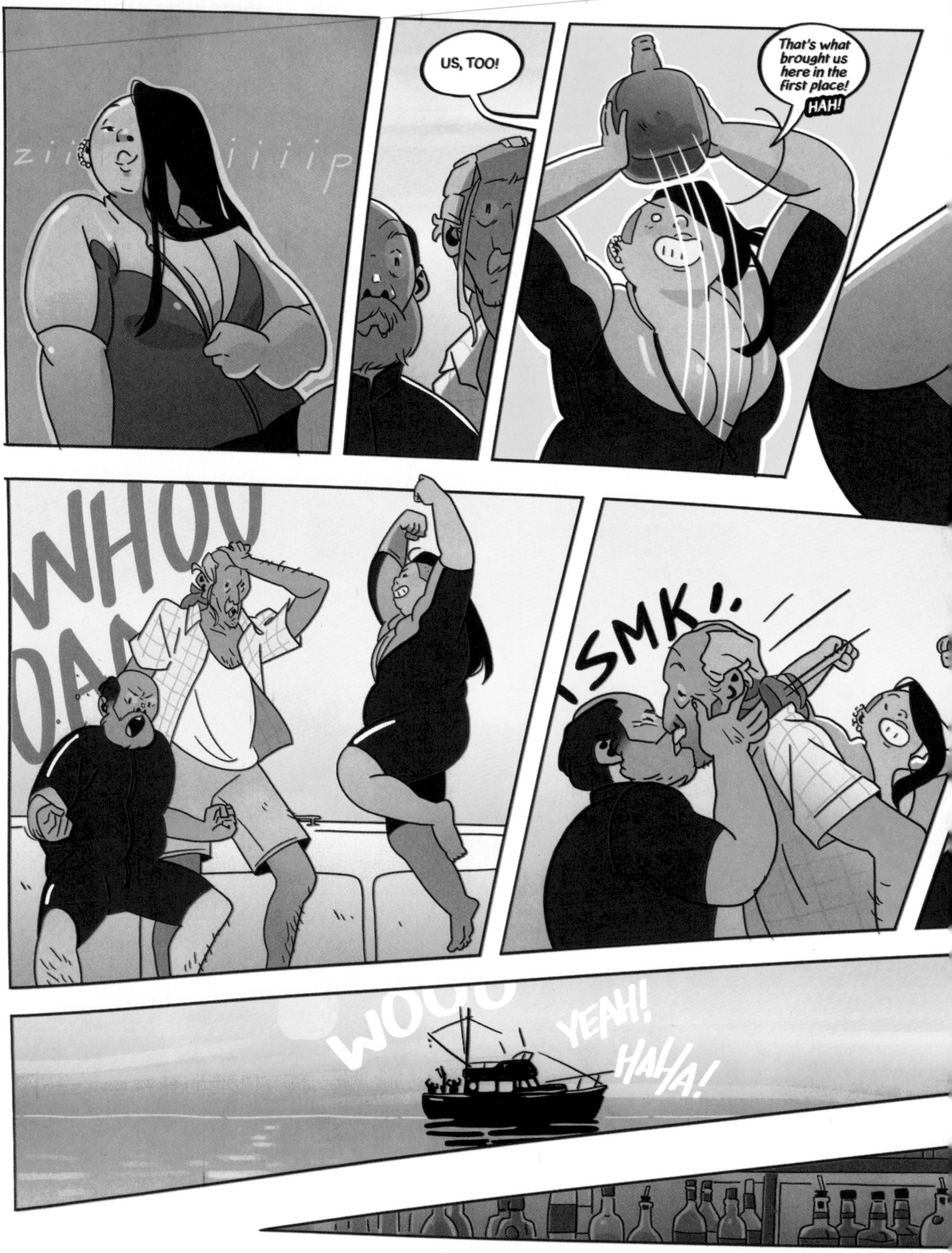
ziiiiiiip
US, TOO!
That's what brought us here in the first place!
HAH!
WHOO OAA
SMK!
WOOO
YEAH!
HAHA!

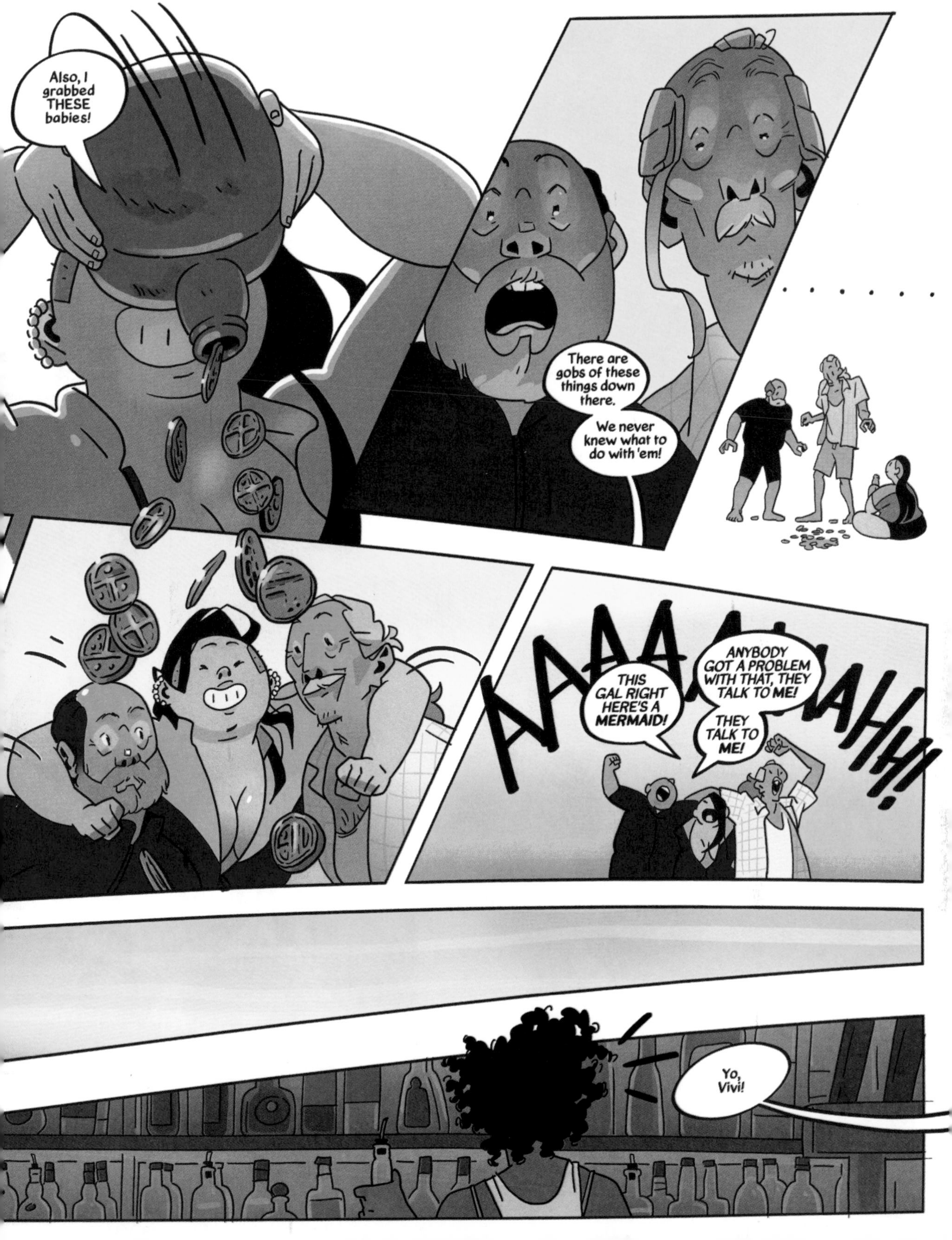
Also, I grabbed THESE babies!
There are gobs of these things down there.
We never knew what to do with 'em!
. . . .
AAAAAHHH!!
THIS GAL RIGHT HERE'S A MERMAID!
ANYBODY GOT A PROBLEM WITH THAT, THEY TALK TO ME!
THEY TALK TO ME!
Yo, Vivi!

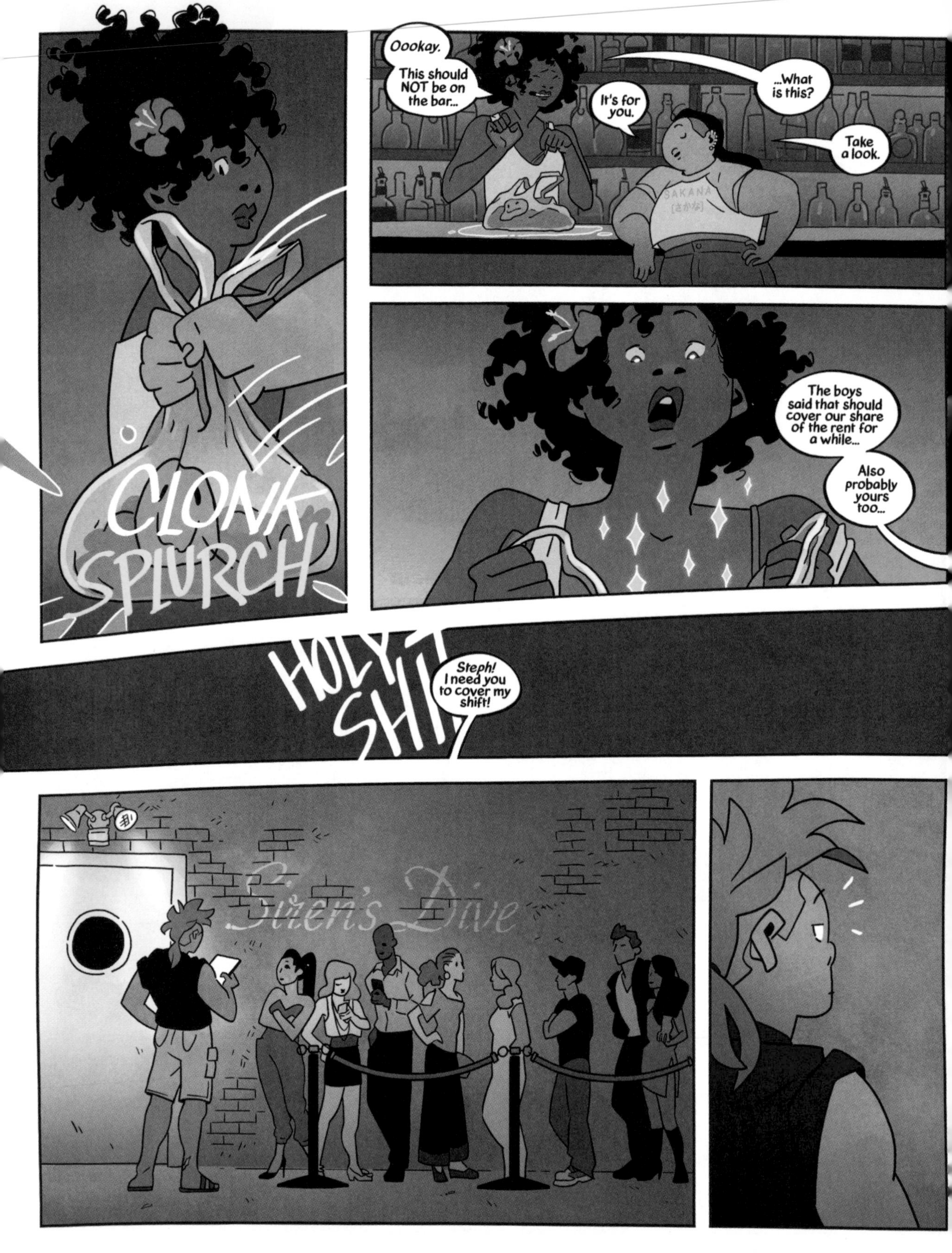
Oookay.
This should NOT be on the bar...
It's for you.
...What is this?
Take a look.
SAKANA
[さかな]
CLONK
SPLURCH
The boys said that should cover our share of the rent for a while...
Also probably yours too...
HOLY SHIT
Steph! I need you to cover my shift!
Siren's Dive

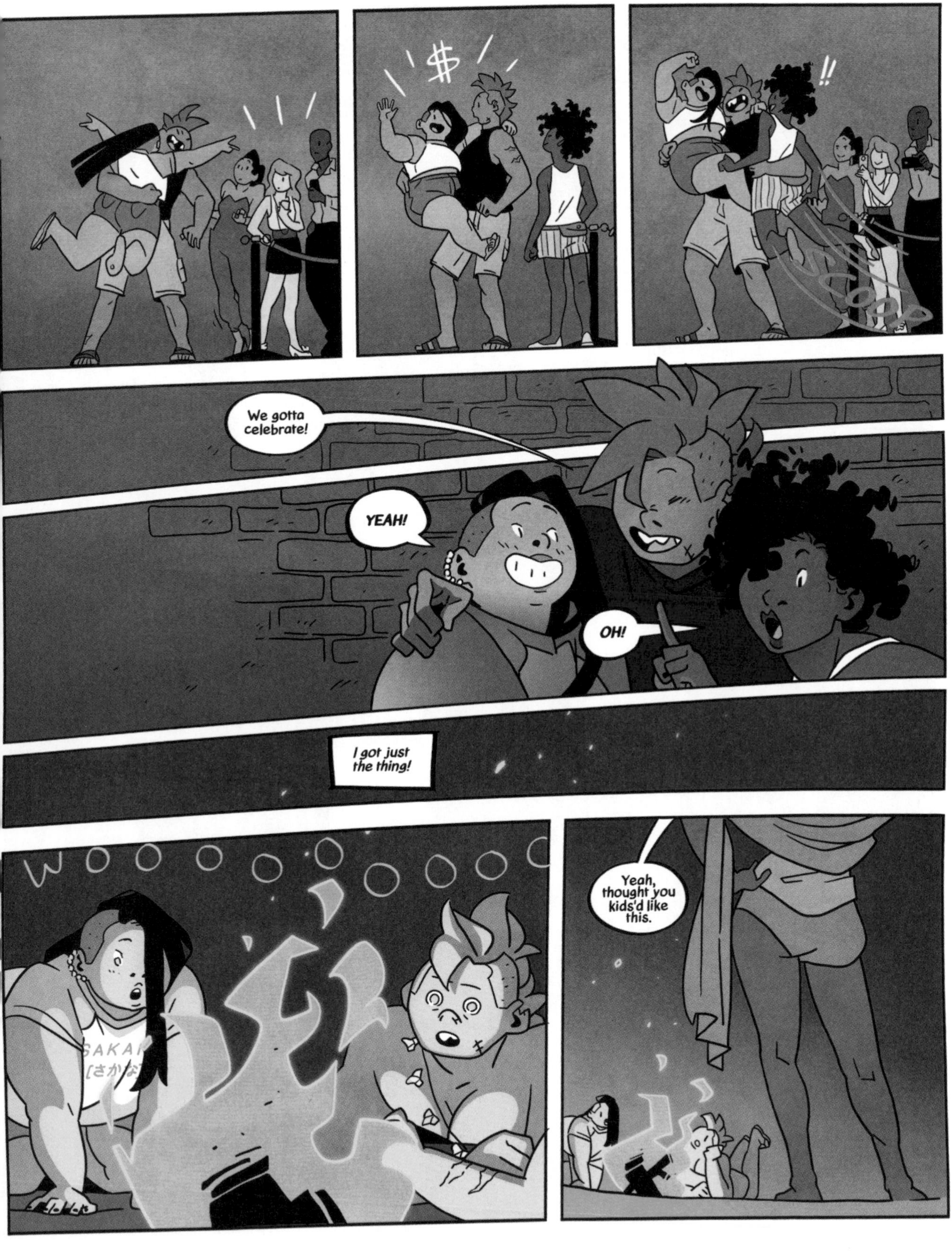
$
We gotta celebrate!
YEAH!
OH!
I got just the thing!
WOOOOOOOOOO
Yeah, thought you kids'd like this.

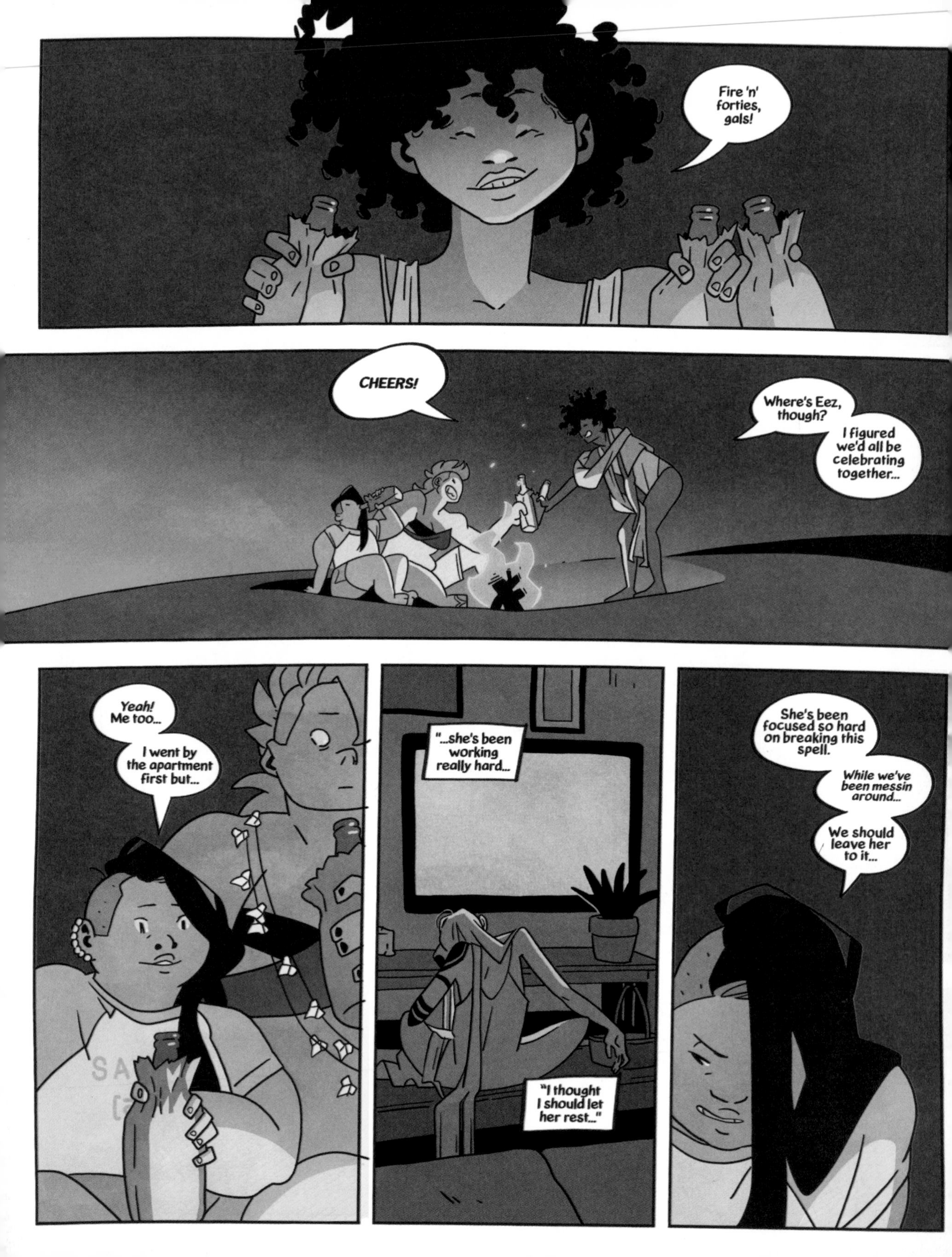
Fire 'n' forties, gals!
CHEERS!
Where's Eez, though?
I figured we'd all be celebrating together...
Yeah! Me too...
I went by the apartment first but...
"...she's been working really hard...
"I thought I should let her rest..."
She's been focused so hard on breaking this spell.
While we've been messin around...
We should leave her to it...

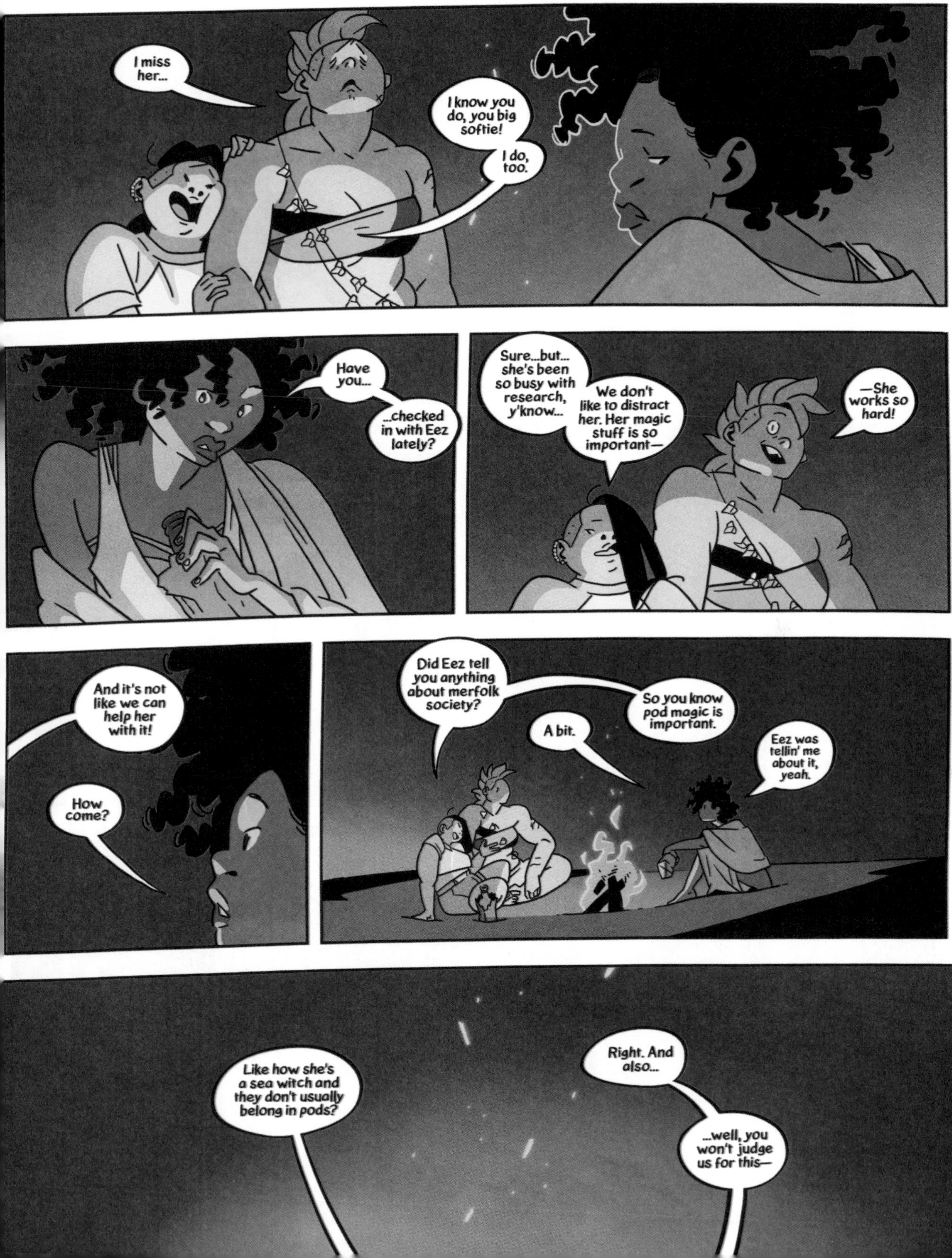
I miss her...
I know you do, you big softie!
I do, too.
Have you...
...checked in with Eez lately?
Sure...but... she's been so busy with research, y'know...
We don't like to distract her. Her magic stuff is so important—
—She works so hard!
And it's not like we can help her with it!
How come?
Did Eez tell you anything about merfolk society?
A bit.
So you know pod magic is important.
Eez was tellin' me about it, yeah.
Like how she's a sea witch and they don't usually belong in pods?
Right. And also...
...well, you won't judge us for this—

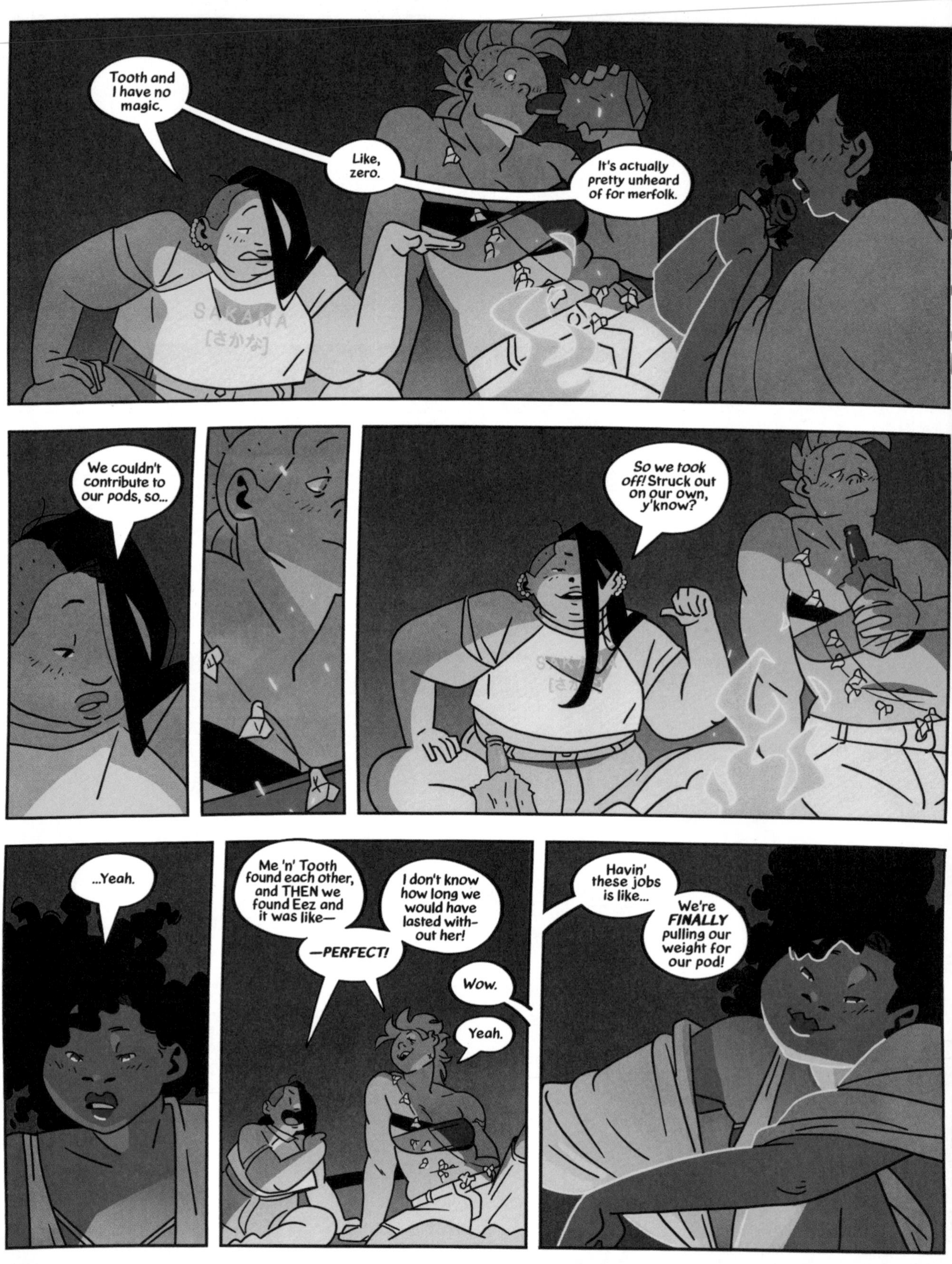
Tooth and I have no magic.
Like, zero.
It's actually pretty unheard of for merfolk.
SAKANA [さかな]
We couldn't contribute to our pods, so...
So we took off! Struck out on our own, y'know?
...Yeah.
Me 'n' Tooth found each other, and THEN we found Eez and it was like—
—PERFECT!
I don't know how long we would have lasted without her!
Wow.
Yeah.
Havin' these jobs is like...
We're FINALLY pulling our weight for our pod!

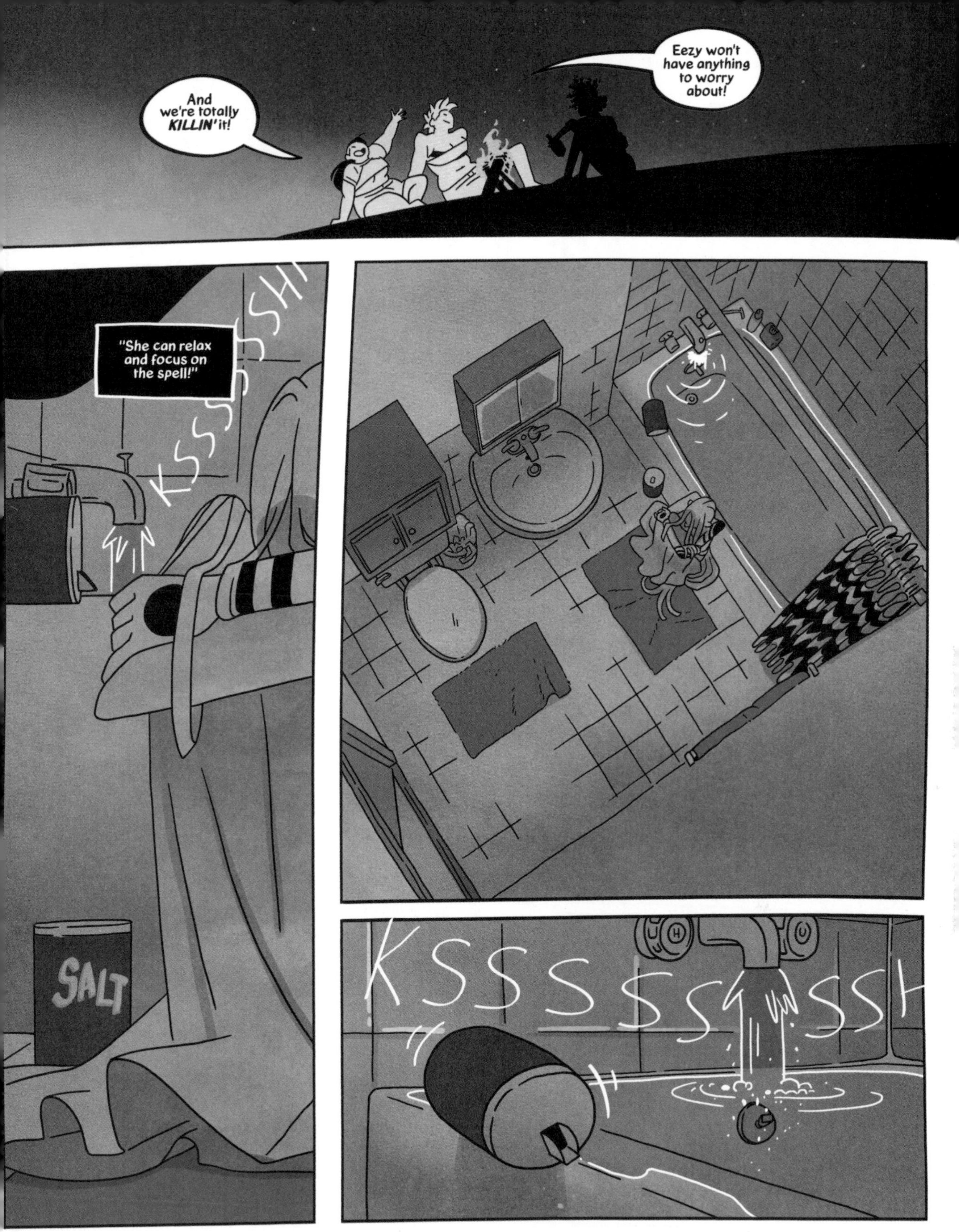
And we're totally KILLIN' it!
Eezy won't have anything to worry about!
"She can relax and focus on the spell!"
KSSSSSSSHH
SALT
KSSSSSSSSH
H

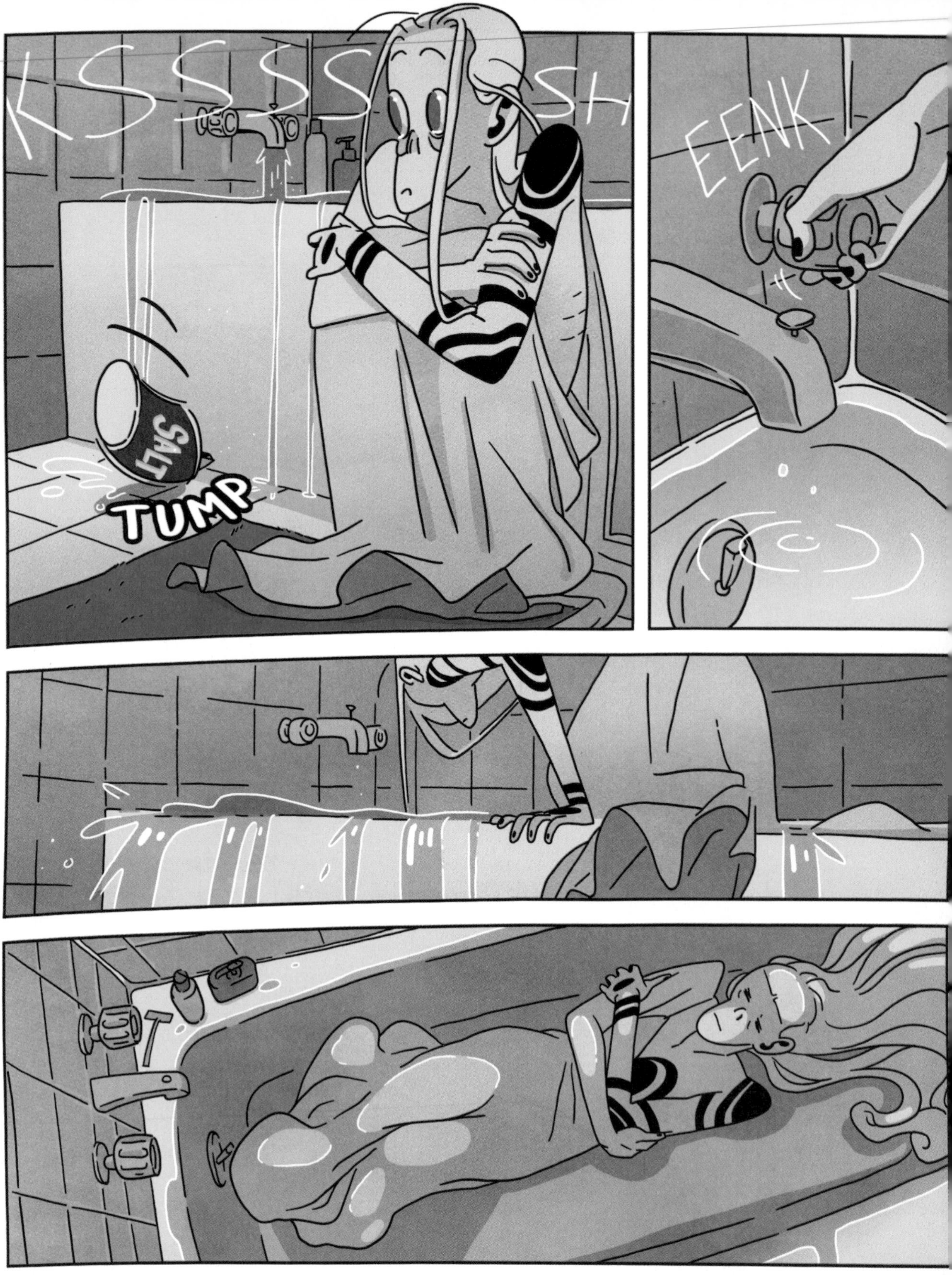
KSSSSSSH
SALT
TUMP
EENK

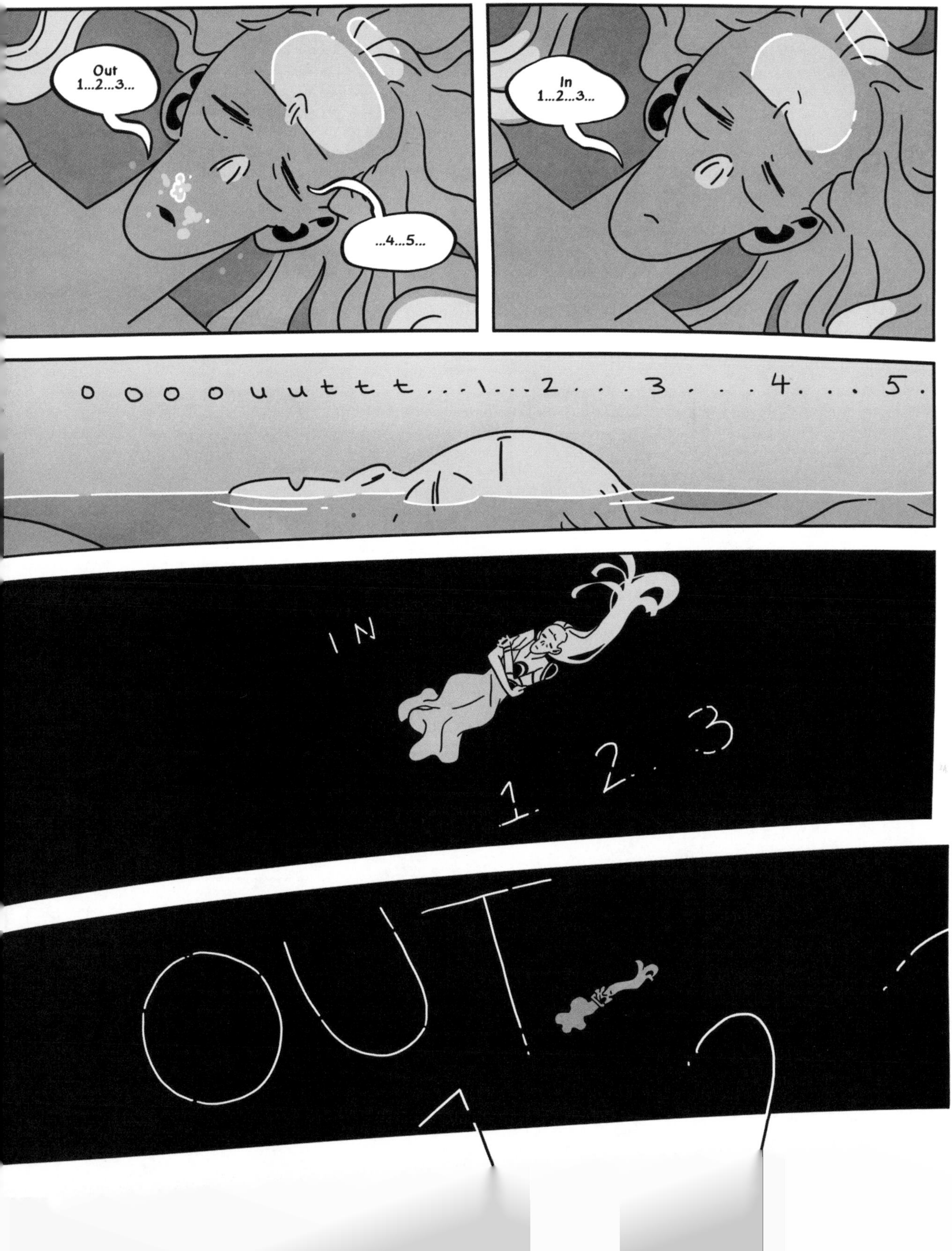
Out
1...2...3...
...4...5...
In
1...2...3...
ooooouuttt...1...2...3...4...5.
IN
1. 2. 3
OUT

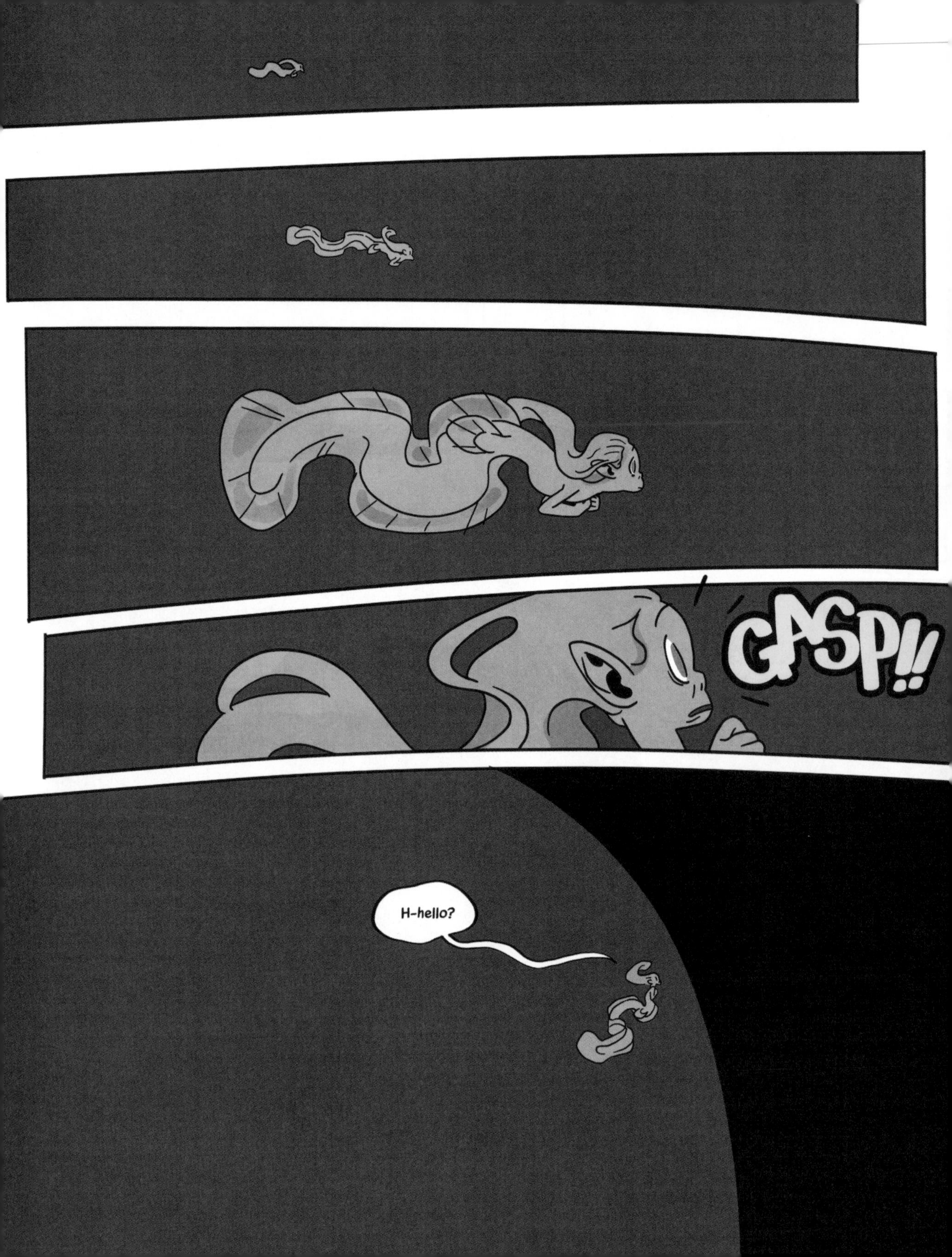
GASP!!
H-hello?

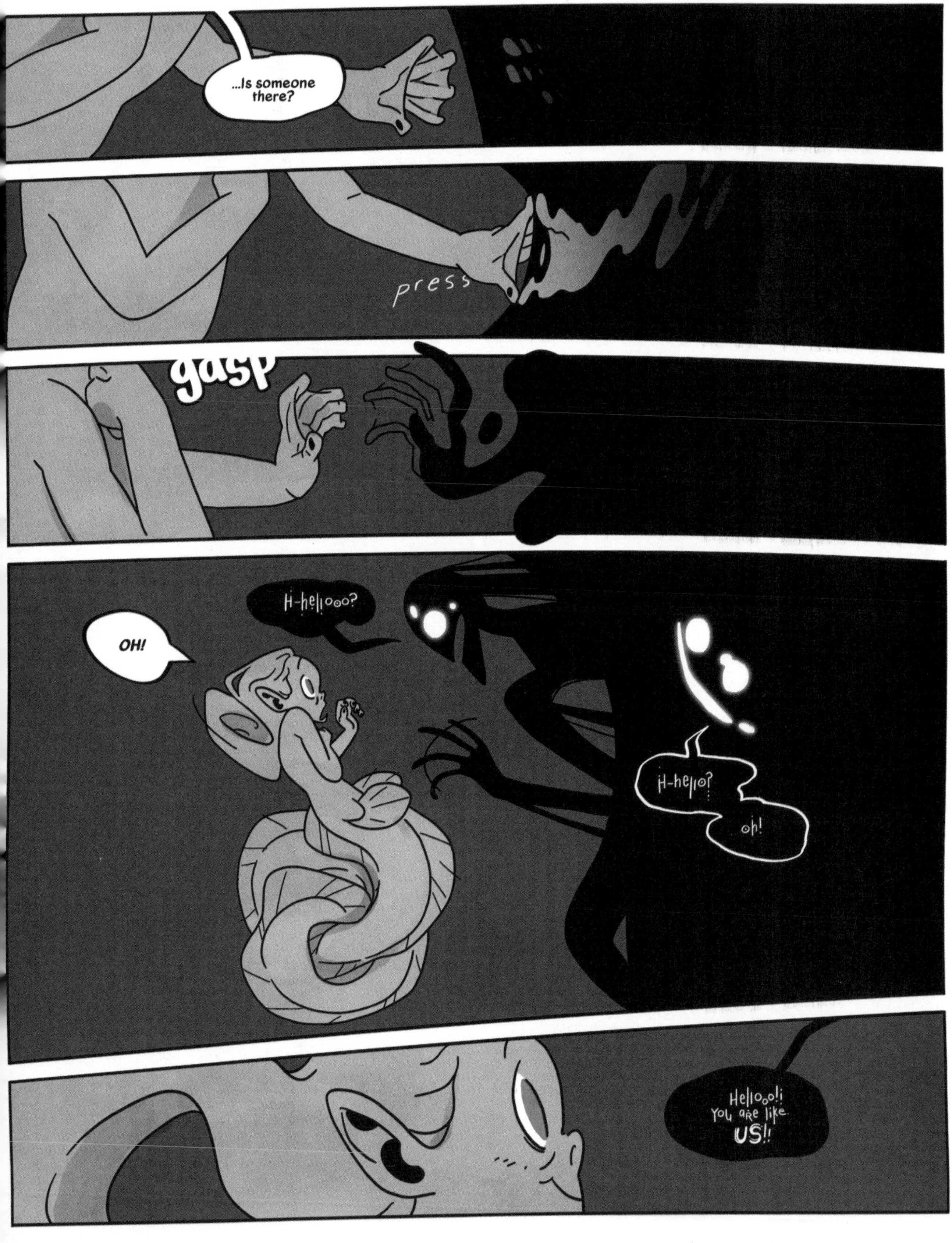

...Is someone there?
press
gasp
H-hellooo?
OH!
H-hello?
oh!
Hellooo!! You are like US!!

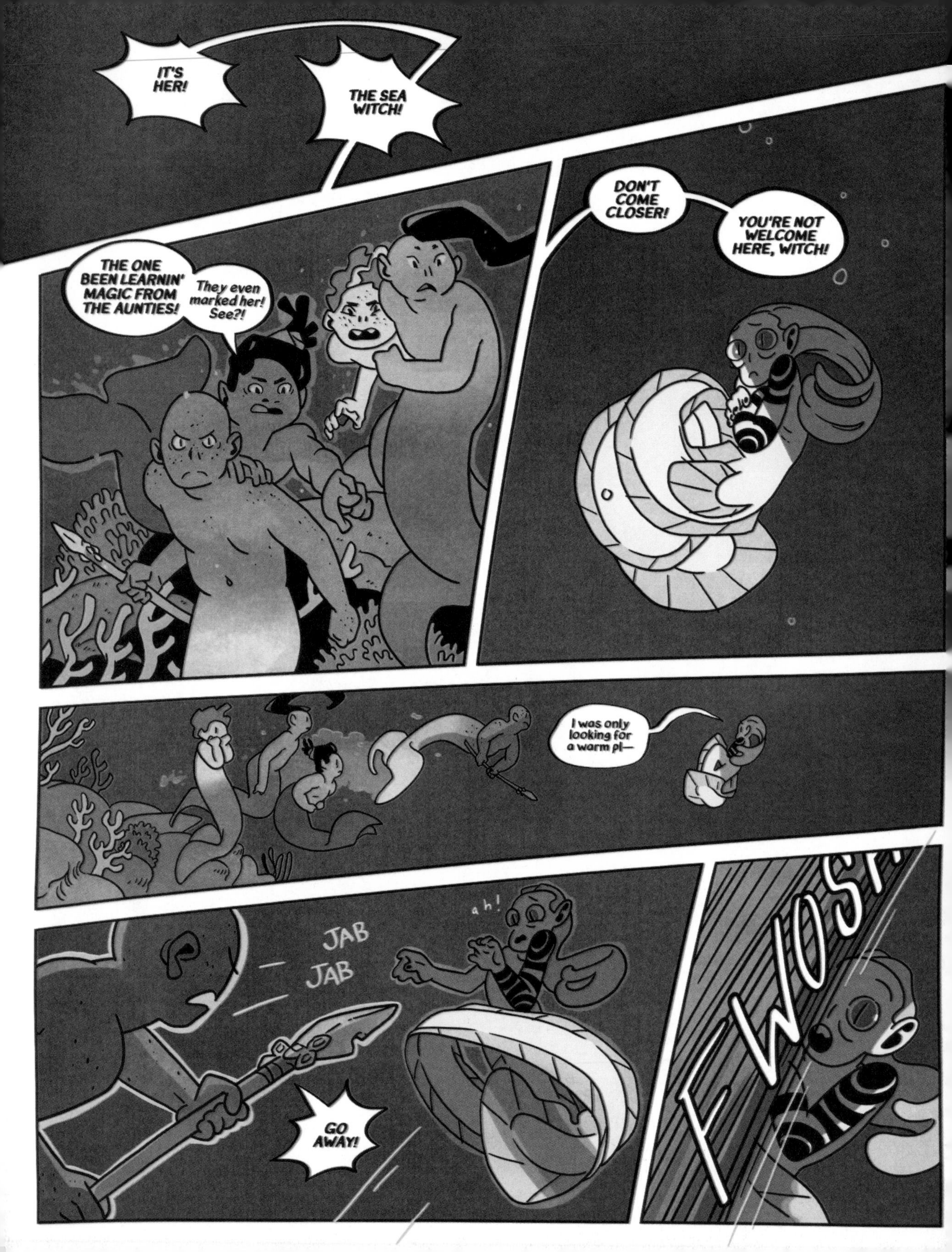

IT'S HER!
THE SEA WITCH!
THE ONE BEEN LEARNIN' MAGIC FROM THE AUNTIES!
They even marked her! See?!
DON'T COME CLOSER!
YOU'RE NOT WELCOME HERE, WITCH!
I was only looking for a warm pl—
JAB
JAB
ah!
GO AWAY!
FWOSH

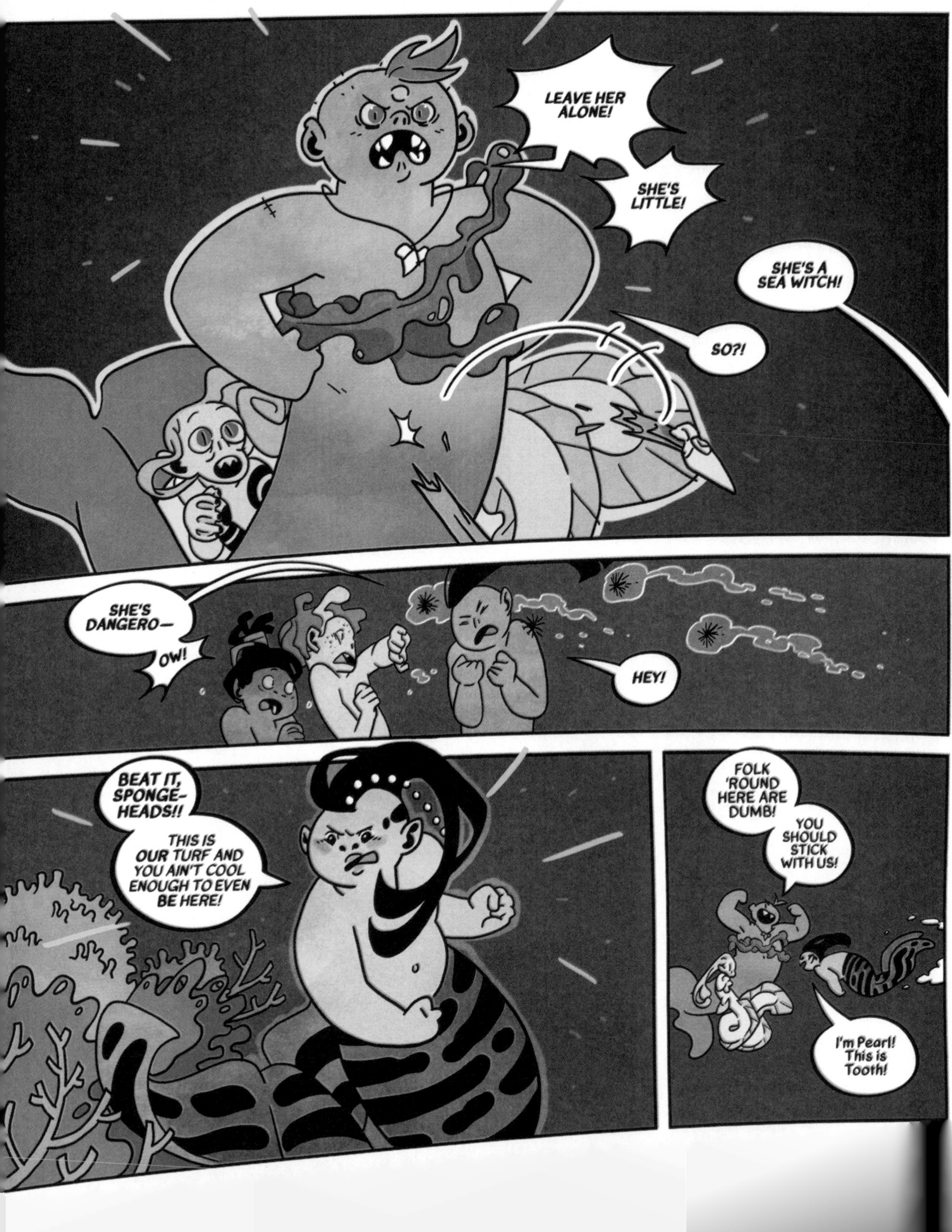
LEAVE HER ALONE!
SHE'S LITTLE!
SHE'S A SEA WITCH!
SO?!
SHE'S DANGERO—
OW!
HEY!
BEAT IT, SPONGE-HEADS!!
THIS IS OUR TURF AND YOU AIN'T COOL ENOUGH TO EVEN BE HERE!
FOLK 'ROUND HERE ARE DUMB!
YOU SHOULD STICK WITH US!
I'm Pearl! This is Tooth!

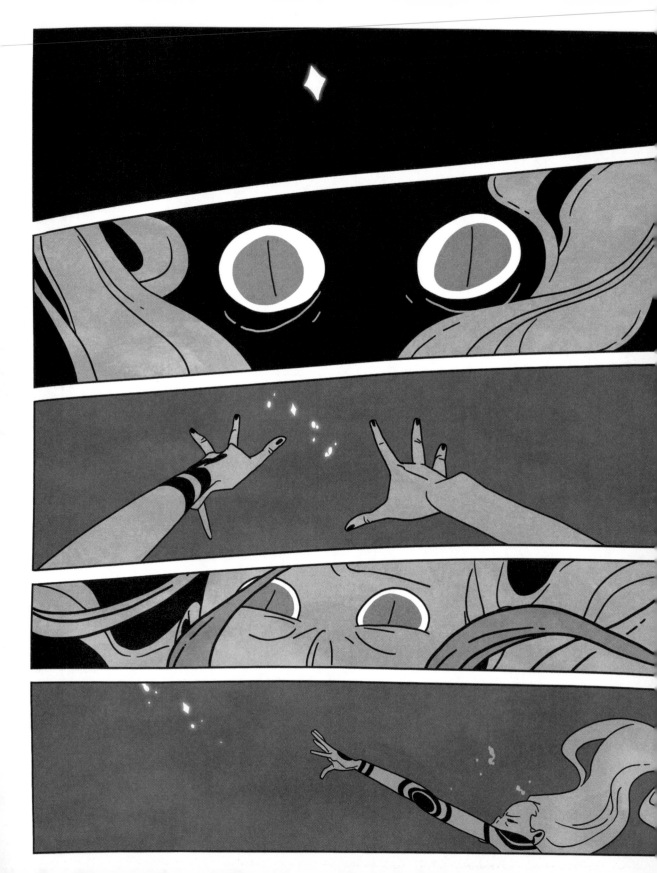

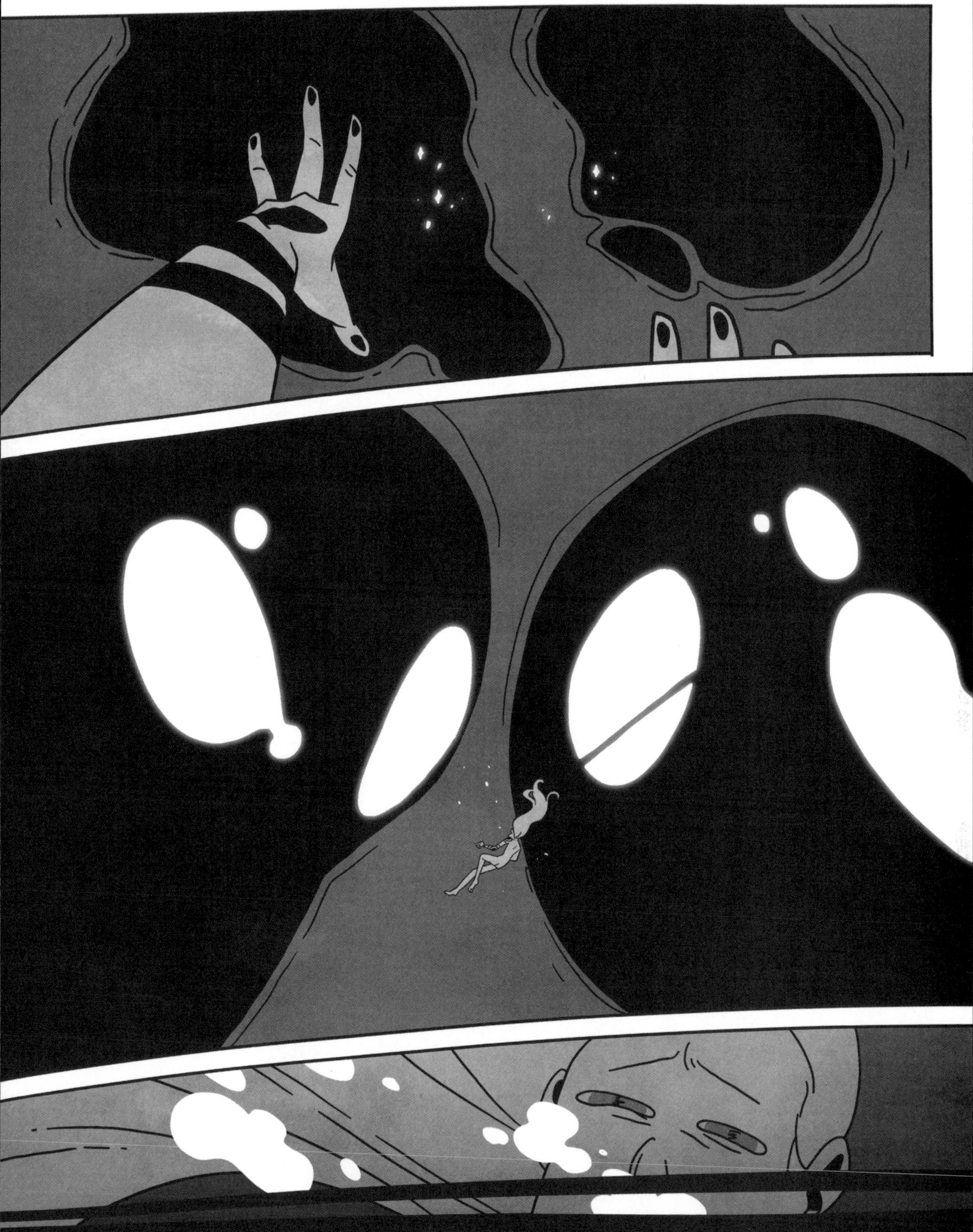

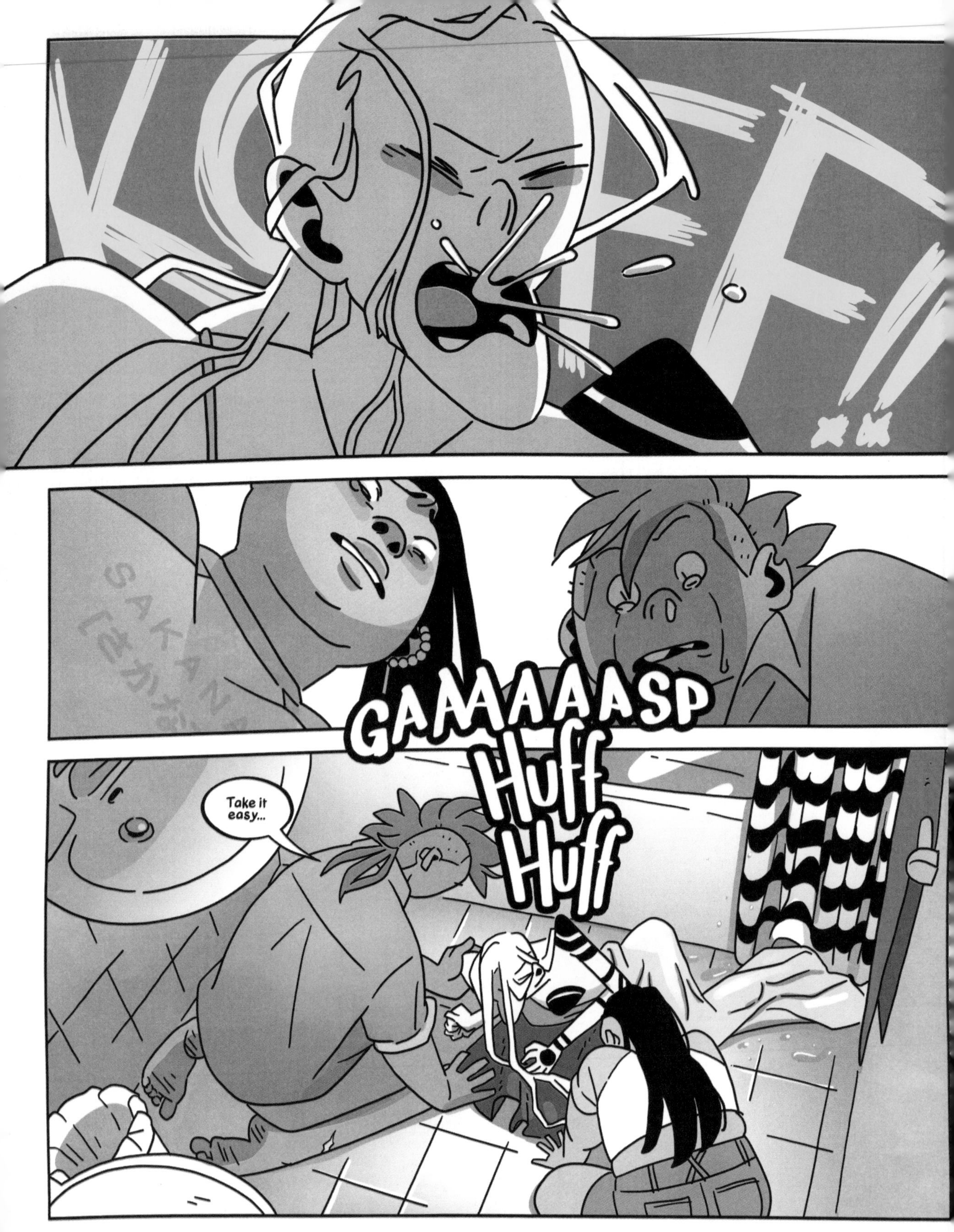
KOFF!!
GAAAAAASP
Huff
Huff
Take it easy...

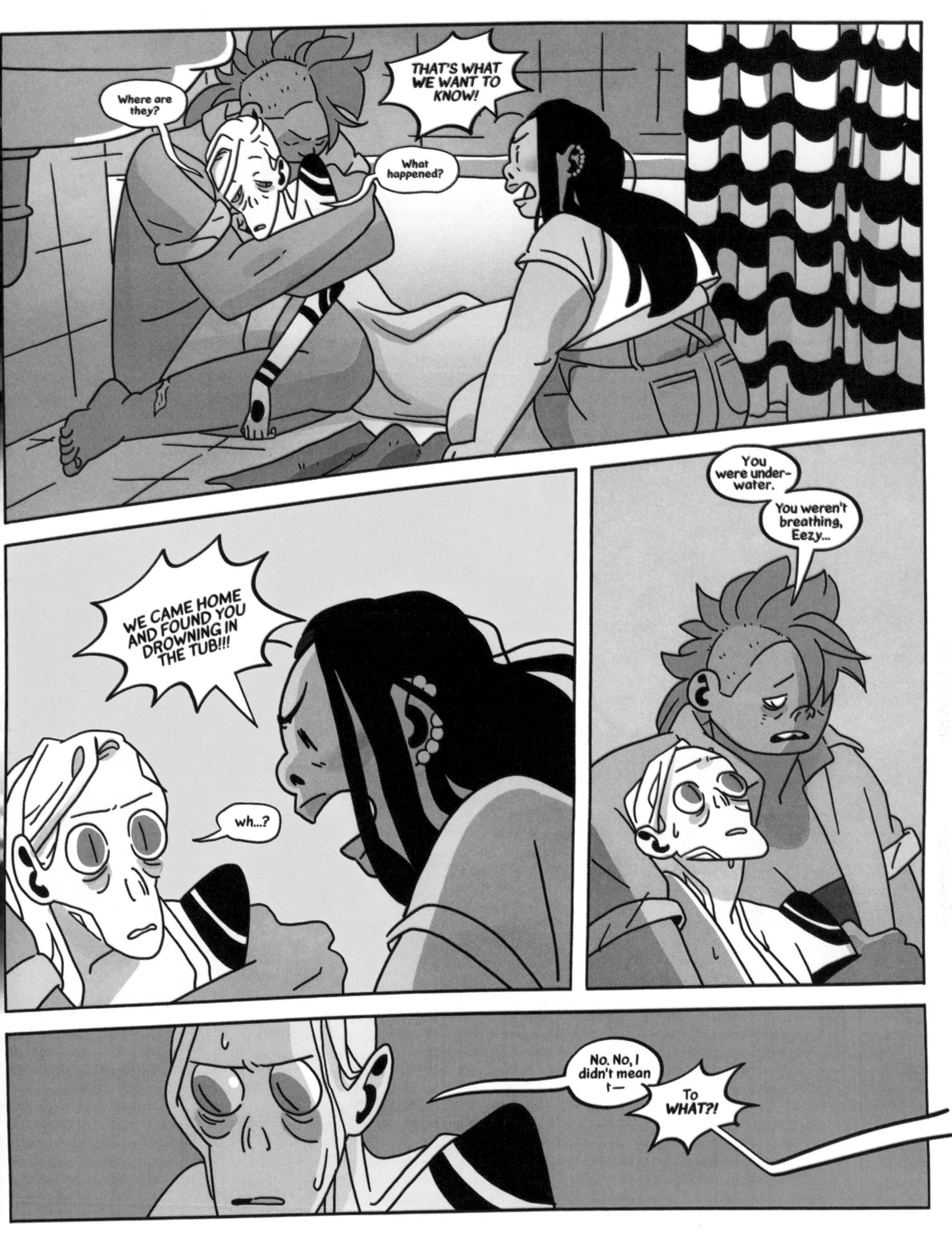
Where are they?
THAT'S WHAT WE WANT TO KNOW!
What happened?
WE CAME HOME AND FOUND YOU DROWNING IN THE TUB!!!
wh...?
You were under-water.
You weren't breathing, Eezy...
No. No, I didn't mean t—
To WHAT?!

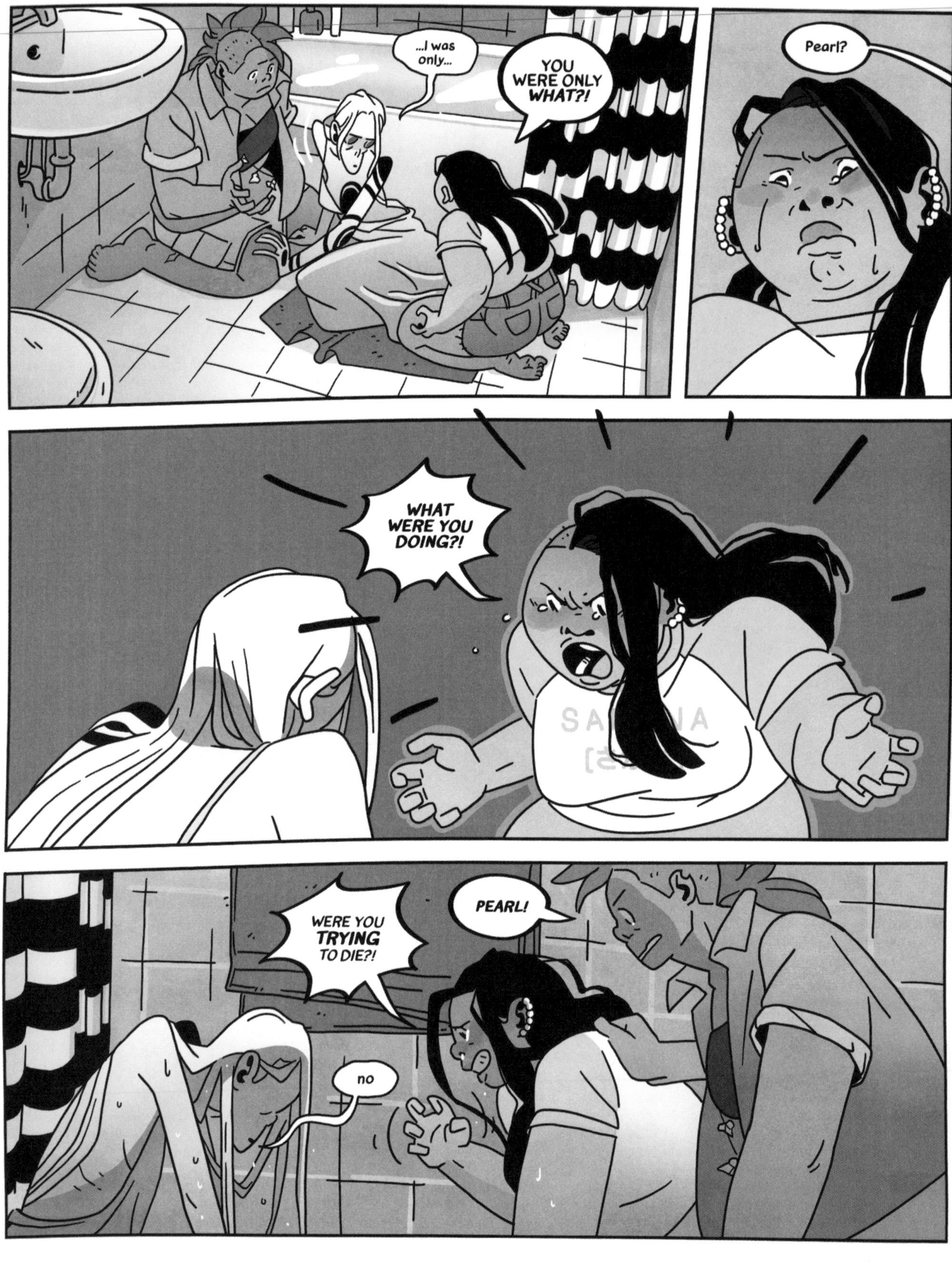
...I was only...
YOU WERE ONLY WHAT?!
Pearl?
WHAT WERE YOU DOING?!
WERE YOU TRYING TO DIE?!
PEARL!
no

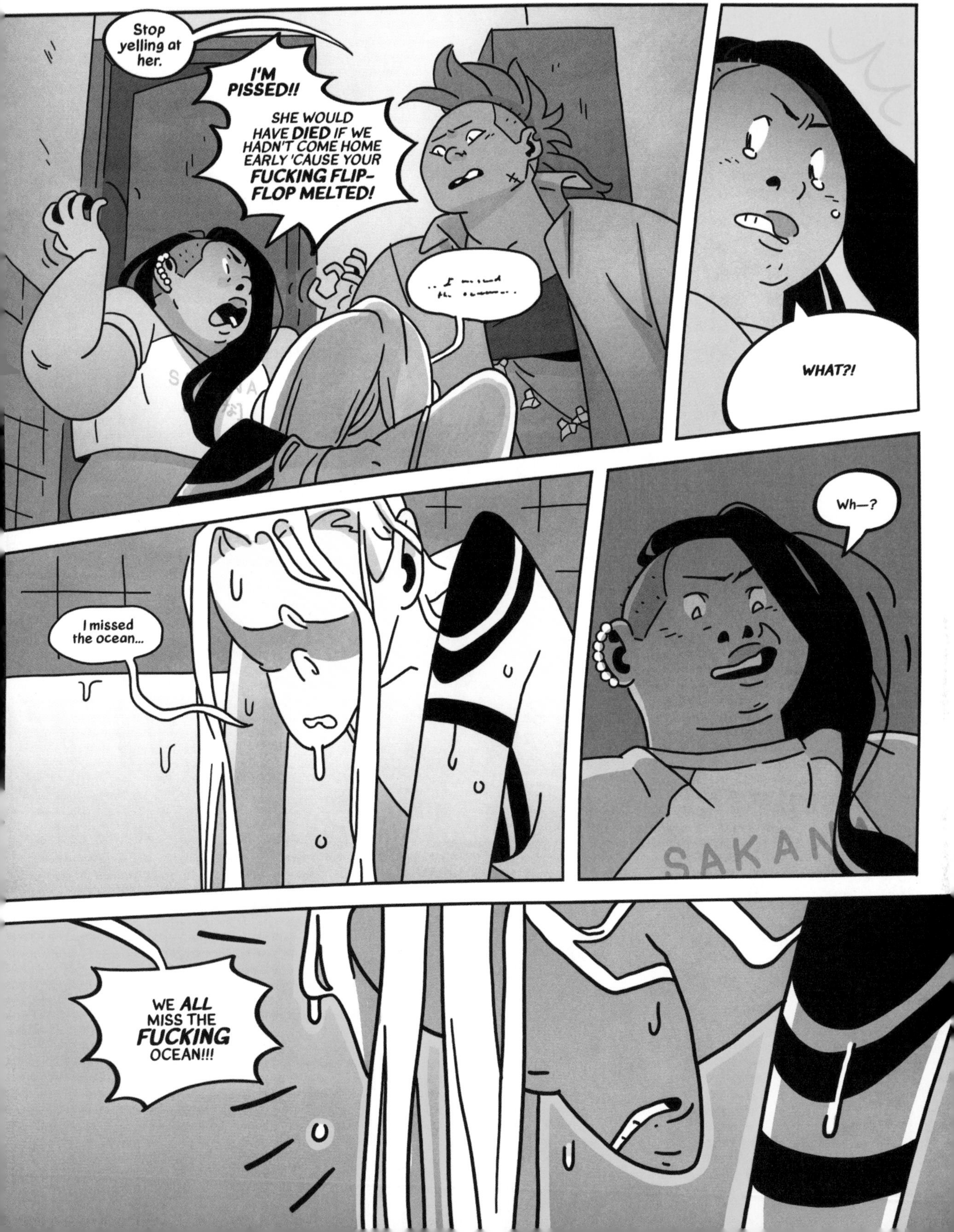
Stop yelling at her.
I'M PISSED!!
SHE WOULD HAVE DIED IF WE HADN'T COME HOME EARLY 'CAUSE YOUR FUCKING FLIP-FLOP MELTED!
WHAT?!
I missed the ocean...
Wh—?
WE ALL MISS THE FUCKING OCEAN!!!

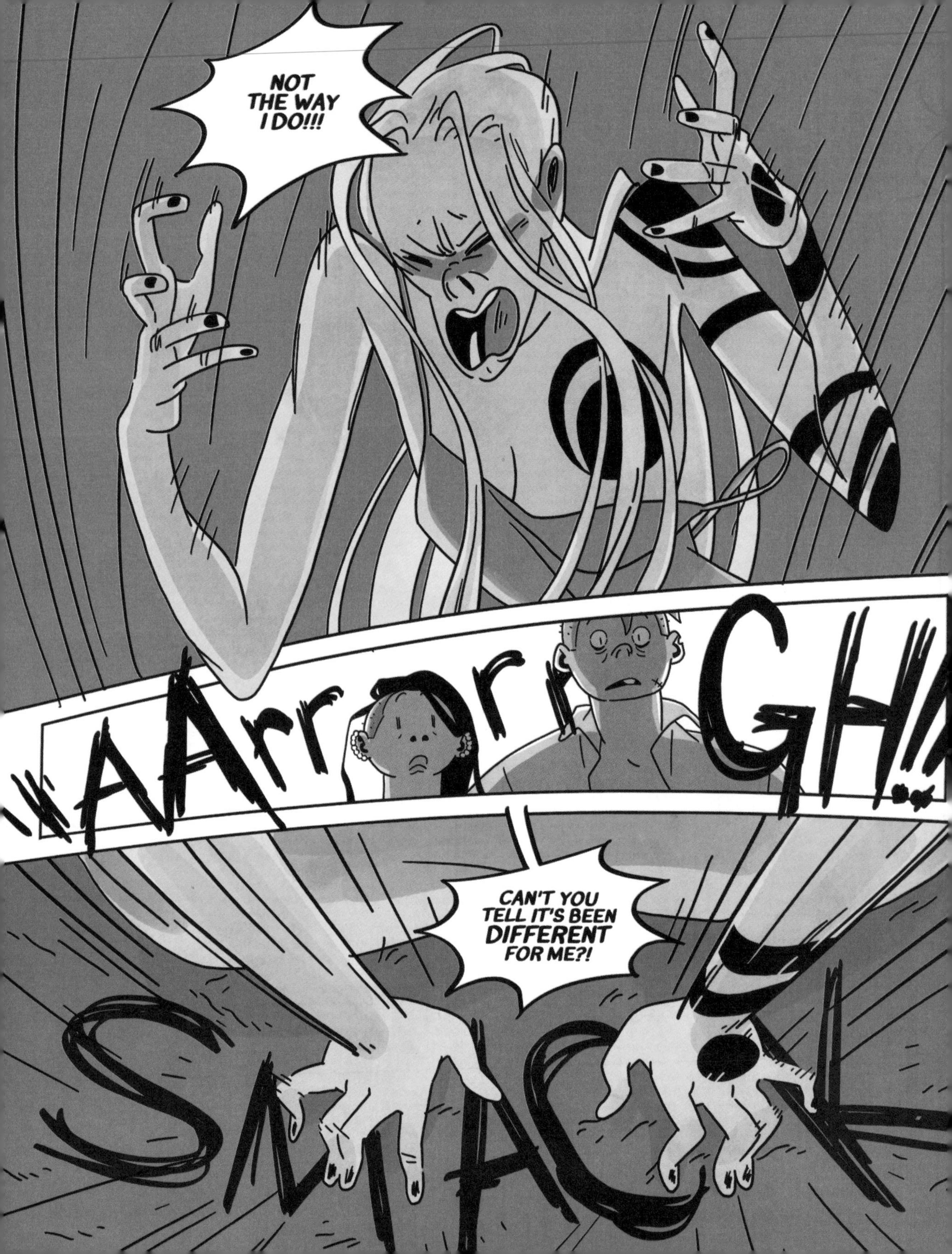
NOT THE WAY I DO!!!
AArrrrrGH!!
CAN'T YOU TELL IT'S BEEN DIFFERENT FOR ME?!
SMACK

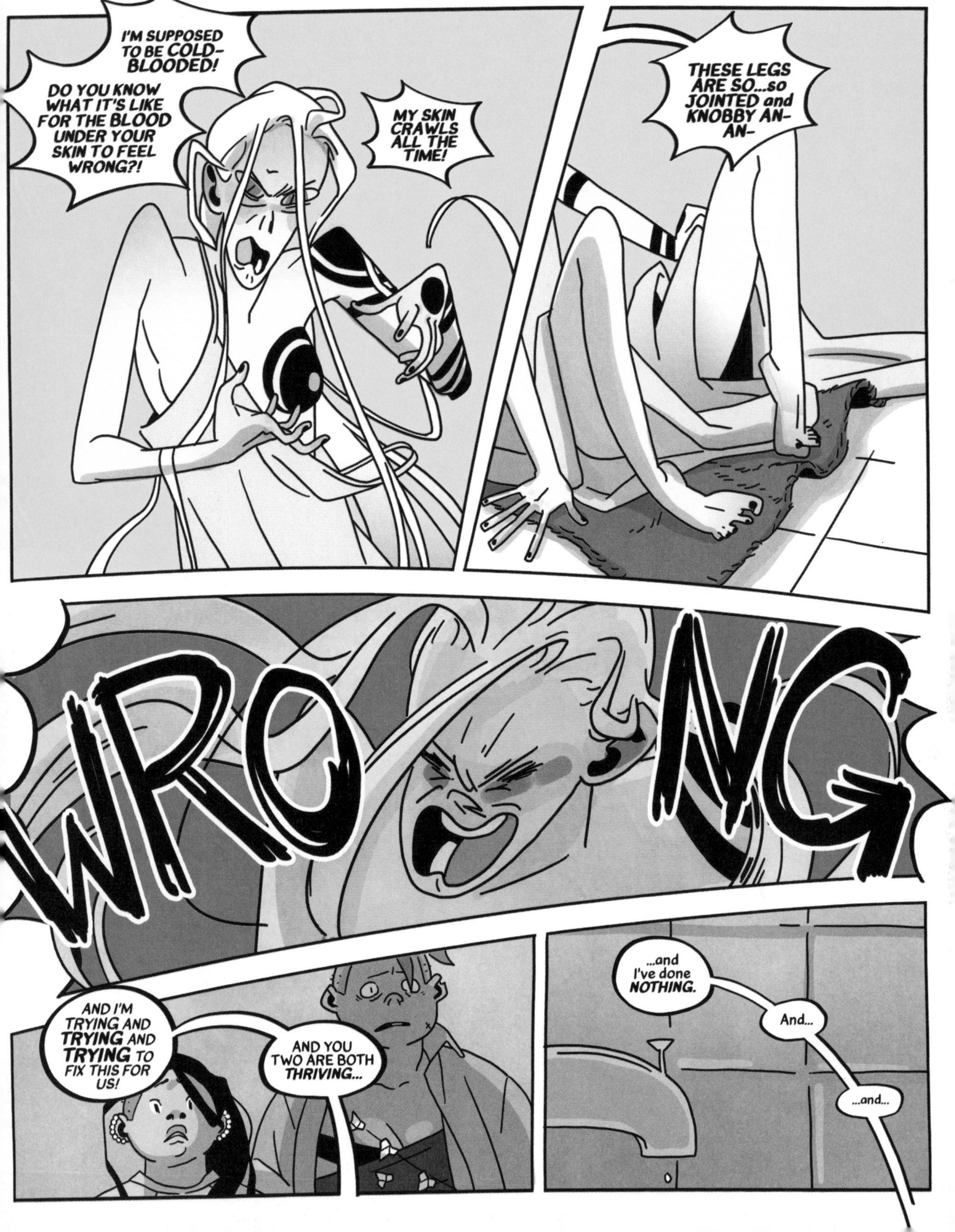
I'M SUPPOSED TO BE COLD-BLOODED!
DO YOU KNOW WHAT IT'S LIKE FOR THE BLOOD UNDER YOUR SKIN TO FEEL WRONG?!
MY SKIN CRAWLS ALL THE TIME!
THESE LEGS ARE SO...so JOINTED and KNOBBY AN-AN-
WRONG
AND I'M TRYING AND TRYING AND TRYING TO FIX THIS FOR US!
AND YOU TWO ARE BOTH THRIVING...
...and I've done NOTHING.
And...
...and...

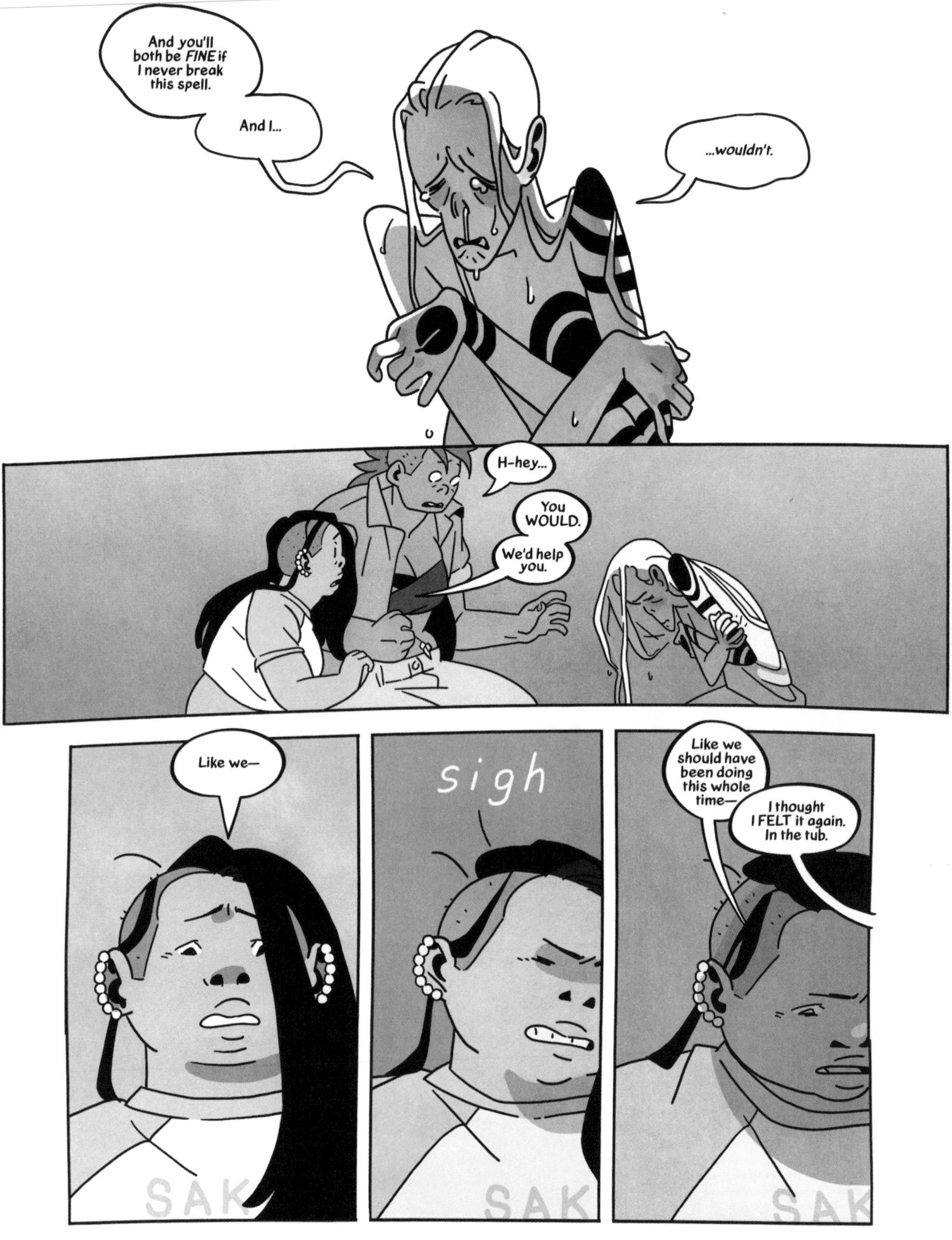
And you'll both be FINE if I never break this spell.
And I...
...wouldn't.
H-hey...
You WOULD.
We'd help you.
Like we—
SAK
sigh
SAK
Like we should have been doing this whole time—
I thought I FELT it again. In the tub.
SAK

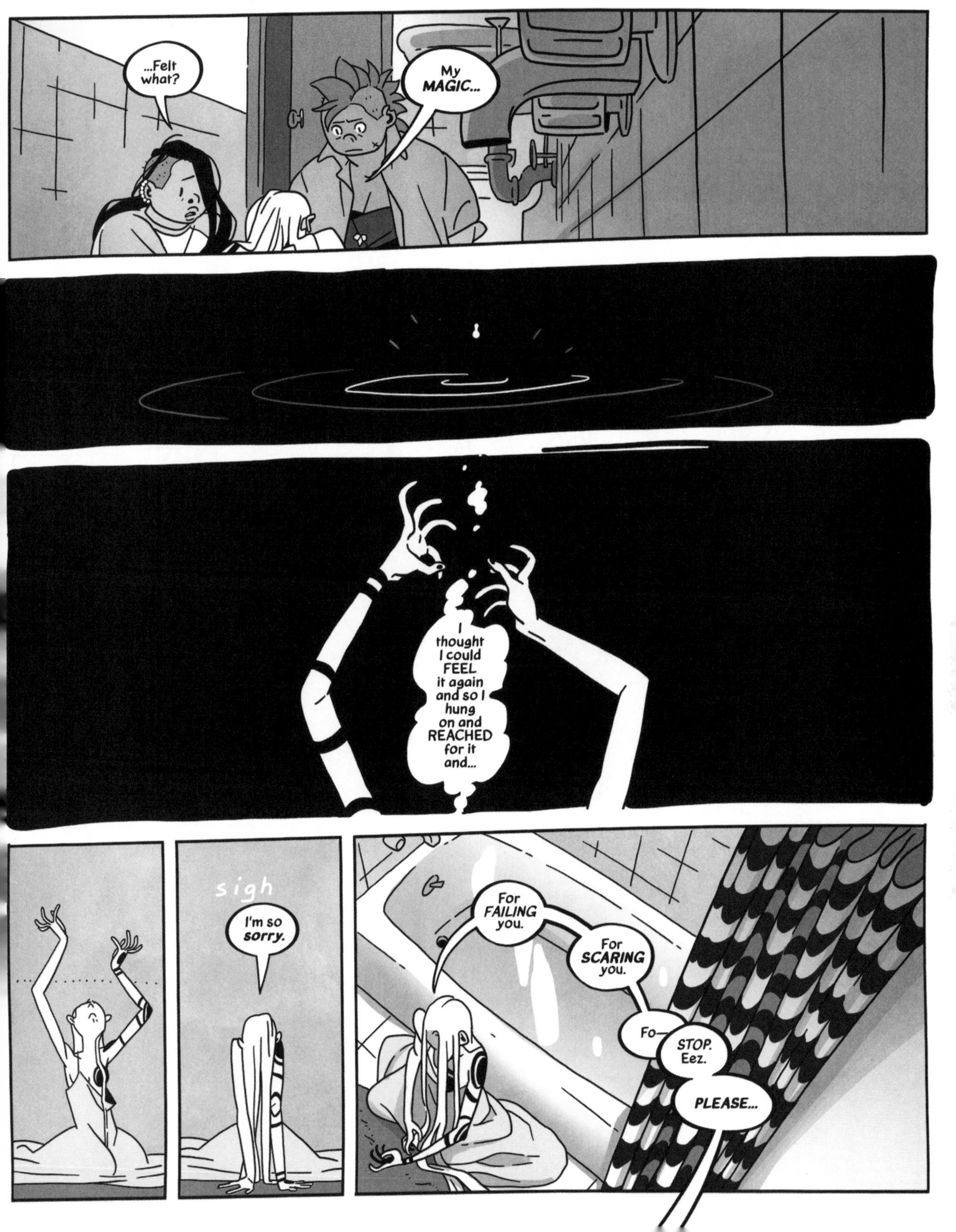
...Felt what?
My MAGIC...
I thought I could FEEL it again and so I hung on and REACHED for it and...
sigh
I'm so sorry.
For FAILING you.
For SCARING you.
Fo—
STOP. Eez.
PLEASE...

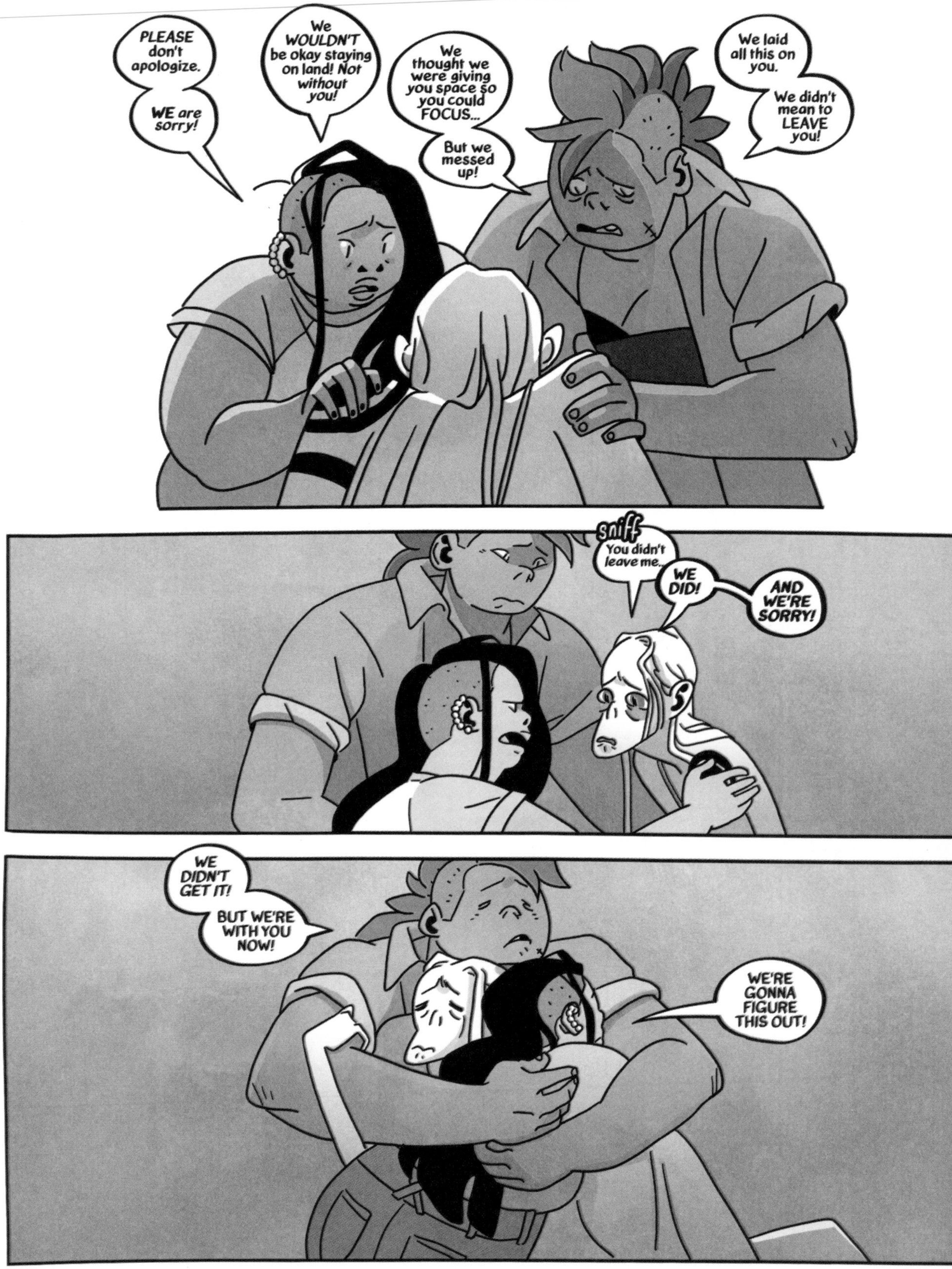
PLEASE don't apologize.
WE are sorry!
We WOULDN'T be okay staying on land! Not without you!
We thought we were giving you space so you could FOCUS...
But we messed up!
We laid all this on you.
We didn't mean to LEAVE you!
sniff
You didn't leave me..
WE DID!
AND WE'RE SORRY!
WE DIDN'T GET IT!
BUT WE'RE WITH YOU NOW!
WE'RE GONNA FIGURE THIS OUT!

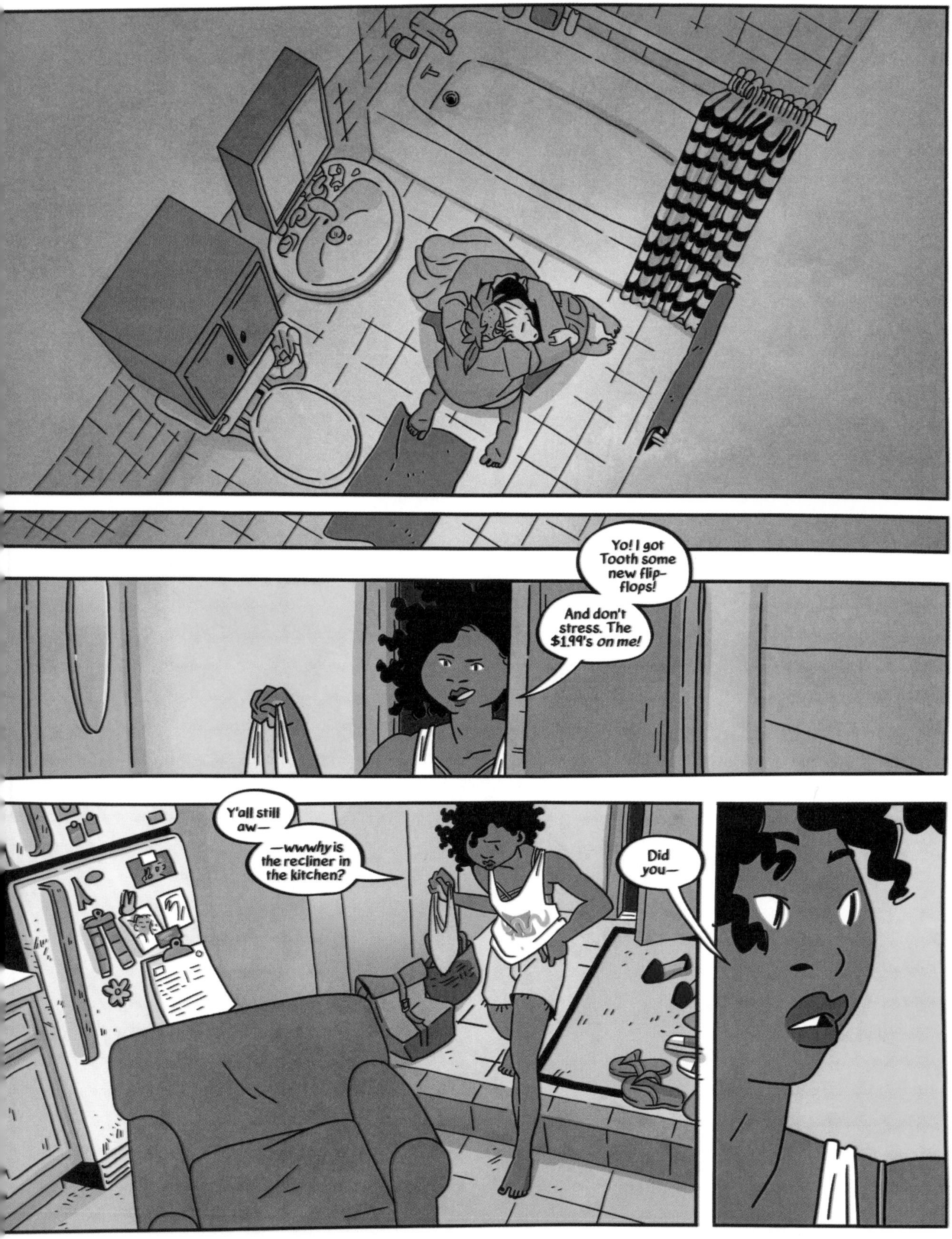
Yo! I got Tooth some new flip-flops!
And don't stress. The $1.99's *on me!*
Y'all still aw—
—*wwwhy* is the recliner in the kitchen?
Did you—

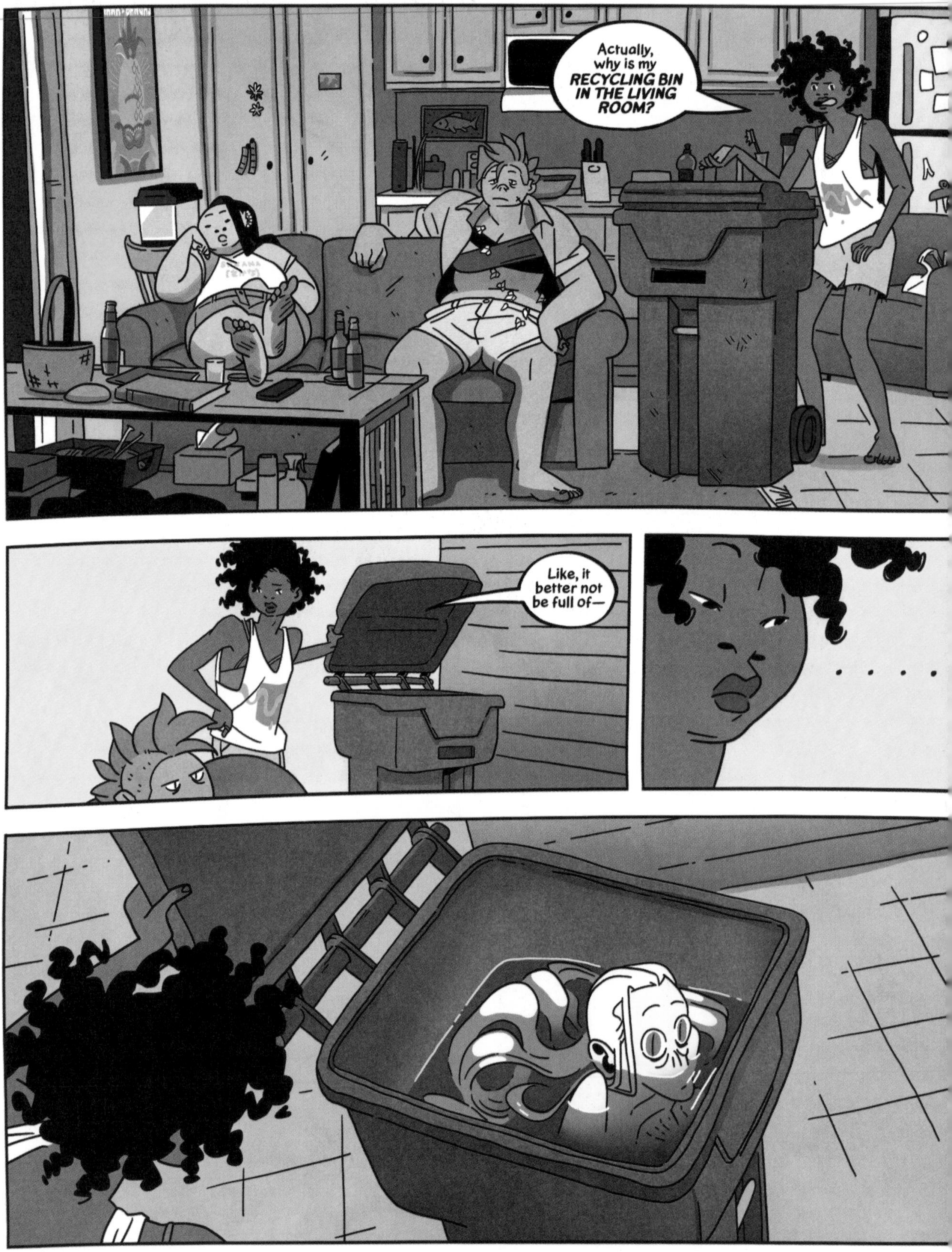

Actually, why is my ***RECYCLING BIN IN THE LIVING ROOM?***
Like, it better not be full of—
. . . .

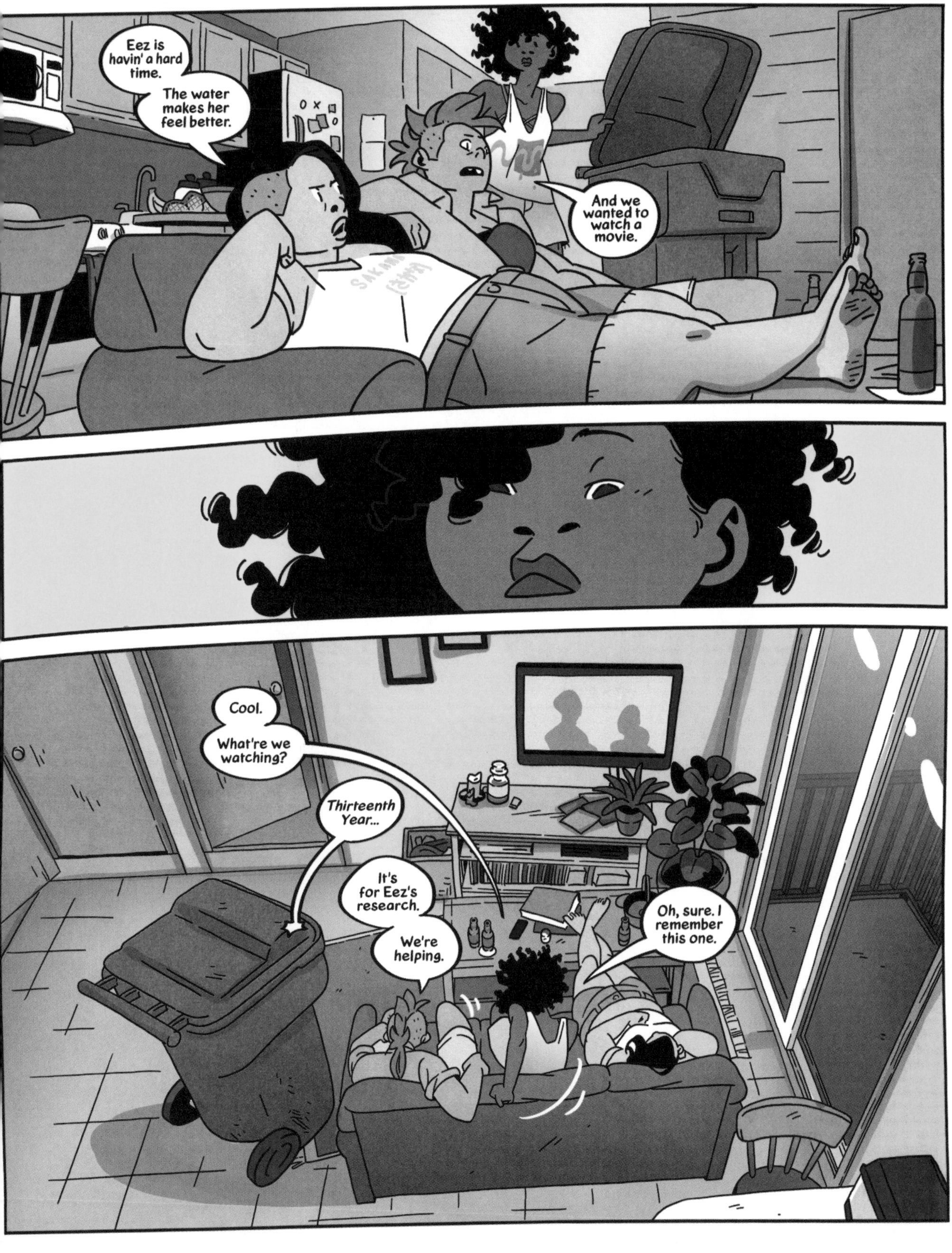
Eez is havin' a hard time.
The water makes her feel better.
And we wanted to watch a movie.
Cool.
What're we watching?
Thirteenth Year...
It's for Eez's research.
We're helping.
Oh, sure. I remember this one.

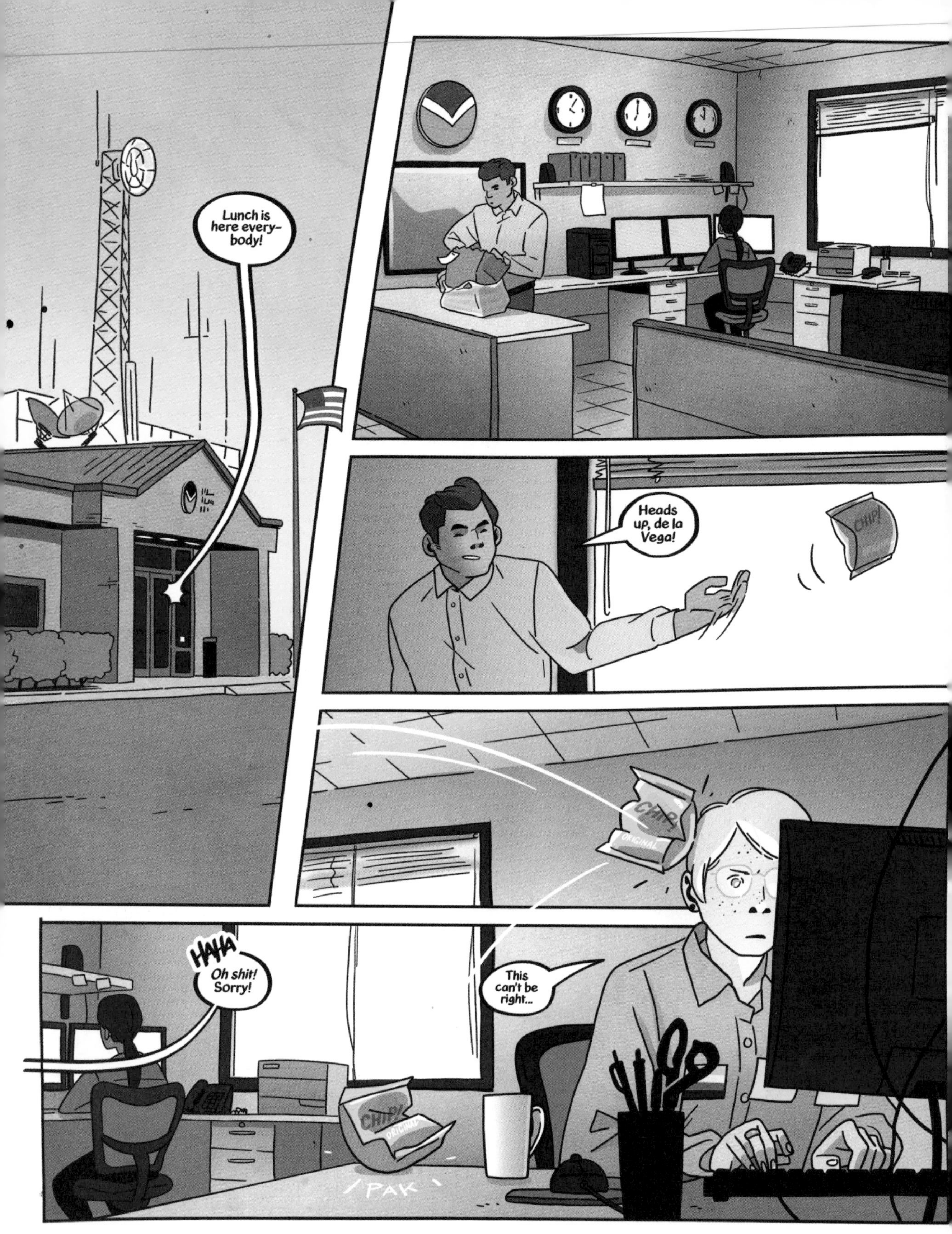
Lunch is here every-body!
Heads up, de la Vega!
CHIP!
CHIP! ORIGINAL
This can't be right...
HAHA
Oh shit! Sorry!
CHIP! ORIGINAL
PAK

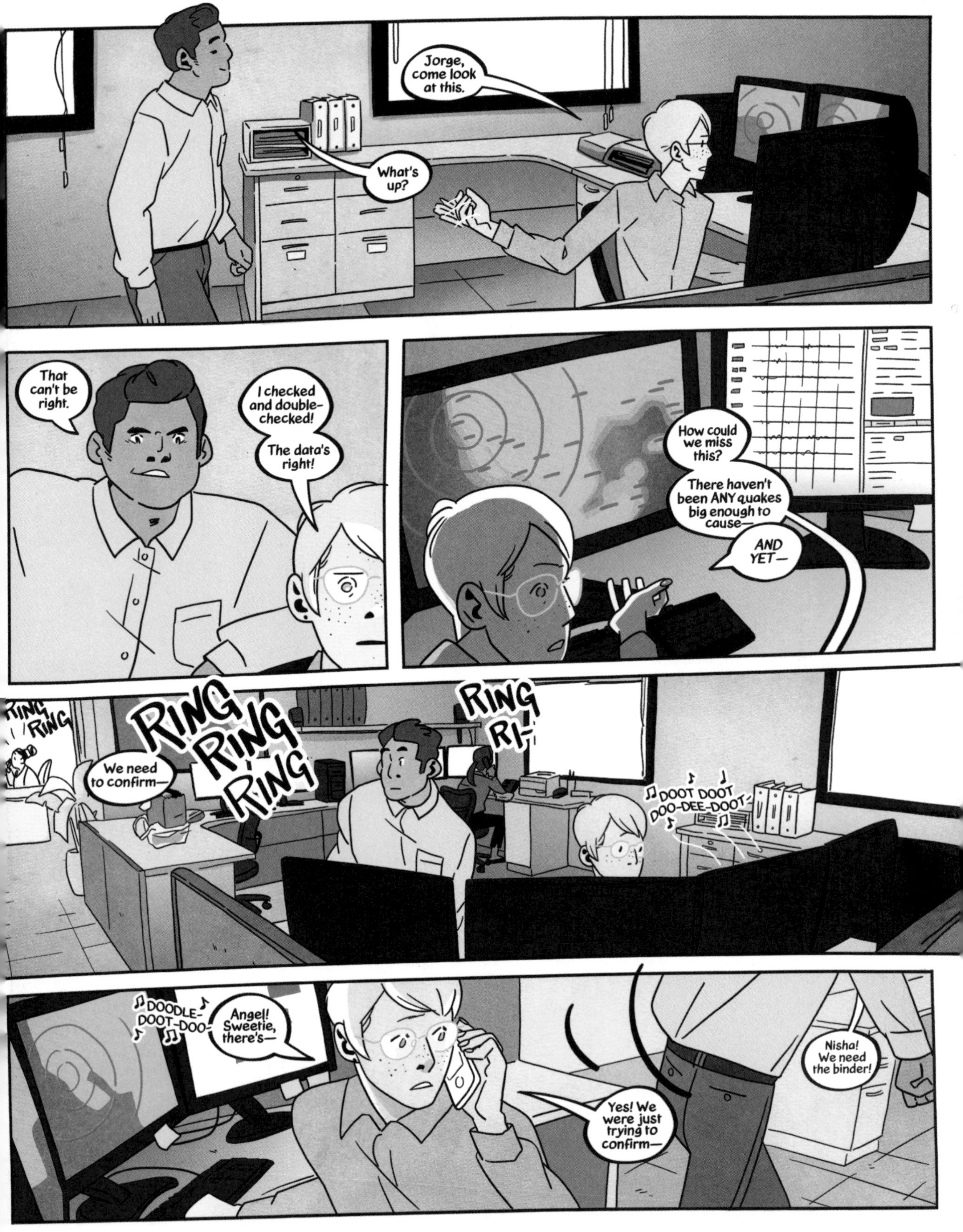

Jorge, come look at this.
What's up?
That can't be right.
I checked and double-checked!
The data's right!
How could we miss this?
There haven't been ANY quakes big enough to cause—
AND YET—
RING RING
RING RING RING
RING RI-
We need to confirm—
DOOT DOOT DOO-DEE-DOOT
DOODLE-DOOT-DOO
Angel! Sweetie, there's—
Nisha! We need the binder!
Yes! We were just trying to confirm—

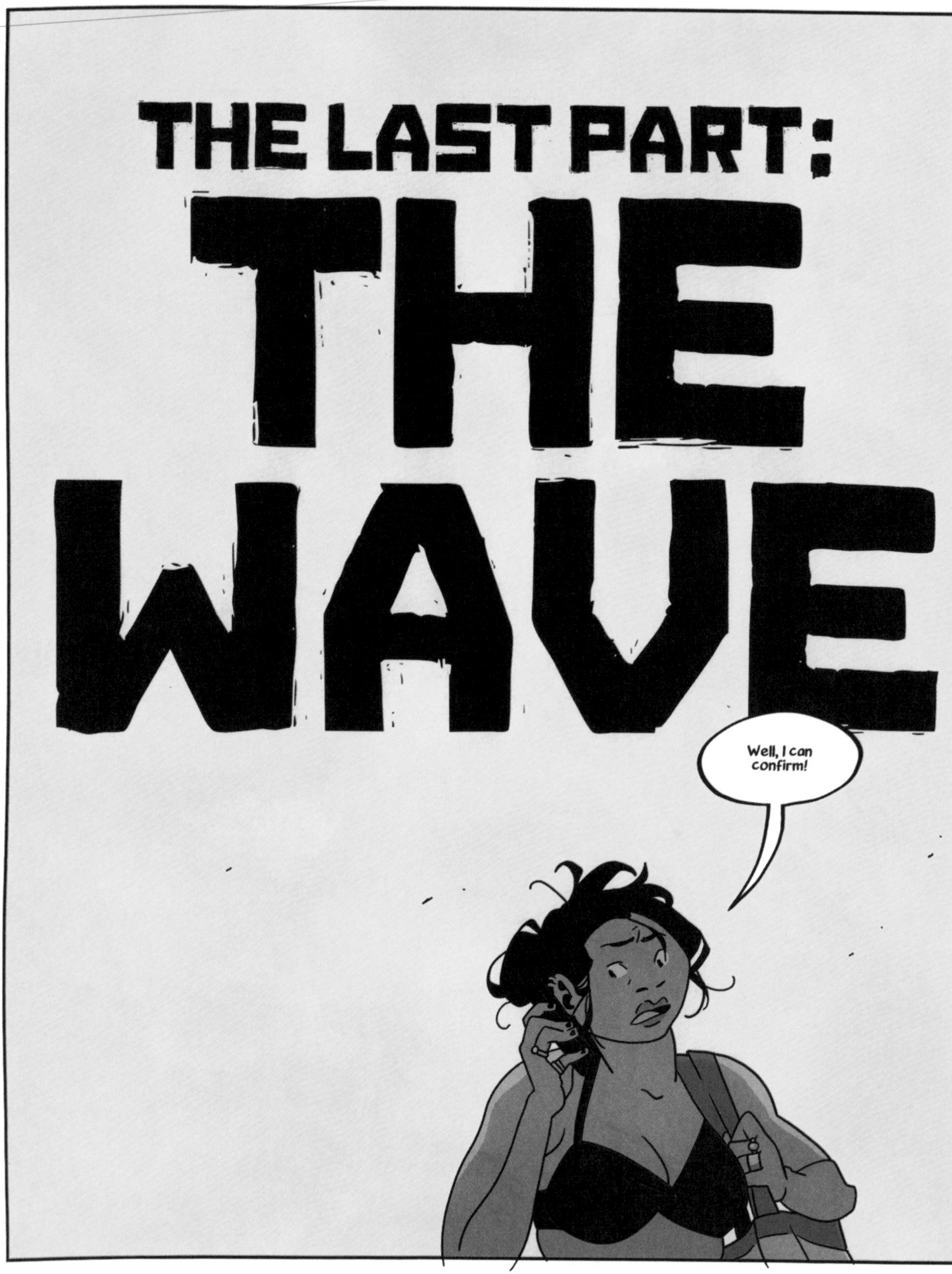
THE LAST PART:
THE WAVE
Well, I can confirm!

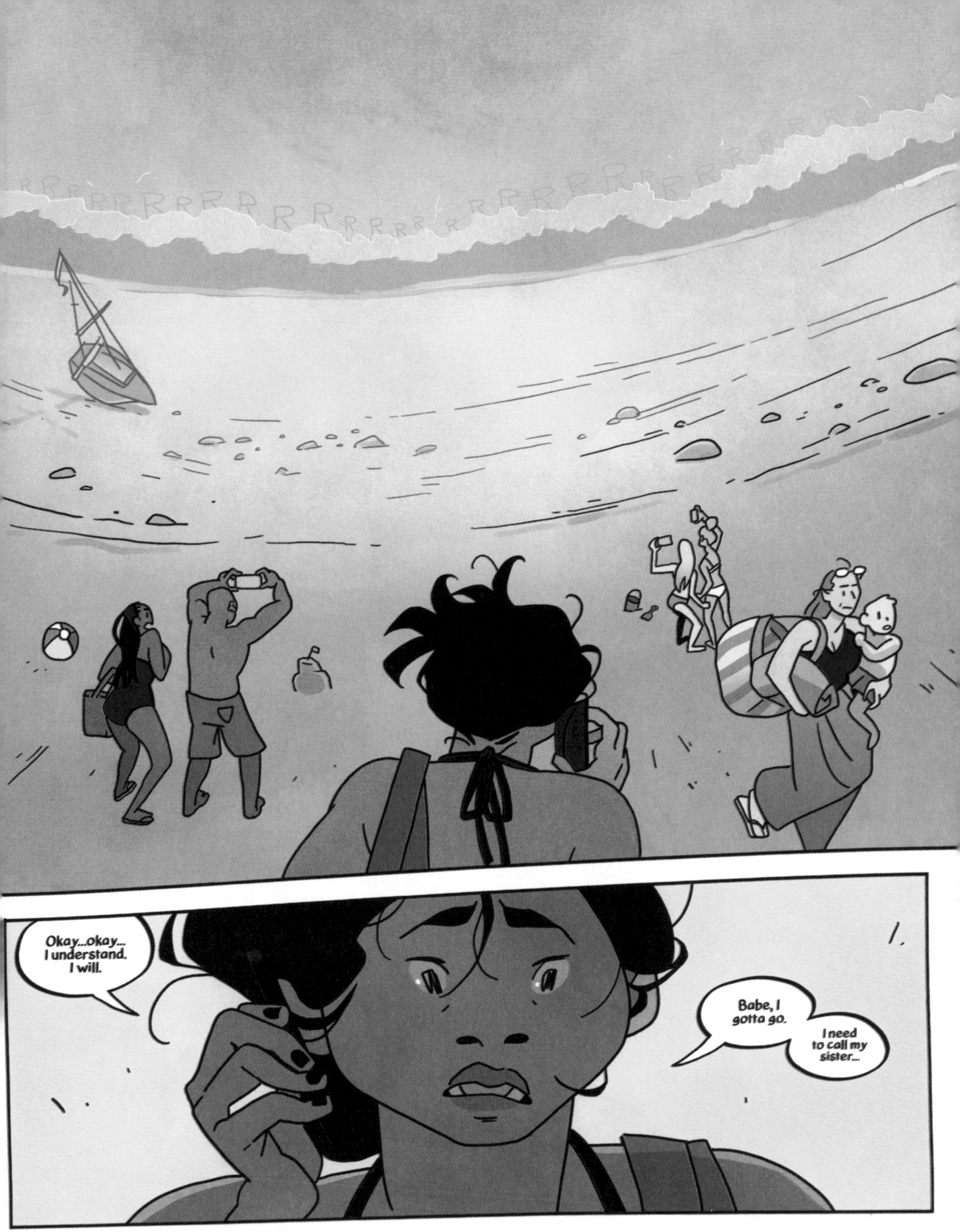
Okay...okay... I understand. I will.
Babe, I gotta go.
I need to call my sister...

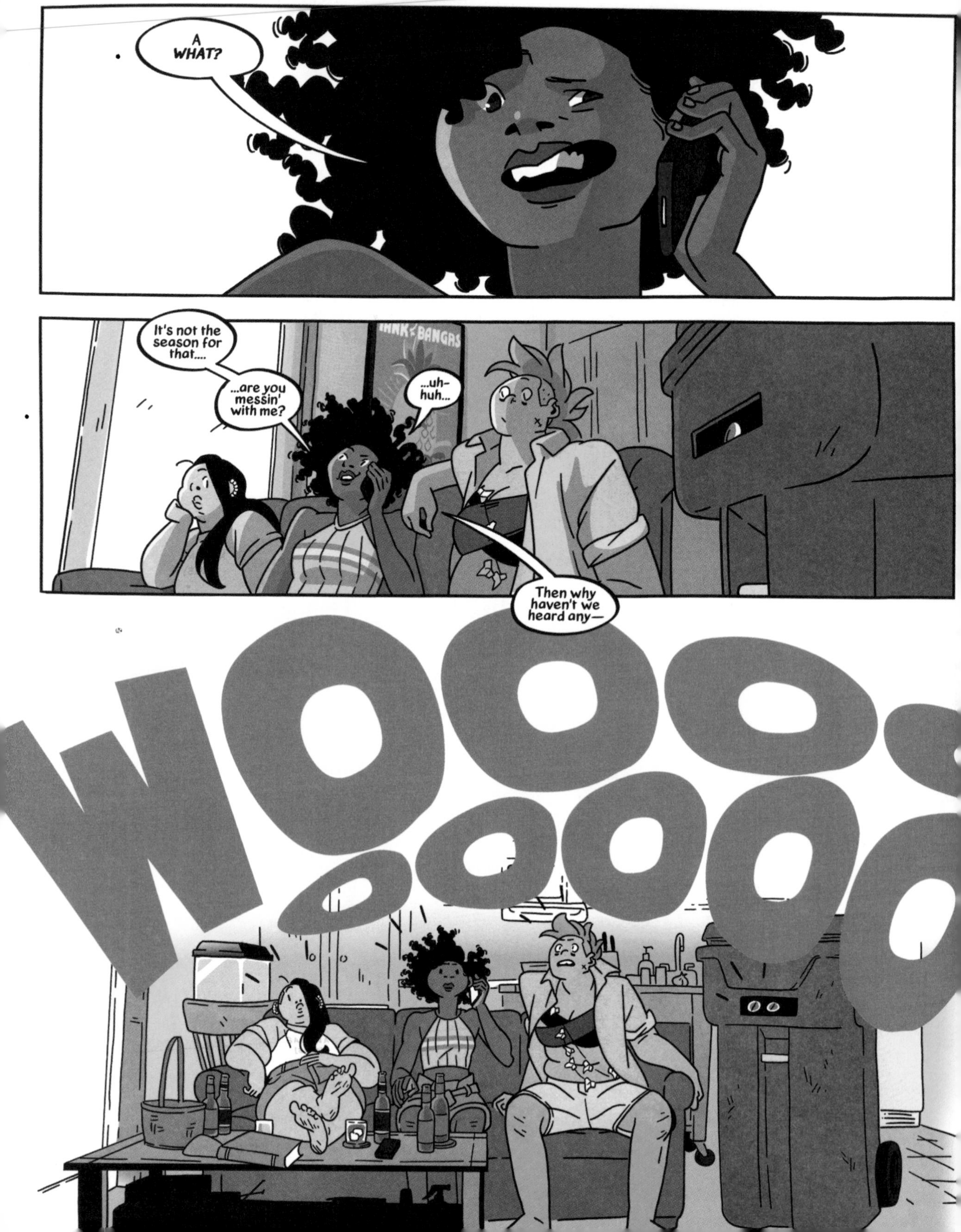
A WHAT?
It's not the season for that....
...are you messin' with me?
...uh-huh...
Then why haven't we heard any—
WOOOOOOOOO

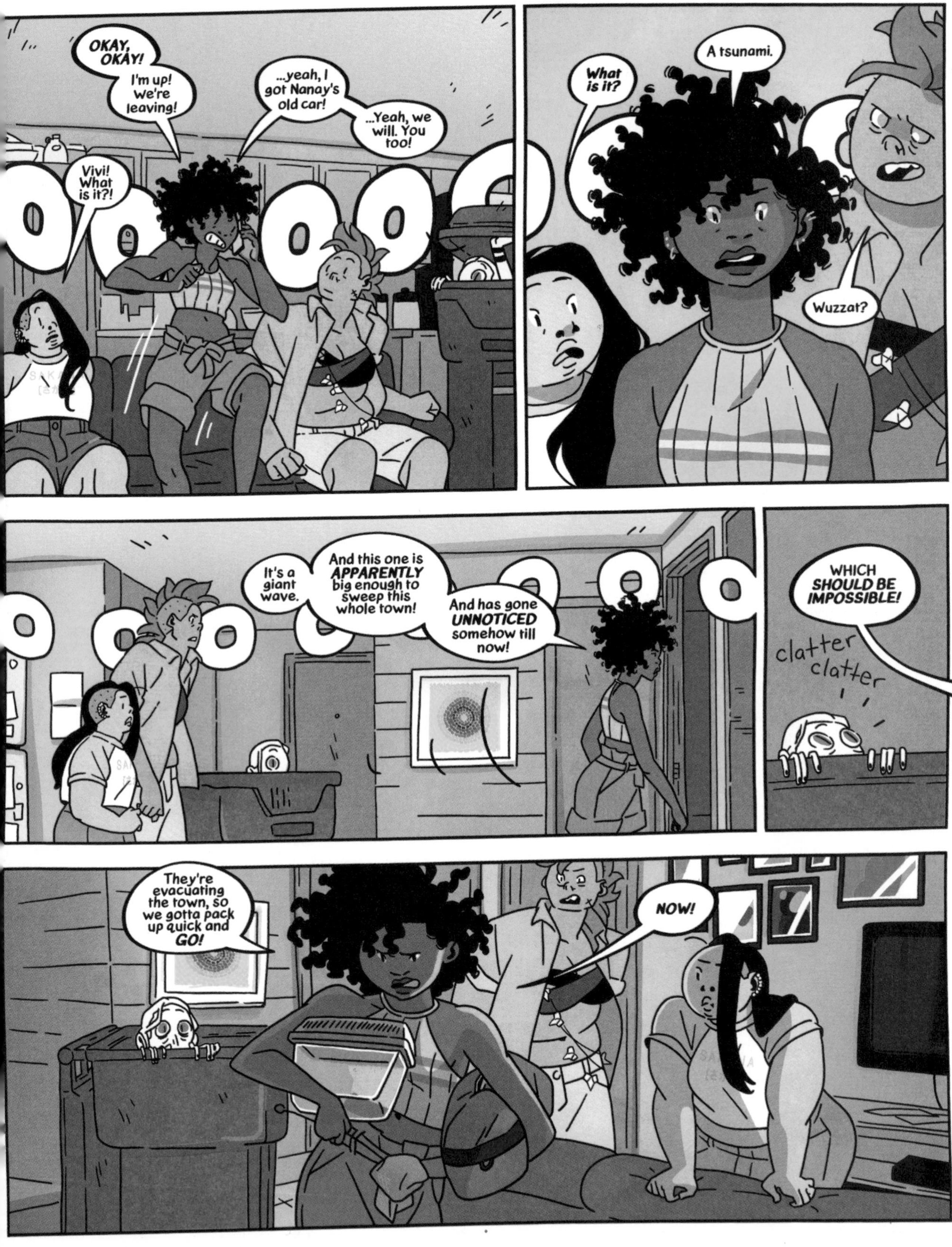

OKAY, OKAY!
I'm up! We're leaving!
Vivi! What is it?!
...yeah, I got Nanay's old car!
...Yeah, we will. You too!
What is it?
A tsunami.
Wuzzat?
It's a giant wave.
And this one is APPARENTLY big enough to sweep this whole town!
And has gone UNNOTICED somehow till now!
WHICH SHOULD BE IMPOSSIBLE!
clatter clatter
They're evacuating the town, so we gotta pack up quick and GO!
NOW!

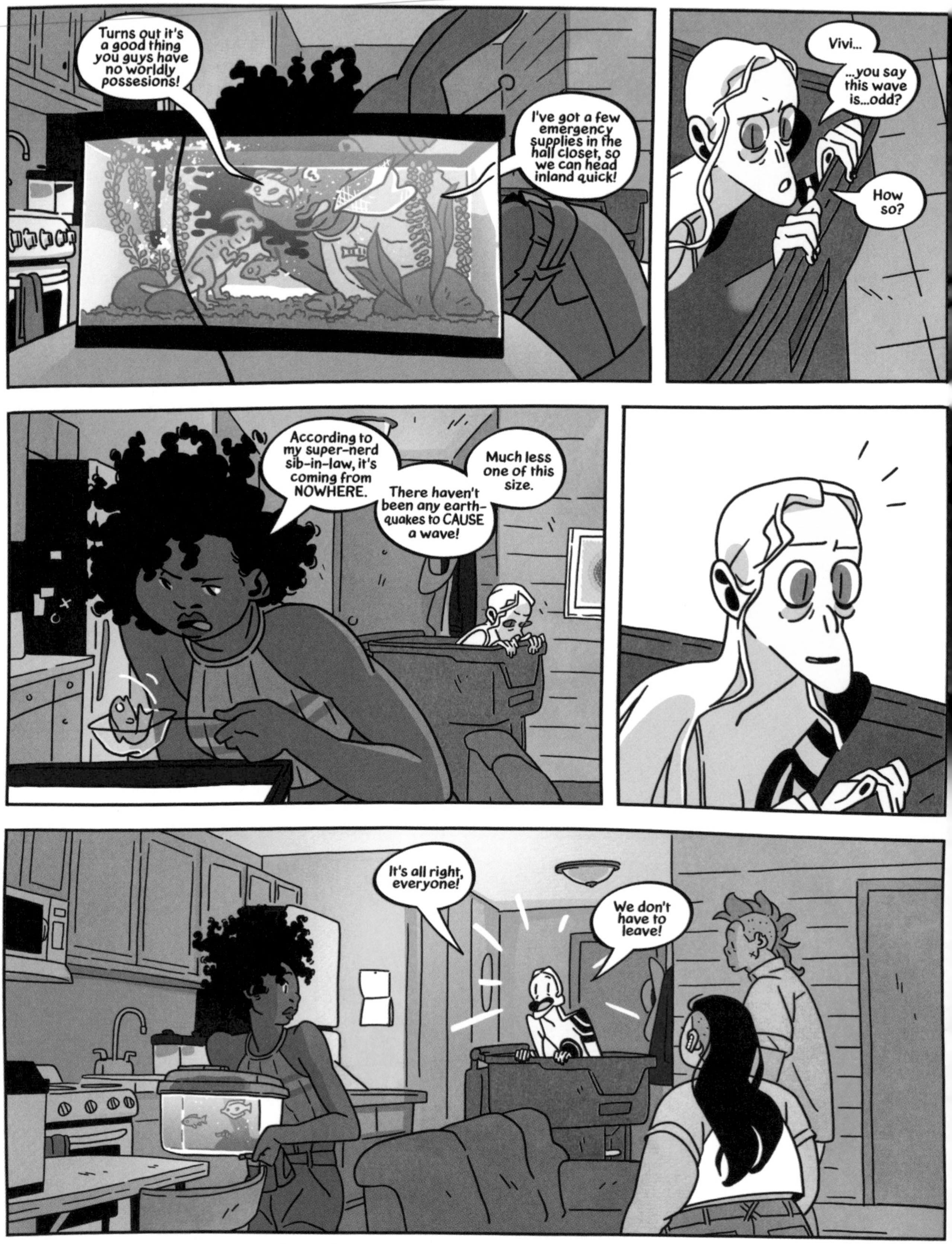

Turns out it's a good thing you guys have no worldly possesions!
I've got a few emergency supplies in the hall closet, so we can head inland quick!
Vivi...
...you say this wave is...odd?
How so?
According to my super-nerd sib-in-law, it's coming from NOWHERE.
There haven't been any earth-quakes to CAUSE a wave!
Much less one of this size.
It's all right, everyone!
We don't have to leave!

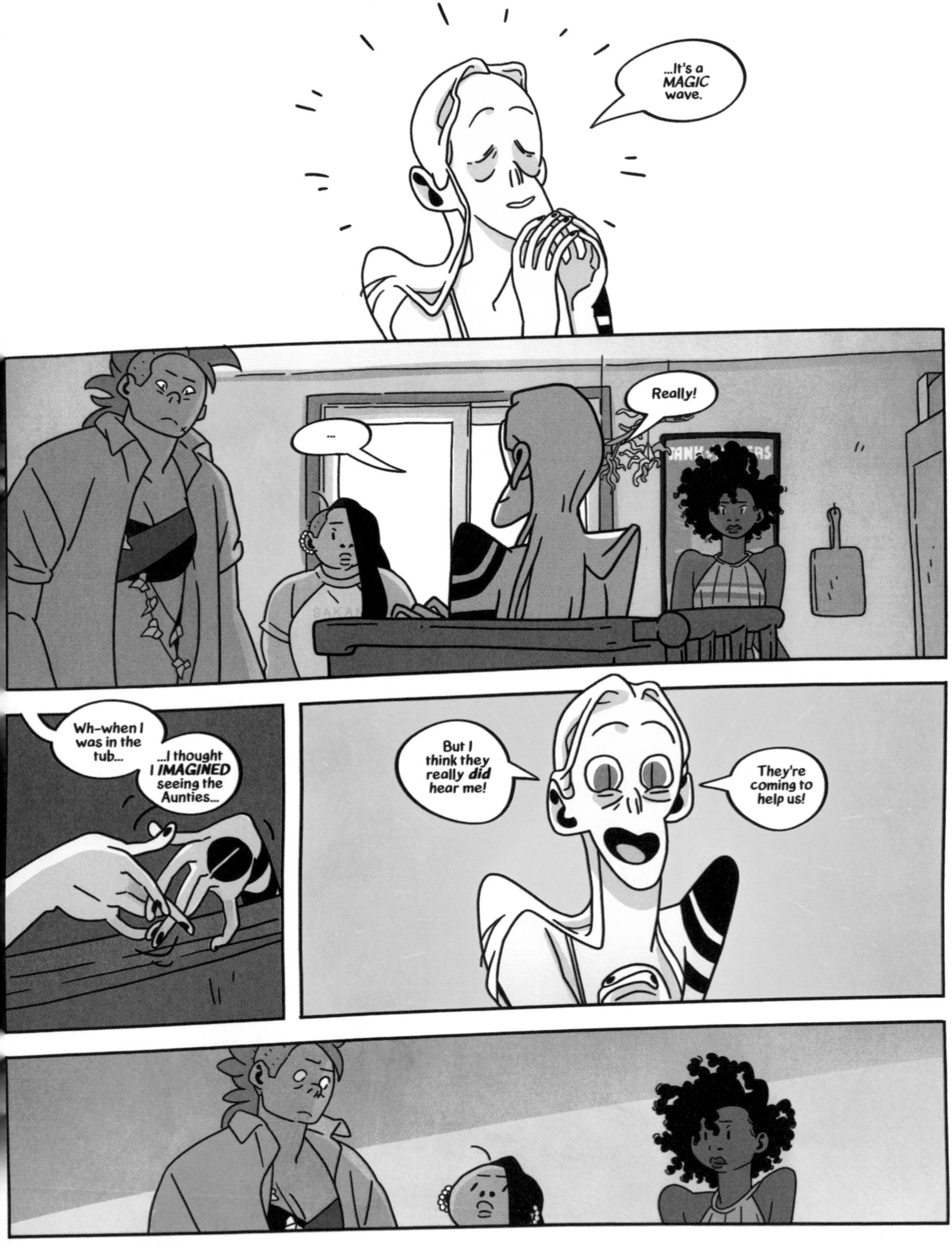

...It's a MAGIC wave.
...
Really!
Wh-when I was in the tub...
...I thought I IMAGINED seeing the Aunties...
But I think they really did hear me!
They're coming to help us!

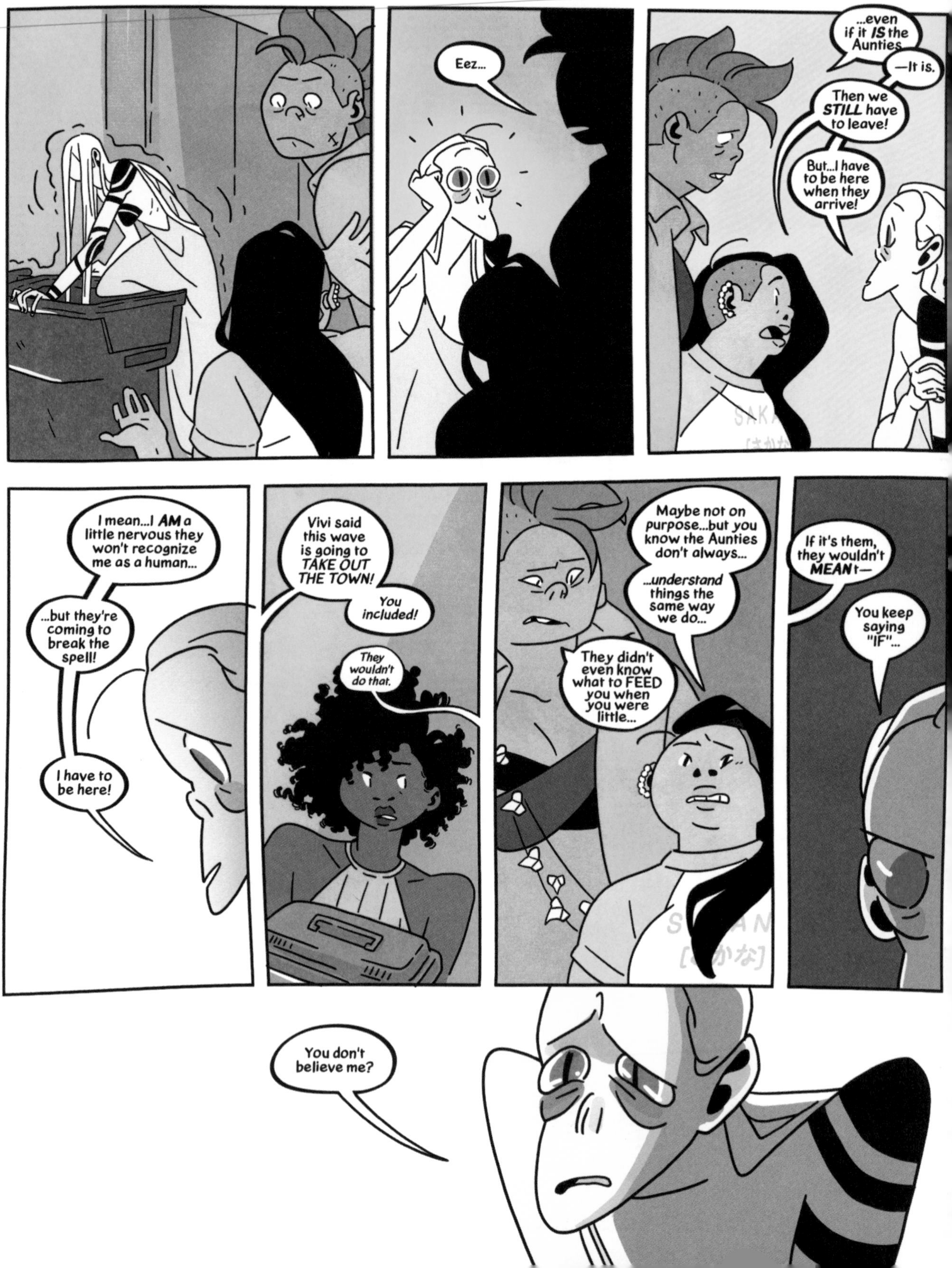

Eez...
...even if it IS the Aunties
—It is.
Then we STILL have to leave!
But...I have to be here when they arrive!
SAKA
I mean...I AM a little nervous they won't recognize me as a human...
...but they're coming to break the spell!
I have to be here!
Vivi said this wave is going to TAKE OUT THE TOWN!
You included!
They wouldn't do that.
Maybe not on purpose...but you know the Aunties don't always...
...understand things the same way we do...
They didn't even know what to FEED you when you were little...
If it's them, they wouldn't MEAN t—
You keep saying "IF"...
You don't believe me?

You were **DROWNING,** Eez!

What if it **WAS** just a dream?

Eez. If you're absolutely sure it's them...

...I. Will. **STAY.**

But if there's a **CHANCE** you're wrong...

We'd die.

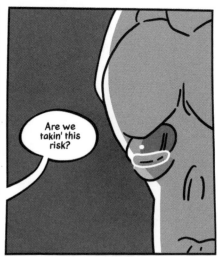

Are we takin' this risk?

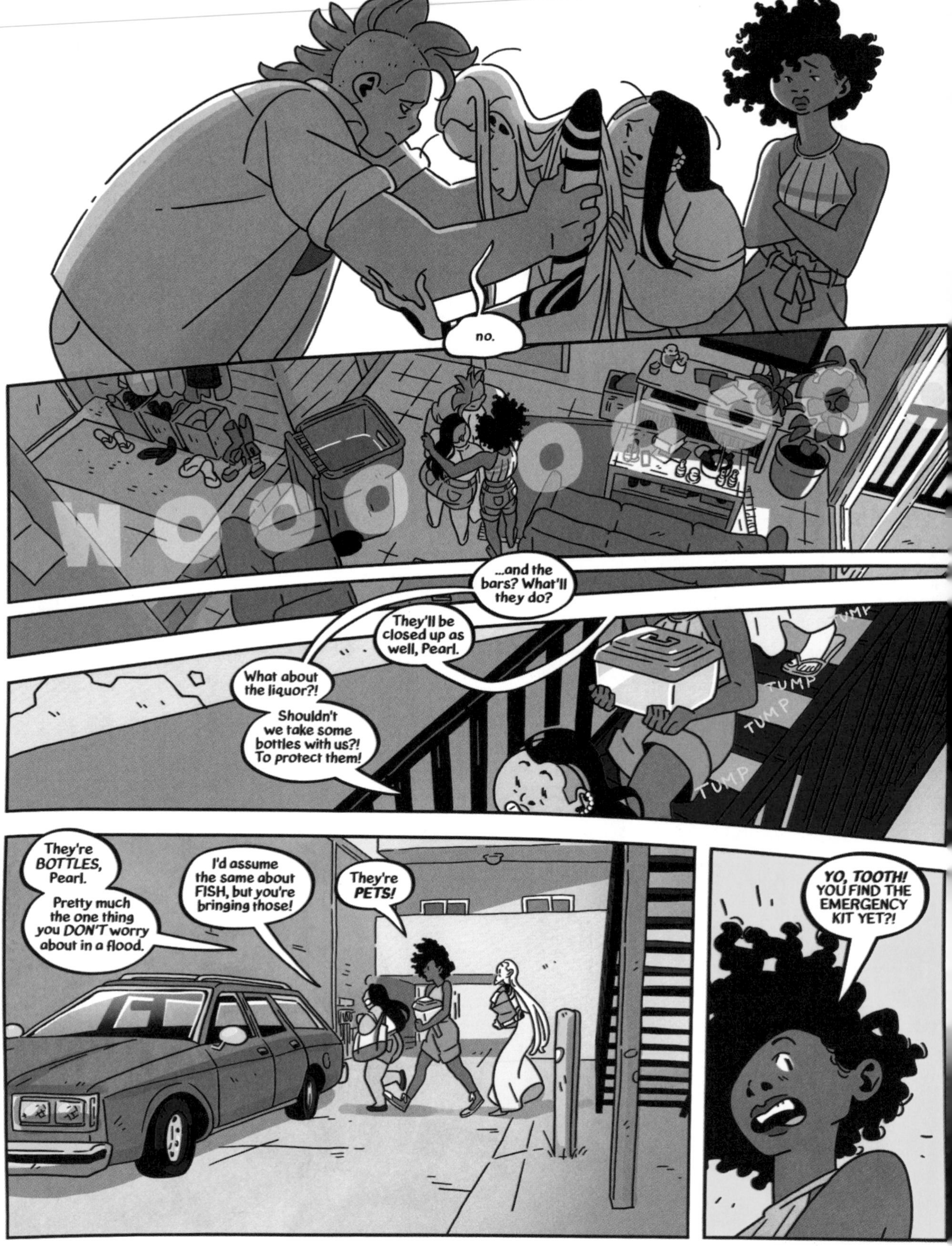
no.
WOOOOOOOOOO
...and the bars? What'll they do?
They'll be closed up as well, Pearl.
What about the liquor?!
Shouldn't we take some bottles with us?! To protect them!
TUMP
TUMP
TUMP
TUMP
They're BOTTLES, Pearl.
Pretty much the one thing you DON'T worry about in a flood.
I'd assume the same about FISH, but you're bringing those!
They're PETS!
YO, TOOTH! YOU FIND THE EMERGENCY KIT YET?!

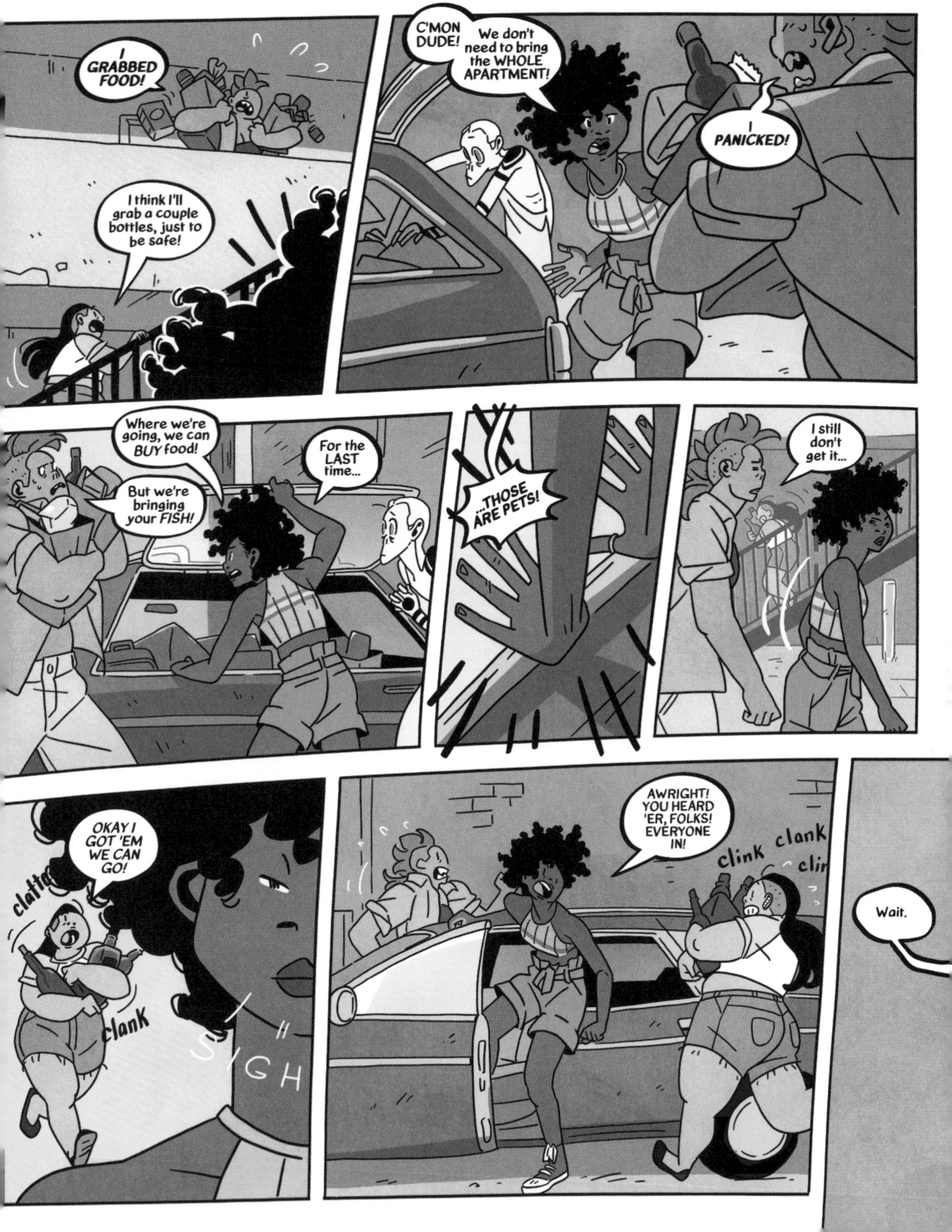
I GRABBED FOOD!
I think I'll grab a couple bottles, just to be safe!
C'MON DUDE!
We don't need to bring the WHOLE APARTMENT!
I PANICKED!
Where we're going, we can BUY food!
But we're bringing your FISH!
For the LAST time...
...THOSE ARE PETS!
I still don't get it...
OKAY I GOT 'EM WE CAN GO!
clank
SIGH
AWRIGHT! YOU HEARD 'ER, FOLKS! EVERYONE IN!
clink
clank
Wait.

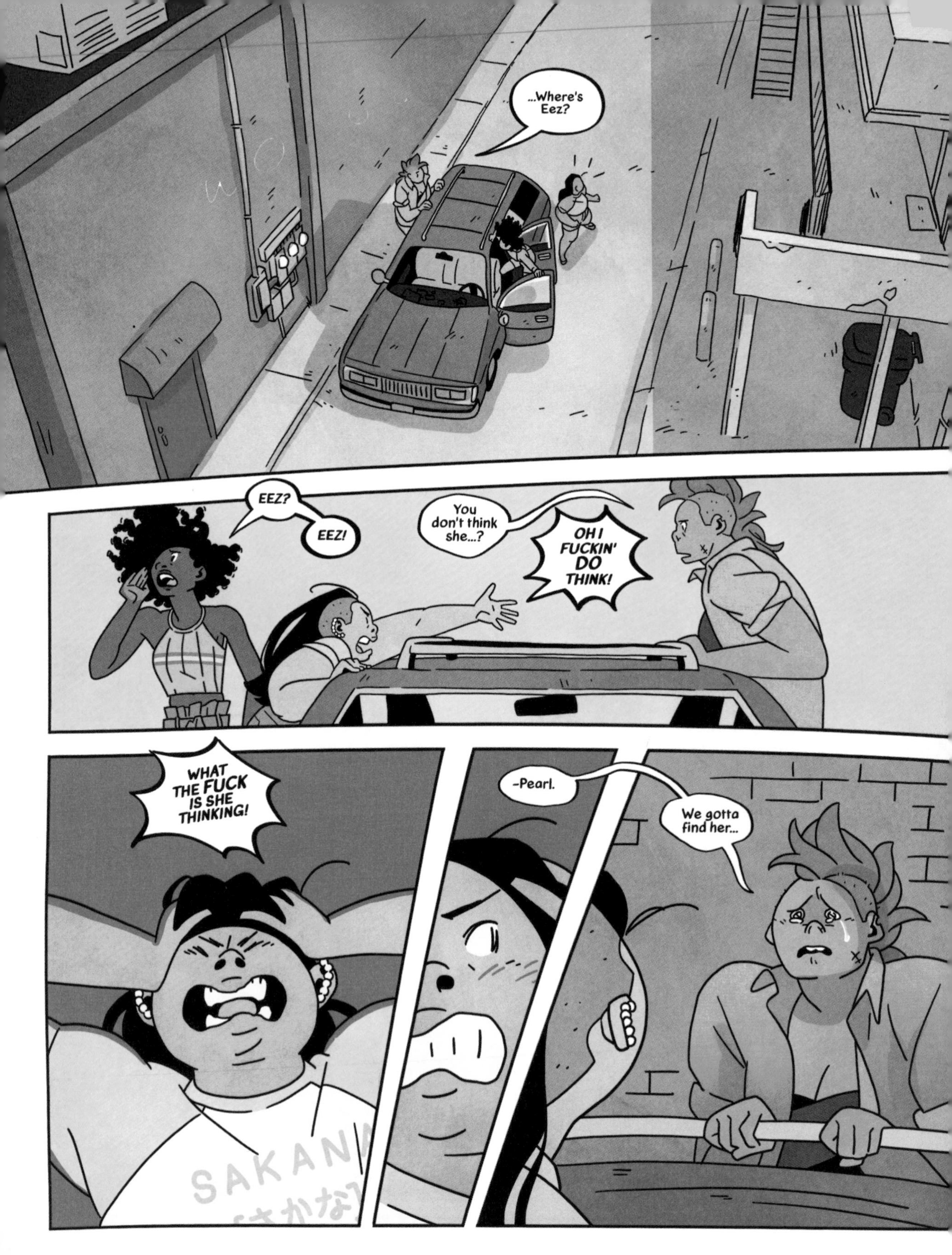
...Where's Eez?
EEZ?
EEZ!
You don't think she...?
OH I FUCKIN' DO THINK!
WHAT THE FUCK IS SHE THINKING!
SAKAN
-Pearl.
We gotta find her...

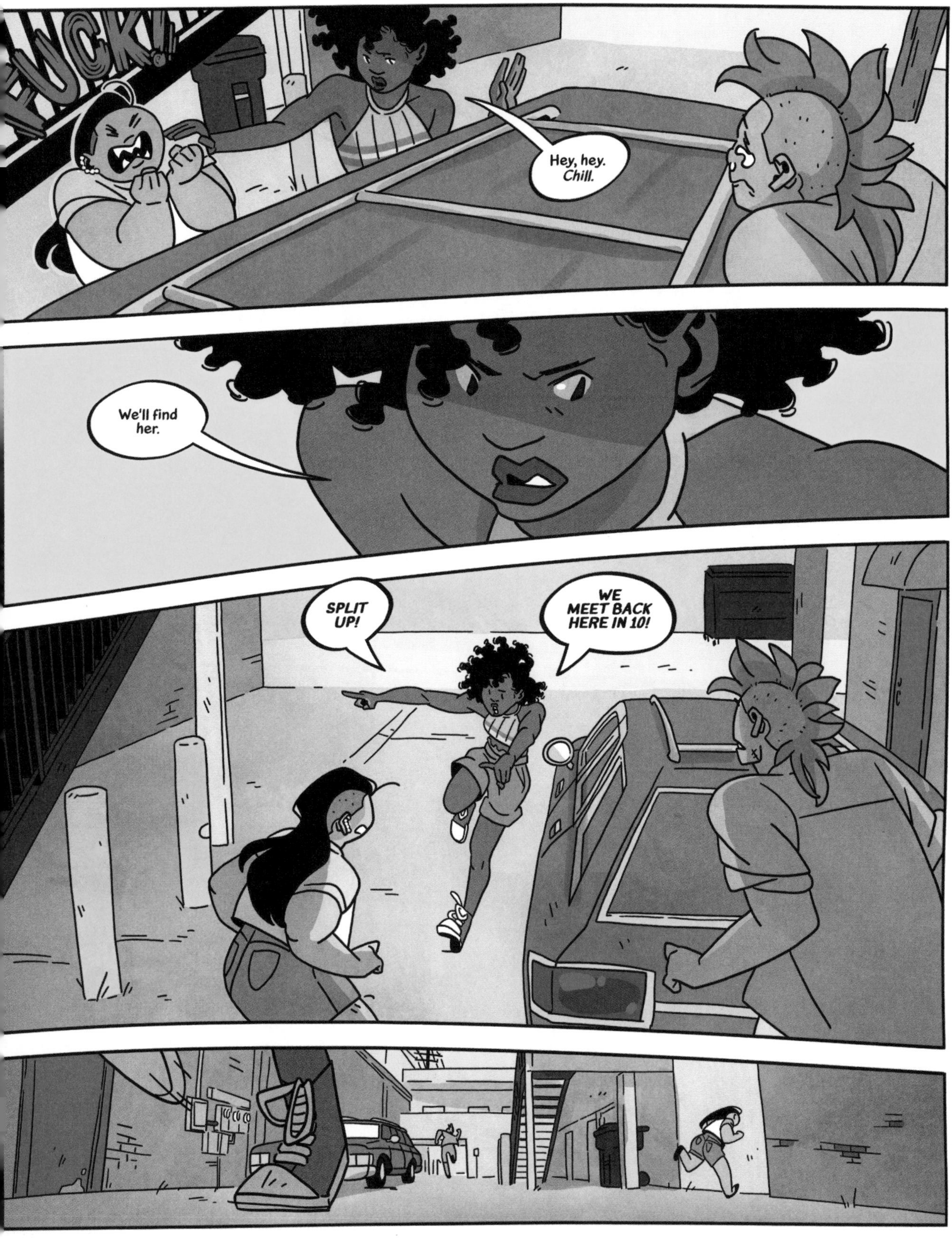
FUCK!!
Hey, hey. Chill.
We'll find her.
SPLIT UP!
WE MEET BACK HERE IN 10!

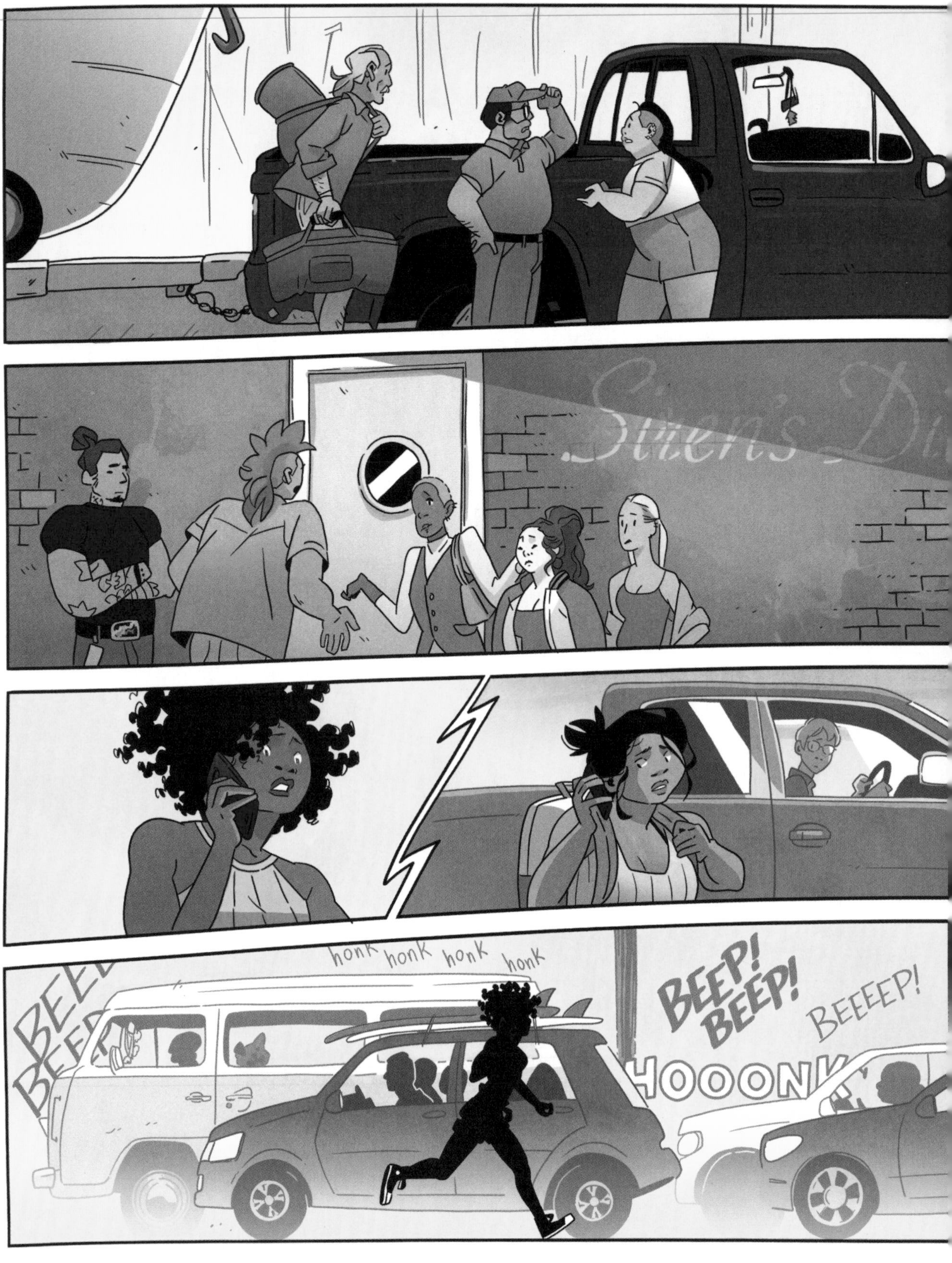
Siren's Di
honk honk honk honk
BEEP! BEEP!
BEEEEP!
HOOONK

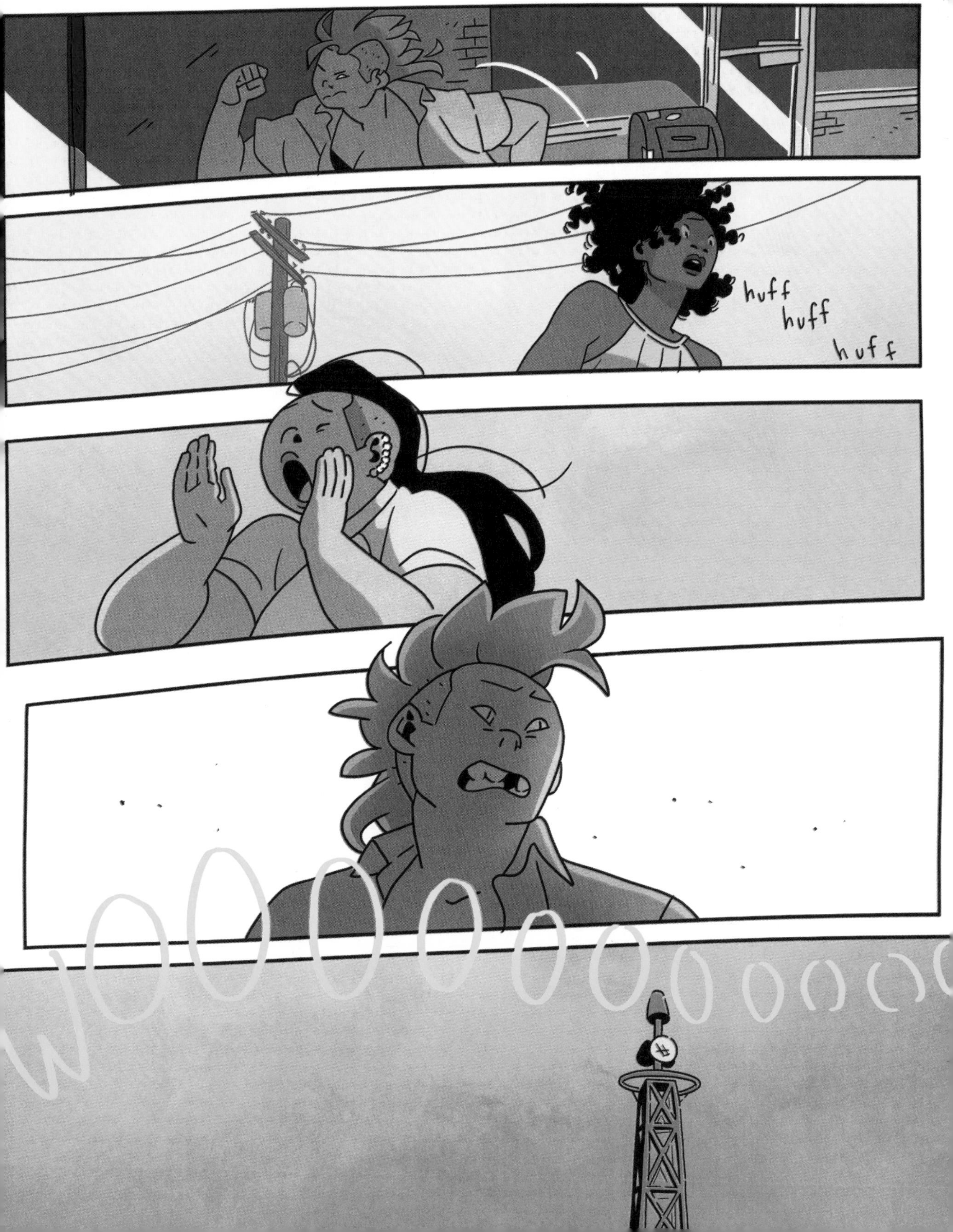

huff
huff
huff
WOOOOOOOOOOO

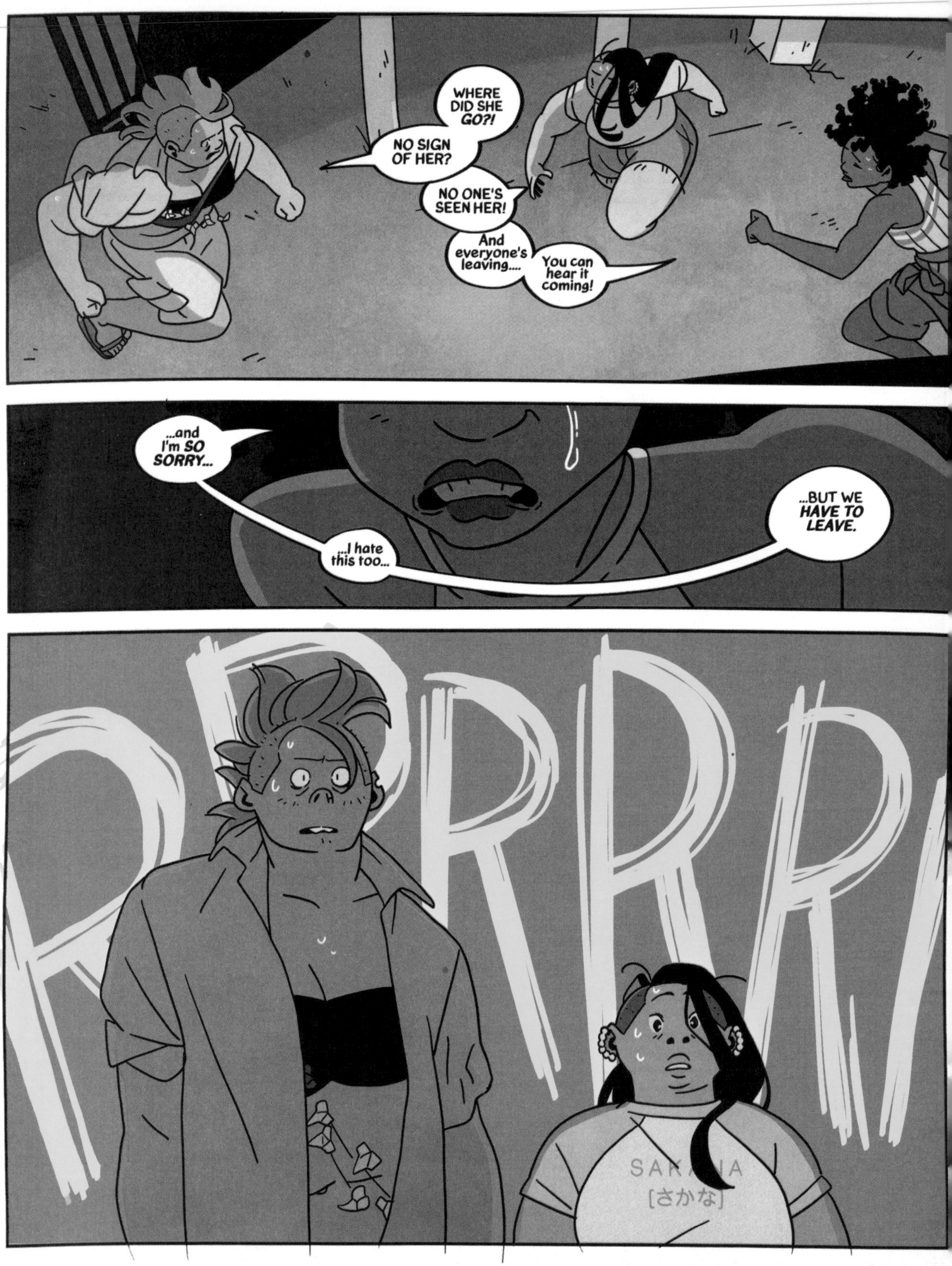

WHERE DID SHE GO?!
NO SIGN OF HER?
NO ONE'S SEEN HER!
And everyone's leaving....
You can hear it coming!
...and I'm SO SORRY...
...I hate this too...
...BUT WE HAVE TO LEAVE.
RRRRR
SAKANA
[さかな]

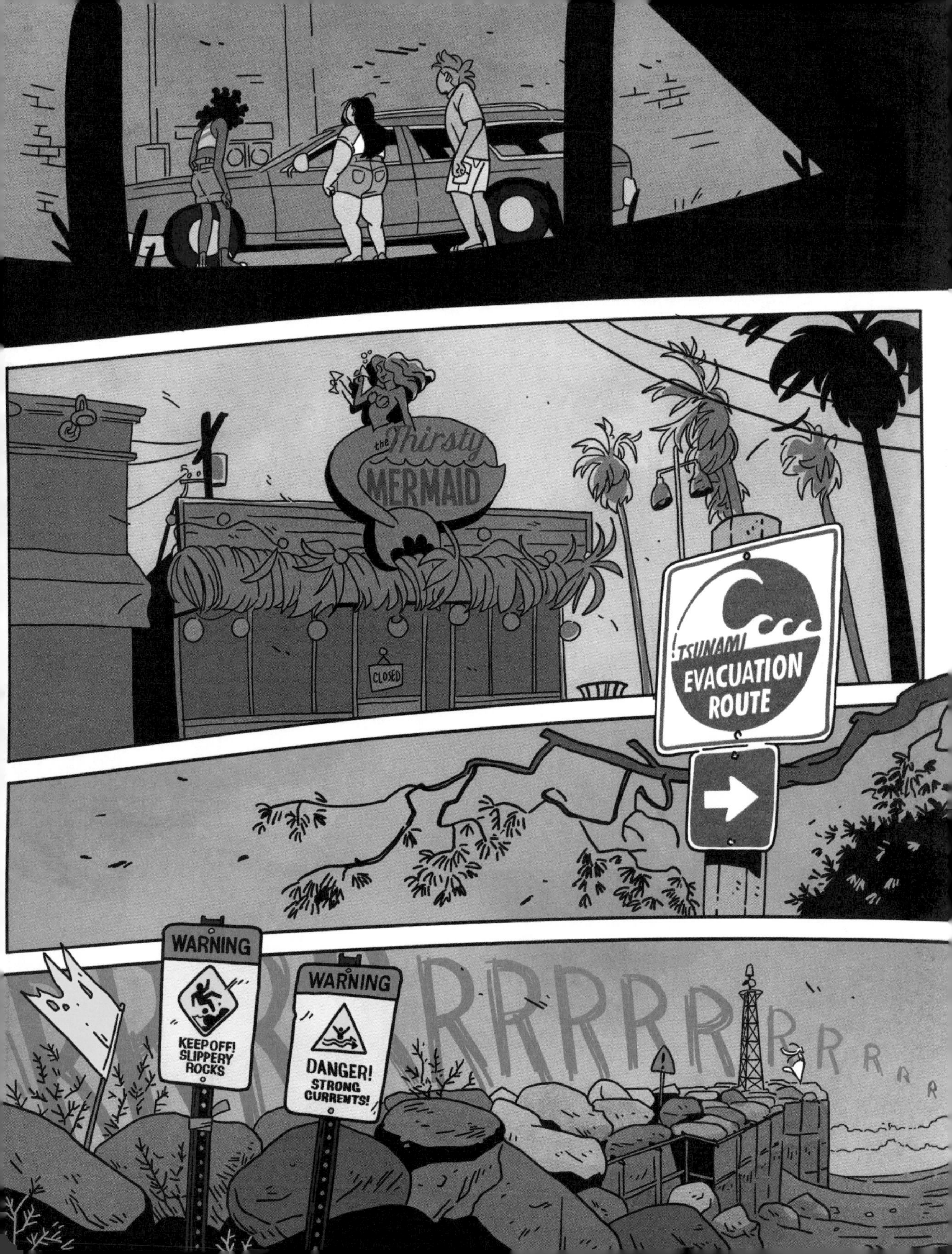

the Thirsty MERMAID
CLOSED
TSUNAMI EVACUATION ROUTE
WARNING
KEEP OFF! SLIPPERY ROCKS
WARNING
DANGER! STRONG CURRENTS!
RRRRRRRRRRRRRR

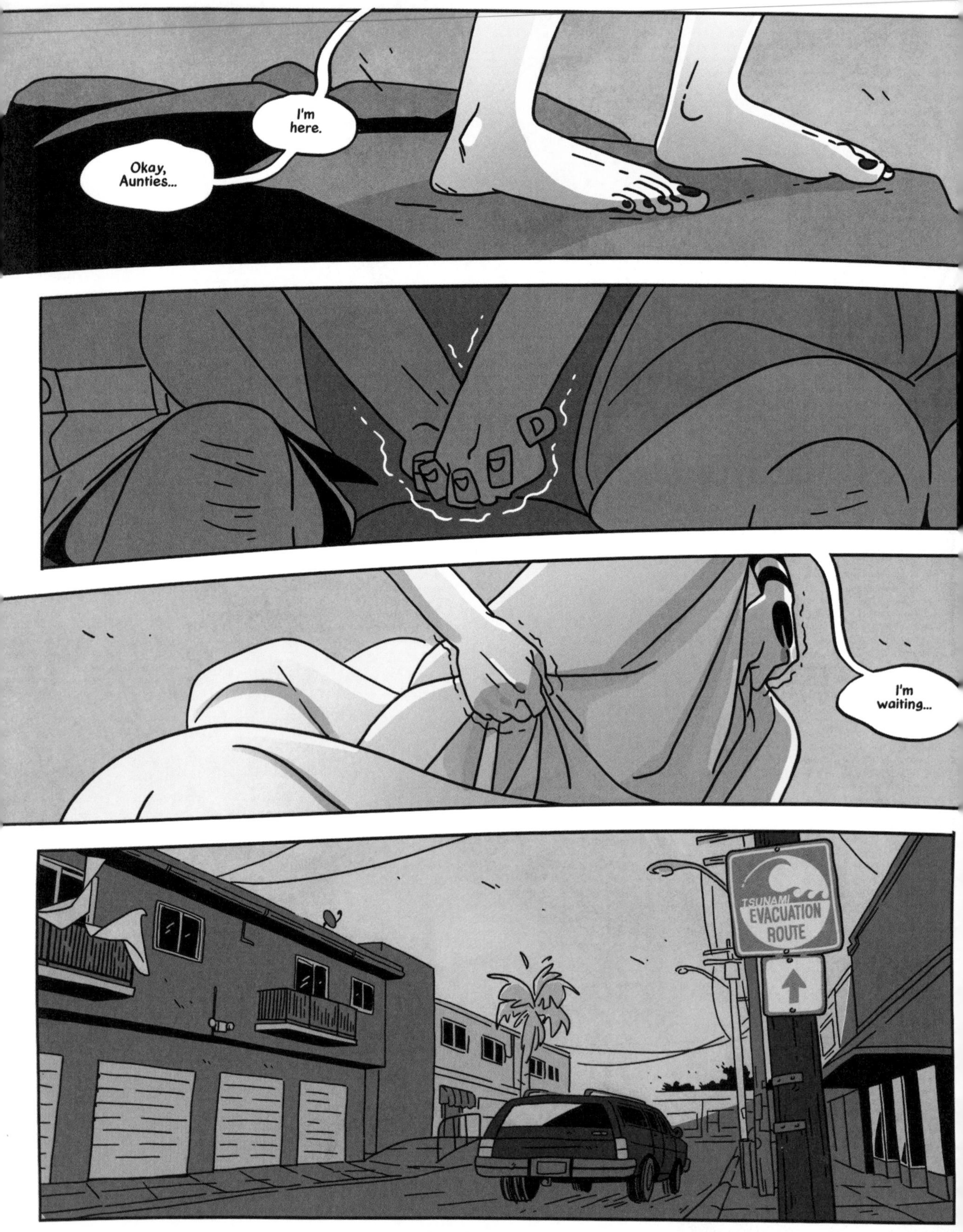
Okay, Aunties...
I'm here.
I'm waiting...
TSUNAMI
EVACUATION ROUTE

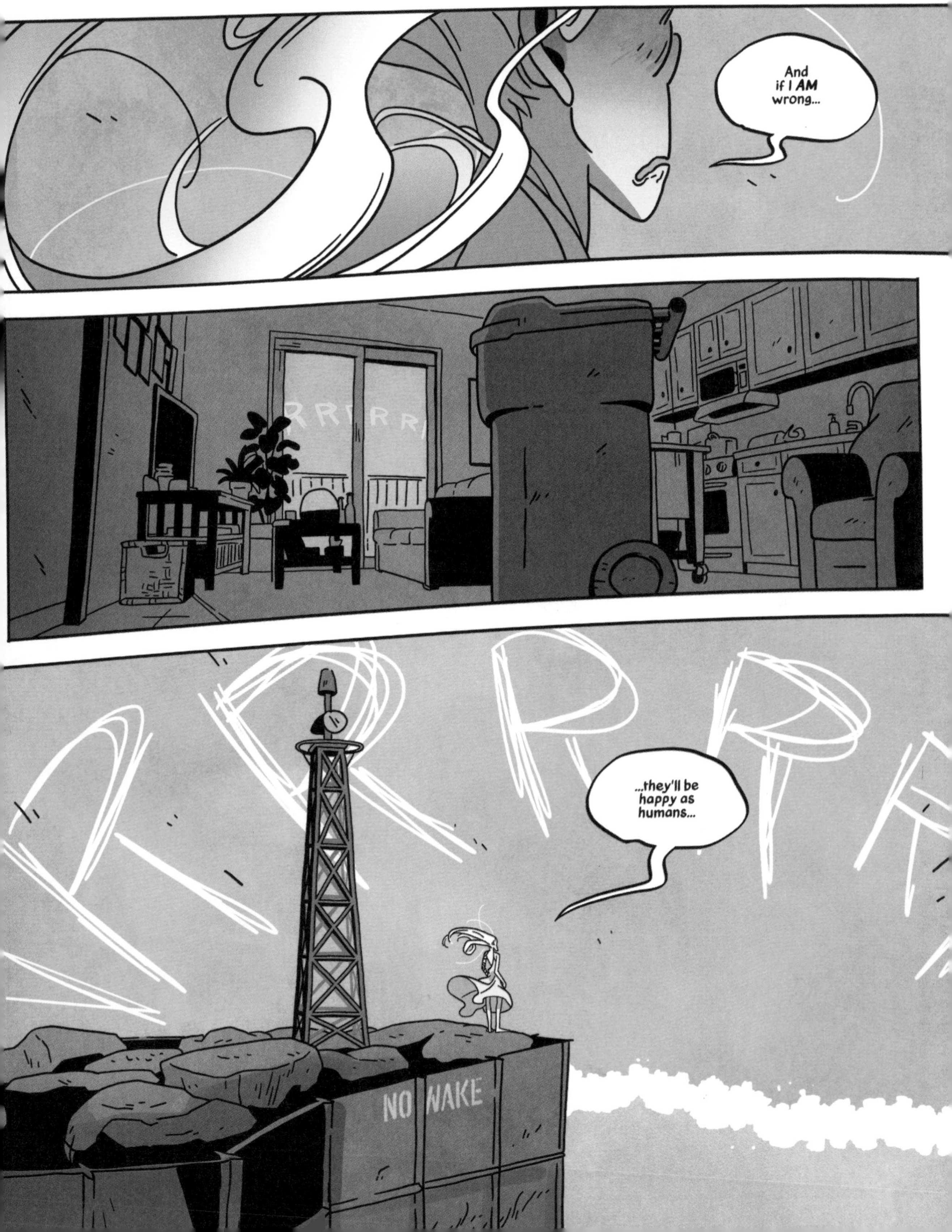
And if I AM wrong...
RRRRRR
...they'll be happy as humans...
NO WAKE

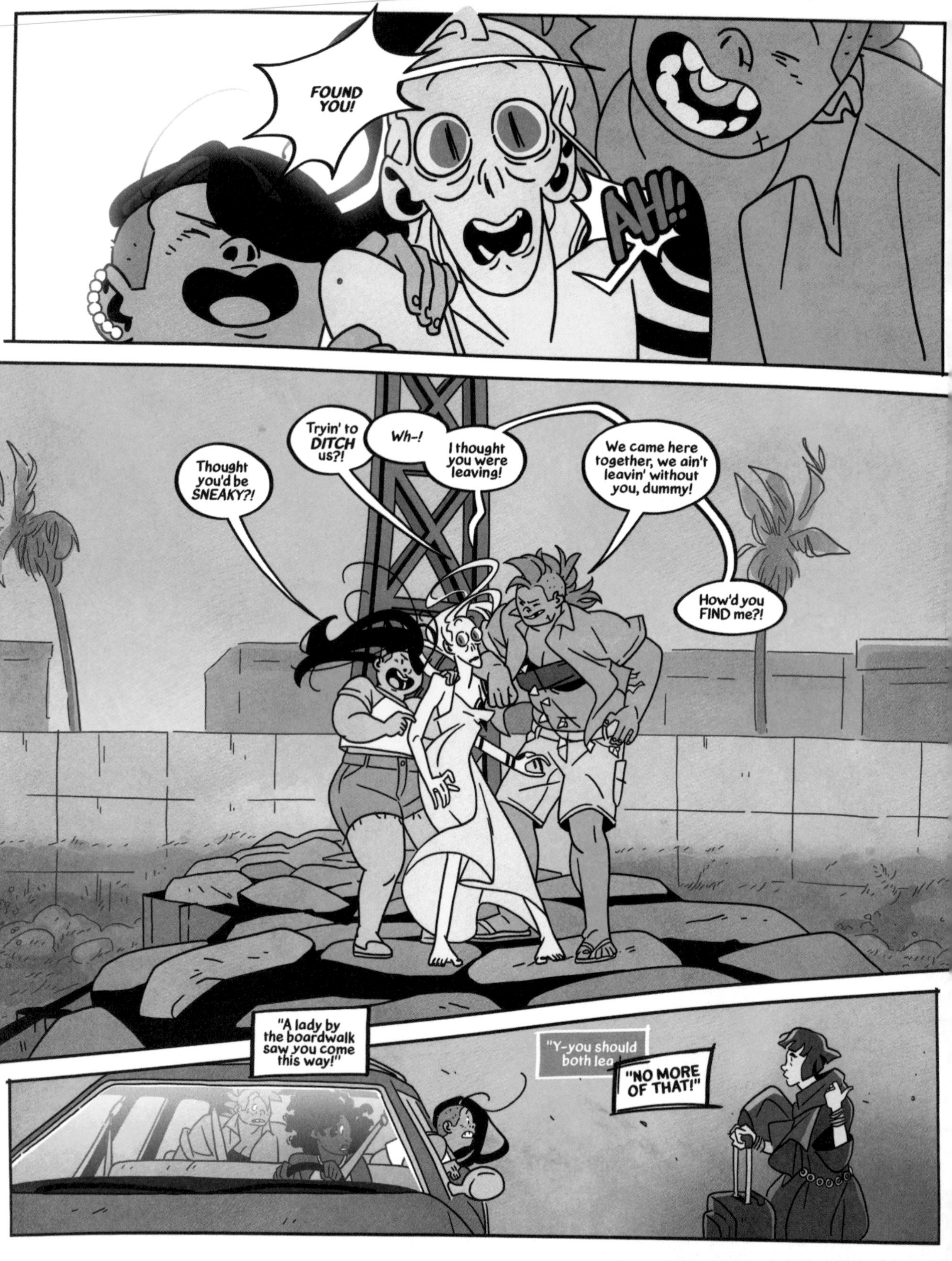
FOUND YOU!
AH!!
Thought you'd be SNEAKY?!
Tryin' to DITCH us?!
Wh-!
I thought you were leaving!
We came here together, we ain't leavin' without you, dummy!
How'd you FIND me?!
"A lady by the boardwalk saw you come this way!"
"Y-you should both lea
"NO MORE OF THAT!"

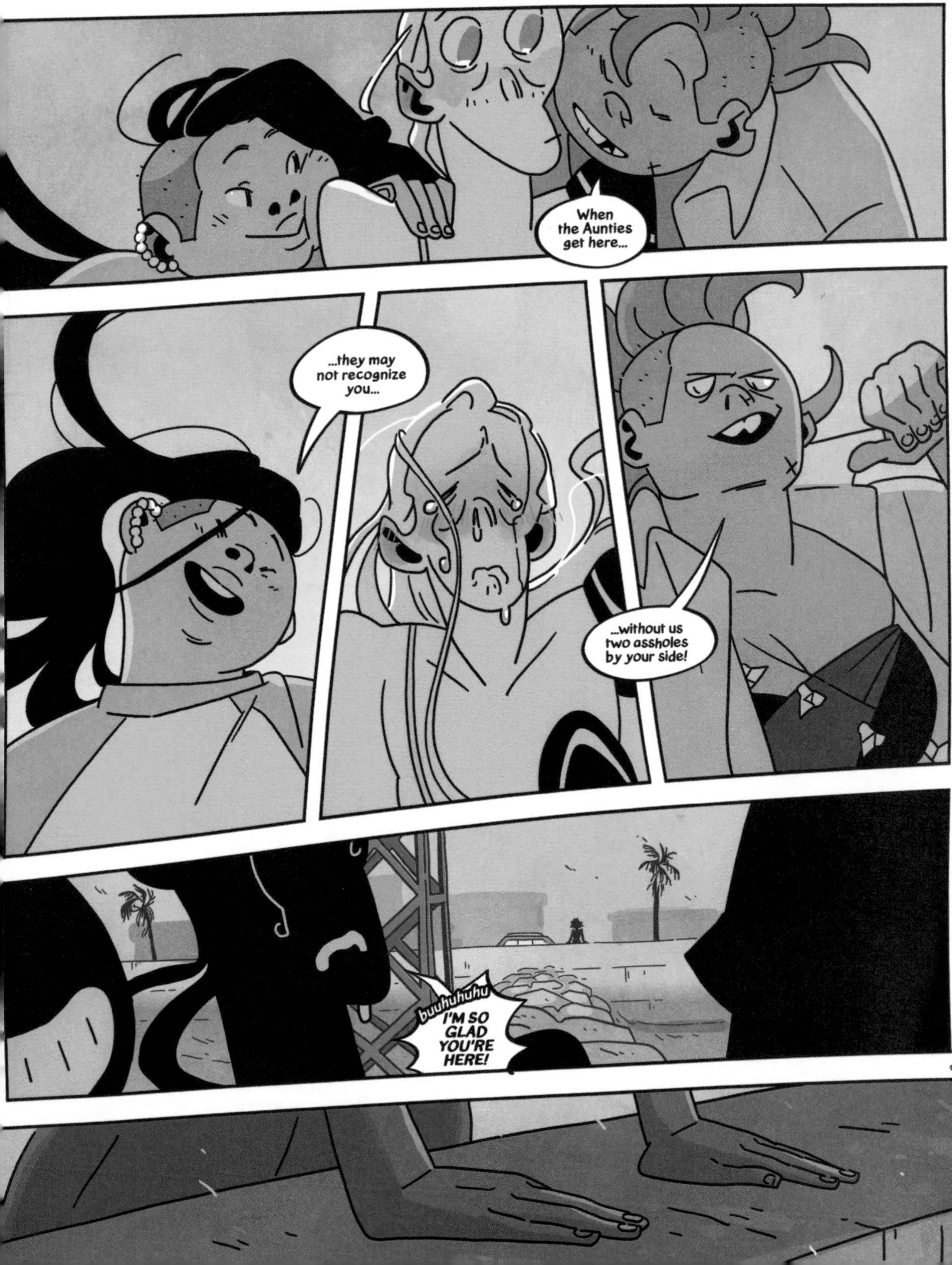
When the Aunties get here...
...they may not recognize you...
...without us two assholes by your side!
buuhuhuhu
I'M SO GLAD YOU'RE HERE!

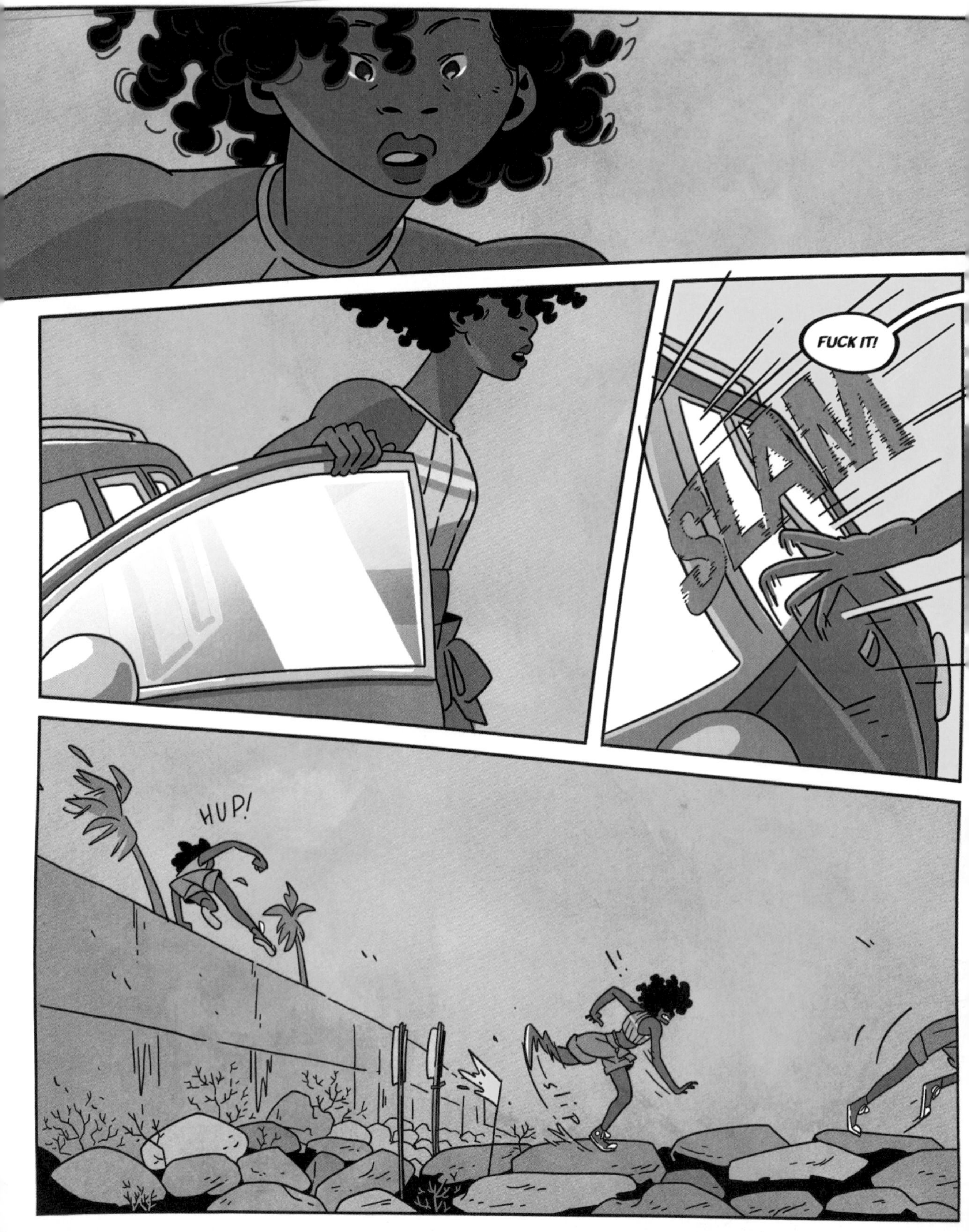
FUCK IT!
SLAM
HUP!
!!
SLIP

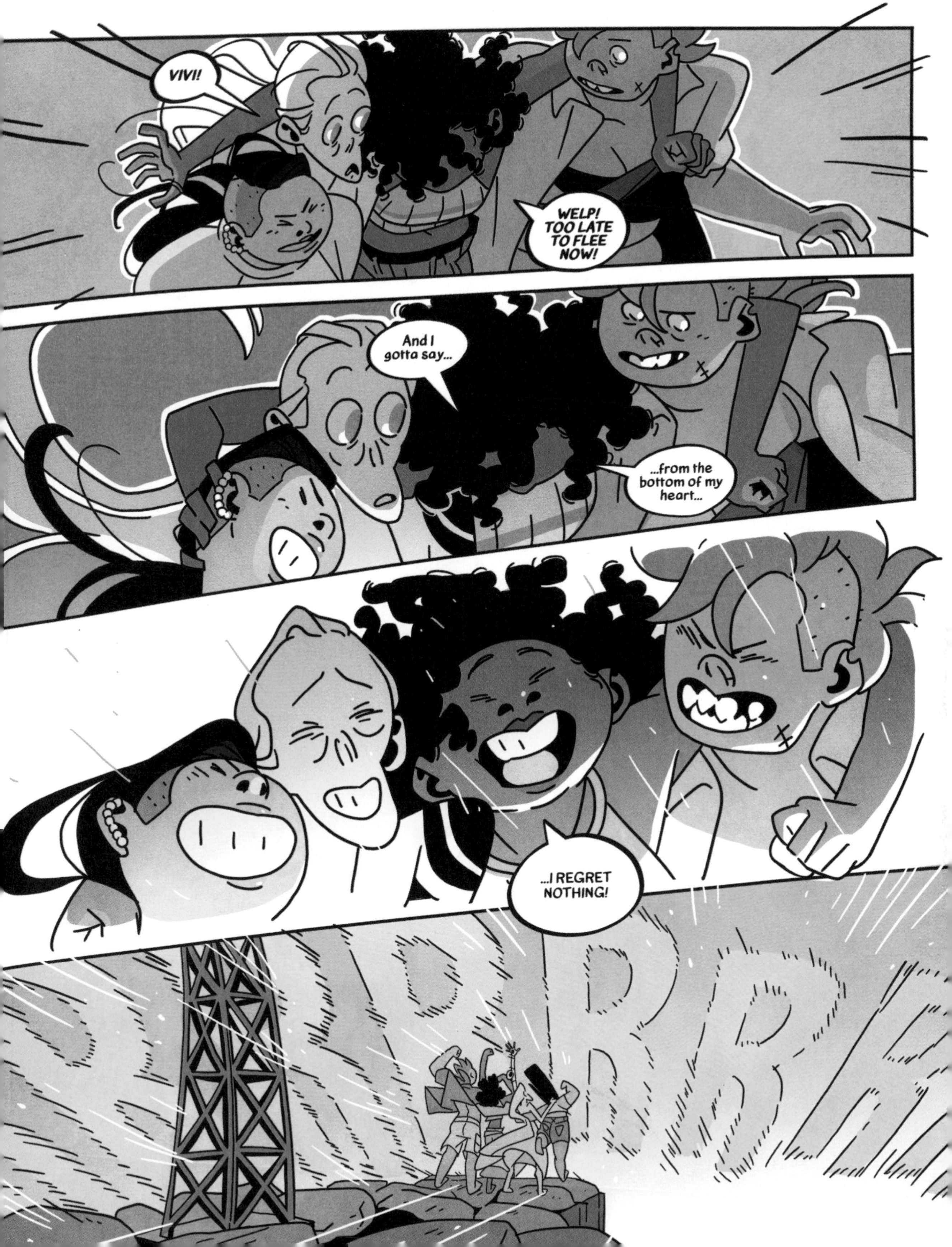
VIVI!
WELP! TOO LATE TO FLEE NOW!
And I gotta say...
...from the bottom of my heart...
...I REGRET NOTHING!

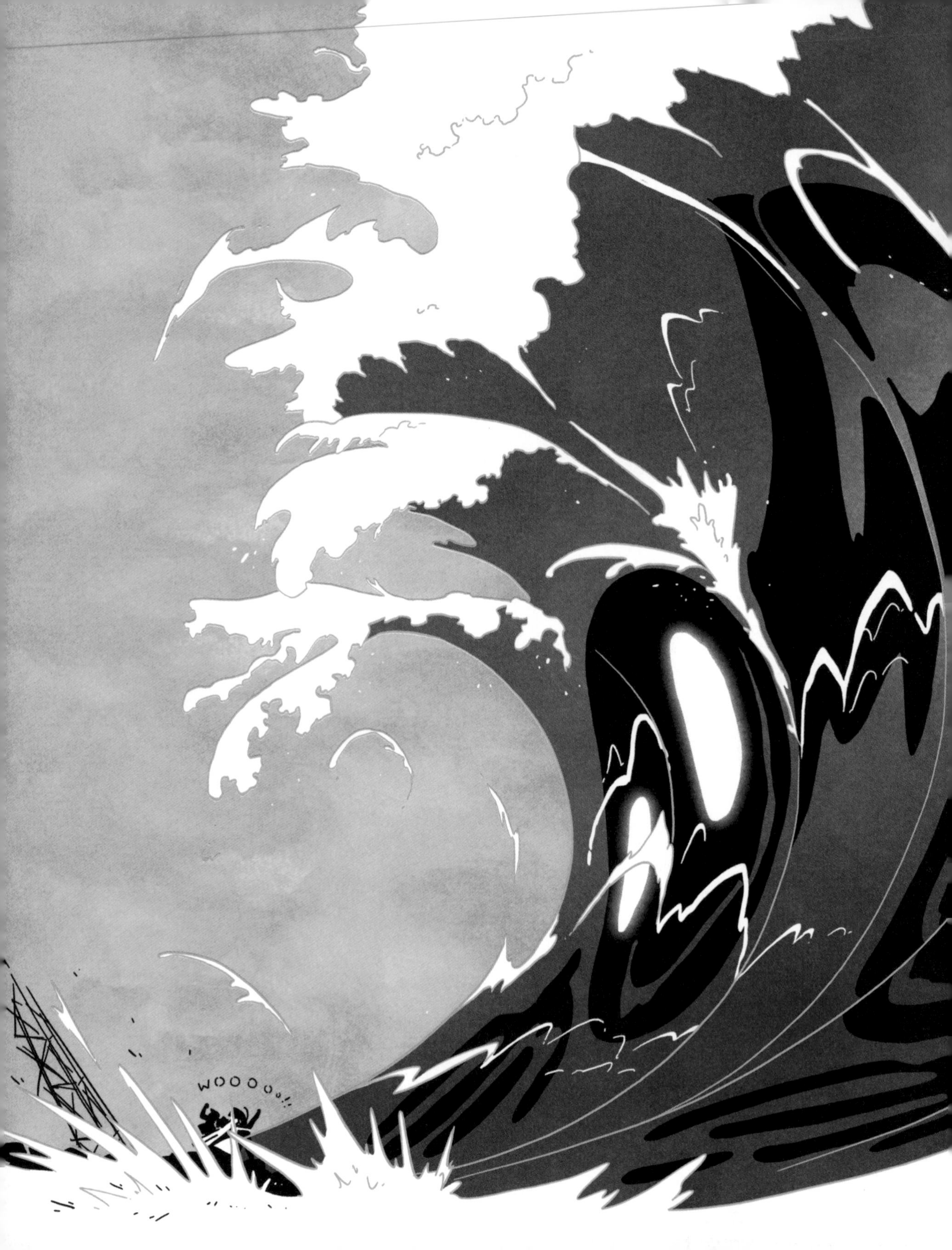
WOOOOo!!

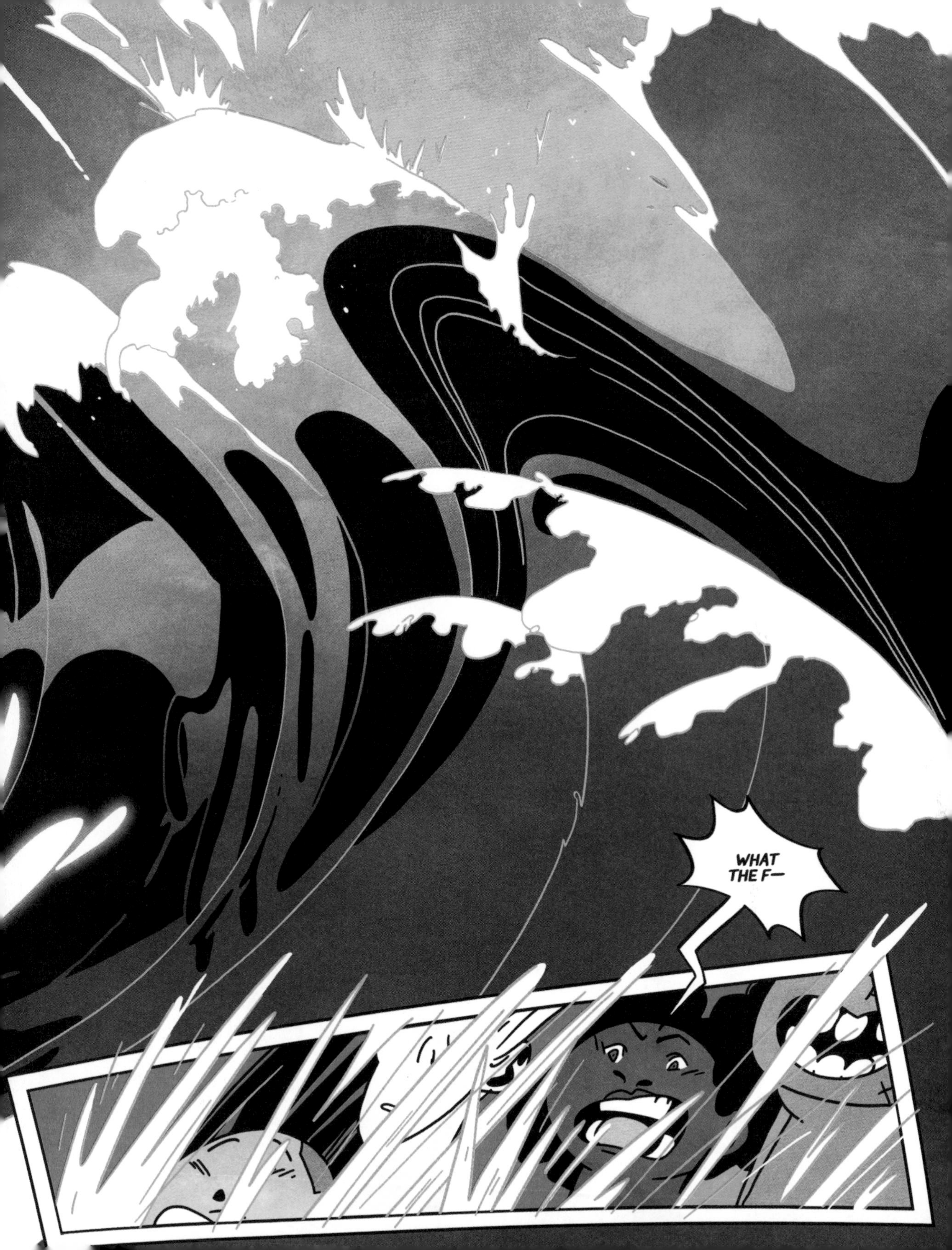
WHAT THE F—

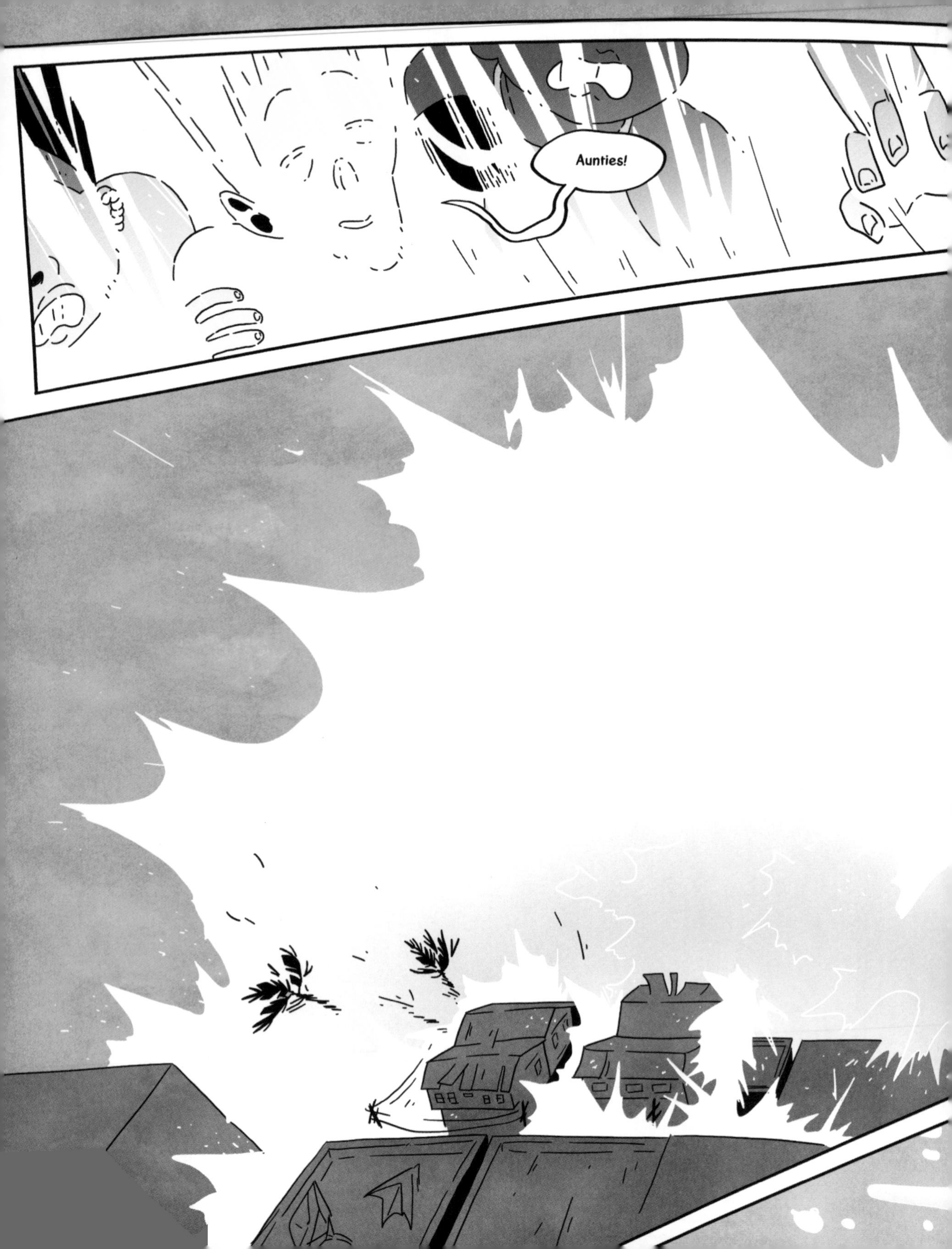
Aunties!

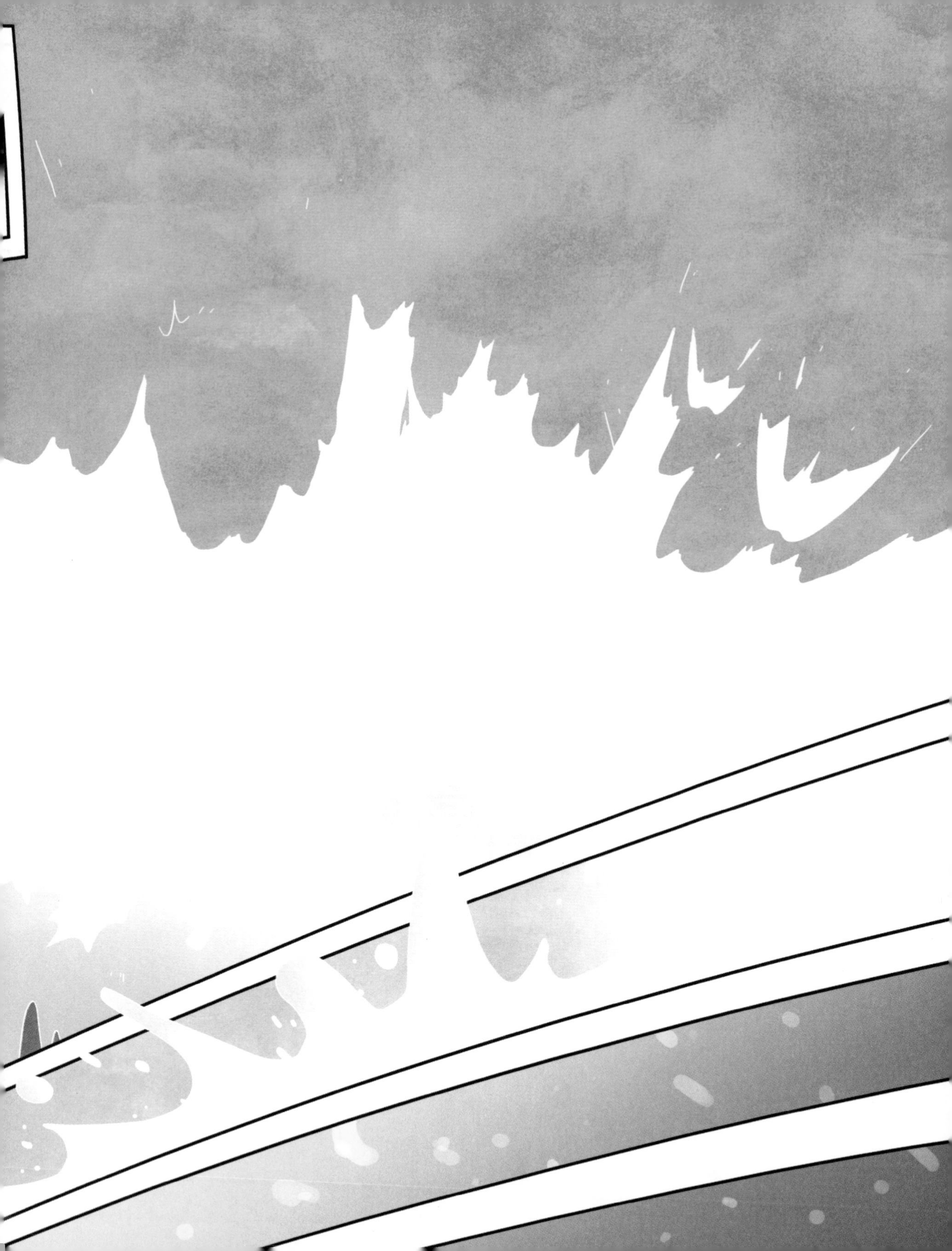

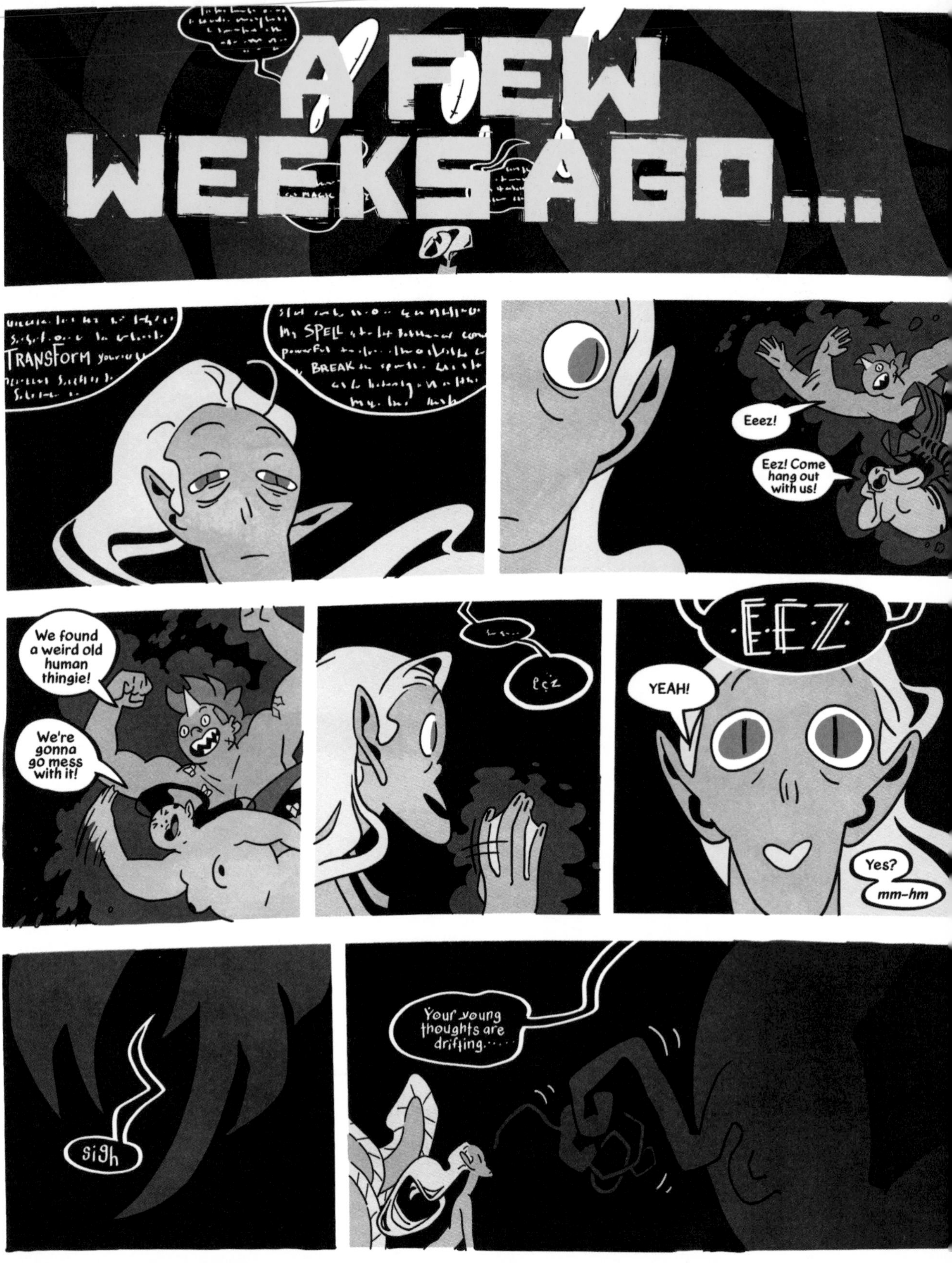
A FEW WEEKS AGO...
TRANSFORM
SPELL
BREAK
Eeez!
Eez! Come hang out with us!
We found a weird old human thingie!
We're gonna go mess with it!
EEZ
YEAH!
Yes?
mm-hm
sigh
Your young thoughts are drifting.....

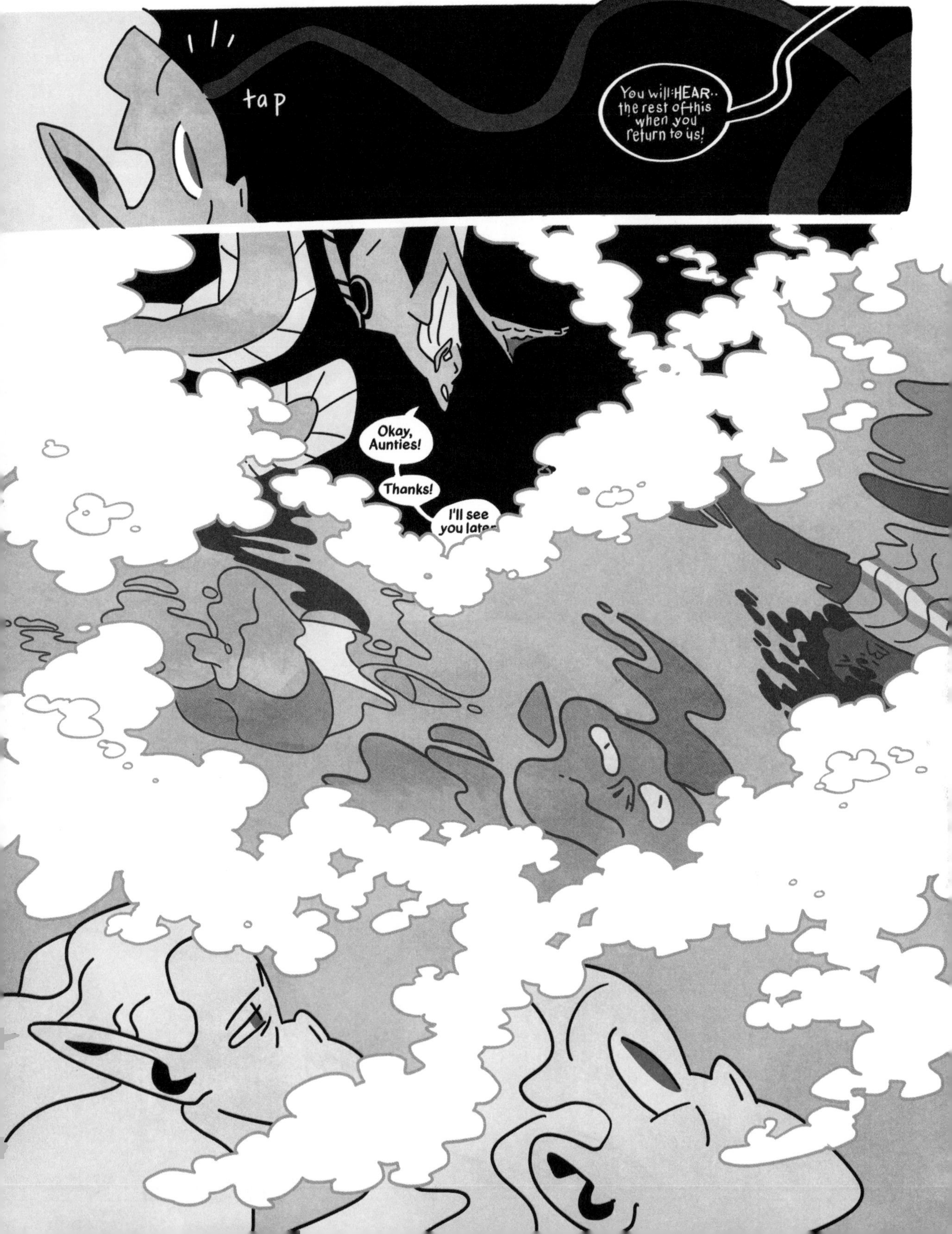
tap
You will HEAR..
the rest of this
when you
return to us!
Okay, Aunties!
Thanks!
I'll see
you later

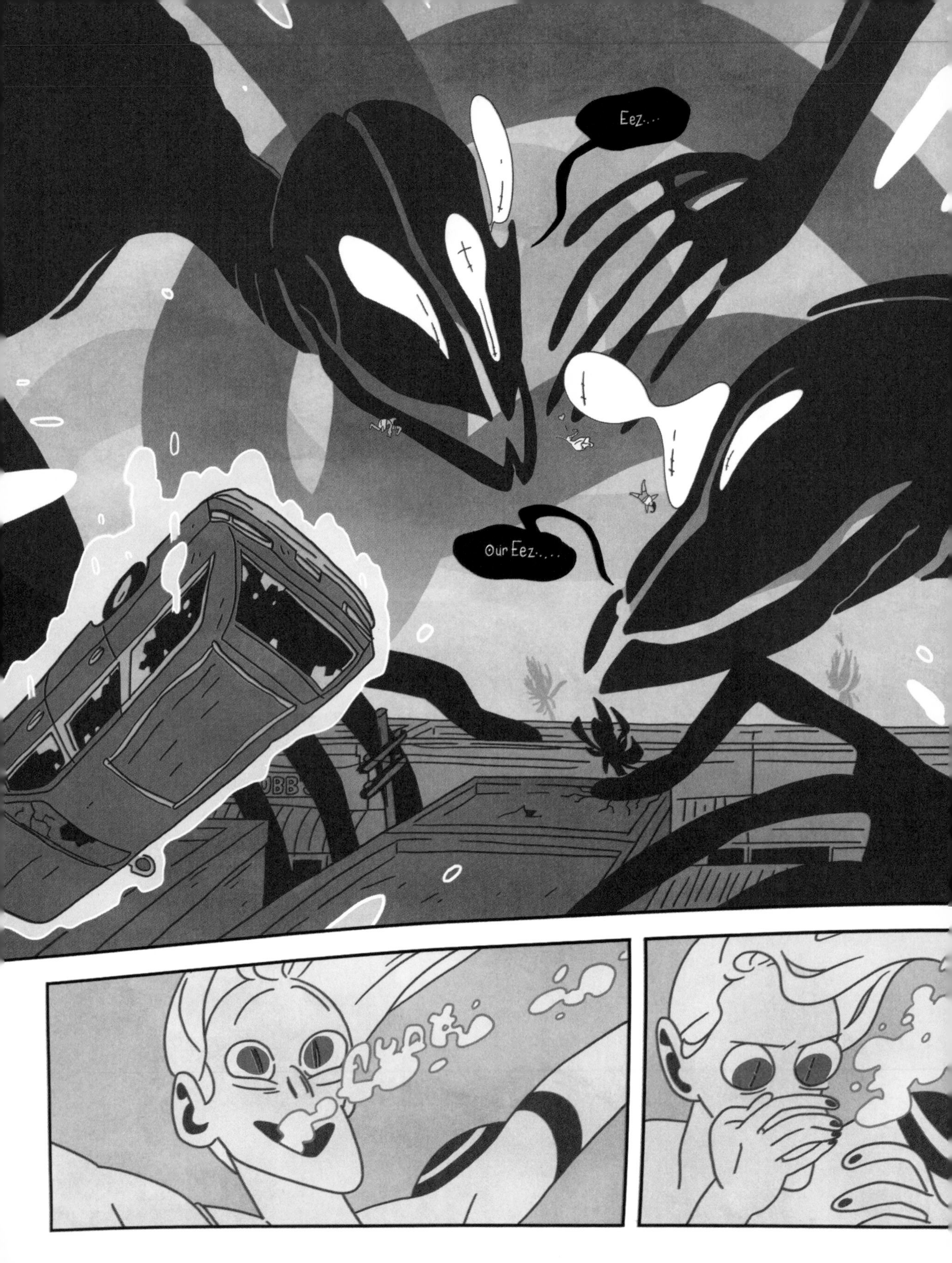
Eez...
Our Eez....

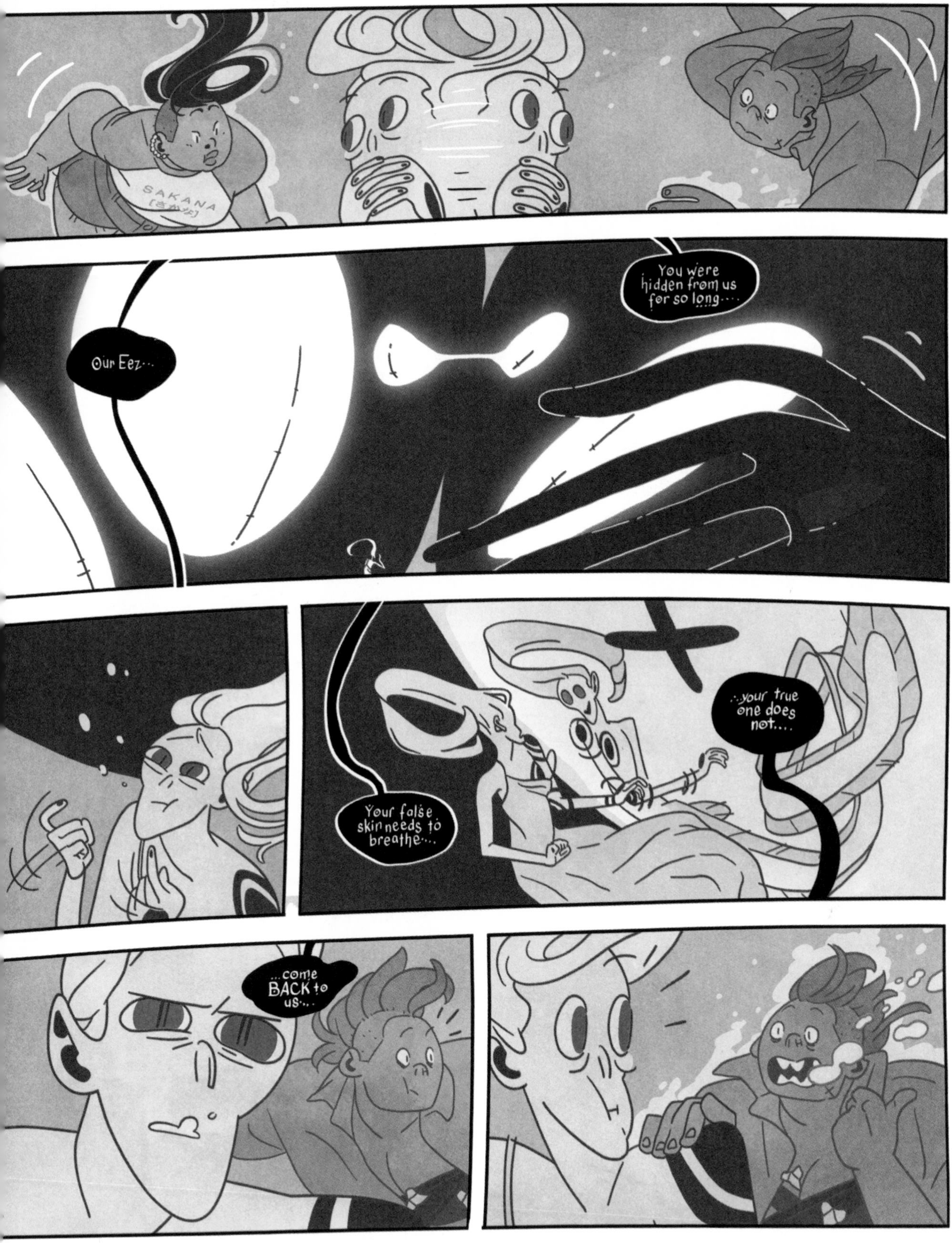
SAKANA
Our Eez...
You were hidden from us for so long....
Your false skin needs to breathe...
...your true one does not....
...come BACK to us...

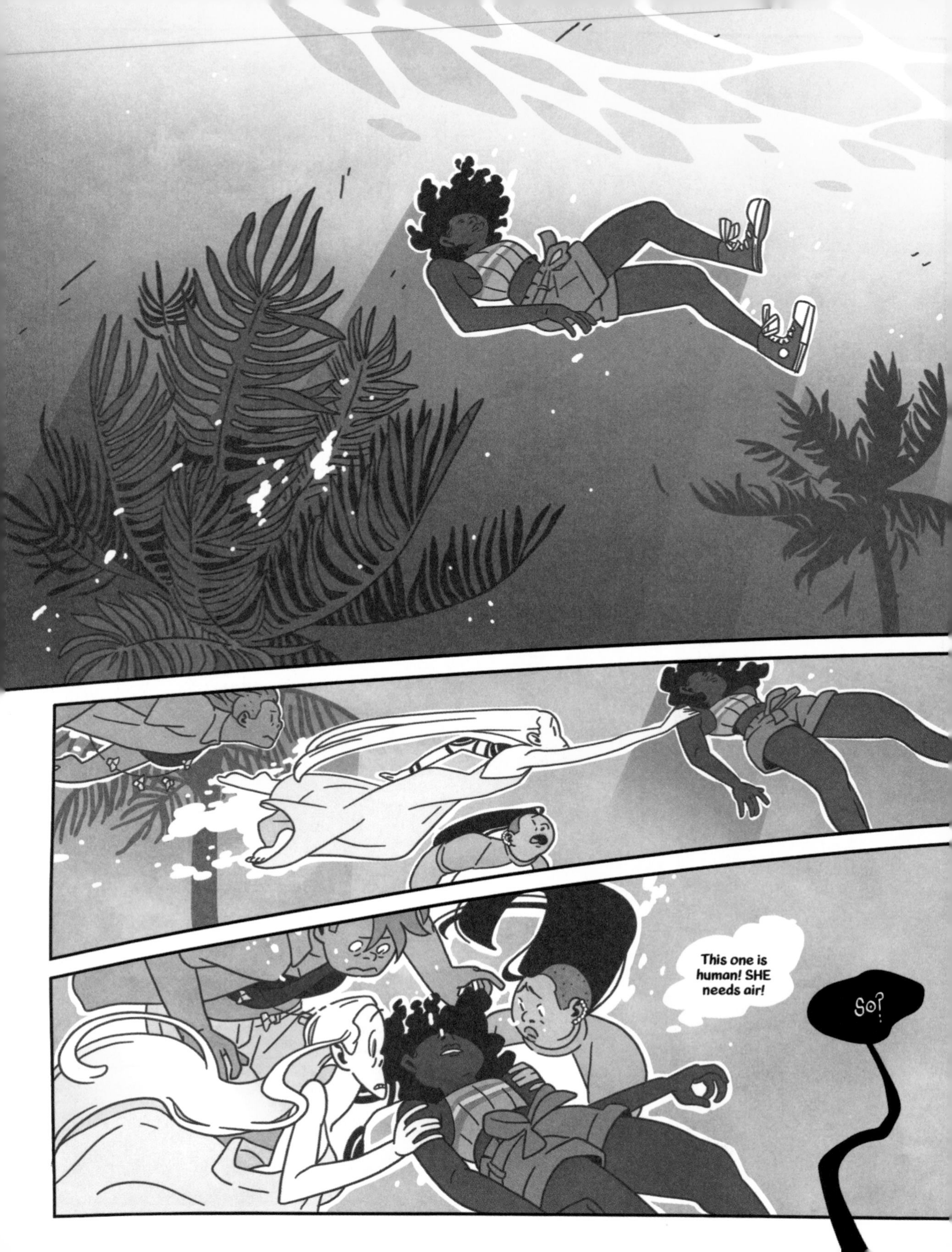
This one is human! SHE needs air!
SO?

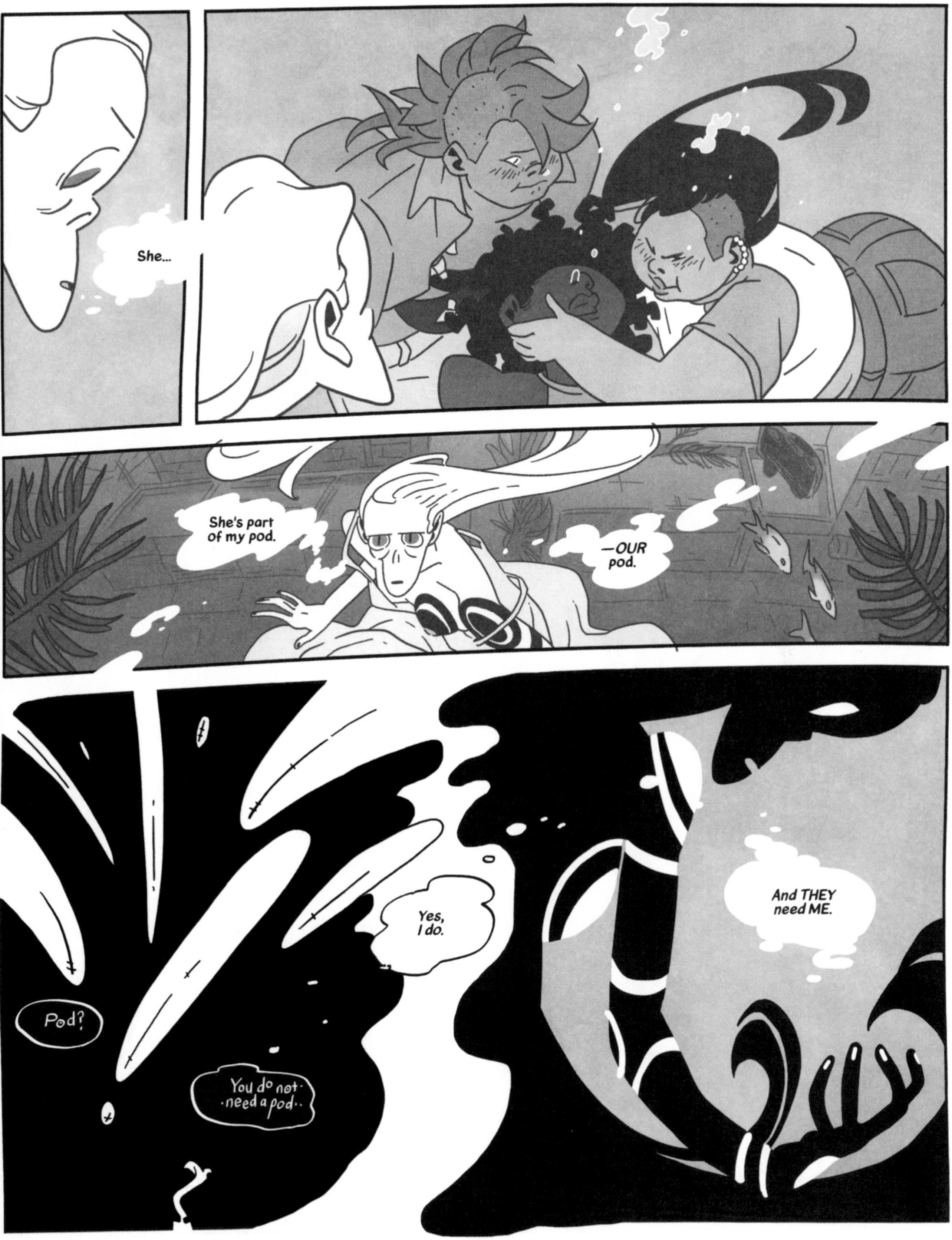
She...
She's part of my pod.
—OUR pod.
Pod?
You do not need a pod.
Yes, I do.
And THEY need ME.

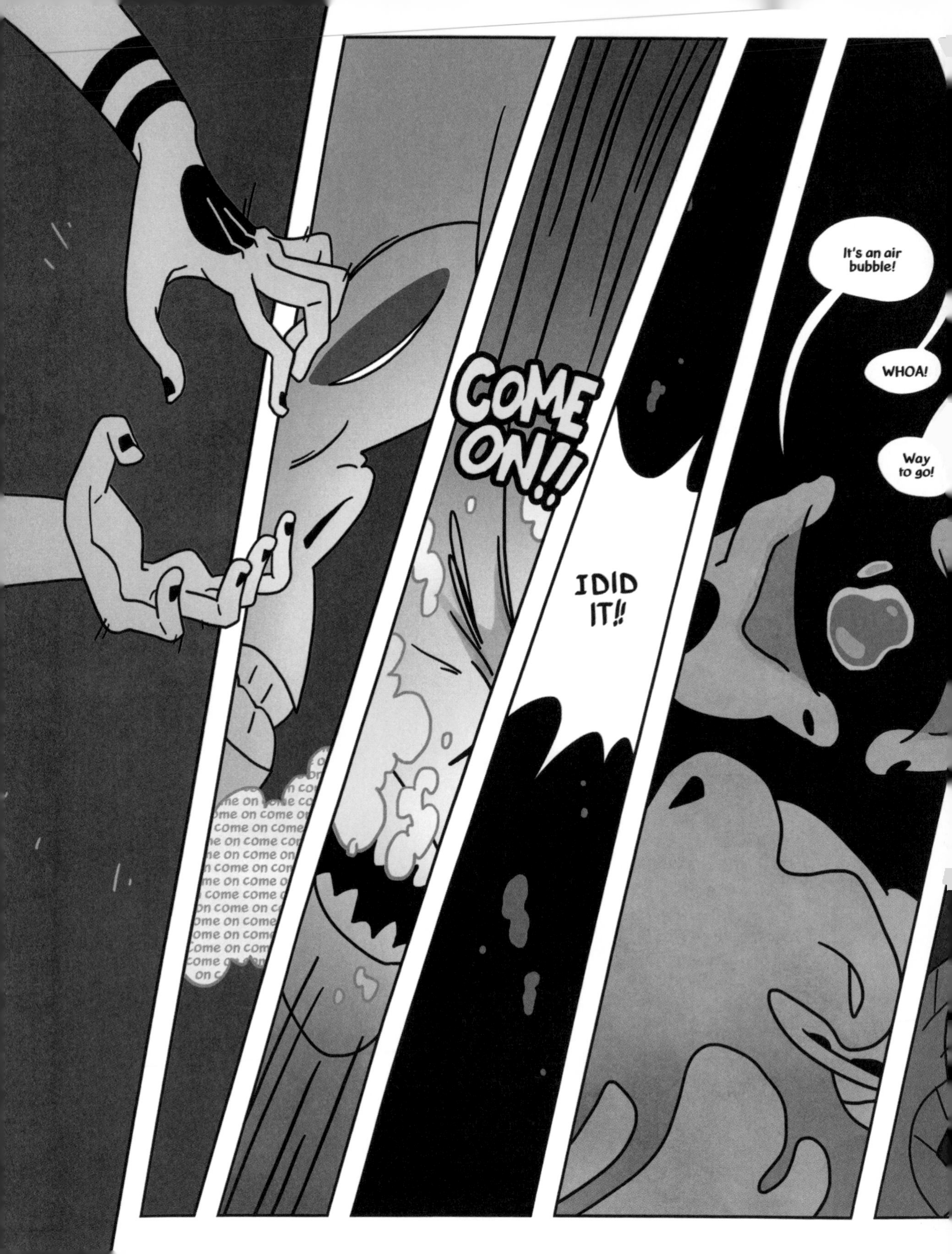
come on come on come on come on come on come on come on come on come on
COME ON!!
I DID IT!!
It's an air bubble!
WHOA!
Way to go!

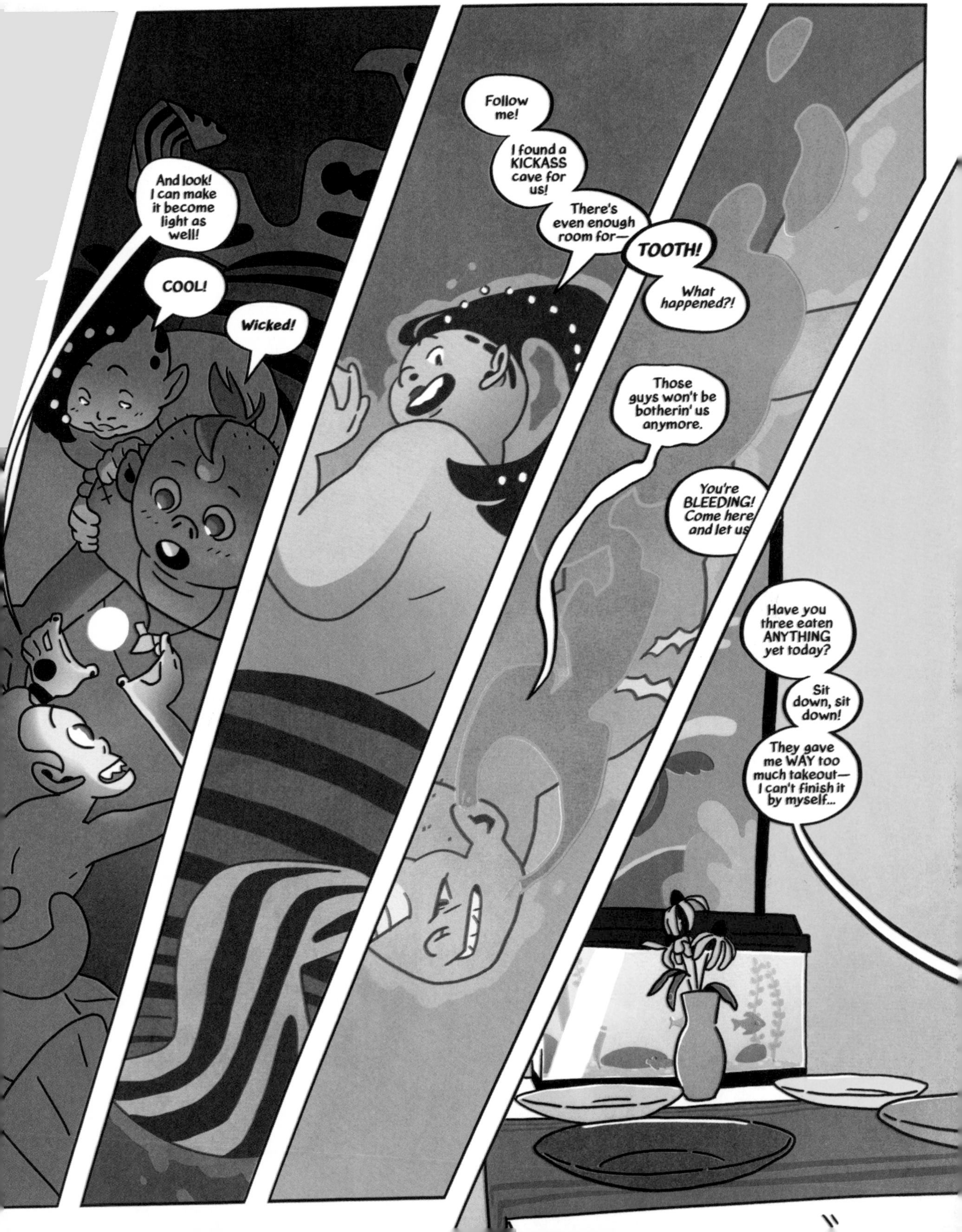
And look! I can make it become light as well!
COOL!
Wicked!
Follow me!
I found a KICKASS cave for us!
There's even enough room for—
TOOTH!
What happened?!
Those guys won't be botherin' us anymore.
You're BLEEDING! Come here and let us
Have you three eaten ANYTHING yet today?
Sit down, sit down!
They gave me WAY too much takeout— I can't finish it by myself...

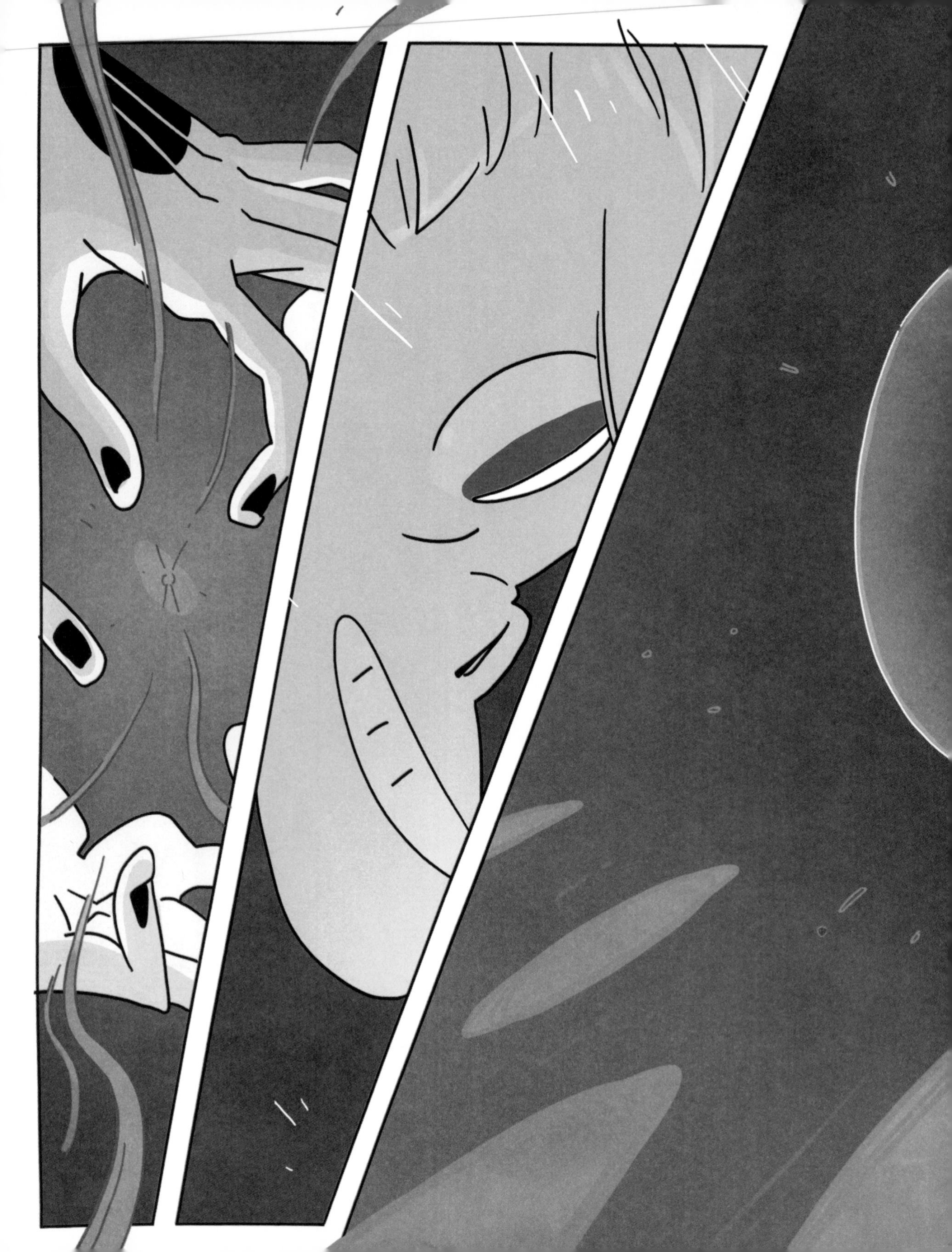

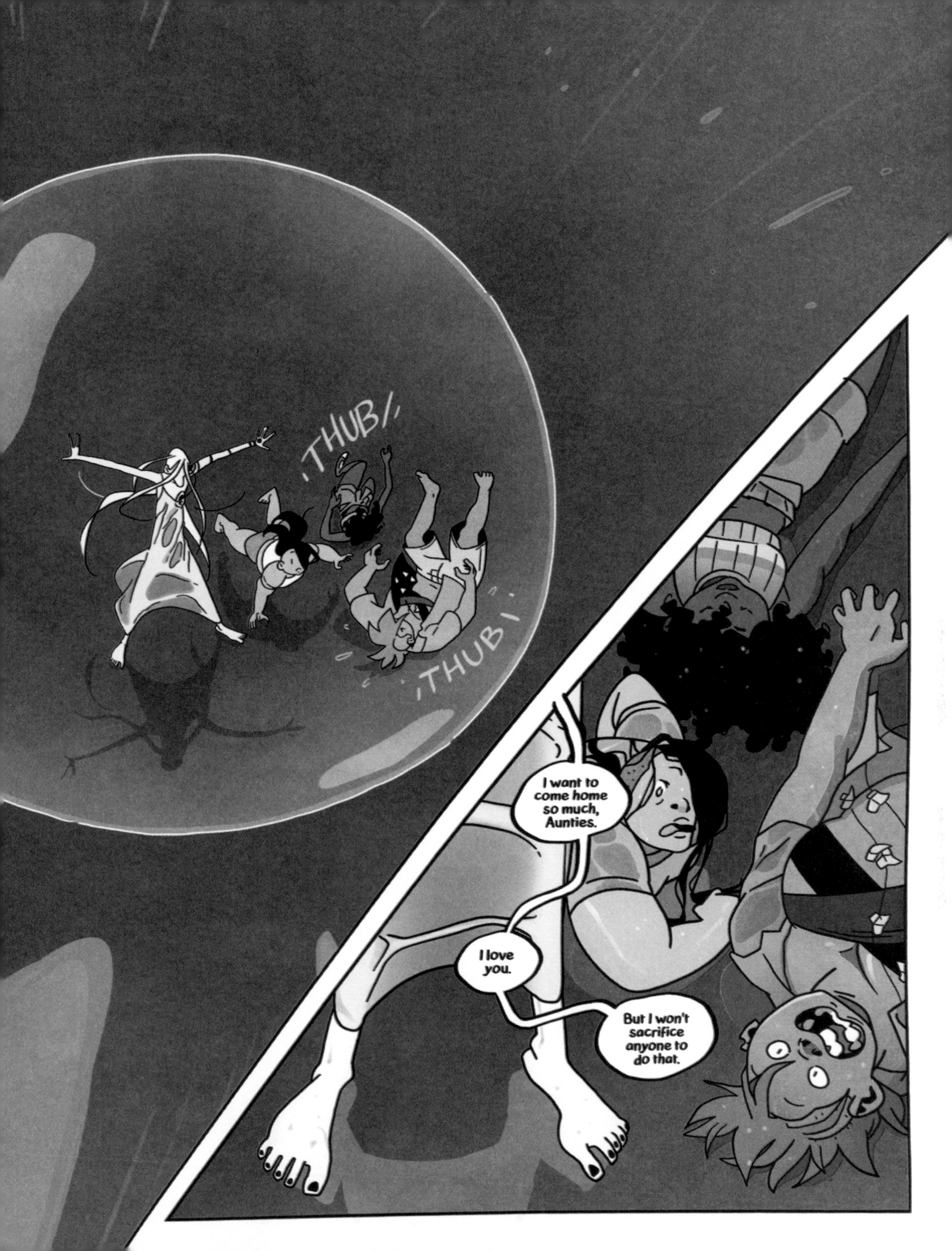

THUB
THUB
I want to come home so much, Aunties.
I love you.
But I won't sacrifice anyone to do that.

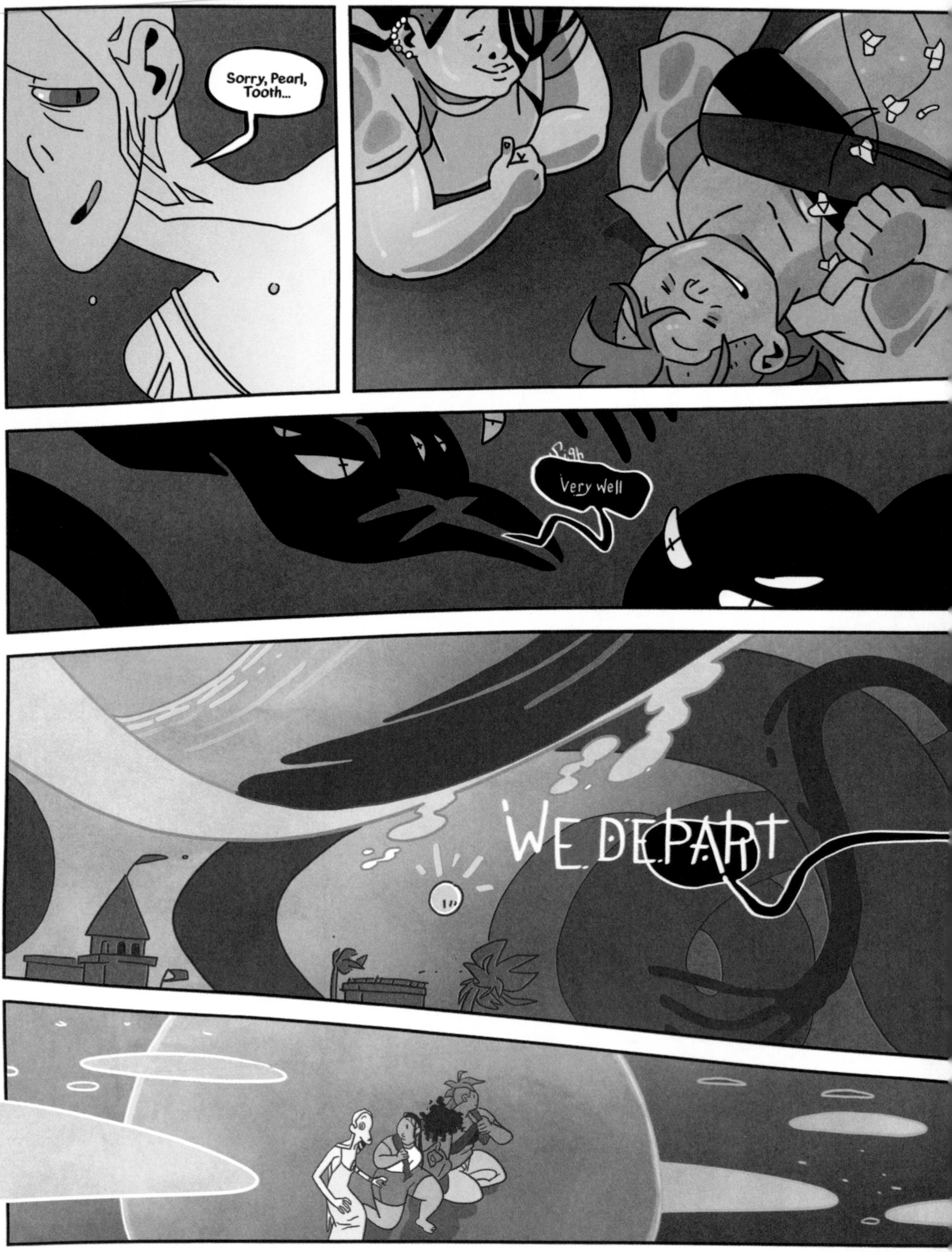
Sorry, Pearl, Tooth...
Sigh
Very Well
WE DEPART

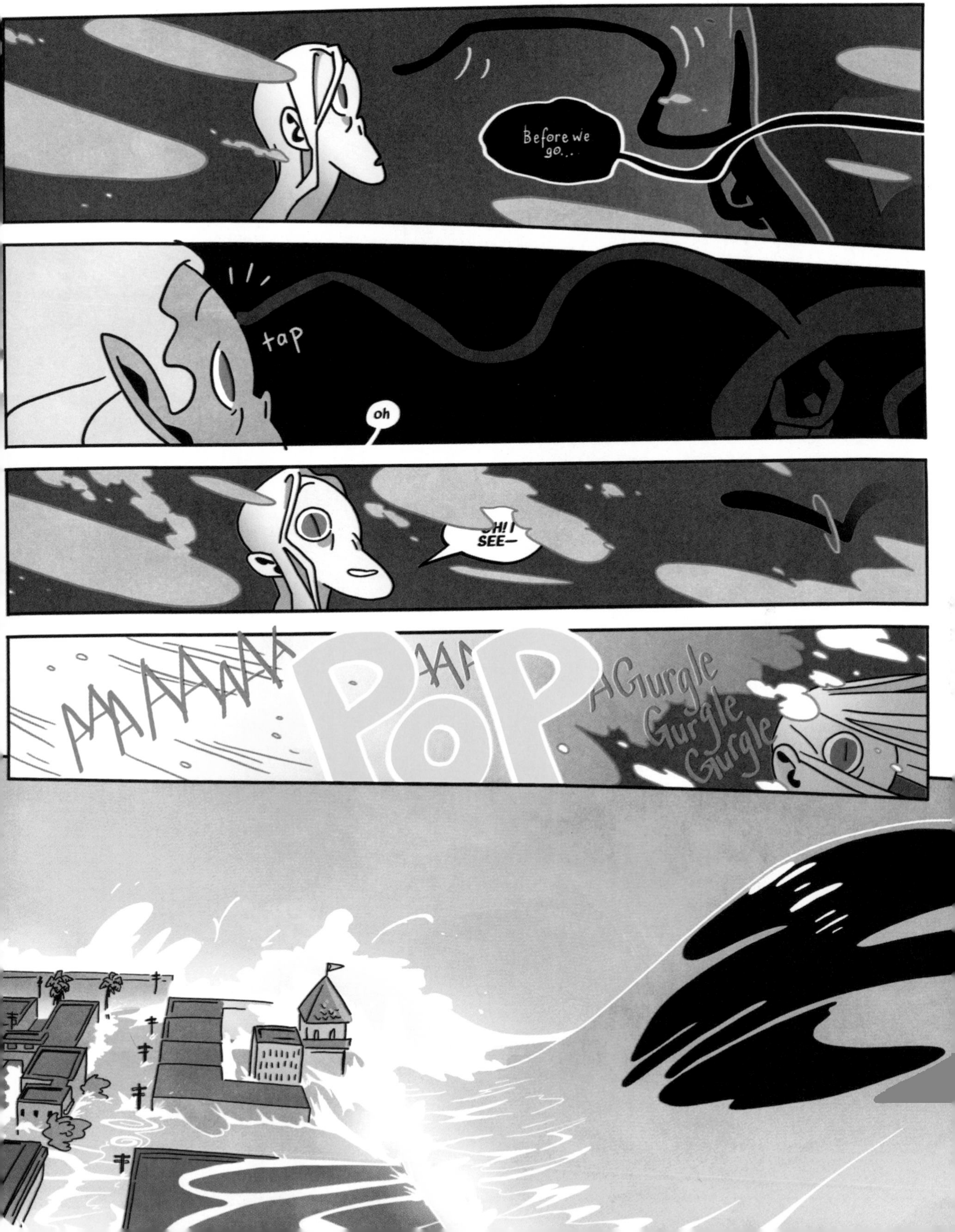
Before we go...
tap
oh
OH! I SEE—
POP
Gurgle
Gurgle
Gurgle
Gurgle

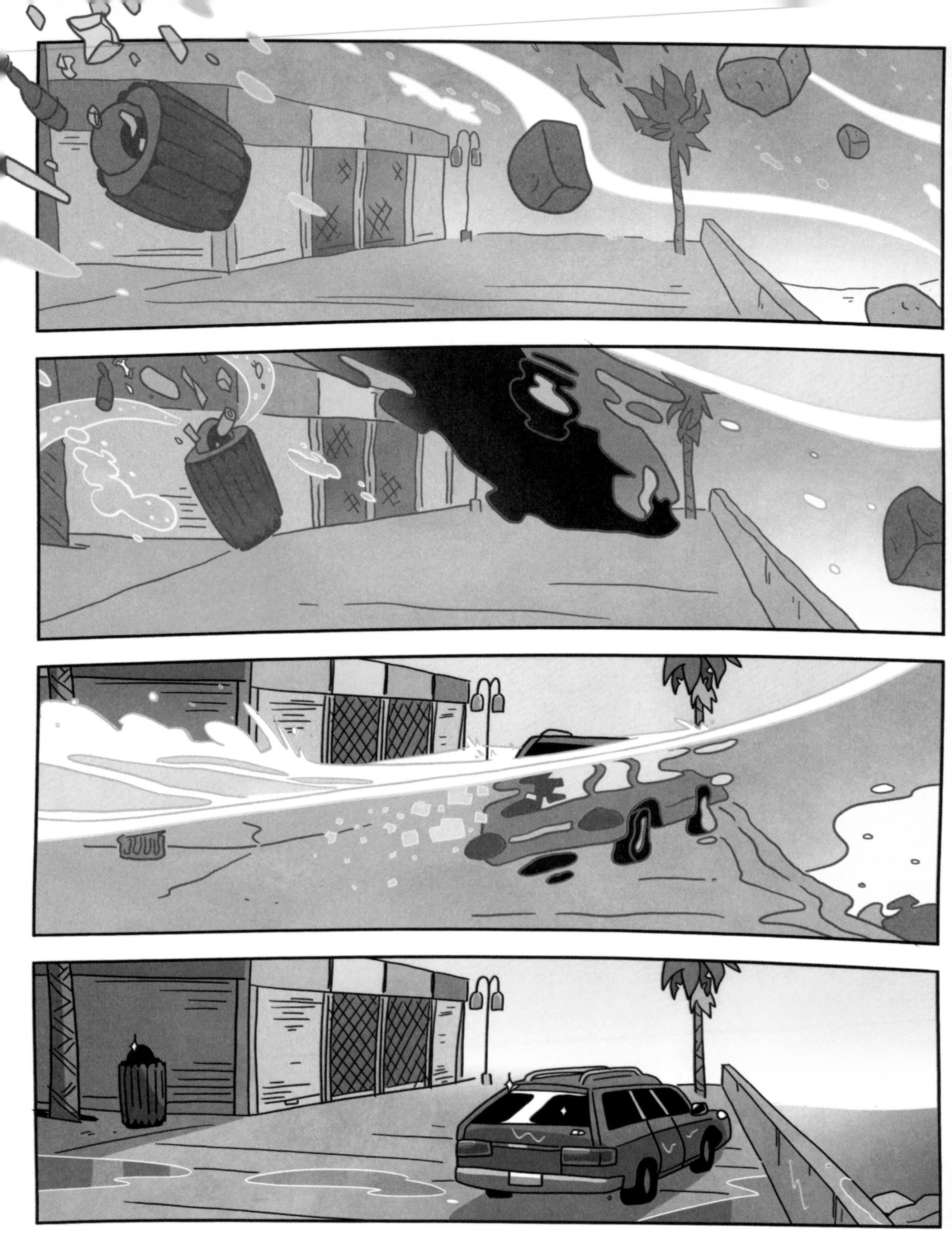

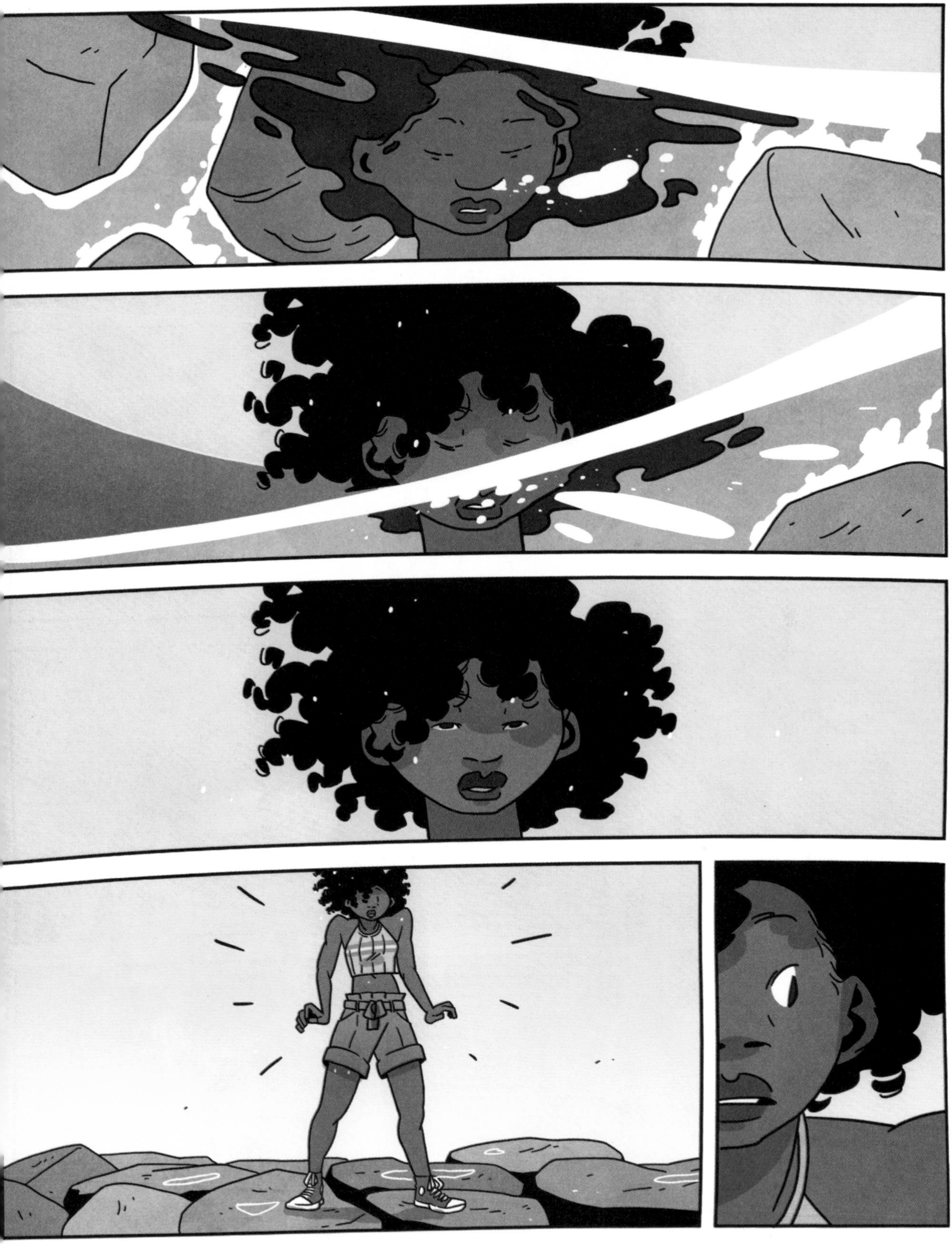

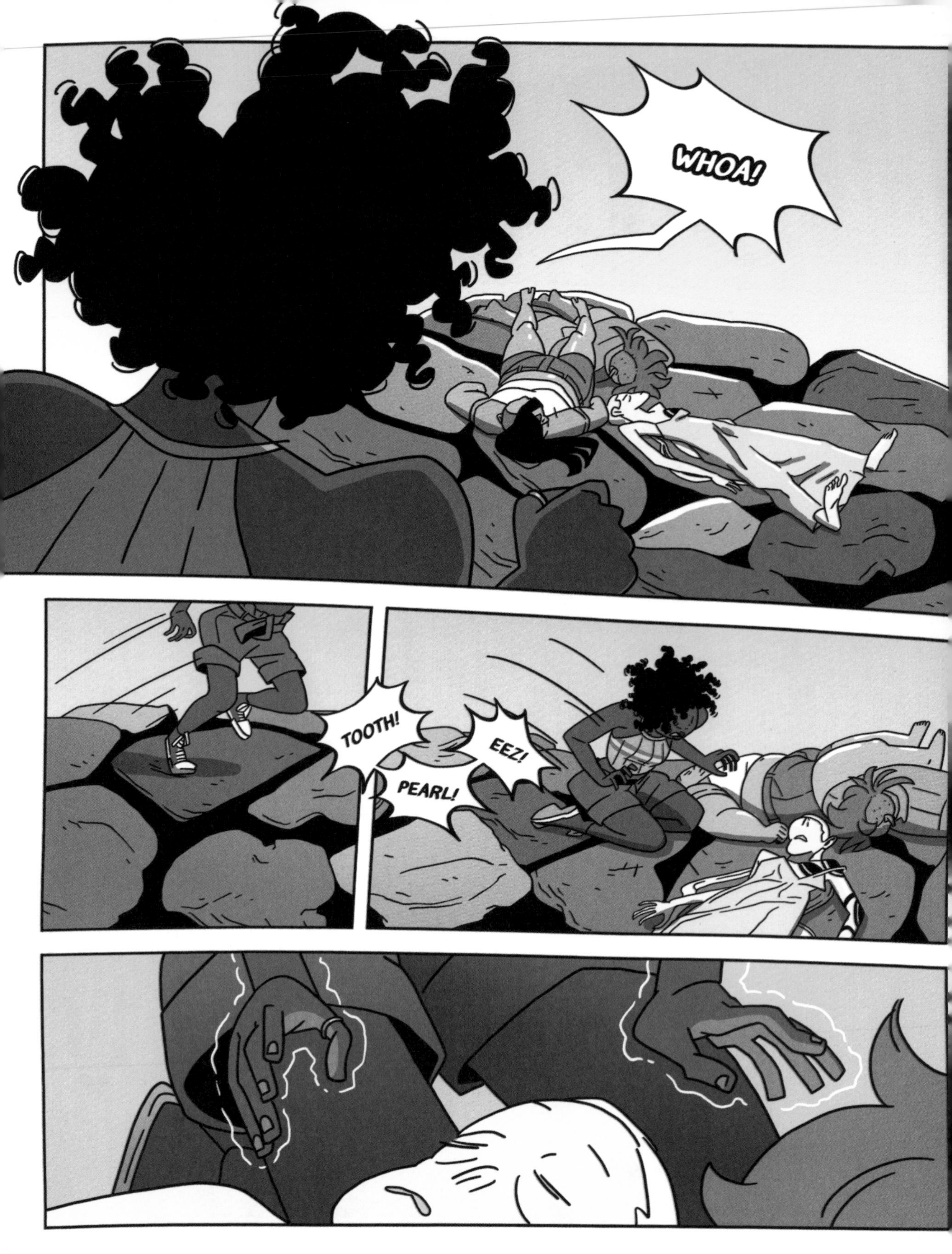
WHOA!
TOOTH!
EEZ!
PEARL!

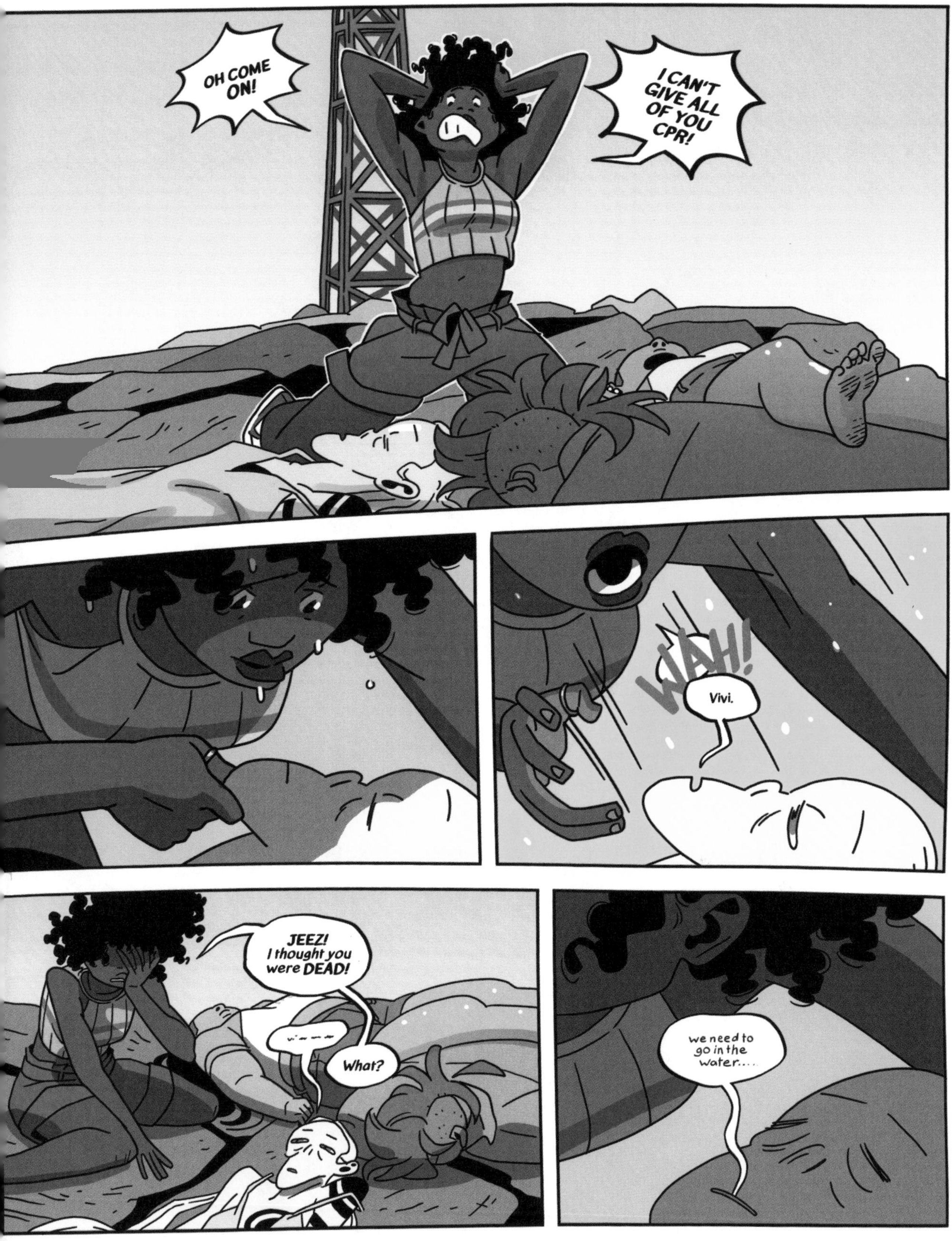
OH COME ON!
I CAN'T GIVE ALL OF YOU CPR!
WAH!
Vivi.
JEEZ! I thought you were DEAD!
What?
we need to go in the water....

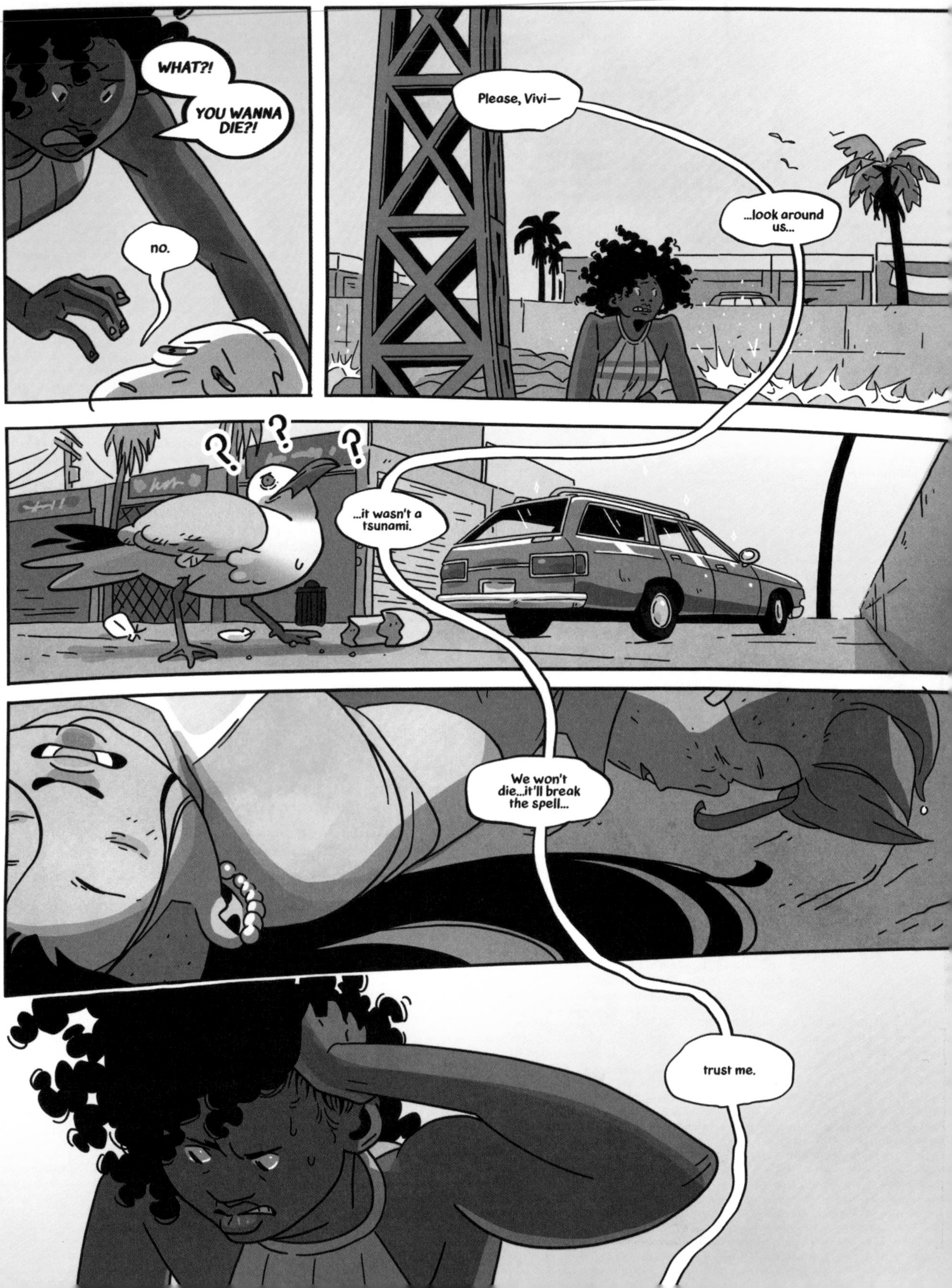
WHAT?!
YOU WANNA DIE?!
no.
Please, Vivi—
...look around us...
...it wasn't a tsunami.
We won't die...it'll break the spell...
trust me.

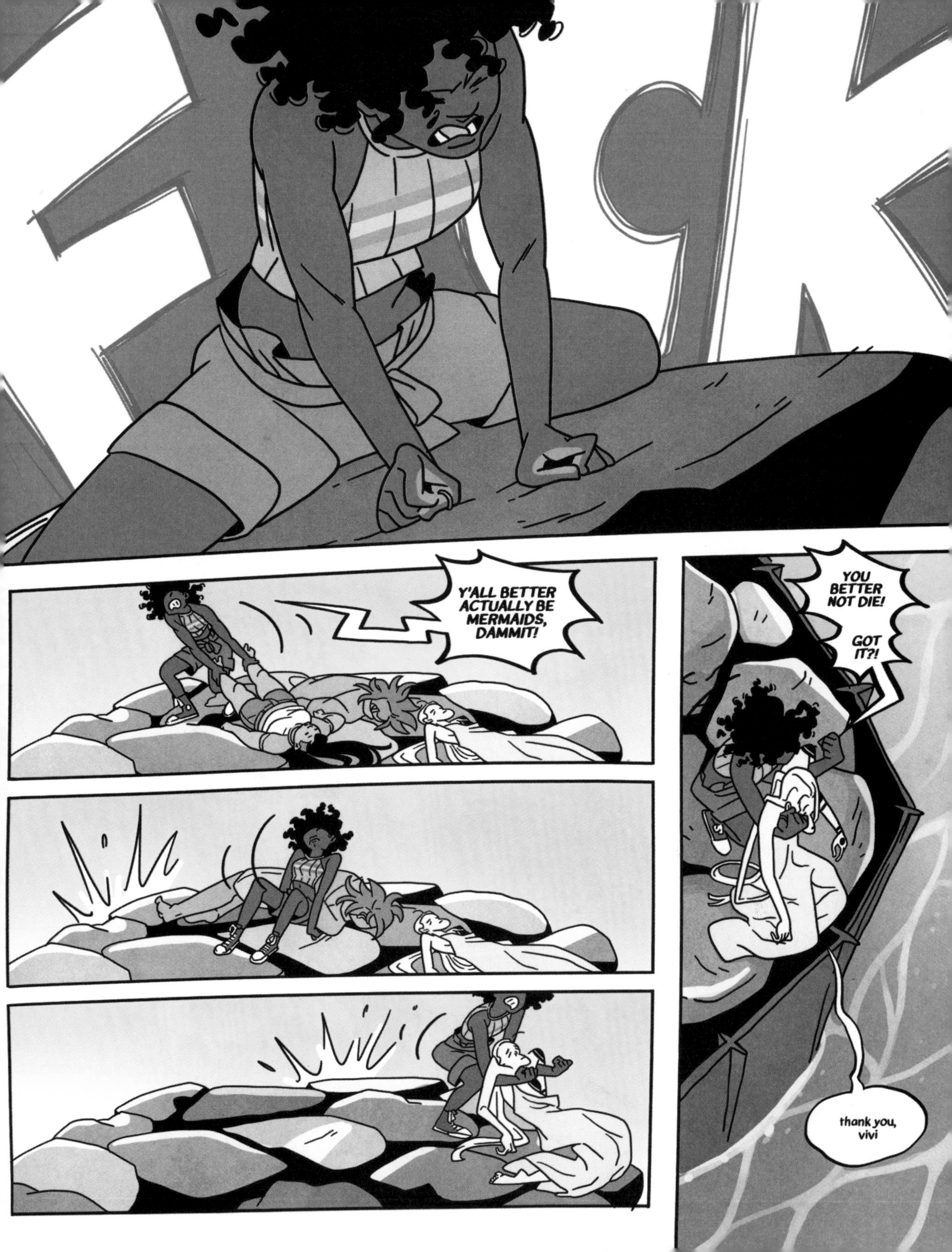
Y'ALL BETTER ACTUALLY BE MERMAIDS, DAMMIT!
YOU BETTER NOT DIE!
GOT IT?!
thank you, vivi

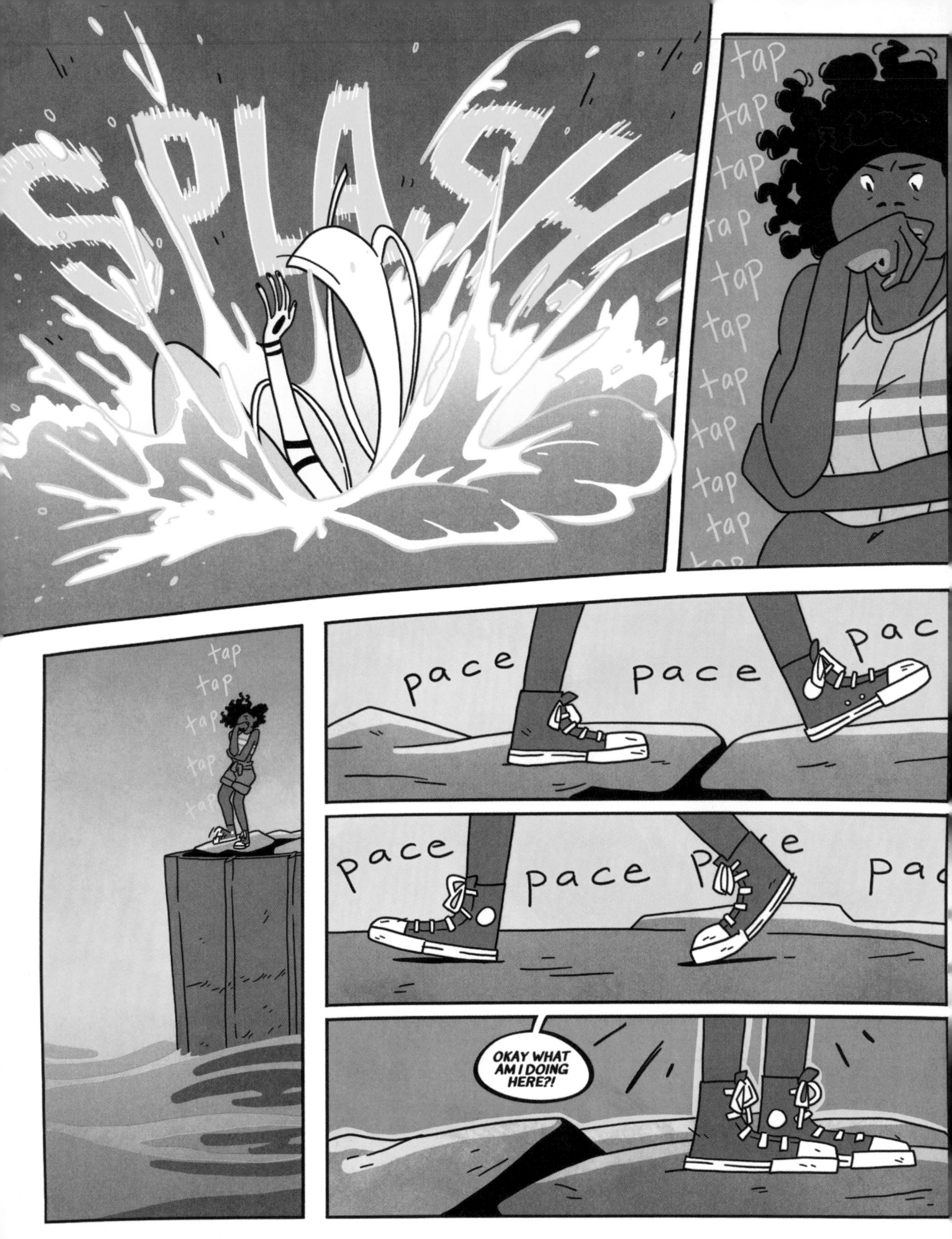
SPLASH
tap tap tap tap tap tap tap tap tap tap
tap tap tap tap tap
pace pace pace
pace pace pace
OKAY WHAT AM I DOING HERE?!

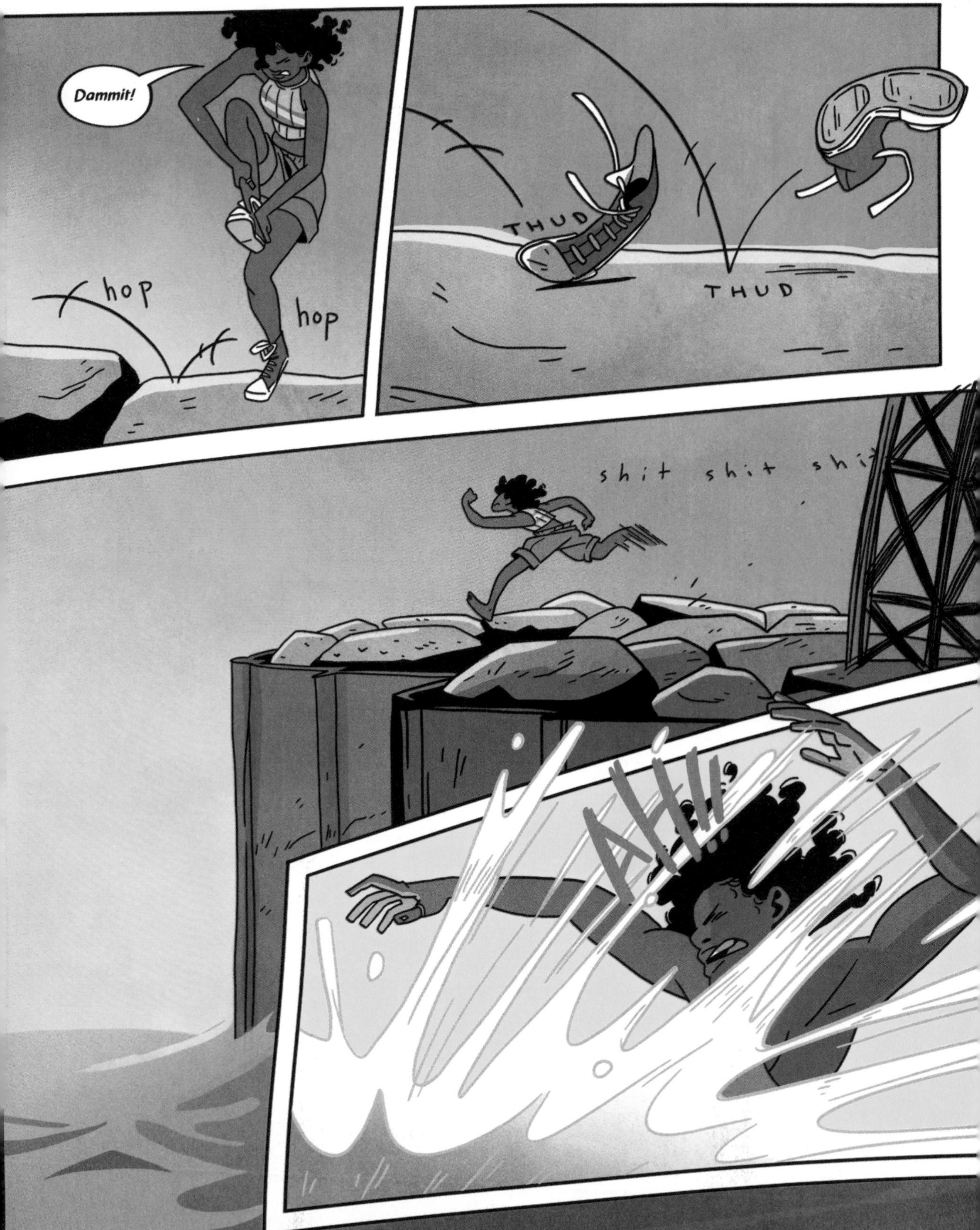
Dammit!
hop
hop
THUD
THUD
shit shit shi
AHH

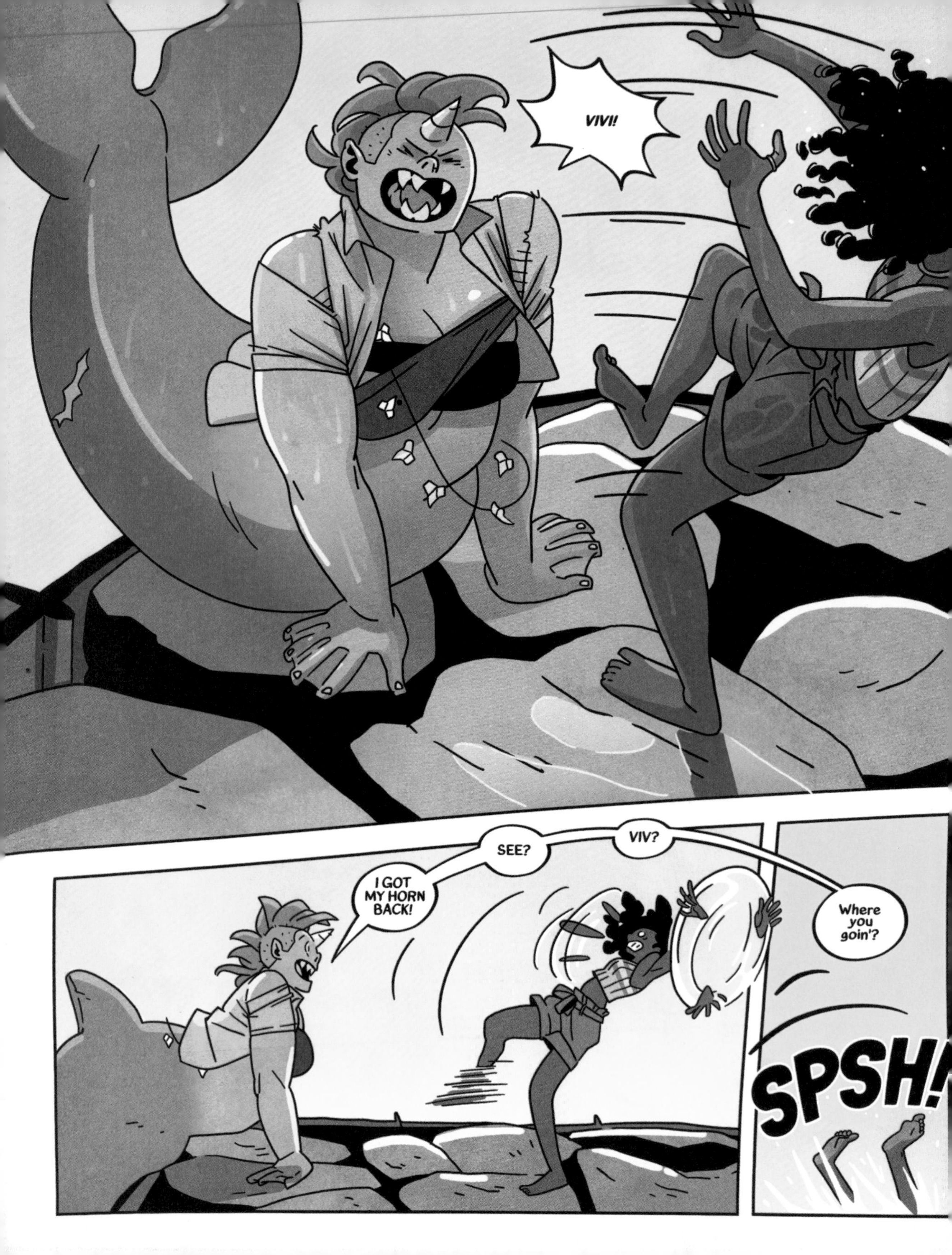
VIVI!
I GOT MY HORN BACK!
SEE?
VIV?
Where you goin'?
SPSH!

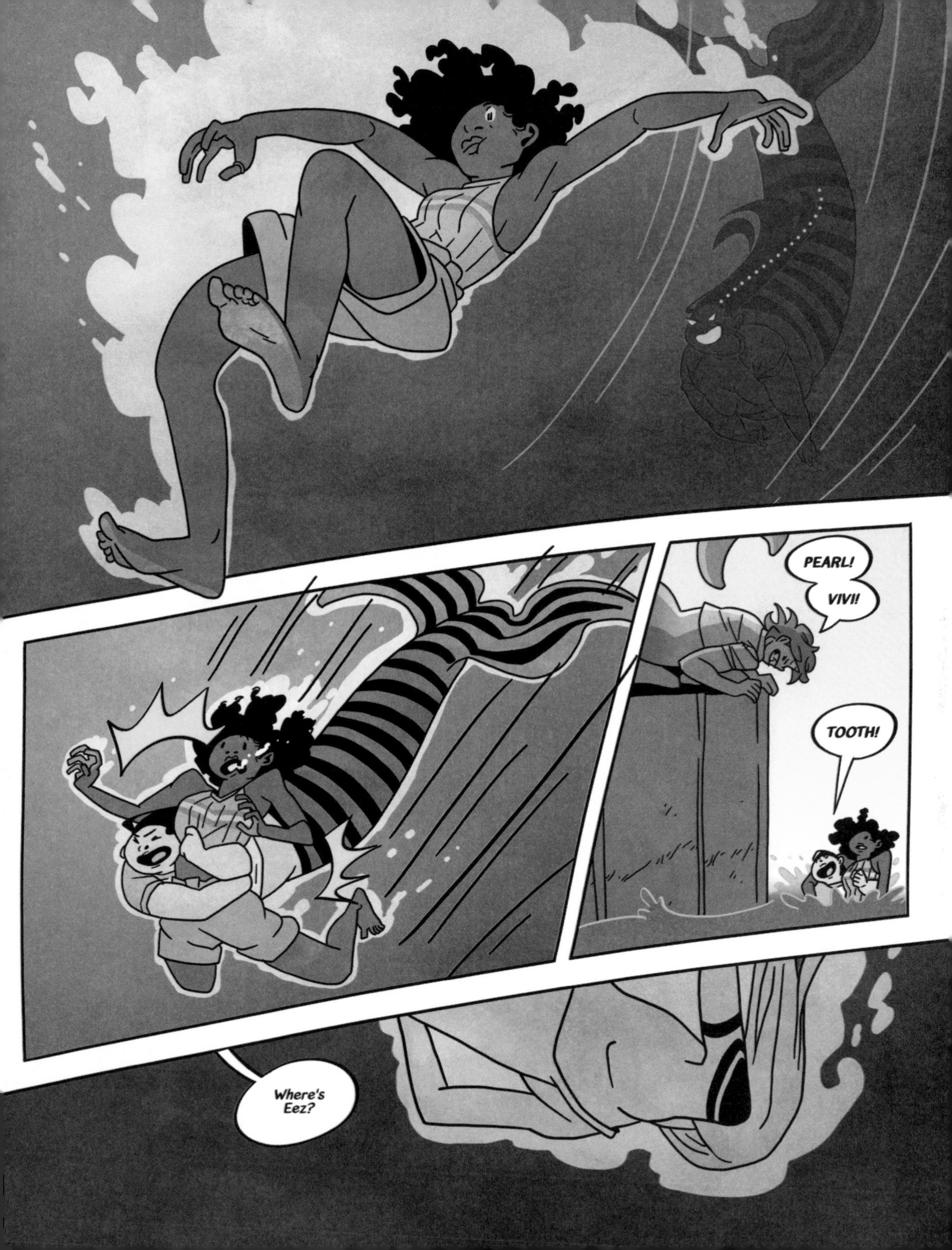
PEARL!
VIVI!
TOOTH!
Where's Eez?

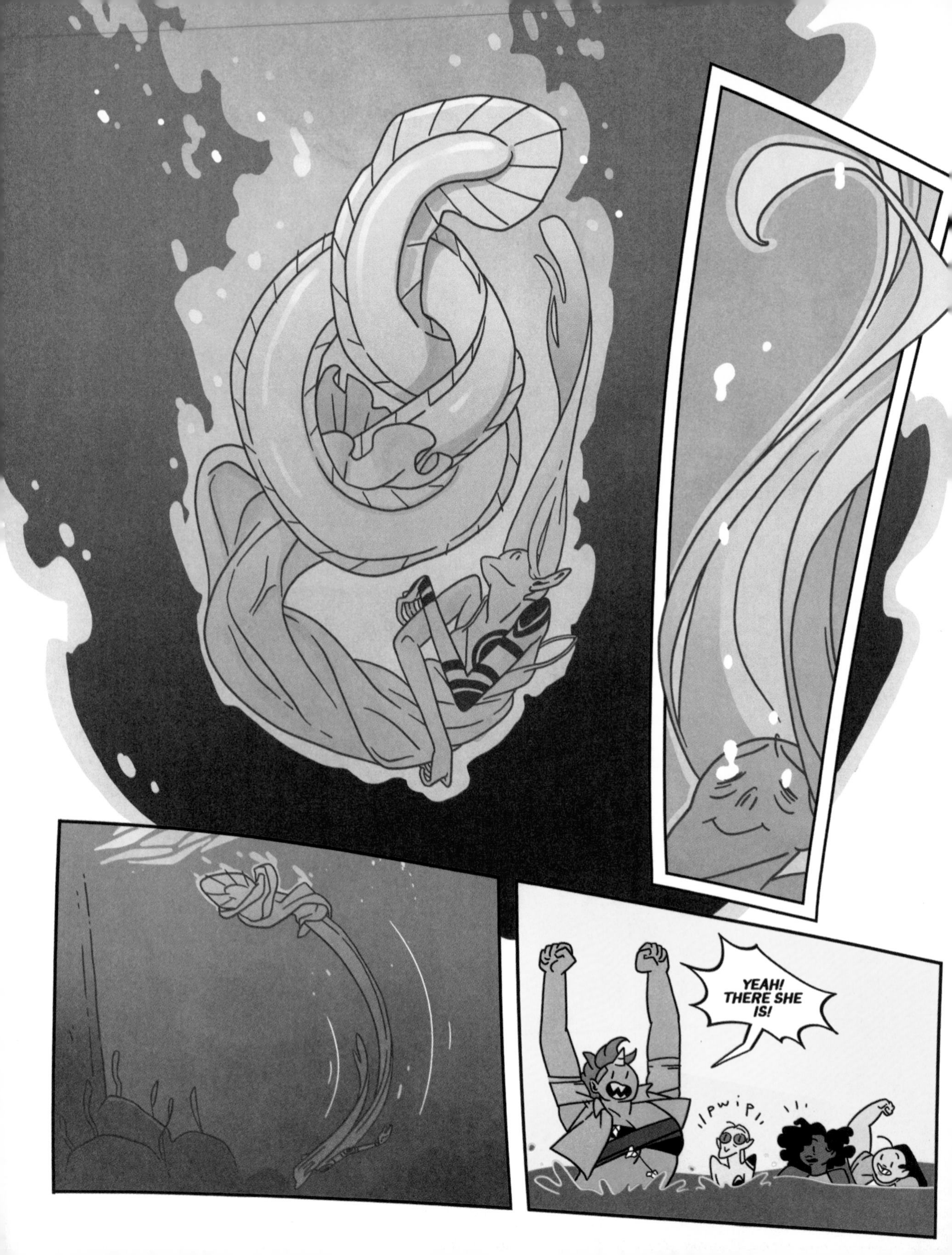
YEAH! THERE SHE IS!
PWIP

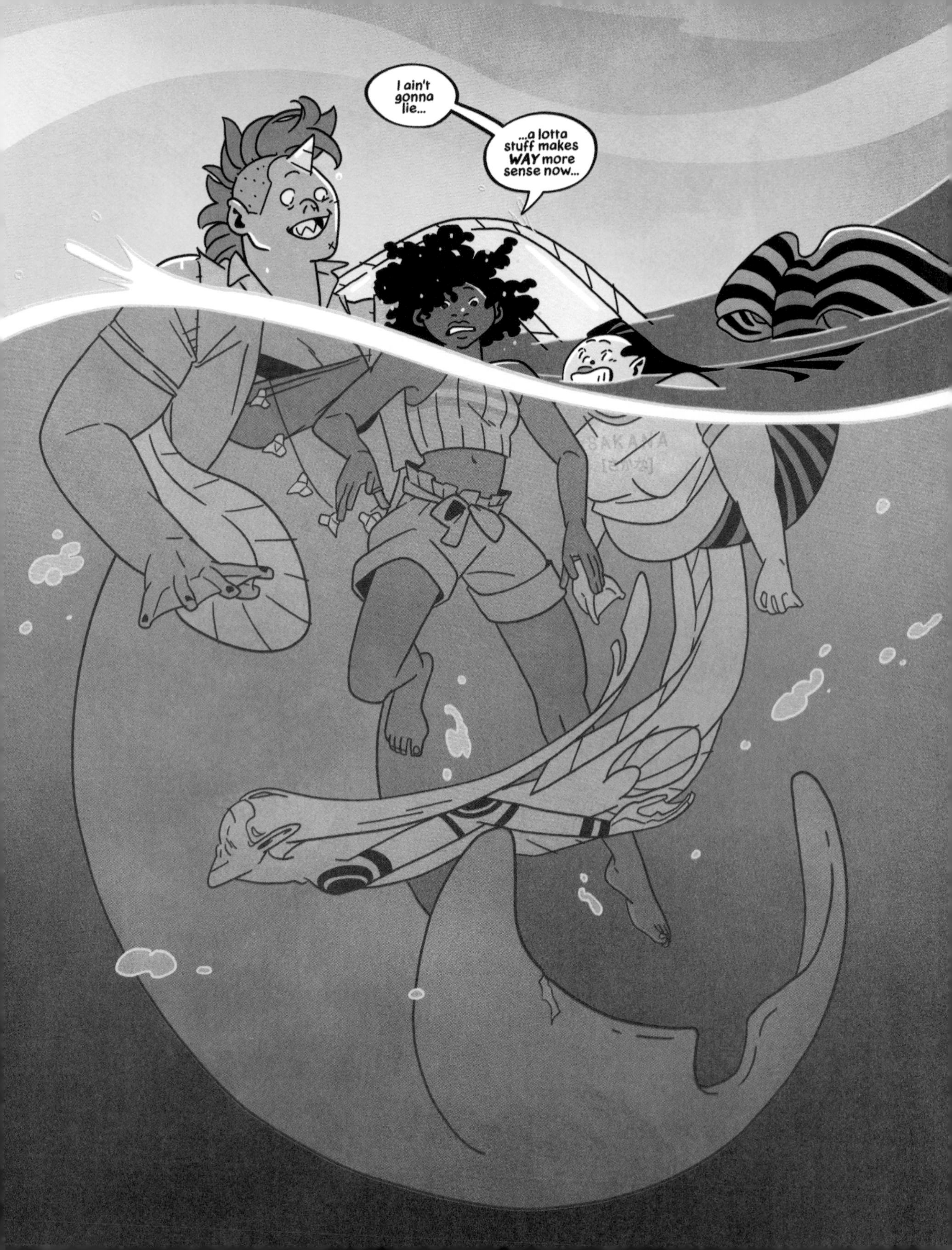
I ain't gonna lie...
...a lotta stuff makes WAY more sense now...
SAKANA
[さかな]

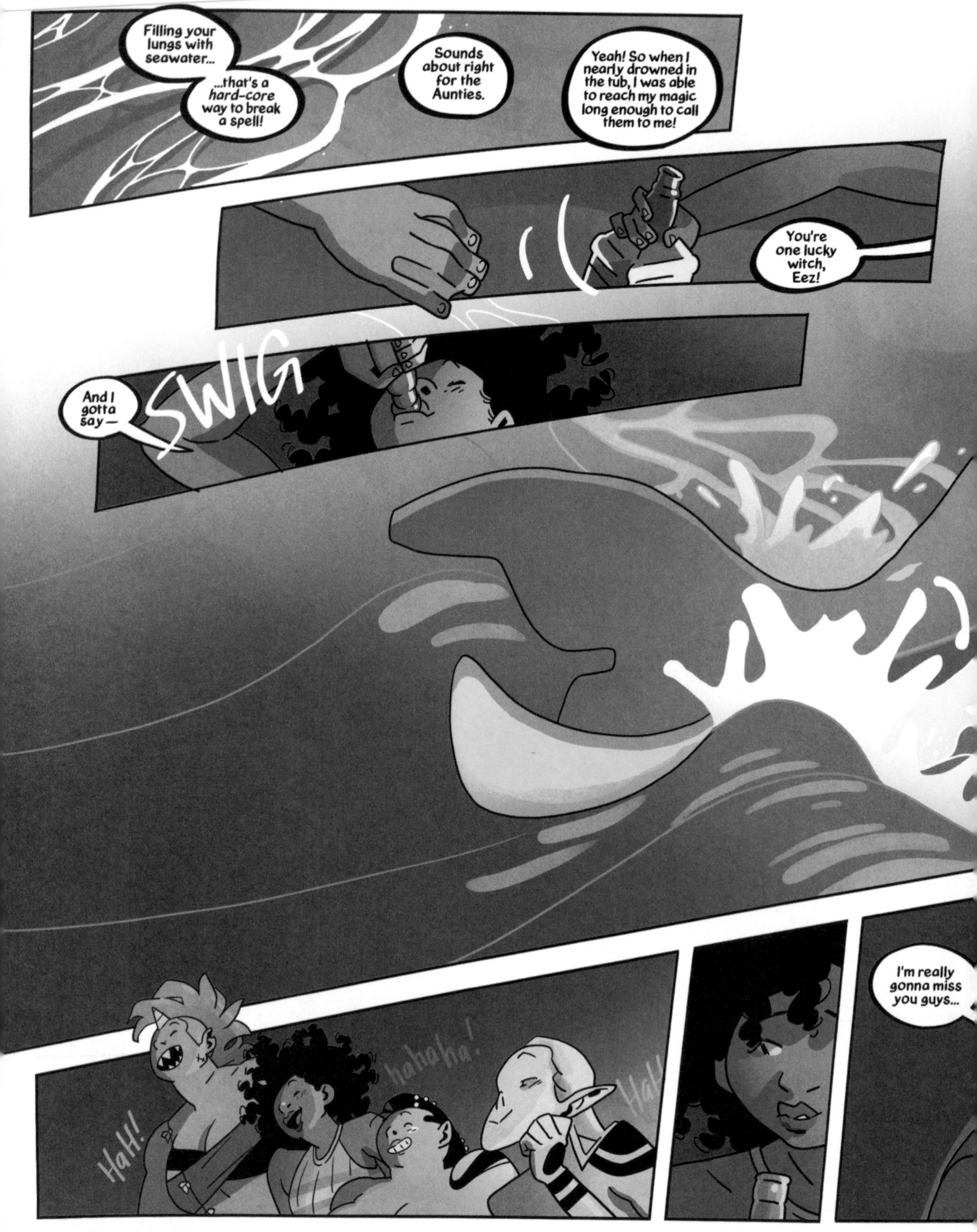
Filling your lungs with seawater...
...that's a hard-core way to break a spell!
Sounds about right for the Aunties.
Yeah! So when I nearly drowned in the tub, I was able to reach my magic long enough to call them to me!
You're one lucky witch, Eez!
SWIG
And I gotta say—
HaH!
hahaha!
HaH
I'm really gonna miss you guys...

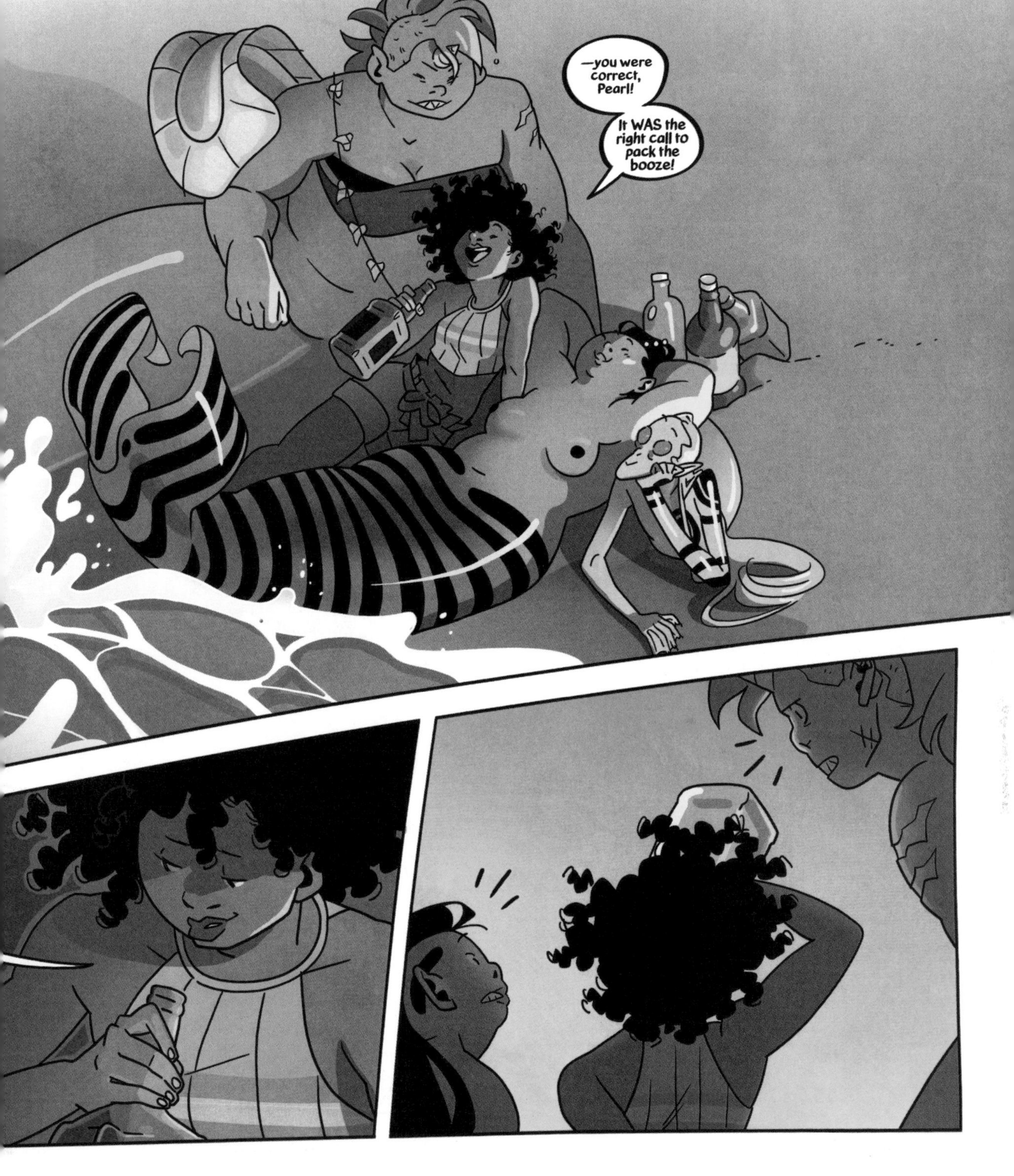
—you were correct, Pearl!
It WAS the right call to pack the booze!

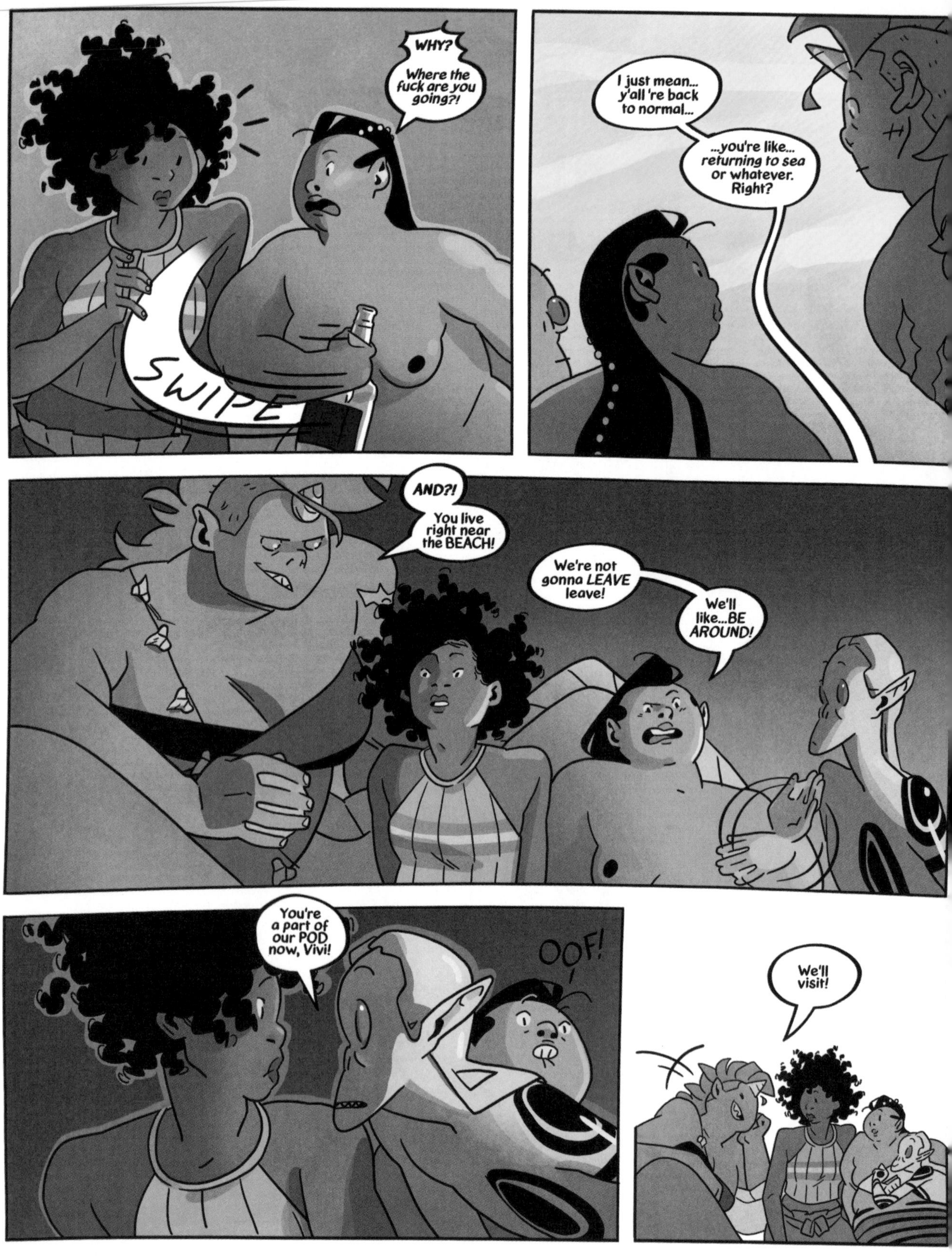
WHY?
Where the fuck are you going?!
SWIPE
I just mean... y'all 're back to normal...
...you're like... returning to sea or whatever. Right?
AND?!
You live right near the BEACH!
We're not gonna LEAVE leave!
We'll like...BE AROUND!
You're a part of our POD now, Vivi!
OOF!
We'll visit!

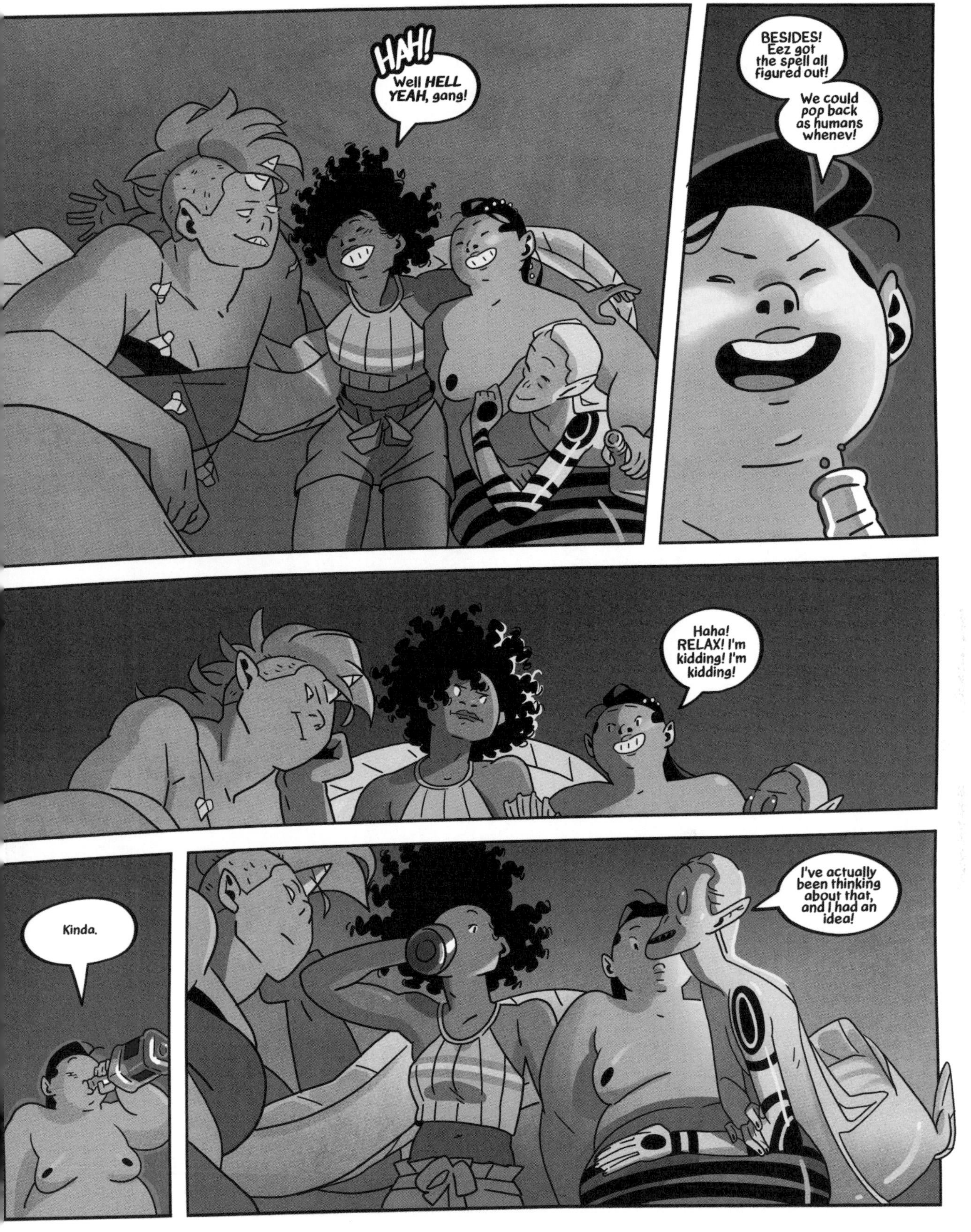
HAH!
Well HELL YEAH, gang!
BESIDES! Eez got the spell all figured out!
We could pop back as humans whenev!
Haha! RELAX! I'm kidding! I'm kidding!
Kinda.
I've actually been thinking about that, and I had an idea!

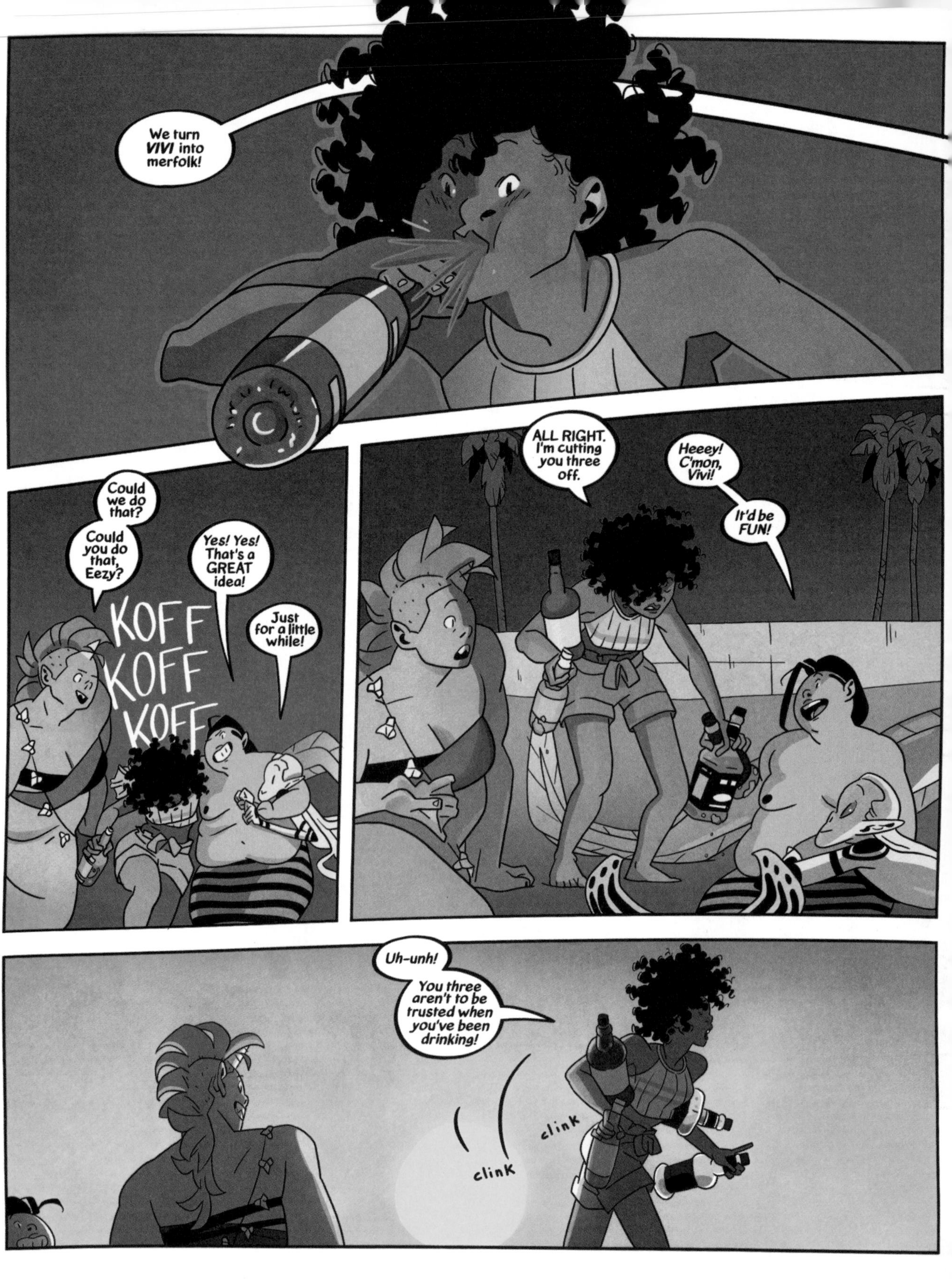
We turn VIVI into merfolk!
Could we do that?
Could you do that, Eezy?
KOFF KOFF KOFF
Yes! Yes! That's a GREAT idea!
Just for a little while!
ALL RIGHT. I'm cutting you three off.
Heeey! C'mon, Vivi!
It'd be FUN!
Uh-unh!
You three aren't to be trusted when you've been drinking!
clink
clink

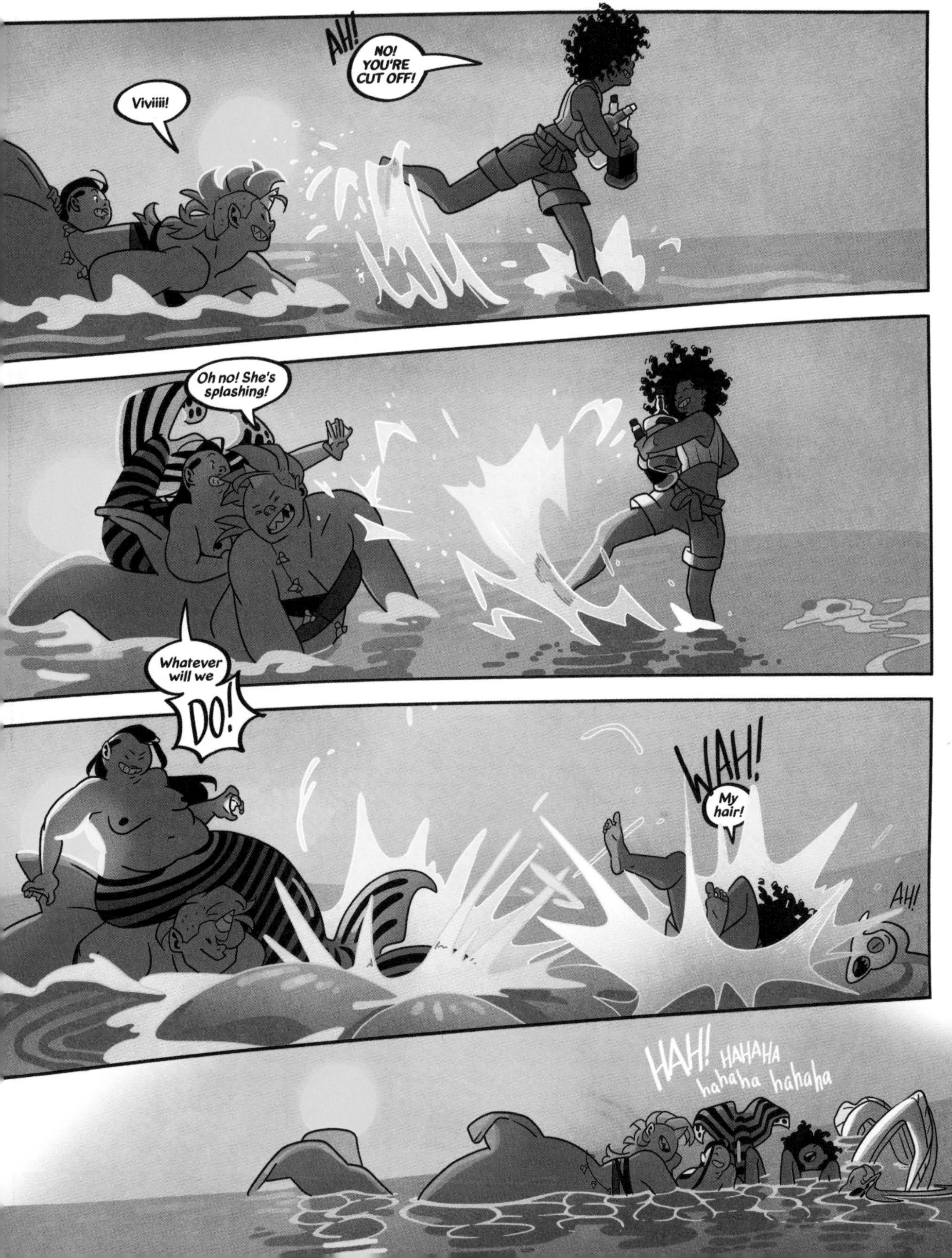

Viviiii!
AH!
NO! YOU'RE CUT OFF!
Oh no! She's splashing!
Whatever will we
DO!
WAH!
My hair!
AH!
HAH! HAHAHA
hahaha hahaha

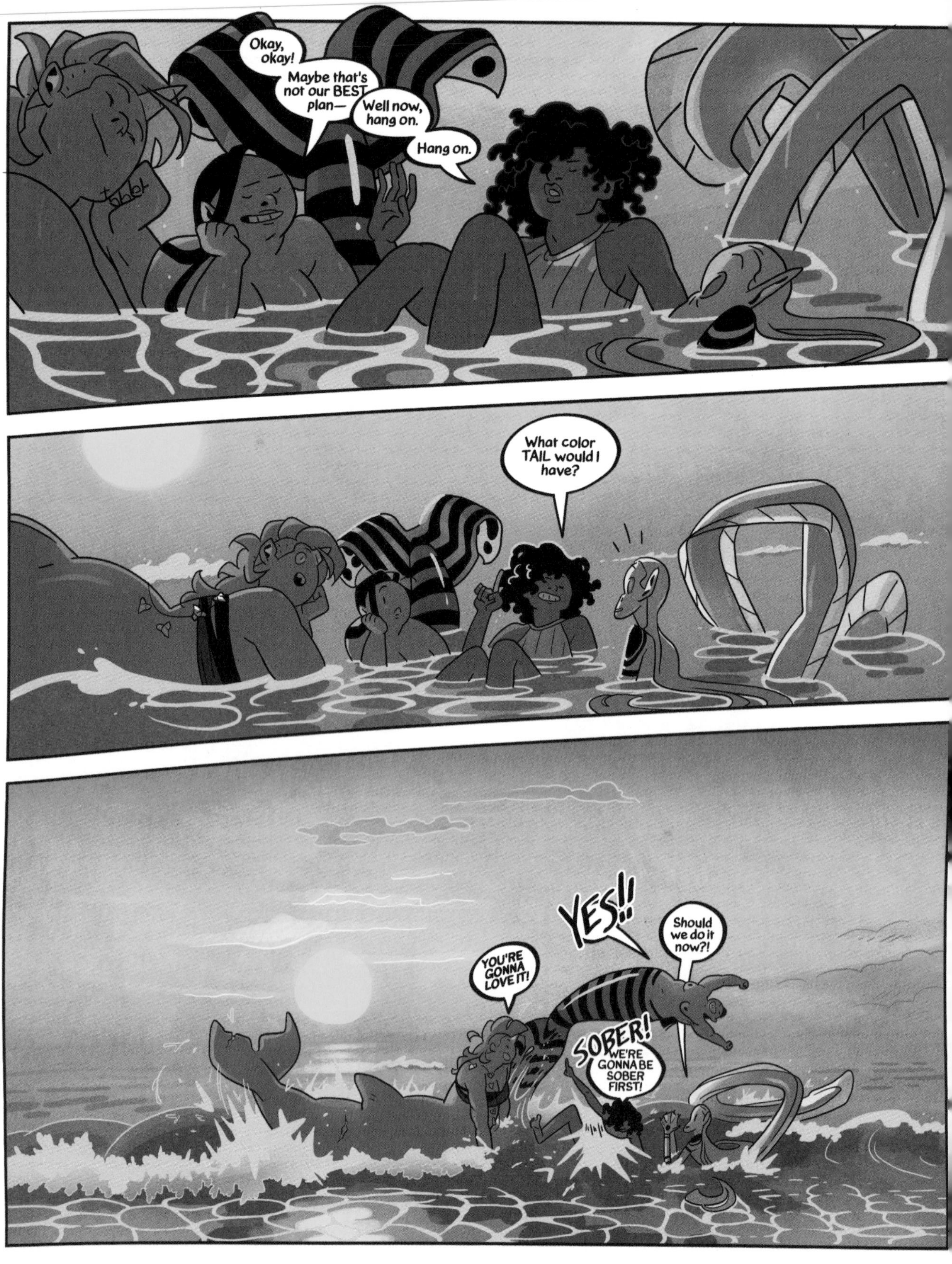
Okay, okay!
Maybe that's not our BEST plan—
Well now, hang on.
Hang on.
What color TAIL would I have?
YOU'RE GONNA LOVE IT!
YES!!
Should we do it now?!
SOBER!
WE'RE GONNA BE SOBER FIRST!

THE
END

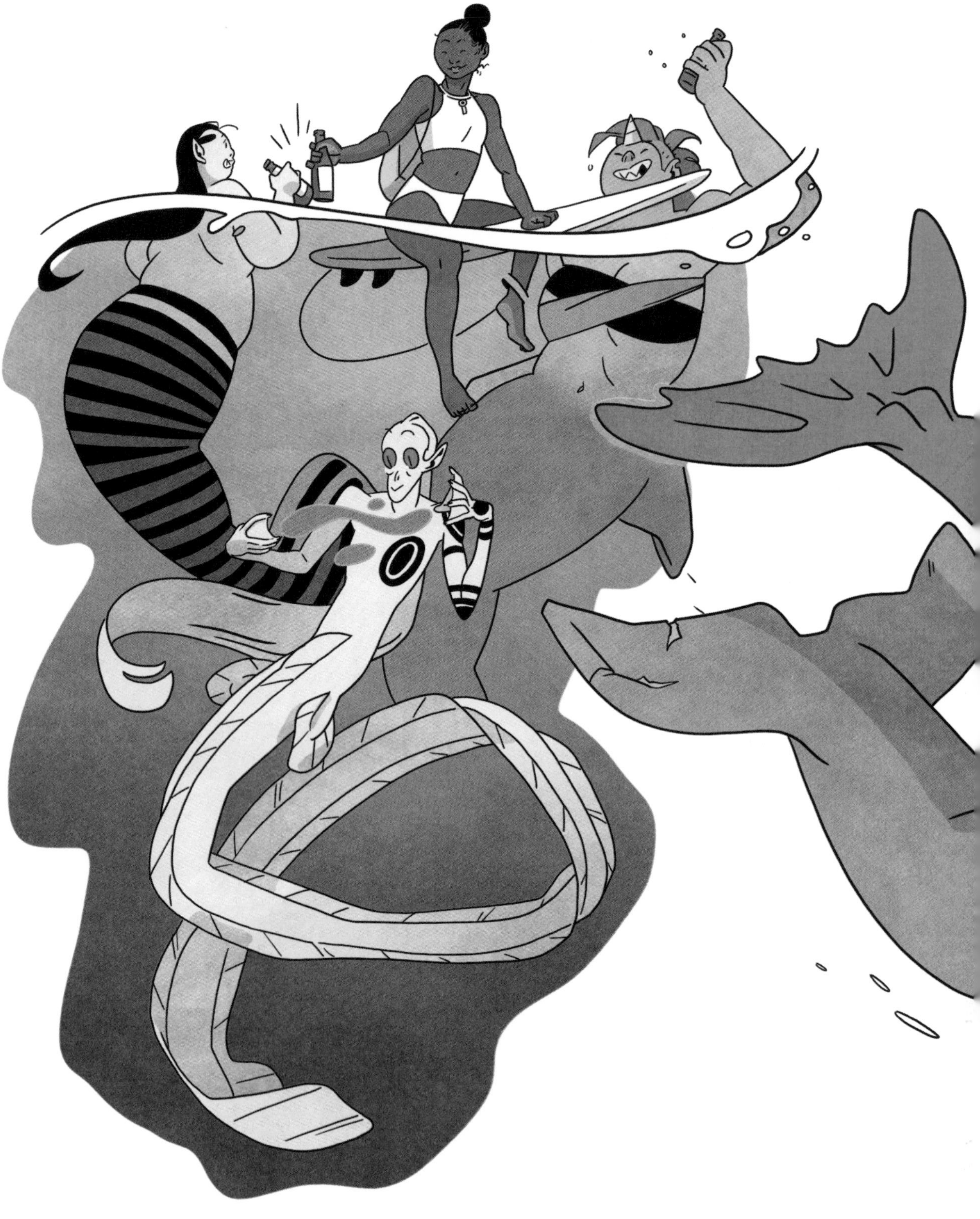

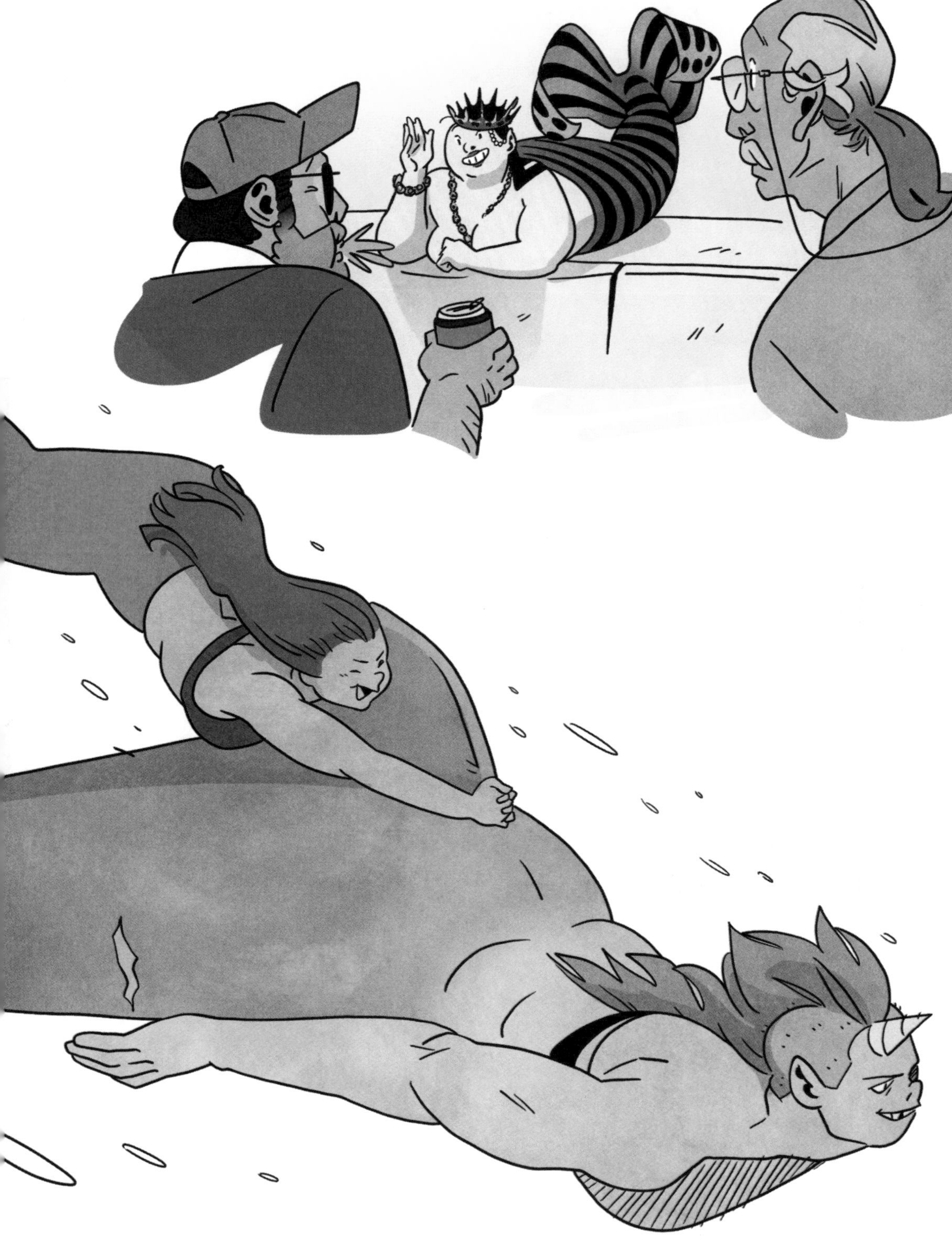

Thanks...

To Coco and Emily for all their love and support.

My agent, Charlie Olsen, for his hard work and encouragement.

@shooglet for their inspirational and beautiful photography Instagram.

Jasmine Lake and Addison Duffy at United Talent.

My editor, Ed Schlesinger, and everyone who worked hard on this book at Simon & Schuster!